MULTIPLE CRITERIA DECISION MAKING

McGraw-Hill Series in Quantitative Methods for Management

Consulting Editor

Martin K. Starr, *Columbia University*

Dannenbring and Starr: *Management Science: An Introduction*
Gohagan: *Quantitative Analysis for Public Policy*
McKenna: *Quantitative Methods for Public Decision Making*
Swanson: *Linear Programming: Basic Theory and Applications*
Zeleny: *Multiple Criteria Decision Making*

MULTIPLE CRITERIA DECISION MAKING

Milan Zeleny

The Joseph A. Martino
Graduate School of Business Administration
Fordham University

McGraw-Hill Book Company

New York   St. Louis   San Francisco   Auckland   Bogotá   Hamburg
Johannesburg   London   Madrid   Mexico   Montreal   New Delhi
Panama   Paris   São Paulo   Singapore   Sydney   Tokyo   Toronto

This book was set in Times Roman by Better Graphics.
The editors were Donald G. Mason and Frances A. Neal;
the production supervisor was Charles Hess.
The drawings were done by ANCO/Boston.
R. R. Donnelley & Sons Company was printer and binder.

MULTIPLE CRITERIA DECISION MAKING

234567890DODO898765432

Library of Congress Cataloging in Publication Data

Zeleny, Milan, date
    Multiple criteria decision making.

    (McGraw-Hill series in quantitative methods for
management)
    Bibliography: p.
    Includes index.
    1. Decision-making—Mathematical models. I.   Title.
HD30.23.Z44   658.4′03   80-23240
ISBN 0-07-072795-3

To Maximilian

CONTENTS

FOREWORD

When Milan Zeleny and I edited Volume 6 of the TIMS Studies in the Management Sciences, entitled *Multiple Criteria Decision Making* and published by North-Holland (1977), we assessed the state of the art as follows:

> Our belief is that MCDM will not continue as a separate field of inquiry. It will be absorbed into the general body of decision studies. Thus, multiple criteria concerns will be part of mathematical programming and part of inventory theory. They will also be applied by managers to finance, marketing, production and other functional areas. Therefore, from a research point of view, MCDM will cease to exist as an alternative approach to SCDM.
>
> . . . The disappearance of a selective interest group may take less time than many of us would wish. The avenues we are following begin to parallel each other as they become increasingly crowded with traffic. Yet many basic enigmas are unresolved, and they promise to remain unresolved as research dedicated to exploring new avenues is supplanted with efforts to apply what exists. There is much benefit to be gained from application, but a danger as well if the techniques require leaps across chasms that are not yet bridged. There may be managerial resistance to employing functions vaguely related to human behavior and the social condition. Such resistance could harden into dismissal. Thus, a managerial flirtation with MCDM might set back potential advances by many years. This pessimistic view of the future is summed up by the question: Are managers better off finding speculative solutions for ill-structured problems than accurate solutions for trivial ones?
>
> The optimistic view of the future requires strong support for continued research. It is facilitated by experimental application, by a willingness to search out dogma and remove it, by an openness to new behavioral knowledge and a blending of that with modeling skills. While the probabilities of the pessimistic or optimistic future are unknown, we believe that the pessimistic scenario has more than a small chance of becoming real history.

Thus, we found that the field was inchoate, but its researchers were striving for a central focus. Yet, we did not believe that it could continue as a separate field of inquiry. Now, some four years later, I believe that we were unduly pessimistic.

What was needed was a basis for identity that would be independent of classical decision analysis. The selective MCDM interest group has steadily grown in size and dedication. Applications have demonstrated sincere managerial involvement rather than flirtations. The optimistic view required strong support for continued research and that has been the case.

The multiple criteria methods were viewed by many as being less rigorous than those of the axiomatic, classical decision analysis field and therefore, not acceptable by the standards of that field. On the other hand, the multiple criteria researchers saw themselves as extending the classical decision analysis to encompass the characteristics of an important set of decision problems.

The resolution of the difference between rigor and reality required establishing MCDM as a unique field—not as an extension of axiomatic optimization. Milan Zeleny's *Multiple Criteria Decision Making* does this.

MCDM opened the door to behavioral inquiry with all its probing but hesitant qualities. Thus, fuzzy set theory and MCDM are joined in a lasting partnership. This is one of several factors leading to the perception of MCDM as a unique field for theoretical and practical applications. What was needed was a sensibly organized taxonomy to reveal the architecture of MCDM and its independence from classical decision analysis. This is a major accomplishment of Milan Zeleny's book.

The book allows MCDM to move into the classroom, as a companion course to classical decision analysis. At the same time, from an application point of view it provides a framework for those interested in problems that fit the MCDM taxonomy, for understanding the state of its art.

A useful consequence may be that MCDM will now be perceived as neither offshoot nor competitor of traditional decision analysis, but rather as a new bridge to behavioral science. We hope that across this bridge will flow increased dialogue between management scientists and behavioral scientists. If, by marching to a different drummer, we can improve our ability to solve a ubiquitous class of problems, Milan Zeleny's contribution will be recognized and appreciated.

Martin K. Starr
Columbia University

PREFACE

Why would anybody decide to *write* a book entitled *Multiple Criteria Decision Making*? There are of course many reasons, and later I will duly list and explain them, but let me share with you a personal one: because I have always wanted to *read* a book with such a title.

An activity in which I engage for most of my waking hours yet know very little about is *decision making*. At every moment of the day I must decide what I am going to do the next moment. Choosing, preferring, and deciding are the commissions which I am obliged to exercise *alone*—no one can perform them for me; no one can take my place. Even when, in desperation, I abandon myself to destiny, I have decided not to decide.

In order to be able to make decisions under increasingly complex circumstances, I must evolve, maintain, and continually update a repertoire of views, values, opinions, and convictions about the world. Such a personal "model" of reality provides the necessary "navigational guidelines," the *criteria* which help to orient me as I face the ever-present dilemma of different possibilities of action.

Decision making is ultimately the most difficult (and potentially the most rewarding) activity because a "model" of any reasonable richness will return *multiple* criteria, forcing us to choose not only among the possible courses of action but also among the means of evaluating such actions.

For example, the process of deciding which automobile to purchase involves not only the actual choice among currently available makes, but, more importantly, the selection of appropriate criteria of choice: price, mileage, projected maintenance costs, horsepower, appearance, expected resale value, overall appeal, and many others.

The alternatives of choice do not usually present themselves nicely ordered and clearly differentiated. Very rarely can we simply choose by saying: "I'll take . . . that one!" But as we invest more in our personal "models" and learn more about our values, needs, and possibilities, our criteria of choice become more reliable and less confusing and we are able to make our choices with greater confidence and understanding.

Decision making is a universal human vocation. While we are generally good at it, some of us are better and some have actually decided to make a living out of it. *This book is for those who are serious about the business of decision making.*

Next, I have some explaining to do about the title and the book's general organization.

Why is it necessary to insert *Multiple Criteria* in front of *Decision Making*? Why not simply call the book *Decision Making*? Is there such a thing as single-criterion decision making? Yes, there is.

In situations of war, emergencies, and disasters, or under extremely time-pressured conditions, our "models" of the world tend to become very simple: win, survive, act—regardless of cost, without concern for the "other side," under any circumstances. Our criteria or objectives become similarly reduced: maximize overall volume of production, minimize delivery time, maximize output per worker, maximize the number of "kills" per area, minimize the costs of raw materials; always minimize *or* maximize something.

Under such conditions, during World War II, the emerging new discipline of operations research and management science (OR/MS) was principally occupied with tactical problems of national defense. In the late fifties OR/MS efforts shifted to industrial-type analyses, with a strong emphasis on *efficiency*, i.e., performing a given task in the best way possible with respect to a single, predefined criterion. Thus, problems of inventory control, production scheduling, transportation, queuing, and resources allocation were prominent.

Managers of the seventies were faced with strategic problems, with a strong emphasis on *effectiveness*, i.e., identifying what should be done and ensuring that the chosen criteria were relevent. They were endeavoring to achieve simultaneously a wide variety of objectives, many of which were in conflict.

Decision makers of the eighties must pay more attention to the "other side"; they are expected, required, and even legally mandated to incorporate a large variety of criteria in evaluating their actions. Their multiple and often incommensurate concerns include economic, political, environmental, social, health, aesthetic, and other categories of criteria. They will have to *compromise*, i.e., search for a proper balance among the many conflicting objectives.

Making a decision, choosing an alternative, is becoming progressively more difficult; yet textbooks on multiple-criteria decision making (MCDM) are virtually nonexistent. Thus, the pressure to apply even inadequate single-criterion methodologies to multiple-criteria problems is still growing.

This book is about decision making as the art of balancing multiple objectives. It is not about a mechanical search for a mathematical maximum or minimum. There are no decision trees or decision matrices in this text. One cannot capture the dynamics of the decision *process* with all its evaluations and reevaluations, value changes, information interpretations, learning and preference adaptations, through such petrified snapshots of a dead "tree."

The process of decision making is a unity of predecision, decision, and postdecision stages. The creative generation of new decision alternatives can be even more important than the careful evaluation of those already existing. A set of alternatives is rarely prespecified or given; *making a decision often means inventing a new alternative*.

I have already mentioned that decision making is a lonely process and that nobody else can make *my* decisions. I do not want to be told what my decisions *should* be—because I bear the ultimate responsibility for them—but I am anxious to learn about *how* I can go about making them myself to my own satisfaction.

No physician can prescribe the correct medicine without first describing the disease and its symptoms. Description means understanding how things *are*; prescription, how they *should* be. *The best prescription comes from a good description*.

Consequently, in this book you also will not find "axioms of rational behavior." Who am I to tell you what is or is not rational? Why can't axioms of rational behavior be irrational? What is so precious about assuming unchanging and continuous preferences, judgmental consistency, transitivity, inflexibility, utility maximization, and an inability to learn? Is it sufficient that such assumptions are easier to handle mathematically?

We shall emphasize *how* and *why* decisions are made. Only after gaining some insight into these questions may we begin to understand how they *should* be made or how to improve our process of making them.

The Need for MCDM Texts

This book is meant to be *companionable*, i.e., suited to be associated with or to complement any standard textbook on operations research, management science, or decision analysis. Most of these books do not provide an adequate treatment of multiple criteria.

The major OR/MS concepts were developed in the fifties in response to problems of the forties. They were further refined, computerized, and applied in the sixties—but not much new material was added that was relevant to the complex problems of the seventies. MCDM is now evolving in response to these more recent practical needs. Education in the eighties, preparing OR/MS students for their decision-making roles in the year 2000, should not be exclusively rooted in the problems of the forties!

Some textbooks have already appeared, dealing with such areas of MCDM as goal programming and multiattribute utility theory. They are rather narrowly specialized and perhaps too technical. Goal programming and multiattribute utility theory appear as separate chapters in this book. But they represent only a small part of the whole story. Few courses deal independently with such specialized topics. But, it is hoped, existing OR/MS courses can be fruitfully complemented by an overview of MCDM and of the recent advances in decision making.

One can also foresee the establishment of introductory courses in multiple-criteria decision making as such. An innovative teacher will find it feasible and rewarding to design such a course in MCDM. In this respect the present text can provide a structure for the initial design of such courses. It contains introductions to even the most advanced concepts and topics of MCDM and provides references to the necessary technical or applicational papers and monographs. Annotated bibliographical notes follow each chapter.

The reader will find frequent critiques and self-critiques, examples and counterexamples, controversial quotations, and generally at least as many questions as answers. This is all by design. In recent years most OR/MS texts have become unduly positive, conflict-free, detailed, and technically polished. They are impressive for their clarity, multicolor exposition, and accompanying educational fringes (slides, video cassettes, self-study guides, and even comic-book versions). Students are expected to master them efficiently and effortlessly—yet, this type of methodological unity, "objectivity," and technical purity seems to lack reality. In an overly careful attempt to avoid subjective "bias," the author often produces a document with no explicit point of view, no "model" of the world. Books begin to resemble each other more and more and a certain intellectual blandness sets in.

One should not teach or conduct decision analyses in an operational setting of a unitary system; rather one should seek a mix of competing and/or complementary systems of methodologies. *There is no single "rational" approach to decision making.*

The Organization of This Book

Although the primary purpose of this book is to complement and extend existing textbooks and courses, I have structured the material in a logical progression as for an independent introductory course in MCDM.

Chapter 1 provides a variety of real-world examples and introduces a discussion of major differences between single-criterion and multicriterion problems. Its goal is to make the reader aware that the decision world is essentially multidimensional and to reinforce commonly shared experiences and intuitions. Chapter 2 provides a short historical framework for MCDM, discusses the concept of optimality, and introduces one of the basic ideas of MCDM: *nondominated solutions.*

Chapters 3 through 7 present various descriptions of decision making as a dynamic process. Chapter 3 discusses the process as a whole, introducing its individual stages (predecision, decision, and postdecision) and summarizing it in a flow diagram. This chapter thus provides a basic framework for the book.

Chapter 4 is concerned with the predecision stage: generation of new alternatives, realization of the predecision conflict, and initiation of resolution efforts. A self-contained theory of *conflict dissolution*, as well as some practical examples of its applicability, are also presented in this chapter.

Not until Chap. 5 is the actual decision-making stage of the process scrutinized. Alternatives are evaluated, preferences measured, and a search for the "best" alternative is triggered. We then show how a decision maker's point of reference, the *ideal alternative*, is used, and how the theory of the displaced ideal naturally emerges from the traditional utility approach. Some axioms of "rational behavior" are examined, such as transitivity of preferences and independence of irrelevant alternatives, and shown to be of limited usefulness in *descriptions* of the decision-making behavior.

Chapter 6 translates the previously described process into quantifiable form and provides a more formal structure for further discussion. The basic notions of *fuzzy sets* is briefly introduced and blended in with no mathematical demands made on the reader. "Good" decisions are then characterized as those *most closely* resembling the ideal alternative. Various numerical and practical examples of this approach accompany the presentation.

Usually decision criteria or objectives are not all equally important. Traditionally, different weighting schemes have been devised to address the problem of differential levels of importance for objectives. Chapter 7 is entirely devoted to discussing such schemes. A new, *entropy-based* concept of weight is introduced, and its numerical properties are explained. It is even proposed that weights might not be the only or the proper way of capturing attribute importance.

Chapters 8, 9, and 10 present more practical and more technical methodologies for decision search: *linear multiobjective programming*, *goal programming*, and *compromise programming* respectively. All three chapters rely on numerical examples, graphic exposition, and discussions of their underlying assumptions. No mathematical theorems and few algorithms are used; they are readily available in the extensive bibliography. Introducing such rigorous material too early could prevent the reader's reaching a full understanding of these techniques. Instead, these chapters concentrate on the differences between constraints, goals, and objectives, showing how the three techniques are interrelated and how they extend traditional linear programming.

Chapter 10, dealing primarily with compromise programming, is complemented by important practical topics on group decision making and game theory. Problems of compromise and *consensus* are revisited but now in terms of collective rather than individual choice and *ordinal* rather than cardinal ranking of preferences. There is also a section on *de novo programming*, concerned with designing an optimal system rather than optimizing a given system.

Chapter 11 goes a step beyond the traditional and generally unsatisfactory single-dimensional measures of *risk*, such as variance, and transforms the *stochastic dominance* criterion into its more practical, partial-information-based form, the prospect ranking vector. This chapter demonstrates how MCDM can be applied to the key concepts of other functional areas of business research to bring about new insights as well as theoretical and practical advances.

Chapters 12 and 13 are devoted to *multiattribute utility theory* and *social judgment theory*. These are more traditional methodologies, prescriptive in nature, which attempt to assess or to capture the decision maker's *utility or preference function*. These topics are presented in some detail and in a more critical mode because they provide an excellent comparative base for MCDM. Without the precision and formalism of such rationalistic theories there would certainly have been less progress in developing descriptive insights.

Chapter 14 emphasizes again that decision making cannot be reduced to an application of a simple logico-mathematical formula. Decision making is a very *human* business, even in the business environment itself. The problems of implementation, decision politics, information, and confidence, as well as the role of intuition, are discussed. This chapter concludes with some reflections on the emerging area of *decision support systems* and the future of MCDM.

Each chapter is preceded by a summary noting its relationship to other chapters. At the conclusion of each chapter, a short Bibliographical Note lists the most important references related to that chapter, and there is also an extensive bibliography at the end of the book.

In order to assist both students and instructors in achieving deeper understanding, problems are appended to each chapter.

To the Reader

Decision making is *not* only the province of operations research, management science, and decision science—it is an activity that *everyone* is interested in. Each student of business, management, government, engineering design, and public policy has to evolve a personal "model" for decision making.

Such a task is not well handled by simply adopting or rejecting complex mathematical prescriptions and their underlying "rational" axiomatic structures. Their stated objectives, the "givens," the constraints, and the assumptions should not be accepted without question or challenge. After all, it is *your* "model" you are searching for!

I have attempted to present concepts and methods that are not yet stripped to their bare mathematical minimum—they still can be molded and shaped to fit a particular reality of a particular decision maker. They still can be doubted and discussed; not only by a simple yes or no, but by a creative personal search for methodological completion.

These concepts have been captured in the *process of becoming* rather than in the *state of being*. Thus, they should be able to withstand the required injections of individualized reality and to accommodate a great variety of value systems and managerial styles.

Thesis—antithesis—synthesis: This book aspires to provide the antitheses that are so crucially needed for a personal synthesis of decision-making theories and practice. One cannot reach satisfactory understanding of a particular methodology without exploring alternative concepts as well. Only through comparison, weighing the advantages and disadvantages of *alternate* conceptual models, is one able to form a truly personal opinion or "model" of reality. To summarize, one has to learn that there are many ways of achieving posted goals, that no way is exclusively "rational" or "irrational," and that unity of purpose *can* emerge from a diversity of views.

Acknowledgments

Although this book may *appear* to be rather individualistic in its tone and emphasis, it is not. I have had the privilege of distilling the views, ideas, and efforts of many great OR/MS colleagues. My confidence has grown out of a fertile and lively background of discussions and experiences, encouragements and discouragements, all equally necessary for the emergence of the final product. My readers, if they enjoy the book, should also have the pleasure of knowing some of my "coauthors"; if they find the book lacking, as they may, let me assure them that *I* have failed in the execution, not my colleagues in their trust, support, and involvement.

I am primarily obliged to Professor Martin K. Starr of Columbia University: the initiator, the mover, and the teacher par excellence. Without his sharing of his deep and sincere concerns about OR/MS and without his indications of possible directions, this book would never even have been attempted.

Professor Richard F. Barton of Texas Tech University, Lubbock, gave me a detailed set of hard comments, illuminating the structure of the entire text, praising Chap. 5, and criticizing the introductory chapters. He really forced me to think harder and write better.

I have received unusually friendly support from Professor Joel N. Morse of the University of Delaware. His involvement went well beyond "professional courtesy"; he has proved to be a colleague of exceptional concern, and his contributions to the book are sincerely appreciated. I hope that his personal sacrifice of effort and time were not in vain.

Professor Daniel P. Loucks of Cornell University and Dr. Ben Hobbs of Brookhaven National Laboratory jointly stressed the need for including more interactive programming features in the book; they also caused me to rewrite Chapters 7 and 12. Their insight and wealth of practical experience should help to make the book more attractive to practitioners. I am a rather poor match for them in matters of application and I hope that references to their work will compensate the reader in that respect.

Professors Michael J. White of the University of South Florida and Stanley Young of the University of Massachusetts offered very specific and insightful comments on Chapters 11 and 12, respectively. These chapters, although probably still quite controversial, have been greatly moderated by their perceptions. Professor Ronald R. Yager of Iona College read an earlier draft and his input into parts dealing with fuzzy sets is appreciated. Also Professors Rakesh K. Sarin, of the University of California at Los Angeles, and Sandra L. Schwartz, of the University of British Columbia, reviewed the early manuscript.

I am grateful to Professor Erik Johnsen for providing me with a haven in København where I completed the manuscript.

Professors Christer Carlsson and Aimo Törn of the Åbo Akademi have been instrumental in preparing and editing the solutions and discussions of text cases which are presented in the instructor's manual. This invaluable aid is a result of their efforts as well as those of many colleagues whom they persuaded to contribute their solutions: M. A. Benito-Alonso (Université Catholique de Mons), J. P. Dauer (University of Nebraska), M. Despontin (Vrije Universiteit Brussel), P. Devaux (Université Catholique de Mons), F. Droesbeke (Université Libre de Bruxelles), E. Jacquet-Lagrèze (Université Paris), B. Karpak (University of Istanbul), J. S. H. Kornbluth (Hebrew University of Jerusalem), R. J. Krueger (University of Nebraska), R. Mayer (University of Delaware), J. N. Morse (University of Delaware), P. Nijkamp (Free University of Amsterdam), L. F. Pau (E.N.S. Télécommunications), D. E. Sebo (University of Nebraska), J. Spronk (Erasmus University Rotterdam), P. Vincke (Université Libre de Bruxelles), J. Wallenius (Jyväskylän Yliopisto, Finland), J. Wallin (Åbo Swedish University), R. R. Yager (Iona College), and S. Zionts (SUNY at Buffalo). My thanks go to all of them, for their willingness to associate their work with my name. In no way should their participation be interpreted as their endorsement of all ideas expressed in the book.

What else is to be said? I have typed the book myself, with a sense of adventure. I recommend it. I am sure that my wife, Betka, would not. So, let me thank her for her patience and tolerance which can never be repaid. It has disturbed her life and I am sorry for that. I also thank Muco, my friend and companion through the sleepless nights.

Milan Zeleny

MULTIPLE CRITERIA DECISION MAKING

INTRODUCTION
MULTIPLE OBJECTIVES ARE ALL AROUND US

To manage a business is to balance a variety of needs and goals. And this requires multiple objectives.

Peter F. Drucker
Management (1974)

It has become more and more difficult to see the world around us in a unidimensional way and to use only a single criterion when judging what we see. We always compare, rank, and order the objects of our choice with respect to *criteria of choice*. But only in a very simple, straightforward, or routine situation can we assume that a *single* criterion of choice will be fully satisfactory.

We may pick the *largest* apple from a basket (size), the *cheapest* brand of beer (price), the *highest* salary offer (dollar amount), or the *shortest* route home (distance). But often we worry whether the largest apple is the sweetest, the juiciest, the most aromatic, and the freshest, and whether we would enjoy eating the whole thing anyway. We may care not only about our beer's price but also about its taste, caloric content, carbonation, and alcoholic content. We think about whether the highest salary offer is the one also promising the highest rate of salary increase, whether it is accompanied by generous fringe benefits, and whether the job provides comfortable working conditions or sufficient interest and challenge. And choosing the shortest route home? In order to get home at all we often have to consider the safest or the cheapest route, and the choice may be complex and even agonizing.

Routine business problems are sometimes described in terms of a single objective only. For example, profit—or more precisely, net present value of a profit stream—may be the index chosen for maximization. However, the profit-maximization criterion is in fact a simplifying assumption of economic theory rather than a useful guideline for modern business enterprise. We shall look at some relevant studies and opinions of the criterion of profit maximization in Sec. 1-3.

Multiple and conflicting objectives, for example, "minimize cost" and "maximize the quality of service," are the real stuff of the decision maker's or manager's daily concerns. Such problems are more complicated than the convenient assumptions of economics indicate. Improving achievement with respect to one objective can be accomplished only at the expense of another. Decision making can be loosely defined as a struggle to resolve the dilemma of conflicting objectives. The Dean of Columbia Business School puts it in the following way:

As for conflicting objectives—quality vs. lower cost, better product vs. cheaper raw materials, for example—just about any idiot can maximize a single function. Anybody can increase

1

sales. After all, if nothing else matters, you can decrease the price to zero. In fact, you don't have to stop there. If they won't take it at zero, you pay them to take it.[1]

Let us introduce a few examples of multiple objectives as they might appear in a large variety of situations faced by human decision makers. The purpose of this section is to accustom the reader to a multicriterion view of the world around us.

Manufacturing There are many different types of manufacturing firms, and they use different sets of criteria to judge their performance. A steady state manufacturer, facing a constant and reliable demand, is concerned about low cost and rapid delivery. The market-creating firm, in contrast, would typically emphasize reliable delivery and product flexibility. Innovative firms are most likely concerned about high quality, reliable delivery, and the learning capacity of their employees. Additional criteria are taken into account by different firms at different times: consistent quality, low investment, volume flexibility, good working conditions, low pollution, product classification, and some others. Using one or another combination of criteria could affect the success or failure of a firm. Using no criteria or too many criteria are both undesirable extremes and usually signal bad management.

Publishing In deciding how many copies of a book to print, both the publishing company and the book's sponsoring editor face the dilemma of conflicting objectives. The editor is concerned about minimizing the chance of being left with a large unsalable inventory of books. He or she is concerned about establishing a record of credibility, correct judgment, and understanding of the market. Thus there is a tendency on the editor's part to print as few books as possible. On the other hand, from the overall system viewpoint, the publisher should make a decision that maximizes the long-run expected returns to the firm. This criterion exerts considerable pressure to print more books. We shall discuss this particular conflict in more detail in Sec. 1-4.1.

Tax shelters and investment In considering tax shelters one is usually concerned about investments for profits and for reducing income taxes at the same time. The criteria for judging a good tax-sheltered investment are typically the following:

1. Current deductions from taxable income
2. Future deductions from taxable income
3. Capital gain after selling the investment

These are conflicting criteria, and there is rarely a single investment which

[1]*Hermes*, vol. 3, no. 2, Spring-Summer 1975.

maximizes all three components simultaneously. We shall analyze this problem in more detail in Sec. 1-4.2.

Multidimensionality of economic indicators One of the most widely used (and also misused) aggregations of multidimensional information into a single-number index is the *index of leading economic indicators*. This index, which is released monthly, is followed by the federal government as an important barometer of future economic activity.

The index represents a complex weighted aggregate of the following anticipatory measures:

 1. Standard & Poor's 500-stock index
 2. Commodity price changes
 3. Change in liquid assets
 4. Building permits
 5. Money supply (M-1)
 6. Net business formation
 7. Change in inventories
 8. Average work week
 9. Vendor performance
10. Plant and equipment orders
11. Consumer goods new orders
12. New claims for unemployment insurance

Weighted adjustments give more value to larger and more recent gains or losses than to smaller and earlier ones. Consequently, the composite index for any month could show a gain even though a majority of the twelve component indicators declined. This would occur when the combined weight for the fewer rising indicators was greater than the combined weight for the declining indicators.

It is even possible for a new record high for the total index to be reached in a month in which *none* of the twelve components was at a peak. This actually happened in the United States economy in both June 1978 and December 1977. In each case, only six of the twelve indicators rose.

Relying on such an unreliable barometer leads to a failure to anticipate downturns and upturns in United States business activity. The whole frequently does not agree with its parts. For example, while the overall index of leading indicators touched new highs in 1978, eleven of its twelve components had already peaked and started declining.

Indexes are simplifications of complex data systems. Obviously, a single economic index may not be sufficient to provide *full* insight into the quantitative aspects of an economic structure. A system of economic indexes must be considered: a nonaggregated multidimensional vector of indexes rather than their single-dimensional "collapsed" version.

For example, the Bureau of Economic Analysis follows forty-one leading economic indicators in its monthly reports, but only twelve of them are included in the aggregate measure. Thirty of these forty-one indicators had peaked by October 1978, yet the index of leading indicators registered new highs at the end of 1978. The downturn and upturn in the United States economy in 1979 and 1980 could not have been anticipated by relying on such an index only.

Aggregating a system of well-defined indexes leads to a considerable loss of the information contained in its separate components. One must consult all other indexes—systems of indexes provide more information about a data system than a single index does.

Medicine and surgery Much of the effort in modern medicine and surgery is now directed toward improving the quality of life rather than toward saving life. But how do we measure improvement in the quality of life? Increasingly we observe that different therapies produce about the same mortality and morbidity, so our choice of therapies cannot be based on this single criterion anymore. But the choice of therapy bears heavily on the ultimate quality of the patient's life and the lives of the people around the patient. Thus, for proper evaluation of alternative treatments, one must assess the patient's residual symptoms, state of restored health, feeling of well-being, limitations, new or renewed capabilities, and responses to implied advantages or disadvantages of the treatment.

Both objective and subjective appraisals of the patient's quality of life must enter the decision-making process. Neither costs alone, nor the probability of death only, nor any other "objectively measurable" single criterion can replace responsible value judgments by qualified decision makers. The medical profession must tackle the increasing complexity of multicriterion conflicts with all their objective and subjective ramifications. How do we quantify pain, suffering, anxiety, and incapacitation? How do we assess the effects a particular treatment will have on the patient's family? How do we involve the patient in the decision-making process? It would be preposterous to prescribe or dictate which decisions should be made—but it is extremely helpful to attempt to understand and thus improve the physician's method of reaching decisions.

Strategic planning for nuclear power Nuclear energy development options or strategies cannot be evaluated, selected, and pursued on the basis of a single, all-encompassing criterion. The initial technological strategy for nuclear development, evolved within government and industry over a quarter of a century, was based on light-water reactors, recycling of plutonium, and eventual replacement by liquid-metal fast breeder reactors. This strategy has been criticized recently for its failure to score well on the issues of safety, weapons proliferation, uranium-resource conservation, and economics.

Any new strategy will have to be judged on the basis of such multiple criteria and meet them in a balanced way. There are *at least* four criteria that seem to be particularly pertinent:

1. *To minimize or limit the risk of nuclear weapons proliferation.* The major concern is preventing plutonium from seeping into commercial channels by selecting more appropriate fuel cycles and developing adequate safeguards.
2. *To minimize uranium-resource requirements.* There are limits to both cumulative and yearly uranium production. Any long-term nuclear option must hedge against the possibility that U_3O_8 resources are minimal or could become rapidly depleted.
3. *To minimize adverse environmental impacts.* Siting, environmental, and safety problems must be satisfactorily resolved in order to promote a stable and long-term nuclear industry.
4. *To maximize economic efficiency.* The capital cost of fast breeders remains high; this could become a decisive factor in evaluating future strategies.

Assessment of medical technology and procedures In 1978 Congress voted to establish a Center for National Health Care Technology[1] with a mandate to define the safety, efficacy, efficiency, and cost effectiveness of medical technology and procedures. Hidden in this mandate are the multiplicity of criteria and a basic conflict of values. Implementing such a law will be difficult without explicitly considering these conflicts and without applying some acceptable procedures for resolving them.

A particular medical technology may be medically efficacious but economically inefficient. Similarly, safety and efficacy are often in conflict: Technology may produce significant medical benefits but may also carry noteworthy risks, such as pain or disability. How does one put a dollar value on pain, disability, or a change in life expectancy? Or a given technology may indicate a favorable risk-benefit ratio for some classes of patients but not for others. The trade-offs among these objectives are situation-dependent; they cannot be established once and for all. The clinical circumstances of a given decision have to be taken into account.

One could set the minimum standards for safety and medical efficacy. Given these minimum requirements, one could then extend the mandate to minimizing the cost of a given technology or procedure, i.e., maximizing the efficiency for a specific level of quality (safety and efficacy).

But it is cost effectiveness which leads to a conflict in human values. Net medical benefits of a given procedure should exceed or at least equal the cost of achieving it. Net medical benefits must be balanced against the dollars spent on them. Humans have to decide whether the medical benefits are greater than their dollar costs.

Diamond appraisal Farquhar (1977) introduces a diamond-appraisal problem to illustrate multiple criteria. A diamond cutter appraises finished cut diamonds in terms of four criteria:

---

[1]See *House Conference Report on S.2466*, "Health Services Research, Health Statistics, and Health Care Technology," Oct. 13, 1978, 95th Cong., 2d Sess., pt. 2, pp. H12828–H12836 (signed into law Nov. 9, 1978, as Public Law 95–623).

1. Size or weight in carats
2. Quality and type of cut
3. Color
4. Clarity and sparkle

Different levels can be achieved with all four attributes. For example, a 2-carat diamond of AAA expert cut, oval shape, white color, and high clarity might be produced from a given uncut gem. There are many possible outcomes associated with a given group of uncut gems because of the uncertainty in the cutting and polishing process.

Similar decision making and judgment are encountered in wine and food testing, animal breeding, art assessment, etc. Multiple attributes are often officially specified and their different target levels prescribed. Such guidelines and rules are designed to untangle the complexity of multicriterion conflict and to establish standards of quality.

Dog Breeding In the American Kennel Club's *The Complete Dog Book* (1975), there is a section entitled "Multiple Objectives." Some interesting observations and a good "feel" for the multiplicity of criteria are exhibited by these American dog breeders. Theirs is a clear and lucid statement of a general multiple-criteria decision making (MCDM) problem:

> One problem of the dog breeder is that he selects for so many different things that it is difficult to attain perfection in all of them at once. Conformation and behavior are probably first considerations. Freedom from hereditary defects is another. In some breeds, color and patterns of coloration are important.
>
> All of this means that the breeder must compromise when he selects his breeding stock. Maximum perfection in some one objective may tempt the breeder to use an animal that is highly undesirable in another. (p. 609–610.)

The reader can substitute appropriate terms in this statement to describe a variety of additional decision-making situations: an investor scanning investment portfolios, a corporate headhunter procuring executive personnel, one's hopeless search for a perfect mate, or the choice of a place to live.

We can contrast to *The Complete Dog Book* A. Kaufmann's statement, in *Methods and Models of Operations Research* (1963), that the value function associated with a system or an operation is *always unique*, i.e., "there can be only one."[1] Dog breeders do not agree. Do you?

Problems of engineering design Measures of performance for engineering design are usually multiple and conflicting when compared to the "ideal design." For example, engineers are often interested in minimizing both weight and cost but encounter the dilemma that lighter materials are typically more expensive than heavier ones. Therefore, frequently a compromise results between the weight and cost of a given engineering part.

---

[1]Quoted more fully in Sec. 1-3.

Other criteria may also enter the picture: The objectives of weight and costs are minimized with respect to given spatial limitations (maximum diameter, minimum length), required safety factors, etc.

Also, different importance may be assigned to weight and cost from design to design and from designer to designer. The exclusive minimization of weight or the exclusive minimization of costs would be an extreme case. Such situations, where one criterion is so dominant that the other criterion can actually be removed from analysis, are infrequent under normal economic circumstances. They occur mostly under the conditions of war, emergency, or embargo. Then single-objective optimization becomes desirable: the cheapest, the fastest, the most effective, the largest, or some other similar single criterion becomes most useful for resolving conflicts. It is then also that industrial designs become prevalently either very cheap or of very high quality, depending on their particular purpose of usage.

Dr. Norman Hilberry, professor of nuclear engineering at the University of Arizona and previously director of Argonne National Laboratory, puts it most succinctly: "All solutions in engineering are compromises."[1] Engineers are accustomed to studying a system as a whole, in all its dimensions. They work with a time scale and costs, and they look not for perfection but for the best compromise.

Management of fisheries Management of fisheries is not guided by the single goal of ensuring the continuation of the fish stocks and their yields. Fisheries are now viewed as multipurpose enterprises, providing a multitude of economic, recreational, and social benefits. The multiplicity of management objectives has been explicitly anchored in the Fishery Conservation and Management Act (FCMA), Public Law 94-265, passed by Congress in 1976 to prevent future overexploitation of present fisheries and to encourage the development of underutilized fisheries.

The FCMA calls on each fishery to produce the amount of fish, which would, among other objectives, achieve:

1. The greatest overall benefit to the nation in terms of
   a. Food production
   b. Recreational opportunities
2. The maximum sustained yield, modified by the following factors:
   a. Economic: minimize cost, promote efficiency
   b. Social: adhere to conservation rules, promote recreational utilization
   c. Ecological: maintain biological balance

The FCMA requires regional management councils to develop management plans on the basis of these multiple objectives. No single methodology would help to reconcile the conflicts among objectives or determine plans objectively.

In addition to multiple objectives the FCMA contains imprecise, nonnum-

[1]*University of Arizona News Bulletin*, 1978.

erical statements about objectives. "Promote," "insure," "on the average," "overall," and similar "fuzzy" expressions are used in setting the goals.

National economy Multiple objectives appear not only on the microlevel of business and management decision making—individuals, groups, firms, and corporations—but also at the level of macroeconomic policy making.

Current economic theory does not provide for multiplicity of objectives: Objectives are treated either separately, one at a time, or through an abstract concoction called the "aggregate social welfare function." Neither approach is compatible with social and economic reality; both approaches are incapable of addressing multiple economic goals simultaneously.

This state of economic theory is in direct conflict with the needs of governmental decision makers. President Carter, in his 1978 message to Congress on the state of the economy, said,

> The problems we face today are more complex and difficult than those of an earlier era. We cannot concentrate just on inflation, or just on unemployment, or just on deficits in the Federal budget or our international payments. Nor can we act in isolation from other countries. We must deal with all of these problems simultaneously and on a worldwide basis.

Carter said that he has been guided by four objectives for the United States economy:

1. *Employment:* Continue to move steadily toward a high-employment economy in which the benefits of prosperity are widely shared.
2. *Economic growth:* Rely principally on the private sector to lead the economic expansion and to create new jobs for a growing labor force.
3. *Inflation:* Contain and reduce the rate of inflation as we move toward a more fully employed economy.
4. *International harmony:* Act in ways that contribute to the health of the world economy.

President Carter's $500 billion budget for 1979 reflected his intent to strike the best compromise among such disparate and often noncommensurate objectives. Different social constituencies—business, labor, consumers, blacks, etc.—are likely to be critical of such budgets, as each group prefers that only one objective, its own, be given the highest priority.

Carter's 1979 budget projected a real growth rate of 5 percent, an inflation rate of 5 percent, and an unemployment rate of 5 percent. These projections turned out to be incompatible with a bleaker economic reality. One cannot keep switching between the goals in a preemptive fashion. Bringing the three rates down simultaneously not only requires patience, prudence, and wisdom but also presents an ultimate challenge to policy makers and economic theorists.

Marine environmental protection The Federal Water Pollution Control Act accorded the U.S. Coast Guard responsibility and enforcement authority for the protection of the marine environment from discharges of oil and other hazardous materials. The Marine Environmental Protection program was established by the Coast Guard in 1971. The Coast Guard, see Harrald et al. (1978), also established twelve criteria corresponding to its new environmental protection duties:[1]

1. The number of liquid bulk transfer operations involving oil and hazardous substances monitored per period
2. The number of tankships boarded per period
3. The number of barges boarded per period
4. The number of daily daylight water patrols of essential harbor areas per period
5. The number of daily night water patrols of essential harbor areas per period
6. The number of waterfront facilities spot-checked each month
7. The number of waterfront facilities inspected every 6 months
8. The number of waterfront facilities to be surveyed once every 2 years
9. The number of monitors sent to the scene of oil or hazardous substance discharge
10. The number of polluting discharges per period where the Coast Guard is responsible for providing an on-scene coordinator
11. The number of reported polluting discharges per period to which a Coast Guard representative is sent
12. The number of worker-hours in pursuit of a public education program per period

These criteria guide Coast Guard activities subject to constraints on personnel, vehicles, and boats. The criteria are approximately ordered in terms of their relative importance or priorities.

Multiple criteria in business   Multiplicity of criteria occurs in almost every area of business decision making and operations. Examples are numerous and more straightforward than those listed so far. They appear in accounting, finance, operations management, marketing, manpower planning, personnel selection, etc. We shall only sketch some typical situations. By now, the reader should be able to appreciate the multiplicity involved quite readily.

A *break-even analysis* usually deals with one particular product. But that product is typically part of a portfolio of products. A multiproduct break-even analysis would lead naturally to decision making within the framework of conflicting break-even points. In *budgeting*, the multiple criteria may include profits, sales revenues, number of worker-hours, number of people hired, departmental budgets, and so on. Criteria in *audit sampling* decisions include error rate, dollar-value error rate, number of errors remaining, dollar value of unchecked accounts, and dollar value of errors remaining. *Consulting and*

---

[1]Harrald et al. 1978, p. 735.

public accounting firms are concerned about billing rates, gross fees, management-staff ratio, net income, personnel working hours, distribution of clients, overtime, etc.

Working capital management involves profits, cash balances, current ratio and quick ratio, acid test ratio, debt to total assets, bank deposit balances, legal reserves requirements, etc. Bank *assets management* includes federal banking regulations, adequate safety, loan portfolio attributes, securities portfolio attributes, target level of earnings, and many other criteria.

Capital budgeting models represent one of the richest sources of multiple criteria: budget allocation targets, net present value, income growth, cash inflow, liquidity, total cash flow, etc. Similarly, *acquisition investments* can be judged with respect to the internal ratio of return on all acquisition investments, present worth of future revenues, growth potential, amount of debt financing, etc.

Purchasing decisions involve the total cost of purchased items, company requirements, minimum and maximum purchases placed with any supplier, unit requirements per supplier, etc. *Aggregate production planning* is concerned with hirings, layoffs, overtimes, idle times, inventories, shortages, production rates, size of the labor force, job rotation, costs, productive hours available, etc. Similar multicriterion structures can be detected in *scheduling, transportation, network planning*, and other areas of operations management.

Media planning concerns budget overexpense, exposure limits, desired exposure levels for geographic areas, population groups, economic segments, and total exposure. *Marketing planning* deals with the rate of return on investment, wages and salaries, promotional expenditures, annual market growth, volume of advertising, special campaigns, etc. Similarly, problems of *sales effort allocation, equal employment opportunity manpower planning, training programs, manpower assignment, project assignment, aggregate manpower planning*, and others are characterized by multiplicity of criteria.

We could go on and on with such examples. But at this point we just want the reader to acquire the sense of how pervasive multiple criteria are in our decision-making reality. We shall return to specific applications in appropriate later sections.

BIBLIOGRAPHICAL NOTE

In our Introduction we have presented several examples of multiple criteria, goals, and objectives. Mostly we have concentrated on situations where the multiplicity might be less obvious—disguised perhaps—difficult to detect or to quantify because they are burdened with incompatible and incommensurable criteria and qualitative features that are shrouded or hazy. We shall now present other sources where additional examples and applications can be found.

Keeney and Raiffa (1976), in addition to their introductory examples, include about eighty pages of *illustrative applications*, all related to multiple criteria. They include air-pollution control, school budget allocation, fire department operations, evaluation of computer systems, siting of nuclear power facilities, blood-bank operations, sewage sludge disposal, job selection, forest pest management, and many others, plus an extensive case study on airport development.

Another source of good examples is the book on analysis of public systems edited by Drake, Keeney, and Morse (1972). Similarly, Ignizio (1976) and Lee (1972) contain extensive sections on applications of goal programming and areas of future research. Lin (1980) has begun a comprehensive, continuing survey of applications of goal programming. Other examples are usually scattered—one example, one article—and listing them would be prohibitive. The reader is advised to consult any of the comprehensive bibliographies on multiple-criteria decision making: Hwang and Masud (1979), Fishburn (1978), Farquhar (1977), Keeney and Raiffa (1976), Zeleny (1976 and 1973) and that compiled for this text.

American Kennel Club: *The Complete Dog Book*, Howell Book House, New York, 1975, pp. 609–610.

Drake, A. W., R. L. Keeney, and P. M. Morse (eds.): *Analysis of Public Systems*, M.I.T., Cambridge, Mass., 1972.

Drucker, P. F.: *Management: Tasks, Responsibilities, Practices*, Harper & Row, New York, 1974, p. 100.

Farquhar, P. H.: "A Survey of Multiattribute Utility Theory and Applications," in M. K. Starr and M. Zeleny (eds.), *Multiple Criteria Decision Making*, TIMS Studies in the Management Sciences, vol. 6, North-Holland Publishing, Amsterdam, 1977, pp. 59–89.

Fishburn, P. C.: "A Survey of Multiattribute/Multicriterion Evaluation Theories," in S. Zionts (ed.), *Multiple Criteria Problem Solving*, Springer-Verlag, New York, 1978, pp. 181–224.

Harrald, J., et al.: "A Note on the Limitations of Goal Programming as Observed in Resource Allocation for Marine Environmental Protection," *Naval Research Logistics Quarterly*, vol. 25, no. 4, December 1978, pp. 733–739.

Hwang, C. L., and A. Masud: *Multiple Objective Decision Making—Methods and Applications*, Springer-Verlag, New York, 1979, pp. 310–351.

Ignizio, J. P.: *Goal Programming and Extensions*, Heath, Lexington, Mass., 1976, pp. 193–219.

Kaufmann, A.: *Methods and Models of Operations Research*, Prentice-Hall, New York, 1963.

Keeney, R. L., and H. Raiffa: *Decisions with Multiple Objectives*, Wiley, New York, 1976, pp. 354–472.

Krischer, J. P.: "An Annotated Bibliography of Decision Analytic Applications to Health Care," *Operations Research*, vol. 28, no. 1, 1980, pp. 97–113.

Lee, S. M.: *Goal Programming for Decision Analysis*, Auerbach Publishers, Philadelphia, 1972, pp. 191–350.

Lin, W. T.: "A Survey of Goal Programming Applications," *Omega*, vol. 8, no. 1, 1980, pp. 115–117.

Zeleny, M.: "MCDM Bibliography—1975," in M. Zeleny (ed.), *Multiple Criteria Decision Making: Kyoto 1975*, Springer-Verlag, New York, 1976, pp. 291–321.

———: "A Selected Bibliography of Works Related to Multiple Criteria Decision Making," in J. L. Cochrane and M. Zeleny (eds.), *Multiple Criteria Decision Making*, University of South Carolina Press, Columbia, 1973, pp. 779–793.

In the Introduction, we describe a variety of multidimensional situations in order to stimulate the reader's way of seeing social, economic, and business realities. Society wants business to conserve energy, reduce pollution, improve occupational safety, help solve the problems of cities, support worthy causes, enrich jobs. The difficult task of balancing such conflicting objectives falls on the shoulders of middle and top management. The new business graduate must be aware of and able to deal with such demands.

In this chapter we provide the language and basic concepts of multiple-criteria decision making (MCDM). Concepts of criteria, goals, objectives, and attributes are explained and carefully defined. Because the sources of purposeful behavior are the basic needs, drives, and motivations, we take a short excursion into the theory of human needs. It is often argued that human needs and wants form a hierarchy. For example, a farmer's uses for corn might be arranged in the following order of importance: food, seeds for next season, grain for brewing alcoholic beverages, fodder, birdseed. We attempt to show that such wants, even though they are of different importance in different situations, are more simultaneous than sequentially hierarchical.

Various types of decision making—computation, judgment, compromise, and inspiration—are defined and described. We argue that, by definition, making a decision means balancing multiple objectives. The reader is invited to contemplate a technological problem (with a single objective) versus an economic problem (with multiple objectives) in Sec. 1-2. A basic knowledge of utility theory and indifference curves will facilitate the reading.

After discussing the role of profit among the multiplicity of business objectives and criteria of performance, we present three examples of multiobjective conflict which are quite structured and can be analyzed quantitatively. After completing Chap. 1, the reader should be able to differentiate between single-objective and multiobjective situations in any area of personal interest.

MULTIPLE OBJECTIVES OF INDIVIDUALS
AND ORGANIZATIONS

Dear Sir,

In the affair of so much importance to you, wherein you ask my advice, I cannot, for want of sufficient premises, advise you what to determine, but if you please I will tell you how. When those difficult cases occur, they are difficult, chiefly because while we have them under consideration, all the reasons pro and con are not present to the mind at the same time; but sometimes one set present themselves, and at other times another, the first being out of sight. Hence the various purposes or informations that alternatively prevail, and the uncertainty that perplexes us. To get over this, my way is to divide half a sheet of paper by a line into two columns; writing over the one Pro, and over the other Con. Then, during three or four days consideration, I put down under the different heads short hints of the different motives, that at different times occur to me, for or against the measure. When I have thus got them all together in one view, I endeavor to estimate their respective weights; and where I find two, one on each side, that seem equal, I strike them both out. If I find a reason pro equal to some two reasons con, I strike out the three. If I judge some two reasons con, equal to three reasons pro, I strike out the five; and thus proceeding I find at length where the balance lies; and if, after a day or two of further consideration, nothing new that is of importance occurs on either side, I come to a determination accordingly. And, though the weight of the reasons cannot be taken with the precision of algebraic quantities, yet when each is thus considered, separately and comparatively, and the whole lies before me, I think I can judge better, and am less liable to make a rash step, and in fact I have found great advantage from this kind of equation, and what might be called moral or prudential algebra.

Wishing sincerely that you may determine for the best, I am ever, my dear friend, yours most affectionately.

B. Franklin

The letter by Benjamin Franklin was written to Joseph Priestley in 1772. His "moral or prudential algebra" represents one of the first systematic methodologies for solving problems characterized by multiple criteria. Franklin was very much aware of the multiplicity of aspects which must be taken into account if one is to judge better. Concentrating on only one or another aspect is what makes problem solving difficult, because "all the reasons pro and con are not present to the mind at the same time."

In Franklin's letter we find most of the ingredients of multiple-criteria decision making: the weighting of attribute importance, the trading off of one attribute for another, the notion of the balanced solution, even the interaction between human judgment and a formal model. Although one cannot capture human preferences and approximate reasoning with the precision of algebraic quantities, there is a positive enhancement and amplification of judgment when one is able to formulate and use an appropriate "prudential algebra."

Our purpose, the purpose of this book, is very similar to Franklin's. Although we cannot make our readers' decisions for them, by describing the decision process itself we can show our readers, if they are interested, how to go about making a decision.

1-1 ATTRIBUTES, OBJECTIVES, AND GOALS

Descriptions of human decision making are replete with interchangeable terms, the lack of a standard terminology, and few widely accepted definitions. People talk about decision "*criteria*," but also about "yardsticks," "measures of effectiveness," "standards," "gauges," "principles," "norms," "rules," and even "models." They pursue and strive for "*goals*," "targets," "aims," "aspirations," "objects," "*objectives*," "ends," "intents," "purposes," "missions," and "ambitions." They describe and classify the objects of reality in terms of their "characteristics," "aspects," "properties," "qualities," "distinctions," "*attributes*," "traits," and "cues." In considering or carrying out pursuits, people contemplate different "objects of choice," "options," "actions," "*alternatives*," "items," "strategies," "means," and so on.

Why is there this abundance of overlapping terminology? Partly because decision making—certainly one of the oldest and most essential activities for satisfying human needs and desires—has been studied systematically only in the last few decades. The multiplicity of decision criteria, in particular, has received serious attention only since the late sixties. (See the short history of MCDM in Sec. 2-2.) We are in an important, complex, new discipline whose terminology has not yet settled. And although we do not wish to prescribe pedantic terminological norms (a sure sign of scientific and intellectual exhaustion), we shall attempt to reveal at least some order in the apparent chaos.

Our preferred terms are indicated in italics in the first paragraph of this section. Even among our preferences, however, isn't there some overlap? The reader may have felt in earlier pages that the terms "attributes," "objectives," and "goals"—and perhaps "criteria" as well—were synonymous. But as we use the first three terms, a major distinguishing characteristic is the degree to which they embody human needs and desires. The fourth term is a general term encompassing the other three. Let us explain:

Attributes This term refers to descriptors of objective reality. They may be actual objective traits, or they may be subjectively assigned traits, but they are perceived as characteristics of objects in the "outside" world. (They include our own descriptions of ourselves.) Thus, although they cannot be separated from the decision maker's values and model of reality, they can be identified and measured in relative independence from the decision maker's needs or desires.

For example, one's choice among lovers might be described in terms of height, weight, coloring, age, wealth, and other attributes of the kind that are plainly objective: An age of 65 is an age of 65, and neither the decision maker nor the object of desire can do anything about it (one must distinguish between the attributes "age" and "appearance of age"). Other attributes are more subjective: intellect, beauty, figure, companionship, social status, tastefulness, and so on. Less well defined, these attributes are less precisely measurable than objective ones. Despite some difficulties, however, it will be possible to measure or assess the attribute levels of all available alternative lovers as the first step in the decision-making process, and to do this in relative independence from the decision maker's personal desires and needs.

Objectives After attributes are described and measured, the decision maker must decide which attributes, at what levels, to maximize or minimize. It is here, where the decision maker's needs and desires enter, that we can speak of objectives. From a given set of alternative lovers, will the decision maker choose the tallest, the youngest, or the most amiable? That is, will the decision maker choose to maximize height, minimize age, or maximize amiableness? To answer such a question is to specify an objective.

Objectives are closely identifiable with a decision maker's needs and desires; they represent *directions* of improvement or preference along individual attributes or complexes of attributes. There are only two directions: more and less, i.e., maximize and minimize. Thus, height in itself is an attribute but finding the tallest among the choices, or maximizing height, is an objective. Objectives are not themselves attributes, but they derive from one or more attributes.

Let us take another example: The decision maker is selecting a new automobile. The attributes of automobiles are such nonsubjective features as horsepower, weight, price, and color, but also subjective factors such as sex appeal, styling and status image. All these attributes are more or less measurable: in foot-pounds of work per second; pounds or kilograms; dollars or yen; hue, lightness and saturation; but also in grades of intensity, ordinal rankings, or even such scales as "yes–no," "wow–oh, well–hmmm," or "take it–leave it." Maximization or minimization of any of these attributes constitutes an objective, for example, to maximize horsepower or to minimize gas mileage. Many interesting objectives derive from aggregates of attributes; for example, the objective of maximizing prestige may derive from combined attributes of price, horsepower, scarcity, group affiliation, etc. Other objectives deriving from multiple attributes could be maximum security, minimum maintenance costs, and maximum comfort.

To repeat, an attribute becomes an objective when it is assigned a purpose, a direction of desirability or improvement. "To maximize horsepower" is an objective, a direction of search related to the attribute horsepower.

Keeney and Raiffa (1976) provide additional examples of attributes as derived from objectives: The objective "reduce sulfur dioxide emissions" may be measured by an attribute, "tons of sulfur dioxide emitted per year." The objective "minimize total transit time for mail" is based on a rather obvious attribute, "transit time in days from sender to receiver." Although an attribute can be measured rather precisely, an objective involves a change in the attribute and so may be more difficult to measure satisfactorily.

Attributes are inputs for postulating one's objectives. There is an implied hierarchy in this relationship: One or more attributes can form an objective, and two or more objectives can form a higher-level objective. Keeney and Raiffa give a good example of this hierarchy: The objective "improve the well-being of the residents" can be viewed as composed of lower-level objectives, for example, "reduce the emission of pollutants within the city" and "improve the citizens' attitude toward the city's air quality." The first of these subobjectives can be further broken down to "reduce sulfur dioxide emissions," "reduce emissions of nitrogen oxides," and "reduce particulate emissions." These latter three objectives can each be measured in terms of an attribute, for example, "tons of nitrogen oxide emitted per year." (Keeney and Raiffa 1976, p. 32).

In a hierarchical pyramid such as this, the lower objectives (subobjectives) are the "attributes" for the higher objectives. If there is only a single superobjective at the highest level, such as maximization of an overall utility or desirability, then all its inputs (attributes and lower-level objectives) can be regarded as attributes. In such a case, the measurement of the attributes becomes the primary concern. We should then use a term such as "multiattribute utility *measurement*" rather than "decision making": Making a decision requires at least two objectives, as we shall discuss later in this section and also in Sec. 2-5. Problems of multiattribute utility theory (MAUT) are more fully addressed in Chap. 12.

An objective indicates the "direction" of improvement. Very often people specify some particular level of achievement for their objective (or even for attributes). This level serves as a point of reference—a limit or an aspiration. It is to be attained, surpassed, or not exceeded. That is, we do not look for the youngest or the smartest, but we specify that our object of desire should not be more than 6 ft in height, should weigh between 95 and 120 lb, and should be 18 years of age.

The achievement of a goal can be judged per se, regardless of the given set of alternatives. Either there are some lovers who satisfy the goals or there are none. But it is not the same with objectives: An objective can be achieved only with reference to a given set of alternatives. And given a set of alternatives, they can always be achieved; there is always a maximum or a minimum of a given attribute.

Goals Goals are fully identifiable with a decision maker's needs and desires. They are a priori determined, specific values or levels defined in terms of either attributes or objectives. They can be precise, desired levels of attainment or more fuzzily delineated or vague ideals. "Maximizing gas mileage" is a well-stated *objective* in the search for an automobile. "Achieving gas mileage of 26 miles per gallon" is a clearly stated *goal* indicating a specific reference value for that objective.

Reaching the moon by 1970 was a goal, reaching the summit of Mount Everest is a goal, realizing at least 16 percent return on our investment is a goal. Reaching the top of Everest in the shortest possible time is an objective.

Thus, while the distinction between attributes and objectives can sometimes become blurred due to their hierarchical nature, goals refer quite unambiguously to particular target levels of achievement which can be defined in terms of both attributes and objectives.

The reader should now be able to judge what represents the subject matter of such methodologies as multi*attribute* utility theory, *goal* programming, multi*objective* programming, or management by *objectives*.

But what about the term used in the title of our book, *Multiple*-Criteria *Decison Making*? What are criteria?

Criteria Criteria are measures, rules, and standards that guide decision making. Since decision making is conducted by selecting or formulating different attributes, objectives, or goals, all three categories can be referred to as criteria. That is, criteria are all those attributes, objectives, or goals which have been judged relevant in a given decision situation by a particular decision maker (individual or group).

Thus, the term "*multiple-criteria* decision making" (MCDM), indicates a concern with the general class of problems that involve *multiple attributes, objectives, and goals*. "Multi*attribute* utility theory" reflects a preoccupation with *how* to construct objectives from attributes, or more specifically, how to assess a superobjective of utility maximization. "Multi*objective* programming" deals mostly with different objectives and does not attempt to regard them as inputs for forming higher-level objective functions. "*Goal* programming" reflects a concern with the conditions of attainment of particular, prespecified aspiration levels.

All are good terms. And, given the methodological differences they express, it makes sense to talk about goals, objectives, and attributes as more or less specific designations or labels within the general area of our concern: decision making under multiple *criteria*.

It is one thing to acknowledge the existence of different criteria, to classify them, count them, or use them. It is quite another to understand why people use them, what their origins are, and why different sets of criteria are used under the same or different circumstances.

One could ask, Where do all the criteria come from? Why don't we use only one at a time?

Criteria derive from both basic and evolved human needs and values. Because humans need food, they use such criteria as digestibility, taste, accessibility, nutritional value, and safety in classifying the items of reality into "food" and "other things."

Human needs are many and varied. There are basic needs, for example, breathing, eating, and drinking. There are needs for more situation-dependent and individual-specific materialities, such as the needs for sexual gratification, clothing, shelter, and transportation. There are also evolved needs, which are psychologically or socially grounded but no less varied or urgent: the needs for group identification, love, a feeling of usefulness, security, self-esteem, etc. These needs sometimes take precedence before their more "primary" counterparts.

Personally I believe that the *sense of being useful* is ultimately a more important need than any material, physiological, or psychological achievement; it is probably even more important than the need for freedom. Sidney Hook (1967) states four central values that guide, or should guide, human choices: (1) The preservation of life, (2) vocation or calling, (3) responsibility and shared power, and (4) beautifying the natural and social environment. These values are interrelated; they involve each other.

Excluding such human values from economics makes it "value-free," objective, rational, and normative. Value, in economics, is an exchange ratio or trade-off which is usually measured unidimensionally, by money or "utility." But the problem of making a rational decision between alternatives in the real world can rarely be reduced to the problem of ascertaining, by means of straightforward mathematical calculation, which possibility is assocated with the maximum of some single index (utility) of value. Thus, stressing the multiplicity of criteria represents an attempt to avoid using a common measure of value when the choice involves heterogeneous items. Multidimensional values are often nondivisible, and they satisfy needs or interests that may not be substitutable for each other.

In this sense, the objectives of this book are rather modest. We do not claim to provide a deep insight into the functioning of human values, needs, and desires in decision making. We simply point out the multiplicity of criteria which they engender and acknowledge their simultaneity.

In a personal letter Roland Fischer asserts, "human values do not constitute a hierarchy," then provides a beautiful allegory from Raymundus Lullus (born about 1234 in Mallorca) as an illustration. I cannot resist sharing this allegory with my readers. In what may be the first description of the interdependency of values, Lullus personifies the three powers of the soul—memory, understanding, and will—as three noble and beautiful damsels standing atop a high mountain, interacting as follows:

> The first remembers that which the second understands and the third wills; the second understands that which the first remembers and the third wills; the third wills that which the first remembers and the second understands.

In order to work with the multiplicity of criteria, we have to grasp the simultaneity of human needs. To do that, we shall turn to Maslow's widely quoted theory of human needs and attempt a critical reevaluation of it.

1-1.1 Maslow's Hierarchy of Needs

Human motivations, objectives, decisions, and actions are often rationalized by invoking *Maslow's dogma* (1962, 1970), which states that basic human needs are organized in a hierarchy of relative prepotency. That is, as listed below, human needs can be ordered according to their decreasing urgency for satisfaction:

1. Physiological
2. Security (safety)
3. Belonging (affection)
4. Esteem
5. Self-fulfillment (self-actualization)

Maslow's dogma implies that human needs are pursued in a *sequential* order, i.e., the "higher" needs emerge only after the "lower" needs have been sufficiently satisfied. Self-actualization then becomes the ultimate, supreme human need or aspiration.

However, the obvious "prepotency" of the basic prerequisites of life—breathing, eating, drinking, etc.—does not provide a sufficient groundwork for erecting a pyramidal superstructure of needs. There is no apparent hierarchy of human needs. Humans pursue a wide variety of wants, goals, drives, and desires concurrently and seek their balanced, simultaneous satisfaction. The complex of interacting needs is highly interdependent and evolved, mutually consistent, and complementary in all its components. Such a complex system of parallel, concurrent motivations is only poorly represented by the image of a well-greased shifting of gears from lower to higher needs.

The "higher" human needs are in fact organically enmeshed with the "lower" ones. In addition to the need for security, the need for belonging makes people seek common shelters and organized groupings. In addition to physiological needs, the need for esteem and recognition motivates hunters to become more efficient and skillful in securing food for a group. The need for self-fulfillment made hungry, insecure, and unloved "primitives" paint supremely beautiful images in the cave of Altamira. These paintings are full-fledged works of art, radiating a sense of power and depth of experience which is rarely surpassed or even recognized by modern "self-fulfilled" artists. Although the purposes and functions of primeval art are many, an "artistic surplus" seems to arise from the sheer joy of creation, the satisfaction of aesthetic needs, and the clear desire for self-expression.

It is well known that prisoners, labor camp inmates, and other people who are deprived of their "primary" needs turn to gardening, study, drawing, writing, poetry and the acquisition of new skills. There is an old Czech story about a man named Dalibor: blinded, starved, cold, and detained in a tower for life, he taught himself to play the violin. Hence the saying, "Misery taught Dalibor to play a violin."

Difficult though it is to accept, the "higher" needs often come first. Is our inability to see the concurrence and mutual dependency of human needs an inescapable sign of our own "self-attainment"?

Many hungry and lonely people have striven for their self-fulfillment while the well-fed and secure ones only indulged further in satisfying their "primary" needs. Do contemporary "self-actualized" executives and public officials achieve something higher than the deprived craftsmen, artisans, writers, and poets of the past? Does not the self-fulfillment (or self-satisfaction) of one's older years reflect simply the realization that there is no self-actualization in the end? that self-fulfillment derives from the *process* of attaining, and so it increases with the intensity of the pursuit? and that the attainment of anything excludes self-attainment by definition?

Concurrent needs are often *perceived* as being in a continuous state of conflict. Thus the frequent references to multiple *conflicting* objectives or criteria. But the needs themselves are not in conflict. On the contrary, their complementarity, synergy, and symbiosis are one of the most beautiful experiences of human life. But objectives as a whole may be in conflict with the means of their pursuit, for natural, economic, technological, and social constraints do not allow the full and simultaneous attainment of multiple objectives. As we reduce these various constraints, we expand our needs and, consequently, we reinstate a sense of conflict. We strive as much to sustain as to contain the conflict.

Our needs depend on the courses of action open to us; in themselves, they are neither primary nor secondary. Needs are shaped by potential actions and, in turn, determine what actions are taken. The need to act is itself one of our basic motives. Not all acts are purposeful, need-satisfying, or goal-directed. Cognitive acts, for example, often function independently, apart from mechanistic motivations or a priori goals. An option may be taken because "it is there" and rationalized or explained later. Its subsequent adornment with purposeful evaluations, utility measurements, and logical rationalizations is usually ad hoc.

Let us digress briefly to describe the multiplicity of human motives among one group of decision makers: holders of the Master of Business Administration degree.

1-1.2 Multiple Motivations: Needs and Desires of MBAs

Liebling (1978) conducted a survey of about 2,000 MBAs to study their motivational patterns. He found that these university-educated managers are often pursuing different and multiple objectives in their careers. At least six distinct types of MBAs were identified: (1) tranquil conformists, (2) individualistic entrepreneurs, (3) moralistic enthusiasts, (4) aloof conservatives, (5) active power pursuers, and (6) money seekers. Members of these six groups derive their goals and objectives from at least fifteen motivational factors, or needs.

These motivational factors and their relative strengths in affecting personal and career objectives of the six MBA types are summarized in Table 1-1. The numbers within the table indicate the strength of motivational impact on the following scale:

5 = very high   4 = high   3 = average   2 = low   1 = very low

The strongest motivational factor(s) affecting each of the individual groups are marked by appropriately placed circles.

Knowing one's sources of motivation, needs, and desires can lead to a better understanding of personal goal formation and the rationale behind one's objectives, whether they be career, management, or personal. One of the least expected findings of the survey was that the money seekers did not end up with the highest median income; the active power pursuers did. It appears that money is best pursued in a roundabout fashion, not head-on. We shall discuss this phenomenon further in Sec. 1-3, in connection with the problem of viewing profit as the sole criterion of business enterprise. Very often the highest profits have been realized by companies pursuing several other, seemingly unrelated objectives; see especially Fig. 1-4 and 1-5.

Liebling's study found also that moralistic enthusiasts are mostly under 30, represent the largest and possibly an expanding portion of the MBAs, and find their work uplifting and exciting. Observe, in Table 1-1, that members of this group also derive their objectives from the largest number of simultaneous motivational factors. They rank prestige, achievement, affiliation, identity, life structuring, and moral fulfillment among their strongest motives. They also pay a high attention to money. This group of people is most likely to deal with a large number of multiple objectives and goals in their managerial efforts. They would probably find *Multiple Criteria Decision Making* most relevant and helpful.

1-1.3 Basic Modes of Deciding

Since we have already discussed some classifications of decision criteria, we may as well go all the way and introduce a useful taxonomy of different patterns or modes of deciding itself.

Criteria of choice can either be well defined and quantitatively measurable, or they can be mostly qualitative, poorly measurable, and laden with uncer-

Table 1-1 Motivational patterns

Total % in sample: MBA types: Needs and desires	7.8% Tranquil conformists	15.2% Individualistic entrepreneurs	20.2% Moralistic enthusiasts	17.5% Aloof conservatives	19.3% Active power pursuers	20.0% Money seekers
Prestige (high status, famous organization, fame)	1	2	⑤	3	3	3
Achievement (problem solving, challenging tasks)	1	3	⑤	3	3	3
Affiliation (congenial colleagues, group spirit, personal relations)	1	3	⑤	3	3	3
Identity (self-definition, self-expression)	1	3	⑤	3	3	3
Power (responsibility, giving orders, making decisions)	1	3	3	3	⑤	3
Money	3	3	4	1	3	⑤
Entrepreneurship (self-employed, own business)	3	⑤	3	1	4	4
Detachment (emotional separation from one's job)	⑤	3	1	3	3	3
Refuge (sanctuary, escape)	3	1	4	3	2	⑤
Life structuring (structure, order, organization)	1	3	⑤	3	3	3
Moral fulfillment (justify one's work as a moral good)	1	3	⑤	3	3	3
Conservatism (permanent employment, aversion to change)	⑤	1	3	④	3	3
Conformity (conform to demands and expectations)	⑤	1	3	3	2	3
Tranquility (calm, slow, predictable environment)	⑤	3	3	3	1	3
Work activity (need to be active)	1	3	3	3	⑤	3

tainty. In the first case, the alternatives of choice are well described, their consequences are measurable, and their impacts understood. In the second case, the alternatives are only imprecisely characterized by the criteria, their outcomes are uncertain, and the cause-effect relationships are unclear.

A decision maker (in certain cases) may be quite certain of his or her preferences and able to express them as a single, dominant criterion. Alternatively, the decision maker's preferences may have many sides and be describable only through multiple criteria of choice.

The decision maker's tasks of deciding can thus be classified into four basic groups or modes:

1. Clearly defined, certain alternatives, which are evaluated in terms of a single criterion
2. Poorly defined, uncertain alternatives, which are evaluated in terms of a single criterion
3. Clearly defined, certain alternatives, which are evaluated in terms of multiple criteria
4. Poorly defined, uncertain alternatives, which are evaluated in terms of multiple criteria.

Following J. D. Thompson (1964), we may characterize these four modes of decision making respectively as computation, judgment, compromise, and inspiration, as in Table 1-2.

Computation is a typical mode of conventional operations research and decision analysis. A well-defined and quantitatively measurable criterion is used to assign each alternative a single number, and then the alternative with the best value is computed or searched out. The following are examples of problems that respond well to computational analysis: Which of the given production mixes is characterized by the lowest cost? What is the shortest route from a given production facility to a given warehouse? Which investment project is characterized by the maximum net present value of its stream of future returns?

After the decision maker has stated an objective (for example, to minimize cost), the analyst can complete the task quite independently and the decision maker does not have to supply further inputs. Measurement of costs and math-

Table 1-2

		Criteria of choice	
		Single	Multiple
Description of alternatives	Certain	Computation	Compromise
	Uncertain	Judgment	Inspiration

ematical search for the minimum-cost alternative are all that is required. Data analysis, accounting, and econometrics, combined with computer-based numerical algorithms of operations research, are characteristic methodological tools of this type of decision analysis.

Judgment is the dominant concern of social judgment theory and multi-attribute utility theory (these methodologies are discussed in Chaps. 12 and 13). The objective is usually single-dimensional, clearly stated, but poorly measurable. Because of the objective's poor measurability, these approaches often resort to empirical observation and evaluation of a large number of decision situations and attempt a relatively precise formulation through statistical analysis.

Characteristic objectives might be to maximize utility, maximize the quality of life, or to minimize employee dissatisfaction. Since typically we are uncertain which alternative will actually achieve the required level of a given criterion, direct human judgment of the causal relationships between alternatives and outcomes is required. Social judgment theory relies on the statistical analysis of a large number of actual or contrived judgments to describe this relationship more reliably. Multiattribute utility theory resorts to direct questioning or interrogation of the decision maker.

Choosing a candidate for political office is another example of judgment; the preferred alternative may be clear (the "best" person), but the causal relationship between this alternative and the required outcome is uncertain.

Compromise involves multiple criteria: One balances well-defined competing objectives—for example, in choosing a production mix with respect to both cost and production time. Attainment of shorter time is possible only at higher cost. In contrast to the problems of judgment previously discussed, here the causation may be quite clear and each alternative may be easily described in terms of both time and cost; nonetheless, a decision can be made only by some form of compromise.

Such situations fall in the domain of MCDM, especially of its relatively technical versions, such as linear multiobjective programming or goal programming. Computer-based algorithms are now well developed, and some of them include a structured decision maker–analyst interface (see Sec. 10-6). One powerful computer package now being developed, subsumes conventional linear programming, linear multiobjective programming, multiparametric linear programming, preemptive and nonpreemptive versions of goal programming, compromise programming, and interactive programming under one computational routine (see App. B). All of these techniques are dealt with in this book. The package allows the user to employ each of these computational modes either separately or in a combination. As its full commercial development is completed, this computational routine will be able to take on large-scale problems, and it may replace most individual packages.

Each decision alternative is characterized by a multidimensional vector of numbers, and there is usually no prior attempt to reduce the problem to one of its single-dimensional variants. The first step is to identify a set of preferrable or "good" alternatives, and the second step is to reduce this set in a structured way. The decision maker generally remains responsible for making the final choice. Even if the objectives have been clearly identified and their measurement is reasonably reliable, the analyst cannot simply assume the decision maker's final responsibility. The decision maker, however, has the option to delegate parts or even the full task to the system, depending on his or her confidence in it and on the decision circumstances.

Inspiration or intuition represents the most common mode of decision making used at the highest executive levels. Typically the most complex strategic decisions involve a mixture of quantitative and qualitative multiple criteria as well as uncertain and only fuzzily defined causal relationships. Under such conditions it may be difficult to recognize even whether a compromise solution has been reached. Political and implementational issues dominate, and emphasis on human factors and their management is self-evident. Often the decision maker must invent a new alternative, create a new vision, or evolve a new image. Such creative problem solving requires rather heavy reliance upon inspiration and intuition.

Inspiration as a mode of decision making is receiving a great deal of attention within the field of MCDM. In combination with computer-based decision support systems (see for example the introductory book of that title by Keen and Morton, 1978), often accompanied by sophisticated graphic displays, MCDM methods strive to enhance and aid human intuition, not to replace it. Invention and generation of new alternatives become synonymous with decision making under these circumstances. The present book is therefore particularly concerned with the increasingly important issues of conflict dissolution, compromise management, fuzziness, decision dynamics, and creativity. Chapters 4 and 5, especially, address these issues in a nontraditional way.

In summary, the more conventional theories of decision analysis are typically involved with problems which belong in the right-hand column of Table 1-2. Within this column, progress and conceptual advancement generally proceed from top to bottom. The problems in the right-hand column have become the main domain of MCDM's new emerging methodologies. Again, progress and innovation seem to traverse the column from top to bottom.

The current shift of attention away from computation and toward inspiration simply indicates that scientific efforts, computer support, and data assessment are finally moving where they are needed most: from simpler to harder problems, from certain to less certain decision situations, from single to multiple criteria. It also indicates that operations research and management sciences are still young, are full of potential, and have the most rewarding applications ahead of them.

The reality of decision making is of course much more complex than our 2×2 table indicates. Only "models" of reality can be classified in this simple way. Rarely do we encounter problems that are purely computational or purely inspirational. Real problems involve and require *all* four modes of deciding. Computation, judgment, compromise, and inspiration are not independent or self-sufficient methodological entities but the necessary and complementary building blocks for a future synthesis of the art and science of managing human systems.

1-2. TECHNOLOGICAL VERSUS ECONOMIC PROBLEMS

> Reality is mobility, innovation; but our minds are molded to unmovable things. Reality is the sense of relative values, the sense of compromise. We persevere in our pattern of the absolute, of the dogmatic.
>
> Alain Peyrefitte
> *Le Mal français*

Peyrefitte's description of reality reflects the dilemma this book attempts to deal with: multiple objectives in human decision making. Individuals, groups, and organizations, in their decision-making efforts, pursue multiple objectives, set multiple goals, evaluate their options according to multiple criteria. As a consequence, they experience *conflict*. Conflict, both within oneself and with others, appears when one's multiple pursuits do not lead to *simultaneous* satisfaction or gratification.

Human beings want their cake and they want to eat it too. They want both quality and quantity; they call for higher incomes and more free time; they need profits as well as social expenditures, low inflation as well as high employment, and so on. Decision making, under such conditions, is characterized by incessant attempts at conflict resolution and the *simultaneous* attainment of goals.

Milton Friedman, recipient of the 1976 Nobel prize in economic science, emphasizes the role of a multiobjective framework of thought in economics:

> An economic problem exists whenever *scarce* means are used to satisfy *alternative* ends. If the means are not scarce, there is no problem at all; there is Nirvana. If the means are scarce but there is only a single end, the problem of how to use the means is a technological problem. No value judgments enter into its solution; only knowledge of physical and technical relationships. (Friedman 1962, p. 6)

To illustrate, suppose that given means (raw materials, skilled labor, energy, technical know-how) are used to build an automobile of maximum horsepower. This is a single-objective, purely technical problem. But suppose that the "best" automobile is desired. The concept of "best" will involve, under different circumstances and in varying degrees, not only horsepower, but also weight, size, safety, price, maneuverability, maintainability, depreciation rate, and possibly hundreds of other attributes and criteria. There is no longer a single end, no single criterion. Rather we are facing a *multiple-criteria decision-making problem*, or an *economic problem* according to Friedman's definition. Human value judgments, trade-off evaluations, and assessments of the importance of criteria now become an integral part of the problem.

Figures 1-1 and 1-2 will perhaps clarify the distinction between single- and

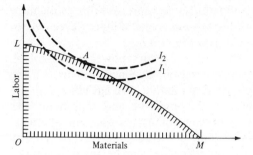

Figure 1-1 Technological problem.

multiple-objective decision making. Assume, for simplicity, only two types of scarce means: raw materials and skilled labor. These can be combined to produce automobiles of different attributes. Maximum availability of labor and materials is indicated by segments OL and OM respectively.

The curve LM indicates a *production-possibility frontier*. That is, combinations of labor and materials inside this curve are possible; those outside it are not. Thus, relating our discussion to Friedman's definitions, the size and shape of the shaded region indicate the nature of "scarcity" of means under given technological conditions. Suppose now that a single "end" or objective, the maximum-horsepower automobile, is represented by a family of indifference curves I_1, I_2, etc. Each curve represents those combinations of labor and materials which produce automobiles of the *same* horsepower. Maximization then corresponds to movement toward a "higher" indifference curve. Point A then corresponds to the maximum-horsepower automobile achievable under the given conditions of resource limitations. Finding such a solution A is a purely technological problem consisting of determining the proper objective function (maximization of horsepower) and searching through the shaded area for its maximum feasible value. No value judgment, no conflict, no decision making need enter the analysis.

Now suppose a second criterion, maximization of safety, that is represented by a second family of indifference curves J_1, J_2, etc. Each curve represents automobiles of the same safety. Figure 1-2 *a* combines both criteria, maximum horsepower and maximum safety, in a single picture.

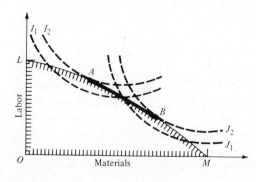

Figure 1-2a Economic problem in terms of inputs.

It is convenient and perhaps more illustrative to represent this problem in terms of output (horsepower, safety) rather than in terms of input (labor, materials). Figure 1-2 *a* becomes transformed into Fig. 1-2 *b*.

The crucial point to observe is that the maximum-horsepower automobile *A* does not coincide with the maximally safe automobile *B*. Since both criteria are important, we are facing a typical multicriterion conflict. We have to *decide*. It is no longer sufficient to determine a single objective and search for the maximizing solution. Human judgment, human values, assessment of trade-offs, and also learning, creativity, and persuasion now enter the picture. A compromise solution that makes best use of technology can be any point on the heavy boundary connecting *A* and *B* in Fig. 1-2 *a* and *b*.

In this book we view the decision-making process from the perspective of the best-automobile solution rather than the traditional maximum-horsepower perspective. We shall deal with problems of multicriterion conflict in economics and show how a purely technological problem of single-criterion optimization is really only a special case of multiple-criteria decision making.

Traditional economics does not perceive problems in terms of alternative ends (despite Friedman's definition quoted earlier). Rather, it usually conceives of problems in terms of single objectives such as utility maximization in decision-making organizations and profit maximization or cost minimization in economic organizations. In this sense only purely technological problems are dealt with by the "dismal science."[1]

The underlying structure of decision making in economics, as well as in operations research and decision theory, is very simple: (1) identify an area of all feasible alternatives; (2) associate each alternative with a single number such that the greater the number, the better the choice; (3) using the existing apparatus of mathematical techniques, search; (4) when you have identified that element represented by the greatest number, stop. The result is often referred to as the solution to the problem.

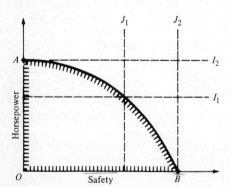

Figure 1-2b Economic problem in terms of outputs.

---

[1]A term coined for economics by one of its most respected early practitioners, A. C. Pigou.

Kenneth Boulding, another famous economist, describes the above principle as follows:

> Decision theory is a large mathematical apparatus resting like an inverted cone on the delicate point that everybody does what he thinks is best at the time; and it is astonishing that a principle apparently so empty could produce such an enormous mass of mathematical context. (Boulding 1967, p. 64)

The "delicate point" on which the "inverted cone" rests is provided by the mathematical concept of optimization, as expressed for example by Arnold Kaufmann:

> Economic function, i.e., the function to be optimized, represents the value associated with the system or the operation. This function is always unique, i.e., there can be only one. (Kaufmann 1963, p. 3)

Such a view of operations research is quite extreme since few problems of significance are truly expressible in terms of a single, unique objective function or criterion. Such problems are usually purely technological in nature: minimization of costs in transporting sand from one place to another, maximization of revenues obtainable from a system at given prices, rearrangement of orders to minimize processing costs, etc. Such single-purpose optimization does not recognize the intricate web of individual goals and aspirations in an organization and can lead to excessive concern with allocative efficiency. Although it is the main preoccupation of economics, operations research, and other disciplines, the exclusive striving for superior allocation of resources is an effort of surprisingly limited significance. Economist Harvey Leibenstein, in his book *Beyond Economic Man*, analyzes allocative efficiency as follows:

> The empirical evidence although far from exhaustive, suggests that welfare gains achieved by increasing *only* allocative efficiency are usually exceedingly small, at least in capitalist economies. In all but one of the cases considered all of the gains are likely to be made in one month's growth. They hardly seem worth worrying about. (Leibenstein 1976, p. 31)

The problem is that production inputs almost never perform at their production-possibility frontier. Workers do not work as hard and effectively as they could, and materials are not employed optimally or fully. Therefore, inputs of fixed specification do not yield a fixed performance. Movement toward the production-possibility frontier requires managerial and decision-making skills, motivation, knowledge, incentives, and organization.

As demonstrated in Fig. 1-3, reallocation of resources alone can be quite insufficient. It may produce a movement from point A to point B along the presently realized production frontier, a small gain in the quality of performance that is represented by the ascent from I_1 to I_2. However, a much larger gain in performance—to point C on the production-possibility frontier, or from I_1 to I_3—can be produced without changing the ratio of inputs, if the inputs are

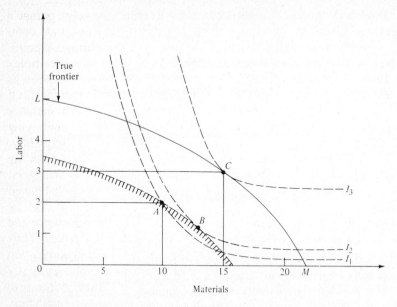

Figure 1-3 Inadequacy of allocative efficiency.

employed optimally. Leibenstein's data suggest that the amount to be gained by increasing effort and motivational efficiency is frequently significant.

Thus, enhancing innovation, creativity, and effective organization must be a concern of managerial decision making. And recognizing multiple "conflicting" objectives among individuals, groups, departments, plants, and companies, then following this recognition up with efforts to manage and resolve the conflicts, is the means to such enhancement.

1-3 OBJECTIVES OF THE FIRM AND THE ROLE OF PROFIT

When we refer loosely to the "objectives" of a firm (or of some other legal or social entity), we should keep in mind that the firm itself is *not* a decision-making entity, nor does it have objectives. And lacking intrinsic objectives, firms as such do not maximize or minimize anything. Professor Leibenstein puts it this way:

> Only individual members of firms have motives, and the meaningfulness and nature of firm motives depend on the study of individual motives. In other words, whether or not it is proper, meaningful, or useful to view firms as profit maximizers becomes a problem to be subjected to analysis and solution and is not something about which we simply make assumptions at the outset. It will all depend on the analysis of individual behavior, of the interaction of individuals within groups, and of the behavior of the groups that constitute the firm which will determine the answer. (Leibenstein 1976, p. 31)

Only individual members of a firm actually have objectives—*they* pursue a complex mixture of parallel and often implicit objectives, *they* negotiate compromises, *they* reach consensus, *they* shift their priorities, *they* engage in political and power persuasion, *they* make decisions. As a result of this complex interaction, there is an observable behavior of the firm that can be *described* as purposeful and that can be characterized by means of explicit objectives. So it is possible and useful to ascribe objectives to a firm as long as we remember that they are in fact undesigned, spontaneous evolutions of the underlying pursuits of individual managers, administrators, and workers. Consequently, when we refer to a firm's objectives it should be understood that we mean the external manifestation of objectives of the individual executives, managers, and workers as they derive from the motivational environment established within the firm.

Researchers and other investigators are often baffled by the reluctance and inability of executives and managers to express their firm's objectives. They usually come up with something as general as survival and profit maximization or even as empty as utility maximization. Such statements seem perfectly appropriate because almost any rational decision or action taken by the firm can be found in harmony with one of these principles. They are nonetheless quite inadequate for our understanding of how group behavior emerges as a result of individual behavior.

Peter F. Drucker considers objectives as the fundamental strategy of business. They should form the basis as well as the motivation for work and achievement. But, most importantly, they should reflect the variety of goals and purposes of a firm's constituents. According to Drucker, *the objectives of the firm must be multiple*:

> Much of today's lively discussion of management by objectives is concerned with the search for "one right objective." This search is not only likely to be as unproductive as the quest for the philosopher's stone; it does harm and misdirects.
>
> To manage a business is to balance a variety of needs and goals. And this requires multiple objectives. (Drucker 1974, p. 100)

It is remarkable that until quite recently the techniques of operations research and management science did not reflect Drucker's insight whatsoever. A definitive textbook, Harvey Wagner's *Principles of Operations Research*, 1969, refers to the existence of multiple objectives only briefly on two out of its thousand pages. This does not mean that the importance of multiple objectives is not recognized by Wagner. It is instructive to quote his references to this problem:

> In some instances he [the decision maker] may test *multiple criteria*, that is, apply several different (perhaps incommensurable) objective functions, to see if they point toward significantly different strategies. (Wagner 1969, p. 61)

And elsewhere we read:

> A few routines also can perform more extensive sensitivity analysis using devices known as *multiple objective functions* and *parametric programming*.
>
> The option of multiple objective functions permits solving a succession of linear programming problems, each with a different criterion function. The computer code optimizes on the first function, then goes on to each other function, one by one, employing the previously optimal basis as an intuitive solution. (Wagner 1969, p. 132)

Since 1969, OR/MS methodologies have made considerable progress. The "option of multiple objective functions" has become a necessity. Multiple criteria are now perceived as part of *all* decision problems rather than merely of "some instances." Parametric programming has become multiparametric programming, and the "one-by-one" approach to multiple objectives has never been given serious consideration.

According to Drucker, the firm should establish multiple objectives in the following key areas:

1. Marketing
2. Innovation
3. Human resources
4. Financial resources
5. Physical resources
6. Productivity
7. Social responsibility
8. Profit requirements

The specific operational objectives and targets that evolve in these key areas will depend on the strategy of the individual business. It is important to note that profit is not on this list. Drucker considers profit not an objective but a requirement: Profit is not so much the *purpose* of business activity as the *means* to achieve other important purposes. And the profit level establishes limits within which the company can set those other objectives. Modifying Drucker slightly, we shall consider profit to be one of the many simultaneous objectives of a firm. Treating profit maximization as the sole objective of a firm precludes the attainment of desired levels of other important objectives, decreases group and individual motivation, and may lead to lower motivational efficiency. On the other hand, insufficient profits will not allow the pursuit of other company objectives either. A simple graphic analysis should resolve the apparent conflict between these statements. In Fig. 1-4, let us assume that two products, A and B, characterize a particular business activity. Different quantity combinations of A and B can be produced. These production possibilities are currently limited to the shaded area. There is a profit function which can be used to evaluate the profitability of each combination of A and B. It reaches its maximum attainable level at point 1. Thus, point 1 is the profit-maximizing production mix of A and B. Other company objectives would reach their maximum at point 2, but they are limited to a much lower value at point 1. Thus, profit as the sole objective, although yielding the profit-maximizing

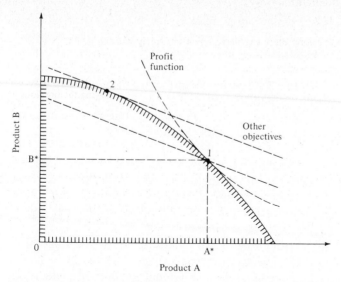

Figure 1-4 Profit as a sole objective.

production mix, could prevent the attainment of other important objectives in the remaining key areas of business.

In Fig. 1-5 we explore a similar situation, but now we shall treat profit as a constraint that limits the area of feasible A and B combinations—i.e., profit as Drucker describes it. Because profit is now a means of reaching other objectives, it need achieve only a minimum rather than a maximum.

Profit constraint limits the shaded area of feasible alternatives in Fig. 1-4 to

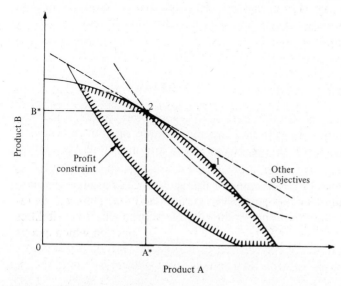

Figure 1-5 Profit as a constraint.

those indicated in Fig. 1-5. "Other" objectives to be maximized reach their extremum at point 2, a new optimal production mix. Observe that actual profit is higher at point 2 than the minimum profit stipulated by the constraint. It is not, however, as high as at point 1.

Comparing point 1 with point 2 we conclude that other company objectives reach their maximum at point 2 and the level of profit is sufficient for their achievement. At point 1 profits are at their maximum, but other company objectives are prevented from reaching more desirable values. Obviously, a trade-off is involved.

Thus, if there is only one single objective, such as profit, it is desirable to maximize it and that should be the end of the discussion. If on the other hand there are multiple objectives, then their replacement by a single function, such as profit, leads to neglect, obscurity, and misunderstanding of the other objectives of the firm.

The problem has shifted from whether to maximize profits or something else, to the question of multiple objectives versus a single objective; which one constitutes the prevailing dilemma of modern individual and corporate decision making?

The answer is necessarily contingent on circumstances. There are situations when both individuals and groups pursue only a single objective at a given time. In other situations those same decision-making agents may engage in complex conflict-resolution efforts with respect to a large variety of objectives.[1] It is important to emphasize, however, that single-objective problems are the exception rather than the rule. Consequently, one should develop a theory, a methodology, and applications to deal with multiple objectives and then derive particular implications for the *special cases* that involve only a single objective. The reverse approach starting from the special case of a single objective and trying to learn from it about the more general case of multiple objectives—has been followed by traditional decision theory and economics but has not been successful.

1-4 EXAMPLES OF MULTIOBJECTIVE CONFLICT

In this text we shall view the conflict between personal and system objectives as essentially analogous to the conflict among multiple objectives within a single person or among individual objectives within a group. In all such situa-

[1] In the increasingly prevailing environment of complexity, turbulence, and stakeholders' pluralism, objectives of the firm are significantly multidimensional. In a recent study, the following objectives were identified: profitability, growth, market share, social responsibility, employee welfare, diversification, efficiency, management development, and multinational enterprise. Among newly emerging objectives were financial stability, resource conservation, and consolidation of activities. The number of declared objectives ranged from 1 to 18, with average of 5 to 6. See Y. K. Shetty: "New Look at Corporate Goals," *California Management Review*, vol. 22, no. 2, 1979, pp. 71-79.

tions we are facing a basic common problem: The available alternatives, strategies, or options are often mutually exclusive.

1-4.1 The Book-Publishing Problem

To demonstrate the difference between the classical single-objective approach and MCDM, we shall adopt an example from a stimulating book by Colin Eden and John Harris, *Management Decision and Decision Analysis* (1975, pp. 227–229). The problem occurs in the book publishing industry and illustrates the essential conflict between multiple personal and system objectives. The question to be decided is how many copies of a particular book should be printed. Let us assume that the selling price has been fixed at $10 and that the cost of production consists of a fixed cost of $2000 plus a variable cost of $2 per book. Thus, if we produce (and sell) 2000 copies, we incur the cost of 2000 + 2 (2000) = $6000 and realize $20,000 in sales and $14,000 in profit.

It is of course quite uncertain how many books are actually going to be sold. We must estimate the demand, which we can do by assigning probabilities to possible demand levels. Let us consider some possible estimates of demand rounded off to whole thousands:

Table 1-3

Demand Level	0	1000	2000	3000	4000	5000	6000+
Estimated probability	.05	.15	.30	.25	.15	.10	.00

Traditional decision theory and its expected-value dogma insist that a "good" decision will be the one which maximizes the long-run expected returns, i.e., the one obtained if all or a large number of decisions of the above type were made in the same manner. For example, assuming zero scrap value for any unsold books, if 2000 books are printed, we would calculate the expected payoff as follows:

The cost, as previously obtained, is $6000. Depending on the level of demand, we would incur a loss of $6000 with probability of 5 percent (i. e., .05), earn $4000 with probability of .15, earn $14,000 with .30, and the same amount of $14,000 at every other level of demand since only 2000 books are printed. Thus, the overall expectation of earnings can be globally summarized as follows:

$$(-6000 \times .05) + (.15 \times 4000) + (.30 \times 14,000) + (.25 \times 14,000) +$$
$$(.15 \times 14,000) + (.10 \times 14,000) + (.00 \times 14,000) = \$11,500$$

Table 1-4 shows this expected value of $11,500 in the third row. All remaining decision alternatives—i.e., the options of printing 0, 1000, 3000, 4000, 5000, and more copies—have been calculated in the same fashion for comparison.

Table 1-4

Demand	0	1000	2000	3000	4000	5000	6000+	
Probability Print	.05	.15	.30	.25	.15	.10	.00	Expected payoff
0	0	0	0	0	0	0	0	0
1000	− 4,000	6,000	6,000	6,000	6,000	6,000	6,000	5,500
2000	− 6,000	4,000	14,000	14,000	14,000	14,000	14,000	11,500
3000	− 8,000	2,000	12,000	22,000	22,000	22,000	22,000	14,500
4000	−10,000	0	10,000	20,000	30,000	30,000	30,000	15,000
5000	−12,000	−2,000	8,000	18,000	28,000	38,000	38,000	14,000
6000+	−14,000+	−4,000+	6,000−	16,000−	26,000−	36,000−	46,000+	12,000−

Observe that the highest expected return is $15,000. According to traditional theory, then, the best decison would be to print 4000 books. But decisions are made by people, and their goals and criteria might differ from those recommended by decision theory.

A decision maker, by printing 4000 books, is running a 70 percent risk that the actual demand will be lower than 4000. Printing 2000 reduces the risk to 50 percent. Of course, printing no books at all would reduce to zero the chance of being left with an unsalable inventory of books. The pressure toward making such a decision (i.e., to print no books) is strong and occurs often. This conflict between system goals (maximizing long-term expected returns) and individual goals (minimizing the probability of misjudging returns) can be resolved by some sort of a *compromise*. It will mean printing some number between 0 and 4000. We shall discuss later several more sophisticated ways of achieving a multiobjective compromise. At this point we simply note that a practitioner might concentrate on the most likely sales of 2000 copies with only a 20 percent chance of not selling the entire production. *This is the kind of solution we want to study, understand, and appreciate in this text*. It is no less optimal than the one that maximizes the expected returns. But if one consistently maximizes expected returns, in the long run one will be wrong in estimating the size of sales 75 percent of the time.

1-4.2 When E. F. Hutton Talks . . .[1]

Another practical example of multiple-criteria conflict arises in investment analysis: the problem of choosing among various *tax shelters*.

Tax shelters or tax-sheltered investments are characterized by opportunities for profit and by provisions for reducing or deferring income taxes at the same time. It is the pursuit of these multiple objectives or criteria which

[1]From an old TV commercial pitch.

makes tax-sheltered investments a risky and complex decision-making endeavor.

According to E. F. Hutton Company (1977), there are three basic benefits associated with tax-sheltered investments:

1. Current deductions from taxable income
2. Future deductions from taxable income
3. Capital gain treatment (low taxation) of profits when investments are sold

Observe that: (1) by focusing on current deductions, one is sheltering current income; (2) future deductions shelter investment income; and (3) there is a lower capital gain tax rate on profits from the sale of an investment.

At E. F. Hutton, the "ideal tax shelter" is defined as a single investment which maximizes all three components (Fig. 1–6). We shall encounter the concept of the *ideal alternative* frequently in this book.

Current deductions come from the way the initial or first-year investment is spent. Since interest expense is an allowed deduction, borrowing may even succeed in causing one's current tax deductions to exceed the amount invested (thus driving out-of-pocket costs to zero or lower). Future deductions are generated through the use of borrowing so that deductions such as depreciation, depletion, and interest will exceed one's actual cash investment. Taxable income can then be less than zero even though a cash income is realized. Finally, there is a lower tax rate on profits from the sale of an investment.

It is virtually impossible to maximize all three tax-shelter components simultaneously. Maximum first-year deductions are usually achieved only

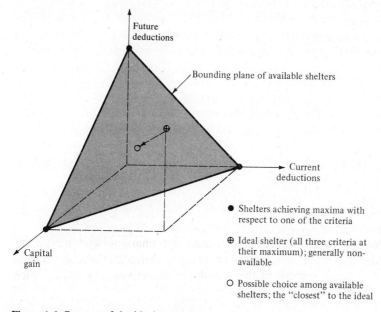

Figure 1-6 Concept of the ideal tax shelter.

through borrowing, and the future operating income is (usually) pledged to repay these borrowed funds. Thus, high, middle, or low first-year deductions usually yield low, middle, or high income shelter, respectively. Maximum capital gain is hard to achieve from an investment that generates maximum first-year deductions. Thus, maximum first-year deductions conflict with maximum income shelter; both conflict with maximum capital gain. Although the ideal alternative is never available, one can attempt to find an investment which comes as close as possible to it.

Let us represent the E. F. Hutton methodology graphically. In Fig. 1-6 each available tax shelter is represented by a point in a space whose three dimensions represent current deductions, future deductions, and capital gain.

1-4.3 The Problem of Profit Planning

Profit planning is a form of operational decision making that requires making choices among such risky alternatives as product mixes, pricing patterns, and volumes of output. It may seem that one is interested only in maximizing the expected value of profit, i.e., a single criterion. Is there any need for multiple criteria?

A so-called "break-even analysis" provides some insight into the relationships among costs, volume of output, revenues, and profits. The purpose is to determine, for each product, the level of output at which total revenues equal total costs. Profits begin to accrue when the level of output exceeds the break-even point. Of course, revenues and costs are random variables, characterized by only imprecisely known probability distributions. Consequently, the profits are also characterized by probability distributions. This is why the expected values and variances of such profit distributions are used as the criteria of choice.

But the variance (or the standard deviation) of the distribution of returns (or profits) does not measure the risk inherent in a given project, as perceived by the decision maker. The variance measures only the variability of returns, something which is only indirectly related to risk.

We shall discuss the issues of risk and perceived riskiness in more detail in Chap. 11. At this point let us simply assert that the riskiness of a project is characterized by at least two other factors:

1. Downside risk: the probability that a profit will be lower than some minimal target level
2. Upside potential: the probability that a profit will be higher than some satisfactory goal level

These three factors—expected return, downside risk, and upside potential—form the so-called prospect ranking vector (PRV), which is discussed in Sec. 11-3.

In profit planning, managers do not consider only expected profits and risks, but also expected cash requirements, return on investment (ROI),[1] and so on. Thus, instead of seeking conventional maximization of expected profits, our decision maker wants to:

1. Maximize the expected value of profit
2. Minimize expected cash requirements
3. Maximize the ROI
4. Minimize downside risk
5. Maximize upside potential

Jan Wallin (1978) has investigated the profit-planning situation of a small ready-made clothing manufacturer with respect to the choice of a production mix for an upcoming season. Two alternatives were defined for each of the following decision areas: production, pricing, marketing, and payment. The two production options were one-product and multiproduct production. The multiproduct option included numerous possibilities, up to twenty-two different product models.

Computer simulation produced a total of eighty alternative solutions. Each of the eighty provided a probability distribution of profit before tax, a forecast income statement, and a report on the profit contribution margins and production volumes per product. Given such information (which is usually necessary for the conventional approach as well) it was possible to measure all five of the stated criteria for all eighty alternatives. Some typical examples of the generated alternatives are given in Table 1-5.

Wallin dropped the upside potential criterion and reduced the eighty alternatives to twelve "interesting" (good) solutions, as shown in Table 1-6.

The smaller group of twelve "interesting" alternatives is characterized by the following property: Among the eighty original alternatives (including the twelve selected) there is none which would attain preferable scores with re-

Table 1-5

Alternative	Expected profit in Finnish Mk	Expected cash requirement (Finnish Mk)	ROI	Downside risk	Upside potential
1	254,148	853,927	29.76	.96	.00
2	330,535	1,111,712	29.73	.10	.54
3	292,815	969,993	30.17	.42	.06
4	344,156	1,140,750	30.22	.08	.66
⋮	⋮	⋮	⋮	⋮	⋮

[1]ROI is *essentially* profit before tax divided by the total cash requirements during the period considered and usually multiplied by 100.

Table 1-6

Alternative	Expected profit before tax	Expected cash requirement	ROI	Downside risk
1	360,986	1,278,789	28.23	.00
2	344,894	1,242,040	27.76	.10
3	334,931	1,236,832	27.10	.02
4	329,930	1,216,557	27.12	.18
5	327,712	1,190,252	27.56	.14
6	315,915	1,076,231	29.39	.18
7	297,365	993,726	29.90	.40
8	292,815	969,993	30.17	.42
9	285,349	936,375	30.52	.54
10	277,583	960,954	28.92	.61
11	267,630	928,464	28.04	.86
12	254,148	853,927	29.76	.96

spect to all four criteria considered. That is, none of the "interesting" solutions is dominated by any other available solution in the sense of preferable performance. Such solutions are called "nondominated" and are studied in Sec. 2-4 in more detail. Whenever one chooses between two nondominated solutions, one always sacrifices at least one preferable score with respect to at least one criterion.

The reader should perhaps try this: From Table 1-6 select any of the twelve solutions listed. Observe that no matter which alternative is chosen, there is at least one other alternative which "performs" better with respect to at least one of the criteria. (For some criteria "better" means minimization and for others it means maximization.)

Technical methods for identifying the nondominated solutions among a given set of alternatives are discussed in Sec. 2-4 and Chap. 8. And after all nondominated alternatives have been identified, how can we assist the decision maker in arriving at the final choice? We shall discuss some possible methods in Sec. 6-5 and Chap. 10.

1-5 BIBLIOGRAPHICAL NOTE

We have tried to trace the *choice* of goals and objectives to basic human needs, wants, and desires. Theories of motivation and needs are abundant, and the reader should do some additional reading before forming his or her own "model" or worldview. The books by Maslow (1962 and 1970) are extremely well written classics for those who want to go deeper into the psychology of human needs. A good and simple comparative analysis of the major theories of human behavior is provided by Ullrich (1972). For economically minded readers, the most sensible discussion of human wants, their hierarchy, and the implied basic principles of subordination, growth, irreducibility, and satiability of wants is provided by Georgescu-Roegen (1954). His article should not be missed under any circumstances.

The interplay between needs and multiple goals and objectives in corporate policy and strategy making has been consistently studied by Barton (1978). His two working papers enrich any reading list on the relationship between MCDM and business policy.

In the latter part of Chap. 1 we have explored the role of profit in the modern enterprise. Drucker's volume on management (1974) provides the basis for our discussion. But additional readings might also be considered. The thought-provoking book by Leibenstein (1976), going well beyond *homo oeconomicus*, and the article by Edwards (1977), describing the firm as maximizing utility through the pursuit of non-profit-maximizing policies, are both worthy of the reader's attention.

Our topic for Chap. 3, decision making as a process, is well foreseen in the books by Harrison (1975) and Eden and Harris (1975). In the latter work, the authors speak about the organization as having a "complex portfolio of multiple and often conflicting objectives." The portfolio concept is a rather interesting one with rich implications for further theoretical and practical development. Quinn (1977) analyzes the role of politics in managerial promotion of corporate goals.

We have also discussed the article by Liebling (1978). Although his study is closely concerned with identifying personality types within groups, it provides a nice example of the multiple and parallel motivational forces experienced by young business managers—potential readers and benefactors from an MCDM text.

Barton, R. F.: "Criteria for Goals: Policy Decisions," College of Business Administration, Texas Tech University, Lubbock, Tex. 1978.
——: "A Multicriterion View of Corporate Strategy," College of Business Administration, Texas Tech University, Lubbock, Tex. 1978.
Boulding, K. E.: "The Basis of Value Judgments in Economics," in S. Hook (ed.), *Human Values and Economic Policy*, New York University Press, New York, 1967, pp. 55–72.
Drucker, P. F.: *Management: Tasks, Responsibilities, Practices*, Harper & Row, New York, 1974.
Eden, C., and J. Harris: *Management Decision and Decision Analysis*, Wiley, New York, 1975.
Edwards, F. R.: "Managerial Objectives in Regulated Industries: Expense-Preference Behavior in Banking," *Journal of Political Economy*, vol. 85, no. 1, 1977, pp. 147–162.
Franklin, B.: "Letter to Joseph Priestley (1772)," *Benjamin Franklin Sampler*, Fawcett, New York, 1956.
Friedman, M.: *Price Theory: A Provisional Text*, Aldine, Chicago, 1962.
Georgescu-Roegen, N.: "Choice, Expectations, and Measurability," *Quarterly Journal of Economics*, vol. 68, no. 4, 1954, pp. 503–534.
Harrison, E. F.: *The Managerial Decision-Making Process*, Houghton Mifflin, Boston, 1975.
Hook, S.: "Basic Values and Economic Policy," in S. Hook (ed.), *Human Values and Economic Policy*, New York University Press, New York, 1967, pp. 246–255.
Hutton, E. F., & Co.: *Understanding the Shelters*, New York, 1977.
Kaufmann, A.: *Methods and Models of Operations Research*, Prentice-Hall, New York, 1963.
Keen, P. G. W., and M. S. Scott Morton: *Decision Support Systems: An Organizational Perspective*, Addison-Wesley, Reading, Mass., 1978.
Keeney, R. L., and H. Raiffa: *Decisions with Multiple Objectives: Preferences and Value Tradeoffs*, New York, 1976.

Leibenstein, H.: *Beyond Economic Man: A New Foundation for Microeconomics*, Harvard, Cambridge, Mass., 1976.

Liebling, B. A.: "Beyond Work Stereotypes," *MBA Magazine*, August-September 1978, pp. 13–25.

Maslow, A. H.: *Toward A Psychology of Being*, Van Nostrand, New York, 1962.

———: *Motivation and Personality*, Harper & Row, New York, 1970.

Quinn, J. B.: "Strategic Goals: Process and Politics," *Sloan Management Review*, Fall 1977, pp. 21–37.

Thompson, J. D.: "Decision-Making, the Firm, and the Market," in W. W. Cooper, H. J. Leavitt, and M. W. Shelly (eds.), *New Perspectives in Organization Research*, Wiley, New York, 1964.

Ullrich, R. A.: *A Theoretical Model of Human Behavior in Organizations: An Eclectic Approach*, General Learning Corp., Morristown, N.J., 1972.

Wagner, H. M.: *Principles of Operations Research: With Applications to Managerial Decisions*, Prentice-Hall, Englewood Cliffs, N.J., 1969.

Wallin, J.: *Computer-Aided Multiattribute Profit Planning*, Skriftserie utgiven av Handelshögskolan vid Åbo akademi, ser. A, no. 19, Åbo, Finland, 1978.

1-6 PROBLEMS

1-1 List two or more equally important criteria which might be considered in each of the following decision situations:

(*a*) Selecting a nuclear plant site in your county, state, or country

(*b*) Choosing a partner in marriage

(*c*) Considering a research and development budget for nuclear versus solar energy for a nation (1) for the next year, (2) for the next ten years, (3) beyond the year 2000

(*d*) The choice of a university in which to pursue your graduate studies

(*e*) The purchase of (1) a house, (2) a car, (3) a new computer system

Substantiate your answers in terms of the equal importance of the criteria.

1-2 For each of the above situations list at least one primary, secondary, and tertiary criterion of choice. Describe the circumstances under which only a single primary criterion might be considered.

1-3 It is often said that bank managers are primarily interested in profits and that they consider liquidity and risk to be important but secondary. Imagine an investment alternative that promises the highest level of profits but also is the most illiquid and risky. Can the criteria be separated? What conditions would justify their separation?

1-4 Consider the following rating of investment opportunities for a bank. Because of budgetary constraints only one of them may be chosen:

Alternatve	Profit ($ million)	Liquidity (capital-adequacy ratio)	Risk (risk-asset ratio)
1	4.248	1.369	8.500
2	4.405	1.603	9.280
3	4.460	1.698	9.592
4	4.482	1.747	9.758
5	4.230	1.486	8.305

Moving from alternative 4 to 3, a reduction in profit of $0.022 million is required in order to achieve reductions in the capital-adequacy (CA) and risk-asset (RA) ratios of 0.049 and 0.166, respectively. Identify and evaluate the trade-offs for moving from 4 to 2, from 3 to 2, from 2 to 1, and from 5 to 1.

Perform the same trade-off analysis while omitting the CA ratio. What are the possible implications for bank decision making when such a criterion is neglected?

1-5 The late Oskar Morgenstern stated, "Present economic theory allegedly deals with *maxima*, e.g., of profit, utility . . . (or *minima*, e.g., of cost, disutility . . .). The fundamental objection is that these *extrema* exist and are attainable only if the individual or firm *controls all variables* on which the maximum depends."[1] Discuss in terms of your own experience.

1-6 "People (i.e., individuals) have goals; collectivities of people do not."[2] This statement of Cyert and March is potentially very significant. How do you reconcile it with the fact that thousands of corporations publish and use goals for the corporation as a whole? Could it be that corporations exhibit behavior which, in hindsight, *appears* as if they were following a set of objectives? More generally, is "purpose" inherent in a system, or is this notion imputed to the system by the observer trying to understand and explain its behavior? What are the implications for business and management if the statement by Cyert and March is true? (Leibenstein [1976] makes a similar observation.)

1-7 Recent studies of fire department operations, intended to establish a policy for measuring and achieving more efficient use of available resources, do so in terms of engine and ladder *response times*. Is this "proxy" attribute sufficiently representative of other attributes, such as fatalities, injuries, property damage, firemen fatigue, and responsiveness to false alarms, and their differential weighting? Are there factors other than response time that affect these latter attributes? Can the "best" way of fighting fires be identified with the fastest response time?

1-8 A farmer uses grain for food, seeds for the next season, making whiskey, cattle fodder, and keeping parrots, in that order. You may use water for drinking, cooking, washing, laundering, and watering the lawn, in that order. Does this imply a hierarchy of needs? What are the conditions of hierarchical and parallel attention to needs?

1-9 A firm is considering four objectives for a given planning period:
> (*a*) Maximize the dividends paid to shareholders
> (*b*) Maximize the net free cash available to the firm
> (*c*) Maximize the value of assets controlled by the firm
> (*d*) Minimize the probability of financial collapse

How are these four objectives related to "maximization of profits"?

1-10 B. Roy[3] suggested the following problem formulations with respect to a given set of alternatives:
> 1. *Choice*: selecting a single "best" alternative
> 2. *Sorting*: segmentation of alternatives into predefined categories
> 3. *Ranking*: ordering of alternatives with respect to given criteria
> 4. *Description*: complete characterization of alternatives in terms of their consequences

(*a*) Give some real-life examples of problems which could be classified within each of the above categories (1) with respect to a single criterion and (2) with respect to multiple criteria.

(*b*) Give examples of problems where some or all of the above formulations would have to be involved.

(*c*) What are the analyst's and decision maker's roles in dealing with these four types of problem formulations?

1-11 According to E. F. Hutton, there are four basic objectives associated with investing in a tax shelter (tax incentive investment):

[1] O. Morgenstern, "Thirteen Critical Points in Contemporary Economic Theory: An Interpretation," *Journal of Economic Literature*, vol. 10 (December 1972), p. 1165.

[2] R. M. Cyert, and J. G. March, *A Behavioral Theory of the Firm*, Prentice-Hall, Englewood Cliffs, N.J., 1963, p. 26.

[3] B. Roy, "The Optimisation Problem Formulation: Criticism and Overstepping," Paper presented at the International Symposium on Extremal Methods and Systems Analysis, University of Texas, Austin, September 13–15, 1977.

(*a*) Tax deferral—postpone payment of taxes
(*b*) Building equity—investment income and capital gains
(*c*) Movement into a lower tax bracket
(*d*) Investment appreciation

Analyze the following investment opportunities in terms of the above criteria (provide their differential rankings):

— Oil- or gas-drilling exploration
— Investing in an apartment complex
— Leasing a railroad car or an offshore oil-drilling rig
— Government-subsidized housing
— Existing shopping center or office building

1-12 West Germany and Japan are pouring research and development money into mass transportation technology called "maglev" (for *mag*netic *lev*itation). The United States government cut such research to the bone in favor of other advanced transit systems. Maglev is developing trains that "fly" at 300 miles per hour and more. Discuss the single-objective (speed) orientation of maglev research in terms of real mass transportation needs (distributed stop-and-go pattern, variable distances and point demands, star-shaped rather than linear or circular commuting patterns, costs, etc.) Is the United States decision wise?

1-13 Some writers insist that reducing unemployment and inflation at the same time are incompatible, conflicting goals (implications of the so-called "Philip curve"). We know that they certainly can move upward together. Is it "rational" to expect that they could move downward as well?

1-14 The most common objectives listed among modern corporate ends are (1) growth, (2) profit maximization, (3) accountability to employees, (4) accountability to the public, and (5) serving the consumer. Identify the conflicting nature of these objectives. Is it desirable for a company to follow conflicting objectives?

1-15 Improving the quality of life is a multiobjective proposition, encompassing areas of health, personality development, employment, working environment, leisure time, goods, services, ecological environment, security, justice, participation in the community, creative fulfillment, mutual understanding and love, and freedom. What would be some personal, community, and national *operational* objectives which would pull toward an improved quality of life?

1-16 Geoffrey Vickers[1] suggested that designing a bungalow could be considered intrinsically more complex than designing the first atomic bomb or landing on the moon. The criteria of success for the latter two are technological and singular (explode or land), while the criteria for even the smallest bungalow could be multiple and conflicting. Many people believe that if we can go to the moon or succeed with the Manhattan Project, we should be able to solve our social problems. Isn't it a matter of criteria? Should we confuse single-criterion vastness with multicriterion complexity?

1-17 If the criterion of "best" is given clearly and unambiguously, the question to be asked is how to achieve it. It is more difficult to deal with a question of *what* is "best" when the criteria are multiple and conflicting and their relative weight must be decided. It is even more difficult to explicate *why* a particular definition of "best" should be used. Comment.

1-18 An individual in business (entrepreneur, retailer, salesperson, etc.) is often said to maximize profit and in doing so to search for *efficiency*. What about the search for *security*, *prestige*, and *comfort*? Are these motivations compatible with the search for efficiency? Give some examples of potential conflicts among them.

1-19 Cost-benefit analysis often requires placing a value on human life. A common measure for this has been estimated life earnings, discounted at a specified interest rate. The resulting figures imply that a 21-year-old male is worth two baby boys or three baby girls. Are there any relevant criteria

[1]G. Vickers, *Making Institutions Work*, Associated Business Programmes, Ltd., London, 1973, p. 111.

missing? Consider a person (perhaps mentally retarded or disabled) whose expected future earnings are zero or negative. Is such a life to be valued at zero? Should parents of such a child actually pay the state for relieving them of the costs if it causes a loss of life? (*Hint*: A Georgia jury awarded $10 for the accidental shooting by the police of a 14-year-old boy with mental problems. The jury argued that his future earnings were not worth more. *New York Times*, July 26, 1980.)

1-20 F. Porsche Aktiengesellschaft stipulated the following objectives of their "long-life car" project:[1]

—Conserve energy resources
—Conserve material resources
—Reduce adverse environmental impacts
—Reduce overall costs
—Improve operational reliability
—Retain established vehicle concept goals

(*a*) What are the conditions of the long-life car's compatibility with the objective of profit maximization? Why would any automobile company be interested in "timeless" design and styling, that is, in qualitative rather than quantitative growth?

(*b*) Suggest some proper *operational* objectives which would reflect the philosophy of Porsche A. G.

1-21 Discuss the alternatives of all-volunteer, conscript, and mixed armed forces in terms of their relevant objectives (for example costs, quality, number of persons prepared, etc.) and situational framework (for example labor-intensive war, capital-intensive war, need for reserves, etc.).

1-22 Discuss the following research and development tax shelters in terms of their relevant objectives and goals:

—John DeLorean sports car
—William P. Lear fan (turboprop aircraft)
—Solar energy projects
—Genetic engineering (for example Genentech, Biogen, Cetus)
—GM Electrovette zinc-nickel batteries

(*Hint*: R&D shelters provide that limited partnerships share R&D costs in return for royalties. Royalties are taxed not as income but as capital gains: as a percentage of the selling price royalties can be a fine hedge against inflation. Do the proper research yourself.)

---

[1] E. Fuhrman: "The Long-Life Car," *Futures*, vol. 11, no. 3, 1979, pp. 216–223.

Multiple-criteria decision making has not been entirely ignored throughout the history of operations research and management sciences (OR/MS). In this chapter we attempt to establish the connection between the two. We use the models of portfolio selection, inventory control, and critical-path analysis as the most useful examples of early OR/MS sensitivity to multiplicity of criteria. These three models also happen to possess great survival value, and their applicability goes well beyond the average OR/MS standard.

The reader is especially invited to study the recurring graphic concept of the *efficient boundary*—one of the most useful tools of modern MCDM analysis. Later, this concept will be formalized and presented as a set of non-dominated solutions, but grasping it intuitively is essential at this stage. It appears in all three of our examples. It is difficult to argue that any "good" solution to a multicriterion problem should *not* lie on an efficient boundary; i.e., any good solution should be nondominated with respect to all relevant dimensions of the problem.

In Sec. 2-2 we present a short history of MCDM. This should provide a time framework and a sense of field dynamics for the reader.

The rest of the chapter deals with the relationship among the concepts of optimization, satisficing, and MCDM compromising with respect to an ideal solution. Nondominance is formally introduced and related to the earlier concepts of classical economics. The reader should pay special attention to these topics, as they represent the conceptual soil in which most of the MCDM reasoning is rooted.

MCDM IN THE MANAGEMENT SCIENCES
AND OPERATIONS RESEARCH

In the world as it is, we are nearly always operating in situations in which we would like to achieve several quite different goals. The conventional way of handling this has been to break our total aspirations down into a collection of sub-goals, and to concentrate on each one of these independently. Whenever we can recognize a NEED, we try to satisfy that NEED, without reference to anything else.

The jargon name for this strategy is "sub-optimization"—which does not mean (as it might do) looking for something below the optimum, but is used to denote a policy of optimizing each sub-goal separately.

Conrad H. Waddington
Tools for Thought (1977)

Conventional OR/MS recognizes the multiplicity of objectives. However, the strategy for dealing with them sets most of their models apart from MCDM. The strategy of *suboptimization* (as described above by one of the founding fathers of operational research) is to select *one* subobjective, and push it to its practical limit, even though doing so might have some unfortunate consequences elsewhere. When the ill effects of such suboptimizing show up, then select another, most pressing subobjective and push that to the limit. This is what Harvey Wagner (1969) probably means by "optimize on the first function, then go on to each other function, one by one, employing the previous optimal basis as an intuitive solution" (p. 132).

Although they acknowledge the multiplicity of criteria, some very good recent OR/MS texts still fail to treat the subject adequately. One author makes the following statement:

First, it is in the nature of things that objectives are usually multidimensional. Thus, the manager must decide which dimension is relevant, what is an appropriate goal (time-oriented target) along each dimension, and what relative weights in terms of importance are to be attached to these goals.[1]

Then, perhaps to motivate his students better, he effectively negates it:

In this book, most of the models that we consider have *single-dimensional objectives that can be stated and measured in monetary terms*.[1]

A *cognitive vacuum* is created by such statements. The perceptive student will ask, "If the first observation is correct, and I want to master managerial tasks, why should I study the models constrained by the second statement?" Perhaps the author believes his readers will be prepared to understand *other*, more realistic models better. But then other texts must fill the vacuum and present the other part of the story of decision making.

2-1 MCDM MODELS—THE OR/MS TRADITION

We have charged conventional operations research and management sciences, perhaps a little unfairly, with preoccupation with single-objective modeling of real-world situations that are essentially multiobjective. Multiple objectives and criteria do however find their way into the OR/MS models. In fact, some of the most useful and popular models are based, implicitly or explicitly, on the multiplicity of objectives.

We shall briefly review several typical OR/MS methodologies. They are well known and yet their dominant feature, the multiplicity of criteria, is rarely recognized explicitly or emphasized by OR/MS instructors. This is actually a good sign: The multidimensionality is neatly blended in; it emerges imperceptibly, as a natural part of the model. People don't even think of setting these models apart from other types of OR/MS cases. They are good models, in the best OR/MS tradition, and they show that the single versus multidichotomy was not an unavoidable historical condition. All OR/MS models could have evolved as multidimensional, and someone wanting *just* to minimize cost or *just* to minimize time would have set n (the number of objective functions in the model) equal to 1.

In peacetime objectives are multiple—individuals and groups are trying to do several things at once. Under war conditions objectives are supposed to be well defined and single. Yet our peacetime OR/MS models recognize mostly single objectives, while the old, World War II operational researchers were dealing with multiple objectives *explicitly*. Somewhere, along the way, we have lost them and their ideas. These facts represent a real dilemma.

Principles of OR/MS decision making were first developed in the form of operational research sections attached to the Royal Air Force during World

[1]N. Paul Loomba, *Management—A Quantitative Perspective*, Macmillan, New York, 1978, p. 43.

War II. These were teams of scientists, drawn from many disciplines, who attempted to help the RAF commander in chief improve his decisions.

What *objective* was the commander trying to achieve? Conrad H. Waddington (1977), one of the participants in the original RAF operational research groups, recalls that even in war it was not easy to answer this question. Although they all had in front of them the straightforward overall objective of winning the war, they could not figure it out operationally: Was the objective to prevent U-boats from sinking their ships, or was it to sink the enemy U-boats? Was the command trying to disrupt industrial productions, or transport; to obliterate homes, or to displace the enemy's military efforts from the front into the interior? Should one make bigger bombs or carry a larger number of them?[1] But perhaps no increase in size or number of bombs would have any effect unless the accuracy of aiming could be increased. Should the bombs be dropped closer together or farther apart? What about the explosion depth of floating mines—should it be minimized to injure ships more efficiently, or maximized to avoid detection?

Such multiple objectives were the true rationale for having *interdisciplinary* OR teams. The OR group should be able to advise the commander whether to call on an optics scientist for improved accuracy, or an explosives expert for better bombs, or a psychologist for better methods of selecting and training air crews, or an engineer for better altimeters to enable aircraft to fly lower without necessarily becoming kamikazes.

Interdisciplinary and multidimensional objectives disappeared from operational research quite soon after the time when C. H. Waddington was young. By the mid-fifties there was only one objective function and OR/MS had itself become a "scientific" discipline. Instead of cross-disciplinary amelioration we have witnessed the emergence of the OR/MS specialist, resourcefully using applied mathematics to perform his quasiconcave dual maximization in a Hilbert space.

Operations research students thus probably know a great deal about large, mixed integer programming start-up computational procedures, Erlang-distributed queues with removable servers and nonremovable customers (analysts), or Lagrange dynamic programming in time-sequential combat games with false contacts. They know much less about risk making and risk taking, conflict management, priority assessments, and the psychology of human judgment. In fact, the discipline of psychology is still considered irrelevant to OR/MS by some down-to-earth, "bottom line" or "quick-and-dirty" operations researchers.

When we talk about the need to restore an interdisciplinary approach in the OR/MS profession,[2] it does not mean that each of us should evolve into a

---

[1] A similar question is of interest to cattle breeders: Should one breed cows which produce more milk per lactation or cattle which live longer and go through more lactations?

[2] Since 1978, operations research, management science, and decision science are often referred to as *Operational Sciences* (OS).

jack-of-all-trades who is master of none, or a "generalist," in the modern managerial jargon. We call not for a renaissance man who can do any number of things reasonably well, but for a person who does one thing extremely well and has developed the capacities, potentialities, and abilities for doing a number of quite different things. These can be called upon when circumstances require, and, perhaps after some interval of "brushing up," they can be put into operation at a masterly level.

2-1.1 Portfolio Selection

In choosing among potential investment prospects, portfolios[1] of securities, or projects, one is primarily concerned about economic (or financial) returns on one's investment. In the case of uncertain prospects (as most investments are), one is concerned about the *expected returns*. It is generally assumed that, other things being equal, an investor would prefer larger expected returns to smaller ones.

Because of an investment's inherent uncertainty, normally the investor is also concerned about the *degree of risk* associated with a given prospect. If we contemplate a set of prospects with the same or practically the same expected return, an investor can be assumed to choose the prospect with the smallest degree of risk.

Thus, the most commonly used portfolio-selection model is based on *two criteria* of investment desirability: expected return and risk. These criteria are then used to rank the components of a given set of available investment opportunities: A portfolio with larger expected return *and* lower risk will be preferred.

Each prospective investment return can be characterized by a probability distribution. That is, each different possible return for a given prospect can be associated with an estimated relative frequency of occurrence, or probability. The distribution mean, a measure of its central tendency, is used to characterize the expected return. The distribution variance, a measure of the dispersion of values around the mean, is used to characterize its riskiness. Graphically, a given set of available portfolios can be represented as a bounded set of feasible points (we assume both the means and the variances of returns to be finite) in the mean-variance two-dimensional space, as in Fig. 2-1.

Each particular portfolio x is described in terms of the corresponding values of two parameters, $E(x)$ and σ_x^2. In Fig. 2-1, observe that the area shaded designates all those portfolios that, with respect to portfolio x, are characterized by larger or equal expected returns *and*, at the same time, smaller or equal grades of riskiness. Portfolio x is *dominated* by all the prospects located in the shaded area; it presents an obviously inferior choice with respect to all of

[1]A portfolio is a detailed list of the investments, securities, and commercial paper owned by a bank, investment organization, or other investor.

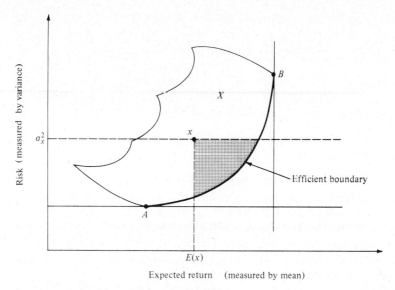

Figure 2-1 Problem of portfolio selection.

them. Note that *all* such prospects (or portfolios) in the interior of the bounded set X are similarly dominated.

Only the points lying on the heavily traced boundary of X, the so-called "efficient boundary" (the set of efficient portfolios), are not dominated by any other prospects in terms of the two selected parameters (E and σ^2). One of the major purposes of this model is to trace the efficient boundary for an investor.

Preference-induced movements along the efficient boundary of X amount to trading off some of the expected returns for some degree of riskiness. One can achieve a higher return on investment at the "price" of higher risk. Conversely, one must "pay" for increased safety by sacrificing some of the returns. It can be hypothesized that risk averters (see Sec. 12-4.5), seeking safety and stability in investment, would tend to locate their preferred choices closer to endpoint A of the efficient boundary. Risk takers, seeking the highest returns and paying less attention to the risk involved, would tend to concentrate their choices closer to endpoint B.

It is one of the main hypotheses of this model that any and all of the points lying on the efficient boundary can conceivably be chosen by at least one rational investor. In more formal terms, there is always a continuous function $u(E, \sigma^2)$, nondecreasing in any of the two arguments, which reaches its maximum somewhere on the efficiency boundary.

As we shall show in more detail in Chap. 11, this hypothesis is false in general, and the efficient boundary and "rational behavior" are in full concordance only under the strictest mathematical conditions. Thus, our argument is not with the model itself, which we consider excellent, but with the concept of measuring the riskiness by σ^2, which we consider insufficient.

After identifying the set of efficient portfolios, the investor is expected to narrow the choices down to some particular subset. The investor must exercise judgment in evaluating the trade-offs between expected return and riskiness, as it is described in Sec. 12-1 and 12-4.6. Observe also that should the full and complete assessment of the function $u(E, \sigma^2)$ become available, the preferred alternative would be implied by definition, and computing the efficient boundary would not serve any immediate purpose (see Chap. 11).

2-1.2 Optimal Inventory Policy Curve

One of the simplest versions of the traditional inventory-control model can be characterized as follows:

Given a rate of demand per time period z, cost per preparing an order C_r, cost per carrying an item (or a dollar's worth of items) in the inventory C_c, and cost of an out-of-stock item to be back ordered C_b, determine the optimal quantity of items to be ordered x^* and the maximum number of items to be kept in the inventory s^* for a given planning period.

The optimal levels x^* and s^* are determined by minimizing the following total-cost function:

$$TC = C_r \frac{z}{x} + C_c \frac{cs}{2} + C_b \frac{x-s}{2}$$

where $\frac{z}{x}$ = number of orders per planning period

$\quad c$ = price of an item

$\quad \frac{cs}{2}$ = average dollar investment in inventory

$\quad \frac{x-s}{2}$ = average number of out-of-stock items per planning period

This model is based on the idea that the sole objective in an inventory problem is to minimize total inventory cost. The cost parameters C_r, C_c, and C_b are to be measured and determined in an a priori way. Estimating them could be unreliable, expensive, or outright impossible, especially for C_b. The minimization of the total cost function TC is usually performed in a trivial, unconstrained way, using the ordinary differential calculus. *But in managerial reality, there are no unconstrained problems.* If there are unconstrained problems, they are not managerial but purely mathematical.

Suppose that there *are* some significant difficulties associated with the measurements of the three types of costs C_r, C_c, and C_b, which are necessary for determining the optimal ordering policy for a given company. Even with no knowledge of C_r, C_c, or C_b whatsoever, we can still proceed with an intelligent analysis of the problem.

Instead of minimizing this vaguely defined, largely unspecifiable, and unconstrained global cost function TC, the same problem can be approached as a multiple-criteria minimization of *three* simultaneous and well-defined objectives:

1. Minimize the number of orders per period:

$$f_1(x) = \frac{z}{x}$$

2. Minimize average dollar investment in the inventory per period:

$$f_2(s) = \frac{cs}{2}$$

3. Minimize average number of out-of-stock items per period:

$$f_3(x, s) = \frac{x - s}{2}$$

The above objective functions are in conflict, under the constraints usually pertaining to the problem: budget limitations, floor-space limitations, employees and machinery available, time constraints, spoilage allowance, desired frequency of orders, and countless others; they all must be explicitly considered.

It is obvious that a department's or company's inventory position can be improved if, for example, we can reduce the average number of out-of-stock items f_3 while maintaining at least the same number of orders f_1 and the average inventory investment f_2 per period.

Let F indicate the set of all feasible (i.e., attainable) values of f_1, f_2, and f_3 with respect to constraints like storage space available, budgeted inventory investment, required order frequency, and acceptable number of shortages per period. Suppose further that the current company inventory policy is characterized by $f_1 = 60$, $f_2 - \$10,000$, and $f_3 = 10$. If we solve the following problem:

$$\text{Minimize } f_3$$

subject to F and

$$f_1 = 60$$
$$f_2 = 10,000$$

and find that $f_3 = 9$ or less, then the current company policy is *dominated*, and the company's inventory position can be improved. That is, a policy triplet (60, 10,000, 10) is dominated by (60, 10,000, 9), because we prefer f_3 to be smaller. By solving a problem of the above type we actually obtain a *nondominated policy*, i.e., one in which any further improvement in one of the objective functions can be achieved only at the "price" of worsening the value of at least one of the remaining objective functions.

The set of all such nondominated policies constitutes the *nondominated surface* of F or, in the Starr and Miller (1962) terminology for a two-objective case, an "optimal policy curve."

For example, suppose that only f_1 and f_2 are being considered. In Fig. 2-2, we present a hypothetical set F and its heavily traced boundary, the optimal policy curve. Observe that if the current company inventory policy is characterized by $f_1 = 10$ and $f_2 = 10,000$, then given the constraints forming the shape of F this policy can be improved by moving to any point within the shaded area associated with f and, preferably, all the way toward one of the nondominated policies on the optimal policy curve itself.

Current policy f is not only inferior to any nondominated policy for a given set of specific costs C_r and C_c; it could not become optimal for *any* conceivable combination of C_r and C_c. We did not even have to know any of the costs to arrive at such a significant conclusion!

Observe in Fig. 2-2 that by minimizing f_1 subject to $f_2 = 10,000$, and by minimizing f_2 subject to $f_1 = 10$, we attain the two nondominated policies designated by points 1 and 2 respectively. In this fashion, by systematically constraining one of the functions and minimizing the other, we could trace out the entire optimal policy curve.

The same curve, or nondominated surface, could also be computed by minimizing

$$TC = \lambda_1 f_1 + \lambda_2 f_2 + \lambda_3 f_3$$

with respect to the F constraints and for all possible values of λ_i such that

$$\sum_{i=1}^{3} \lambda_i = 1 \quad \text{and} \quad \lambda_i \geq 0 \quad i = 1, 2, 3$$

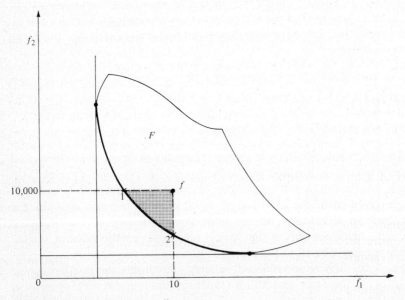

Figure 2-2 Optimal inventory policy curve.

This formulation leads directly to multiobjective programming and multiparametric decomposition, the topics discussed in Chap. 8 and especially in Sec. 8-5. These methodologies allow us to consider any number of objective functions and any number of constraints at the same time.

All the above analysis is simply a matter of information available on λ_1, λ_2, and λ_3. (That is, what do we know about C_r, C_c, and C_b?) If we know all three parameters *precisely*, we replace λ_1 by C_r, λ_2 by C_c, and λ_3 by C_b in function TC, and only one optimal policy is likely to be calculated. Instead of the nondominated surface, we obtain a single point. If only ranges of λ_i's are specified, then some subset of the entire nondominated surface will be obtained. If we know nothing about λ_i's, then we obtain the entire nondominated surface, and any point lying on it could become the solution.

2-1.3 CPM Cost-Time Trade-Offs

Complex projects typically consist of a large number of subprojects and *activities* which have to be organized into technologically feasible and managerially desirable sequences and networks. Examples of complex projects are the construction of a new plant or a new skyscraper, any space program mission, aircraft or missile design and development, and research and development projects in the chemical or drug industry. Because of their complexity and size, performance uncertainties, and the large number of people involved (For example, the Polaris missile program required the coordination of several thousand subcontractors and hundreds of thousands of activities), these projects generally experience tremendous time and cost overruns.

In planning, scheduling, controlling, and evaluating complex projects we are certain to encounter multiobjective conflicts among expected project duration, project costs, utilization of resources, reliability of projected completion dates, and other factors.

Methods of *critical-path analysis* are quite suitable for analyzing complex projects; they are simple in conception and successful in practice. It is obvious that some project activities cannot be started until others have been completed. One does not start assembling a machine before the parts have been received, and they will not arrive before they are ordered. Other project activities can proceed in a parallel fashion; for example, the machine site can be prepared while the orders for machine parts are being processed. So, a complex project will consist of a large network of parallel and interconnected *sequences of activities*.

The principle of critical-path analysis is to decide what is unavoidably the longest sequence (the critical path) of activities which will have to be finished before the entire project can be completed. The critical path determines the *minimum time* required to complete a project. It is thus a particularly good idea to expedite the activities lying on the critical path as much as possible if one is interested in minimizing the duration of the project. But we already know that speeding up an activity costs money—in overtime, more and better workers, more or better equipment, etc. One is trading off time for money, a surefire feature of any successful OR/MS model.

To ensure a successful trade-off, we first describe each activity with two pairs of time and cost estimates, the so-called "normal" and "crash" points. The normal points consist of the *maximum time* and the *minimum cost* for the performance of the activity. The crash points consist of the *minimum time* and the *maximum cost* for the same activity. If we assume a linear relationship between time and cost, then we can compute the cost-time trade-off for each activity as follows:

$$\text{Trade-off coefficient} = \frac{\text{maximum cost} - \text{minimum cost}}{\text{maximum time} - \text{minimum time}}$$

The trade-off coefficient (which will never be negative) indicates how much money it would cost to shorten the activity by one additional unit of time (day, week, hour, etc., depending on the project).

If the relationship between time and cost is not linear, we can still apply the same model by dividing the original activity into several segments and estimating normal and crash points for all segments as if they were different activities. The greater the number of segments in this piecewise linear time-cost function, the more closely it will approximate a nonlinear time-cost curve. Since we know the minimum project-completion time (the duration of the critical path) and we have estimated cost-time trade-off coefficients for all activities, our objective is to design the minimum-cost variant for each particular project-completion time—in other words, a variant which would yield minimum project-completion time with the smallest possible increase in cost over minimum (normal) costs.

The Region P in Fig. 2-3 designates all possible combinations (or variants) in which the project can be planned. Remember that each activity can be characterized by normal point, crash point, or anything in between. Suppose that only two possibilities are allowed for each activity and that there are only ten activities—then P consists of $2^{10} = 1024$ different combinations. Or suppose that each activity can be planned in only two time-cost variants but that the number of activities is a bit closer to reality, say, 400. The number of variants is then 2^{400}, which is approximately equal to 10^{120}. The number of atoms in the known universe has been estimated as something close to 10^{76}!

The critical-path method (CPM) is a good model. It allows the decision maker to cut through a formidable number of combinations within computer-seconds. But how does it work?

Let us explore Fig. 2-3 more carefully. Suppose that *all* activities are performed at their normal points (maximum time and minimum cost). This one particular variant of performance is designated by point A. The corresponding critical path, the normal critical path, represents the maximum duration of the project. Take some other obvious combination: Let all activities be performed at their crash points (minimum time and maximum cost). This is represented by point C. There can be nothing more expensive or shorter in duration.

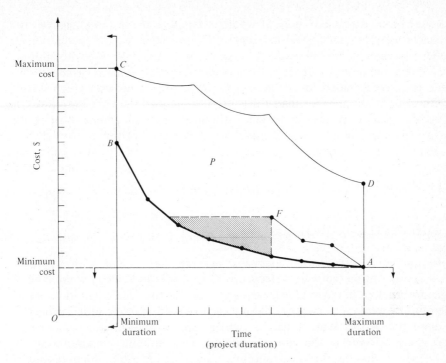

Figure 2-3 Cost-time trade-offs in critical-path analysis.

What about points B and D of region P? How do we interpret them?

Point D corresponds to a combination with the same duration as the one at point A. Thus, all activities on the corresponding critical path must be at their maximum (normal) durations. However, all activities on noncritical paths have been assigned their most expensive options: they are at crash points. Point D is the most expensive combination corresponding to the maximum duration of the project. How undesirable it is!

Point B represents a combination of activities with the same minimum project duration as point C. But it is so much less expensive. All activities on the corresponding critical path are at their minimum (crash) durations. However, all activities on noncritical paths have been relaxed as far as possible— they are performed at their least expensive options, while the minimum project duration is kept intact. Combination B is thus very attractive.

The main task of existing computer algorithms for CPM is to identify the nondominated boundary of P, the heavily traced piecewise linear curve AB, as swiftly and efficiently as possible. These CPM algorithms are based on a truly simple but powerful rule: Always shorten the least expensive activity, the one with the lowest trade-off coefficient, first.

Suppose we are at the point A. There is a sequence of critical-path activities, and in order to reduce the duration of the project we should shorten at least one of the critical activities. If we do not choose the least expensive one first, and thus violate the above-stated principle, we achieve a time reduction at a higher cost than would otherwise be possible. We shall move into the interior of P, let us say to point F. Observe that F represents a *dominated* combination, i.e., its associated shaded area denotes all feasible project variants which would be both shorter and cheaper than F.

Because we rarely want a project to be at its shortest (point B) or at its cheapest (point A), identifying boundary AB makes a lot of sense. How do we choose the final combination, the best project design when we must trade one objective (cost) off for another (time)? That's what this book is all about, in a sense.

2-2 THE HISTORY OF MCDM

People, including professional decision makers, have dealt with multiple criteria for as long as there were decisions to be made. In Chap. 1 we quoted a Benjamin Franklin letter in which we can recognize the idea of multicriterion trade-offs. However, the concept did not receive its first "scientific" articulation until the World War II period, when John von Neumann and Oskar Morgenstern referred to the dilemma of "several conflicting maximum problems" (1944, p. 10–11). But these authors did not pursue the problem of multiple criteria further, developing the unidimensional *game theory* instead—not a bad "trade-off," considering the success of their book!

T. C. Koopmans (1951) first used the concept of the *efficient vector*, i.e., the nondominated solution of modern MCDM. In the same year, H. W. Kuhn and A. W. Tucker formulated the problem of *vector maximization* and derived optimality conditions for the existence of efficient solutions. Their *saddle point theorem* is well known and extends to nonlinear cases. Arrow, Barankin, and Blackwell (1953) pursued a similar direction, exploring the optimality conditions for "admissible" solutions and pointing out the connection between the vector maximum problem and what has become known today as "multiparametric linear programming" (see Sec. 8-5).

To this list of seminal mathematical works we should add the works of Blackwell (1956) and L. S. Shapley (1959) on games with vector payoffs (see Sec. 10-5.2). Unfortunately, none of these leads was followed up by either mathematicians or operations researchers or even the authors themselves!

The practical-minded operations researchers pursued *their* discussions of multiple objectives during the fifties apparently unaware of the already existing mathematical base. These discussions were good on problem recognition but rather limited in terms of methodology. We should mention B. O. Koopman (1953 and 1956), Charles J. Hitch (1953), W. M. Hoag (1956), and C. N. Klahr (1958).

The most tangible outcome of the fifties turned out to be the *goal programming* of Abraham Charnes and William W. Cooper, first introduced in their book (1961), parts of which were based on their earlier article (1957). The idea of goal programming was originally a restatement of T. C. Koopmans' earlier "efficiency" concept and was treated neither prominently nor extensively by the authors. They even outlined a procedure, the *spiral method*, for identifying all "efficient" solutions to a linear programming problem. Unfortunately this lead was not followed up by the authors either. Other books, Karlin (1959) and Hanssmann (1962), also took up the problem of multiobjective conflict, but still in the sketchy and uncommitted fashion of the fifties.

On a different front, the foundations of what is today known as "multiattribute utility theory" (see Chap. 12), were being laid down in the works of May (1954), Adams and Fagot (1959), and especially Yntema and Torgerson (1961), who introduced *utility function decomposition* both with and without interactive terms. But even in this area, there was a scientific pause and no significant follow-up work.

Miller and Starr revived the whole thing again in their book *Executive Decisions and Operations Research* (1959). But as before, no significant follow-up work resulted. Apparently the OR/MS world was too much preoccupied with refining computer-based mathematical algorithms and a little overwhelmed by the mathematical successes and elegance of single-criterion models.

Peter Bod (1963) laid the foundations of linear multiobjective programming and of what has today become known as the "multicriterion simplex method." It was, however, another ten years before working algorithms were actually developed.

In the mid-sixties Kuhn-Tucker's vector maximum theory experienced a short revival, this time by engineers: especially notable were Lotfi Zadeh (1963), of the later *fuzzy sets* fame; Klinger (1964), and Da Cunha and Polak (1966).

Also in the mid-sixties, multiattribute utility decomposition received more significant attention. Fishburn (1965) and Pollak (1967) stated the necessary and sufficient conditions for additive utility decomposition. Less mathematical but more practically appealing is a widely quoted work of Eckenrode (1965) and the less-quoted effort of Briskin (1966). Shepard's extremely stimulating, empirical paper (1964) confirmed that human performance, in trading off several attributes simultaneously, is not very impressive and implied that some sort of "aid" should be provided.

One of the most influential papers on multiattribute utility theory in the sixties was Howard Raiffa's RAND memorandum of 1969. A similarly influential RAND report, and one of the first overviews of multiattribute utility theory, was MacCrimmon (1968). We should also mention Keeney's first paper on quasiseparable utility functions (1968).

The true foundations for the serious and continuous study of problems with multiple conflicting objectives were laid by Erik Johnsen in his voluminous monograph, *Studies in Multiobjective Decision Models* (1968).

Goal programming had in the meantime received further elaboration and application (this time in the field of accounting) by Ijiri (1965), and later it acquired its preemptive weights version in the book by Lee (1972).

Multiobjective programming reemerged with new strength in the work of Saska (1968), which was based on the articles by Radzikowski (1967) and Jüttler (1967). Geoffrion's doctoral work (1965) should also be mentioned. Dinkelbach (1971) and Dinkelbach and Dürr (1972) provided further extensions of the vector maximum problem. Philip (1972), Evans and Steuer (1973), and the Zeleny monograph (1974) brought *linear multiobjective programming* firmly into existence.

The time was ripe for the First International Conference on Multiple Criteria Decision Making, held at the University of South Carolina on October 26 and 27, 1972. Sixty-three papers were presented and 250 people attended. The papers were collected in a volume edited by Cochrane and Zeleny (1973). This "big book" has become a classic of sorts; it contains an almost inexhaustible wealth of research and application ideas. The name of the conference, and its acronym MCDM, have since become the identifying marks of this new field of inquiry.

The South Carolina conference represented a turning point in MCDM research and applications. Many already famous and soon-to-be-famous researchers in MCDM participated: Churchman, Dawes, MacCrimmon, Fishburn, Keeney, Blin, Roy, Dyer, Yu, Zeleny, Dinkelbach, Isermann, Steuer, Ijiri, Green, Zadeh, Easton, Briskin, Wagner, and Ben-Israel, to name just a few. An explosive growth of MCDM literature followed in the seventies.

The Seventies MCDM was unquestionably the fastest growing and the most innovative OR/MS field of the seventies. The number of articles and books was well above 1000, and this growth is expected to continue well into the eighties. It was not until the late seventies that a large variety of practical applications began to appear, thus assuring a further growth of MCDM.

Because there is no way to do justice by a simple listing of all those who contributed to MCDM research in the seventies, we provide here a short review of only the most representative works. In this and the Bibliographical Notes after each chapter, we endeavor to build up a picture of "who's who" in MCDM today and who might be worth watching in the next decade.

The seventies witnessed a large number of conferences and published proceedings. Most were of high quality and represent a rich source of theoretical and practical material. *Multiple Criteria Decision Making: Kyoto 1975*, the proceedings of the TIMS/ORSA conference, was edited by Zeleny (1976) and contains contributions by Marschak, Rapoport, Charnes, Cooper, Hammond, Polak, Johnsen, Dawes, and others. It also contains Zeleny's first exposition of the theory of the displaced ideal. Other significant published proceedings include the volumes edited by Thiriez and Zionts (1976), Leitmann and Marzollo (1975), Leitmann (1976), Zionts (1978), Wendt and Vlek (1975), and Bell, Keeney, and Raiffa (1977).

Certain journals published special issues devoted to MCDM: *Management Science*, edited by Starr and Zeleny (1977), and *Computers & Operations Research*, edited by Zeleny (1980). These volumes contain methodological advances of significance to MCDM research and applications in the eighties.

Many journals now print articles on MCDM on a regular basis: *Omega*, *Computers & Operations Research*, *European Journal of Operational Research*, *Journal of the Operational Research Society*, *Journal of Optimization Theory and Applications*, *Water Resources Research*, *Mathematical Programming*, *Journal of Mathematical Analysis and Applications*, and even *Management Science* and *Operations Research*.

Several significant monographs and books also appeared during the seventies. A version of goal programming was covered by Lee (1972) and Ignizio (1976). More specialized treatment of multicriterion problems appeared in Easton (1973), Green and Wind (1973), Haimes, Hall, and Freedman (1975), Keeney and Raiffa (1976), Miller (1970), Wallenius (1975), Wilhelm (1975), Sfeir-Younis and Bromley (1977), and the survey of MCDM by Hwang and Masud (1979). An excellent, textbook exposition of multiobjective programming, *Multiobjective Programming and Planning*, was published by Cohon in 1978. Nijkamp and Spronk edited *Multiple Criteria Analysis: Practical Methods* (1980), Fandel and Gal the proceedings of the MCDM conference in Königswinter, Germany (1980), Morse those from Delaware (1980), and Colson and Zeleny published their monograph on multicriterion concept of risk (1979).

By the end of the seventies MCDM had become established as one of the most dynamic and widely applied areas of OR/MS. At the present time, research and applications of MCDM are continuing. Interactive programming, descriptive decision models, interfaces with decision support systems and judgmental psychology, multidimensional risk analyses, and applications to strategic management and economic policy making represent the major trends.

Lively scientific interest in MCDM is likely to continue well into the eighties. International MCDM conferences are now occurring on a yearly basis. For example, the American Association for Advancement of Science (AAAS) is sponsoring a major MCDM symposium in Washington, D.C., in January 1982. Other recent MCDM places of meetings include Newark, Delaware, in 1980; Laxenburg, Austria, in 1981; and, possibly, Mons, Belgium, in 1982. Preparations are going on for a 1982 conference and MCDM decennial volume entitled "MCDM 1982—Ten Years After," a recapitulation of the ten years since the first South Carolina conference of 1972. The number of regional and local conferences, seminars, and workshops is staggering. For example, European Working Group on MCDM is staging its conferences twice a year—more than twelve meetings up to 1980.

Interestingly enough, most of the MCDM activities take place outside and independently of the official OR/MS undertakings. MCDM is now able to stand on its own and bring its research results directly to practicing managers and decision makers. Activities are going on to establish an MCDM journal as well as an MCDM society which would evolve in parallel to the single-criterion pursuits of operations research and management sciences.

2-3 WHAT IS AN OPTIMUM?

One speaks of an "optimum" when one compares decision alternatives according to a *single* measure of merit. Conventional utility function (either single- or multiattribute) can provide such an external yardstick, as can some other convenient global measures, like profits, costs, sales, and growth. The emphasis is on the singleness or uniqueness of any given measure at any given time. When only one global criterion of choice is involved, any two alternatives can be compared, and one of the alternatives is preferred or the decision maker is indifferent.

More formally, the concept of optimum can be defined as follows: Given a fixed set of alternatives X, then $x^1 \in X$ indicates that alternative x^1 is feasible, i.e., it belongs to X. Any two alternatives x^1 and x^2 can have their utility (or other single measure of merit) compared in any of the following ways:

$$u(x^1) > u(x^2)$$ implies that x^1 is preferred to x^2

$$u(x^2) > u(x^1)$$ implies that x^2 is preferred to x^1

$$u(x^1) = u(x^2)$$ implies that the decision maker is indifferent between the two alternatives.

The above comparisons are transitive over all available alternatives; i.e., $u(x^1) > u(x^2)$ and $u(x^2) > u(x^3)$ imply that $u(x^1) > u(x^3)$ is also true.

A similar implication can be postulated for the relation of indifference. Any alternative $x^* \in X$ is *optimal* if and only if for *any* other alternative $x \in X$ the following is true: $u(x^*) > u(x)$ or $u(x^*)=u(x)$. *Given a fixed set* X *and a point function* u, *there is always at least one optimum* x*.

This technical notion of optimality has dominated operations research for most of its history.[1]

Roy (1979) cautions that the reality of executive decision making is quite different. Real decisions are based on a progressive comparison of the preference systems of *multiple* actors, in a generally fuzzy environment, evolving through interactions within the sphere of different political, value, and power frameworks. The preferences themselves are also fuzzy, incompletely formulated, nontransitive, and often inconsistent and conflicting. They differ from one actor to another, and throughout the decision-making process they change with new circumstances and information.

To quantify and aggregate such a variety of factors into a single objective function, a single criterion of choice, represents an undesirable reduction of reality.

Keen (1977) provides an excellent overview of the evolving concept of optimality. He notes that optimization in the traditional mathematical sense is impossible if multiple criteria are involved. Designing, for example, an optimal health care policy on the basis of conventional cost-benefit analysis means defining optimality with the single measuring rod of money. For example, Rice (1966) measured the "cost" of death from illness by computing earning expectancies. His tables showed that the life of a 20-year-old male "is worth the life of

---

[1]One should be able to understand the difference between "optimum" and "maximum" (or "minimum"). Optimum human body temperature is about 98.6°F. Maximum body temperature is likely to kill you.

two babies if they are boys and three if they are girls.'' The optimization paradigm has thus stalled on ''the curse of multidimensionality,'' as it was once characterized by Richard Bellman.

Keen calls for a new definition of optimality based on what is feasible and desirable for decision makers, especially in a political and social context. Simon's concept of *satisficing*, which makes clear that certain cognitive limits lead decision makers to think in terms of a *bounded rationality*, is often viewed as a suitable extension and modification of the concept of optimization. As we shall argue later, the notion of satisficing is only superficially compelling.

Both optimization and satisficing follow Tinbergen's dogma that the choice of goals and the analysis of means must be kept separate in economic policy planning. Both concepts generally ignore the dynamic interaction between means and ends. In Chap. 5 we treat the problem of means-ends dependency in an explicit and operational way.

With complex policy-planning issues, always marked by multiple criteria, decision makers are often more concerned with resolving conflict, reducing risk, and managing cognitive strain than with optimizing solutions. The MCDM model becomes a methodology supporting the problem-solving process of the decision maker.[1] The role of the analyst should not be to force prescriptions and recommendations—there is no solution independent of the decision maker's judgment.

Does this mean that the ''best'' solution is whatever the decision maker declares to be the best?[2] Before answering this question, let us attempt to resolve the issue of optimization versus satisficing.

Optimization versus satisficing   Herbert A. Simon, the 1978 Nobel laureate in economic science, has written that ''no one in his right mind will satisfice if he can just as well optimize.''[3] Yet Simon also suggests that the choice to satisfice, or to accept the ''good enough,'' is generally more realistic than the choice to optimize the satisfaction or utility of the decision maker. Is Simon suggesting that we abandon the state of being in our right mind? Let us explore the apparent dilemma of these statements in more detail, with two arguments: First, there is a confusion between so-called ''bounded'' rationality and satisficing. Second, satisficing is often interpreted as an attempt to attain prespecified aspiration levels or goals with respect to given criteria when in fact, satisficing is the outcome or end result of an incomplete or unsuccessful at-

---

[1]Compare with the statement of ORSA President Seth Bonder: ''I believe OR research should have an inward focus with the objective not one of helping the decision-maker but, more introspectively, of helping itself.'' (*Operations Research,* vol. 27, no. 2, 1979, p. 218.)

[2]We use the term ''best'' instead of ''optimal'' in order to avoid the latter's connotation of objectivity and to stress the subjective underpinnings of the former. Also, we try to avoid some confused extensions of ''optimal,'' like ''multicriteria optimization,'' which are contradictory and inadequate in this context. MCDM methodologies strive for subjectively ''best'' or compromise solutions, optimization techniques search for mathematically optimal solutions.

[3]H. A. Simon, *Science of the Artificial*, MIT Press, Cambridge, 1969.

tempt at optimization. Satisficing is not a major guiding principle of human decision making.

The idealized concept of rationality assumes maximization of a fixed or relatively stable objective, a known set of relevant alternatives and their outcomes, and a skill in computation that allows one to reach the highest attainable point with respect to the objective.

In reality, objectives are dynamic rather than static, information is seldom perfect, and alternatives, along with human cognition, are incomplete and limited. There are obvious time and cost constraints on the amount of effort that can be spent in the search for the optimum. Alternatives characterized by multidimensional consequences do not lend themselves to a well-organized and easily quantified preference ordering. Environmental forces, implementation issues, and one's confidence in the decision present additional limitations.

An ideal objective rationality is therefore unattainable; the capacity of the human mind to formulate and solve complex problems is inadequate with respect to objectively defined rational behavior. Decision makers can operate on the principle of limited or bounded rationality only.

The point is that neither maximization nor optimization is incompatible with bounded rationality. Given all the constraints and limitations indicated above, one can still pursue a given maximizing objective *subject to constraints*. Unconstrained, unbounded optimization is rarely postulated in any economic theory; it is a mathematical artifact. *Bounded optimality*, i.e., optimization under all the constraints and limitations of the human mind, would be a suitable term for human decision making. People always do the best that they can or that they wish to under the circumstances.

Note that satisfactory or good-enough solutions are the result of bounded optimization—they are good enough with respect to existing and currently considered constraints. They become acceptable under given decision circumstances, but they are not a priori postulated aspiration levels or guidelines for decision-making behavior.

Figure 2-4 demonstrates this argument graphically. Let X denote the complete, full-information base set of available alternatives. Then maximization of a single objective leads to its highest possible value u. This is of course an idealized, objectively rational solution. In reality, the limitations of bounded rationality will allow us to perceive only a small fraction of relevant alternatives correctly. Let us denote this limited set as X'. Maximizing our objective under these conditions will lead to a bounded optimum, characterized by value u'.

Achievement u' could be satisfactory or good enough with respect to the absolute (and unknown) maximum u. Or u' might not be acceptable and we would have to search for more information and extend the current feasible set X'. In either case, the satisfactory or good-enough solution is the *result* of bounded optimization.

Suppose not only that u' is satisfactory but that even u'' is satisfactory. The decision maker has defined u'' as the satisfactory aspiration level. He or she

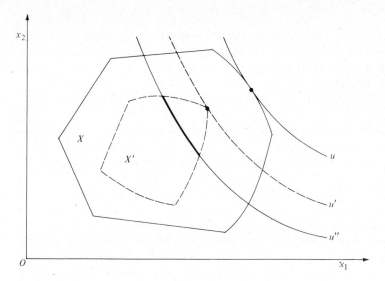

Figure 2-4 Bounded rationality and optimization.

engages in a search activity and ascertains that u'' is indeed feasible—good-enough solutions (the heavy section of curve u'' in Fig. 2-4) are available. Being a satisficer in the Simon sense, he is satisfied with the outcome u'' when he might have achieved u'.

The reader can now appreciate better the warning that people in their right mind will not satisfice if they can just as well optimize. One can and should always optimize in a bounded sense. In fact, most of us normally do practice bounded optimization, with rare exceptions such as the cautious gambler who sets a limit of $100 on winnings and does not try for more in fear of losing it, or the worker who works only to secure subsistence food, clothing, and shelter and then stops.[1]

The problem with satisficing is not that performance can fall short of the level of aspiration but that the level of aspiration can be set too low. One cannot establish a good and practically attainable aspiration level without first exploring the limits of X'. That can be achieved only via bounded optimization over X'. Then why not set the aspiration level arbitrarily large so that it will never be achieved at the first approximation? Because this is too clumsy. One would then have to adjust the level downward and search for feasible alternatives to provide the newly targeted performance. If none were found, this process of

---

[1]Even here I am not sure that we observe satisficing rather than bounded optimization. Obviously, the costs (time, energy, risk, etc.) of searching for a better "solution" must be taken into account. If they are perceived to be higher than the expected marginal return, one may stop searching. It appears *as if* one satisfices—due to the bounded insight and understanding of the observer.

adapting aspirations to performance could continue indefinitely. Bounded optimization achieves the desired result much more efficiently and elegantly.

Ackoff and Sasieni identified the weaknesses of satisficing early, clearly, and succintly:

> Satisficing is usually defended with the argument that it is better to produce a feasible plan that is not optimal than an optimal plan that is not feasible. This argument is only superficially compelling. Reflection reveals that it overlooks the possibility of obtaining the best feasible plan. Optimality can (and should) be defined so as to take feasibility into account, and the effort to do so forces us to examine the criteria of feasibility that are seldom made explicit in the satisfaction process. Furthermore, the approximate attainment of an optimal plan may be more desirable than exact attainment of an inferior one. Not surprisingly, this type of planning seldom produces a significant break with the past. . . . It appeals to planners who are not willing to stick their necks out. (Ackoff and Sasieni 1968, p. 443)

Beyond satisficing So far we have compared optimization and satisficing within the single-objective framework. While optimization methodologies are exclusively connected with a single criterion, satisficing concepts have been stretched to include multiple criteria as well. This had led to the concept of *goal programming*, where target or goal levels are predetermined for each of the criteria or objectives involved. We deal with this methodology in detail in Chap. 9. At this point let us simply state that all the difficulties associated with the single-objective concept of satisficing are only magnified when applied to the multicriterion case.

From a purely computational viewpoint, under single or multiple criteria, *satisficing is more demanding and less expedient than bounded optimization*. The set of available alternatives has to be identified in both cases—how else would one be able to ascertain that a given solution is feasible? The objectives must be operationally defined—how else would one be able to compute goal-attainment levels that are appropriate for a given solution? But satisficing requires more: an intelligent setting of aspiration levels prior to the analysis and prior to exploring the limits of a feasible set. These levels are hard to obtain and their purpose is obscure; if they are set incorrectly one has to engage in a step-by-step adaptation process to finally bring the goals (if everything goes well) to the levels corresponding to those of bounded optimization.

Then what about the "best" solution in the multicriterion case? Optimization is a technical concept, inapplicable in situations where conflict, ambiguity, multidimensionality, and qualitative judgment are dominant. Thus, in such situations, there can be no absolute definition of optimality—it is contingent on the type of problem, on the decision maker's purpose, ability, and needs, and on the context of the problem. In other words, the "best" solution to a multicriterion problem is that which is judged such by the decision maker. It is the solution which is preferred, understood, accepted, supported, and implemented *with confidence*.

The confidence of the decision maker that the best solution has been found is crucial. The analyst can help to build up such confidence or gather arguments to weaken it. Törn (1978) even argues it does not matter what this best solution is—it could be satisficing or maximizing, compromising or arbitrary—the only thing that matters is that the decision maker is confident that the best solution has been obtained.

MCDM methodologies and analyses are intended to support and develop the decision maker's confidence in a contemplated "best" solution. Many conventional OR/MS analyses fail because the issue of building up the decision maker's confidence has been ignored. The normative OR/MS solution prescribes how things *should* be, and if the decision maker expresses doubts, his or her rationality may be questioned. Decision makers are expected to have confidence in the analyst and the analyst's tools rather than in themselves.

If the problem to be solved is the rare purely technical, single-dimensional one, no problem of confidence is likely to arise. The optimal solution will also be the best solution and thus will command the decision maker's highest confidence. But such confidence in the problem's solution actually derives from the problem's formulation: In a single-criterion problem, the solution more or less follows from the formulation, and therefore if decision makers have confidence in the formulation, they are bound to have confidence in the solution.

Such is not the case with multiple-criteria problems: Even if the problem is correctly formulated, there is no guarantee of the decision maker's confidence in the solution. But MCDM resolves this difficulty with a solution concept that delivers a high level of confidence similar to that experienced with single-objective optimization. For if there is a high level of confidence in the formulation of the problem, then a solution which optimizes all criteria simultaneously, a so-called "ideal solution," will be accepted with the highest level of confidence. This ideal solution is normally unattainable, and the decision maker attempts to maintain confidence by considering the feasible solutions closest to the perceived ideal. The proximity to the ideal guarantees that a high-confidence "best" solution can be identified. To be as close to the perceived ideal as possible is then identical with confidence maximization and thus constitutes an operational criterion for deciding when the "best" solution has been achieved.

A decision maker's confidence that a solution is the best depends on a large variety of factors:

1. The larger the imprecision, uncertainty, and fuzziness of a problem, the smaller the confidence in its solution
2. The smaller the correspondence between problem formulation and the real characteristics of the problem, the smaller the confidence in its recommendations
3. The larger the number of alternatives of comparable performance, the less confidence in the final choice
4. The greater the correspondence between the model's analytical recommendations and the decision maker's intuitive judgments, the higher the level of confidence
5. The larger the number of feasible alternatives evaluated in the process of choice, the larger the confidence in the final choice

The higher confidence in a given solution, the greater the motivation to its commitment and successful implementation. Some of these factors are potentially in conflict because of the multidimensionality of confidence itself. Take factors 1 and 2, for example. A well-defined, well-structured problem commands a high level of confidence. But a well-defined, well-structured *formulation* of a problem commands little confidence if the real, underlying problem is ill-structured, complex, and fuzzy.

In summary, the good-enough or satisfactory solution appears to be the outcome or result, not the input, of decision analysis. One does not know what is satisfactory until one has explored the available alternatives. One has to reach for the unreachable, the ideal. As William Blake put it, "You never know what is enough unless you know what is more than enough."

2-4 NONDOMINANCE AND PARETO OPTIMALITY

An interesting feature recurs in all the concepts discussed in Sec. 2-1. We introduced the efficiency frontier, the optimal policy curve, and the cost-time trade-off curve, and we could have continued with the additional concepts of bargaining set, admissible set, sets of nondominated solutions, etc. All these solution sets consist of points or elements having a simple and highly desirable property: nondominance.

A point within such a set is nondominated in that no other point is feasible at which the *same or better* performance could be achieved with respect to *all* criteria (dimensions), with at least one being strictly better.

The nondominance solution concept, originating with Pareto (1906), has been one of the cornerstones of traditional economic theory. Rarely disputed, it is advanced by almost every writer in the economic literature. It is usually stated as the Pareto principle or Pareto optimality principle: a state of the world *A* is preferable to a state of the world *B* if at least one person is better off in *A* and nobody is worse off. This is a strong normative statement with high intuitive appeal to economists. It defines a state compared with which there is no other state in which one consumer can obtain higher satisfaction without at the same time lowering the satisfaction of at least one other consumer.[1]

T. C. Koopmans, the 1975 Nobel prize winner in economics, has extended Pareto optimality to *productive efficiency*, a state in which productive activity has been so organized that, within the given limitations of resources and technology, there is no other way of producing more of some desired commodity without reducing the output of some other desired commodity. This productive efficiency is achieved at the production-possibility frontier, and there is not much difference between the two concepts.

---

[1]Free agents (individuals who can possess wealth and enter into contracts) will "make deals" until no contract can be proposed that is satisfactory to *all* the contracting parties. This state is Pareto optimal. But note that the model depends on an initial distribution of wealth and subsequent bargaining skills.

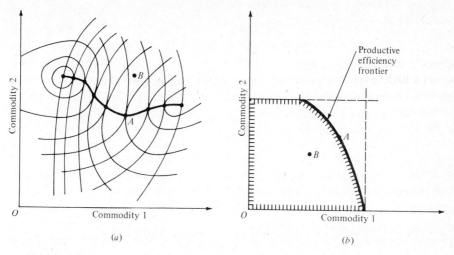

Figure 2–5 (a) Pareto optimality—contract curve. (b) Productive efficiency frontier.

Fig. 2-5 presents graphic representations of both interpretations. In Fig. 2-5a combinations (or bundles) of two commodities are being ranked by two individuals according to their corresponding families of indifference curves. Observe that Pareto-optimal bundles lie on the curve passing through the points of tangency of both indifference-curve systems. Any point off the connecting line (contract curve) is dominated. The preferred movement is from B to A.[1]

In Fig. 2-5b the shaded area delimits the set of technologically feasible production mixes of two commodities. The heavily traced boundary corresponds to those mixes for which there is no other way of producing more of one commodity without reducing the output of the second commodity. The preferred movement is again from B to A. All production mixes off the heavy boundary are deemed "inefficient."

For our purposes we simply substitute criteria, attributes, or objective functions for persons or commodities, and decision alternatives or solutions for states of the world: Solution B is dominated by solution A if by moving from B to A we improve at least one objective function while leaving others unchanged. Solution A is nondominated if there is no other solution which would improve at least one objective function and not worsen any other.

It is useful to express nondominance in terms of a simple vector comparison. Let x and y be two vectors of n components, $x_1, \ldots, x_n$ and $y_1, \ldots, y_n$ respectively. Thus,

$$x = (x_1, \ldots, x_n) \quad \text{and} \quad y = (y_1, \ldots, y_n)$$

[1]If two individuals start with the same bundle, and if the bundle is on the heavy curve, they won't "make a deal" to exchange goods. Heterogeneous individuals issued homogeneous bundles will in general *not* be Pareto optimal *except* when on the heavy curve, e.g., POWs issued a pack of cigarettes and candy bars by the Red Cross.

We say that x dominates y if

$$x_i \geq y_i, \qquad i = 1, \ldots, n$$

and $x_i > y_i$ for at least one i.

We may compare x and y directly and say that x dominates y if $x \geq y$ and $x \neq y$.

Let us assume that x belongs to a set of feasible solutions or feasible decision alternatives, designated X. Then x is nondominated in X if there exists no other $\bar{x}$ in X such that $\bar{x} \geq x$ and $\bar{x} \neq x$. The set of all nondominated solutions in X is designated N. The main property of N is that for every *dominated* solution (i.e., feasible solution *not* in N) we can find a solution in N at which no vector components are smaller and at least one is larger. Figure 2-6 provides some graphic explanation of the above concepts. (For a numerical example of dominance-nondominance relations the reader should return to Sec. 1-4.3, The problem of profit planning.) Feasible set X, the shaded area in the two-dimensional space of points $x = (x_1, x_2)$, consists of feasible combinations of x_1 and x_2. For example, x_1 and x_2 could represent production levels of product 1 and product 2 respectively. As objective functions, they would correspond to "maximize production of product 1" and "maximize production of product 2."

Observe the point x in X *is dominated by all points in the shaded subregion of X*, indicating that the levels of both components can be increased simultaneously. Only for points in N does this subregion of improvement extend beyond the boundaries of X into the infeasible region. Thus the points in N are the only points satisfying our definitions, and they make up the heavy boundary of X. All other points of X are dominated.

The set of nondominated solutions is often referred to in the literature as the "efficient set," the "admissible set," the "noninferior set," the "Pareto-optimal set," etc. We shall use the term "nondominated" because of its clear, unambiguous meaning and because it best describes what such points really are: not dominated by other points.

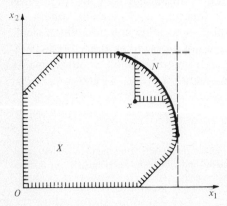

Figure 2-6 Set of nondominated solutions.

Finding N on X is one of the major tasks of multiobjective programming, and we shall deal with many of its technical aspects later. At this point we shall make some comments about the usefulness of nondominated solutions. Among the advantages of N are the following:

1. Multiple objectives are often incommensurate, both quantitative and qualitative, and carry different weights of importance. This leads to a complex problem of trade-off evaluation using the decision maker's utility or preference function. Reliable construction of a utility function may, however, be too complex, unrealistic, or impractical. The set of nondominated solutions then provides a meaningful step forward under such conditions of relative ignorance.

2. If more is always preferable to less, then any solution which maximizes the utility function of a *rational* decision maker must be nondominated: If more is preferred to less then only higher or equal utility may be derived from the increased levels of corresponding attributes or criteria of choice. Such a utility function is said to be nondecreasing in its arguments; that is,

$$u(x_1 + \Delta_1, x_2 + \Delta_2) \geq u(x_1, x_2) \qquad \text{for } \Delta_1, \Delta_2 \geq 0$$

Thus, regardless of the specific mathematical form of u, we know that its maximum will be reached at a nondominated point.

3. If N consists of only a relatively small number of solutions or alternatives of choice, there is no need to search for the decision maker's utility function. Consequently it makes sense to explore X and characterize its N *before* engaging in the assessment of u. It is not wise to gather and process all the information needed for utility assessment without finding the approximate size of N first. It is even possible that an alternative will emerge, such as shown in Fig. 2-7.

   Observe that N consists of a single point only, that such a point will *always* be the choice under the assumption of nondecreasing utility functions, and

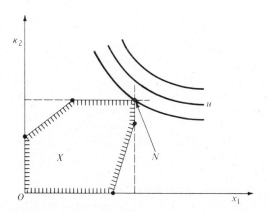

Figure 2-7 Conflict-free solution.

that an assessment of u for this particular X would constitute an effort of considerable redundancy.

4. The set of nondominated alternatives can be useful in dealing with more complicated types of X, for example, discrete point sets or nonconvex sets of feasible alternatives. Figure 2-8a shows seven distinct alternatives. The nondominated ones are indicated by heavy dots. Observe that only points 3 and 6 are dominated by some other available points, while the nondominated set comprises points 1, 2, 4, 5, and 7. In Fig. 2-8b observe that the nondominated boundary is not necessarily continuous, especially in the presence of "gaps" in X (nonconvex cases of X). Both these cases are more difficult to handle analytically, and we shall deal with them separately later on.

A careful review of the figures displaying two-dimensional nondominated sets would reveal that *a nondominated solution is a feasible solution for which an increase in value of any one criterion can be achieved only at the expense of a decrease in value of at least one other criterion.* This definition leads naturally to the concept of *value trade-offs*: How much achievement with respect to criterion 1 are we willing to sacrifice in order to gain a particular achievement with respect to criterion 2? The nondominated boundary is sometimes characterized as the "trade-off curve."

We must emphasize the importance of a priori knowledge of N in this context. In Fig. 2-9 observe that depending on the position of x^* and the curvature of the nondominated boundary in its immediate neighborhood, we can make a pretty good, nonsubjective assessment of the worthiness of x^* with respect to value trade-off. Assume that there are two *fixed* alternatives x^1 and x^2, while x^* is allowed some flexibility of displacement. Observe that as x^* is displaced further in the northeast direction, less and less can be gained by

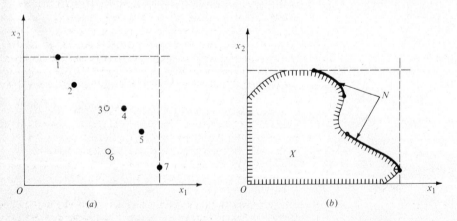

Figure 2-8 (a) Nondominance on a discrete point set. (b) Nondominance on a nonconvex set.

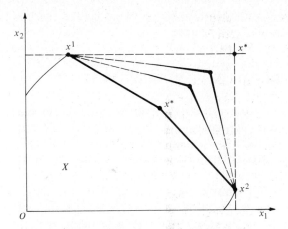

Figure 2-9 Value trade-off under the displacement of x^*.

giving up more and more in trading off the achievements with respect to both criteria. We must sacrifice progressively more of x_1 to gain progressively less of x_2 (and vice versa) when moving even slightly from x^*. Ultimately, at its extreme position, point x^* cannot be abandoned at all because an infinitely large sacrifice is needed to obtain an infinitely small gain.

Thus, the question we posed earlier: "How much achievement with respect to criterion 1 is the decision maker willing to give up in order to improve achievement on criterion 2?" is incorrect because it all depends on the position of x^*, the point at which such a question is asked. In other words, even though it is subjective, criteria value trade-off is not a fixed and easily accessible quantity, but rather it is a situation-dependent, dynamic, and ever-changing descriptor of immediate circumstances. To gain a *fixed* amount of x_1 the decision maker will have to give up more and more of x_2 as x^* moves in the northeast direction. Thus, the decision maker will be less and less willing to move away from x^* as its worthiness increases. Observe that the value trade-off question then reflects subjective judgment and personal differences to a lesser degree. Regardless of the personal value structures involved, point x^* becomes more and more acceptable for a widening variety of decision makers.

Why is it so important to discuss all this at an early stage of our journey? Just imagine that the consecutive displacements of x^* in Fig. 2-9 actually represent the creative generation or unfolding of new, previously unavailable alternatives of action. The utmost importance of generating new alternatives would then become indisputable and its place in the decision-making *process* almost mandatory. We shall devote a whole chapter specifically to this issue, even though the concept itself permeates the whole book. We want to avoid the self-imposed limitation of Keeney and Raiffa in their recent book on *Decisions with Multiple Objectives*: "We talked about the importance of generating imaginative alternatives but then we said that in this book we would not stress this point, no matter how important it may be'' (Keeney and Raiffa 1976, p. 545).

2-5 CAN THERE BE SINGLE-OBJECTIVE "DECISION MAKING"?

The reader has already probably encountered the difficulty of finding suitable examples of problems with purely unidimensional decisions. Even profit maximization ceases to retain its singularity when one starts to think about it. It has been well established—see, for example, Gordon (1961)—that nonfinancial attractions and criteria frequently outrank business profits as the primary incentive for the majority of top executives in large corporations. In ''maximizing'' profits the executive must consider the firm's goodwill, the reputation of its brand name, lawful and conventionally acceptable ways of making profits, and many other criteria. Many business owners might try to avoid unusually high profits for fear of taxes or government regulation. In short, in most situations business executives and managers deal with multiple criteria even though they may use a single criterion as a proxy descriptor of a complex situation.

Truly singular objectives or criteria usually occur under extreme conditions of time pressure, emergency, or crisis. Under such conditions, one often concentrates on a single criterion in order to simplify, speed up, or control the decision process itself. Another rationale for the singular objective is that the singularity itself can become an objective. One can pursue profits for profits' sake, just as one can try to construct the fastest car or traverse a distance in the minimum of time.

We shall now challenge the reader with the following statement: No decision making occurs unless at least *two* criteria are present. If only one criterion exists, mere measurement and search suffice for making a choice.

If you are asked to select the biggest apple from a basket, the tallest man from a group, the heaviest book from a shelf, or the best-paying job, are you engaged in decision making? Or is it sufficient to measure the attribute in question and search for the maximal alternative? This reasoning does not imply that measurement and search are simple and easy activities. Often the attribute in question is difficult to measure, resulting in an unreliable, fuzzy, or ambiguous evaluation. How does one measure utility, leadership, creativity, or future profitability? Sometimes we can measure quite precisely, but the search itself is difficult because of the large number of alternatives. For example, which combination of integers x_1 and x_2 will maximize the expression $(x_1 - x_2)^3 x_2$?

Theoretically then, if there is only a single criterion which can be perfectly measured and efficiently searched for, indeed no decision making is involved. Even if two alternatives attain precisely the same scores, no decision making is needed: Either one will do. (Remember that nothing else matters; therefore, no additional criteria should be brought into the analysis.) If our criterion is not perfectly measurable, then the evaluation and comparison of alternatives is correspondingly difficult. One has to resort to judgment (see Sec. 1-1.3), not to decision making. Decision making occurs only as additional dimensions, such as an estimated reliability, a judge's credibility, or the cost of erroneous judgments, are brought in. In essence, then, no unidimensional decision problem can exist!

But when we face multiple criteria, even if our measurement is perfect and the search along each dimension is fully efficient, there is still a need for deciding. The choice is not implicit in the measurement.

The previously introduced concept of nondominated solutions supports our argument on more technical grounds. A family of multiattribute utility functions, monotonically nondecreasing in all of their variables, is characterized by a corresponding set of nondominated solutions. Given such a family of utility functions, all rational decision makers would prefer a nondominated choice. (It is interesting to contemplate that price often serves as a tool to bring a dominated alternative into a nondominated set, at least in competitive markets.) It is obvious that only if there are at least two nondominated solutions is any decision to be made. The unidimensional or aggregage utility functions usually provide a nondominated set of dimension zero, i.e., exactly one point (not one choice, for one choice is no choice). Even if there are multiple solutions of equal utility, they are fully substitutable, and unless some additional dimensions are brought in, one solution is as good as any other.

Even if we relax the monotonicity restriction for the utility function (i.e., more is better, or at least not worse) and allow an ideal point or points to exist along the utility scale, no unidimensional choices appear. For example, assume that three lumps of sugar in my coffee is the optimal alternative (an ideal point). But if that alternative is not available, would I prefer one lump or five? If the utilities of one and five lumps of sugar are perfectly measurable and different, then the choice is obvious and no decision making is needed. If their utilities are precisely the same, then it does not matter and I can simply toss a coin.

The reader might wonder about the importance of these semantic distinctions between decision making and measurement-search activities. Is it necessary to spend so much time on making this point, even if correct? We believe it is important to be able to identify whether a given difficulty is due to inadequate measurement, inefficient search, or incompetent decision making. Also one should be able to determine in which of these areas help might be needed. Most importantly, good measurement and efficient search are necessary to but certainly not sufficient for decision making in the presence of multiple criteria.

We have said that at least two criteria are necessary for decision making to occur. We should add that the multiplicity of criteria, although also a necessary condition, is not a sufficient condition for decision making. There are situations—quite rare to be sure—when one of the available alternatives attains the highest scores with respect to *all* criteria, i.e., there is only one nondominated solution. For example, if you are seeking a spouse and there is one person of the opposite sex who is the most intelligent, physically the most attractive, the richest, the most lovable—and, most importantly, if this person wants to marry you—no decision making is usually necessary.

2-6 BIBLIOGRAPHICAL NOTE

In the history of MCDM, there is a conspicuous absence of economists concerned about the multiplicity of human objectives, with one notable exception: Nicholas Georgescu-Roegen, an economist's economist, called in 1954 for "a theory of entrepreneurial decisions under multiple criteria." His article, "Choice, Expectations, and Measurability," provides an adequate background for evolving a new theory of economic behavior which would transcend that untenable artifact, *homo oeconomicus*. It is unfortunate that the foundations laid by Georgescu-Roegen have apparently been overlooked by a generation of economists—the work is still to be done and the challenge involved is considerable. So are the potential rewards for an able student taking up the challenge.

In Sec. 2-2, we carefully review the history of MCDM and list a large number of representative writings and publications which have enriched it. We cannot analyze these works one by one, but note that often the original exposition of an approach is still stimulating and full of ideas which are waiting yet for their elaboration. For the serious student of MCDM, going back to the sources is highly recommended.

In this chapter we deal with some classical OR/MS topics: portfolio selection, inventory control, critical-path analysis. These are well covered in most current OR/MS texts. Out of the hundreds of textbooks devoted to single-criterion analysis, we can recommend the charming and simple introduction by Waddington (1977), the rigorous and complete compendium by Wagner (1969), and the appealing intermediate text by Loomba (1978).

For the student who would like to study some of these areas in more detail, we recommend the specialized books by Markowitz (1959, 1970) and Sharpe (1970) on portfolio selection, Starr and Miller (1962) on models for inventory control, and Moder and Phillips (1964) on critical-path analysis.

Our discussion of satisficing versus optimization should be complemented by readings from the books of Simon (1957, 1960) and the article by Keen (1977). The book by Ackoff and Sasieni (1968) is another lasting classic which provides a sensible discussion of operations research and the paradigm of optimization.

The bibliographical listing for this chapter is quite extensive and the space available does not allow for a more detailed commentary by this author. It is hoped that both students and instructors will be able to make their own choices. We provide detailed comments on some of the books and articles in the Bibliographical Notes to later chapters.

Ackoff, R. L., and M. W. Sasieni: *Fundamentals of Operations Research*, Wiley, New York, 1968.

Adams, E. W., and R. Fagot: "A Model of Riskless Choice," *Behavioral Science*, vol. 4, 1959, pp. 1–10.

Arrow, K. J., E. W. Barankin, and D. Blackwell: "Admissible Points of Convex Sets," in H. W. Kuhn and A. W. Tucker (eds.), *Contributions to the Theory of Games*, Princeton, Princeton, N.J., 1953, pp. 87–91.

Bell, D. E., R. L. Keeney, and H. Raiffa (eds.): *Conflicting Objectives in Decisions*, Wiley, New York, 1977.

Blackwell, D.: "An Analog of the Minimax Theorem for Vector Payoffs," *Pacific Journal of Mathematics*, vol. 6, no. 1, Spring 1956, pp. 1–8.

Bod, P.: "Lineáris programozás több, egyidejüleg adott célfüggveny szerint," *Publications of the Mathematical Institute of the Hungarian Academy of Sciences*, ser. B, vol. 8, no. 4, 1963, pp. 541–544.

Briskin, L. E.: "A Method of Unifying Multiple Objective Functions," *Management Science*, vol. 12, no. 10, 1966, pp. B406–B416.

Charnes, A., and W. W. Cooper: *Management Models and Industrial Applications of Linear Programming*, vols. 1 and 2, Wiley, New York, 1961.

———and———: "Management Models and Industrial Applications of Linear Programming," *Management Science*, vol. 4, no. 1, 1957, pp. 81–87.

Cochrane, J. L., and M. Zeleny (eds.): *Multiple Criteria Decision Making*, University of South Carolina Press, Columbia, 1973.

Cohon, J. L., *Multiobjective Programming and Planning*, Academic Press, New York, 1978.

Colson, G., and M. Zeleny, *Uncertain Prospects Ranking and Portfolio Analysis under the Conditions of Partial Information*, Mathematical Systems in Economics no. 44, Oelgeschlager, Gunn & Hain Publishers, Cambridge, Mass., 1979.

Da Cunha, N. O., and E. Polak: "Constrained Minimization under Vector-Valued Criteria in Finite Dimensional Spaces," Electronic Research Lab. Rep. ERL-188, University of California, Berkeley, 1966.

Dinkelbach, W.: "Über einen Lösungsansatz zum Vektormaximumproblem," in M. Beckmann (ed.), *Unternehmensforschung Heute*, Springer-Verlag, Berlin, 1971, pp. 1–13.

———and W. Dürr: "Effizienenzaussagen bei Ersatzprogramen zum Vektormaximumproblem," in R. Henn, H. P. Künzi, and H. Schubert (eds.), *Operations Research-Verfahren*, vol. 12, Verlag Anton Hain, Meisenheim, 1971.

Easton, A.: *Complex Managerial Decisions Involving Multiple Objectives*, Wiley, New York, 1973.

Eckenrode, R. T.: "Weighing Multiple Criteria," *Management Science*, vol. 12, no. 3, 1965, pp. 180–192.

Evans, J. P., and R. E. Steuer: "A Revised Simplex Method for Linear Multiple Objective Programs," *Mathematical Programming*, vol. 5, no. 1, 1973, pp. 54–72.

Fandel, G., and T. Gal (eds.), *Multiple Criteria Decision Making, Theory and Application, Königswinter 1979*, Springer-Verlag, New York, 1980.

Fishburn, P. C.: "Independence in Utility Theory with Whole Product Sets," *Operations Research*, vol. 13, 1965, pp. 28–45.

Franklin, B.: "Letter to Joseph Priestley (1772)," *The Benjamin Franklin Sampler*, Fawcett, New York, 1956.

Geoffrion, A. M.: "A Parametric Programming Solution to the Vector Maximum Problem, with Applications to Decisions under Uncertainty," Operations Research Program Tech. Rep. 11, Stanford University, February 1965.

Georgescu-Roegen, N.: "Choice, Expectations and Measurability," *Quarterly Journal of Economics*, vol. 68, no. 4, 1954, pp. 503–541.

Gordon, R. A.: *Business Leadership in the Large Corporation*, University of California Press, Berkeley, 1961, pp. 312–313.

Green, P. E., and Y. Wind: *Multiattribute Decisions in Marketing: A Measurement Approach*, Dryden Press, Hinsdale, Ill., 1973.

Haimes, Y. Y., W. A. Hall, and H. T. Freedman: *Multiobjective Optimization in Water Resources Systems, The Surrogate Trade-off Method*, Elsevier, New York, 1975.

Hanssmann, F.: *Operations Research in Production and Inventory Control*, Wiley, New York, 1962.

Hitch, C. J.: "Sub-Optimization in Operations Research," *Operations Research*, vol. 1, no. 3, 1953, pp. 87–99.

Hoag, W. M.: "The Relevance of Cost in Operations Research," *Operations Research*, vol. 4, no. 3, 1956, pp. 448–459.

Hwang, C. L., and A. Masud: *Multiple Objective Decision Making—Methods and Applications*, Springer-Verlag, New York, 1979.

Ignizio, J. P.: *Goal Programming and Extensions*, Lexington Books, Lexington, Mass., 1976.

Ijiri, Y.: *Management Goals and Accounting for Control*, North-Holland Publishing, Amsterdam, 1965.

Johnsen, E.: *Studies in Multiobjective Decision Models*, Studentlitteratur, Lund, Sweden, 1968.

Jüttler, H.: "Lineinaia modelj s neskolkimi celevimi funkciami," *Ekonomika i Matematicheskoe Metody*, vol. 3, no. 3, 1967, pp. 397–406.

Karlin, S.: *Mathematical Methods and Theory in Games, Programming and Economics*, vol. 1, Addison-Wesley, Reading, Mass., 1959.

Keen, P. G. W.: "The Evolving Concept of Optimality," in M. K. Starr and M. Zeleny (eds.), *Multiple Criteria Decision Making*, TIMS Studies in the Management Sciences, vol. 6, North-Holland Publishing, Amsterdam, 1977, pp. 31–57.

Keeney, R. L.: "Quasi-Separable Utility Functions," *Naval Research Logistics Quarterly*, vol. 15, 1968, pp. 551–565.

———and H. Raiffa: *Decisions with Multiple Objectives: Preferences and Value Tradeoffs*, Wiley, New York, 1976.

Klahr, C. N.: "Multiple Objectives in Mathematical Programming," *Operations Research*, vol. 6, no. 6, 1958, pp. 849–855.

Klinger, A.: "Vector-Valued Performance Criteria," *IEEE Transactions on Automatic Control*, AC-9, no. 1, 1964, pp. 117–118.

Koopman, B. O.,: "Fallacies in Operations Research," *Operations Research*, vol. 4, no. 4, 1956, pp. 422–426.

———: "The Optimum Distribution of Effort," *Operations Research*, vol. 1, no. 2, 1953, pp. 52–63.

Koopmans, T. C. (ed.): *Activity Analysis of Production and Allocation*, Cowles Commission Monograph 13, Wiley, New York, 1951, pp. 33–97.

Kuhn, H. W., and A. W. Tucker: "Nonlinear Programming," in J. Neyman (ed.), *Proceedings of the Second Berkeley Symposium on Mathematical Statistics and Probability*, University of California Press, Berkeley, 1951, pp. 481–492.

Lee, S. M.: *Goal Programming for Decision Analysis*, Auerbach Publishers, Philadelphia, 1972.

Leitmann, G. (ed.): *Multicriteria Decision Making and Differential Games*, Plenum, New York, 1976.

——— and A. Marzollo (eds.): *Multicriteria Decision Making*, Springer-Verlag, New York, 1975.

Loomba, P. N.: *Management—A Quantitative Perspective*, Macmillan, New York, 1978.

MacCrimmon, K. R.: "Decision Making Among Multiple-Attribute Alternatives: A Survey and Consolidated Approach," RAND Memorandum RM-4823-ARPA, Santa Monica, Calif., 1968.

Markowitz, H. M.: *Portfolio Selection: Efficient Diversification of Investments*, Cowles Foundation Monograph 16, Wiley, New York, 1959, 1970.

May, K. O.: "Transitivity, Utility, and Aggregation in Preference Patterns," *Econometrica*, vol. 22, 1954, pp. 1–13.

Miller, D. R., and M. K. Starr: *Executive Decisions and Operations Research*, Prentice-Hall, Englewood Cliffs, N.J., 1959, 1969.

Miller, J. R.: *Professional Decision Making: A Procedure for Evaluating Complex Alternatives*, Praeger, New York, 1970.

Moder, J. J., and C. R. Phillips: *Project Management with CPM and PERT*, Van Nostrand Reinhold, New York, 1964.

Nijkamp, P., and J. Spronk (eds.), *Multiple Criteria Analysis: Practical Methods*, Gower Press, Inc., London, 1980.

Pareto, V.: *Manuale di economia politica, con una introduzione ulla scienza sociale*, Societa Editrice Libraria, Milan, Italy, 1906.

Philip, J.: "Algorithms for Vector Maximization Problems," *Mathematical Programming*, vol. 2, no. 2, 1972, pp. 207–229.

Pollak, R. A.: "Additive von Neumann-Morgenstern Utility Functions," *Econometrica*, vol. 35, 1967, pp. 485–494.

Radzikowski, O.: "Die Berücksichtigung mehrerer Zielfunktionen bei Aufgauben der linearen Optimierung," *Wirtschaftswissenschaft*, no. 5, 1967, pp. 797–806.

Raiffa, H.: "Preferences for Multi-Attributed Alternatives," RAND Memorandum RM-5868-DOT, Santa Monica, Calif., 1969.

Rice, D. P.: *"Estimating the Cost of Illness,"* U.S. Department of Health, Education, and Welfare Public Health Service Publication 947-6, 1966.

Roy, B.: "The Optimisation Problem Formulation: Criticism and Overstepping." Paper presented at the International Symposium on Extremal Methods and Systems Analysis, University of Texas, Austin, September 13–15, 1977.

Saska, J.: "Lineární Multiprogramování," *Ekonomicko-Matematický Obzor*, vol. 4, no. 3, 1968, pp. 359–373.

Sfeir-Younis, A., and D. W. Bromley: *Decision Making in Developing Countries—Multiobjective Formulation and Evaluation Methods*, Praeger, New York, 1977.

Shapley, L. S.: "Equilibrium Points in Games with Vector Payoffs," *Naval Research Logistics Quarterly*, vol. 6, no. 1, March 1959, pp. 57–61.

Sharpe, W. F.: *Portfolio Theory and Capital Markets*, McGraw-Hill, New York, 1970.

Shepard, R. N.: "On Subjectively Optimum Selections Among Multi-Attribute Alternatives," in M. W. Shelley and G. L. Bryan (eds.), *Human Judgments and Optimality*, Wiley, New York, 1964, pp. 257–281.

Simon, H. A.: *Administrative Behavior*, Free Press, New York, 1957, 1976.

———: *The New Science of Management Decision*, Harper & Row, New York, 1960.

Starr, M. K., and D. W. Miller: *Inventory Control: Theory and Practice*, Prentice-Hall, Englewood Cliffs, N.J., 1962.

———and M. Zeleny (eds.): *Multiple Criteria Decision Making*, TIMS Studies in the Management Sciences, vol. 6, North-Holland Publishing, Amsterdam, 1977.

Thiriez, H., and S. Zionts (eds.): *Multiple Criteria Decision Making: Jouy-en-Josas, France*, Springer-Verlag, New York, 1976.

Törn, A.: "Optimality by Means of Confidence," Working Paper 25, School of Economics, Åbo Swedish University, Åbo, Finland, 1978.

Von Neumann, J., and O. Morgenstern: *Theory of Games and Economic Behavior*, Princeton, Princeton, N.J., 1944.

Waddington, C. H.: *Tools for Thought*, Basic Books, New York, 1977.

Wagner, H. M.: *Principles of Operations Research*, Prentice-Hall, Englewood Cliffs, N.J., 1969.

Wallenius, J.: *Interactive Multiple Criteria Decision Methods: An Investigation and Approach*, Helsinki School of Economics, Helsinki, 1975.

Wendt, D., and C. Vlek (eds.): *Utility, Probability, and Human Decision Making*, D. Reidel Publishing, Boston, 1975.

Wilhelm, J.: *Objectives and Multi-Objective Decision Making under Uncertainty*, Springer-Verlag, New York, 1975.

Yntema, D. B., and W. S. Torgerson: "Man-Computer Cooperation in Decisions Requiring Common Sense," *IRE Transactions on Human Factors in Electronics*, HFE-2, 1961, pp. 20–26.

Zadeh, L. A.: "Optimality and Nonscalar-Valued Performance Criteria," *IEEE Transactions on Automatic Control*, AC-8, no. 1, 1963, pp. 50–60.

Zeleny, M. (ed.): *Computers and Operations Research: Special Issue on Mathematical Programming with Multiple Objectives,* vol. 7, no. 1–2, 1980.

———: *Linear Multiobjective Programming*, Springer-Verlag, New York, 1974.

Zionts, S. (ed.): *Multiple Criteria Problem Solving: Proceedings, Buffalo, N.Y. (U.S.A.), 1977*, Springer-Verlag, New York, 1978.

2-7 PROBLEMS

2-1 From your personal experience, list and describe the circumstances of decision problem situations that involved a single criterion of choice. Be aware of possible hidden or implicit criteria. Consider the time available for a decision as one of the influencing factors.

2-2 To exercise your graphic intuition, consider a convex polyhedron X of feasible solutions in two dimensions and two objective functions f_1 and f_2 to be minimized. If both f_1 and f_2 are linear, then the nondominated set consists typically only of boundary points of X. Sketch graphically the following situations:

(a) Both f_1 and f_2 are linear, but also interior points of X are nondominated. Can the entire feasible set X be nondominated? When?

(b) f_1 is linear and f_2 is quadratic, but only boundary points of X are nondominated.

(c) Both f_1 and f_2 are quadratic, but the nondominated set consists only of boundary points of X.

(d) Both f_1 and f_2 are quadratic, but the nondominated set consists of interior *and* boundary points of X.

(e) f_1 is linear and f_2 is quadratic, but the nondominated set consists of interior *and* boundary points of X.

(f) Both f_1 and f_2 are quadratic, but the nondominated set consists only of interior points of X.

Can you form any conjectures about the properties of nondominated sets on the basis of the insights gained from (a) to (f)? *Hint*: Quadratic functions are for example $f_1 = (x_1-3)^2 + (x_2-4)^2$ or $f_2 = (x_1 - 2)^2 + (x_2 - 3)^2$. Observe that the respective unconstrained minima are self-evident. What are they?

2-3 The considerations of Prob. 2-2 gain a definite content when we construct a simple model of *portfolio selection*. Let $x_1, x_2, \ldots$ denote fractions of the portfolio invested in security 1, 2, etc. If μ_i is the expected return on the ith security, then $E = \mu_1 x_1 + \mu_2 x_2 + \cdots$ is the expected return on the whole portfolio (a linear function to be maximized). If σ_{ij} denotes *covariance* between the returns of the ith and jth securities, then the variance of the return on portfolio is a quadratic function:

$$V = \sigma_{11}x_1^2 + \sigma_{22}x_2^2 + 2\sigma_{12}x_1x_2 + \cdots$$

which is to be minimized. Maximizing linear E *and* minimizing quadratic V over a set of constraints imposed on x_i's, say X, lead to identification of a so-called "efficiency frontier" (set of nondominated solutions). Provide these new interpretations to cases (b) and (e) of Prob. 2-2.

2-4 The *present value* rule, i.e., summing of the future cash-flows weighted by a priori assigned weights (discounting factors), does not discriminate between projects having the same present value but different time patterns of their cash-flow streams. Form a numerical example of such a situation and comment on the significance of this statement.

2-5 Consider the following seven alternatives evaluated with respect to four criteria:

	f_1	f_2	f_3	f_4
1	2	2	2	2
2	3	3	0	0
3	0	0	3	3
4	0	3	3	0
5	0	3	0	3
6	3	0	3	0
7	3	0	0	3

Which of the seven alternatives are nondominated?

2-6 The choice of nondominated alternative A over B implies an acceptable trade-off between the corresponding levels of criteria. Exploring such trade-offs, and therefore analyzing the nondominated set, are undoubtedly important. What if, however, in a complex situation, there is a suspicion that an important criterion could have been omitted? It is said that by introducing an additional criterion the most preferred solution could lie in the *dominated* region of the initial formulation.

(*a*) Show the effects of adding or deleting a criterion with respect to the nondominance in the original formulation.

(*b*) If an alternative is nondominated, then it remains nondominated when additional criteria are introduced. True or false? Why?

(*c*) If an alternative is nondominated, then deleting some of the initially considered criteria could make it dominated. True or false? Why?

(*d*) Under what conditions would examining the *dominated* region of solutions be desirable? Give examples.

2-7 The principle of satisficing postulates that a decision maker sets target values of individual objectives, the attainment of which he or she considers satisfactory.

(*a*) What does the satisficer do when there are *no* "satisfactory" solutions? If the satisficer is forced by circumstances to choose a "nonsatisfactory" solution, does this imply that his or her aspiration levels (and sense of "satisfactory") have been lowered?

(*b*) In attempting to attain aspiration-level targets as closely as possible, does not the satisficer become an optimizer? What if the satisficer selects the "best" among satisfactory solutions?

2-8 When dealing with capital budgeting problems, the criterion of net present value is often used to rank investment alternatives. There are, however, other important characteristics of capital investments: compatibility with present activities, impact on community relations, impact on employee working conditions, environmental impact, company image, effects on earnings per share, etc. How can such criteria enter into net present value computations? Should they be used in conjunction with net present value?

2-9 In production scheduling, the objectives of cost minimization shift toward those of utilizing existing company resources of space, labor, raw materials, plant capacity, and machine availability. Can such criteria be expressed in meaningful cost terms? How would their measurement differ from that of production and storage costs? How are the two categories (fixed and variable) interrelated?

2-10 Is the following an acceptable definition of nondominance: A solution is *nondominated* if, and only if, there is no other feasible solution which would lead to an improvement in at least one criterion without simultaneously degrading at least one other criterion.

2-11 Britain's National Radiological Protection Board published a cost-benefit analysis of nuclear safety based on financial valuation of human lives. Its argument was that any decision which can be evaluated in terms of costs and lives saved—and such decisions are made every day—puts an implicit price on human life. It is only necessary to make explicit the implied cost per life saved. When analyzing a series of governmental decisions, the Board found these "prices" of human life to vary from $2,200 to 20,000 times that amount! It seems that there is no "price" of human life like, for example, that of a tomato. Discuss the above approach. How does it differ from maximizing lives saved instead? What are the moral and humanistic implications of each approach?

2-12 What, if anything, is wrong with the reasoning in the following statement: People do not maximize utility or average utility—most likely, they don't even know that such things exist. People try to satisfy or maximize the attainment of their needs, wants, desires, goals, or objectives. As the preferences of a person are observed, a utility function can sometimes be established, and the person *seems* to be maximizing it. The person is *not* trying to maximize utility but may act *as though* he or she were maximizing a utility function.

2-13 It is possible to analyze game-theoretical conflict situations, even if outcomes are only numerically ranked. For example, in the table below, each player ranks the outcomes as 1, 2, 3, or 4 in increasing order of preference:

Player B

		Strategy 1	Strategy 2
Player A	Strategy 1	3, 3	1, 4
	Strategy 2	4, 1	2, 2

where the first outcome refers to player A and the second outcome to player B for each pair of strategies.

(a) What is the likely outcome if both players are "rational" in choosing their strategies? Could they both do better if they were "irrational"?

(b) Would the outcome be changed if they were allowed to communicate? For example, player B tells A that B will play strategy 1. Should A trust B? Why should not player A play strategy 2 in any case?

(c) In experimental situations players often choose strategy 1. What could be their rationale? Observe that any communications, negotiations, etc., which may precede the actual choice of strategy are irrelevant to rational players.

(d) Suppose there are two societies. In one society, the above conflicts are always solved rationally; in the other, irrationally. Which society would have more chances for survival?

2-14 The Pareto principle (Sec. 2-4) implies that a state of the world A is preferable to a state of the world B if at least one person is better off in A and nobody is worse off. Consider a community of economic agents characterized by the following distribution of resources among individuals:

$$A = (1000, 1000, \ldots, 1000)$$

This community has an opportunity to induce a societal transition towards one of the following states of the world:

(a) $B = (10,000, 1000, \ldots, 1000)$
(b) $C = (20,000, 1001, \ldots, 1001)$
(c) $D = (1001, 1001, \ldots, 1001)$
(d) $E = (1000, 1000, \ldots, 999)$

Compare B, C, D, and E with A in terms of Pareto optimality. Compare also B, C, D, and E among themselves. Predict the most likely voting preferences of the community with respect to the four alternative future scenarios of resource distribution. Do you have any difficulties with applying the Pareto principle?

2-15 Consider Prob. 2-14 again and assume that redistribution of resources (or compensation) is feasible and enforceable within the community. Does this assumption change the ranking of the states of the world considered?

2-16 Suppose that utility maximization *does* underly human behavior. How would you go about testing such a hypothesis? Pay special attention to the following: In order to derive an individual's utility function from the individual's observed behavior, one has to invoke the maximization hypothesis; in order to test the maximization hypothesis, one has to apply an individual's utility function. Can one test a hypothesis by assuming its a priori validity? In order to establish that human behavior is guided by utility maximization, can we use the utility functions obtained from observing human behavior? (*Hint:* We have to be able to derive utility function through other means, without relying on observations of behavior.)

2-17 Is it entirely obvious that only nondominated solutions should be considered? If there is a large number of criteria for which more is always preferred to less, than a vector of scores,

$$A = (500, 5, 5, \ldots, 5)$$

clearly dominates

$$B = (5, 5, 5, \ldots, 5)$$

(a) Consider a single decision maker: Is it necessarily true that A will be preferred to B? What if a balance between criteria scores is of value?

(b) Consider multiple decision makers (A and B are vectors of single-dimensional returns to multiple decision makers): Is it necessarily preferable when one person attains an extremely high score even if the others are not worse off?

(c) Can the ambiguities in (a) and (b) be resolved by introducing an additional criterion measuring the equity or balance inherent in A and B? Is the principle of nondominance preserved?

2-18 Attempt to find the interpretation and real-life examples of usefulness for the following solution concepts:

(a) A solution that dominates the greatest number of feasible solutions

(b A solution that is dominated by the smallest number of infeasible solutions which do not exceed maximum feasible values with respect to any criterion

2-19 On p. 5 we discussed a diamond cutting example as a multicriterion problem. Diamond High Council of Antwerp developed an internationally accepted multicriterion system of grading diamonds according to four Cs: carat weight, color, clarity, and cut. A computer is used to evaluate the design possibilities of the uncut diamond. Pertinent information on the rough stone is fed into a computer which then calculates the optimum weight, size, and parameters for the finished cut stone. Each criterion has many possible levels or scores. For example, the principal diamond cuts are: round brilliant, pear-shaped brilliant (pendeloque), emerald, marquise (navette), oval brilliant, baguette, and heart-shaped brilliant. Discuss the measurability of all the criteria involved in terms of precision, ambiguity, uncertainty, qualitative versus quantitative measures, and so on. How do you envision the functioning and use of Antwerp's computer system for diamond design?

CHAPTER
THREE

This short chapter is one of the most important in the entire book. It departs from the static view of decision making as an *act* of selecting the most desirable alternative and treats it, instead, as a *process*: a dynamic and interrelated unity of predecision, decision, and postdecision stages. Such a view implies that decision making's normative aspect—the question of how decisions *should* be made—is a natural outgrowth of its descriptive aspect—the question of how decisions are made. Without this connection, normative emerging out of descriptive reasoning, the present book would be an unpersuasive exercise in static mathematical formalism.

In a chapter on the stages of the decision process, *decision trees* might usually be introduced. Although such a logical and temporal structuralization of decision making is quite useful and instructive for dealing with simple problems, it is not adequate for dealing with complexity. Decision trees are well covered in most standard texts on decision making (see the Bibliographical Note); we shall not pause to discuss them here.

The chapter concludes with a diagram of the decision-making process. This diagram is by no means a unique representation; many different versions are possible. However, it provides a basic conceptual model that can be modified for more particular situations. The reader is invited to study the diagram, run a few imaginary decisions through it, and modify it as necessary.

It is hoped that the reader will study this chapter several times. It has been made intentionally short to allow such repeated passes through before one plunges into the next couple of chapters.

> *The real decision taking process involves a lot of people, and the whole*
> *structure is redolent with feedback. At every decisive moment, of which*
> *there will be great many* within *the total decision, we range ahead and back*
> *and sideways. We gauge the effect of this sub-decision on everything we*
> *have tentatively decided already, and on the sub-decisions left to take. This*
> *is why I think the decision tree is an artefact, and of little use to us. You*
> *cannot isolate these nodes either in time or in logical connectivity, and*
> *anyone who has ever taken a complicated decision knows this.*

> *Stafford Beer*
> *Platform for Change (1975)*

3-1 TWO BASIC APPROACHES TO DECISION MAKING

There are essentially two basic approaches to modeling human decision making:

1. The *outcome*-oriented approach, based on the view that if one can correctly predict the outcome of the decision process, then one obviously understands the decision process. The decision outcome and its correct prediction are at the center of this approach. Normative decision analysis, single- and multiattribute utility theories, etc., are examples of this orientation, which asks questions like what and when rather than how.
2. The *process*-oriented approach, based on the view that if one understands the decision process, one can correctly predict the outcome. Essentially descriptive, this approach has prescriptive and normative features as well: Knowing how decisions are made can teach us how they should be made; the reverse causal linkage, unfortunately, does not follow.

It is important to distinguish between the processes of measurement and search on the one hand and decision making on the other. What is traditionally presented as decision theory is in fact mostly concerned with measurement of comparative indexes of merit. If one obtains a correct measure of the total attractiveness of each available alternative, one can predict with confidence that the most attractive one will be chosen. It is remarkable how much can be built upon such a simple and trivial tautology.

Technical measurement, followed by mechanical search, designed to predict the most attractive alternative, here in fact become a substitute for decision making and its theory. For if an adequate measurement of net attractiveness is obtained, i.e., a single number evaluates each alternative, the decision has implicitly been made, and its subsequent discovery is relatively trivial: Find the largest (or the smallest) number and select the corresponding alternative. Thus, the technical problem of mechanical search has replaced the actual decision-making process.

It is important to realize that whenever we face a single attribute, an objective function, a utility function, or any other single aggregate measure of merit, there is no decision making involved. The decision is implicit in the measurement, and it is made explicit by the subsequent search, as we asserted in Sec. 2-5.

It is only when facing multiple attributes, objectives, criteria, functions, etc., that we can talk about decision making and its theory. As alternatives of choice become more complex and are characterized by multiple attributes as well as multiple objectives, the problem of combining these various aspects into a single measure of utility becomes more difficult and less practical.

Decision making is a dynamic process: a complex search for information, full of detours, enriched by feedback from casting about in all directions, gathering and discarding information, fueled by fluctuating uncertainty, indistinct and conflicting concepts—some sharp, some hazy; the process is an organic unity of both predecision and postdecision stages overlapping within the region of partial decision making. Man is a reluctant decision maker, not a swiftly calculating machine.

The reader should not infer from this characterization that decision making has no structure or that no formalization of the process can be attempted. But surely, it cannot be captured by a decision tree, by a decision table, by a single mathematical function, or by other simple mechanistic artifacts. Its structure is functional, capable of generating its own path toward the decision. The final decision unfolds through a process of learning, understanding, information processing, assessing, and defining the problem and its circumstances. The emphasis must be on the *process*, not on the *act* or the *outcome* of making a decision; hence the orientation of this book is on the second or process approach to decision making.

The decision-making process consists of *predecision, decision,* and *postdecision* stages. These stages are interdependent; the postdecision phase often coincides with the predecision preparations for the next decision. Each decision stage is itself composed of a series of *partial decisions,* characterized by their own pre- and postdecision stages. We shall first describe these main stages of the decision-making process verbally. Later on we shall present a symbolic equivalent of the decision process, a mathematical model, in Chap. 6.

3-2 THE PREDECISION STAGE

First there is a sense of conflict. Conflict provides the decision-motivating tension, a frustration and dissatisfaction with the status quo. The underlying source of the predecision conflict is the *nonavailability of suitable alternatives* and particularly the *infeasibility of the ideal alternative*. While the main criteria are being selected, the decision maker immediately examines and evaluates the various alternatives in their light.[1] It is soon realized that the ideal alternative is not feasible (see Sec. 1-4.2).

Experiencing conflict, the decision maker starts searching for new alternatives, preferably for those approximating the ideal. The limits of individual attribute levels are soon attained. A first, tentative ideal image may be displaced during the process and the conflict amplified further.

As the component values of the ideal alternative become stabilized and clearly perceived, the decision maker recognizes its infeasibility, and the conflict between the achievable and the available sets in. The search for alternatives continues, but now it becomes purposefully directed toward the point of reference—the established ideal alternative. We know the attribute mixture of this desired alternative; is there one which is also empirically realizable? Or, at least, is there one close to it?

The evaluation of alternatives becomes more systematic as the decision maker realizes that a choice among alternatives already generated, rather than a discovery of new alternatives, will dominate the process toward the conflict resolution. Observe that if the ideal alternative became a feasible choice, the decision process would cease and the conflict would be fully resolved. Because such conditions are quite rare, an effort toward conflict resolution is replaced by an attempt at conflict reduction or, in many cases, at conflict containment. The decision maker asks the question, Which alternative will reduce the conflict to an acceptable level?

The process of careful reinterpretation and reassessment of alternatives ensues. The decision maker seeks a greater divergence in attribute scores of attractiveness. The greater the divergence, the more information is transmitted by each attribute, and the sounder the basis for a decision. A small divergence of values, nondistinct evaluations, and equal attractiveness of alternatives, render decision making difficult. Recall the fable of Buridan's ass, which starved to death while facing two readily available but precisely equidistant stacks of hay.

The *divergence process* leads to a search for new information, not only outside the system but also hidden, implicit within the system. Raw score measurements are checked; subjective assessments are scrutinized; prefer-

---

[1] It is important to be able to trace the conflict to the set of available alternatives if one is to avoid treating conflict symptoms only, such as cognitive differences, multiobjective disparity, an abstract "need," and subjective perception.

ences are questioned. Additional decision makers may be brought into the picture as the decision maker reaches for a consensus of opinion.

This information-gathering and evaluation process is highly objective and impartial at first. But as the decision maker realizes that additional information is unlikely to reverse or appreciably influence the existing order of preference, the process becomes more biased and subjective. Then only particular pieces of information are admitted; some information is consciously or unconsciously ignored; some may be reinterpreted or even dismissed. Festinger (1964) provides experimental evidence that the closer the alternatives in their attractiveness and the more varied the information acquired, the greater the amount of information that will be sought before a decision is taken. There is less need for additional information if the alternatives are sufficiently divergent and the information is uniform and single-dimensional. As the predecision process becomes stabilized, a partial decision can be made.

3-3 PARTIAL DECISIONS

Partial decisioning includes a directional adjustment of the decision situation. Such an adjustment may consist of discarding alternatives that at the moment appear obviously inferior, returning previously rejected alternatives to the feasible set, and adding or deleting criteria.

As all alternatives are compared with the ideal, those which are the farthest away are removed from further consideration. There are many important impacts of such partial decisions. First, discarding an alternative may shift the maximum available score to its next lower feasible level. Thus, the ideal alternative is displaced closer to the feasible set. Such displacement induces further changes in evaluation, attribute importance, and ultimately in the preference ordering of the remaining alternatives. All alternatives are now compared with respect to the new, displaced ideal. This dynamic process is illustrated in Fig. 3-1. The ideal ★ and its subsequent displacements are numbered sequentially.

Another important consequence of a partial decision, or of any decision, is the cognitive dissonance that emerges after the decision has been taken. Festinger (1964) shows that the longer and more difficult the predecision stage, the greater the dissonance that follows. Thus, there is a tendency to justify the partial decision just made, i.e., to reduce the resulting dissonance. The decision maker initiates a process of subjective reevaluation of attributes. This evaluation is carried out in such a way that the attractiveness of discarded alternatives is diminished and that of the retained alternatives is amplified. After each partial decision there is still some residual conflict, the displaced ideal alternative is still infeasible, and a new predecision stage is entered.

The question often arises of whether the divergence process, the spreading apart of the attractiveness of individual alternatives, occurs mainly in the predecision or the postdecision period. We maintain that these two stages of the

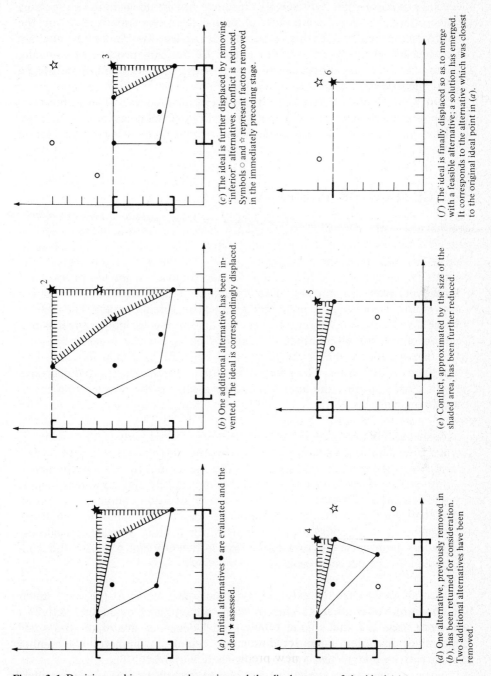

(a) Initial alternatives ● are evaluated and the ideal ★ assessed.

(b) One additional alternative has been invented. The ideal is correspondingly displaced.

(c) The ideal is further displaced by removing "inferior" alternatives. Conflict is reduced. Symbols ○ and ☆ represent factors removed in the immediately preceding stage.

(d) One alternative, previously removed in (b), has been returned for consideration. Two additional alternatives have been removed.

(e) Conflict, approximated by the size of the shaded area, has been further reduced.

(f) The ideal is finally displaced so as to merge with a feasible alternative; a solution has emerged. It corresponds to the alternative which was closest to the original ideal point in (a).

Figure 3-1 Decision-making process dynamics and the displacement of the ideal (★).

decision process are not dynamically different. Any postdecision stage is also a predecision stage in the continuum of partial decisions traversed before the final decision is reached. In this sense, the "act of decision," or better, the "act of partial decision," is not critical within the decision process as a whole. Similar or even identical psychological processes occur both before and after a partial decision.

But what about the endpoints of the decision process? That is, how significant are the predecision stage before the first partial decision and the postdecision stage after the last partial decision, i.e., the final decision? We attempt an answer in the next section.

3-4 THE FINAL DECISION STAGE

We have already described the predecision conflict as originating from the perceived infeasibility of the ideal alternative. This conflict is initially sufficiently large to trigger the decision process. After the first partial decision the conflict is reduced by the ideal being displaced closer to the set of available alternatives. However, the cognitive dissonance, which was not operating initially, is now increasingly compounded with the residual conflict. The conflict and the dissonance tend to reinforce each other. At the beginning, the iterative deletion of inferior alternatives is relatively easy, but the process becomes more and more difficult as the number of alternatives diminishes and their attractiveness converges. The greater the difficulty in making partial decisions and the closer together the alternatives, the greater is the postdecision cognitive dissonance.

> **Postulate** The overall level of a decision maker's dissatisfaction, which is necessary to trigger and maintain the process of decision making, consists of two components: *predecision conflict*, generated by the infeasibility of the ideal, and *postdecision dissonance*, induced by making a decision. At the beginning of the decision process the predecision conflict almost completely dominates, while at the end the cognitive dissonance completely dominates. As the dissonance increases, the conflict decreases, while the overall intensity of dissatisfaction stays sufficiently high to assure the completion of the decision process.

Let us summarize the essential dynamics once more: At the start, under the conditions of conflict, the information-gathering and evaluative activities are quite impartial and objective. As partial decisions are made and some alternatives discarded, cognitive dissonance begins to dominate. The number of alternatives diminishes, and so does their variability. The process of divergence becomes more subjective and biased toward the few remaining alternatives. The information gathering and interpretation also become biased and directional. When the final decision unfolds, the ideal alternative has been displaced entirely in the direction of the chosen alternative, and the predecision conflict has been fully resolved. However, the magnitude of the postdecision dissonance is at its highest level and completely dominates. The divergence process still continues, but it now becomes biased toward the chosen alternative. All impartiality or objectivity is abandoned; there is no need for it, the decision has been made. (We assume, of course, the irreversibility of the decision. Otherwise, it would be only a partial decision, and previously described processes would be at play.)

Observe that dissonance-reduction processes become stronger as the number of alternatives still in the running becomes smaller. The decision maker becomes more and more committed to a smaller number of options, which in turn move closer to each other in attractiveness. The level of commitment reaches the highest point when the final decision has been made.

3-5. THE POSTDECISION STAGE

The dissonance-reduction process should not be viewed as one of distortion and biased judgment. Rather, it is the gradual process of reevaluation, reassessment, and cognitive "tune-up." The information search and processing is, however, directional. The decision maker enhances the attractiveness of preferred alternatives and reduces that of rejected alternatives. The objective predecision information search is gradually replaced by a selective postdecision information search. For example, after we purchase a new automobile, the advertisements we read tend to support our choice. We experience a clear preference for reading "own car" ads.

The presence of cognitive dissonance leads to a selective exposure to information. Consonant information is favored over dissonant. Dissonance-increasing information is not simply avoided or ignored but rather tends to be reinterpreted and incorporated in the direction of the chosen alternative.

In summary, we have shown how the predecision and postdecision stages of the decision process are interrelated and how the act of decision both evolves from the predecision stage and influences the postdecision stage. The transition occurs gradually through a series of partial decisions. As soon as the decision has been made, all the negative aspects of the chosen alternative and all the positive aspects of the rejected alternative become salient to the decision maker. As the choice is forced on smaller and smaller subsets of alternatives contrasting less and less, there is a tendency to counteract the increasing postdecision dissonance expected by succumbing to increasingly stronger postdecision regret. Leon Festinger states this effect as follows:

> Avoiding post-decision dissonance can also be accomplished to some extent by psychologically revoking the decision as soon as it is made. (Festinger 1964, p. 99)

Postdecision regret simply manifests the fact that the dissonance has suddenly become salient. Then there is a tendency to reverse one's decision immediately after making it. This period, when the chosen alternative seems to be inferior to the rejected one, is followed by the dissonance-reduction process described earlier.

Postdecision regret and dissonance are strongest at the end of the decision process. This complements the fact that the predecision conflict has been resolved by displacing the ideal, i.e., by lowering one's aspiration level. In this sense the conflict, although resolved, has not been actually removed or dissolved but rather transformed into postdecision dissonance. A theory of conflict dissolution is discussed in Sec. 4-2.

Obviously, the final choice—say, between two remaining and equally attractive, although not identical, alternatives—is the most difficult to make. Postdecision regret is maximal; the tendency to reverse to the other alternative is uncomfortably strong.[1] After the final decision has been made, the level of cognitive dissonance is the highest. Moreover, the decision maker continues to seek new information. Its purpose now is to increase the decision maker's confidence and to reduce postdecision regret and dissonance.

Thus, the postdecision stage of the decision process is extremely important for an understanding of the decision-implementation process. This implementation phase is an organic continuation of the process of decision making. A good decision is not independent of its implementation attributes. Implementation activity can be viewed as the final postdecision process, characterized by the maximum of dissonance and a full commitment to the chosen alternative. The information gathered is biased in favor of the alternative being implemented; it is intended to increase the decision maker's confidence, which is necessary for an effective implementation through negotiation, team building, and action taking.

3-6 THE DECISION PROCESS: A DIAGRAM

Figure 3-2 summarizes the stages and dynamics of the decision process in a fluid and imprecise flow diagram. This is not intended as the only possible representation of the decision process; obviously, many alternative descriptions are possible. But we want to stress the *process* quality of human decision making, the interrelatedness of its stages, and the evolutionary nature of its main outcomes, i.e., decisions. One should imagine that all of the activities described are more or less parallel and mutually dependent.

There is another kind of "parallelism" involved: No individual decision making is completely independent of the social or collective framework in

---

[1]In comparing two otherwise identical alternatives, their potential for allowing changing one's mind, to reverse a decision, becomes a very salient attribute. There is a tendency to postpone final choice and to preserve the ability to "switch" as long as one can.

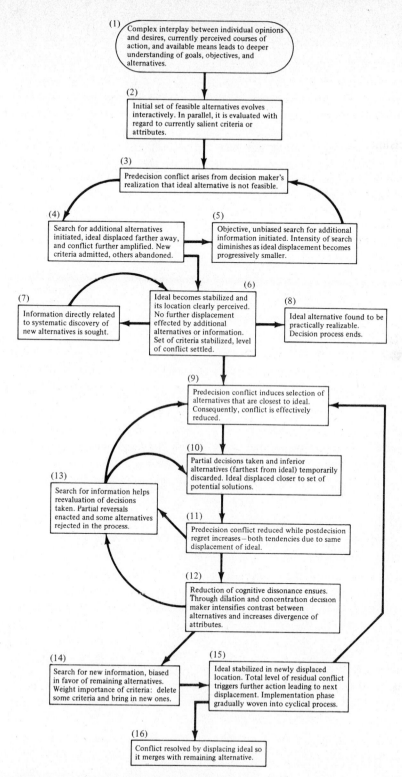

(1) Complex interplay between individual opinions and desires, currently perceived courses of action, and available means leads to deeper understanding of goals, objectives, and alternatives.

(2) Initial set of feasible alternatives evolves interactively. In parallel, it is evaluated with regard to currently salient criteria or attributes.

(3) Predecision conflict arises from decision maker's realization that ideal alternative is not feasible.

(4) Search for additional alternatives initiated, ideal displaced farther away, and conflict further amplified. New criteria admitted, others abandoned.

(5) Objective, unbiased search for additional information initiated. Intensity of search diminishes as ideal displacement becomes progressively smaller.

(6) Ideal becomes stabilized and its location clearly perceived. No further displacement effected by additional alternatives or information. Set of criteria stabilized, level of conflict settled.

(7) Information directly related to systematic discovery of new alternatives is sought.

(8) Ideal alternative found to be practically realizable. Decision process ends.

(9) Predecision conflict induces selection of alternatives that are closest to ideal. Consequently, conflict is effectively reduced.

(10) Partial decisions taken and inferior alternatives (farthest from ideal) temporarily discarded. Ideal displaced closer to set of potential solutions.

(13) Search for information helps reevaluation of decisions taken. Partial reversals enacted and some alternatives rejected in the process.

(11) Predecision conflict reduced while postdecision regret increases—both tendencies due to same displacement of ideal.

(12) Reduction of cognitive dissonance ensues. Through dilation and concentration decision maker intensifies contrast between alternatives and increases divergence of attributes.

(14) Search for new information, biased in favor of remaining alternatives. Weight importance of criteria: delete some criteria and bring in new ones.

(15) Ideal stabilized in newly displaced location. Total level of residual conflict triggers further action leading to next displacement. Implementation phase gradually woven into cyclical process.

(16) Conflict resolved by displacing ideal so it merges with remaining alternative.

Figure 3–2 A diagram of the decision process.

which it takes place. Other people, their values, objectives, and constraints, interact with the individual decision-making process. Rarely can we concentrate on the pursuit of our own objectives without acknowledging the impact of our decisions on others, or without understanding how actions taken elsewhere influence the effectiveness of our efforts. Directly or indirectly, the diagram is a part of a larger, interdependent network, of a collective decision-making process. But at this stage we should not complicate the diagram any further. We shall attempt to make this diagram operational in the next sections, particularly in Chaps. 5 and 6.

3-7 BIBLIOGRAPHICAL NOTE

In this chapter we have characterized decision making as a process. The literature dealing with such a dynamic view of decision making is still rather sparse. One of the best descriptive books is Janis and Mann, *Decision Making: A Psychological Analysis of Conflict, Choice, and Commitment* (1977), in which the student will find process diagrams similar to the one presented here. Janis and Mann is strongly recommended as a supplementary reading for this chapter. It contains a wealth of descriptive material, examples, and empirical findings which provide a rationale for the type of analysis used here.

The first process view of decision making was advanced by Festinger (1957, 1964). His theories of cognitive dissonance and conflict resolution, his empirical experiments supporting the process view, and his careful analysis of postdecision regret are the foundation for current descriptive methodologies.

Stafford Beer in his *Platform for Change* (1975) also subscribes to the process view of decision making and criticizes the static methodology of decision trees rather persuasively. His view of decision making as a process "redolent with feedback" has become a classic. Brehm, *A Theory of Psychological Reactance* (1966), is a classic in the theory of descriptive decision making.

In the OR/MS literature, the process view of decision making is mostly maintained in the works of Zeleny (1976, 1977, 1979), Yu (1977), and Roy (1977).

Readers who are unfamiliar with the methodology of decision trees will find the necessary information in any standard OR/MS text. But perhaps going back to one or both of the original articles by Magee (1964) would be even better.

Beer, S.: *Platform for Change*, Wiley, New York, 1975.

Brchm, J. W.: *A Theory of Psychological Reactance*, Academic, New York, 1966.

Festinger, L. (ed.): *Conflict, Decision and Dissonance*, Stanford, Stanford, Calif., 1964

———: *A Theory of Cognitive Dissonance*, Row Peterson, Evanston, Ill., 1957.

Janis, I. L., and L. Mann: *Decision Making: A Psychological Analysis of Conflict, Choice, and Commitment*, Free Press, New York, 1977.

Magee, J. F.: "Decision Trees for Decision Making," *Harvard Business Review*, July-August 1964.

———: "How to Use Decision Trees in Capital Investment," *Harvard Business Review*, September-October 1964.

Roy, B.: "A Conceptual Framework for a Prescriptive Theory of 'Decision Aid'," in M. K. Starr and M. Zeleny (eds.) *Multiple Criteria Decision Making*, TIMS Studies in the Management Sciences, vol. 6, North-Holland Publishing, Amsterdam, 1977, pp. 179–210.

Yu, P. L.: "Decision Dynamics with an Application to Persuasion and Negotiation," in M. K. Starr and M. Zeleny (eds.), *Multiple Criteria Decision Making*, TIMS Studies in the Management Sciences, vol. 6, North-Holland Publishing, Amsterdam, 1977, pp. 159–177.

Zeleny, M.: "Adaptive Displacement of Preferences in Decision Making," in M. K. Starr and M. Zeleny (eds.), *Multiple Criteria Decision Making*, TIMS Studies in the Management Sciences, vol. 6, North-Holland Publishing, Amsterdam, 1977 pp. 147–157.

———: "Descriptive Decision Making and its Applications," in R. L. Schultz (ed.), *Applications of Management Science*, vol. 1, JAI Press, Greenwich, Conn., 1980.

———: "The Theory of the Displaced Ideal," in M. Zeleny (ed.), *Multiple Criteria Decision Making: Kyoto 1975*, Springer-Verlag, New York, 1976, pp. 153–206.

3-8 PROBLEMS

3-1 Decision makers attempt to approximate their perceived ideal as closely as possible. If the set of choice alternatives is fixed, one can manipulate the decision maker toward choosing a particular alternative by causing him or her to perceive the ideal as being properly displaced. Analyze the following manipulative tactics:

(*a*) When a fear or uncertainty is intensified, one can sell more smoke detectors, life insurance, lock alarms, etc.

(*b*) When a "bargain," a "steal," or a "windfall" is offered, people will be more likely to buy an item, even though the reference price was previously inflated by the same amount as (or even more than) the "bargain" gain.

(*c*) A boss will be more likely to accept a recommendation if it is documented by computer-generated "evidence."

(*d*) "Condition" a seller by making a series of ridiculously low insincere offers. Then offer slightly more and watch the seller sell, perhaps way below actual market value.

3-2 There are times when people will avoid making a decision, even though they have a preference among alternatives.

(*a*) A person in a restaurant, after staring at the menu for some time, may show considerable relief if a companion offers to order for both.

(*b*) A student faced with a choice between two colleges will ask both parents and peers to name a choice.

What are the possible explanations for this tendency to avoid decision? Could there be any hidden criteria of choice?

3-3 Kenneth J. Arrow explains *independence of irrelevant alternatives* as follows: "Since the chosen element from any environment is completely defined by knowledge of the preferences as between it and any other alternative in the environment, it follows that the choice depends only on the ordering of the elements of that environment." Consequently, "the choice made does not depend on preferences as between alternatives that are not in fact available in the given environment, nor, and this is probably more important, on preferences as between elements in the environment and those not in the environment."[1]

(*a*) Obviously our concept of using an unavailable "ideal" as a reference point against which preferences are measured is completely at odds with the above statement. Are there any logical weaknesses in Arrow's argument? (We submit that he substitutes consequence for cause and arrives at a tautology.)

(*b*) There is a strong intuitive sense that it is never necessary to compare available alternatives with those not available at that moment in order to arrive at a decision. State pros and cons derived from your own decision-making experience.

3-4 Individual decision processes often require a considerable span of time before the various stages are traversed and a final decision emerges. Good biographical accounts of the decision-making stages are given in R. H. Grossman (ed.), *The God That Failed,* Harper & Row, New York, 1949. Try to analyze these accounts, identify the stages, and interpret them in view of the theory presented. Draw diagrams for comparison and possible generalizations.

3-5 Janis and Mann (1977, p. 172) identified five basic stages of decision making: appraising the challenge, surveying alternatives, weighing alternatives, deliberating about commitment, adhering despite negative feedback. Compare these stages with the theory presented in Chap. 3 by superimposing them on Fig 3-2. Discuss their compatibility and implications for group decisions.

---

[1]K. J. Arrow, "Public and Private Values," in S. Hook (ed.), *Human Values and Economic Policy*, New York University Press, New York, 1967, p. 6.

3-6 Use the insights gained from Prob. 3-5 for analyzing the stages of human decision-making response to startlingly new circumstances or information, as manifested in the following cases:

(a) Taking of the United States hostages by Iran in 1979.

(b) Soviet intervention in Afghanistan in 1979.

(c) Appearance of the first Soviet Sputnik in 1959.

(d) The Cuban missile crisis in 1962.

(e) OPEC oil embargo in 1972.

In the above situations, gather relevant information, identify the decision maker(s), classify the events and responses according to stages traversed, and discuss the process-nature of the decision making involved.

Having presented a general diagram of the decision-making process, we are ready to explore and expand its first stage: evolving the initial set of feasible decision alternatives. This is a new area of research in the art and science of problem solving. Invention of new alternatives is now generally recognized as being of decisive importance, but so far it has received only precursory treatment in the literature. Therefore, this is a rather experimental and searching chapter, and the reader is asked to extend to the author more than the customary dose of patience and cooperation.

The concepts of strategies, alternatives, and variants are first discussed and demonstrated in simple examples. Alternatives are not simply means of achieving given ends: Both "means" and "ends" are intrinsically related and evolve through their mutual interaction. An alternative is a particular realizable form of the relationship between means and ends.

Although the invention or generation of new alternatives is and will remain an art, the process may be aided by computer in some fairly well defined technical situations. The computer-based generation of alternatives is therefore briefly outlined.

The first part of this chapter concludes with a discussion of *technological forecasting* and its possible relationship to what we term a "technologically closed" set of alternatives.

In the second part of Chap. 4 we apply the method of inventing new alternatives to the problem of *conflict dissolution* in decision making. Because we define conflict as the absence of a prominent or ideal alternative, the search for a highly desirable alternative becomes the most effective approach to conflict management. One can attempt to solve conflicts, resolve them, contain them, remove them, or ignore them, but it is their dissolution which becomes worthy of the art of problem solving. A conflict is dissolved when the very circumstances that produced it are changed in such a way that the conflict becomes irrelevant or disappears. Some typical examples of conflict dissolution are given at the end of the chapter, and the reader will surely be able to generate a large variety of additional cases. A perceptive decision maker should be able to start applying the principles of conflict dissolution right away in daily personal and professional problem solving. Newly gained confidence and a new attitude toward decision making will be an asset in reading the remaining sections of the present book.

INVENTION OF ALTERNATIVES AND CONFLICT DISSOLUTION

The new idea does not have to be preceded by years of work in the field, for dissatisfaction with the old idea may happen much more quickly than that. Indeed, such years of work may even make new ideas more hard to come by, since over the years the usefulness of the old ideas may be reinforced if they have any usefulness at all. The scientific world is full of hard-working scientists who lack nothing as regards the logic of their approach and the meticulousness of their work, yet new ideas may for ever elude them.

Edward De Bono
New Think (1967)

How does one get a new idea? How does one invent an alternative? In order to make an intelligent decision, to arrive at a best choice, one has to start with good "raw material," i.e. a good set of available options. If the set of alternatives is poor, no significant decision-making process can commence; instead, the decison maker faces frustration and circular agonizing. By a good set of alternatives, we do not mean a large number of options—that can also be very frustrating—but a reasonable number of sufficiently different alternatives pro viding the best possible information about the attainable limits of all relevant dimensions, criteria, or objectives. Such alternatives must be invented.

Creativity and invention have to do with breaking out of old, self-perpetuating patterns and generating new ways of looking at things. De Bono (1973) describes the use of *lateral thinking* in the generation of new ideas. Lateral thinking is based on biological information-processing principles which differ from the mechanistic information-processing principles of mathematics, logic, and computers that are the basis of vertical thinking. Vertical thinking follows the most obvious and probable line of reasoning. Lateral thinking seeks to get away from the patterns that lead in one definite direction, to break out of one's habitual domain. In solving a problem, usually all thoughts, all information gathering and interpretation, and all search soon begin to pull in one direction—the solving process gets "locked in." It builds up logically on all previously established stepping-stones. Yet the solution may require a sideways move in another direction.

Ackoff (1978) puts lateral thinking to good use in the area of managerial decision making. He considers creativity the most essential characteristic of good management. His examples provide a wealth of decisions arrived at by breaking away from obvious and well-established patterns. In the *Art of Problem Solving* he relies on a number of concepts that are central in our text as well:

1. Ends and means are interdependent: Every means can play the role of an end, and every end that of a means. Investment is a means for getting profit, an end. Profit is a means for expanding one's operations through investment, an end.
2. An ultimately desired outcome is called an "ideal." If one formulates a problem in terms of approaching an ideal solution, one minimizes the chances of overlooking relevant consequences in decision making. Seeking the ideal is the best way to open and stimulate the mind to creative activity.
3. The assumption of "rational behavior" is a limiting and arrogant artifact, a curse of decision making and problem solving. Ackoff distills this notion in the following moral: "Irrationality is usually in the mind of the beholder, not in the mind of the beheld."
4. Conflicts are often a consequence of the scarcity of appropriate courses of action. One can dissolve a conflict by changing the environmental constraints, by inventing new alternatives in the direction of an ideal alternative.

The reader will find the principles listed above are woven into this text and form the basis of the multicriterion approach.

4-1 GENERATION OF DECISION ALTERNATIVES

4-1.1 "Given a Set of Viable Action Alternatives . . . "

Traditional decision-analysis literature is replete with weathered variations of one rather inconspicuous word: "given." For example, "Given a set of viable action alternatives," the analyst assures us, "I'll assist you in selecting the best choice or I'll recommend the best solution." The reason is simple: The invention and generation of decision alternatives have been traditionally associated with creativity, intuition, and insight. If the alternatives are given, then the analyst, assisted by the modern mathematical and statistical "toolbox," can employ a simple rational process to assign each alternative a single number.

But most decision-making problems are not resolved by agonizing between alternatives A *and* B, *but through the discovery of* C. The assumption that alternative decision options are prespecified is one of the most serious misrepresentations of real-world decision making that formal decision analysis makes. Preanalysis or predecision stages are rarely completed; rather, they represent the most active and important part of the decision-making process. Assuming otherwise leads to suboptimization, inflexibility, and poor adaptability. Making a decision often means inventing a creative new alternative, not just choosing one among the "givens."

The importance of generating imaginative alternatives cannot be overemphasized. Although formal multiattribute utility analysis might help in finding a new superior alternative—as Keeney and Raiffa admit, that may be the single most important way it *can* help (1976, p. 546)—a more straightforward and operational recognition of the function of generating imaginative alternatives is needed.

Let us illustrate. When looking for appropriate investment opportunities, one may consider a set of feasible decision alternatives: different types of savings accounts, stocks and bonds, condominium houses or apartments, undeveloped vacation land, etc. After we consider all major feasibility constraints—the amount of capital available, current and projected interest rates, legal restrictions, technical requirements, etc.—we usually identify the initial set X of alternatives to choose from. During this process some additional alternatives may have been suggested, and they too will be included in set X.

Very soon we realize that new alternatives are being generated at a slower rate. More and more information must be processed, often at high costs, in return for less and less differentiated alternatives or variants. We may decide that no additional worthwhile alternatives exist or are worth seeking. The set X is thus closed, and we switch our focus from generating alternatives to choosing among those we already have. Refer to our discussion in Chap. 3.

There is a danger that the decision maker might settle upon a given set of alternatives too fast. Many options are obvious, habitually made, or automatically included in X, even before one explores their natures or defines them properly in context. One cannot make great decisions by concentrating on casually made or easily generated options.

Great decisions are accomplished only through purposefully challenging and *extending one's habitual domain*, as P. L. Yu (1977) describes it; otherwise, one cannot expect an unusual outcome. Searching for an ideal, breaking self-imposed constraints on creativity, learning to invent, evolving and unfolding one's options as well as one's decision criteria—these seem to be the most important ingredients of a successful generation of alternatives.

True, some decision makers (or analysts) are satisfied with mediocre, habitual solutions, or they are looking only for corroboration or confirmation of the status quo.

There even exists a hypothesis to condone that kind of "decision making": *satisficing*. According to this theory, explored in Sec. 2-3, it is sufficient to look for "good enough" solutions, satisfying some a priori determined goals or arbitrarily lowered aspiration levels. No creative generation of alternatives is involved, no search for excellence is encouraged. H. A. Simon describes satisficing as "the behavior of human beings who satisfice because they do not have the wits to maximize" (1976, p. xxviii).

Some people use a simple satisficing approach when they face relatively unimportant, trivial, or inconsequential decisions. Others satisfice because they do not have the "wits" to do otherwise: an MBA settling for the first available job that meets certain minimal requirements—acceptable salary, good location, and the promise of advancement; an investor taking the first option which will bring in a "satisfactory return"; a person marrying the first "acceptable" mate. No search for superior alternatives, no genuine search for information, and no commitment to decision-making excellence is involved.

It quickly becomes evident that alternatives and criteria unfold jointly, in mutual causal interdependence. New alternatives often render certain previously unconsidered attributes very important, while other criteria may be dropped. Such changes in the criteria set throw a new light on the existing alternatives, possibly leading to the exclusion of some of them from current consideration. These changes in the set of feasible alternatives in turn affect the criteria set, and so the process continues.

In human decision making there can be no separation of means and ends, alternatives and objectives. Both sides of the decision process—analysis of what is available and analysis of what is desirable—are equally important, interdependent, and interactive. Neither aspect is primary. We cannot generate our alternatives without having some notion of our objectives or goals. Similarly, we cannot determine the criteria of choice without having some notion of what is available. One can recall the "let me see what they have and I will tell you what I need" attitude of a young shopper.

Neither means nor ends are determined independently of each other. Objectives evolve on the basis of available alternatives which, in turn, are adjusted and generated in accordance with existing objectives. Modeling of decision processes and economic behavior must take into account the fact that the mathematically convenient separation of means and ends does not accurately describe the way in which people typically approach decisions.

This view may seem hopelessly intractable if one is to evolve a useful operational decision support system. Its dynamics and adaptive interactions contrast strongly with the well-defined task of replacing a prespecified set of attributes or criteria with a single utility number and then assigning such numbers to a given set of alternatives.

But we do not want to *prescribe* how the decision maker should structure the decision-making process or what solutions to adopt, because we do not know. Since we, as analysts, do not have the final responsibility for particular decisions taken, we shall never know.[1] Rather, we are trying to *describe* what has been done in the past and then to improve and support the decision processes of the future. By learning more about how people actually arrive at

---

[1]Important *ethical* issues are involved. Excessive emphasis on "rationality," characterized by efficiency, consistency, and optimal calculations, i.e., by the efficiency with which means are used to attain ends, avoids the judgment of ends themselves. Can one plan, rationally, to commit a crime? The "goodness" of objectives and goals must be of paramount concern to decision analysts.

decisions, we hope to make them more skillful and confident about what decisions they should make in the future. Prescriptions, if any, should concern the ends rather than the means.

In fact, our approach cannot be classified as purely descriptive or prescriptive. To prescribe without understanding is arrogant and foolish. To describe without attempting to improve or suggest better goals is incomplete and ineffective. Thus, we are going to muddle through even though our task seems to be mathematically intractable and possibly inelegant.

Matters of elegance should be left to the tailor and the cobbler, as Albert Einstein was fond of saying.

4-1.2 Strategies, Alternatives, and Variants

In this section we are mainly concerned with decision *alternatives*, i.e., the mutually exclusive sets of means engaged toward achieving the stated objectives and prespecified goals or targets. It will be useful to define and clarify the related concepts of *strategies* and *variants*, as the three terms are often used interchangeably by different authors. We wish to avoid any serious terminological and analytical confusion which could occur when special attention is paid to the processes of generating new alternatives. The reader will encounter other terms as well: "options," "actions," "acts," "ways," etc., are used throughout the text but only as metaphoric substitutes for "alternatives."

Let us introduce the necessary distinctions with a simple example. We shall then summarize all three concepts at the end of this section. Suppose that our purpose is to travel from New York to Boston. There are different means or ways of acting on that purpose, i.e., many *strategies* we could employ: We could walk, bicycle, or drive an automobile or motorcycle, if we had such means at our disposal. Or we could take a regularly scheduled airline, air taxi, helicopter, bus, or train, or combinations of these.

At this point we have no way of evaluating these strategies. No specific objectives or goals have yet been formulated, and the stated purpose is too general and compatible with most of these means of transportation.

Let us assume that one of the goals is to traverse the New York to Boston distance in less than 2 hours. Not all the listed strategies remain alternatives. Going by bus, automobile or train, is incompatible with this goal. *Alternatives* represent means of achieving a given goal or goals: in this case regular airlines, air shuttles, air taxis, helicopters, etc.

Alternatives are usually *mutually exclusive* activities, objects, projects, or modes of behavior among which a choice is possible. In the decision literature, an alternative is often identified with one and only one set of means, and no real distinction is made between the concepts of a strategy and an alternative.

The extended notion of alternative reflects not only a given set of means (a strategy) but also a set of goals or criteria according to which each strategy can be evaluated and judged. Strategies themselves cannot be compared until at least a preliminary set of goals is determined, i.e., until they become alternatives. We could select travel time, cost, comfort, safety, or other criteria and thus generate different alternatives of traveling to Boston.

Essentially alternatives are *goal-feasible strategies*—feasible not only with respect to constraints but also with respect to goals and objectives.

Suppose that our second goal is to travel for under $100 of total cost. To go by bus, automobile, and train are now available alternatives.[1] The same strategy can become two different alternatives with respect to two different goals. Strategies and alternatives are not necessarily identical. An alternative is a strategy employed toward achieving a known objective.

New alternatives can be generated in three different ways:

1. By inventing or introducing new strategies
2. By modifying existing strategies in order to achieve new goals
3. By creating or introducing new goals or criteria

If we consider a two-dimensional goal, e.g., traversing the New York to Boston route in less than 2 hours *and* for less than $120, then only the regularly scheduled flight and the air shuttle constitute feasible alternatives of choice.

In summary, we have generated *three* sets of alternatives so far:

1. Travel by regular airline, air shuttle, air taxi, or helicopter in less than 2 hours
2. Pay under $100 by using bus, automobile, or train
3. Pay under $120 by using bus, automobile, train, regular airline, or air shuttle

If the three goals above are considered separately, then all the corresponding means constitute alternatives because they allow attainment of a goal.

But note that if we combine the three goals to create a multiple goal, the number of alternatives dwindles. There are none which would be compatible with the first two and the last two goals as pairs. The first and the third goals are reachable by traveling on a regular airline or air shuttle.

New alternatives can be generated by the introduction of either new strategies, new criteria, or new levels of aspiration with respect to existing criteria. For example, taking a taxi from New York would be a new strategy which is incompatible (costs over $120 and takes over 2 hours) with any of the above-listed goals. This strategy could, however, form the basis for a new alternative.

Similarly, introducing a new criterion or changing the level of a given goal could lead to a new alternative. For example, traveling for less than $20 is a goal achievable by private car, motorcycle, bicycle, hitchhiking, walking, etc.

---

[1] We do not consider walking, bicycling, or motorcycling, say, because heavy luggage must be carried, constraining our choices.

The reader can explore other combinations of strategies and goals and generate new options.

Before explaining the notion of a *variant* we shall discuss some important implications of what has been said about strategies and alternatives so far.

"Alternatives," as the word itself strongly suggests, must be *at least two*, and they should be *mutually exclusive*. That is, a single alternative does not allow us any choice.[1] Similarly, the choice process may not proceed satisfactorily if accepting one alternative does not exclude accepting the remaining ones. This condition is less severe, however, and it is sufficient to state that *at least* one alternative must be mutually exclusive with *at least* one other alternative in a given set of options. Often we select five best projects, five hundred best applicants, or in some cultures, two or more spouses.

Quite often the stated objectives or goals admit of only one strategy to form an alternative. When we set our objectives singularly as maximization or minimization, we are creating the conditions for one and only one alternative to be admitted. For example, if we want to travel from New York to Boston so as to minimize the costs, i.e., in the cheapest way and with no other criteria applying, then there is only one way of doing it: the cheapest. There is no decision making when there is only one alternative to choose from. We just have to find the cheapest alternative through a search procedure which is necessary and sufficient for the task. Recall our discussion in Sec. 2-5.

Similarly, if we state our goals in a crisp, precise manner, such as spend exactly $24, or if we set our aspiration level too high, e.g., travel in less than 1 hour, there may be only one (or even no) alternative available. Again, no choice is possible; we just have to search for that one alternative, if it can be found. The process of search, e.g., for the profit-maximizing production mix at General Motors, is not necessarily trivial, however.

True decision alternatives are generated only if our goals are technologically achievable and directional, not strictly predetermined (i.e., they should be "at least" and "at most" types, providing ranges, limits, or intervals of values rather than a single "crisp" number). When we deal with objectives such as maximization and minimization, only multiple objectives allow at least two alternatives to compete and an actual decision-making process to take place. (We could, of course, have a *single* criterion which is so fuzzily defined and so hard to measure that the appropriate ranking of alternatives is difficult to attain).

If our objectives are to minimize costs and to minimize travel time, then we could search for the two minimizing alternatives, maybe hitchhiking and renting a jet respectively, and face the kind of genuine conflict which triggers the decision-making process. If we consider only one of the objectives or if there is an "ideal alternative" which minimizes both objectives at the same time, then there is no implicit conflict, and no decision making would have to take place.

[1]To be allowed not to choose is also an alternative. No decision is itself a decision.

Our search would result in only one alternative, and the choice would be trivial. We do not mean to imply that the *search* is trivial; quite often it is time-consuming and costly, and computerized search procedures (operations research algorithms) must be employed, especially because of measurement difficulties.

Let us return to our example again and assume a multidimensional goal: travel to Boston in less than 2 hours *and* under $120. From the three sets of alternatives generated earlier we select regular airline and air shuttle as the only remaining and mutually exclusive means of achieving the goal. Essentially, a new set of alternatives has been created:

1. Pay under $120 *and* travel in less than 2 hours by regular airline or air shuttle

The regular airline is cheaper, but the air shuttle is faster, and thus a multiobjective conflict is established. We have to choose. Apparently our goals are stated too loosely, but we could resolve the dilemma by changing our goals, introducing new criteria, or considering additional strategies, such as

2. Secure a medium level of comfort by going to a midtown hotel or by staying with a friend

The whole problem now consists of two parts: deciding about the means of travel and deciding about the overnight stay. Suppose that we want to get to Boston for under $120, in less than 2 hours, and enjoy a medium level of overnight comfort. Selecting the air shuttle and a midtown hotel would constitute a *variant* of our plan. Other variants are regular airline and midtown hotel; air shuttle and friend's house; and regular airline and friend's house.

Note that variants are generated by selecting the appropriate strategies from the available sets of alternatives. The sets of means constituting individual variants are not necessarily mutually exclusive, as was the case with alternatives. Variants tend to establish interaction among selected alternatives, and their composite effect becomes important.

The generation of new variants is accomplished by introducing changes in strategies or attainable levels and numbers of attributes. New alternatives imply new variants. But also within a given set of alternatives, new variants can be generated when one attempts different selections or combinations of strategies.

We can summarize the three discussed concepts as follows:

Strategies are *the means* determined by the prevailing level of technological development. Examples of strategies are go by bus, develop the SST, invest in project A, lower taxes, relocate the plant, close the production line, etc.

Alternatives are *strategies employed toward achieving given goal(s)*—for example, go by bus in less than 6 hours, invest in A for 15 percent return, close the production line to minimize costs, produce x amount of A to maximize profits, etc.

Variants are *combinations of alternatives* employed toward achieving different *sets* of goals or objectives—for example, go by bus in less than 6 hours *and* pay less than $20 for an overnight stay, invest in *A* for a 15 percent return *and* do not invest more than $50,000, etc.

An example from production, usually described by a linear-programming model, is also helpful. Suppose that products *A* and *B* are both produced in plants 1 and 2. Within given technological constraints we can produce different amounts of *A* and *B* in both plants. These different combinations of *A* and *B* (including the possibility of *A* or *B* only) are available *strategies* we can use toward achieving our objectives. Suppose that in plant 1 we want to produce *A* and *B* so that total profits will reach at least $100,000 per month. There will be one or more mutually exclusive *alternatives* to achieve such a goal. If we produce one combination of *A* and *B*, we cannot produce any other. One combination will be chosen.

In plant 2, because of the environmental conditions there, we are looking for the strategies (combinations of *A* and *B*) that would provide the largest possible production of *A* and *B* at a level of pollution fines not exceeding $1000 per month. There will be at least some combinations of *A* and *B* compatible with our goals, and they form our decision *alternatives* at plant 2.

If only one alternative is available at each plant, then only one variant of the production plan can be created for both plants. If at least two alternatives are available in at least one of the plants, then at least two variants of the production plan can be created.

Strategies, alternatives, and variants represent different levels of the decision process. Before a particular set of goals or objectives evolves to guide their unfolding, new strategies are created through technological development, relaxation of constraints, or expansion of possibilities. As soon as one sets the criteria and aspiration levels, at least some of the strategies become alternatives. As one extends decision-making concerns to interrelated sets of decision problems, one starts to evaluate different variants of a solution. In this book we are mostly concerned with the intermediate level—the generation of alternatives.

4-1.3 The Generating Process

Each alternative may be represented by its vector of attainable attribute levels, $x = (x_1, x_2, \ldots, x_n)$. To distinguish among them we shall simply number them in the superscript: $x^1, x^2, \ldots$, etc. Thus, x_1^1 represents the level of the first attribute attainable by the first alternative, x_2^1 is the second attribute by the first alternative, x_1^2 is the first by the second, and so forth.

Because the attribute levels are expressible in cardinal scales, we can imagine that they are characterized by different positions in the geometric space of attributes. For two attributes x_1 and x_2 we could represent two alternatives x^1 and x^2 as in Fig. 4-1.

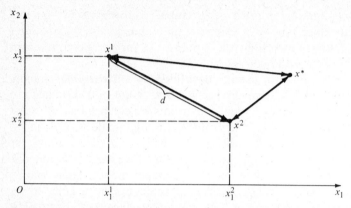

Figure 4-1 Concept of distance in the attribute space.

Although we can draw such pictures only up to three dimensions (three attributes), this geometric concept can be readily extended to all higher-dimensional cases.

Observe that a distance between the two points, $x^1 = (x_1^1, x_2^1)$ and $x^2 = (x_1^2, x_2^2)$ is a well-defined and natural concept of the attribute space. For example, the euclidean distance between x^1 and x^2 is given by

$$d(x^1, x^2) = \sqrt{(x_1^1 - x_1^2)^2 + (x_2^1 - x_2^2)^2}$$

We shall discuss other suitable distance measures in Sec. 6-5.2. Now we need to establish that the notion of distance is useful and that it makes sense to characterize two alternatives as being "close," "very far," or "almost identical" with respect to each other.

Any two alternatives can be compared in the attribute space and their distance measured. Also, all alternatives can be compared according to their respective distances from a given point(s) of reference. In Fig. 4-1 we have chosen x^* as such a point of reference, and we see that $d(x^1, x^*) > d(x^2, x^*)$, i.e., x^2 is closer to x^* than to x^1.

Starr and Greenwood (1977) explored the computer-based generation of alternatives and suggest a signaling system which would inform the decision maker that the number of existing alternatives is sufficiently representative and that the available resources should be diverted to more productive areas. In this case the process should move from the alternative-creation phase to subsequent stages of the decision-making process.

This signaling system should indicate when (1) a new decision alternative is not sufficiently different from another decision alternative; or, (2) the creation of any new alternatives is unlikely to be productive; or both (1) and (2).

As an appropriate measure which may be used as the cutoff criterion, Starr and Greenwood suggest the cumulative entropy of successive distance measures of decision alternatives from each other. When the increases in entropy become negligible, the creation of new options should be stopped. For a detailed explanation of entropy see Sec. 7-1.2.

Let us number all generated alternatives with $j = 1, 2, \cdots , k, k + 1$, and designate any two successively generated alternatives with k and $k + 1$. Thus we generate $x^1, x^2, x^3, \cdots , x^k, x^{k+1}$. After generating each x^j, we can calculate the corresponding value of the cumulative entropy measure, $H(x^j)$:

$$H(x^j) = -\frac{1}{A}\sum_{k=1}^{j} d(x^k, x^{k+1}) \, [\log d \, (x^k, x^{k+1}) - \log A]$$

where $d(x^k, x^{k+1}) = \sqrt{\sum_{i=1}^{n} (x_i^k - x_i^{k+1})^2}$

$A = $ a normalization constant, e.g., the maximum-distance value minus the minimum-distance value generated so far.

$H(x^j) = $ the cumulative entropy up to the jth alternative.

When the cumulative entropy of the system is increasing, the decision-alternative set covers a greater and greater variety of situations, and it is therefore productive to continue the generating process. Once the rate of increase in $H(x^j)$ approaches zero, the addition of further decision alternatives does not add to the variety of the system, and the additional alternatives do not provide any significantly new information. For example, using three successive increases of less than 1 percent in the cumulative entropy is one possible version of the cutoff criterion.

Applying the stopping rule does not mean that the alternative invention procedure should not be invoked on a local basis at some future stages of the decision process. Once the preferred alternative has been selected, decision-alternative generation should resume in its neighborhood on a much tighter search trajectory. The purpose is either to confirm or further refine the selection or to reject it by opening up a previously unexplored region of possibilities.

One can generate a new alternative from the existing one by taking into account all relevant technological constraints and possibilities that were not adequately considered before. The incorporation of new technical, scientific, and organizational knowledge will be reflected in the inclusion of additional strategies, the attainment of new attribute levels, and ultimately in the generation of a new alternative.[1]

---

[1]The approach described here is similar to the so-called *morphological analysis* (MA); see for example, Jantsch (1967). Instead of attributes or criteria, MA employs a narrower set of basic engineering *parameters*. All possible combinations are formed by varying the parameters within technological limits. Jantsch describes an analysis of chemical jet propulsion which yielded 25,344 possible configurations. Under the parameter "medium in which the jet is operating," water and earth appeared beside the more obvious air and vacuum. Several versions of a "hydro-jet" and of a "terra-jet" were discovered.

Technological closure If we start with an obviously inferior alternative that does not fully exploit the existing technological possibilities, there is much room for improvement. The new alternatives will be generated relatively fast and without excessive effort or creative strain. As the process continues and the new alternatives approach technological boundaries with respect to an increasing number of criteria, the alternatives will become closer to each other, and their further generation will require considerable outlays of additional effort and time. Achievable attribute levels become less distinct; distances between subsequent alternatives tend to be smaller or approach zero; the process converges to a final limiting alternative. Any further effort expended in the same direction would be misplaced. A new direction must be chosen and explored.

We say that a set of alternatives is *technologically closed* in a given direction if it contains at least one sequence of alternatives converging to a limiting alternative. A technologically closed set of alternatives reflects the fact that a certain stage of technological development has been recognized as completed and that the decisions will have to be made within its framework. At least one limiting alternative must be generated before the set of feasible alternatives can be considered technologically closed.

A set of alternatives is technologically open if the limiting alternatives have not yet been generated. In that case, one needs to intensify the search process, to broaden information gathering, and, possibly, to increase research and development efforts. The purpose of generating new alternatives is, then, to achieve technological closure with a given set of alternatives. By finding at least one converging sequence, one discovers a developmental tendency and can contemplate its future extrapolation. A technologically open set is typically characterized by a broad scattering of alternatives all over the space with no tendencies being apparent. If alternatives are uniformly or randomly scattered in this way, it becomes very difficult to establish goals or targets.

In order to set one's aspiration levels intelligently, one has to acquire at least some understanding of the major stages of the relevant technological development as well as its orientation for the future. Only a technologically closed set of alternatives is helpful in the later goal- and target-setting process. Goals and targets must not only correctly reflect the current stage of technological development, they must also take into account estimates of future developmental tendencies. Not least, they must stimulate further innovations and encourage increased research and development efforts.

An estimate of the limiting alternative forms the necessary base for establishing good strategic goals and targets. The transformation of a technologically open set into a closed one can be achieved by generating new options in such a way that a converging sequence of alternatives is safely recognized and quickly extended to its limiting point.

It is not sufficient to keep increasing the *number* of options, but it is necessary to explore particular directions in a purposeful, nonrandom way. Redefinition and reformulation of goals and targets may be required during this process. Assuming new criteria and objectives will facilitate the opening of alternative directions and the developing of additional options. Restructuring of the problem can be achieved by temporarily discarding some less important or ineffective criteria.

Let us consider a simple example illustrating the concept of a technologically closed set of alternatives. In Fig. 4-2 alternative engine designs are represented by points on a two-dimensional plane. The evaluative criteria are mileage and horsepower. Other possible criteria are weight, cost, durability, speed, etc. The maximum-horsepower engine is associated with low mileage; high mileage requires lower horsepower. Starting from design 1, one can unfold two basic sequences of alternatives toward exploiting current technological limits (indicated by the dashed lines perpendicular to the respective axes). One might concentrate either on horsepower or on mileage and arrive at two limiting alternatives, 2 and 3. The set of alternatives is technologically closed if at least one of the points, say 2 or 3, is feasible. There are other possible technological sequences, including an extension toward the ideal-design alternative. Let alternative 4 represent a technologically limiting combination of horsepower and mileage. Obviously, the set of alternatives is technologically closed, and only alternatives 2, 3, and 4 are of interest. Since we cannot move beyond point 2 or 3 in their respective directions, the further generation of alternatives would entail opening new sequences in the direction (indicated by the dotted arrows) of the ideal design.

In contrast, when such discernible sequences are nonexistent and the process of technological development does not converge to one of the limiting alternatives, we encounter a technologically open set, as depicted in Fig. 4-3. Any decision making based on a technologically open set is necessarily suboptimal and short-term. Creating a technologically closed set of alternatives is one of the main prerequisites of good decision making. Yet this point is usually ignored in the decision-analysis literature, and a rather complex and precise

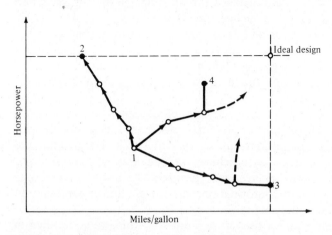

Figure 4-2 Technologically closed set of alternatives.

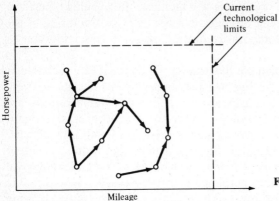

Figure 4-3 Technologically open set of alternatives.

battery of mathematical tools and algorithms is applied to a "given" set of alternatives. Technological closure of the given set is usually left to the "less important" stages of the analysis.

Figure 4-4 captures the main stages of the alternative-generation process. Some of the features of the diagram have been adapted from Klusoň (1976). We start with an initial set of alternatives X and attempt to characterize it in terms of its technological limits. It is important to note that the set of criteria is still very crude and the number of criteria very small. Only as we reach closure in at least some of the directions do we proceed to finalize the relevant set of goals and criteria. That is, both the alternatives and the criteria evolve at the same time and in mutual interdependency. Observe also that technological development in the direction of the ideal design is the most efficient form for research and development efforts. It leads directly toward multicriterion conflict resolution. On the other hand, extending the limits vertically or horizontally beyond points 2 or 3, as in Fig. 4-2, would displace the ideal design further away and thus set the aspiration levels even higher. This latter strategy is not usually attractive to a company's research and development department, but it is often adopted in response to external pressures and regulations. It represents a long-term version of new-strategy generation. Within existing technological states of the art, movement toward the ideal design is the most effective direction for generating new options.

An ideal design is the best the designers can conceptualize *now*. It is not utopian because it is capable of being improved or modified. It is ideal only with respect to a particular set of circumstances. Ackoff (1978) asserts that the purpose of an idealized design is *not* to achieve an ideal state or system but to establish an *ideal-seeking* state or system. The ideal is subject to continual revision in light of newly acquired information, knowledge, and understanding: The ideal is a guide for action.

An ideal is like a good plan for the future—not something to be fulfilled in detail and slavishly followed, but there to be aborted, as Stafford Beer used to

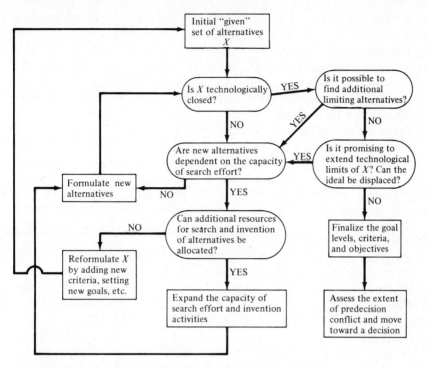

Figure 4-4 Stages of the alternative-generation process.

say, to be surpassed, redesigned, and changed. A plan is a learning matrix for management; only through its ultimate negation can a reality be mastered. Yet without it, without its frame of reference, our activities would be chaotic, purposeless, and inaccessible to evaluation and comparison. If a plan is followed slavishly as a directive, then there is a pretense that one has the final answers to all questions. Such a plan becomes absolute, final, or fixed. *But just as no good plan can serve well unless it can be changed in the course of its pursuit, no ideal design can remain ideal for long.*

4-1.4 Technological Forecasting

We have introduced the notion of the *technologically closed* set of alternatives. Such a set takes into account all relevant technological constraints and possibilities and incorporates the most recent technical, scientific, organizational, and managerial knowledge. A large amount of scientific and technological information must be processed, interpreted, and evaluated. Trends and directions must be inferred and future impacts assessed. Therefore, some forms of *technological forecasting* are needed.

Jantsch (1967) identifies about a hundred systematic, semiscientific, and intuitive techniques for forecasting the future. These include trend-curve extrapolation, relevance trees, goal hierarchies, morphological analysis, gaming simulation, scenario writing, Delphi techniques, cross-impact matrices, and even brainstorming.[1]

Technological forecasting is concerned with trying to work out the nature and efficiency of anticipated technological advances. It provides a basis for *technology assessment*, an attempt to foresee the side effects and secondary repercussions of new technologies.

Let us take supersonic-aircraft technology as an example. One has to forecast the prospects for such a technology being able to transport people and cargo from one place to another. What are the speed and distance? What are the costs? What is the reliability of this new technology? These are the concerns of technological forecasting. What are the secondary consequences: pollution of the stratosphere, sonic booms, monopolistic concentration, social impacts, political impacts, military potentials, etc. These are the questions of a technology-assessment effort.

Technological forecasting and technology assessment aim at making explicit comparisons between alternative technologies. They aid in developing a technologically closed set of available alternatives—or, because of the imperfection of the alternatives and the uncertain nature of forecasting itself, something which resembles such an ideal set as closely as possible.

Frequently there is criticism, cautiousness, or skepticism concerning one or another approach to technological forecasting. All approaches are inadequate and unreliable. But their use assures that an organized effort to think about the alternatives has been made. At least *possible* impacts may have been foreseen, even if no one can assure us whether or not particular impacts will actually occur.

4-2 THEORY OF CONFLICT DISSOLUTION

"An intelligence which aims at the definitive resolution (that is, suppression) of conflict," is not worth defending, according to Susan Sontag. We agree. In this age of conflict suppression and conflict resolution, we witness the proliferation of conflict in a large variety of forms and intensities: between individuals and groups, between social classes, within families, between business and government, among nations, etc.

In an era of information processing and unprecedented communication capabilities, and after decades of collective bargaining, negotiations, and mediation efforts, few conflicts are actually resolved or even temporarily "swept under the rug." Our society is not very effective in dealing with conflictual situations. Wars, police actions, uninvited "fraternal assistance," threats, ter-

---

[1]A short review of more recent techniques, including scoring models, dimensional analysis, trade-off surface forecasting, etc., can be found in J. P. Martino: "Technological Forecasting—An Overview," *Management Science*, vol. 26, no. 1, 1980, pp. 28–33.

ror strikes, boycotts, and "official silence" seem to be still the most effective means of conflict "resolution." Propaganda, persuasion, brainwashing, and "logical reasoning" a close second in popularity. Is it possible that our theories of conflict and its resolution are inadequate and one-sided? Can an alternative theory be advanced?

4-2.1 Symptoms of Conflict

Conflict, in psychology, is a situation in which two or more motives are partially blocking each other. It is often assumed that the prime source of conflict lies in the *cognitive domain*, in cognitive differences in perception or interpretation of the components of a given decision situation. Conflict thus becomes *cognitive* conflict, generated by poor communication, misunderstanding, ideological inflexibility, etc. Its resolution is sought in *cognitive change* induced through discussion, argumentation, persuasion, negotiation, "shuttle diplomacy," and other means of temporary conflict confusion and concealment.

But are perceived cognitive differences the causes or the symptoms of the underlying conflict?

It is a gross simplification to assume that conflict arises only because of inadequate communication, value confusion, and mutual misunderstanding. Such an approach implies that there is no *real* conflict at the bottom of human problems; all is due to our stubbornness, ignorance, and ill-conceived goals. Conflict resolution is then simply a matter of skillful persuasion, consciousness raising, intensive propaganda, strategic threats, or diligent learning. To be sure, most of these devices attack real inadequacies, which contribute to our feeling of discomfort and urgency about most conflicts. *But no disease can be cured by removing its symptoms. It can only be temporarily concealed and obscured to our senses.*

Thus communication does not appear to be essential for conflict resolution. It might be necessary—but not sufficient. In fact, one could submit that excessive communication may even hamper efforts at conflict resolution. The amount and intensity of conflict in modern society seem to increase with advances in the means of communication. Moreover, the most stable, lasting, and effective agreements are frequently results of tacit and implicit understandings, often without explicit communication. We may observe many cases of commonly shared values among people who are essentially noncommunicative, as well as increasingly divergent values among people who intensify their communication.

Decision making can be described as a process of searching for the "right" alternative(s). It is remarkable that so little attention has been devoted to the generation of new alternatives.[1] Yet, quite often, the decision process can be

---

[1]Recent papers by Starr and Greenwood (1977), Shocker and Srinivasan (1974), Kluson (1976), and this author are notable exceptions.

completed when a new, prominent alternative is generated, i.e., long before the full set of feasible alternatives has been evaluated. Such a crucial aspect of decision making should not be summarized under the label "given."

4-2.2 Conditions of Conflict

Conflict occurs when two or more distinct *strategies*, selected as the means of achieving given goals or objectives, are mutually exclusive—that is, when the strategies become mutually exclusive *alternatives*, each capable of satisfying only a portion or a particular aspect of a given goal complex.

The following are *necessary* conditions of a potentially conflicting situation:

1. One or more *decision subjects*, i.e., organisms or machines capable of making a choice: human decision makers, Buridan's donkeys, Skinner's rats, or decision-forming contrivances
2. *Two* or more available *alternatives* of choice, including a "no choice" alternative or a "no preference" vote
3. One or more objectives or *criteria* of choice, including rules, programs, needs, instincts, motives, or other concepts which are used to evaluate the decision subjects' choices

We shall designate a *conflict-free state* between two decision subjects, with respect to a given criterion, as the state where no further action is being considered by either party.

Next, we shall attempt to induce a conflict between two subjects, M and F. Suppose that both M and F share an identical objective: to spend their vacation together in the most pleasurable way. Both subjects are currently considering only two alternatives: either Miami Beach or Las Vegas. If M selects Las Vegas and F prefers Miami as the means of maximizing or achieving the given goal, we have obtained the necessary conditions for a classical case of conflict.

How could we restore a conflict-free situation? Assuming no changes or relaxations in both parties' criterion, we could invent and introduce a new, third option, as for example going to Spain. A trip to Spain may represent a point of maximal pleasure for both subjects. No communication, persuasion, or marital (or martial) discussion need be involved.

Now we can demonstrate why the mutual exclusivity of alternatives is the main prerequisite for conflict. If we remove the mutual exclusivity in our example, by changing the criterion to spending their vacations in the most pleasurable way and separately, then M can go to Las Vegas and F to Miami, and each of them will be happy. No conflict is present.

What about the second necessary condition, i.e., the stipulation of at least two alternatives? The condition implies that if there exists only one alternative there cannot be any conflict (recall that "no choice" is also an alternative), because mutually exclusive choices cannot appear.

There can be two-alternative situations in which one option so completely dominates the other that the situation is perceived as a single-alternative one. For example, the choice between life and death, ceteris paribus, does not usually generate conflict.

Let us turn to the third necessary condition. So far we have assumed a single, jointly shared (or common) objective or criterion. Yet we observe that, even in the absence of multiple objectives, two or more decision subjects can generate a large variety of conflictual situations. Each decision subject can make a choice by employing different multiple objectives, but according to our concept of conflict, the similarity, identity, or distinctiveness of objectives might have nothing to do with the presence or absence of conflict.

Conflict can be characterized as induced by the mutual exclusivity of distinct alternatives which are selected by different decision subjects. We now provide a concise and general definition of *conflict*: *the perceived absence of a prominent alternative.*

4-2.3 Dissolving versus Resolving the Conflict

We shall now represent conflict graphically to support the definition just given. Because graphic analysis is limited to two-dimensional geometry, only the following cases can be represented: (1) one decision subject with two objectives, and (2) two decision subjects with a single, shared objective. The number of decision alternatives can be as large as desired in both cases.

Let us first represent two decision subjects with a common single objective, as were M and F in our earlier example. In Fig. 4-5 observe that M and F *maximize their criterion at points x^2 and x^1 respectively.* Even though they share a common objective and we do not assume any special cognitive differences, errors, misinformation, or insufficient communication, there is a conflict.

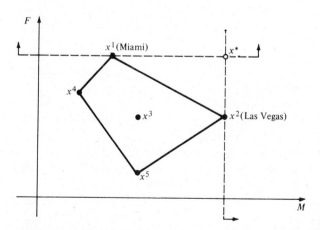

Figure 4-5 Classical case of conflict.

The prominent alternative x^* either is nonexistent or has not yet been "discovered" by either M or F. It is the *absence* of x^* which causes the conflict to appear. Note that if alternative x^* became feasible, the conflict would be fully dissolved. Both M and F would maximize their pleasure at x^*.

In Fig. 4-6 we offer a more general representation of conflict. Let $X = \{x^1, x^2, x^3, \ldots, x^m\}$ denote the set of feasible alternatives, and M and F the two decision subjects, each employing a single objective function.

The heavily traced boundary of X, consisting of nondominated solutions (see Sec. 2-4.), represents a *region of compromise*, a bargaining set. Observe that no compromise solution x^s, including even both extremes x^1 and x^2, removes or resolves the underlying conflict. Conflict resolution via compromise represents only a temporary disguise of the absence of x^*. At any compromise point x^s, located on the heavily drawn boundary of X, there is at least one decision subject (or at least one of the multiple objectives) that stays unsatisfied with respect to what is actually achievable. Even if M "persuades" F to go along with him and accept alternative x^2, and even if F is genuinely convinced that such a negotiated outcome is the best for both M and F, *the conflict has not been removed*. Sooner or later the suppressed perceptions and value judgments will claim their toll; conflict will emerge again; hasty agreements will not be honored; deceit and treason may appear. In the words of a popular television commercial, "you can't fool Mother Nature"—in this case the culturally based, deeply entrenched set of preferences and values. These values do not change overnight.

"Conflict resolution" does not remove conflict; it may not even reduce conflict. For example, if x^{ss} is chosen as a satisfactory level of achievement (the solution of satisficing or its technical model, goal programming), the parties would move even farther away from x^*, and the shaded region between the solution in X and x^* would increase. The shaded region roughly indicates the

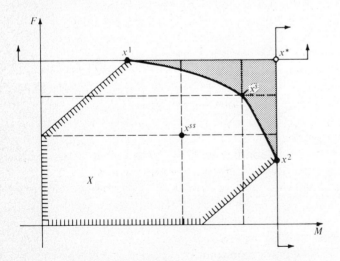

Figure 4-6 Satisficing, compromise, and conflict dissolution.

extent of present or remaining conflict. The larger it is the more intense is the conflict; as it gets smaller or as it disappears, the conflict is dissolved.

The only way to dissolve conflict is to find or invent x^*.

The only way to decrease the intensity of conflict is to generate alternatives in the shaded area of Fig. 4-6, i.e., those which are as close as possible to x^*. Points x^s, x^{ss}, etc., temporarily disguise the absence of x^*. They indicate a lack of the innovation and creativity needed for "inventing" x^*.

4-2.4 Implications of Conflict Dissolution

Negotiators, persuaders, diplomats, and bargaining experts still devote most of their efforts to inducing a cognitive change in the adversary party, to making the adversary see the problem from their point of view. When the powerful ones, the skillful ones, and the slick ones succeed, they reap the glory of temporary conflict "resolution." But the sources of conflict will have been left largely untouched. At the first opportunity, as the threats and power domination abate, the conflict will burst out with renewed vigor. Throughout history, only the greatest statesmen and decision makers knew the secret of finding the prominent alternative and were able to dissolve conflicts for generations to come.

Human objectives, values, perceptions, cognitive differences, etc., are the result of extremely complex evolutionary processes. Such deeply ingrained characteristics as the interactions of genetic, cultural, environmental, and educational experiences, or as the unique and nonreproducible evolution of an individual, group, nation, or society—are they reversible and adaptable during the course of a few days or weeks? Is the art of compromise just a euphemism for the skill of persuasion? We don't think so.

Compromise involves the art of finding or creating a prominent conflict-free alternative. Only a few practitioners are still applying this art.

One of the most persistent and frustrating conflicts in the United States is that between blacks and whites. The symptoms of this conflict are obvious: racism, segregation, intolerance, discrimination, hate, etc. But we don't cure the disease by removing its symptoms. We cannot ban the symptoms. We don't remove conflict by persuasion, communication, or reeducation. It is difficult to educate patients by teaching them that fever is not good for them. We are borrowing time by avoiding the conflict. Busing, quotas, goals—none of these artificial remedies will remove the conflict.

It is much harder to *dissolve* a conflict than to "resolve" it. It is much easier to suppress the symptoms than to cure the disease. Thus we have many expert and fast "problem solvers," "troubleshooters," and professional "activists," and we only rarely encounter the more contemplative, patient, and wise conflict managers.

Paul Robeson recognized that persuasion and mere removal of symptoms are very inadequate tools for conflict dissolution. Although he was never popular for the hard and painful solutions he suggested, he was nevertheless correct: "My problem is not to counteract the white man's prejudice against the Negro. That does not matter. I have set myself to educate my brother to believe in himself."

Truly, cognitive differences or cultural prejudices are not what matter in the end.

The preferences of two (or more) opposing decision subjects are not necessarily in contradiction. The preferences can be traced to their roots in the subjects' cultural, social, and psychological histories, which offer clues to their underlying value system. Then the individual sets of preference can be restated as the opposition of these underlying value systems. At least some of the assumptions will be common to both systems—otherwise there would be no basis for the conflict or opposition in the first place. This commonality of assumptions suggests that there must exist a suprasystem that implies *both* opposing systems of assumptions. The discovery of this suprasystem is similar to the discovery of a prominent alternative x^*. The new preference statements derived from the suprasystem will be consistent and conflict-free and will render the original conflicting preferences irrelevant.

4-2.5 Significance of Conflict

Conflict provides the decision-motivating tension, the sense of frustration and dissatisfaction with the status quo. Since the underlying source of a predecision conflict is the nonavailability of a prominent alternative, one must first attempt to create one.

We usually know the attribute measurements of alternative x^*. Is there any possibility for its empirical realization? Or, at least, something close to it? The shaded area in Fig. 4-6 provides good normative guidance with respect to what kinds of alternatives should be generated. One forms a "model" of a desirable alternative while it is still in the early stages of its development and well before excessive costs have been incurred toward its elaboration and physical development. Measures of distances between the most preferred levels of attributes (prominent point x^*) and the potential new alternatives are then used to evaluate the latter's merits. A complete formalization of this dynamic model is presented in Chap. 6 as a part of the theory of the displaced ideal.

Distance is a natural concept in conflict modeling. If a skinnerian rat is taught to approach food at the end of a long corridor and then is shocked while retrieving it, thereafter, upon repeating the procedure, the rat will stop at a certain distance from the goal. If released nearer the food, the rat will retreat to the same distance as before. The conflict is thus modeled by an increase both in attraction to the goal and in the tendency to retreat as the goal is approached.

The same model applies to any human decision subject. Consider the example of a single decision subject M facing two different objectives, maximized at x^1 and x^2 respectively. As M approaches x^1, M is also being painfully reminded of the discomfort of being too far away from x^2. After a while, M settles at a certain distance from both competing tendencies—a compromise solution, say x^s. If there are no other real alternatives except x^1 and x^2, M might avoid or delay the choice by staying put at the compromise distance from x^1 and x^2. Depending on the actual circumstances—for example if x^1 and x^2 are mutually exclusive and precisely equal, the decision can be made only once, and the consequences are uncertain and serious in their impact—the decision maker may try to avoid the choice. Or, if the consequences are negligible, the decision maker might toss a coin. If the same decision is to be made repeatedly, the decision maker might oscillate between x^1 and x^2 in the decision sequence.

Since genuine conflict resolution is impossible and conflict dissolution may mean a very lengthy process of invention, innovation, and discovery, the decision maker can attempt *conflict reduction*, i.e., reduce the distance between x^* and the contemplated compromise solutions. Such partial reduction of conflict intensity is termed "conflict management." We emphasize again that no traditional compromise solution actually removes the conflict. The only way to dissolve a conflict is through the creation of x^*.

Management scientists should learn how to dissolve the *essential* underlying conflict through the identification of prominent alternatives, not how to remove the *apparent* conflict through persuasion or advocacy. Most of the current available models start with, "Given a set of feasible alternatives X . . . " Not enough. Because making a decision, as a means of conflict dissolution, reduction, or resolution, is tantamount to generating a prominent alternative, one would expect that normative generation of new alternatives should become a primary concern of the management sciences.

4-2.6 Prominent Alternative

The concept of a prominent alternative is not entirely new. See for example the stimulating work of Schelling (1960), introducing the idea. What is new is the recognition that the *absence* of a prominent alternative constitutes the source of most conflicts.

Alternative x^* represents a point at which all multiple objectives would be optimized: an overall optimum, *optimum optimorum*, an unattainable ideal. But this does not mean that the ideal cannot serve as a norm or a rationale directing and facilitating human choice and decision making. An external, generally nonaccessible alternative has been shown by Leon Festinger and his colleagues (1964) to assume the important role of a point of reference against which choices are measured.

If we cannot achieve x^*, we should at least attempt to move *as close as possible* to it. Its unattainability should not serve as an excuse for trying to achieve the attainable only. Ignoring the ideal and settling down to what is "good enough" does not remove the conflict, and it is incompatible with management *sciences*. "Satisficing" means "resolving" the conflict by simply ignoring its extent and scope. Point x^s in Fig. 4-6 represents such a good-enough solution, satisfying a priori determined goals and arbitrarily lowered aspiration levels. Even worse, a satisficer may set goals still lower, choose point x^{ss}, and live happily ever after.

Schelling (1960) observed that most stable agreements and conflict resolutions are not conspicuously fair or conspicuously in balance with estimated bargaining powers; they are just plain conspicuous. Their focal points and conspicuous features are very similar to the prominence of x^*. Schelling demonstrated that people watch each other's choices if a prominent option exists that can serve as an anchor or tacit agreement. The prominence principle can be viewed as a strategic principle, as a means of implementing tacit agreements among decision subjects with at least partially coinciding motives in situations where explicit conflict-free compromise is not possible.

The task of looking for a prominent alternative does not reduce the need for bargaining and negotiating skills. Rather than being used to persuade or induce cognitive changes, they become displaced to the domain of problem definition, formulation, and expansion. The identification of new and prominent alternatives, along with their subsequent incorporation in a decision situation, is more than a skill: It is an art.

4-2.7 Examples of Conflict Dissolution

It is of course very important to be able to identify the cases of conflict dissolution and distinguish them from the more common compromises, negotiated agreements, or other conflict "resolution" outcomes. We shall list several illustrations of the conflict-dissolution principle.

The following cases are meant to serve as illustrations of the potential usefulness of searching for new alternatives. They demonstrate both the high resolution power of a prominent alternative and the need to break out of one's habitual domain of thought. But, in the end, explaining conflict dissolution seems to be simply an attempt to explain the functioning of human "common sense."

1. Alan C. Filley (1976) relates a case of eighteen top prison officials meeting to design an ideal correctional institution. A member of the security group proposed that uniforms for guards be eliminated in the new institution. The group then began a lengthy argument about whether or not uniforms should be worn. Finally, one of the officials said, "Look, let's settle this democratically; let's take a vote." As a result, six people voted to eliminate uniforms and three voted in favor of their use.

   The winning members appeared pleased; their position had prevailed. The losing members got angry or withdrew from the discussion. One complained that they were turned into a bunch of "social workers." New alternative solutions were then generated with the help of a consultant. Ten solutions were suggested. The outcome was the recommendation that guards wear casual clothes and name tags, while guard captains wear uniforms. The guards were known to the inmates anyway, they said, but the captains were not, and the uniform would serve a useful purpose in that case. The solution was acceptable to everyone and received full support.

2. In the well-publicized controversy about the SST Concorde service to New York City, the two opposing parties quickly locked themselves into considering only two possible alternatives: to land or not to land. Instead of arguing about the desirability of allowing the SST to land at Kennedy airport and trading off the noise pollution against the economic benefits, a vigorous search for a prominent third alternative should have been attempted. For example, the SST could land on a floating platform anchored and self-stabilized a few miles offshore, or on a special landing strip located in the New Jersey interior and approached over unpopulated swamp areas. Helicopter services could then shuttle the passengers directly to Manhattan. It now takes almost 1 hour by taxi from Kennedy to Manhattan anyway.

   Instead, this dilemma was handled through typical means of conflict "resolution": One side gave in, and the other side's solution has been temporarily accepted. But none of the initial arguments and issues have been resolved. The special requirements of the SST Concorde continue to plague airport traffic; the service is becoming substandard, and the time savings for passengers are negligible.

3. New York City is infamous for its high incidence of false fire alarms. Analysts have been consulted, and operations researchers have suggested the optimal distribution and deployment of fire engines so that an efficient response pattern to some 204,000 false alarms per year can be figured out and implemented. A suggestion has been made that, to identify or deter the culprits, street alarm boxes be furnished with cameras and voice- and fingerprinting devices.

   Instead, the city should consider removing the red alarm boxes from the streets altogether. They were quite useful in the pretelephone days of the nineteenth century. No other big city has them, and none needs them. Yet, cutting the false alarms down would mean that a large number of unionized firemen would have to be laid off. Hence the dilemma.

4. One recent and quite impressive case of group conflict *dissolution* was the election of a Pole, Cardinal Karol Wojtyla, as the new Pope of the Roman Catholic Church in 1978. Choosing a Supreme Pontiff is a multiple-criteria problem and not a simple task. There were 111 electors locked up in the Sistine Chapel, and they had no other choice than to reach a consensus.

   Several basic criteria were applied by the electors: The Pope should be an Italian, of respectable age, held in high esteem, reasonably conservative or liberal (depending on the values of individual electors), and so on. A classical case of conflict evolved: Cardinal Giuseppe Siri of Genoa, the conservative condidate, and Cardinal Giovanni Benelli of Florence, a liberal candidate, each got between twenty-five and thirty-five votes on the first ballot. With the criterion of Italianism met, the electors concentrated on the conservative-liberal issue.

A deadlock settled in: Each side was determined to block the other side's candidate at all costs. Negotiations, discussions, and politicking only led to even more inflexible and determined positions. Even a compromise choice was impossible to achieve: Both sides actually offered other alternatives: Cardinal Giovanni Colombo of Milan and Cardinal Ugo Poletti of Rome. But these "new" choices were perceived as simple replacements, with neither side giving up anything in terms of the conservative-liberal criterion. On the fifth ballot there was a firm deadlock, and a long, trying session of negotiation and persuasion was in the offing for the conclave.

The only way to dissolve the conflict was to bring forward a new, refreshing and nonobvious alternative. One cannot invent a new Cardinal, but a new alternative can be "created" by concentrating on a new dimension, a new criterion of choice. The issue of Italianism was reconsidered, and suddenly good new options started to appear. On the seventh ballot, Cardinal Wojtyla moved well ahead, and on the eighth ballot he received 104 votes and the three puffs of white smoke. He was an ideal alternative: non-Italian, neither liberal nor conservative, young and vigorous, intellectual, worldly, and somebody who really knew what lack of freedom meant.

14-2.8 Concluding Remarks

We have been concerned with the dissolution of conflict and neglected the other ways of dealing with conflicting situations. These other approaches are usually well covered in the literature, and a detailed review of them would detrimentally increase the size of this book. Let us provide only a short summary.

Ackoff (1978) enumerates three ways of dealing with conflict and thus with problems in general: *solution*, *resolution*, and *dissolution*. We might also add *neglect*, *containment*, *control*, and *denial* as additional strategies employed by people under different circumstances. These seven or so approaches comprise our repertoire for conflict *management*. Each approach has its merits if applied properly under proper circumstances; each approach can become seriously dangerous if applied improperly or arbitrarily.

The last four strategies are often used but difficult to formalize or study in a structured way. One can of course ignore conflict, neglect it, let it run its course. Two drunks are fighting on the corner; two nations are at war; my mother-in-law does not like me—so what? Let it be. One can also attempt to contain conflict, freeze it in its progress, to gain time and let heads cool off. A temporary cease-fire, a cooling-off period, a "quiet" household, "let's not talk about it now"—these are also admirable strategies if properly used. A conflict is not a well-defined, crisp, and unambiguous state of affairs. It is fuzzy, due to incomplete information, wrong perceptions, or lack of development. It often makes sense to contain it and think.

One can also choose to control conflict—making sure that it runs its course within certain limits, according to some rules. The referees of professional hockey often let the players fight off their aggravations so that they don't have to carry them off the ice. They control the conflict by making sure that nobody gets hurt, that it does not last too long, and that the parties will be able to shake hands afterward. Competition is often characterized as constrained conflict—constrained by rules. Two tennis players are in a conflict constrained by rules. In controlling the conflict one recognizes a higher objective or purpose which is achieved more efficiently through the conflict than through direct pursuit, be it the interests of consumers or more intense exercise or a heightened recreational experience.

Finally, one can choose to deny conflict's existence or reality. This is not the same as ignoring or neglecting a conflict. One acknowledges that a certain situation exists but then advances a different, often very imaginative interpretation in conflict-free terms. The two drunks at the corner are not fighting but engaging in manly play; she said "no" but meant "yes"; apparent political disagreements are simply reflections of a dialectical dialogue or of a "There is no bread? Let them eat cake" attitude of enlightened monarchy. Conflict denial requires the use of persuasion, propaganda, brainwashing—and lies.

Let us turn to more structured and tangible ways of dealing with conflict: solution and resolution. One can *solve* a conflict by acknowledging and accepting the conditions that produced it, then seek a way of getting out of it—or of getting out of it what one wants. The other side does not matter. One attempts to win it, by either force, gamesmanship, or elimination of the opponent. One can cut the Gordian knot. One can give money to the poor while accepting the causes of their poverty; one can bus children to better schools without trying to improve the bad ones; one can relocate the plant rather than deal with dissatisfied employees. Solving a conflict is characterized by a single party's single objective, and its maximization or optimization is the sole criterion for action.

To resolve a conflict, by definition, involves the consideration of multiple objectives: Resolution pays attention to the "other side." Nonetheless, it accepts the conditions which created the conflict. It seeks a compromise, a settlement, or a consensus. Each party usually gives up something it originally desired. Both parties strive for a "fair" distribution of gains and losses. Negotiation, bargaining, and arbitration are common tools for seeking conflict resolution. As we have argued earlier in the chapter, conflict resolution by compromise reduces conflict and diffuses it temporarily. But resolution does not affect the conditions which produced the conflict; it does not dissolve it.

There is an extensive literature dealing with conflict resolution. There is even a specialized journal, the *Journal of Conflict Resolution*, devoted solely to this topic. Also, the theory of games studies the mathematical conditions under which settlement solutions can be attained in simple parlor games. (See Sec. 10-5.2.) We cannot afford to pay much attention to these topics, as our main interest lies in the theory of conflict dissolution.

4-3 BIBLIOGRAPHICAL NOTE

Invention of viable alternatives for action requires creativity—it is an art. Yet, creative talents can be dormant and may need some stimulus to be awakened. Often, reading a good book on creative thinking will heighten a student's receptivity to and interest in the material presented in a chapter like this one. Start with De Bono: his earlier *New Think* (1967) and the subsequent *Lateral Thinking* (1973) are very simple, very readable, and very useful—exactly what our future executives need to know about creativity. Those who long for a truly remarkable experience should read Arthur Koestler's *The Act of Creation* (1973).

For some good narratives about the ingenious uses of creativity, insight and common sense in approaching seemingly perplexing managerial and business problems, the best source is Robert E. D. "Gene" Woolsey's "Fifth Column" pieces in *Interfaces*, commencing about 1976. Another good collection of fables can be found in Ackoff's *Art of Problem Solving* (1978).

Many authors agree that the search for alternatives and the exploration of their feasibility are the primary purpose of MCDM. Papers by Church and Cohon (1976) and Cohon and Marks (1975) not only support this orientation but describe some interesting applications as well. The author has also found useful the good discussion of the role of alternatives in strategic decison making and planning provided by Kluson (1976). Unfortunately this article is in Czech and not readily available. Papers by Yu (1977), Starr and Greenwood (1977), and Shocker and Srinivasan (1974) represent a cross section of the technical trends within this new concern about the invention, generation, and identification of new ideas and alternatives.

The best review of technological forecasting is the classical study by Jantsch (1967). A short and lively introduction can be found in the paperback by Waddington (1977). An excellent introduction and guide to brainstorming, a methodology for groups to generate new ideas, is provided by Osborn (1949).

Festinger, Schelling, and Filley provide the background on which the theory of conflict dissolution hinges. The first explicit treatment of conflict dissolution is Zeleny (1976). This article also describes *conflict algebra*, a tool for identifying and analyzing a large variety of types of dissolvable conflict. A good discussion of the role of conflict dissolution in practice can be found in Ackoff (1978).

Ackoff, R. L.: *The Art of Problem Solving*, Wiley, New York, 1978.

Church, R., and J. Cohon: "Multiobjective Location Analysis of Regional Energy Facility Siting Problems," Brookhaven National Lab. Rep. BNL-50567, 1976.

Cohon, J., and D. Marks: "A Review and Evaluation of Multiobjective Programming Techniques," *Water Resources Research*, vol. 2, no. 2, 1975, pp. 208–220.

De Bono, E.: *Lateral Thinking*, Harper & Row, New York, 1973.

———: *New Think*, Basic Books, New York, 1967; reprint, Avon Books, 1971.

Festinger, L.: *Conflict, Decision, and Dissonance*, Tavistock Publications, Ltd., London, 1964.

Filley, A. C.: *Interpersonal Conflict Resolution*, Scott, Foresman, Glenview, Ill., 1975.

Jantsch, E.: *Technological Forecasting in Perspective*, Organization for Economic Co-operation and Development, Paris, 1967.

Keeney, R. L., and H. Raiffa: *Decisions with Multiple Objectives: Preferences and Value Tradeoffs*, Wiley, New York, 1976

Klusoň, V.: "Tvorba cílů a množiny variant rozvoje plánového systému," *Ekonomicko-matematický Obzor,* vol. 12, no. 3, 1976, pp. 294–310.

Koestler, A.: *The Act of Creation*, Dell, New York, 1973.

Osborn, A.: *Your Creative Power*, Scribner, New York, 1949.

Schelling, T. C.: *The Strategy of Conflict*, Harvard, Cambridge, Mass., 1960.

Shocker, A. D., and V. Srinivasan: "A Consumer-Based Methodology for the Identification of New Product Ideas," *Management Science*, vol. 20, no. 6, 1974, pp. 921–937.

Simon, H. A.: *Administrative Behavior: A Study of Decision-Making Processes in Administrative Organization*, 3d ed. Free Press, New York, 1976.

Starr, M. K., and L. Greenwood: "Normative Generation of Alternatives with Multiple Criteria Evaluation," in *Multiple Criteria Decision Making*, TIMS studies in the Management Sciences, vol. 6, M. K. Starr and M. Zeleny (eds.), North-Holland Publishing, Amsterdam, 1977, pp. 111–127.

Waddington, C. H.: *Tools for Thought*, Basic Books, New York, 1977.

Yu, P. L.: "Decision Dynamics with an Application to Persuasion and Negotiation," in M. K. Starr and M. Zeleny (eds.), *Multiple Criteria Decision Making,* TIMS Studies in the Management Sciences, vol. 6, North-Holland Publishing, Amsterdam, 1977, pp. 111–127.

Zeleny, M.: "Conflict Dissolution," *General Systems Yearbook*, vol. 21, 1976, pp. 131–136.

4-4 PROBLEMS

4-1 "Conflict is dissolved if the desired region (goals) and /or the feasible region (alternatives) is expanded so that they have at least one point in common." Discuss the significance of "and /or" in this statement. Prepare a real-life example of conflict dissolution and describe its attainment in the *three* different modes implicit in this statement.

4-2 It is often said that to give the consumer the best possible product at the lowest possible price is a "rhetorical" objective which has no operational meaning and cannot be acted upon; there must be a trade-off between price and quality. Analyze the objective in the framework of the ideal solution. Do you agree with the statement?

4-3 Mitroff poses a "wicked" question: "How do we select a criterion for resolving multicriterion conflict? Can we sensibly treat the problem of selecting a criterion for multicriterion decision making as a multicriterion decision problem itself?" [See Starr and Zeleny (eds.), 1977, p. 299.]

(*a*) What is one to do about the infinite regress implied by Mitroff's question?

(*b*) The multicriterion problem is *not* fundamentally technical in character but deeply philosophical. Comment.

(*c*) Would the concept of conflict dissolution, i.e., inventing a new, "conflict-free" alternative, provide the answer to the dilemma?

4-4 There are two levels of conflict: One arises when parties are constrained to choose among mutually exclusive alternatives, none of which is fully acceptable to all. The second level arises when such a conflict is not resolved and contained. Then different values, emotions, and hostilities are allowed to manifest themselves overtly.

(*a*) Give examples of both types of conflict. Under what conditions is the first level transformed into the second level?

(*b*) Shortages of food in wartime, as during the siege of Leningrad or the blockade of Britain, have not led to second-level manifestations. Were such conflicts resolved, contained, or dissolved? Are there any differences among these three modes of response, i.e., resolution, containment, and dissolution?

4-5 Someone has said that conflictual situations are the hallmark of human life and that conflict resolution and containment are the basic art of human life. How does the concept of conflict dissolution modify this perception? Consider the role of the time dimension and the need to balance disparate criteria through time.

4-6 In utility theory there is something called "persistence of choices" (from T. C. Koopmans). Basically it illustrates that if one prefers

$$(x_1, x_2, a, x_4, x_5) \quad \text{to} \quad (x_1, x_2, b, x_4, x_5)$$

then one *should* also prefer

$$(y_1, y_2, a, y_4, y_5) \quad \text{to} \quad (y_1, y_2, b, y_4, y_5)$$

(*a*) Consider a situation where one contemplates possible vacations during the next 5 years. Let x_1 through x_5 represent vacation places in Italy and y_1 through y_5 vacation places in the United States. Let a and b refer to places in the United States and Italy respectively in a given year. Would Koopmans' axiom of persistence of choice necessarily be preserved among travel packages (vectors)? What if the decision maker is concerned about variety among the packages?

(*b*) Form other examples as in (*a*), and discuss the conditions under which persistence of choice could not be maintained. For example, what about future income streams?

4-7 Discuss the ethical issues inherent in decision analysis or cost-benefit analysis. As one computes the total benefits (or overall utility) for each alternative, one is expected to recommend the alternative with the maximum *total* benefit. What about the *individuals* affected or the impact on various component criteria? Should one be hurt to help many? How would you go about dealing with such conflict? (*Hint*: Consider a criterion of *equity*. How equitably are benefits, losses, and risks distributed? How would one reconcile equity criterion with total measures?)

4-8 Many conflicts are being perceived as being related to product quality:

(*a*) Quality goals are being viewed by production managers as directly conflicting with shipping schedules, budgetary constraints, and distribution requirements.

(*b*) Managers often insist that there is a direct trade-off between costs and quality of a given product.

(*c*) A goal of matching rather than exceeding the competition's quality is often a matter of policy even in respectable business firms.

(*d*) Consumers often perceive quality as being lower than it actually is.

Discuss the above phenomena in terms of their true "conflicting" nature and attempt to work out some policy- or strategy-related solutions. Are these phenomena interconnected?

(Consider the following: If one can decrease quality and increase costs, or increase both unemployment and inflation at the same time, why should the possibility of reverse movement be excluded a priori?)

The interdependency of means and ends, the search for an ideal outcome or solution, the generation of new alternatives—such are the ingredients of the decision-making process as we have described it so far.

In this chapter we explore the dynamics of the ideal, its displacement, and how it affects our preferences and ultimate choice.

New means, new alternatives, may imply a redefinition of the ideal, i.e., new ends and new goals.

Ideals are often unattainable or infeasible. Yet they are not irrelevant—they are major ingredients in shaping human choice and preferences. Ideals are approachable, and their pursuit is a motivating force of primary importance. Human beings derive as much satisfaction from the pursuit of objectives as from their attainment. This is why every attainment leads to the setting of new goals, to a new pursuit. Without this remarkable mechanism there would be no progress, no achievement, no striving for improvement in the human condition.

Because of the dynamic interplay between means and ends, their mutual determinancy, and their parallel, interdependent evolution, human preferences cannot be fixed and transitive. We discuss the issues of the transitivity of preferences in Sec. 5-3.3. Our conclusion is that intransitivity of preferences is an integral part of human decision-making strategy.

We attempt to explain intransitivity as a result of the consistent pursuit of a moving target: the ideal solution. Especially in dealing with a large number of multidimensional alternatives, there is a tendency to simplify the task by engaging in pairwise comparisons only. This leads to a more frequent displacement of the ideal, and thus the intransitivity of preferences is more likely to manifest itself as well.

Chapters 3, 4, and 5 represent the conceptual core of our approach. After Chap. 5, the reader should attempt a synthesis of these three chapters before proceeding to Chap. 6, which provides a more formal model of the concepts covered so far.

THEORY OF THE DISPLACED IDEAL

In the realm of values, the highest *values are the measuring unit. Things can only be correctly evaluated by comparing them with the most valuable. In proportion as the really topmost values are suppressed in the perspective of values, those next in line assume this highest rank. The heart of man does not tolerate an absence of the excellent and supreme.*

José Ortega y Gasset
Revolt of the Masses (1964)

We have already discussed the importance of creating new decision alternatives and the major properties they should have: They should be technologically closed and as close as possible to the ideal alternative (point x^*). Next, we shall discuss the dynamics of the ideal alternative: its perceived or real displacement, and the impact of its "movement" on human preferences. We shall attempt to tie some of the loose ends into a coherent descriptive theory of human decision making. Let us start with several preliminary notions.

5-1 MEASUREMENT OF PREFERENCES

The first important prerequisite is to acquire some understanding of the scales of measurement of human preferences, utilities, and subjective probabilities. All three notions are crucial for the so-called "Von Neumann—Morgenstern utility theory" and its major normative dictum: *maximize expected utility*.

The above "golden rule" stands rather firmly at the core of modern decision analysis and its most lively derivative, multiattribute decision theory (MAUT), as it is discussed in Chap. 12.

Two basic ways of measuring preferences can be expressed by notions of ordinal and cardinal scales. *Ordinal* scales are purely relational; objects are rank-ordered, and no other meaningful numerical properties can be assigned to them. We can say only that object A is preferred to B, that A is equal to B, or that B is preferred to A, but we cannot say by how much; the intensity of preference is not apparent from ordinal scales.

Ordinal scales can be expressed through numerical or verbal rankings, e.g., 1, 2, 3, 4, etc., or "bad," "average," "good," "excellent," etc. A special case of an ordinal scale would be a boolean variable, i.e., assigning 1 to preference and 0 otherwise. Ordinal numbers are those for which the intervals (differences) between them are meaningless. That is, if $7 - 5 \neq 4 - 2$, then all algebraic manipulations of such numbers are meaningless as well, and the numbers can be replaced by ordinal ranking. For example, if A is preferred to B, B to C, C to D, and so on, and if 2, 4, 5, 7 are respective ordinal evaluations of A, B, C, and D, then the following scale results:

Rank	1	2	3	4	. . .
Evaluation	2	4	5	7	. . .
Object	A	B	C	D	. . .

Cardinal scales *do* assign meaningful numerical values (numbers, intervals, ratios, etc.) to the objects in question. Intervals or differences between cardinal numbers are meaningful, for example, $7 - 5 = 4 - 2$, and addition, subtraction, and multiplication by a constant are allowable operations.

Cardinal scales can be further divided into interval and ratio scales. *Interval* scales are characterized by the allowance of an arbitrary zero point so that only addition, subtraction, and multiplication by a constant are well defined. The Fahrenheit and Celsius scales of measuring temperature are typical examples. *Ratio* scales are characterized by a nonarbitrary zero point, as for example in the Kelvin temperature scale. Here the multiplication by interval-scaled variables is allowed, i.e., the ratios of individual scale values have meaning.

Consider the following cardinal ranking of objects on an interval scale with arbitrary zero:

Scale	2	4	5	7	. . .
Object	A	B	C	D	. . .

Observe that the intervals (the differences between values) do not change by redefining the zero arbitrarily, for example by subtracting 2:

Scale	0	2	3	5	. . .
Object	A	B	C	D	. . .

However, the ratios have changed: For B/A from $\frac{1}{2}$ to ∞, for D/B from $\frac{7}{4}$ to $\frac{5}{2}$ (i.e., from 1.75 to 2.5), etc. That is, if "6" is to be twice as much as "3," one has to use a ratio-preserving scale with nonarbitrary zero.

The intensities of preference are often measured on a scale from 0 to 1. For example, the intensities of preferrring A to B, B to C, C to D, etc., could be:

Intensity	0.6	0.5	0.45	0.2	. . .
Object	A	B	C	D	. . .

Observe that cardinal ordering would be meaningless unless the interval 0 to 1 were specified. Without such reference points, or *anchor points*, we could not make any sense out of, for example, preference intensity 0.45. Similarly, a temperature of $36°$ means nothing until we specify anchor points, say, the freezing and boiling points of water, and assign them 0 and 100 respectively.

Although anchor points can be chosen arbitrarily (we could very well measure the intensities of preference on a 0 to 100 scale and temperature on a 0 to 1 scale), there are some choices that are better than others. And often an anchor point is implied uniquely and unequivocally by a given physical situation. We shall argue later that, especially in human decision making and assessment of intensities of preference, reference objects are not selected arbitrarily but are characterized by distinct desirable properties.

Even ordinal scales can be anchored, i.e., furnished with convenient reference points. Dalkey (1976) introduces the example of the Mohs hardness scale. If object x scratches object y, then x is harder than y, or by analogy, x is *preferred* to y. The following is one particular version of the Mohs hardness scale:

Rank	Object
1	Talc
2	Gypsum
3	Calcite
4	Fluorite
5	Apatite
6	Orthoclase
7	Quartz
8	Topaz
9	Corundum
10	Diamond

The higher numbered mineral always scratches, i.e., is preferred to, the lower-numbered mineral. The associated numbers are purely ordinal; they indicate rank and nothing more. All other objects can be compared with the above set of reference objects and their hardness thus established. For example, we may say that the hardness of window glass is between 5 and 6, fingernails between 2 and 3, etc.

When people are called upon to make assessments, they tend to anchor their judgments in some initial point of reference. Tversky and Kahneman (1975) describe many experiments demonstrating "anchored" judgment, including the following:

People were randomly placed in two groups and assigned a number between 0 and 100 that was determined by the spin of a wheel of fortune made in their presence. They were told to assume this number was an initial estimate of the percentage of African nations in the United Nations. Their task was to adjust this figure to reflect their own estimate of the correct percentage.

Although the two groups were homogeneous and therefore might have been predicted to arrive at close estimates, the roulette values turned out to have a marked effect. The group whose roulette value was 10 percent estimated the

African nations at 25 percent; the other group, with a roulette value of 65 percent, estimated African membership at 45 percent!

Anchoring also occurs in intuitive numerical calculations. For example, within 5 seconds try to estimate the product:

$$1 \times 2 \times 3 \times 4 \times 5 \times 6 \times 7 \times 8$$

Now, independently of the above answer, evaluate the following product:

$$8 \times 7 \times 6 \times 5 \times 4 \times 3 \times 2 \times 1$$

In experiments, the median estimate for the second sequence was 2,250, while the median estimate for the first sequence was 512. The correct answer to both, of course is 40,320.

What seems to happen is that anchors influence judgments in such an important and often unconscious manner that even when they are selected openly and arbitrarily, as with the wheel of fortune, they can exert a profound influence.

We should not strive for elimination of the anchoring bias.[1] Most of the existing as well as future models in management sciences and psychology depend on some sort of subjective input: judgment, estimate, assessment, or evaluation. All these inputs are going to be anchored, and we should at least recognize the fact in our theories. Decision makers can learn how to make their biases work for them, just as in jujitsu one tries to use an opponent's strength to one's own advantage. There is nothing wrong with anchored judgment, except when the anchors are incorrect and misleading.

Anchoring can hamper judgment only when it is unrecognized and, as a result, applied in a possibly detrimental way. Correctly used, it is likely to improve judgment. Let's say you wish to make an investment in a business or stock. You could simply go ahead and try picking one which, in itself, seems best to meet your criteria for profitability, safety, etc. On the other hand you could attempt to anchor your decision by consciously selecting an ''ideal'' investment, one with a mix of profitability, safety, and other factors that you would consider best. Then you would try to approach this ideal point as closely as possible. Recall our E. F. Hutton example in Sec. 1-5.2. Successful investors and consultants use ideal alternatives intuitively. We shall attempt to make decision reference points explicit.

Anchored scales are important because people usually express their preferences only with respect to a given reference point (or points). The choice of appropriate anchors will influence the intensity or even rank order of preferences. It is not sufficient to ask, Do you prefer A to B? One must know with respect to what. What is the point of reference, the framework of inquiry? Is it

---

[1]Further discussion of why ''failures'' of human intuition should not necessarily be removed, and why ''debiasing'' procedures should be viewed with caution, is available in M. Zeleny, ''Intuition—Its Failures and Merits,'' in B. Persson (ed.) *Surviving Failures*, Humanities Press, Atlantic Highlands, NJ, 1979, pp. 172-183.

point C? Or is it D? Does it make any difference for the choice of A versus B? Yes, it does.

5-2 HOW RELEVANT ARE "IRRELEVANT" ALTERNATIVES?

Arrow's axiom of the independence of irrelevant alternatives (1967) represents one of the many conditions of prescribed rational behavior. It is not only the most important but also the most controversial axiom in decision theory.

In essence, the axiom states that a choice made from a given set of alternatives depends *only* on the ordering made with respect to the alternatives in that set. That is, only available or feasible alternatives have a bearing on the choice to be made.

The problem with this axiom is that although it is theoretically appealing and logically acceptable, it lacks strong pragmatic justification. Empirical experience does not generally support it. It is true that, for example, when choosing among candidates for an elected office, all one is asked for are one's preferences among the actual candidates, not among other individuals who are not candidates or not available for the office. This should not be interpreted to mean that noncandidates and their attributes do not affect voters' preferences among the actual candidates. When the electorate chose between Reagan and Carter, was the fact that Ford did not run irrelevant? Is it true that Kennedy, although finally not a candidate but always a potential candidate or at least a point of reference, had no effect on the choice between Reagan and Carter? Do not people choose among the available so as to emulate as closely as possible the preferred nonavailable? Or to move as far away as possible from the one considered mediocre?

Leon Festinger and his colleagues (1964) conducted a series of experiments which affirmed that when comparing A with B the outcome is likely to be influenced by whether C or D is the point of reference.

Festinger established that a large portion of "decision" time is not spent on collecting and evaluating information but on trying to discover *new* alternatives that are not currently available. Considerable time is spent devising ways to turn better but unavailable alternatives into available ones.

If one has to choose between two alternatives which are both far from the "ideal," one first attempts to make some *third* alternative available for consideration. One will explore, vigorously, the "irrelevant" alternatives of Arrow. Only when convinced of the unavailability of the ideal alternative will one settle down to the choices currently presented.

In Festinger's experiments, the subjects were given a choice among attractive but imperfect alternatives. In one situation, prior to the decision, they were first shown a "perfect" alternative that was not available to them. In another situation they were first shown a much worse alternative. It was concluded that a difference exists in the attractiveness of available alternatives, depending upon whether the unavailable alternative is ideal or mediocre.

In this case 127 boys from the second and third grades of two Palo Alto schools rated five toy race cars, each with a windup motor. Each of the toys was different from the others in color and detail. Also, each had a slight defect: scratches, loose wheels, a missing steering wheel, and the like. The ideal toy was a rather large, red race car, powered by a gasoline engine. The mediocre one was an ordinary blue sedan with no motor at all. Figure 5-1 portrays the situation graphically.

All toys were rated on a scale from 1 ("Really crazy about this toy; the nicest one I've ever seen") to 6 ("Just hate it; the worst toy I've ever seen").

The average rating given to the ideal car was 1.1, an almost perfect rating. The average rating given to the mediocre blue sedan was 3.1. The overall average rating for the five slightly damaged racers was 2.1.

The average rating given to the five slightly damaged racers by those (75 subjects) who saw the ideal car first was 2.2; the corresponding average rating given by those (52 subjects) who saw the mediocre car first was 1.9. Although the differences themselves do not approach statistical significance, Festinger found a clear difference in the subjects' recall of positive and negative characteristics of the toys. In the "ideal" situation they recalled 1.9 more negative than positive characteristics of the five racers. The corresponding figure for the "mediocre" situation was only 1.1. *The difference between the "ideal" and the "mediocre" conditions was significant at the 2 percent level.* The quality of the irrelevant (unavailable) alternative was very relevant to the evaluation of available options.

We should keep in mind that Festinger and Walster (his colleague in this experiment) actually tried to show that such an effect was not present. They considered it undesirable:

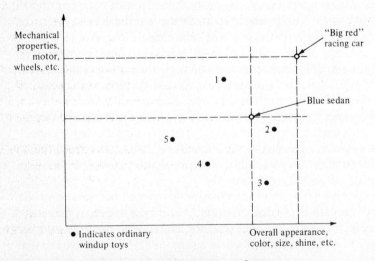

Figure 5-1 The impact of reference points on preferences.
● available alternatives; ○ unavailable alternatives.

> We must accept the conclusion that a difference probably exists in the attractiveness of the available alternatives, depending upon whether unavailable alternative was "ideal" or "mediocre." In other words, we cannot maintain, unfortunately, that the same decision situation was present psychologically in all conditions. (Festinger 1964, p. 139)

Although Festinger and Walster failed to see the significance of their experiment in clarifying the role of reference points in human decision making, they suggested the following idea:

> Usually, when we think about a situation in which a person must decide among two or more alternatives, we analyze the situation, and theorize about it, in terms of the characteristics of the alternatives and the person's behavior with respect to these alternatives. The Walster and Festinger experiment shows, however, that this is too narrow a framework within which to reach an adequate description of pre-decision cognitive processes. The behavior of the person, his considerations and his thought processes, are not confined to the alternatives between which he must decide. Factors outside this narrow realm also affect what he does. (Festinger 1964, p. 144)

Unfortunately, Walster and Festinger never pursued the above line of thought, and this type of experiment has not been reported since, possibly because Arrow's axiom has become a widely accepted dogma of rational decision making.

5-3 ADAPTIVE DISPLACEMENT OF PREFERENCES

5-3.1 Means and Ends

In human decision making there should not be any isolated treatment of means and ends or strategies and objectives. We have already combined the two aspects within the extended concept of alternatives introduced earlier: strategies compatible with a particular set of goals. Now we shall extend the concept of *means-ends interdependency* and attempt its operational expression.

Both sides of the decision process, i.e., analysis of what is available and of what is desirable, are to be carried out jointly, without establishing any clear primacy for either side. The available means often determine our needs or goals. One can recall the "let me see what they have and I will tell you what I need" attitude of some shoppers.

Neither means nor objectives are determined independently of each other. Objectives evolve on the basis of available alternatives which are, in turn, adjusted and generated in accord with existing objectives. Modeling of decision processes and economic behavior must take into account the fact that the means-ends dichotomy is not how people typically approach decisions. For further elaboration of these notions consult Leibenstein (1976) and Ward (1972).

As we have shown in our discussion of the nature of conflict, the insufficiency of means (the absence of a prominent alternative) is at least as important as the "incompatibility" of objectives. Sharp separation of ends and means precludes any meaningful conflict resolution, since it relegates conflict to the realm of conflicting values. But there is *no* conflict per se between the objectives of increasing energy consumption and of decreasing environmental pollution; the apparent conflict quickly dissolves as soon as solar energy is effectively harnessed. Only in the absence of such an "ideal" alternative does there *appear* to be a permanent conflict between the two objectives so that the notion of trade-off must be entertained. The conflict exists only between our ends and *currently available means*, not among the ends themselves.

5-3.2 Traditional Utility Approach

We shall briefly review some relevant utility theory concepts.

Consider the preference space in Fig. 5-2. Both axes x and y may represent a number of things: amounts of available goods, attribute scores, criteria levels, preferences of two different individuals, and so on.

Maximum utility is achieved at M, the "point of bliss." Obviously, M is preferred to all points on lower indifferrence curves, that is, $M > I_n > \cdots > I_2 > I_1$; toward points on the same curve, like A and B, the decision maker is assumed to be indifferent (that is, $A \sim B$, where the symbol $\sim$ indicates indifference). In the absence of any availability constraints (or production-possibility boundary), point M would always be the choice; no conflict is present and no decision making is needed.

Oskar Morgenstern (1972) criticizes the indifference-curve analysis as introduced above. If x and y denote respective amounts of goods in one's possession, then one could move from B to M directly by disposing of (freely or at

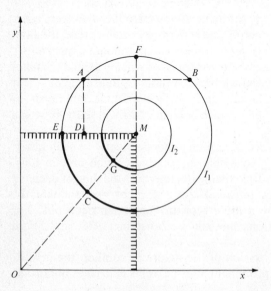

Figure 5-2 Unconstrained utility space.

costs) excess amounts of x and y. One cannot similarly go from A to M. It is thus difficult to maintain indifference between A and B; actually $B > A$. Similarly, $F > A$, $A > E$, etc. It turns out that indifference curves seem to be valid only in the shaded subregion of Fig. 5-2. Hidden assumptions, discreteness of economic goods, etc., are not explicitly treated in the analysis.

Most utility theory assumes that all alternatives are comparable in the sense that given any two alternatives, one or the other is either strictly preferred or the two are seen as being preferentially equivalent, i.e., choice-indifferent. If one is presumed not to be able to express the intensity of one's preference, as is assumed in the ordinal utility model, then also the notion of indifference, which is the most precise expression of preference intensity (i.e., the one of intensity zero), becomes difficult or impossible to estimate: an artifact.

If the decision maker does not strictly prefer one alternative to another, the absence of strict preference should not imply indifference. As Roy (1977) emphasizes, certain pairs of alternatives are noncomparable because the decision maker (1) does not know how to, (2) does not want to, or (3) is not able to compare them. To confound such noncomparability with indifference represents a considerable simplification of the decision-making process. In Fig. 5-2 one is not expected to be able to state how much G is preferred to C (only that $G > C$), and yet one is assumed to be quite capable of stating how much C is preferred to E. One is assumed to be able to determine the indifference between C and E with absolute precision!

Indifference, as the extreme and the most precise expression of the intensity of preference, is, correspondingly, the most difficult to assess explicitly.

The relation of preference is assumed to be transitive: If $B > A$ and $A > D$, then $B > D$. Some writers, for example, Fishburn (1973), do not however assume indifference relations are necessarily transitive. That is, $B \sim A$ and $A \sim D$ are not assumed to imply $B \sim D$ in all cases. In spite of this confusion, utility-maximization theory requires that at least preference relations are transitive; it would not work otherwise.

In real situations intransitivities of preferences occur sufficiently often to be a curse upon modern decision theory. Notwithstanding that transitive relations are far more mathematically tractable than intransitive ones, one must recognize that they exist and provide a theory which would take them into account.

5-3.3 Transitivity of Preferences

The economic preference of A to B implies and is implied by the fact that A has higher utility than B. This is the utility-maximization assumption. All such preferences must be *transitive*; i.e., preferring A to B and B to C implies that one also prefers A to C, because A *must* have higher utility than C. The two assumptions, utility maximization and the transitivity requirements, are inseparable.

Ward Edwards (1954) provides an excellent review of the theory implied by these twin assumptions. He finds the notion of maximization psychologically unobjectionable: So many different kinds of functions can be maximized that almost any available choice alternative can be declared a maximum of some sort. Thus, the notion of maximizing *something* is relatively harmless, general, and undoubtedly correct. It is when we attempt to determine *what* is being maximized that the notion becomes powerful, specific, and possibly wrong.

In contrast to the assumption of utility maximization, the assumption of transitivity can be empirically tested. K. O. May (1954) suggests that intransitive choices may be expected to occur whenever more than one dimension exists in the attributes along which people order their choices. If we allow the choice ordering to be only unidimensional, e.g., utility function, profit function, net present value, etc., there can be no intransitivity of choices—unless we assume that the ordering function itself has changed during the process.

In his experiment, May requested a classroom group to perform pairwise choices among three potential marriage partners who were identified only by their descriptions with respect to three attributes: intelligence, physical attractiveness, and wealth. No judgments of indifference were permitted. The results were that 27 percent of the students managed to generate intransitive triads of choices!

It can always be argued that the students may have changed their tastes, i.e., their utility schedules, between the first choice and the third. However, unless we assume at least a temporary constancy of tastes, decision theory in its entirety would become an exercise in futility. Utility maximization will stay meaningful only if the transitivity of choices is preserved or if intransitivities are rare enough to be designated as errors in rational judgment.

What are the possible ways out of our twin dilemma of maximization and transitivity? Let us list the most obvious ones:

1. Assume stability in tastes and consider the utility function to be independent and unchanging. Declare the intransitive choices as falling outside the realm of one's interest, i.e., exclude multidimensional choices. Be concerned only with behavior which is transitive.
2. Assume stability in tastes and independent, unchanging utility function. Declare the intransitive choices to be stochastic in nature, infrequent deviations from the norms of rational behavior, brought about by ignorance or insufficient information. Transitive description is then taken as a close approximation of reality.
3. Assume changing tastes and an unstable, fluctuating utility function. Then anything, even the intransitivities, can be accommodated. But the theory will be empirically untestable, and thus empty, unless the nature of such utility changeovers is fully understood.
4. Assume stability in tastes and in the utility function. Postulate transitivity of preferences because transitive relations are far more mathematically tractable than are intransitive ones.

5. Declare that utility maximization and transitivity of choices are indicative of how people *should* behave. Ignore how they actually behave. This is the so-called "normative" approach, directed toward teaching decision makers how they should make their decisions.
6. Assume a basic stability in tastes and postulate the utility function as being dependent on a set of external parameters. Although the function itself is temporarily fixed, its parameters could change and as a result some intransitive choices might appear.

It is the sixth resolution, a particular and simplified version of it, that we shall introduce in the next section. We attempt to preserve maximization while allowing for intransitivities.

The multidimensional rationalization of intransitivities was first asserted as May's law: *Intransitivities occur when there are conflicting stimulus dimensions along which to judge*. But May's suggestion was not acceptable to decision theorists, and his serious study of multiple-criteria phenomenon was often lightheartedly dismissed. Luce and Raiffa characterized it as follows:

> The idea is that each alternative invokes "responses" on several different "attribute" scales and that, although each scale itself may be transitive, their amalgamation need not be. This is the sort of thing which psychologists cryptically summarize by terming it a multidimensional phenomenon. (Luce and Raiffa 1957, p. 25)

Although May's idea is captured by Luce and Raiffa rather accurately, in reading them one has to ignore the tone of heavy sarcasm and realize what has happened to May's idea between 1957 and today.

Decision alternatives are often viewed as multidimensional bundles of attributes. In addition to maximization and transitivity a third important assumption arises under such conditions: *The utility of a commodity bundle or multiattribute alternative is an aggregate of the utilities of its components*. This decomposition hypothesis lies at the core of multiattribute utility theory, discussed in Chap. 12. All three basic assumptions—maximization, transitivity, and decomposability—are interdependent. For example, if people exhibit intransitive behavior, then both maximization and decomposability might be violated.

Adams and Fagot (1959) empirically tested the validity of the most widely used decomposition hypothesis, the additive model. Each of twenty-four subjects was asked to play the role of a personnel manager for a large corporation and choose among hypothetical applicants, two at a time, for an executive position. The applicants were described in terms of two attributes: "intelligence" and "ability to handle people." Each of these attributes was distinguished at four different levels, so the total number of combinations (alternatives) was sixteen. Analysis of the data showed that only six subjects out of twenty-four perfectly satisfied the additive model. It was established that all the violations were *due to the intransitivity of pairwise comparisons*.

Conventional wisdom would have it that transitivity is a simple condition which we should expect to be satisfied, whereas additivity is a more complex requirement about which we should be doubtful. Adams and Fagot found that transitivity implies additivity and not vice versa. The transitivity requirement seems to be the most important of our triad of assumptions, and thus it should be better grounded empirically.

It could be argued that a good normative model should respect, at least partially, the most essential descriptive findings about human behavior. If intransitivity does occur frequently, and even appears to be an integral part of human decision-making strategy, then it should be incorporated into our models as well. Unfortunately, it cannot simply be defined away.

5-3.4 The Ideal Point

C. H. Coombs (1958) assumes that there is an ideal level of attributes for objects of choice and that the decision maker's utilities decrease monotonically on both sides of this *ideal point* (corresponding to our point M in Fig. 5-2). Coombs shows that probabilities of choice depend on whether compared alternatives lie on the same side of the ideal point, or whether some lie on one side of the ideal and some on the other. This is compatible with the discussed difference between points A and B in Fig. 5-2.

In technologically constrained situations, as in Fig. 5-3, attainment of M becomes an unrealistic goal over a given planning time horizon. The set of available alternatives is much too limited by the production-possibility boundary P. Conflict between what is preferable (the ends) and what is possible (the means) is thus established, and a decision-making process may take place. Because M is not a clearly defined point or a crisply delineated region but rather a fuzzy "cloud" of preferred levels of attributes, the conflict is perceived

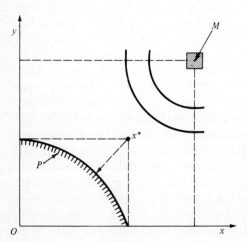

Figure 5-3 Constrained utility space.

by humans only as a fuzzy sense of conflict—initially neither well understood nor operational.

As the decision maker attempts to grasp the extent of the emerging conflict between means and ends, he or she explores the limits attainable with each important attribute. The highest achievable scores with all currently considered attributes form a composite, an *ideal alternative* x^*. Figure 5-3 shows both M and x^*. Whereas M is almost always too difficult to identify, x^* is easier to conceptualize because all its characteristics can be directly experienced and derived from the existing alternative choices. These individual attribute maxima can be found (perhaps by using operations research optimization techniques), quantified, and made fully operational. Point x^* serves as a good temporary approximation of M in decision making.

The general infeasibility or nonavailability of x^* creates a predecision conflict and thus generates the impulse to move as closely as possible toward it. Because of the conflict experienced, the decision maker starts searching for new alternatives, preferably those which are the closest to the ideal one. We have discussed this in Sec. 4-2.

It should be noted that if such an ideal alternative is created, that is, if point x^* becomes feasible, then there is no need for further continuation of the decision process. Conflict will have been dissolved, and x^* will automatically be selected since it is unquestionably the best of the currently available choices, provided that the set of alternatives is technologically closed.

Note that in contrast to the relative stability of M, ideal point x^* can be and is frequently displaced. It is responsive to changes in the available set of alternatives, objectives, evaluations, measurements, and even errors. It responds to new technological advances, inventions, and discoveries of oversights. It becomes a moving target, a point of reference which provides an anchor for human adaptivity, intransitivity, and dynamic adjustment of preferences.

5-3.5 Displacement of Preferences and Intransitivity

As all alternatives are compared with the ideal, those farthest away are removed from further consideration. There are many important consequences of such partial decisions. First, whenever an alternative is removed from consideration there could be a shift in a maximum attainable score to the next lower feasible level. Thus, the ideal alternative can be displaced *closer* to the feasible set. Similarly, addition of a new alternative could displace the ideal *farther away* by raising the attainable levels of attributes. Such displacements induce changes in evaluations, attribute importance, and ultimately in the preference ordering of the remaining alternatives.

In Fig. 5-4 and Table 5-1 we explore a simple case of such displacements and their impact on the subsequent displacement of preferences. We assume that the decision maker attempts to choose an alternative which would be as

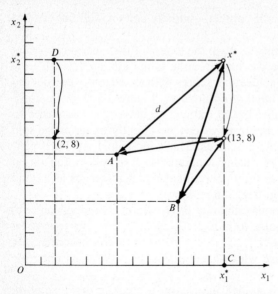

Figure 5-4 Displacement of x^* as presented in Table 5-1.

close as possible to the ideal. As a proxy measure of distance we shall employ again the euclidean measure:

$$d = \sqrt{(x_1^* - x_1)^2 + (x_2^* - x_2)^2}$$

Some additional measures of distance will be discussed later.

In the first case the ideal point is $(x_1^*, x_2^*) = (13, 13)$, and it induces the following order of preference: $A > B > D > C$. Let us assume that point D has been shifted from $(2, 13)$ to $(2, 8)$. This shift can be due to an error in measurement, the replacement of one alternative by another, a change in the perception

Table 5-1

Alternatives	1st case		2nd case	
	Attribute values	Euclidean distance from the ideal	Attribute values	Euclidean distance from the ideal
	x_1 x_2		x_1 x_2	
A	6 7	9.2195	6 7	7.0710
B	10 4	9.4868	10 4	5.0000
C	13 0	13.0000	13 0	8.0000
D	2 13	11.0000	2 8	11.0000
Ideal	13 13	0.0000	13 8	0.0000

Note: The ideal is chosen as the best x and y values from the competing alternatives.

of x^*, etc. As a result, there is a new ideal point $(x_1^*, x_2^*) = (13, 8)$. Recall that the ideal is defined as consisting of the best x_1 and x_2 values from all the available alternatives. The same euclidean distance measure now induces the following ranking: $B > A > C > D$.

Notice in Fig. 5-4 that the preference between A and B has been reversed because of the change in D.

Let us consider the second case independently of the first one. Note that B is the most preferred, followed by A, C, and D. We shall expand the second set of four available alternatives by adding a fifth one, say $E = (2, 13)$, as summarized in Table 5-2. Although E is not the best alternative, the optimality ranking of all previously considered alternatives has now been reversed: $A > B > E > D > C$. *A nonoptimal alternative* A *has been made optimal by adding nonoptimal* E *to the feasible set.*

This result is in violation of a fundamental axiom which reflects the course of development of traditional decision analysis:

If an alternative A *is nonoptimal, it cannot be made optimal by adding a new alternative to the problem.*

On the face of it this axiom makes sense. But as in preceding (and following) examples the axiom is too restrictive to be of any use to the decision maker.

Starr and Zeleny (1977) illustrate the fallacy of the axiom with an example in a probabilistic setting of expected utility:

Let us design two alternatives A_1 and A_2 such that one is always dominated by the other with respect to all possible expected utilities obtainable with all different combinations of probabilities p_1 and p_2, $p_1 + p_2 = 1$. As shown in Table 5-3, A_1 pays \$4 when state of nature O_1 occurs and \$2 when O_2 occurs. Similarly, A_2 pays \$6 when O_1 occurs and \$4 when O_2 occurs. The probabilities of O_1 and O_2 occurring are p_1 and p_2, respectively, but they are presently unknown.

Table 5-2

Alternatives	Attribute values		Euclidean distance from the ideal
	x_1	x_2	
A	6	7	9.2195
B	10	4	9.4868
C	13	0	13.0000
D	2	8	12.0845
E	2	13	11.0000
Ideal	13	13	0.0000

Table 5-3

	p_1	p_2
	O_1	O_2
A_1	4	2
A_2	6	4
A_3	4	3
A_4	6	0
A_5	$3\frac{1}{3}$	$3\frac{1}{3}$

Calculate the respective expected utilities:

$$A_1 \quad p_1\ (\$4) + p_2\ (\$2) = p_1\ (\$4) + (1 - p_1)\ (\$2)$$
$$= p_1\ (\$2) + \$2$$

$$A_2 \quad p_1\ (\$6) + p_2\ (\$4) = p_1\ (\$6) + (1 - p_1)\ (\$4)$$
$$= p_1\ (\$2) + \$4$$

Obviously, A_2 dominates A_1 for *all possible values* of p_1.

Next, let us alter the set of feasible alternatives by adding A_3 and A_4. Then the expected utilities are:

$$A_3 \quad p_1\ (\$4) + p_2\ (\$3) = p_1\ (\$4) + (1 - p_1)\ (\$3)$$
$$= p_1\ (\$1) + \$3$$

$$A_4 \quad p_1\ (\$6) + p_2\ (\$0) = p_1\ (\$6) + (1 - p_1)\ (\$0)$$
$$= p_1\ (\$6)$$

Obviously, A_3 is superior to A_4 over 60 percent of the range of p_1, that is, for p_1 between 0 and 0.6. At $p_1 = 0.6$ both alternatives have identical expected utilities:

$$A_3 \quad 0.6\ (\$1) + \$3 = \$3.6$$

$$A_4 \quad 0.6\ (\$6) = \$3.6$$

A_4 is superior to A_3 for p_1 between 0.6 and 1, i.e., over only 40 percent of the p_1 range. According to expected-utility theory, one should select A_3 as the superior strategy because if p_1 is chosen at random, A_3 would be the "winner" 60 percent of the time in a large number of hypothetical trials.

Unfortunately, a risk analysis such as this is not compatible with the axiom cited earlier. The addition of a new, nonoptimal alternative *can* convert a previously nonoptimal alternative into an optimal one. For example, consider a new alternative A_5 with the following expected utility:

$$A_5 \quad p_1\ (\$3\tfrac{1}{3}) + p_2\ (\$3\tfrac{1}{3}) = p_1\ (\$3\tfrac{1}{3}) + (1 - p_1)\ (\$3\tfrac{1}{3}) = \$3\tfrac{1}{3}$$

Now both A_3 and A_5 are dominant 30 percent of the time, while A_4 is dominant 40 percent of the time. *Thus*, A_4, *a previously nonoptimal strategy, has become optimal with respect to riskiness*.

Let the expected utilities represent the expected speeds of five racehorses. Track conditions are assumed to be the major determinant of racing speed. Further, if p_1 is the probability that the track will be dry, and p_2 is the probability that it will be wet, then horse A_2 has a higher expected speed than horse A_1. Thus, it is expected that A_2 will always win over A_1, regardless of track conditions.

With A_3 and A_4, it is a real horse race. When A_4 wins, it does so at a greater speed than A_3. However, since p_1 (and p_2) are unknown, A_3 has a greater chance of winning the race. The addition of A_5 further changes the odds. The new entry is better than A_3 on a wet track. This decreases the probability of A_3 winning to the point where A_4 has a higher probability.

Let us return to Table 5-2. What is implied by the reversal from $B > A > C > D$ to $A > B > E > D > C$? In comparing A with B the decision maker uses x^* as a point of reference. Points A and B are rarely compared directly with each other. Rather, A is compared with x^* and B is compared with x^*, each separately. The comparison of A and B is an indirect consequence of this process.

The sequential nature of these comparisons leads to corresponding changes in the number and the nature of alternatives comprising the available set. Thus, a different ideal might be involved in the different stages of the comparison process. Intransitivity of choices can then appear as a natural consequence of a consistent and rational decision-making process.

Consider the first case in Table 5-1 once more. We shall now explore a particular triad of options, say (A, B, D), shown in Fig. 5-5.

Assume that the decision-making process unfolds in stages and that inferior

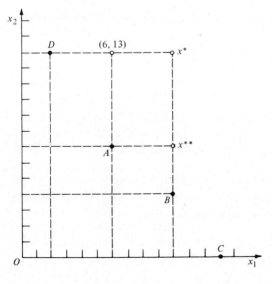

Figure 5-5 Sequential choice among three alternatives excerpted from Table 5-1.

alternatives can be sequentially screened and removed from immediate consideration. For example, if $A > B$ and B and D have already been compared, then we can discard B temporarily.

After comparing B and D one concludes that $D > B$. Next, observe that $A > D$ and thus D can also be discarded. To complete our triple comparison we evaluate A and B and conclude that $B > A$ because the removal of D has induced the displacement of x^* to x^{**}, a new point of reference. Thus, in three stages, the decision maker expresses a preference as follows: $A > D$, $D > B$, and $B > A$.

There is nothing inconsistent about the intransitivity of these preferences. The decision maker consistently minimizes the distance from the ideal. It is the partial decisions about individual pairs of alternatives that lead to a corresponding displacement. Observe that not all such triads would be characterized by intransitivity and that the sequential order of pairwise comparisons does matter. For example, if we start the process with $A > D$, we then establish that $A > B$ and finally that $D > B$. Similarly, the sequence $A > B$, $D > B$, $D > A$ presents yet another, fully *transitive* ordering. In this case the removal of B would shift x^* to point (6, 13), and $D > A$ simply follows.

We can conclude that in situations involving sequential displacements of the ideal there is a possibility of emerging intransitivity, especially if a sequence of pairwise comparisons is performed. If asked to compare all four alternatives *as a whole*, the decision maker would confirm that $A > B > D > C$, as derived earlier.

As the number of alternatives to be compared as a whole and nonsequentially, increases, there is a tendency toward partial decisioning and reducing the task to a set of pairwise comparisons. This leads to more frequent displacements of x^*, and the intransitivity of preferences would also appear more frequently.

For example, if we expand (A, B, D) into (A, B, C, D) and then perform the sequence of comparisons $A > C$, $B > C$, $D > C$, observe that C can be removed at this stage. Then, continuing the process, establish $D > B$ and $A > D$. At this point D can be removed. Finally, $B > A$.

There is a large variety of ways in which the decision-making sequence can be performed. A number of preference orderings can be generated on the same set of alternatives. Any number of alternatives is difficult to assess as a whole if the number of attributes is large. It is therefore possible to establish a link between the incidence of intransitivity and the attribute dimensionality of a given problem.

Because the choice between A and B is affected by the position of x^* (and therefore by some other, x^*-defining alternatives as well), observe that Arrow's axiom of the independence of irrelevant alternatives is ineffective in describing human selection of choices. Recall the empirical experiments of Festinger and his colleagues: So-called "irrelevant" alternatives suddenly become very relevant.

5-4 BIBLIOGRAPHICAL NOTE

There is one reference in this chapter which *must* be read by all serious students of economics and decision making: the late Oskar Morgenstern's *Thirteen Critical Points*. In December 1972, Morgenstern, like a contemporary Martin Luther, nailed his thirteen theses to the gates of the besplendored cathedral of economic science. His parting message has been mostly ignored—nobody dared to criticize it openly; nobody dared to support it openly. One finds again and again that young students of economics and business must go through their studies in pristine ignorance of such names as Oskar Morgenstern, Nicholas Georgescu-Roegen, and Herbert A. Simon. So, dear reader, don't let wisdom pass you by, don't get left behind, don't stand in the dark corner of the cathedral.

We started this chapter with some comments on the measurement of preferences through cardinal and ordinal scales. For further reading, one should consult Dalkey (1976) or Hobbs (1978). Both discussions are in the framework of MCDM and relatively simple.

Many of the references in this chapter can be acquired quite simply by buying one paperback, *Decision Making*, edited by Edwards and Tversky (1967). This collection of articles contains the classical overview of decision theory by Edwards (1954), an axiomatic treatment of utility by Luce and Raiffa (1957), the seminal treatment of preferential inconsistency by Coombs (1964), and the first article on multiattribute utility decomposition by Adams and Fagot (1959). If you acquire the paperback, please also read the paper by Shepard (1964), which provides a beautiful raison d'être for MCDM; the selection by Yntema and Torgerson (1961), on further extensions of utility decomposition and a discussion of a role of computers in decision making; and Tversky's introductory comments to part 3, "Riskless Choice."

People's behavior has been found to deviate significantly from the "rational" axioms of utility theory. They do not maximize expected utility; they anchor their judgments in external points of reference; they often disregard prior knowledge and equally often ignore new evidence; and so on. There is a wealth of interesting readings related to these issues: Tversky and Kahneman (1975), Kahneman and Tversky (1973), Tversky (1977), and Kunreuther et al. (1978) represent a good sampling of this literature.

The issues of intransitivity of preferences are well elucidated in May (1954). The independence of irrelevant alternatives of Arrow (1959, 1967) is also criticized by Blin (1976). Papers by Roy (1977), Starr and Zeleny (1977), and Zeleny (1977) provide the MCDM framework in which Chap. 5 was conceived.

Adams, E. W., and R. Fagot: "A Model of Riskless Choice," *Behavioral Science*, vol. 4, 1959, pp. 1–10.

Arrow, K. J.: "Public and Private Values," in S. Hook (ed.), *Human Values and Economic Policy*, New York University Press, New York, 1967, pp. 3–21.

———: "Rational Choice Functions and Orderings," *Economica*, vol. 26, 1959, pp. 121–127.

Blin, J.-M.: "How Relevant are 'Irrelevant' Alternatives?," *Theory and Decision*, vol. 7, 1976, pp. 95–105.

Coombs, C. H.: "Inconsistency of Preferences: A Test of Unfolding Theory," in C. H. Coombs, *A Theory of Data*, Wiley, New York, 1964, pp. 106–118.

———: "On the Use of Inconsistency of Preferences in Psychological Measurement," *Journal of Experimental Psychology*, vol. 55, 1958, pp. 1–7.

Dalkey, N. C.: "Group Decision Analysis," in M. Zeleny (ed.), *Multiple Criteria Decision Making*: *Kyoto 1975*, Springer-Verlag, New York, 1976, pp. 45–74.

Edwards, W.: "The Theory of Decision Making," *Psychological Bulletin*, vol. 51, no. 4, 1954, pp. 380–417.

——— and A. Tversky (eds.): *Decision Making: Selected Readings*, Penguin, Baltimore, 1967.

Festinger, L.: *Conflict, Decision and Dissonance*, Tavistock Publications Ltd., London, 1964.

Fishburn, P. C.: *The Theory of Social Choice*, Princeton, Princeton, 1973.

Hobbs, B. F.: Analytical Multiobjective Decision Methods for Power Plant Siting: A Review of Theory and Applications," Policy Analysis Div., Brookhaven National Lab., Upton, N.Y., 1978.

Kahneman, D., and A. Tversky: "On the Psychology of Prediction," *Psychological Review*, vol. 80, 1973, pp. 237–251.

Kunreuther, H., et al.: *Disaster Insurance Protection*: *Public Policy Lessons*, Wiley, New York, 1978.

Leibenstein, H.: *Beyond Economic Man*, Harvard, Cambridge, Mass., 1976.

Luce, R. D., and H. Raiffa: "An Axiomatic Treatment of Utility," *Games and Decisions: Introduction and Critical Survey*, Wiley, New York, 1957, pp. 23–31; reprinted in Edwards and Tversky (1967), pp. 111–120.

May, K. O.: "Intransitivity, Utility, and the Aggregation of Preference Patterns," *Econometrica*, vol. 22, 1954, pp. 1–13.

Morgenstern, O.: "Thirteen Critical Points in Contemporary Economic Theory: An Interpretation," *Journal of Economic Literature*, vol. 10, December 1972, pp. 1163–1189.

Ortega y Gasset, J.: *Revolt of the Masses*, Norton, New York, 1964.

Roy, B.: "A Conceptual Framework for a Prescriptive Theory of 'Decision Aid'," in M. K. Starr and M. Zeleny (eds.), *Multiple Criteria Decision Making*, TIMS Studies in the Management Sciences, vol. 6, North-Holland Publishing, Amsterdam, 1977, pp. 179–210.

Starr, M. K., and M. Zeleny: "MCDM—State and Future of the Arts," in M. K. Starr and M. Zeleny (eds.), *Multiple Criteria Decision Making*, TIMS Studies in the Management Sciences, vol. 6, North-Holland Publishing, Amsterdam, 1977, pp. 5–29.

Tversky, A.: "On the Elicitation of Preferences: Descriptive and Prescriptive Considerations," in D. E. Bell, R. L. Keeney, and H. Raiffa (eds.), *Conflicting Objectives in Decisions*, Wiley, New York, 1977, pp. 209–219.

——— and D. Kahneman: "Judgment under Uncertainty: Heuristics and Biases,"*Science*, vol. 185, 1975, pp. 1124–1131.

Walster, E., and L. Festinger: "Decisions Among Imperfect Alternatives," in L. Festinger, *Conflict, Decision and Dissonance*, Tavistock Publications Ltd., London, 1964, pp. 129–145.

Ward, B.: *What's Wrong with Economics?*, Basic Books, New York, 1972.

Zeleny, M.: "Adaptive Displacement of Preferences in Decision Making," in M. K. Starr and M. Zeleny (eds.), *Multiple Criteria Decision Making*, TIMS Studies in the Management Sciences, vol. 6, North-Holland Publishing, Amsterdam, 1977, pp. 147–157.

5-5 PROBLEMS

5-1 An MBA student said, "A dollar is a dollar." Her statement implied the extreme suitability of monetary units for aggregating multiple criteria, in terms of overall profit, for example. But compare the following dollars:

    (*a*) A dollar today, last year, next year, and 10 years hence

    (*b*) The first dollar, the one hundredth, and the ten thousandth

(c) A dollar given, earned, stolen, and borrowed

(d) A dollar earned on product sales, liquidation of equipment, and sale of stocks

(e) The federal government dollar, county government dollar, and town government dollar

In each case, are the "dollars" any different? What is lost (or gained) by adding them together? Can you reconcile your conclusions with the initial statement?

5-2 Kenneth J. Arrow considered maximization of function $U(x)$, utility indicator, over a universe of commodity bundles x. Let X be a convex feasible set. If x^0 belongs to X and $U(x^0) \geq U(x)$ for all x in X, then x^0 is *optimal* in X. Arrow calls x^* a "point of bliss" if $U(x^*) \geq U(x)$ for all x. Explain the difference between x^0 and x^*, and their relationship. How is the *point of bliss* related to the *ideal point*? *Hint*: There *is* a difference among the three concepts.

5-3 Form a universe of objects, a set of decision or choice alternatives, and classify them into two groups: "preferred" and "not preferred." Can you think of objects and circumstances which would not allow you to use this two-way classification? Are you sometimes obliged to say "it depends," when asked to express your preference? "It depends" on what?

5-4 Intransitive preferences can be visualized by considering the children's game, paper-scissors-stone. Paper covers stone, stone breaks scissors, scissors cut paper. That is, A is preferred to B, B is preferred to C, C is preferred to A. In this game, the preference depends entirely on what the other players do—on the circumstances under which a preference is expressed. Give some examples from your own experience of intransitive preferences. What would a strict and complete *transitivity* of preferences imply for human choice behavior? Under what conditions could a strict transitivity be postulated?

5-5 Consider the following situation: You offer to buy two animals (the most you can afford), cats or dogs, for your mother. You want to sketch your mother's preference function, so you ask her a few questions. You collect the following insights into her preferences: She would like to have some animal(s); she is entirely indifferent between two dogs and two cats; she strongly prefers having two animals of the same kind to having one of each; she even prefers having a single animal to having one of each; she reluctantly admits that she prefers one of each to nothing.

(a) Sketch her preference map over all possible bundles of commodities (cats, dogs).

(b) How would your "map" change if she preferred nothing to one of each, ceteris paribus?

(c) What would be the ideal and anti-ideal in both situations? Compare "as close as possible to the ideal" with "as far as possible from the anti-ideal."

5-6 Suppose that you are a professor in midcareer considering a new teaching position, and trying to decide among four institutions on the basis of salary and teaching load.

Institution	Salary	Teaching load (hours per week)
A	20,000	9
B	30,000	12
C	30,000	9
D	40,000	12

(a) What can be said about your trade-offs and preferences if you choose C?

(b) If C and D are no longer available and you choose A, what can you say about your trade-offs?

(c) Suppose there is a new prospect E, characterized by a salary of $80,000 and a 12-hour load. You take it. What does this say about your trade-off function between salary and teaching load? Can you apply it to situations (a) and (b)?

5-7 "If you prefer steak to lamb chops, that preference should not be affected by whether or not salmon is on the menu." Discuss the conditions under which this statement might not be true.

5-8 Is it safe to say that a house costing $30,000 is half as expensive as a house costing $60,000? What if the most expensive house in the set of those you could possibly afford is $65,000? What if it is $120,000? Is $60,000 simply twice as much as $30,000 in both situations?

In dealing with large-scale decision problems involving possibly hundreds of alternatives and scores of criteria or objectives, it is obviously necessary to perform computations and quantitative assessments. The theory of the displaced ideal, as presented so far, is not yet fully operational—it cannot be "computed."

In this chapter, first we present the axiom of choice, a fundamental observation about human choice behavior on which all subsequent modeling and formalism are founded. This axiom derives from the descriptions and experiments described in preceding chapters. In some sense it is a distillate of these chapters.

Next, we develop our formal model within the framework of the *theory of fuzzy sets* in order to be able to deal with the basic ambiguity, fuzziness, and uncertainty characterizing complex decision situations and reflected in managerial language. Only the most fundamental features of the theory are explained, and their presentation is closely interwoven with actual multicriterion analysis.

After introducing some basic measures of closeness to the ideal, we will be in a position to introduce the concept of *compromise solutions*. This is one of the key concepts in MCDM. An entire computational methodology, *compromise programming* (discussed in Chap. 10), derives from it.

We also explore the notion of an *anti-ideal*: the worst possible outcome that could be conceptually associated with a given decision situation. Does one strive to be as close as possible to the ideal, or as far as possible from the anti-ideal? We attempt to provide an answer.

We conclude this chapter with a comprehensive flow diagram, a formal version of its more qualitative counterpart presented at the end of Chap. 3.

DISPLACED IDEAL: AN OPERATIONAL MODEL

> *But a consequence cannot be ultimate if it is attainable, because it could be a means to a further consequence. Therefore, an ultimate end must be unattainable, but it must also be continuously approachable, otherwise it would not be an end at all. A maximally desired ultimate outcome is called an* ideal. *An ideal is the only kind of end that can have purely intrinsic value, that can be a pure end-in-itself.*
>
> *Therefore, the extrinsic value of any end that is less than an ideal must lie in the amount of* progress *toward one or more ideals which its attainment brings about.*
>
> Russell L. Ackoff
> A Concept of Corporate Planning (1970)

In this section we provide a symbolic model of the previously discussed decision-process hypothesis. Our paradigm will thus become computationally accessible, quantifiable, and operational. Numerical examples will be introduced to demonstrate the most important concepts.

6-1 HISTORICAL NOTE

The theory of the displaced ideal has evolved from ideas that were floating around MCDM circles for some years. Its main concept, the *ideal solution*, has been disguised under many different labels, and the exposition of this concept has often been indirect, tentative, or timid. Its short history can be traced through a large variety of working papers, theses, articles, and most significantly, authors of truly different backgrounds. The idea seems to possess the exciting and elegant quality of a paradigm.

At this time, the evolution of the ideal-solution concept cannot be established safely or accurately. Nor is the following historical sketch based on an extensive search of the literature. It thus represents only the limited knowledge of the author.

It seems that the appearance of the concept of the ideal solution is due to parallel searches in the early sixties for an approach to multiobjective conflict resolution. The idea was actually temporarily abandoned in favor of the nondominated solutions concept. It is now slowly working its way back into focus.

The concept was briefly introduced by Geoffrion (1965) as the "perfect solution." Other initiatory traces appear in works of Radzikowski (1967) and Jüttler (1967). It was originally conceived as a technical artifact, a fixed point of reference, facilitating the choice of a compromise solution. The first fully operational use of the concept occurs in the linear multiprogramming methodology of Saska (1968). Dinkelbach (1971) reviewed the concept in the same spirit.

The ideal solution soon became known under the term "movable target." The progressive orientation procedure, designed by Benayoun and Tergny (1969), and its further elaboration known as STEM, published by Benayoun, de Montgolfier, Tergny, and Larichev (1971), are the earliest sources to use this term.

The same concept appears, now as the "shadow minimum," in the exterior branching algorithm devised by Aubin and Näslund (1972) in the game-theoretical framework.

Zeleny (1973, 1974) introduced the concept of the compromise set and developed the method of the displaced ideal. Sequential displacements of the ideal solution also form the basis for evolutive target procedure, introduced by Roy (1977).

The concept appears to be general enough to encompass problems involving multiple decision makers as well. Some initial thoughts on this possibility are advanced by Yu (1973) who uses the term "utopia point." One is also reminded of Arrow's "point of bliss" in a slightly different context (see Chap. 5).

It is our opinion that the concept of the ideal solution and its displacement represent more than a convenient technical tool. It is a hypothesis about the rationale underlying human decision-making processes. As such it deserves a full axiomatic development, empirical testing, and interdisciplinary cross validation. This section is designed to motivate such developments. It does not represent a mathematical theory in itself, but it is about one which is evolving. It is neither normative nor descriptive but rather a blend of these two basic (and extreme) views of the world.

6-2 KEY CONCEPTS AND NOTATION

Recall that $X = \{x^1, x^2, \ldots, x^m\}$ denotes the set of initial feasible alternatives and that each alternative is characterized by n attributes. For example, the kth alternative can be written as

$$x^k = (x_1^k, x_2^k, \ldots, x_n^k) \qquad k = 1, \ldots, m$$

Individual x_i^k designate the level of attribute i attained by alternative k, where $i = 1, \ldots, n; k = 1, \ldots, m$.

Note We let x_i^k represent the kth alternative in terms of both the attributes *and* the objectives or criteria. There is a slight difference, as we discussed earlier. Attributes are the physical or physiological characteristics, the scores which can be obtained through an objective measurement (e.g., horsepower, mileage, size, weight, color, etc.), while objectives or criteria originate subjectively and are not necessarily inner properties of the objects considered. In some sense, they are imputed from without (security, prestige, image, comfort, ready transportation), although heavily influenced by actual attributes. Objectives could be, of course, reflected in a particular decision maker's *selection* of salient attributes, and thus the difference is often inessential.

Thus, x^k is simply a vector of n numbers, assigned to each x^k and summarizing the available information about x^k in terms of incommensurable, quantitative and qualitative, objective and subjective, attributes and criteria. We have thus established what is often called a "multiattribute alternative" in decision theory or a "commodity bundle" in economics.

Let us look at the ith attribute in isolation. The set X generates m numbers, a vector

$$x_i = (x_i^1, \ldots, x_i^m)$$

representing the currently achievable scores or levels of the ith attribute. Their simplest interpretation occurs when we assume that more is always preferred to less (or vice versa). Because

$$\operatorname*{Min}_{k} x_i^k = \operatorname*{Max}_{k} (-x_i^k) \qquad k = 1, 2, \ldots, m$$

i.e., finding the minimum of the m numbers is identical to finding the maximum of these numbers taken with negative signs, we shall agree to treat both cases as maximization.

There are of course situations when the extremal *achievable* scores of an attribute are not desirable. That is, as Coombs argues (1964), there is an ideal value of sugar or degrees of temperature, and desirability decreases monotonically on both sides of this ideal point.

Note that if this ideal point happens to lie outside the feasible set (i.e., it is not currently achievable), then the assumption of straightforward maximization again applies. We shall make this simplifying assumption in all cases where the explicit treatment of Coombs' ideal value is not essential.

Among all achievable scores for any ith attribute, see vector x_i, there is at least one extreme *or* ideal value that is preferred to all others. We shall call it an "anchor value," denoted x_i^*. That is, we can write

$$x_i^* = \operatorname*{Max}_{k} x_i^k \qquad i = 1, 2, \ldots, n$$

with the understanding that the above "Max" operation is only a simplification, since *both* maximum and ideal values are included in the concept of an anchor value.

We shall call the collection of all such anchor values the "ideal alternative" or the "ideal" denoted as

$$x^* = (x_1^*, \ldots, x_n^*)$$

The ideal plays a prominent role in decision making. Suppose, for example, that there exists x^k in X such that $x^k \equiv x^*$, for example, the ideal is attainable by the choice of x^k. There is no decision to be made. Any conceivable (but rational) utility function defined over an n-tuple of numbers $(x_1, \ldots, x_n)$ would attain its maximum value at x^* and consequently at x^k. *The ideal is, however, not feasible in general*, or if feasible, it soon becomes infeasible as the decision maker raises aspiration for just one x_i.

The difference between Coombs' concept of the ideal point and the concept of the ideal alternative introduced here is crucial, and any tendency to confuse the two should be avoided. As discussed in Sec. 5-3.4, Coombs' ideal is the absolute, unconstrained "point of bliss," denoted by M. Our ideal is dependent on the current limits and constraints of technological and economic nature.

6-3 AXIOM OF CHOICE

Alternatives that are closer to the ideal are preferred to those that are farther away. To be as close as possible to the perceived ideal is the rationale of human choice.

The fuzzy language employed in the axiom of choice— "as close as possible," "closer," "farther," etc.—reflects the reality of the fuzziness of human thought, perception, and preferences. It is actually more precise than the artificial precision and rigor of mathematical formalism. Before we engage in further elaboration of the axiom, let us clarify a few minor points.

First, we have implicitly assumed that there exists a single anchor value of any attribute, except possibly in the case of identical scores. For example, the attribute "body temperature" would have its anchor value somewhere around 37°C, with the attractiveness of numerical scores decreasing in both directions. But what about the attribute "water temperature in °C," when the objective is to minimize water density? This is achieved at both 2°C and 6°C, at 0.99994 kgm dm^{-3}, implying two anchor values. Similarly, hot or cold tea might be preferred to tepid tea. Multiple anchor values are therefore a real possibility.

These examples also demonstrate the relationship between attributes and objectives. Observe how the scores of the same attribute, say water temperature, can be evaluated quite differently when various objectives (usage for swimming, drinking, chemical purposes, etc.) are applied. Needless to say, different individuals could locate their anchor values at different points on the scale.

Finally, it is quite obvious that "preference" can be expressed as an "as far as possible" concept as well, employing an anti-ideal as the point of reference.

In fact, we shall show that the two concepts are closely interrelated and complementary in Sec. 6-6.2

6-4 A SINGLE ATTRIBUTE

We explore the case of a single attribute first, mainly to emphasize its inclusion as a special case of the presented theory.

Given that the anchor value of a single attribute has been successfully located, the decision problem is trivial: choose the anchor value. Construction of a utility function seems superfluous. Neither the choice nor the ordinal order would be affected.

In order to express the intensities of preference for all alternatives (especially if a selection of multiple alternatives is intended) and to demonstrate the use of the axiom of choice in this special case, a cardinal analysis is essential.

6-4.1 The Fuzziness of Managerial Language

Since the ideal point and the anchor value are now identical, the alternatives close to x^*_i are preferred to those farther away. Consider the following:

> Three different alternatives are to be evaluated with respect to a single, simple attribute, say "dollar return." For example, a three-dimensional vector of returns might describe the alternatives (5, 10, 500). Obviously the first two values are quite far from 500, with 10 being a little closer then 5. Observe that 500 is the anchor value and, in this case, the ideal. Let us assume that the lucrative third alternative has turned out to be infeasible and was replaced by a new alternative, thus generating a modified vector (5, 10, 11). This change in the anchor value has also caused 10 to be much closer to the ideal than 5. The difference between 5 and 10 has changed from negligible to substantial.

There are two important points made by this example: The intensities of preference change with the situation, and they are expressed in fuzzy terms.

We shall employ the *linguistic approach* developed by Zadeh. The essence of the linguistic approach is best captured in Zadeh's principle of incompatibility:

> As the complexity of a system increases, our ability to make precise and yet significant statements about its behavior diminishes until a threshold is reached beyond which precision and significance can no longer coexist. (Zadeh 1973, p. 688)

The complexity of human preferences is unquestionable, and it is amplified further by the dominant role of judgment, perception, and emotions. In contrast, to create units of measurement for preferences—such as "utils," in analogy with mechanistic systems—may allow for precise mathematical treatment but diminishes understanding of human preferences. The key elements in human thinking are not numbers but *labels of fuzzy sets*, i.e., classes of objects in which the transition from membership to nonmembership is gradual rather than abrupt.

For example, to designate a color by a natural linguistic label, such as "red," is often much less precise than to apply the numerical value of the appropriate wavelength. Yet it is far more significant and useful in *human* affairs. Similarly, we tend to assign a linguistic rather than a numerical value to the intensity of our choice preferences.

In order to amplify the relationship between fuzziness and precision in human deliberations, we shall elaborate the example of labeling of colors in the following short digression.

Fuzziness and precision: an example of colors Fuzzy linguistic labels, rather than "precise" numerical measurements, are often successfully used by large numbers of people with no apparent handicap or uncertainty. A typical example concerns our way of defining *colors*.

It would be most precise, a scientist might argue, to associate each color with its particular wavelength, as registered by the human retina, and measure it in angstroms to as many decimal places as desired. Yet nobody has ever suggested such nonsense, even though the wavelengths of colors are in principle measurable. (It is apparently more acceptable to measure human preferences in utils to three or four decimal places).

The reason for using linguistic labels for designating color is the need for a system which is acceptable and usable in science, sufficiently broad for art and industry, and sufficiently familiar to be understood by the public. Nothing less will do. Such diverse needs are well met by the *Munsell color system*.

According to this system, each color can be described in terms of three basic attributes: *hue*, *lightness*, and *saturation*. *Hue* names can be used as both nouns and adjectives: "red," "reddish orange," "orange," "orange yellow," "yellow," etc. The hues include black, gray, and white. The terms "light," "medium," and "dark" designate decreasing *degrees of lightness*. The adverb "very" then extends the lightness scale from "very light" to "very dark." Finally, the increasing degrees of color *saturation* are labeled with the adjectives "grayish," "moderate," "strong," and "vivid." Additional adjectives cover combinations of lightness and saturation: "brilliant" for light and strong, "pale" for light and grayish, and "deep" for dark and strong.

Combining the agreed upon linguistic labels (standardized by the ISCC-NBS system), one can specify about 267 visually distinguishable colors, for example, vivid purple, brilliant purple, very light purple, very pale purple, very deep purple, very dark purple, but also dark grayish purple, very light purplish gray, and strong purplish pink. Most of these colors can be recognized and their differences remembered by scientists, artists, professionals, and the public alike.

The Munsell system also fixes the boundaries of each color name. These boundaries are then translated into numerical scales of hue, lightness, and saturation, and each color can thus be expressed as accurately as desired.

Definition A fuzzy subset A of a set of objects U is characterized by a membership function f_A which associates with each element x of U a number $f_A(x)$ in the interval $[0, 1]$, which represents the grade of membership of x in A.

We shall use this definition to exemplify the meaning of "as close as possible" in the axiom of choice. Consider vector x_i of available scores of the ith attribute over m alternatives. We shall define the *degree of closeness* of x_i^k to x^*_i as

$$d(x_i^k, x^*_i) \equiv d_i^k$$

where $d_i^k = 1$ if $x_i^k = x^*_i$ and otherwise $0 \leq d_i^k < 1$.

6-4.2 Membership Functions

Essentially the ith attribute's scores are now viewed as a *fuzzy set*, defined as the following set of pairs:

$$\{x_i^k, d_i^k\}\; i = 1, \ldots, n$$
$$k = 1, \ldots, m$$

Where d_i^k is a *membership function* mapping the scores of the ith attribute into the interval $[0, 1]$. For example, the scores generated by available alternatives might be labeled with respect to the ideal as *"close," "not close," "very close," "not very close," "distant," "not distant," "not very distant," "not close and not distant,"* etc.

The membership function of a fuzzy set can be defined by a *fuzzy recognition algorithm*, a procedure suggested by Zadeh (1974). At this stage let us simply introduce a few plausible functions yielding the degree of closeness to x^*_i for individual alternatives:

1. If x^*_i is a maximum, then

$$d_i^k = \frac{x_i^k}{x^*_i}$$

2. If x^*_i is a minimum, then

$$d_i^k = \frac{x^*_i}{x_i^k}$$

3. If x^*_i is a feasible goal value (or Coombs' ideal value), for example, x^*_i is preferred to all x_i^k smaller *and* larger than x_i^k, then

$$d_i^k = \left[\tfrac{1}{2} \left(\frac{x_i^k}{x_i^*} + \frac{x_i^*}{x_i^k} \right) \right]^{-1}$$

4. If, for example, the most distant feasible score is to be labeled by zero regardless of its actual closeness to x_i^*, we can define:

$$x_{i*} = \underset{k}{\text{Min}}\ x_i^k$$

and write d_i^k as

$$d_i^k = \frac{x_i^k - x_{i*}}{x_i^* - x_{i*}}$$

The above four functions d_i^k indicate that x^j is preferred to x^k when $d_i^k < d_i^j$.

To gain a proper numerical grasp of the functions d_i^k introduced so far, let us evaluate a simple vector of ten numbers with respect to their distances from different anchor values x_i^* (and x_{i*}), as shown in Table 6-1.

Implication Preference ordering among available alternatives is transitive with respect to a *single* attribute.

We can iteratively change the actual values of d_i^k even in the course of their analysis. This is due to learning, sharpened perception, changed situation, and other dynamic factors. The following two operations are then useful (the symbol $\rightarrow$ means "is replaced by"):

1. Concentration:

$$d_i^k \rightarrow (d_i^k)^\alpha \qquad 0 < \alpha < 1$$

Table 6-1

	k	1	2	3	4	5	6	7	8	9	10
(a)	x_i^k	6	7.5	15	32	33	36	36.8	50	70	⑨⑨
	d_i^k	0.060	0.075	0.152	0.323	0.333	0.363	0.371	0.505	0.707	1.000
(b)	x_i^k	⑥	7.5	15	32	33	36	36.8	50	70	99
	d_i^k	1.000	0.800	0.400	0.187	0.181	0.167	0.163	0.120	0.086	0.060
(c)	x_i^k	6	7.5	15	32	33	36	36.8	㊿	70	99
	d_i^k	0.237	0.293	0.550	0.908	0.920	0.949	0.955	1.000	0.946	0.805
(d)	x_i^k	⑥	7.5	15	32	33	36	36.8	50	70	⑨⑨
	d_i^k	0.000	0.016	0.097	0.279	0.290	0.322	0.331	0.473	0.688	1.000

Note: The corresponding x_i^*, and x_{i*} in case (d), are circled.

2. Dilation:

$$d_i^k \rightarrow (d_i^k)^\alpha \qquad \alpha > 1$$

where α is the power of d_i^k. Observe that concentration leads to the increasing equalization of initial d_i^k's as α changes from zero to 1. On the other hand, dilation lessens the larger values less and the smaller values more. Consequently, the differences between d_i^k's are increased by applying a large α (or by a repeated application of a particular α). We say that dilation leads to *attribute contrast intensification*, or to "spreading apart of values," in Festinger's terminology.

Let us demonstrate the above with a simple numerical example. Consider a vector of score perceptions along an attribute:

$$d_i = (d_i^1, \ldots, d_i^m) = (0.2, 0.6, 0.65, 0.9, 1)$$

representing the degrees of closeness to the anchor value of five alternatives. We are interested in the changes induced by both concentration and dilation:

1. Concentration with $\alpha = 0.9$, $\alpha = 0.5$, and $\alpha = 0.01$ yields the following three vectors respectively:

$$
\begin{array}{ll}
\alpha = 0.9 & (0.23, 0.63, 0.68, 0.91, 1) \\
\alpha = 0.5 & (0.45, 0.77, 0.81, 0.95, 1) \\
\alpha = 0.01 & (0.98, 0.99, 0.99, 0.99, 1)
\end{array}
$$

Observe the decreasing contrast intensity, the equalization of values.
2. Dilation with $\alpha = 1.1$, $\alpha = 1.5$, and $\alpha = 2$ yields the following three vectors respectively:

$$
\begin{array}{ll}
\alpha = 1.1 & (0.17, 0.57, 0.62, 0.89, 1) \\
\alpha = 1.5 & (0.09, 0.46, 0.52, 0.85, 1) \\
\alpha = 2.0 & (0.04, 0.36, 0.42, 0.81, 1)
\end{array}
$$

Observe the tendency to spread out the values. For a more distinct example, $(0.9, 0.91, 0.92, 0.98, 1)$ can be dilated, by using $\alpha = 10$, to $(0.35, 0.39, 0.43, 0.81, 1)$.

Note that the extreme values of α, $\alpha = 0$ and $\alpha = \infty$, transform any vector into $(1, 1, \ldots, 1)$ and $(0, 0, \ldots, 1)$ respectively; i.e., they make the choice among alternatives either impossible or trivial.

6-5 MULTIPLE ATTRIBUTES

Degrees of closeness d_i^k are not of great value in the case of a single attribute. The transitivity of preferences is preserved along a single dimension, and the ordinal ranking of alternatives is not influenced by changes and adjustments in degrees of closeness.

Alternatives are usually characterized by multiple attributes, i.e., by vectors $x^k = (x_1^k, \ldots, x_n^k)$, $k = 1, \ldots, m$. We can represent n independent attributes as in Table 6-2.

In each column we locate an anchor and then transform the scores into the corresponding degrees of closeness, i.e., all x_i^k's would be changed into d_i^k's according to a particular membership function, as for example, the four function types shown earlier.

We now ask, How close is the kth alternative to the anchor along the ith attribute? That is n questions for each alternative. If we were to assume independency among the individual columns of Table 6-2, this approach would be quite straightforward. There is, however, usually some interdependence among the attributes in the sense that a particular value of, say d_1^k restricts or even determines the possible values of d_2^k, d_3^k, etc.

Let us assume that attributes are generally *dependent* on each other in a complex, dynamic, and highly subjective way. This subjective nature of attribute dependency makes an interaction between person and model almost mandatory. Let us now review briefly some traditional notions of attribute dependency, as they can be derived from the multiattribute utility literature discussed in Chap. 12.

6-5.1 Multiple Attribute Dependency

Most theories of multiattribute utility first define strict independence conditions for a decision maker's preferences for different levels of a given set of attributes while the levels of the remaining attributes are held fixed. It is often assumed that when the levels of the other attributes shift, the initially derived preferences stay unaffected.

The two basic types of attribute dependency are value dependency and preferential dependency:

1. *Value Dependency*. A set of attributes is value-dependent if the measurement of numerical scores (either objective or subjective) with respect to

Table 6-2

Attributes / Alternatives		x_i			
		x^1	x_2	$\cdots$	x_n
x^k	x^1	x_1^1	x_2^1	$\cdots$	x_n^1
	x^2	x_1^2	x_2^2	$\cdots$	x_n^2
	$\vdots$	$\vdots$	$\vdots$		$\vdots$
	x^m	x_1^m	x_2^m	$\cdots$	x_n^m

one attribute implies or restricts a particular attainment of scores by all other attributes of the set. Typical examples are water temperature and water density, cost and price, and size and weight.

2. *Preferential dependency*. A set of attributes is preferentially dependent on other attributes if preferences within the set depend on the levels at which the scores of other attributes are fixed. For example, the preference for the removal or nonremoval of one kidney depends on the performance score achieved by the other; the preference for speed in an automobile depends on safety; the preference for life depends on its quality; etc.

These two essential types of attribute dependency form a base for an array of more specific technical derivatives of dependency conditions. Current multiattribute utility theory offers, for example, utility dependency, parametric dependency, diagonal dependency, fractional dependency, semicube dependency, quasipyramid dependency, as well as generalized versions of all of the above! They are usually referred to as "independence" conditions, see Sec. 12-4.2.

It is probably futile to handle attribute dependency this way. Note that value dependency and preferential dependency are themselves interdependent. That is, the scores of the attributes cannot be fixed at any particular level without simultaneously "fixing" all value-dependent attributes as well. Preferential changes are thus induced in response to different *subsets* of the value-dependent set, and consequently they are extremely difficult to trace.

We shall attempt to suggest a simpler and, at the same time, a more flexible way of dealing with the dependency problem. Let us start with a few examples.

Consider two alternatives providing an identical income of $100. With an anchor value of, say, $200, both alternatives can be considered equally close to the anchor. However, let us also assume that with respect to some other attribute, say the cost of living, the two alternatives, for example two identical incomes in Frankfurt and Nicosia, differ substantially. This fact influences our perception of $100 and causes one $100 to be perceived as closer to $200 than the other.

Another example: Even though Sam and Charley are of exactly the same height, I could label them differently, say, "tall" and "quite tall," simply because the two men are of different girths.

Similar interdependence exists across the alternatives. I can consider both Sam and Charley to be quite sturdy, until I have seen Jim. That is, the availability of a particular alternative in a given set influences a particular assignment of linguistic labels.

Observe that the problem with these three examples lies in the proper specification of attributes. Instead of "income" and "cost of living," we could use "real income," and in the case of the two men, we could judge their "bodily structure" rather than anything else. The problem is that the number of attributes increases, and such composite attributes are often difficult to quantify and even to conceptualize.

Only in the last example is there an interdependence worthy of serious consideration. Traditionally, dependency has been treated as *separable* from a particular set of feasible alternatives. Thus, if the intensity of preference for a given level of one attribute systematically changes with respect to all achievable levels along the second attribute, then all the conditional or parametric preferential functions must be assessed a priori.

Let us focus on X, the set of all initially feasible alternatives. Each k induces a particular vector x^k consisting of the scores attained with respect to all salient attributes. In this sense we can say that all attribute scores are fixed for a given alternative. That is, x_1^k comes only with x_2^k and not any other value. There is no point in talking about evaluating x_1^k with respect to all achievable scores along the second attribute. The two levels x_1^k and x_2^k are not separable, and they *both* characterize a particular alternative in a vector sense. Consequently, the value dependency, as defined earlier, does not require any special attention.

For example, a particular type of automobile is characterized by certain levels of horsepower and mileage. Another alternative, a different type of car, is characterized by a distinctly different combination of horsepower and mileage. One can choose one such combination of attributes or the other; barring the creation of a new alternative one cannot cross-combine their specific attribute levels. It is meaningless to keep horsepower constant and ask about preferences for different levels of mileage—there may not be any real alternatives providing such preferential "crossbreeds." Abstract assessment of preferences without consideration of the actual bearers of particular attribute levels, the alternatives, is an empty and pointless exercise. People choose the alternatives, and their preferences concern the alternatives and not some imaginary ranges of conditional attribute levels.

Instead of making an a priori assessment of attribute dependency, we incorporate its impact implicitly into the dynamic process of partial decision making. As an alternative, say the kth, is removed from further consideration, the set of n attribute scores $(x_1^k, \ldots, x_n^k)$ is removed as well. The initial evaluation is performed on a more or less complete set X, and the attribute interaction demonstrates itself only as the alternatives (and the appropriate attribute scores) are being progressively removed (or added back). The impact of removing an alternative k is essentially twofold:

1. The variety and contrast of the currently achievable attribute scores is diminished.
2. The ideal alternative can be displaced if the removed alternative contained at least one attribute anchor value.

Consequently, the removal of any alternative affects the ranking of the remaining alternatives in terms of their closeness to the ideal. It also affects the discriminatory power of the attributes and thus their relative importance as well. Finally, if the ideal is displaced, the actual distances of the remaining alternatives must also be recomputed. As some attribute scores become unavailable, the preferences for the remaining levels have to be interactively reassessed.

Attribute levels do not increase or decrease per se, by decree or by an analyst's "fixations." There is always the underlying alternative or a set of alternatives being made available or unavailable. No significant understanding of preferences, their intransitivities and reversals, can be achieved without analyzing the dynamics of the set of feasible alternatives.

We introduce the simple notion of attribute dependency, reflecting the conditions of choice discussed above:

Anchor dependency A set of attributes is anchor dependent if the degrees of closeness assigned within the set depend on the corresponding anchor values as well as on the degrees of closeness associated with other attributes in the set.

We shall, then, interactively adjust all degrees of closeness each time an anchor is displaced.

The question, How close is alternative k to the ideal?, can be viewed as a *composite question*, a collection of constituent questions, How close is alternative k to the ith attribute anchor value? The answer to the composite question can be derived from the answers to its constituent questions. The nature of this dependency, i.e., the manner in which the constituent questions are combined to form a composite question, is explored next.

6-5.2 Composite Membership Functions

Both the constituent and the composite questions are "classificational" in the sense of Zadeh (1974). Their answers represent the grade of membership of k in the fuzzy set "as close as possible," expressed either numerically or linguistically. Answering a classificational question thus corresponds to assigning a value to the membership function. The answer set may be the unit interval [0, 1] or a countable set of linguistic labels defined over [0, 1].

Let d_i^k represent the degrees of closeness of x_i^k to x_i^*, as in Sec. 6-4.1. Observe that the set of feasible alternatives X has been mapped through d_i^k's into a "distance" space. Let us denote the space of all d_i^k's generated by X as D.

Note also that the ideal alternative is now translated into a unitary vector, $d^* = (d_1^*, \ldots, d_n^*) = (1, \ldots, 1)$, because if

$$x_i^k \equiv x_i^* \quad \text{then} \quad d_i^k = d_i^* = 1$$

To determine the degree of closeness of any x^k to x^* in terms of d^k and d^*, let us define an appropriate family of distance *membership functions* as follows:

$$L_p(\lambda, k) = \left[\sum_{i=1}^{n} \lambda_i^p \, (1 - d_i^k)^p \right]^{1/p}$$

where $\lambda = (\lambda_1, \ldots, \lambda_n)$ is a vector of *attribute attention levels* λ_i, and the power p represents the *distance parameter* $1 \leq p \leq \infty$. Thus $L_p(\lambda, k)$ evaluates the distance between the ideal alternative d^* and the actual vector of degrees of closeness induced by an alternative d^k.

Observe that for $p = 1$, and assuming $\Sigma_{i=1}^n \lambda_i = 1$, we can write $L_p(\lambda, k)$ as

$$L_1(\lambda, k) = 1 - \sum_{i=1}^{n} \lambda_i d_i^k$$

Similarly for $p = 2$, we obtain

$$L_2(\lambda, k) = \left[\sum_{i=1}^{n} \lambda_i^2 (1 - d_i^k)^2 \right]^{1/2}$$

and for $p = \infty$:

$$L_\infty(\lambda, k) = \max_i \{\lambda_i (1 - d_i^k)\}$$

In order to appreciate the numerical differences between $L_1(\lambda, k)$, $L_2(\lambda, k)$, and $L_\infty(\lambda, k)$, we shall consider ten alternatives evaluated with respect to *two* attributes. Numerical values are given in Table 6-3.

Observe that $x_1^* \equiv x_1^{10} = 99$ and $x_2^* \equiv x_2^8 = 15$. Therefore, $x^* = (99, 15)$ is the (infeasible) ideal point.

We have used

$$d_1^k = \frac{x_1^k}{x_1^*} \quad \text{and} \quad d_2^k = \left[\tfrac{1}{2} \left(\frac{x_2^k}{x_2^*} + \frac{x_2^*}{x_2^k} \right) \right]^{-1}$$

for transforming attributes 1 and 2 into the distances from their respective anchor points, $x_1^* = 99$ and $x_2^* = 15$. For example,

$$d_1^6 = \frac{x_1^6}{x_1^*} = \frac{36}{99} = 0.3636$$

Table 6-3

k	1	2	3	4	5	6	7	8	9	10
x_1^k	6	7.5	15	32	33	36	36.8	50	70	⑨⑨
x_2^k	3	3.5	4	5	6	10	14	⑮	8	5
d_1^k	0.060	0.075	0.152	0.323	0.333	0.363	0.371	0.505	0.707	1.000
d_2^k	0.385	0.443	0.498	0.600	0.689	0.923	0.998	1.000	0.833	0.600
L_1	0.777	0.741	0.675	0.538	0.489	0.357	0.315	0.247	0.230	⓪.⑳⓪
L_2	0.562	0.540	0.493	0.393	0.368	0.320	0.315	0.247	⓪.①⑥⑧	0.200
L_∞	0.470	0.462	0.424	0.338	0.333	0.318	0.314	0.247	⓪.①④⑥	0.200

and

$$d_2^6 = \left[\tfrac{1}{2}\left(\frac{x_2^6}{x_2^*} + \frac{x_2^*}{x_2^6}\right)\right]^{-1} = \left[\tfrac{1}{2}\left(\frac{10}{15} + \frac{15}{10}\right)\right]^{-1} = 0.9230$$

Note that only x^8, x^9, and x^{10} are not dominated by any other alternative in the set of ten. Applying the three measures of distance we derive the closeness of each x^k to x^*. We assume that both attributes are equally important, that is, $\lambda_1 = \lambda_2 = 0.5$. For example,

$L_1(\lambda, 6) = 1 - (\lambda_1 d_1^6 + \lambda_2 d_2^6) = 1 - (0.5 \times 0.363 + 0.5 \times 0.923) = 0.357$

$L_2(\lambda, 6) = [\lambda_1^2(1 - d_1^6)^2 + \lambda_2^2(1 - d_2^6)^2]^{1/2} = [0.25(1 - 0.363)^2 + 0.25(1 - 0.923)^2]^{1/2}$
$\qquad\quad = 0.320$

$L_\infty(\lambda, 6) = \text{Max}\,\{\lambda_1(1 - d_1^6);\, \lambda_2(1 - d_2^6)\}$

$\qquad\qquad\quad = \text{Max}\,\{0.5(1 - 0.363);\, 0.5(1 - 0.923)\}$

$\qquad\qquad\quad = \text{Max}\,\{0.318;\, 0.038\} = 0.318$

Observe that x^{10} is the closest to x^* with respect to L_1, while x^9 is the closest with respect to L_2 and L_∞. Both compromise solutions x^9 and x^{10} are encircled in Table 6-3.

6-5.3 Compromise Solutions

Thus we can define the closest alternatives to the ideal as those minimizing $L_p(\lambda, k)$ with respect to some p. If

$$\underset{k}{\text{Min}}\; L_p(\lambda, k)$$

is achieved at $x^{k(p)}$, then $x^{k(p)}$ (or $d^{k(p)}$) is called the "compromise alternative with respect to p." Let C denote the set of all such compromise alternatives for $p = 1, \ldots, \infty$.

Compromise solutions enjoy a number of interesting and useful properties; see for example the excellent discussion by Yu (1973). We are interested in the following:

1. For $1 \leq p \leq \infty$, since there is no x^k in X such that $d_i^k \geq d_i^{k(p)}$ for all i and $d^k \neq d^{k(p)}$, $x^{k(p)}$ and $d^{k(p)}$ are *nondominated*. It can also be shown that *at least one* $x^{k(\infty)}$ (and $d^{k(\infty)}$) is nondominated.
2. For $1 < p < \infty$, $x^{k(p)}$ (and $d^{k(p)}$) is the *unique minimum* of $L_p(\lambda, k)$ on X.

It can be shown that $L_p(\lambda, k)$ is a strictly increasing function of

$$L_p'(\lambda, k) = \sum_{i=1}^{n} \lambda_i^p\, (1 - d_i^k)^p$$

and thus $x^{k(p)}$ minimizes L_p if and only if it minimizes L_p'. Note that $L_p'(\lambda, k)$ is a strictly convex function and thus it gives a unique minimal point on X for $1 \leqq p < \infty$.

It is important to realize that the membership functions L_p and L_p' are not independent of a positive linear transformation of individual degrees of closeness; see Yu (1973). For example, let $\mathbf{d}_i^k = \alpha_i d_i^k$, $\alpha_i > 0$. Then

$$\mathbf{d}_i^* = \alpha_i d_i^* = \alpha_i,$$

and

$$L_p(\lambda, k) = \left[\sum_{i=1}^{n} \lambda_i^p (\mathbf{d}_i^* - \mathbf{d}_i^k)^p \right]^{1/p}$$

transforms into

$$L_p(\lambda, k) = \left[\sum_{i=1}^{n} \lambda_i^p (\alpha_i - \alpha_i d_i^k)^p \right]^{1/p}$$

$$= \left[\sum_{i=1}^{n} \lambda_i^p \alpha_i^p (1 - d_i^k)^p \right]^{1/p}$$

Thus changing the scale of the degrees of closeness has the same effect as changing the attention levels λ_i in L_p and L_p'.

The above observation is potentially very important. It suggests that the degrees of closeness (as well as any other perceptions of attribute scores, e.g., utilities) are interrelated with the weights of importance. It seems that their compounding effect must be clearly understood to avoid "double weighting." We should concentrate on manipulating either d_i^k or λ_i, only exceptionally on both. The assignment of a particular set $(d_i^1, \ldots, d_i^m)$ already implicitly contains and reflects the importance of the ith attribute. We need to understand how much d_i^k reflect the underlying objective measurements and how much they are products of a subjective reinterpretation. Otherwise, additional weighting by λ_i could only obfuscate the problem.

Before we explore the problem of weights in greater detail, let us gain some understanding of the distance parameter p. So far we have worked with $p = 1, 2, \infty$. Because we may disregard the power $1/p$, let us use L_p' and substitute $v_i = 1 - d_i^k$:

$$L_p'(\lambda, k) = \sum_{i=1}^{n} \lambda_i^p v_i^{p-1} (1 - d_i^k)$$

Observe that as p increases, more and more weight is given to the largest deviation $(1 - d_i^k)$. Ultimately the largest deviation completely dominates, as when $p = \infty$ in L_∞ and L_∞'. We conclude that p weights the individual deviations according to their magnitudes and across the attributes, while λ_i weights deviations according to the attributes and irrespective of their magnitudes.

The compromise with respect to p then indicates a particular form of conflict resolution between the available alternatives and the infeasible ideal. Ob-

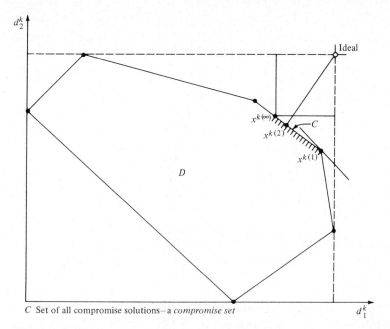

C Set of all compromise solutions—a *compromise set*

Figure 6-1 Typical compromise solutions and a compromise set.

serve that for $p = 1$ the minimization of $L'_p(\lambda, k)$ reflects our extreme disregard for individual deviation magnitudes—it is their total sum we are after. On the other hand, for $p = \infty$ we try to minimize the maximum of the individual deviations. All attributes are thus considered to be of comparable importance, and the compromise deviations are equalized as much as possible.

What about the cases of $0 < p < 1$? Because the values of d_i^k are normalized between zero and 1, observe that the emphasis is reversed: As p changes from 1 to zero, the smallest deviation is given relatively larger and larger weight in the total sum, while the larger deviations are adjusted relatively slightly. Figure 6-1 shows typical compromise solutions.

6-6 ADDITIONAL TOPICS CONCERNING THE "IDEAL"

6-6.1 Solution Pocket

It has become an accepted belief that nondominated solutions provide a good general starting point (or sometimes even the endpoint) of rational decision analysis. So far, we have not used the concept of nondominance explicitly, and now we shall actually dispute its general usefulness and discuss its inferiority to the concept of compromise solutions introduced earlier.

If there is no j and x^j in X such that $d_i^j \geqq d_i^k$ for all i's and $d_i^j \neq d_i^k$, then k represents a *nondominated alternative* x^k, which generates a nondominated outcome d_i^k in the above sense. That is, x^k is nondominated if, and only if, there is no other feasible alternative generating an outcome which can dominate it. Quite often we conclude that a good decision must yield a nondominated outcome, and many authors actually start their procedures by eliminating all dominated x^j from X.

At least two objections can be raised against such a conceptual framework:

1. If more than one alternative is required for a solution (e.g., problems of capital budgeting, portfolio selection, consumer brand choice), then the second and subsequent choices are not necessarily nondominated. The concept of nondominated solutions is fully viable if and only if a single solution is required.
2. If a ranking of alternatives is desired, then the set of all nondominated solutions does not provide a good basis for the ranking. Even if only a single solution is the target, subsequent rankings of alternatives serve as an important intermediate orientation tool, helping the decision maker to explicate preferences.

The above points are of course only additional to such obstacles as computational difficulties, nondominated sets that are too large, and nonlinearity gaps. Yet they are much more important, since they do not allow us to generalize the concept. These objections, however, do not dispose of the fact that a single or the first selection is always to be nondominated. It is only the tendency to work exclusively with nondominated solutions which is questionable.

In Fig. 6-2 the shaded boundary of D, denoted N, represents the set of all nondominated solutions. Recall that all compromise solutions, denoted C, are nondominated by definition. Since C is always smaller or equal to N, the selection of a single solution is thus greatly simplified. If we are concerned about the *second best* alternative to $d^{k(2)}$, it can be assumed that the kth alternative is the next closest to the ideal. Observe that d^k is obviously dominated by $d^{k(2)}$, and yet its initial omission could significantly distort our final choice of the second best. Correct ranking of alternatives, even if only partial, provides the essential information for the intermediate as well as the final stages of a decision process.

In Fig. 6-3 we illustrate a new solution concept. The *solution pocket*, designated $\mathscr{P}$. All desirable *multiple* solutions are likely to be found in the pocket. Its shape and ''depth'' will depend on the particular location of the ideal. Its advantages arise fully in dealing with nonconvex, discrete sets, integer programming frameworks, and severe nonlinearity gaps.

6-6.2 Anti-Ideal

A concept similar to the ideal alternative, its mirror image, the *anti-ideal*, can be defined on any properly bounded set of feasible alternatives.

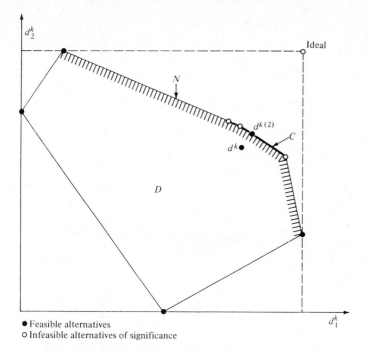

● Feasible alternatives
○ Infeasible alternatives of significance

Figure 6-2 The problem of the second best.

Among all achievable scores, for any ith attribute, there is at least one extreme value which is *the least preferred* in relation to all remaining values. Let us define:

$$x_{i*} = \operatorname*{Min}_{k} x_i^k \qquad i = 1, \ldots, n$$

and the collection of all such minima, the anti-ideal alternative, as:

$$x_* = (x_{i*}, \ldots, x_{n*})$$

The anti-ideal might be either infeasible or feasible; in either case it could serve as a point of reference during the process of decision making. The question is, *Do humans strive to be as close as possible to the ideal or as far away as possible from the anti-ideal?* Our answer—*both*. As matter of fact we propose that humans are capable of switching between the two regimes according to the given circumstances of the decision process.

Since all alternatives are compared with the ideal (rather than directly among themselves), it is obvious that the ideal's usefulness will depend on its discriminatory power, i.e., how well it aids the decision maker in distinguishing among the alternatives.

Let us return to the simple example of three alternatives, evaluated along a

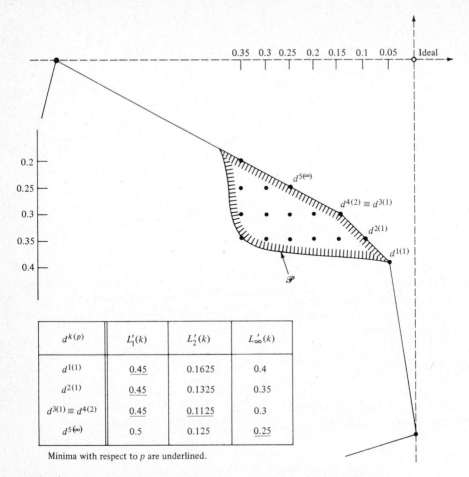

$d^k(p)$	$L_1'(k)$	$L_2'(k)$	$L_\infty'(k)$
$d^1(1)$	0.45	0.1625	0.4
$d^2(1)$	0.45	0.1325	0.35
$d^3(1) \equiv d^4(2)$	0.45	0.1125	0.3
$d^5(\infty)$	0.5	0.125	0.25

Minima with respect to p are underlined.

Both axes are scaled according to $(1 - d_i^k)$ and only the relevant portions are shown. Observe that feasible members of the compromise set are characterized by the following vectors: (0.45, 0.1625, 0.4), (0.45, 0.1325, 0.35), (0.45, 0.1125, 0.3), (0.5, 0.125, 0.25).
All remaining points ● inside the pocket $\mathscr{P}$ are nondominated with respect to the above three-dimensional compromise vectors.

Figure 6-3 The solution pocket.

single dimension, generating a vector of scores (5, 10, 11). Our task is to choose among the first two alternatives, 5 and 10, using the third one, 11, as the ideal. To transform the scores into the corresponding degrees of closeness we shall assume that a simple seminal function x_i^k/x_i^* provides a good approximation. We shall displace the ideal farther and farther away from the two values in question, as in Table 6-4.

Observe that in the last two columns, the discriminatory power of the ideal diminishes as its value approaches large numbers. Under such conditions a person might attempt to use the anti-ideal since its discriminatory power would still be preserved.

Table 6-4

No.	Vector	$\dfrac{x_i^k}{x_i^*}$	$(x_i^* - x_i^k)$
1	(5, 10, 11)	(.45, .9, 1)	(6, 1, 0)
2	(5, 10, 20)	(.25, .5, 1)	(15, 10, 0)
3	(5, 10, 100)	(.05, .1, 1)	(95, 90, 0)
4	(5, 10, 500)	(.01, .02, 1)	(495, 490, 0)
5	(5, 10, 1000)	(.005, .01, 1)	(995, 990, 0)
.	.	.	.
.	.	.	.
.	.	.	.
∞	(5, 10, ∞)	(0, 0, 1)	(∞, ∞, 0)

Naturally, the compromise set based on the ideal is not identical with the compromise set based on the anti-ideal. This fact can be used in further reducing the set of available solutions by considering the intersection of the two compromises. This possibility is illustrated in Fig. 6-4.

6-6.3 Perception of the Ideal

Quite often the decision maker or analyst is unable to measure or specify the ideal point in an exact way. Not being able to obtain a point-valued estimate one must deal with a fuzzy-valued assessment of its location.

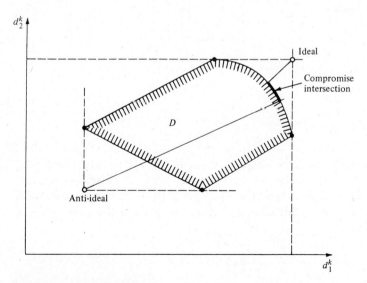

Figure 6-4 Ideal and anti-ideal.

That is, instead of stating that the maximum value of an attribute is, for example, equal to 100, we learn that it is somewhere in *the vicinity of 100*, *not much larger than 100*, or *quite beyond 100*. Again, fuzzy intervals must be set up, and the corresponding membership functions established. The ideal "point" is not then perceived as a point but rather as a cloud, larger or smaller according to given circumstances.

Because the axiom of choice refers to the *perceived* ideal, the fuzziness of the ideal's definition will have a considerable impact on its discriminatory power, as well as on the choice ultimately derived from it.

Observe that fuzzy intervals should not be confused with a priori probabilities. It is becoming increasingly clear that in many real-world decision situations fuzziness rather than randomness is the major source of imprecision. Thus the point-valued probabilistic evaluations of multiple criteria should not be substituted for the fuzzy-valued nature of a decision problem in general. In Fig. 6-5 we introduce the *hazy cloud*, which describes the ideal point in more complex cases.

The fuzziness of the ideal point's definition allows it to be perceived as being displaced when it is actually not displaced and vice versa. As Professor Dawes has suggested in a personal exchange, it can also be utilized as a tool for manipulating and influencing human choices. If a "phony displacement" of the ideal can be successfully implanted in human minds, via advertising, promotion, or persuasion, people will be subtly forced to make choices they would not make if the location of the ideal alternative could be safely determined.

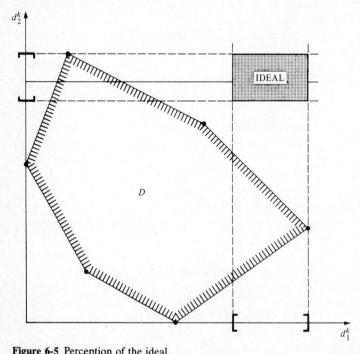

Figure 6-5 Perception of the ideal.

Through indirect and implicit manipulation of "unavailable alternatives," people can be skillfully led against their true wills. The axiom of choice has often been subconsciously utilized by successful advertisers.

A better understanding of these mechanisms will help decision makers to recognize phony displacements and to search for the true location of the ideal before completing the path toward a decision.

6-6.4 Concluding Remarks

The concept of an ideal is becoming a powerful paradigm competing with the traditional concept of optimality. Engineers and planners use it in the guise of ideal system or idealized design, and organizational theorists talk about an ideal organization: establishing a point of reference against which human values and preferences can be measured. Yet the concept itself is often misunderstood.

It is not the main purpose of the ideal-seeking process to produce a utopia, an ideal system. It is the *progress* toward one or more ideals, not its absolute attainment, that brings about the instrumentality and expressibility of values. It is the amount of progress toward an ideal which can be measured. Establishing an ideal stimulates creativity and invention of new means and alternative ways to approach it. It gives direction to the process of generating new alternatives.

The displacement of an ideal reflects continuing change and adjustments characterizing human values and preferences. In one sense, an ideal can never be reached: it is being displaced by the very process leading to its attainment. It is the best *ideal-seeking* system, not the ideal itself, which is to be the outcome of our design and decision-making efforts.

Modern decision theory is directed toward understanding and description of the ideal-seeking decision dynamics. We cannot understand the "it" without understanding the "process leading to it." All decisions and all solutions are relative to the process and circumstances bringing them about and to the ideal which both characterizes the current situation and reflects our immediate preferences and values. Good decision makers search for and try to attain ideals, but are not reluctant to displace them when circumstances change. Good decision makers create good ideal-setting and ideal-seeking systems; neither dreaming of utopia and absolute truth nor embracing mediocrity of satisfaction. An ideal-seeking system is not short-term oriented. It has been said that in the long term we are all dead. True. Seeking a long-term, shifting ideal, however, does not rob you of short-term benefits and pleasures, which are still there, but now they acquire a framework in which they can be historically placed and understood—they acquire meaning.

We have talked about anti-ideal, the fuzziness of perceiving an ideal, its frequent displacements. The multiplicity of ideals is at least a potential. Any alternative dominating the ideal, a supra-ideal, could serve as a point of reference. Any anti-ideal could serve as a point of departure. There are now theories which show that *any* point of reference could order our preferences in a consistent manner. Humans seem to entertain, at any one time, many ideals defined on nonintersecting sets of criteria. You might seek cost-profit ideal *and*

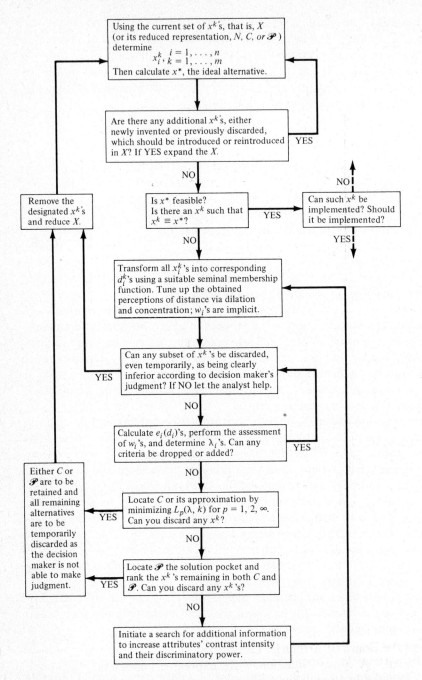

Figure 6-6 Flowchart of the ideal-seeking decision process. *See Sec. 7-1.1 for appropriate definitions.

beauty-fulfillment ideal at the same time. Although such ideals are interconnected, through a supra-ideal of sorts, one does experience conflict between ideals as often as conflict between available alternatives and the ideal. Again, "the process leading to it" is often more important than the "it" itself.

As we shall see in Chapter 10, searching for an ideal is not just a matter of setting the ideal, but also of measuring the distance to it and its re-definition or displacement. Decision making is a process, a search-learning process of considerable challenge.

We conclude this chapter by presenting a flowchart of the ideal-seeking decision process in Fig. 6–6. This diagram represents a more operational extension of the decision process displayed in Sec. 3–6. The reader is advised to compare Figs. 6–6 and 3–2 in order to appreciate how operational models can be built from conceptual models. It is important to realize that the diagram in Fig. 6–6 is only one of many possible models of the underlying decision process.

6-7 BIBLIOGRAPHICAL NOTE

Models related to the approximation and displacement of the ideal solution are consistently treated in the works of Zeleny (1973, 1974, 1975, 1976, 1977, and 1981). This approach departs from classical utility maximization quite substantially, and many researchers view the ideal solution as a source of some arbitrariness in the modeling. Nevertheless, the author continues to find it conceptually sound, descriptive, flexible, dynamic, and capable of a large variety of extensions and adaptations. Recent works of Gearhart (1979), Roy (1977), Yager (1978), and Ackoff (1978) attest to its increasing viability and acceptance. It is very likely that this approach will become the core of a new theory of economic behavior of individuals and firms.

For further study of fuzzy sets, the reader should consult the early works of Zadeh (1973, 1974). And the seminal article on the application of fuzzy sets in decision making, by Bellman and Zadeh (1970), is a must. It is one of the few "fuzzy" papers to find its way into *Management Science*. As of today there are no textbooks or monographs which can be recommended without reservations—the articles mentioned are still the most inspiring, most illustrative, and written in readable English. In this case at least, the master is still better than his apprentices. (There is even a journal, *Fuzzy Sets and Systems*, for those who would really like to get into the thing).

What about the practice of "fuzzy management"? Robert K. Mueller, Chairman of the Board of Arthur D. Little, Inc., starts his recent book with a chapter entitled "A Fuzzy Situation." He expresses hopes that "someday managers will be able to use the fuzzy set theory to help to provide a better grammar for conflict dissolution" [sic].

A direct application of the theory of fuzzy sets in the theory of MCDM can be found in a rare and unusual review of Blin (1977). Some previous knowledge of fuzzy sets is necessary for its comprehension. It is important to note that the theory of fuzzy sets has become very popular in Japan, the U.S.S.R., Romania, France, and Germany. Interest in the United States, especially among OR/MS researchers, is still lacking.

Ackoff, R. L.: *A Concept of Corporate Planning*, Wiley, New York, 1970.
———: *The Art of Problem Solving*, Wiley, New York, 1978.
Aubin, J. P., and B. Näslund: "An Exterior Branching Algorithm," Working Pap. 72-42, European Institute for Advanced Studies in Management, Brussels, November 1972.
Bellman, R., and L. Zadeh: "Decision-Making in a Fuzzy Environment," *Management Science*, vol. 17, no. 4, pp. B141-164.
Benayoun, R., and J. Tergny: "Critères multiples en programmation mathematique: une solution dans la cas linéaire," *Revue Française d'Automatique, d'Informatique et de Recherche Opérationelle*, vol. 3, no. V-2, 1969, pp. 31-56.
———, J. de Montgolfier, J. Tergny, and O. Larichev: "Linear Programming with Multiple Objective Functions: STEP Method (STEM)," *Mathematical Programming*, vol. 1, no. 3, 1971, pp. 366-375.
Blin, J. M.: "Fuzzy Sets in Multiple Criteria Decision-Making," in M. K. Starr and M. Zeleny (eds.), *Multiple Criteria Decision Making*, TIMS Studies in the Management Sciences, vol. 6, North-Holland Publishing, Amsterdam, 1977, pp. 129-146.
Coombs, C. H.: "On the Use of Inconsistency of Preferences in Psychological Measurement," *Journal of Experimental Psychology*, vol. 55, 1958, pp. 1-7.
Dinkelbach, W.: "Über einen Lösungansatz zum Vektormaximumproblem," in M. Beckmann (ed.), *Unternehemensforschung Heute*, Springer-Verlag, Berlin, 1971, pp. 1-13.
Gearhart, W. B.: "Compromise Solutions and Estimation of the Noninferior Set," *Journal of Optimization Theory and Applications*, vol. 28, 1979, pp. 29-47.
Geoffrion, A. M.: "A Parametric Programming Solution to the Vector Maximum Problem, with Applications to Decisions under Uncertainty," Operations Research Program, Tech. Rep. 11, Stanford University, February 1965, p. 2.
Jüttler, H.: "Lineinaia Model s Neskolkimi Celovimi Funkciami, *Ekonomika i Matematicheskoe Metody*, vol. 3, no. 3, 1967, pp. 397-406.
Mueller, R. K.: *Career Conflict: Management's Inelegant Dysfunction*, Heath, Lexington, Mass., 1978.
Radzikowski, W.: "Die Berücksichtigung Mehrerer Zielfunktionen bei Aufgaben der Linearen Optimierung," *Wirtschaftswissenschaft*, vol. 5, 1967, pp. 797-806.
Roy, B.: "A Conceptual Framework for a Prescriptive Theory of 'Decision Aid'," in M. K. Starr and M. Zeleny (eds.), *Multiple Criteria Decision Making*, TIMS Studies in the Management Sciences, vol. 6, North-Holland Publishing, Amsterdam, 1977, pp. 179-210.
Saska, J.: "Lineární Multiprogramování," *Ekonomicko-matematický Obzor*, vol. 4, no. 3, 1968, pp. 359-373.
Yager, R.: "Competitiveness and Compensation in Decision Making: A Fuzzy Set Based Interpretation," Iona College Tech. Rep. RRY 78-14, New Rochelle, N.Y., 1978.
Yu, P. L.: "A Class of Solutions for Group Decision Problems," *Management Science*, vol. 19, no. 8, 1973, pp. 936-946.
Zadeh, L. A.: "A Fuzzy-Algorithmic Approach to the Definition of Complex or Imprecise Concepts," Electronics Research Lab. Memorandum ERL-M474, College of Engineering, University of California, Berkeley, 1974.
———: "Outline of a New Approach to the Analysis of Complex Systems and Decision Processes," in J. L. Cochrane and M. Zeleny (eds.), *Multiple Criteria Decision Making*, University of South Carolina Press, Columbia, 1973, pp. 686-725.
Zeleny, M.: "Descriptive Decision Making and its Applications," in R. L. Schultz (ed.), *Applications of Management Science*, vol. 1, JAI Press, Greenwich, Conn., 1981, pp. 327-388.
———: "Adaptive Displacement of Preferences in Decision Making," in M. K. Starr and M. Zeleny (eds.), *Multiple Criteria Decision Making*, TIMS Studies in the Management Sciences, vol. 6, North-Holland Publishing, Amsterdam, 1977, pp. 147-157.

———: "The Theory of the Displaced Ideal," in M. Zeleny (ed.), *Multiple Criteria Decision Making: Kyoto 1975*, Springer-Verlag, New York, 1976, pp. 153–206.

———: "Compromise Programming," in J. L. Cochrane and M. Zeleny (eds.), *Multiple Criteria Decision Making*, University of South Carolina Press, Columbia, 1973, pp. 262–301.

———: "The Attribute-Dynamic Attitude Model (ADAM)," *Management Science*, vol. 23, no. 1, September 1976, pp. 12–26.

———: "A Concept of Compromise Solutions and the Method of the Displaced Ideal," *Computers and Operations Research*, vol. 1, no. 4, 1974, pp. 479–496.

6-8 PROBLEMS

6-1 Can you explain the difference between fuzziness and probability? Consider the following: There are four persons, aged 16, 28, 35, and 45. Which one of them is *young*? Can any of them be more or less young (not "younger") than another? Is a person either young or not-young? The probability of selecting a particular person at random (e.g., by lottery drawing) is .25. What is the probability of selecting a young person? What is the probability that a given person is young? What is the possibility that a given person is young? Is there any difference between probability and possibility? (If you prefer you can replace "young" with "tall," "red," "very young," etc.)

Would your assessments of fuzziness change if the 45-year-old person in the group were replaced by an 85-year-old? Would it affect your thinking about the situation? How? What if the 85-year-old replaced the 16-year-old?

6-2 Your boss asks you to provide a rough assessment of the budgetary requirements for a future project in order to find out whether the cost will be low, medium, or high. You estimate that anything below $5000 would be "low" and above $10,000 would be "high." A cost in between would be "medium." Of course, you are quite uncertain about the true amount; this is why the boss asks for only a verbal evaluation.

(*a*) What about $4990, $5010, and $9990? Which ones are low and which ones are medium? What about $1000? Is that also "low"?

(*b*) How would you go about preparing the report for your boss? Could the theory of fuzzy sets be of any use?

(*c*) Analyze similar situations involving age (old or young), income (low, medium, high), and education (low, high levels). Are there any differences among the three attributes? How would you handle them in combination?

6-3 Consider the following eight alternatives evaluated with respect to three criteria:

	f_1	f_2	f_3
1	66	31	−12
2	48	60	12
3	36	12	72
4	24	66	66
5	60	20	−20
6	15	−15	75
7	30	30	15
8	20	80	20

Any set of rows in this matrix is called a "primitive subset" of the matrix if (1) the column minima of the subset occur in distinct rows, and (2) no row of the matrix strictly dominates (i.e., *all* its components are larger than) the row of subset minima. For example, form a subset from rows 3, 4, and 7.

	f_1	f_2	f_3
3	36	(12)	72
4	(24)	66	66
7	30	30	(15)

The minima are circled. Verify that rows 3, 4, and 7 form a primitive subset.

(a) Do rows 1, 3, and 5 and rows 1, 3, and 4 form primitive subsets?

(b) Verify that the rows forming a primitive subset (and their corresponding alternatives) are nondominated.

(c) What is the significance of (b)? Rom and Hung[1] suggest that the concept of nondominance is thus extended from being a property of a point to being a property of a set of points. How are the components of a primitive subset interrelated? Interpret the primitive subsets of a nondominated set as potential solution clusters to the MCDM problem.

6-4 With reference to Prob. 6-3, consider the following exercises:

(a) Can the definition of a primitive subset be restated in terms of *maxima* rather than minima?

(b) Can the concepts of the ideal and anti-ideal be usefully incorporated?

(c) Devise a criterion which would differentiate or rank individual primitive subsets of a given matrix. For example, rows 3, 4, and 7 form a subset in which each of the rows is inferior with respect to a different attribute.

6-5 Let f^*_i and f_{i*} denote the ideal and anti-ideal values respectively. What are the implications of the following relationship:

$$\frac{f^*_i - f_i}{f^*_i - f_{i*}} + \frac{f_i - f_{i*}}{f^*_i - f_{i*}} = 1$$

where f_i is any value between f_{i*} and f^*_i.

(a) Devise a graphic two-dimensional analysis of the above relationship.

(b) Consider two problems:

$$\text{Minimize the maximum of } \left(\frac{f^*_i - f_i}{f^*_i - f_{i*}}\right) \quad \text{for } i = 1, 2$$

$$\text{Maximize the minimum of } \left(\frac{f_i - f_{i*}}{f^*_i - f_{i*}}\right) \quad \text{for } i = 1, 2$$

over a graphically chosen polyhedral feasible region. Do the two problems have a common solution? Under what conditions?

6-6 Consider a fuzzy subset of the set of human ages ranging from 0 to 100. Let us refer to this subset as "young." Obviously young is a fuzzy subset of [0, 100] because we cannot specify precise and unambiguous boundaries (e.g., age 35) which would separate youngs from nonyoungs. We can only assess a *degree of compatibility* of a particular age, say 28, with the fuzzy label "young." That is, "John (who is 28) is *young*" is a true proposition to a degree, say 0.7 on a scale from 0 to 1. Number 0.7 is referred to as a "degree of membership" of an object (John) in a fuzzy subset (young).

---

[1] Rom, W. O., and M. S. Hung: "Application of Primitive Sets to Multi-Criteria Optimization Problems," *Journal of Mathematical Economics*, vol. 7, no. 1, 1980, pp. 77–90.

(a) A possible membership function can be defined as follows:

$$m_{\text{young}}\,(\text{age}) = 1 - f(\text{age}) = 0 \qquad\qquad\quad \text{for age} \leqq 20$$
$$= 2\left(\frac{\text{age} - 20}{40 - 20}\right)^2 \qquad \text{for } 20 \leqq \text{ age} \leqq 30$$

$$\text{where} \qquad f\,(\text{age}) = 1 - 2\left(\frac{\text{age} - 40}{40 - 20}\right)^2 \qquad \text{for } 30 \leqq \text{ age} \leqq 40$$
$$= 1 \qquad\qquad\qquad\quad \text{for age} \geqq 40$$

Numbers m associate a degree of membership in "young" for each age. Draw a graphic representation of function m_{young} (age).

(b) Evaluate the following group of people (their ages given) with respect to their compatibility with the designation "young" according to the function postulated in (a):

(Karen, 18; Martin, 20; John, 28; Leo, 29; Joe, 30)

(c) If John is young to a degree 0.68, consider the following:
You heard that John is "young"; what is the *possibility*, given that statement, that John is 28? Could the degree of possibility be 0.68? Interpret. What can be said about the *probability* that John is 28, given that he is young?

6-7 The following table of "social indicators," measured for eighteen metropolitan areas, was published in *The New York Times* of October 21, 1973:

	Unemployment	Poverty	Income level	Housing	Health	Mental health	Public order	Racial equality	Community concern	Citizen participation	Education	Transportation	Air quality	Social disintegration
New York	9	9	4	17	9	1	18	1	18	14	9	1	10	7
Los Angeles	18	15	3	10	2	17	11	3	17	11	3	7	8	3
Chicago	2	5	5	13	18	3	14	6	15	2	7	13	16	1
Philadelphia	7	9	14	9	17	13	6	9	10	8	13	2	15	-
Detroit	17	3	1	5	12	15	17	8	7	5	13	8	14	-
San Francisco	16	17	2	14	2	18	13	2	13	7	2	16	1	5
Washington	1	2	8	11	5	7	15	7	16	18	1	10	3	6
Boston	4	1	17	18	6	10	3	-	12	2	6	15	5	4
Pittsburgh	14	12	13	3	11	11	5	5	2	2	13	3	17	-
St. Louis	10	13	12	8	10	4	9	11	6	11	17	14	18	2
Baltimore	5	11	16	4	15	14	16	4	14	14	18	9	11	-
Cleveland	12	7	9	15	8	16	10	12	1	9	9	6	13	-
Houston	5	17	11	1	16	12	12	10	11	16	9	17	5	-
Minneapolis	14	4	6	6	1	5	7	-	5	1	3	11	2	-
Dallas	3	16	7	2	14	6	8	-	9	16	3	4	3	-
Milwaukee	10	5	15	16	4	8	1	-	8	5	7	4	11	-
Cincinnati	7	14	10	7	7	9	2	-	3	11	13	12	9	-
Buffalo	12	8	18	12	13	2	4	-	4	10	9	18	5	-

In this table, the numbers represent *rankings* of the areas in terms of their "desirability": 1 is the best; 18 is the worst. (Dashes in the table indicate that data were not available.) These rankings were derived from statistical data; e.g., mental health was measured by reported suicides per 100,000 population, educational attainment by median school years completed by adults, etc.

(a) How meaningful would it be to combine the data into some overall index of the quality of life? Why is it important to keep the dimensions separate? Or is it?

(b) Suppose that the criteria used are the ones of importance to you and that you accept their underlying statistical measurements. Prepare an analysis which would support your choice of the "best" metropolitan area.

(c) What are the nondominated areas? Which area is the closest to the ideal city?

6-8 Let us test your understanding of *possibility* and *probability* and their relationship. Consider the following fuzzy statement: "John had *a few* drinks before dinner." In the universe of a possible number of drinks [1, 2, 3, 4, . . .] "a few" refers to its particular fuzzy subset. In the table below some degrees of possibility and probabilities are given:

Number of drinks	1	2	3	4	5	6	7	8	. . .
Degree of possibility	.8	1	1	.8	.6	.1	.01	0	. . .
Probability	.1	.7	.2	0	0	0	0	0	. . .

Degrees of possibility refer to such modifiers as "quite possible" (.8), "very possible" (1.0), "slightly possible" (.6), etc.

(a) Do "highly possible" and "highly probable" mean the same thing? If so, under what conditions?

(b) If an event is impossible, it is bound to be improbable, *not vice versa*. True or false?

(c) Consider: "John had *quite a few* drinks." How might the degrees of possibility be affected? How might the probabilities be affected?

6-9 Consider two groups of people with their ages given:

$$A \text{ (Karen, 18; Martin, 20; John, 28; Leo, 29; Joe, 30)}$$

$$B \text{ (Janice, 26; Joe, 30; John, 28; Hans, 45; Lotfi, 50)}$$

Consider the statement, made independently within the context of each group, "John is *very young*."

(a) Is it likely that the statement would carry the same connotation within the contexts of A and B? That is, is the compatibility of "very young" with 28 unaffected by the context?

(b) Consider a simplified membership function for "very young":

$$m_{very \ young} \ (age) = \frac{age_{max} - age}{age_{max} - age_{min}}$$

where age_{max} and age_{min} refer to the extreme ages characterizing each group. Interpret both groups with respect to this function. What if the two groups are combined into one group?

(c) Relate the results in (b) with the theory of the displaced ideal. Is there any connection?

6-10 Consider two points $x = (14, 13)$ and $y = (4, 4)$ in a two-dimensional space. Employing the following general measure of "distance" between x and y.

$$d_p = \left\{ \sum_{i=1}^{n} |x_i - y_i|^p \right\}^{1/p}$$

explore the behavior of numerical values of d_p for parameter p changing from 1 to ∞.

(*a*) Draw a diagram of function $d_p = f(p)$. What are the general properties of such a function?

(*b*) Perform the same analysis for p changing from 0 to 1 and also from $-\infty$ to 0. Do these cases allow any meaningful interpretation?

(*c*) A more difficult but very rewarding exercise: Do these distance measures, especially for p between 1 and ∞, correspond to any particular subfamily of utility (or preference) functions? Can you identify such a subclass?

(*d*) Perform the following graphic exercise: Define a point $y = (0, 0)$ in a two-dimensional space. Plot all such points x whose distance from y is equal to a fixed number r, that is, $d_p = r$. (Choose r equal to 1 or 10.) Draw such loci of points x for p ranging from 1 to ∞. (Pay special attention to $p = 1, 2, \infty$.) Do the resulting "shapes" suggest any connection with utility functions?

(*e*) Are there some points in (*d*) which have the same distance from point y regardless of the value of p? What are the other characteristics and possible interpretations of such points?

By the very nature of most MCDM techniques, individual dimensions, criteria, and objectives are weighted according to their relative importance. The alternative would be to consider all criteria to be of equal importance or salience.

It seems obvious that people attach different importance to different attributes. They say, "Looks are not as important as personality and intelligence," or, "I have to pay attention to price as much as to quality," or, "Increasing market share is now more important than profits," etc. How can these weights be elicited, quantified, and used operationally?

In this chapter, we review first some classical methods of deriving weights of attribute importance through more or less elaborate batteries of questions and interviews. Although some of these techniques are widely used, they have not proven to be adequate and reliable in capturing what is needed.

We then relate the concept of attribute importance to the amount of information which can be transmitted to the decision maker through a given attribute variable. This amount of information can be measured by a suitably adapted *entropy measure*. There is a short digression on entropy, a simple and nontechnical introduction to the concept.

Several numerical examples showing how to calculate weights of importance via entropy also show how attribute importance can be intrinsically related to a given, particular set of decision alternatives. Any changes in the set of alternatives are then translated into the corresponding changes in the weights of importance.

We conclude this chapter with a rather extensive discussion of the potential usefulness of the information-related concept of attribute weights in studying consumer behavior and advertising implications. Understanding why people consume alcoholic beverages, particularly beer and wine, how they choose their preferred brands, and why the answers are not often what they seem to be—that is our task.

MEASURING ATTRIBUTE IMPORTANCE

There are no irrational customers, there are only lazy merchants. If the customers don't behave the way you think they should behave, don't say, "They're irrational." And don't start "reeducating" them–that's not the merchant's job. His job is to satisfy customers and to make them want to come back. If they don't behave rationally, go out and look at the store and the merchandise through the customers' eyes. You'll always find that they behave rationally, only their reality is different from yours.

Uncle Henry[1]

A consumer, as a decision maker, asserts that price is of primary importance among the attributes characterizing a given product, and then chooses the most expensive item; a professor declares that it is the prestige of a prospective university which is most important to him, and then chooses one which pays more; an executive insists on maximizing profits, and then invests in a project promising the safest return—how can we predict such shifts in what is considered an "important" attribute? How do we measure importance? How is the notion of attribute importance dependent on a particular choice situation?

Can the "inconsistent" behavior described above be considered irrational? Well, "Uncle Henry" does not think so—and he knows!

What is then a correct weight of importance? Is it the one stated by the decision maker *before* facing the choice situation, or is it the one implied by the real act of choice, i.e., confirmable only *after* the choice is made?

Corresponding to these two possibilities, there are two fundamentally different ways of eliciting weights of attribute importance: (1) *direct explication,* through interviews, questionnaires, preference or trade-off interrogation, and similar approaches (we shall deal with some of them in Chap. 12, especially in Sec. 12-4.5); (2) *indirect explication*, in which the decision maker performs a series of overall evaluations of a number of alternatives, e.g., ranking. Through the multiple regression approach, weights are then explicated. The decision maker's overall evaluations are related to the corresponding attribute levels of the alternatives. We shall deal with this approach more fully in Chap. 13.

[1]As quoted in Peter Drucker's *Adventures of a Bystander,* Harper & Row, New York, 1979, p. 200.

Both approaches are based on the belief that weights of attribute importance are somehow fixed (at least temporarily) in the decision maker's head, independently of the actual decision situation. Therefore, they can be "extracted." What are some of the classical approaches of extraction?

The simplest approach is to have the decision maker rank the attributes in order of their importance, e.g., low importance—1, average importance—2, high importance—3, utmost importance—4, etc. Such ranking of importance can be either *preemptive* or *additive*. Preemptive ranking means that only the highest ranked attribute is considered, and all the remaining ones are excluded from the analysis—they are assumed not to be important at all. After the highest ranked attribute has been fully analyzed, one then moves to the next highest one, and so on. This approach is dealt with in some detail in Chap. 9. Additive ranking (or weighting) means that all weights have a simultaneous effect. They can be summed and normalized. That is, each weight can be divided by the sum of all relevant weights so that they add to unity. As one can readily see, ranking has nothing to say about the differences in importance of attributes. The fifth-ranked is always five times as "important" as the first-ranked attribute, regardless of the actual differences.

A special case of ranking is *rating*, which asks questions such as, What is the relative importance of a given attribute on a scale of 1 to 5? This method is almost as simple as ranking and equally inadequate.

Or, in order to capture the differences among weights, we may ask, How many times is attribute i more important than attribute j? A decision maker is then being asked to determine the *ratio* of importance for every conceivable pair of attributes.

A matrix of these ratios can be formed—see Saaty and Khouja (1976)—and the eigenvector of the matrix then provides the set of weights that is most consistent with those ratios. But the number of comparison ratios needed can become excessive, and there is no assurance that what have been derived are actually weights of attribute importance.

One can also ask the decision maker to *allocate* (say, 100 points) among the available attributes. One has to make sure that the weights derived add up to 100.

It is disturbing that each of these methods would elicit a different set of attribute weights from an identical group of respondents.

A sophisticated extension of the rating approach was provided by Churchman and Ackoff (1954) in their *successive comparison* technique. This is an arbitrary, cumbersome, and hard to understand weight-elicitation approach—readers are invited to judge the reference for themselves.

Even more sophisticated is the *indifference trade-off* method; for example, see, Keeney and Nair (1977). One attempts to establish so-called "marginal rate of substitution" between two attributes. The type of question asked is, What is the maximum amount of attribute i that you would be willing to give up in order to obtain a (prespecified) additional amount of attribute j?

A probabilistic version of the trade-off method is the *lottery* method used in decision analysis (see Sec. 12-4.5 for a quick overview). This approach is based on the assumption that decision makers behave in accord with the maximization of the von Neumann-Morgenstern expected utility—but this presupposition has not yet been empirically verified. One could always say that they *should* behave this way, but thinking about hypothetical lotteries or gambles is foreign, unrealistic, and inappropriately difficult in the view of most decision makers; see, for example, Otway and Edwards (1977), or our illustration in Sec. 12-6.

Among the methods of indirect explication of weights, the most prominent are so-called "policy capturing" techniques (see Chap. 13). A decision maker must evaluate a large number of alternatives—at least as many as there are attributes, but preferably many more—and these "holistic" evaluations are then regressed against attribute scores, usually via linear regression. A major problem arises when there is some dependency among the attributes: Different sets of weights will be derived if global evaluations are made over different sets of alternatives by the same decision maker. We address this issue in Sec. 13-4.

All the approaches discussed so far assume that the weights of attribute importance are purely subjective and can thus be extricated in relative independence from a particular choice situation. In the next section we shall introduce an "objective" or external factor of attribute importance. That is, attribute importance is as much a property of an attribute as it is of a decision maker. If all available alternatives score about equally with respect to a given attribute, then such an attribute will be judged unimportant by most decision makers. Such an attribute does not help in making a decision.

7-1 WEIGHTS AND THEIR ASSESSMENT

Membership functions L_p and L_p' discussed in Chap. 6 contain explicit parameters λ_i, the weights of attribute importance. It is reasonable to assume that attributes do weigh differently on the outcome of the decision-making process. The problem is, can the differences in attribute importance be captured fully by λ_i's, or are they implicitly reflected in the assignment of d_i^k, or are they to be derived as a combination of both concepts? Beckwith and Lehmann state:

> Thus we conclude that individuals do tend to spread their perceptions more on the attributes which they consider to be more important. We would expect that differential weights might be more useful than uniform weights in cases where the measured attributes are objective rather than subjective, as respondents might reflect their weights less in the dispersion of their perceptions. (Beckwith and Lehmann 1973, p. 144)

This hypothesis of course had already originated with Festinger:

> Evaluation of the alternatives in the pre-decision period is a very systematic affair in the course of which the alternatives are reinterpreted so as to produce greater and greater di-

vergence in attractiveness. When the divergence becomes great enough, the person is finally able to make a decision. (Festinger 1964, p. 4)

Let us view decision making as an information-processing activity. Decision-relevant information about the available alternatives is transmitted, perceived, and processed via their attributes. In this sense the attributes serve as *information sources*. The more information is emitted by the ith information source (i.e., the ith attribute), the more relevant (or the more salient) is the attribute in a given decision situation.

How does this information concept relate to the subjectively assessed and a priori determined notion of attribute importance? Moinpur and Wiley (1974) report that good predictions were obtained using unweighted scores on important attributes, but *also* using such scores on attributes nominally declared unimportant. In fact, in some situations, accurate predictions can be made from given attribute scores at all levels of importance.

Obviously, most a priori declared weights are independent of the actual attribute information transmitted. *In that sense they are to be used for the initial selection of salient attributes only.* From the entire universe of relevant attributes we select a smaller number, usually five to nine, by assigning weights w_i. This *primary weighting* is intended to identify which attributes will be considered initially. Then these attributes again become undifferentiated in terms of their importance. Scores are then assigned and evaluated with respect to a particular set of alternatives. Their informational significance is thus established and a *secondary weighting* (actually the more important one) can take place. Some of the initially important attributes might "fail" the information criterion and later be discarded. Under special circumstances (e.g., when most a priori important attributes do not transmit sufficient decision information) some originally nonsalient attributes can be added to the initial set.

Definition A *weight of attribute importance* λ_i, assigned to the ith attribute as a measure of its relative importance in a given decision situation, is directly related to the average intrinsic information generated by the given set of feasible alternatives through the ith attribute, and, in parallel, to the subjective assessment of its importance, reflecting the decision maker's cultural, psychological, and environmental history.

Observe that two components enter into the formation of λ_i:

1. A relatively stable concept of a priori attribute importance w_i, reflecting an individual's cultural, genetic, psychological, societal, and environmental background.
2. A relatively unstable, context-dependent concept of informational importance, say $\bar{\lambda}_i$, based on a particular set of feasible alternatives, a given decision situation. These weights are sensitive to any changes in both feasible sets X and D, and thus to fluctuations in the average intrinsic information generated by both.

7-1.1 Entropy Measure of Importance

The above definition of attribute importance becomes operational only if the average intrinsic information transmitted to the decision maker through the ith attribute can be measured. We can adjust the traditional entropy measure to suit this purpose. If you are not familiar with the entropy concept, please consult Sec. 7-1.2 first.

The more distinct and differentiated are the scores, i.e., the larger is the *contrast intensity* of the ith attribute, the greater is the amount of "decision information" contained in and transmitted by the attribute.

Recall that a vector $d_i = (d_i^1, \ldots, d_i^m)$ characterizes the set D in terms of the ith attribute. Let us define:

$$D_i = \sum_{k=1}^{m} d_i^k \qquad i = 1, \ldots, n$$

Then the entropy measure of the ith attribute contrast intensity is

$$e(d_i) = -K \sum_{k=1}^{m} \frac{d_i^k}{D_i} \ln \frac{d_i^k}{D_i}$$

where $K > 0$, ln denotes natural logarithm, and

$$0 \leq d_i^k \leq 1$$
$$e(d_i) \geq 0$$

If all d_i^k become identical for a given i, then $d_i^k/D_i = 1/m$, and $e(d_i)$ assumes its maximum value, that is, $e_{\max} = \ln m$. Thus, by setting $K = 1/e_{\max}$ we achieve $0 \leq e(d_i) \leq 1$ for all d_i's. Such normalization is needed for comparative purposes.

We shall also need a *total entropy* of D, defined as

$$E = \sum_{i=1}^{n} e(d_i)$$

Observe that the larger $e(d_i)$ is, the less information is transmittted by the ith attribute. Actually, if $e(d_i) = e_{\max} = \ln m$, the ith attribute would not transmit any useful information at all. It can be removed from further decision consideration at that time.

Because weights $\tilde{\lambda}_i$ are reversely related to $e(d_i)$, we shall use $1 - e(d_i)$ rather than $e(d_i)$ and normalize to assure that $0 \leq \tilde{\lambda}_i \leq 1$ and $\sum_{i=1}^{n} \tilde{\lambda}_i = 1$:

$$\tilde{\lambda}_i = \frac{1}{n - E} [1 - e(d_i)]$$

Note that any dynamic changes in X or D could lead to a displacement of the ideal point. This, in turn, would induce further changes in d_i^k's and the corresponding changes in their relative contrast intensities. Ultimately such changes get reflected in a new set of $\tilde{\lambda}_i$'s. For example, a removal or an addition of a particular alternative could increase the contrast intensities and thus produce additional decision information. Or the opposite could occur: The informational richness could be diminished by such events. Similar effects can be achieved by actually removing or adding an attribute.

The less divergent the scores d^k_i are, the smaller is $\tilde{\lambda}_i$, and the less important the ith attribute becomes. If all the attribute scores are equal, then $\tilde{\lambda}_i = 0$. The difference between w_i and $\tilde{\lambda}_i$ is clarified in the following example.

Example Let us assume that fluoride content has been designated as the most important attribute on which the decision to select a toothpaste brand should be based, say $w_i = 1$. If it happens that X consists only of brands that are virtually equal with respect to this particular attribute, we see that the "most important" attribute does not allow the decision maker to make a choice on its basis. The ith attribute transmits *no information* to the decision maker, and $\tilde{\lambda}_i = 0$. Some may argue that one can flip a coin in such a situation. Not true. To avoid cognitive dissonance, new attributes must be sought instead. The influence of $w_i = 1$ is entirely negated, and fluoride content becomes the least important attribute. (It could, of course, regain its importance if some brands low in fluoride were added to X.) Thus, the decision maker, in spite of a priori claims and beliefs, might base the *actual* choice on some new attribute—say, taste—which would now become the most important one.

Clearly, both w_i and $\tilde{\lambda}_i$ are determinants of importance in a parallel fashion. If $w_i = 0$, then even $\tilde{\lambda}_i = 1$ does not justify making the ith attribute salient. Similarly, if $\tilde{\lambda}_i = 0$, then even the attribute with $w_i = 1$ becomes irrelevant for making a decision. *The most important attribute is always the one having both w_i and $\tilde{\lambda}_i$ at their highest levels possible.*

Note One possible hypothesis of attribute overall importance weight λ_i can be formulated as follows:

$$\lambda_i = \tilde{\lambda}_i \cdot w_i$$

or after normalization:

$$\lambda_i = \frac{\tilde{\lambda}_i \cdot w_i}{\sum_{i=1}^{n} \tilde{\lambda}_i \cdot w_i} \qquad i = 1, \ldots, n$$

Some numerical examples of how to calculate entropy-based weights of importance can be found in Zeleny (1974) and in Sec. 7-1.3.

7-1.2 A Digression on Entropy

Since we are using the concept of entropy several times in this book (Sec. 4-1.3, 7-1.1, 7-1.5, 10-1, and 11-1 in particular), we shall provide a nontechnical introduction to this simple but powerful *measure of the amount of information* conveyed by a given information source (message, report, measurement, etc.).

The occurrence of any event can usually be estimated by its probability p ($0 \leqq p \leqq 1$). For example, the probability of rain in Moscow for today was estimated to be 20 percent, i.e., $p = .2$. Now, let us suppose that you have just received a message: Yes, it did rain in Moscow today. How much information is contained in that received "yes" (or "no"), and can it be measured? Many would say that such a message carries the same information no matter what; it says that it rained, and there is no need to measure it. But we are interested in the *relative* information conveyed, which might depend on our previous state of uncertainty, ignorance, or confidence.

Suppose that the estimated $p = .001$. Then the message "yes" would cause you quite a surprise. Suppose that $p = 1.0$, that is, it was predicted that it would *certainly* rain. Your reaction to "yes" might be something like "Oh, well"; no surprise. The smaller the probability, the larger the surprise. The amount of surprise, newness, or newsworthiness elicited by the arrival of the message is concomitant with the amount of relative information conveyed by it.

Any function which would decrease as p increased and increase as p decreased would be a candidate as a measure of this relative information. This function should be 0 if $p = 1.0$ and ∞ for $p = 0$. One such function is $h(p) = -\ln p$, that is, a negative natural logarithm, one with the base $e = 2.71828\ldots$. One can check a few values on a pocket calculator. For example $\ln(.25) = -1.386$ and $h(.25) = -(-1.386) = 1.386$. Similarly, $h(.5) = 0.693$, $h(1) = 0$, $h(0.0000000001) = 23$, and $h(0) = \infty$.

Sometimes $\log_2 (p)$ is used, and results appear in bits (*binary digits*) of information. We shall stick with the natural logarithms.

But we are interested in evaluating the information content of a message not after but before its arrival. That is, what is the *expected information content* of a message to be received?

Suppose again that $p = .2$. Then, of course, the probability of no rain is $1 - p = .8$. The message we are going to receive will be either "yes" (it did rain) or "no" (it didn't). The information content of "yes" would be $h(.2) = 1.6$, and the information content of "no" would be $h(.8) = 0.223$. Because of the forecast, $p = 20$ percent, we can expect to receive "yes" with probability $p = .2$ and "no" with probability $1 - p = .8$. So the *expected* information content of the message, regardless of whether it is "yes" or "no," can be computed as follows:

$$H = ph(p) + (1-p)h(1-p) = (.2)(1.6) + (.8)(.223) = 0.498$$

or $\quad H = -p \ln p - (1-p) \ln (1-p)$

$$= -(.2)(-1.6) - (.8)(-.223) = 0.498$$

Given such a measure H of the relative expected information content of a message to be received, we can compare the worthiness of a given message under different *uncertainty conditions*. Let us start with certainty, $p = 1$. Then $H = 1h(1) + 0h(0) = h(1) = 0$. What if $(1 - p) = 0$? Then, $H = 0h(0) + 1h(1) = h(1) = 0$. When we are *certain* that it will or will not rain, then receiving a message confirming the certainty does not carry any information: $H = 0$ in both cases.

Under which conditions would the message convey the largest amount of information? Let us compute H for some representative values of p and $1 - p$:

p	0	.1	.2	.3	.4	.5	.6	.7	.8	.9	1
$1 - p$	1	.9	.8	.7	.6	.5	.4	.3	.2	.1	0
H	0	.325	.5	.61	.673	.693	.673	.61	.5	.325	0

Observe that the highest value of H is .693, that is, when $p = (1 - p) = .5$. That is, Max $H = ph(p) + (1-p)h(1-p) = -2ph(p) = -2(.5)(-\ln .5) = 0.6931471806$.

The next question is, How does one tell whether a given H—say, $H = 0.61$—is large or small? What is its relative magnitude with respect to the largest possible H? For purely comparative purposes we shall measure the amount of information not by H but by $\mathbf{H}$:

$$\mathbf{H} = \frac{H}{H_{\max}}$$

where $H_{\max}$ denotes Max H. With the help of $\mathbf{H}$ we now reevaluate the above table for the rain-no rain message:

p	0	.1	.2	.3	.4	.5	.6	.7	.8	.9	1
$H/H_{\max}$	0	.469	.722	.88	.971	1	.971	.88	.722	.469	0

Observe that $\mathbf{H}$ now reaches its maximum at 1 and its minimum at 0, while all other numbers reflect the degrees of closeness to the maximum as numbers between 0 and 1.

So far we have dealt with only two possible states of nature, rain and no rain. Entropy measure H can of course be generalized to include any finite number of states of nature. Let us illustrate with the following example: The United States dollar can go up, go down, or stay unchanged with respect to the Japanese yen on tomorrow's money market. The probabilities have been assessed as $p_1 = .25$ for up, $p_2 = .05$ for unchanged, and $p_3 = .7$ for down. What is the expected amount of information to be received from our broker in London? Remember that the broker can wire "up," "unchanged," or "down." The overall entropy is:

$$H = -p_1 \ln p_1 - p_2 \ln p_2 - p_3 \ln p_3$$

$$= -(.25) \ln .25 - (.05) \ln .05 - (.7) \ln .7$$

$$= -[(.25)(-1.386) + (.05)(-2.996) + (.7)(-0.357)]$$

$$= -(-0.3465 - 0.1498 - 0.2499) = 0.7462$$

The maximum entropy of the message would be attained if the initial probabilities of "up," "unchanged," and "down" were equal, $p_1 = p_2 = p_3 = \frac{1}{3}$. Then $H_{max} = -3(\frac{1}{3})(-\ln\frac{1}{3}) = 1.0986$. Then **H** = 0.68.

In general, if there are ℓ states of nature with estimated probabilities $p_1, \ldots, p_\ell$, then

$$H = -\sum_{i=1}^{\ell} p_i \ln p_i$$

where Max H is defined when all p_i are equal to one another, that is, $p_i = 1/\ell$ for $i = 1, \ldots, \ell$. Then

$$H_{max} = -\sum_{i=1}^{\ell} 1/\ell \ln 1/\ell$$

Because $\ln 1/\ell$ is a constant, we can put it in front of the summation sign:

$$H_{max} = -\ln 1/\ell \sum_{i=1}^{\ell} 1/\ell = \ln \ell$$

because $\ln 1/\ell = -\ln \ell$. The finding that $H_{max} = \ln \ell$ greatly simplifies our computations.

Entropy[1] is a good measure to be used for evaluating the relative worthiness of different tests or assessment procedures. Suppose that the decision maker is facing ten nondominated solutions from which the best one is to be chosen. They are all equally probable to be the best. A decision analyst suggests a procedure which ascertains which of the ten alternatives is the best. Thus, we have received $\ln 10 = 2.3$ pieces of information. (These "pieces" are called "bits" if $\log_2 10$ is used; we might call them "nits" if natural logarithms, $\log_e 10 = \ln 10$, are used.) Another decision analyst introduces a procedure which reduces the number of nondominated solutions to four. If the best alternative is then pointed out, the amount of information received is $\ln 4 = 1.386$. Consequently, the procedure provided $2.3 - 1.386 = 0.914$ pieces of information. Different "solution pruning" techniques can be evaluated on this basis.

The question of "pruning" or "filtering" of solutions is taken up in greater detail in Sec. 10-6, dealing with interactive procedures. Very often there are too many solutions that are too "close" to each other in the sense of performing almost equally well with respect to the criteria involved. Such *clusters* of solutions can be represented by a typical solution characterizing the cluster and thus only solutions that are sufficiently different can be submitted to the decision maker for assessment.

---

[1] From German *Entropie*; Greek *en* − (in) and *tropē* (a turning, change). Entropy is often interpreted as a measure of the randomness, disorder, or chaos in a system. An interesting treatment of entropy as a measure of disorder brought about by economic activity can be found in J. Rifkin and T. Howard, *Entropy*, Viking, New York, 1980.

7-1.3 A Numerical Example of Entropy Calculations

Consider $k = 1, 2, 3, 4; i = 1, 2, 3;$ and x_i^k's representing measured scores of four alternatives on three attributes, as summarized in Table 7-1.

Table 7-1

k \ i	1	2	3
1	7	(100)	4
2	8	60	4
3	8.5	20	(6)
4	(9)	80	2

Note: Maximum attribute values are circled.

Because the x_i^k's in Table 7-1 are noncommensurable (dollars, points, pounds, etc.), we transform them into degrees of closeness to the point $x^* =$ (9, 100, 6). Using $d_i^k = x_i^k/x_i^*$ we obtain Table 7-2.

Table 7-2

k \ i	1	2	3	Σ
1	.778	(1)	.667	2.445
2	.889	.6	.667	2.156
3	.944	.2	(1)	2.144
4	(1)	.8	.334	2.134
D_i	3.611	2.6	2.668	

Let us assume that the d_i^k's in Table 7-2 are to be left unchanged and their differential contribution is to be modeled by λ_i's. First we calculate $e(d_i)$, the entropy measure of the ith attribute. The results are given in Table 7-3.

Table 7-3 contains the information necessary for calculating $e(d_i)$. We know that $e_{max} = \ln 4 = 1.3863$, and we set $K = 1/e_{max} = .7213$. For $i = 1$ we obtain:

$$e(d_1) = -(.7213) [.216 (\ln .216) + .246 (\ln .246) + .261 (\ln .261) + .277 (\ln .277)]$$

$$= -(.7213)[.216(-1.532) + .246(-1.402) + .261(-1.343) + .277(-1.284)]$$

$$= -(.7213)[-.331 - .345 - .350 - .356] = -(.7213)[-1.382] = .997$$

Table 7-3

k \ i	$\dfrac{d_i^k}{D_i}$			$\dfrac{d_i^k}{D_i\,(\ln d_i^k/D_i)}$		
	1	2	3	1	2	3
1	.216	.385	.25	− .331	− .367	− .347
2	.246	.231	.25	− .345	− .338	− .347
3	.261	.007	.375	− .350	− .197	− .368
4	.277	.307	.125	− .356	− .363	− .260
Σ	1	1	1	− 1.382	− 1.265	− 1.332

In summary, we have calculated:

$$e(d_1) = .997 \qquad e(d_2) = .913 \qquad e(d_3) = .954$$

and E, the sum of all $e(d_i)$, is 2.864. Substituting in the formula for $\tilde{\lambda}_i$ we obtain:

$$\tilde{\lambda}_1 = .022 \qquad \tilde{\lambda}_2 = .64 \qquad \tilde{\lambda}_3 = .338$$

measuring the intrinsic average information transmitted by attributes 1, 2, and 3 respectively.

Let us assume that the w_i's have been separately determined as:

$$w_1 = .8 \qquad w_2 = .1 \qquad w_3 = .1$$

Comparing $\tilde{\lambda}_i$'s and w_i's we see that the relatively large w_1 will be offset by small $\tilde{\lambda}_1$. Since the two remaining attributes are about equally important in terms of w_i, we expect the second attribute to remain the most important one. Using the formula for λ_i we get:

$$\lambda_1 = .153 \qquad \lambda_2 = .555 \qquad \lambda_3 = .292$$

Observe that the assignment of w_i's does not perceptibly influence the relative weights $\tilde{\lambda}_i$'s. However, if $w_1 = .05$, $w_2 = .15$, and $w_3 = .8$, then $\tilde{\lambda}_i$'s are adjusted to $\lambda_1 = .003$, $\lambda_2 = .261$, and $\lambda_3 = .736$.

The values of λ_i's are then substituted directly into $L_p(\lambda, k)$. We shall calculate compromise solutions for $p = 1, 2, \infty$. We transform the table of d_i^k's, Table 7-2, into a table of deviations, Table 7-4.

Table 7-4

k \ i	$(d_i^* - d_i^k)$			$(d_i^* - d_i^k)^2$			$\text{Max}(d_i^* - d_i^k)$
	1	2	3	1	2	3	
1	.222	0	.333	.05	0	.11	.333
2	.111	.4	.333	.01	.16	.11	.4
3	.056	.8	0	.003	.64	0	.8
4	0	.2	.666	0	.04	.443	.666

Next we multiply the deviations by λ_i's, as prescribed by $L_p(\lambda, k)$, and sum the products. The results are summarized in Table 7-5.

Table 7-5

| | $\lambda_i(d^*_i - d^k_i)$ | | | | $\lambda^2_i(d^*_i - d^k_i)^2$ | | | | |
| | 1 | 2 | 3 | Σ | 1 | 2 | 3 | Σ | $\text{Max}\{\lambda_i(d^*_i - d^k_i)\}$ |
k									
1	.034	0	.097	$\boxed{.131}$	.001	0	.009	(.01)	(.097)
2	.017	.222	.097	.336	.000	.049	.009	.058	.222
3	.009	.444	0	.453	.000	.197	0	.197	.444
4	0	.111	.194	.305	0	.012	.038	.05	.194

The minimum values are circled. The first alternative is the closest to the ideal with respect to all p. For comparison purposes let us compute the closest alternative with w_i or $\tilde{\lambda}_i$ instead of λ_i and $p = 1$, as in Table 7-6.

Table 7-6

| | $w_i(d^*_i - d^k_i)$ | | | | $\tilde{\lambda}_i(d^*_i - d^k_i)$ | | | |
k	1	2	3	Σ	1	2	3	Σ
1	.178	0	.033	.211	.005	0	.113	(.118)
2	.089	.04	.033	.162	.002	.256	.113	.371
3	.045	.08	0	.125	.001	.512	0	.513
4	0	.02	.066	(.086)	0	.128	.255	.383

In Table 7-6 observe that w_i's alone would select the fourth alternative as the closest one, while $\tilde{\lambda}_i$'s conform with the choice due to λ_i's, that is, the first alternative.

According to the theory, there is a possibility of weighting the attributes implicitly by contracting or dilating d_i's and then using unweighted $L_p(k)$ instead of $L_p(\lambda, k)$. Note that the initially unadjusted values x^k_i's, assuming $p = 1$, would lead to the choice of the first alternative again. If we are guided by w_i's, that is, $w_1 = .8$, $w_2 = .1$, and $w_3 = .1$, we would dilate the first attribute and contract the other two. Let us use $\alpha = 2$ for dilation and $\alpha = \frac{1}{2}$ for concentration and summarize the results in Table 7-7.

Table 7-7

k	i $(d^k_i)^2$	$(d^k_i)^{1/2}$	$(d^k_i)^{1/2}$	
	1	2	3	Σ
1	.605	1	.817	2.422
2	.79	.775	.817	2.382
3	.891	.447	1	2.338
4	1	.894	.578	(2.472)

Comparing this and the previous results, we see that the implicit weighting (biased toward w_i's) has switched the closest alternative from the first to the fourth, as expected. If the adjustment is guided by $\tilde{\lambda}_i$'s, we would reinforce the choice of the first alternative.

7-1.4 Explicit and Implicit Use of Weights

Observe that d^k_i's represent degrees of closeness to the corresponding anchor value, that is, d^k_i's are derived from the ideal point and thus cannot be determined without its previous specification. Consequently, d^k_i's differ from x^k_i's mainly in the following sense:

The x^k_i's are directly observed attribute scores scaled in dollars, points, degrees, rank, and other units of measurement. They could include both objectively measured and subjectively assigned values, independent of the ideal point. The d^k_i's are, on the other hand, anchor- and ideal-dependent. They must be recalculated after each change in a decision situation. The axiom of choice necessitates that x^k_i's be expressed in terms of d^k_i's, that is, the degrees of closeness to the anchor value.

Weights of attribute importance can enter in many different ways, both explicit and implicit. For example:

1. Obtain x^k_i's and transform them into d^k_i's according to some suitable seminal function, as in Sec. 6-4.2. Then calculate λ_i's in dependency on both $\tilde{\lambda}_i$ and w_i. Observe that human judgment enters on the level of w_i's and, while d^k_i's are kept relatively stable, the necessary flexibility is achieved by manipulating λ_i's in L'_p.
2. Obtain x^k_i's and transform them into d^k_i's *directly*, i.e., as subjective assessments of a distance. Operations of concentration and dilation are then used to interactively "tune up" their values: The important attributes are dilated, and the less important attributes are concentrated. The resulting adjusted d^k_i's are then substituted in $L'_p(k)$ below, and no weights are calculated implicitly:

$$L'_p(k) = \sum_{i=1}^{n} (1 - d^k_i)^p$$

3. Use w_i's to determine salient attributes, i.e., all the attributes that are to be considered initially as relevant to the decision process. Obtain x^k_i's and transform them into d^k_i's. Adjust d^k_i's through dilation and concentration to reflect the implicit w_i's only. Then calculate $\tilde{\lambda}_i$'s and substitute in $L'_p(\tilde{\lambda}, k)$ below:

$$L'_p(\tilde{\lambda}, k) = \sum_{i=1}^{n} \tilde{\lambda}^p_i (1 - d^k_i)^p$$

All adjustments are made through $\tilde{\lambda}_i$'s, while w_i's are not explicitly substituted.

It is too early to state which of the three approaches, if any, will prove to be the most realistic. Each has its appeal, advantages, and disadvantages. It is our impression, however, that a robust decision support system will not be overly sensitive to any one particular approach we use.

7-1.5 Example of Beer

Beer provides a good illustration of the entropy theory of attribute importance. Ackoff and Emshoff (1975) present quite controversial theories of advertising and drinking, which have generated widespread discussion and debate within marketing circles. Beer, in the Ackoff and Emshoff two-part report, is subject to many different interpretations. Our quite different explanation is, we hope, equally appealing. It is important that the discussion of vital ideas move beyond arguments about levels of statistical significance, estimator biases, unexplained variance, and four-decimal-places as in Allaire (1975) and Ackoff and Emshoff (1975). The issues are much too important.[1]

Typically the choice among available brands of beer, as with most other consumer products, is based on a perceived set of salient attributes and criteria. Some of beer's obvious *primary attributes* are, for example, distinct taste, lightness, alcoholic content, quality of ingredients (water, hops, yeast, barley, etc.), acidity, yeastiness, carbonation level, draft or bottled, price, reputation, complementary foods, and type of retail outlet.

The choice among brands becomes more difficult as perceived differences along individual attributes become less pronounced.

The closer together the alternatives (brands of beer) are in their attractiveness, the more information a person seeks out before being ready to arrive at a decision. If the alternatives score about the same along a particular attribute, the information transmitted by the attribute is low, and the attribute does not contribute to a resolution of the predecision conflict.

---

[1]The Ackoff-Emshoff article has been reprinted in R. L. Ackoff, *The Art of Problem Solving*, Wiley, New York, 1978, pp. 162–188. We shall refer to it in this latter form.

Average intrinsic information can be measured through the traditional *entropy measure*. Note that the more distinct and divergent are the scores, i.e., the larger is the *contrast intensity* of the attribute, the greater is the amount of "decision information" contained in and transmitted by the attribute.

Any reevaluation or reinterpretation of attribute scores or perceptions, any addition or removal of brands (alternatives), etc., will change the contrast intensities and thus will be reflected in changed entropies of the attributes. Attribute importance thus changes dynamically with circumstances.

Example Let us assume that consumers have designated that caloric content is the most important attribute in selecting a brand of beer. If it happens that the set of available alternatives consists only of brands that are virtually equal in caloric content, individuals are unable to make a choice based solely on the "most important" attribute. The attribute transmits no information to the decision maker. Either the decision is then forced and a strong postdecision dissonance must be faced, or more likely, *additional, more discriminating attributes must be sought out*. (A more detailed, technical exposition of entropy measure of attribute importance can be found in Sec. 7-1.1.)

There is often a *dynamic shift of salience* to attributes which offer a more substantial differentiation among brands. As a choice based on taste or quality becomes virtually impossible, new attributes and criteria will be brought into the picture. Competition then causes most brands to become equalized and undifferentiated with respect to these additional attributes as well, and the search goes on. The process becomes more difficult and more costly. New attributes, new marks of distinction and criteria, must be created artificially, from without rather than from within the product itself. These *derived attributes* could be quite alienated from the beer itself: package impact, status image, peer association, advertising exposure, social and racial identification, brand-name appeal, personality types, social occasions, etc. The emphasis shifts from natural to artificial attributes; the art of beer making is replaced by the art of beer selling and image making.[1] See also Probs. 7-14 and 7-17.

Because of their alienation from primary product attributes, derived attributes maintain their differentiating power with great difficulty, brand loyalty is not stable, and continuous advertising pressure is required. After brands have become equalized with respect to their primary attributes, it becomes instructive to distinguish between the *numerousness* and *variety* of brands. There is no question that the number of American beers is staggering; hundreds of brands

---

[1]For example, Anheuser-Busch Brewing Company, in trying to expand into England and Germany, is concentrating on advertisements, label and libel suits, and price cutting rather than on trying to match European quality. They are facing Budweiser Budvar Co. of Czechoslovakia, distributing the famous *Budvar* ("Bud") and *Budweiser* (from a thirteenth-century Bohemian brewing town Budweis, now Budějovice). Czechs also produce the original *Pilsner Urquell*, quite different from a variety of light "pils" beers. Even the *Michelob* label derives from an old Bohemian brew, "Michelské."

are available to beer drinkers. Yet the variety of American beers is probably one of the lowest among beer-producing countries. Most brands have no intrinsic, primary characteristics of distinction: They are bland, watery, light, bubbly, low in alcohol—lawn mowers' beers. Over the years American beer drinkers have become conditioned to relying mostly on derived attributes.

In one experiment, Ackoff and Emshoff offered *the same brew*, presented as four different, newly developed brands, to 250 regular United States beer drinkers. The only basis for an intelligent judgment was exposure to commercials extolling a derived attribute, such as personality type. *All* subjects believed that the brands were substantially different!

Two main points were established by this experiment. As primary attributes become retarded,

1. Artificially created attributes are readily substituted
2. The sensitivity of beer drinkers to primary attributes becomes retarded as well

Beer drinkers can be induced to shift from primary to secondary attributes and thus perceive differences which do not exist. The experiment did *not* show that they could be similarly induced not to perceive differences that do exist. That is, should the primary attributes be truly differentiating, the drinkers would presumably be able to make up their own minds, as they did with respect to secondary attributes.

Ackoff and Emshoff interpret this experiment as confirming the following hypothesis of *why* people drink: "Alcoholic beverages are used to produce short-run transformations in personality of the same type produced by maturation in the long run" (Ackoff 1978, p. 184). That is, introverts and extroverts drink to become more introverted or extroverted, and mixed personalities drink to become more "centraverted. [sic]" And you thought that you drank wine because it goes with cheese, or beer because it goes with pork, or simply because your taste buds crave pleasant stimulation!

Obviously, with some people in some situations, the purpose of drinking is the short-run transformation of personality. Alcohol then serves a similar purpose to drugs or intense psychological stimulation. But what about the normal use of alcoholic beverages?

The implications of the personality-transformation view of drinking are profound. If it is accepted, advertising will concentrate more and more on personality segmentation of the market, and advertising messages will stress the personality-transformation capabilities of products. In production, the shift from primary to secondary attributes will progress further. Unable to differentiate along primary attributes, drinkers will be forced more and more to consider personality-related attributes. They will be forced to drink less because they like the beverage and more because of the transformations in personality it promises. There will be more and more drinking of products that are less and less differentiated in terms of quality. The so-called "drinking problem" is thus further intensified rather than ameliorated.

One way of ameliorating the drinking problem is to return to primary attributes and allow consumers to differentiate products at a basic level. The imbibing of high-quality beverages then becomes a part of culinary art and dining culture. Low-quality, undifferentiated, "popular" brews, however, are often drunk only to transform one's personality; encouraging such a trend is more than unfortunate.

Traditional beer-drinking countries produce a large variety of beers, although the actual number of brands may be relatively low. Czechoslovakia, for example, has one of the highest consumptions of beer per capita in the world. It has no significant amount of beer advertising. It offers a large *variety* of beers (insufficient quantity, however) with about twenty brands. They range from light to heavy, from sweet to bitter, from pale to black, from 5 to 18 degrees of the sugar-alcoholic content. A similar situation exists in Belgium and many other countries. Because market shares are based on primary attributes, they are quite stable, brand loyalty is high, and the effects of personality advertising are low. In fact, this type of beer advertising is virtually nonexistent, as is the case with most better wines, even in the United States.

People drink beer *primarily* because they like it—as they drink wine or eat cheese and salami. Only if the primary attributes are retarded and nondifferentiating do the reasons for drinking become associated with derived attributes: Then, some may even drink beer to produce "short-run transformations in personality," as Ackoff and Emshoff suggest.

At one point, there is a significant shift of focus in the Ackoff and Emshoff theory of drinking: "We would not be able to evaluate advertising messages adequately without knowing *why* people drink beer and, more generally, alcoholic beverages" (Ackoff 1978, pp. 176). Beer drinking is thus considered to be on a par with consuming whiskey, gin, vodka, or absinthe. Even hashish, LSD, or grass have similar effects. Even though the reasons for alcoholism and drug addiction are mostly psychological, i.e., related to personality transformation, French and Italian wine drinkers and Czech, Belgian, Danish, and German beer drinkers still enjoy their indulgence for earthier reasons. American beer drinkers are probably not too different. But the simultaneous impact of the numerousness of brands in the hundreds and a variety close to zero leads to frustration of choice and forced reliance on psychological rather than primary attributes.

It is important to note that the situation with American wines is quite different. Around the midsixties, American wineries achieved a quality of vintage similar to that produced prior to Prohibition, and are now approaching the quality of French wines. Reliance on primary attributes is still high; the need for media advertising is quite low. The few television advertisements for wine mostly tout third-rate sangrias and light, sparkling fruit wines of no distinction. Variety has kept pace with numerousness.

7-2 CONCLUDING REMARKS

Weighting multiple criteria and objectives, as it can be surmised from this chapter, is a vexing business. Differential importance of decision criteria derives from the very fact that we consider or select some criteria and not others: most criteria, although considered simultaneously, are not of equal importance. That much can be asserted.

But their importance is relative, changing, situation-dependent, and difficult to measure. We have discussed earlier how deceptive it is to rely on decision makers' context-free expressions of criteria importance. The selection of criteria is itself a form of assessing their differential importance. Yet we are inclined to assign weights to a *given* set of criteria or objectives and not pay enough attention to the selection process as such. As with the "given" alternatives, the problem of generating viable and valid criteria is an integral part of a decision process. Criteria themselves are not simply given, predetermined, or reliable: even the best MCDM methodologies will fail if applied to a "wrong" set of objectives and goals. Yet we still know little about the process of stating objectives and setting goals.

Let us demonstrate the difficulty with a short anecdote. A class of MBA students was grappling with a real-life problem of assigning parking lots to the tenants of a high-rise building in New York. There was obvious consensus that the distance walked by tenants to their cars should be minimized. The discussion quickly focused on the technical matters of measuring the distance. Should we minimize the overall distance walked by all tenants? Or some sort of average distance? Or the maximum distance walked by any individual?

MBA students quickly seized on the idea, and rather heated discussions, conveying the sense of involvement and "expertise," ensued. One student, an operations research major, recommended that the sum of squares of distances should be minimized. This would give larger weight to larger distances and relatively lower weight to shorter distances. In pursuing this idea, the instructor suggested that perhaps fourth powers or sixth powers of the distances should be summed up. But the student knew only of linear or quadratic programming methodologies and was unable to justify his choice of squares beyond the obvious computational expediency.

The discussion shifted toward the definition of a distance. Should it be measured from each individual apartment, from floor elevators or from several building entrances? Should it be measured in absolute terms, or as a percentage of the longest possible distance or perhaps some other "point of reference"? Should we agree on one single measure to be minimized, or should we consider a variety of measures at the same time and strive for a compromise? A new set of questions emerged about the relative weights of importance to be assigned to individual measures and about the ways of defining the compromise. The discussions were lively, technically well argued, and thoroughly in the operations research tradition. But one could not escape the impression that it was the existence or nonexistence of particular OR/MS methodologies which dictated the perception of criteria.

The problem was that each objective function and each way of measuring the distance resulted in a different assignment of parking lots. A large variety of solutions came out of the students' efforts. Which one was correct? Which one should have been recommended and implemented? Would it be acceptable to the tenants?

It was only at this stage that the possible preferences and desires of the tenants entered into the discussions. The field tests showed that most of the solutions were unacceptable and the rest encountered lukewarm acceptance or courteous indifference. The students were disappointed. The problem of solution implementation was driven home clearly and unforgivingly.

Some students consulted OR/MS implementation literature and engaged in a political process of persuasion, education, and advocacy. They prepared careful analyses of potential benefits of recommended solutions and skillful arguments as to why the tenants should accept them. This led to a disaster: the students' consulting help was rejected, and the operations research studies of budding MBAs went into the case library to be used for teaching future generations of students.

Further investigations showed that the criteria (which seemed so obviously valid at the time) were wrong, not the techniques. The tenants' major criterion, although never explicitly stated, was the ability to *see* their parked automobiles from their windows! Second in importance was that daily commuters should park closer to the main parking lot entrance while occasional users should be further away. A third criterion concerned handicapped tenants. The question of walking distance was not of interest although not objectionable per se.

This brief example illustrates the importance of searching for valid, context-dependent criteria even though they may be qualitative, ambiguous, or difficult to measure. An approximate solution to the right problem is infinitely more desirable than a precise solution to the wrong or irrelevant problem.

Criteria, objectives, or goals are not inherently important or unimportant; they acquire their importance or weight within the context of the problem and through the process of searching for its solution. Only rarely can they be ascertained a priori.

It appears that the greater the number of "givens" required by our modeling efforts: given alternatives, given criteria, given weights of importance, given preferences, and so on, the less relevant and useful such models are in aiding the decision-making process. Breaking out of deeply entrenched modeling habits is not going to be easy—as this book itself stands witness.

7-3 BIBLIOGRAPHICAL NOTE

A good, detailed overview of various classical MCDM weighting techniques, evaluated in terms of their theoretical validity, flexibility, and ease of use, can be found in the survey by Hobbs (1978). Hobbs concludes that the choice of weighting technique could make as much difference in the weights as the choice of person to be asked. A similarly good study is Eckenrode (1965).

For entropy-based measures of importance one should consult Zeleny (1974, 1976). For further information on the use of entropy in business, consult Starr (1971), and Rifkin and Howard (1980).

Moinpur and Wiley (1974) is an interesting study of attribute importance in marketing models of consumer attributes. The authors confirm that weighting of attributes, as currently used, contributes little to the predictive power of the models. Because of this finding, some researchers have even recommended using arbitrary equal weights. See, for example, Einhorn and Hogarth (1975), or the interesting study by Einhorn and McCoach (1977) evaluating the overall performance of players in the National Basketball Association. They compared ranking, rating, and equal-weights methods in predicting the all-star teams for two seasons: All three methods showed remarkable similarity in their predictive power. We provide our own version of equal-weighting interpretation in Sec. 13-4.1.

The beer example comes from a two-part article by Ackoff and Emshoff (1975), later reprinted in Ackoff (1978). The first part of the article is also of interest as a study of the effect of advertising on sales: Reduction in advertising, under certain conditions, produces an increase in sales. The subsequent interchange between Allaire (1975) and Ackoff and Emshoff (1975) makes enlightening but sobering reading.

At the beginning of Chap. 7 we quoted from a recent book by Peter F. Drucker (1979). Although not related to MCDM, it is worth reading for its insights into the human side of decision making, learning, and observing.

Ackoff, R. L.: *The Art of Problem Solving*, Wiley, New York, 1978.
────── and J. R. Emshoff: "Advertising Research at Anheuser-Busch, Inc. (1963–68)," *Sloan Management Review*, vol. 16, Winter 1974, pp. 1–15.
────── and ──────: "Advertising Research at Anheuser-Busch, Inc. (1968–74)," *Sloan Management Review*, vol. 16, Spring 1975, pp. 1–16.
────── and ──────: "A Reply to the Comments of Yvan Allaire," *Sloan Management Review*, vol. 16, Spring 1975, pp. 95–98.
Allaire, Y.: "A Multivariate Puzzle: A Comment on 'Advertising Research at Anheuser-Busch, Inc. (1963–68)'," *Sloan Management* Review, vol. 16, Spring 1975, pp. 91–94.
Beckwith, N. E., and D. R. Lehmann: "The Importance of Differential Weights in Multiple Attribute Models of Consumer Attitude," *Journal of Marketing Research*, vol. 10, May 1973, pp. 141–145.

Churchman, C. W., and R. L. Ackoff: "An Approximate Measure of Value," *Operations Research*, vol. 2, 1954, pp. 172–191.

Drucker, P. F.: *Adventures of a Bystander*, Harper & Row, New York, 1979.

Eckenrode, R. T.: "Weighting Multiple Criteria," *Management Science*, vol. 12, no. 3, 1965, pp. 180–192.

Einhorn, H. J., and R. M. Hogarth: "Unit Weighting Schemes for Decision Making," *Organizational Behavior and Human Performance*, vol. 13, 1975, pp. 171–192.

—— and W. McCoach: "A Simple Multiattribute Utility Procedure for Evaluation," in S. Zionts (ed.), *Multiple Criteria Problem Solving*, Springer-Verlag, New York, 1978, pp. 87–115.

Festinger, L.: *Conflict, Decision and Dissonance*, Tavistock Publications Ltd., London, 1964.

Hobbs, B. F.: "Analytical Multiobjective Decision Methods for Power Plant Siting: A Review of Theory and Applications," Policy Analysis Div., Brookhaven National Lab., 1978.

Keeney, R. L., and K. Nair: "Nuclear Siting Using Decision Analysis," *Energy Policy*, September 1977.

Moinpur, R., and J. B. Wiley: "Application of Multi-Attribute Models of Attitude in Marketing," *Journal of Business Administration*, vol. 5, no. 2, 1974, pp. 3–16.

Otway, H., and W. Edwards: "Application of a Simple Multi-Attribute Rating Technique to Evaluation of Nuclear Waste Disposal Sites: A Demonstration," IIASA Res. Memorandum RM-77-31, Schloss Laxenburg, Austria, June 1977.

Rifkin, J., and T. Howard: *Entropy,* Viking, New York, 1980.

Saaty, T., and M. Khouja: "A Measure of World Influence," *Journal of Peace Science*, vol. 2, no. 1, 1976.

Starr, M. K.: *Management: A Modern Approach*, Harcourt Brace Jovanovich, New York, 1971.

Zeleny, M.: "The Attribute-Dynamic Attitude Model (ADAM)," *Management Science*, vol. 23, no. 1, September 1976, pp. 12–26.

——: *Linear Multiobjective Programming*, Springer-Verlag, New York, 1974.

7-4 PROBLEMS

7-1 "Attributes evaluation scores may in fact be 'weighted judgments'; hence, multiplying by independently derived 'weights' would serve only to doubly weight the attribute scores." This statement is offered as an explanation of why certain "unweighted" (or equally weighted) models of attributes lead to the same or even better predictions than carefully weighted models. Analyze this statement. On the basis of your own decision-making experience, do you agree with it?

7-2 It is often said that Americans are unable to distinguish among the different brands of beer they drink. Do the following experiment: Collect several nationally marketed brands of beer (preferably of the "light" variety) and have a group of subjects taste them. Then introduce the same batch, with labels covered, and ask the tasters to identify the brands. (Another variation is to have two identical sets of brands, with labels covered, offered in sequence. Ask the subjects to rank them in terms of preference and then compare both rankings.)

(*a*) Identify the attributes of importance in the subjects' judging and ranking of brands in the absence of any brand-identifying information.

(*b*) Perform the same experiment with regional beers (e.g., Fyfe & Drum, Rolling Rock, Genesee Cream Ale, Rainier Ale, Hamm's, Iron City, and the like).

(*c*) Perform the same experiment with foreign beers (e.g., Pilsener Urquell, Heineken, Guinness, Würzburger, St. Pauli Girl, Kirin, etc.).

(*d*) Perform the same experiment with a balanced mixture of all categories; consider similar experiments with wines or mineral water brands.

(*e*) Write a paper about your findings, emphasizing the role of primary, secondary, and, perhaps, tertiary attributes; the question of numerousness versus variety; comparison with wine brands.

7-3 The so-called "*eigenvector prioritization method*"[1] is often suggested for deriving the weights of importance for individual criteria. Assume that ℓ criteria are assigned weights of importance w_1, $w_2, \ldots, w_\ell$. A decision maker must determine the *ratio* of importance for every possible pair of criteria, thus forming the following matrix:

	1	2	3	$\cdots$
1	$\dfrac{w_1}{w_1}$	$\dfrac{w_1}{w_2}$	$\dfrac{w_1}{w_3}$	
2	$\dfrac{w_2}{w_1}$	$\dfrac{w_2}{w_2}$	$\dfrac{w_2}{w_3}$	
3	$\dfrac{w_3}{w_1}$	$\dfrac{w_3}{w_2}$	$\dfrac{w_3}{w_3}$	
$\vdots$				

The entries in this matrix W are denoted as $W_{ij} = w_i/w_j$, where $i, j = 1, \ldots, \ell$. The *eigenvector* of matrix W is the set of weights w satisfying $Ww = \lambda w$ in matrix notation. (Note that ratios W_{ij} are estimated *directly*, that is, w_i are unknown variables.) Constant λ is called the "eigenvalue." The eigenvector is found by solving the following set of equations:

$$W_{11}\,w_1 + W_{12}\,w_2 + W_{13}\,w_3 = \lambda w_1$$

$$W_{21}\,w_1 + W_{22}\,w_2 + W_{23}\,w_3 = \lambda w_2$$

$$W_{31}\,w_1 + W_{32}\,w_2 + W_{33}\,w_3 = \lambda w_3$$

where λ is the corresponding eigenvalue.

[1]A good discussion of priority theory appears in F. A. Lootsma, "Saaty's Priority Theory and the Nomination of a Senior Professor in Operations Research," *European Journal of Operational Research,* vol. 4, 1980, pp. 380–388.

(*a*) Consider the following matrix W of estimated ratios:

	1	2	3	4
1	1	5	6	7
2	$\frac{1}{5}$	1	4	6
3	$\frac{1}{6}$	$\frac{1}{4}$	1	4
4	$\frac{1}{7}$	$\frac{1}{6}$	$\frac{1}{4}$	1

Verify that $w_1 = 0.62$, $w_2 = 0.23$, $w_3 = 0.10$, and $w_4 = 0.05$ constitute the eigenvector and $\lambda = 4.39$ the eigenvalue.

(*b*) Construct your own matrix of ratio estimates and attempt to recover the weights.

(*c*) Matrix W is consistent, that is, W_{ij} are logically related rather than randomly chosen, if $\lambda = \ell$. Increasing "inconsistency" is indicated by values $\lambda > \ell$. Could this be a criterion for revising the original judgments about W_{ij}? Discuss.

7-4 The ELECTRÉ (E*limination et choix traduisant la réalité*) method[1] is based on a pairwise comparison of alternatives. For each pair (i, j) of the universe of alternatives we compute two indexes:

1. *Concordance index*—a sum of weights corresponding to all criteria for which j dominates i.

2. *Discordance index*—calculated as follows: Identify all criteria for which j is dominated by i; weight the differences between values of j and i divided by the overall range of values corresponding to a given criterion; select the *maximum* of these weighted relative differences.

In the above computations we assume that the criterion weights are nonnegative and add up to 1. (More complicated versions of the indexes have been developed in the literature.) An alternative i is said to "outrank" an alternative j when the concordance index is $> p$ and the discordance index $< q$, where p and q are thresholds specified by the decision maker.

(*a*) Assume that all criterion weights are equal. Consider the following universe of (three) alternatives:

$$i: \quad (50, 20, 60, 40, 70)$$

$$j: \quad (90, 30, 20, 70, 50)$$

$$k: \quad (80, 10, 80, 50, 30)$$

Comparing i with j, verify that the concordance index is 0.6, and the discordance index is 0.133.

(*b*) Complete the evaluation for all pairs of alternatives in (*a*). Consider $p = 0.7$ and $q = 0.3$ and identify the outranking relations.

(*c*) Interpret the reasoning behind ELECTRÉ. Under which conditions would the discordance index be equal to 0 and 1 respectively? How does the choice of p and q affect the outranking?

[1]See for example P. Nijkamp and A. van Delft, *Multi-Criteria Analysis and Regional Decision-Making*, Martinus Nijhoff, Leiden, 1977.

7-5 The so-called "STEM method" views the weights of criterion importance w_i as being proportional to the difference between the ideal and the anti-ideal values attainable with respect to criterion i, that is, $f^*_i - f_{i*}$. Cohon and Marks comment as follows:

> "The interactive methods also do not explicitly capture the trade offs between objectives. The weights in no way reflect a value judgment on the part of the decision maker. They are artificial quantities, concocted by the analyst to reflect deviations from an ideal solution, which is itself an artificial quantity. This definition of weights serves to obscure rather than capture the normative nature of the multiobjective problem."[1]

(*a*) Relate your understanding of the STEM weighting procedure to this critique.

(*b*) In view of the Cohon and Marks statement, what is your attitude toward the ideal-solution concept and its corresponding idea of criterion importance (e.g., entropy-based)? What is the difference between the STEM and the displaced ideal approach?

7-6 Throughout the book we argue against pairwise comparison of alternatives. Consider the following three alternatives evaluated with respect to three criteria:

	f_1	f_2	f_3
A	100	0	50
B	50	100	0
C	0	50	100

Assume that the three criteria are equally important.

(*a*) Compare A with B, B with C, and finally A with C on the basis of the *concordance index*. If you assumed the *transitivity* of preferences, would the comparison of A with C be necessary? (You can also think of the problem as if f_1, f_2, and f_3 represented three committee voters, and the numbers were their voting preferences with respect to A, B, and C: 100 is preferred, 50 is mediocre, 0 is unacceptable.)

(*b*) Perform this "voting" comparison for all possible pairs of A, B, and C.

7-7 "If all plans are equally or near equally successful at meeting certain criteria, those criteria will not affect the decision and can be eliminated." True or false? What are the conditions for your answer? How is the importance of such criteria dependent on the decision maker's a priori judgment of their importance?

[1] J. L. Cohon and D. H. Marks, "A Review and Evaluation of Multiobjective Programming Techniques," *Water Resources Research*, vol. 11, no. 2, 1975, p. 217.

7-8 Consider three plans evaluated with respect to nine criteria, all of which are to be maximized:

	1	2	3	4	5	6	7	8	9
A	O.K.	40	15	100	Good	−3.15	14	200	300
B	O.K.	42	20	90	Poor	−3.07	6	180	270
C	O.K.	41	30	91	Good	−3.05	13	183	272

(a) Under what conditions can we drop criteria 1 and 2? If they are eliminated, what is the status of plan B?

(b) Can we eliminate criteria 5 and 7 on the basis of (a)?

(c) Complete the evaluation of the plans with a MCDM approach of your choice.

7-9 In this chapter we have used the entropy measure of attribute intrinsic importance. It has often been suggested that a standard deviation measure

$$\sqrt{\frac{1}{n} \sum_{i=1}^{n} (d_i^k)^2 - \frac{1}{n} (D_i)^2}$$

would do as well. Compare the two measures, especially in relation to the scaling of numerical data.

7-10 The *preemptive weighting* of goals was first proposed by Ijiri.[1] Its simplicity is often stressed: The decision maker only has to rank the objectives in terms of priority and find the goal levels for them. The goals and objectives do not have to be commensurate as long as they refer to different priority levels. However, depending on the feasible set, small sacrifices in connection with one objective could produce sizable effects on other objectives. How is this situation handled within the preemptive framework?

7-11 Consumer products are characterized by multiple attributes. If we assume a relatively stable set of weights that individuals apply to these attributes, we would expect that consumers would be likely to identify their most preferred brand. Yet, a widespread phenomenon of brand switching exists. Why do consumers switch their preferences between brands? Consider the following explanations:

1. There is a random component in their choice behavior—consumers seek and derive satisfaction from a variety of brands.
2. Brand switching reflects errors of consumer choice stemming from incomplete information and vaguely defined preferences. If they had all the data, they would be able to identify "their" brand. That is, brand switching is somewhat irrational.

[1] Y. Ijiri, *Management Goals and Accounting for Control*, North-Holland Publishing, Amsterdam, 1965.

3. Consumers buy two or more brands in order to achieve the most preferred balance of attributes—that is, brand switching reflects the search for complementarity of brands with respect to their attributes.

4. In a given situation a consumer faces a host of new and unplanned factors which intervene between the preferred and the actual choice. If the consumer were able to account for *all* the factors a priori, the most preferred brand would be identified.

5. Consumer preferences and attribute weights are situation-dependent. There is no "most preferred" brand but only a "most preferred brand in a given situation." Thus a consumer always chooses the "most preferred brand" under the given circumstances, and the switching reflects the changes in these circumstances. Uncertainty and incompleteness of information are only secondary intervening factors.

Analyze the hypotheses proposed in (1) to (5). Provide comparative evaluations on the basis of your own experience as a consumer. How would the individual hypotheses be modeled?

7-12 The farther the achieved score is from the ideal score, the more important the criterion in question will become. As we move closer to the ideal along that criterion, its significance and our immediate attention devoted to it will diminish. Weights of importance are thus functions of alternatives currently considered, ideal alternatives, and their relative positioning in space and time as perceived by a particular decision maker. Explain your understanding of criterion importance in plain English.

7-13 Mr. Clean Sweep, the owner of a laundry, is about to open a new launderette. The neighborhood demand requires installation of some twenty washing machines. He has found that there is a wide selection of machines available. Among their attributes, in addition to price, he considers washing time and consumption of electricity and water to be the most important.

Mr. Sweep has collected data on four attributes and thirty-three types of machine. The figures are given in the table below.

The table of alternatives and their descriptions do not give Mr. Sweep any hint of how to make his choice. After studying the table for some time, he turns for help to a management scientist. The latter identifies the situation as an MCDM problem.

Mr. Sweep explains that he wants to reduce the number of alternatives to no more than five. He feels he could not handle more, for in arriving at his final choice he must consider many attributes which cannot be expressed numerically.

He further explains that since he has already invested a lot of money in the launderette, a low price of machine is important. A short washing time is desirable in order to attract customers and to be able to serve more customers per time period. He would also like to minimize both electricity consumption and water consumption for reasons of economy, energy conservation, and environmental protection.

Imagine that you are the management scientist. Can you help Mr. Sweep analyze the situation and arrive at a decision? This is a broadly stated problem and your approach and reasoning are more important than any particular result. You may yourself provide Mr. Sweep's answers to any questions that you wish to ask him. [This case is from Prof. A. Törn of Åbo Akademi, Finland.]

Machine type	Price, $	Total washing time,[1] min	Electricity consumption,[1] kwh	Water consumption,[1] liters
1	509	74	1.5	114
2	425	80	1.5	110
3	446	72	1.6	135
4	564	65	1.6	118
5	547	53	1.8	140
6	450	68	1.6	135
7	473	65	1.6	130
8	484	56	1.7	115
9	456	68	1.6	130
10	488	72	1.6	114
11	530	55	1.7	135
12	477	76	1.5	110
13	589	53	1.6	130
14	534	61	1.4	122
15	536	57	1.7	110
16	494	71	1.5	135
17	425	65	1.8	120
18	555	53	1.7	125
19	543	57	1.6	120
20	515	68	1.5	130
21	452	76	1.5	112
22	547	68	1.5	120
23	421	76	1.4	130
24	498	68	1.6	120
25	467	65	1.7	130
26	595	50	1.8	135
27	414	68	1.7	125
28	431	66	1.7	110
29	452	72	1.5	115
30	408	77	1.6	119
31	478	59	1.8	110
32	395	76	1.5	120
33	543	57	1.5	135

[1]For the most frequently used program.

So far, we have dealt mostly with decision alternatives which were discrete, i.e., they could be listed separately one by one, forming countably small sets of "points" in the multidimensional space of attributes or criteria. There are many types of problems in which not only every discrete point but also every feasible combination of them identifies a decision alternative. Thus, there could be an infinite number of possible courses of action. Their analysis by simple enumeration, as we usually can do with discretely defined alternatives, would be prohibitively time-consuming, costly, or just plain impossible. One needs a more efficient method.

A suitable methodology for handling such problems is called "linear multiobjective programming" (LMP). Through a series of simple numerical and graphic examples in this chapter, we introduce the reader to different kinds of programming formulations. After mastering the logic of model construction, the reader can proceed to study the multicriterion simplex method, a technique for identifying and calculating all nondominated solutions of a given problem. This is a rather complex, technical task, but it represents a potentially worthwhile intellectual investment. The reader will acquire not only this particular method but also the simplex method of traditional linear programming, as well as a good computational base for goal programming, compromise programming, and many other approaches that are based on similar solution logic.

Later, we explore an important accompanying concept, multiparametric decomposition. This approach is very useful for performing sensitivity analysis of obtained nondominated solutions; it allows additional flexibility through differential weighting of multiple objective functions and provides a good base for person-machine interaction.

We also devote considerable space to a transportation problem with multiple objectives, an interesting special case of LMP. Traditional linear programming (LP) and its derivatives in turn represent the simplest special case of LMP. By studying LMP directly, the reader acquires a good, nonmechanistic knowledge of LP as a fringe benefit. The other way of proceeding, from LP to LMP, is considerably more cumbersome.

Throughout the chapter we also deal with some special versions of LMP, such as integer programming and fractional programming.

LINEAR MULTIOBJECTIVE PROGRAMMING

Programming sticks upon the shoals
Of incommensurate multiple goals
And where the tops are no one knows
When all our peaks become plateaus
The top is anything we think
When measuring makes the mountain shrink.

The upshot is, we cannot tailor
Policy by a single scalar,
Unless we know the priceless price
Of Honor, Justice, Pride, and Vice.
This means a crisis is arising
For simple-minded maximizing.

Kenneth Boulding[1]

Before introducing the methodologies of linear multiobjective programming, goal programming, and compromise programming, we introduce a simple example of how a multiobjective program may arise and how it can be typically formulated.

Because this text is intended to complement existing books and to extend some of the traditional concepts of decision analysis, management sciences, and operations research, we will not discuss the theory of linear programming and "simple-minded maximizing" in detail. The following two sections should be sufficient to establish the basic ideas. The reader should consult any introductory text on linear programming for technical details. Some of the suitable textbooks are listed at the end of this chapter. They all deal with a single objective function maximization or minimization. We start with multiple objectives.

---

[1]A poem introducing the paper by A. Charnes and W. W. Cooper, "Constrained Extremization Models and Their Use in Developing Systems Measures," in M. D. Mesarović (ed.), *Views on General System Theory*, Wiley, New York, 1964, p. 61.

8-1 ABE REAM'S DISBURSEMENT PROBLEM

Abe Ream is the new manager of a *federal funds disbursing system*. He has to distribute funds to five political localities. For each federal dollar it receives, locality 1 will add $0.20 as its matching contribution. Localities 2 to 5 will add $0.25, $0.33, $0.40, and $0.50, respectively.

Mr. Ream manages a budget of $10 million. Since he would like to receive at least the same amount for the next year, he feels that he should spend at least 95% of this year's budget, or even exceed it by up to 20% if he can do so without getting into trouble.

Each of the localities faces a separate economic rate of return on funds committed to local projects. These rates are currently estimated to be 0.30, 0.25, 0.22, 0.20, and 0.15 for localities 1 to 5, respectively.

Mr. Ream would like to maximize the *total* return for every dollar invested. He is also under pressure to obtain the highest rate of return for each federal dollar invested in local projects. Political considerations also require that federal funds be spread more or less evenly among individual localities.

Finally, all funds distributed through this system must be audited. On the basis of historical records, Mr. Ream has estimated the following hours of audit time required for each $1000 invested in localities 1 to 5: 0.02, 0.03, 0.08, 0.10, and 0.12. Ream's audit staff has only 800 hours available per year.

We can summarize Mr. Ream's objectives and constraints as follows:

Let x_j indicate the total amount of federal funds allocated to locality j for this year, $j = 1, \ldots, 5$. Then, $x = (x_1, \ldots, x_5)$ is a solution vector satisfying the following objectives, goals, and constraints:

Total return in dollars to be maximized:

$$\text{Max } (0.30)(1.2)x_1 + (0.25)(1.25)x_2 + (0.22)(1.33)x_3 + (0.20)(1.4)x_4 \\ + (0.15)(1.5)x_5$$

Rate of return on federal dollars to be maximized:

$$\text{Max } 0.30x_1 + 0.25x_2 + 0.22x_3 + 0.20x_4 + 0.15x_5$$

Even distribution. Let d_j denote the deviation over $2 million, i.e., when each locality obtains exactly the same allotment (Let $\bar{x} = 10{,}000{,}000 / 5 = 2{,}000{,}000$). That is,

$$x_j - d_j \leq 2{,}000{,}000 \qquad \text{for } j = 1, \ldots, 5$$

Abe Ream considers two ways of equalizing the allocation. First:

$$\text{Min } d_1 + d_2 + d_3 + d_4 + d_5$$

subject to $x_j - d_j \leq \bar{x} \qquad j = 1, \ldots, 5$

and second

$$\text{Min}_{X} \text{ Max}_{j} \; d_j \quad j = 1, \ldots, 5$$

that is, minimize the maximum of the five deviations.

There is one more aspect which Abe Ream cannot neglect: Each locality contributes a different amount, and supporting such local activity is of importance. Some bonus for a locality's own contribution is in place, but this policy partially conflicts with efforts for even distribution. Abe would like to explore this conflict:

Local support bonus:

$$x_1 - \frac{.20}{.25} x_2 \leq 0$$

$$x_2 - \frac{.25}{.33} x_3 \leq 0$$

$$x_3 - \frac{.33}{.40} x_4 \leq 0$$

$$x_4 - \frac{.40}{.50} x_5 \leq 0$$

Budget constraints:

$$x_1 + x_2 + x_3 + x_4 + x_5 \geq 9,500,000$$

$$x_1 + x_2 + x_3 + x_4 + x_5 \leq 12,000,000$$

Audit constraint:

$$.02x_1 + .03x_2 + .08x_3 + .10x_4 + .12x_5 \leq 800,000$$

Your task is to advise Abe Ream of the best ways to allocate his budget for this year.

Mr. Ream has established two maximization *objectives*: total dollar return and rate of return on federal dollar invested; five *goals*: \$2 million for each of the five localities; and two minimization *objectives*: total sum of deviations over the five goals and/or the maximum of all deviations. There are also some *constraints*: local support bonus constraints, budget and audit constraints—seven altogether. All functions involved are linear.

Mr. Ream's problem, however, is *not* one of linear programming. The LP methodology relates to only one specific form: A single objective function to be maximized (or minimized) with respect to a set of constraints. Mr. Ream faces more than one objective, and he is not generally willing to choose only one of them exclusively. By minimizing the sum of deviations:

$$\text{Min} \sum_{j=1}^{5} d_j$$

subject to

$$x_j - d_j \leq \bar{x} \qquad j = 1, \ldots, 5$$

or minimizing the maximum deviation:

$$\text{Min } d$$

subject to

$$x_j - d \leq \bar{x} \qquad j = 1, \ldots, 5$$

where d (different from the previous d_j!) is the largest (or maximum) deviation satisfying the goal constraints; both problems can be solved by *goal programming*.

Numerical example Minimization of the maximum deviation by the above-mentioned method is sometimes difficult to grasp intuitively. First, let us consider a solution, say, $x = (x_1, x_2, x_3, x_4, x_5) = (1900, 1980, 2100, 2050, 2000)$ and disregard the other constraints for the time being. Because $\bar{x} = 2000$ and d_j's are defined as deviations *over* 2000, otherwise $d_j = 0$, we can write:

$$1900 - d_1 \leq 2000 \qquad (d_1 = 0)$$
$$1980 - d_2 \leq 2000 \qquad (d_2 = 0)$$
$$2100 - d_3 \leq 2000 \qquad (d_3 = 100)$$
$$2050 - d_4 \leq 2000 \qquad (d_4 = 50)$$
$$2000 - d_5 \leq 2000 \qquad (d_5 = 0)$$

The sum of all deviations for this particular solution x is

$$\sum_{j=1}^{5} d_j = 0 + 0 + 100 + 50 + 0 = 150$$

We are then looking for a solution x which would minimize the above sum with respect to all constraints.

Next, let us find d which would satisfy all five goals *at the same time* for the same solution x. Obviously, that d is the maximum of all d_j's, that is, $d = \underset{j}{\text{Max}}\{d_j\} = \underset{j}{\text{Max}}\{0; 0; 100; 50; 0\} = 100$, because:

$$1900 - 100 \leq 2000$$
$$1980 - 100 \leq 2000$$
$$2100 - 100 \leq 2000$$
$$2050 - 100 \leq 2000$$
$$2000 - 100 \leq 2000$$

Thus, $d = 100$ in this case. Then we look for a solution which would provide the minimum d. That is, we solve

$$\underset{X}{\text{Min}} \ \underset{j}{\text{Max}} \ d_j$$

subject to a set of constraints X.

Neither linear programming nor goal programming can handle *multiple* objectives, such as total dollar return, rate of return on federal dollars, sum of deviations, and maximum deviation, all at the same time. Such a problem can be dealt with by linear multiobjective programming and compromise programming, our next major topics of interest. Linear programming and goal programming are viewed as special cases of these two methodologies, suitable only for specific and limited applications. They are no good for Mr. Ream's problem.

8-2 GASOLINE PRODUCTION PROBLEM—OVERVIEW OF BASIC FORMULATIONS

Assume two distinct technological processes 1 and 2 available for the production of two basic types of gasoline X and Y. Both technologies should be utilized because they are capable of producing different proportions of quantities X and Y: The first process is X-efficient while the second one is Y-efficient. There are two basic inputs of crude oil, A and B. Our task is to determine the number of units of two-gasoline mixtures x_1 and x_2 to be produced by the two processes respectively. Several constraining conditions must be taken into account: There are only 100 units of crude A and 150 units of crude B available for each production run. The company must produce at least 200 units of X and 75 units of Y, because of previous sales commitments.

The technological requirements are as follows:

1. *The first process x_1:* 1 unit of A plus 3 units of B will produce 5 units of X and 2 units of Y
2. *The second process x_2:* 4 units of A plus 2 units of B will produce 3 units of X and 8 units of Y

Observe that x_1 and x_2 can be interpreted as follows: For $x_1 = 1$ we use up 1 unit of A and 3 units of B to produce 5 units of X and 2 units of Y. Thus, x_1 indicates the number of units of a 5-and-2 mix of X and Y. If $x_1 = 2$, we get 10 of X and 4 of Y, or two times 5 of X and 2 of Y. A similar computation can be done for x_2.

Thus, at the unit levels of x_1 and x_2 we use 1 unit of A in process 1 and 4 units of A in process 2. Observe that

$$x_1 + 4x_2 \leq 100$$

because we have only 100 units of A available per run. Similarly,

$$3x_1 + 2x_2 \leqq 150$$

because only 150 units of B are available.

For example, producing 40 units through the first process and 10 units through the second process, $x_1 = 40$ and $x_2 = 10$, would have the following consequence with regard to the availability of A:

$$40 + 4(10) = 80$$
$$= 100 - 20$$

That is, this solution is feasible with respect to the first constraint and 20 units of crude A are still left. What about the second constraint? We face the following limitation:

$$3(40) + 2(10) = 140$$
$$= 150 - 10$$

That is, 10 units of crude B are left unused.

How does the solution $x_1 = 40$ and $x_2 = 10$ translate into amounts of X and Y? Recall that $x_1 = 40$ represents 40 units of a 5-and-2 mix of X and Y, that is, 200 units of X and 80 units of Y. Similarly, $x_2 = 10$ represents 30 units of X and 80 units of Y.

What about the sales commitments? We have to supply at least 200 units of gasoline X. That is,

$$5x_1 + 3x_2 \geqq 200$$

must be satisfied. Using the solution at hand, we get:

$$5(40) + 3(10) = 230$$
$$= 200 + 30$$

That is, 30 units of X are in excess of our lower limit of 200.

The amount of gasoline Y to be supplied is 75 units. That is,

$$2x_1 + 8x_2 \geqq 75$$

must be satisfied. Let us substitute $x_1 = 40$, $x_2 = 10$ again:

$$2(40) + 8(10) = 160$$
$$= 75 + 85$$

That is, 85 units of Y in excess of 75 are produced.

We can summarize all our constraints as follows:

$$x_1 + 4x_2 \leqq 100 \qquad \text{availability of crude } A$$

$$3x_1 + 2x_2 \leqq 150 \qquad \text{availability of crude } B$$

$$5x_1 + 3x_2 \geqq 200 \qquad \text{sales commitment on gasoline } X$$

$$2x_1 + 8x_2 \geqq 75 \qquad \text{sales commitment on gasoline } Y$$

$$x_1 \qquad \geqq \quad 0 \qquad \text{no negative amounts can be}$$

$$x_2 \geqq \quad 0 \qquad \text{produced}$$

All solutions (x_1, x_2) must satisfy the above set of inequalities (as $x_1 = 40$ and $x_2 = 10$ does).

The set of feasible pairs of x_1 and x_2 can be displaced graphically by checking the amount of x_1 on the horizontal axis and the amount of x_2 on the vertical axis of Fig. 8-1. See Sec. 8-4.1 for details of graphic analysis.

All constraints are drawn in Fig. 8-1. For example, $x_1 + 4x_2 = 100$ is represented by the line passing through points ($x_1 = 100, x_2 = 0$) and ($x_1 = 0, x_2 = 25$). The direction of feasibility $\leqq$ is indicated by shading the corresponding half plane. Similarly for all other constraints. The shaded quadrangle represents all feasible points (x_1, x_2) with (40, 10) located in its interior. The four corner points A to D—(40, 15), (50, 0), (40, 0), and (29.412, 17.647), respectively—are also indicated in the graph.

At the beginning we said that our task was to determine the amounts x_1 and x_2, but we have not yet specified the criterion by which one solution (x_1, x_2) would be judged better than another. We have not specified our objectives.

Depending on a given objective or criterion we could formulate several problems:

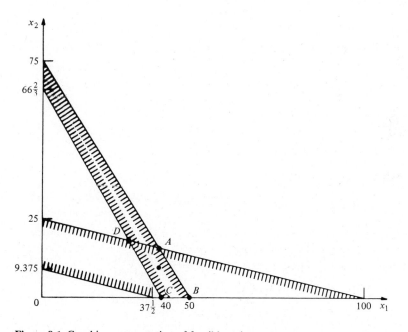

Figure 8-1 Graphic representation of feasible points (x_1, x_2).

1. Maximize the production of gasoline X:

$$\text{Max } 5x_1 + 3x_2$$

subject to
$$x_1 + 4x_2 \leqq 100$$
$$3x_1 + 2x_2 \leqq 150$$
$$5x_1 + 3x_2 \geqq 200$$
$$2x_1 + 8x_2 \geqq 75$$
$$x_1 \qquad \geqq 0$$
$$x_2 \geqq 0$$

The optimal solution is B, $x_1 = 50$, $x_2 = 0$, i.e., 250 units of X (and 100 units of Y) are produced.

2. Maximize the production of gasoline Y:

$$\text{Max } 2x_1 + 8x_2$$

subject to
$$x_1 + 4x_2 \leqq 100$$
$$3x_1 + 2x_2 \leqq 150$$
$$5x_1 + 3x_2 \geqq 200$$
$$2x_1 + 8x_2 \geqq 75$$
$$x_1 \qquad \geqq 0$$
$$x_2 \geqq 0$$

The optimal solution is now either

$$D = (x_1 = \tfrac{500}{17}, x_2 = \tfrac{300}{17})$$

$$\text{or } A = (x_1 = 40, x_2 = 15)$$

or any linear combination of these two corner points. That is, 200 units of Y are produced at the most:

$$2\left(\frac{500}{17}\right) + 8\left(\frac{300}{17}\right) = 200 = 2(40) + 8(15).$$

Let us try a combination, say, midway between the two corner points

$$\tfrac{1}{2}\left(\frac{500}{17}, \frac{300}{17}\right) + \tfrac{1}{2}(40, 15) = \left(\frac{590}{17}, \frac{277.5}{17}\right),$$

giving

$$2\left(\frac{590}{17}\right) + 8\left(\frac{277.5}{17}\right) = 200.$$

A and *D*, and the whole section *AD*, are so-called "alternative optimal solutions" in linear programming. If there are at least two such optima, then there must be an infinite number of them, because an infinite number of linear combinations can be formed.

3. Maximize total profits to be derived from the sale of both types of gasoline using both technological processes. If the unit profit margins for both technologies were p_1 and p_2 respectively, then

$$\text{Max } p_1 x_1 + p_2 x_2$$

subject to the same constraints would do the trick. For example, $p_1 = \$2$ and $p_2 = \$4$ would lead to maximization of $2x_1 + 4x_2$ at $x_1 = 40$ and $x_2 = 15$, that is, \$140 of profits. Observe that the production of gasoline *Y* is also maximized at this point.

All three of the above cases are examples of the classical linear-programming approach. Many more variations could be generated. What would maximization of x_1, that is, Max x_1, mean in this context? What about Max x_2, Max $x_1 + x_2$, etc.?

Next, we shall consider various *multiple* objectives or goals.

4. Maximize the production of gasoline *X* and the production of gasoline *Y*. That is,

$$\text{Max } \begin{cases} 5x_1 + 3x_2 \\ 2x_1 + 8x_2 \end{cases}$$

subject to the same constraints. This is a problem of linear *multiobjective programming*. We could first determine all nondominated solutions, for example by using the multicriterion simplex method (discussed in Sec. 8-4). Solutions $B = (50, 0)$ and $A = (40, 15)$ are the only nondominated corner points, and their combination represents the nondominated set *N*, the edge *AB* in Fig. 8-2. Observe that point *D*, although maximizing one of the objectives in separation, must be excluded from *N*. The nondominated set of solutions can be further reduced by considering different weights of importance assigned to gasolines *X* and *Y*, via *interactive programming* or by iterative "shrinking" of the size of *N*. See the discussion in Sec. 10-6.

5. Maximize the utilization of the reserve of crude oil *A* while saving as much available crude oil *B* as possible. At the same time, maximize the production of gasoline *X*.

First, the utilization of a resource is measured by a deviation from its available quantity:

$$x_1 + 4x_2 + d_1^- = 100$$

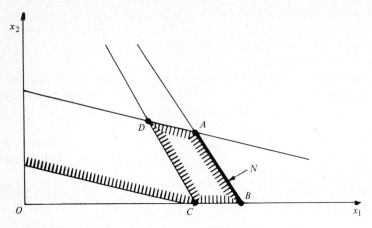

Figure 8-2 An example of the nondominated set.

Because of our goal, we want to minimize deviation d_1^-. We want to make it zero if possible.

Second, to save the available crude oil B, we introduce deviation d_2^-:

$$3x_1 + 2x_2 + d_2^- = 150$$

and attempt to *maximize* d_2^-.

Thirdly, we maximize production of gasoline X, that is, $5x_1 + 3x_2$. In summary,

$$\text{Min } d_1^- - d_2^-$$
$$\text{Max } 5x_1 + 3x_2$$

subject to
$$x_1 + 4x_2 + d_1^- = 100$$
$$3x_1 + 2x_2 + d_2^- = 150$$
$$5x_1 + 3x_2 \geqq 200$$
$$2x_1 + 8x_2 \geqq 75$$
$$x_1 \geqq 0$$
$$x_2 \geqq 0$$

The above problem is a mixture of multiobjective programming and goal programming.

6. A typical *goal-programming* formulation would be associated with the following set of goals. At the highest priority maximize the utilization of crude oil A; if this goal is achieved, minimize the overproduction of gasoline Y, because there is no apparent demand for Y beyond those commited sales of 75 units:

$$\text{Minimize } P_1 d_1^- + P_2 d_4^{+1}$$

subject to
$$
\begin{aligned}
x_1 + 4x_2 + d_1^- &= 100 \\
3x_1 + 2x_2 &\leq 150 \\
5x_1 + 2x_2 &\leq 200 \\
2x_1 + 8x_2 - d_4^+ &= 75 \\
x_1 &\geq 0 \\
x_2 &\geq 0
\end{aligned}
$$

7. Maximize the production of gasoline X *and* the production of gasoline Y, as we have done in case 4. But instead of multiobjective programming, let us use *compromise programming*.

   Production of X is maximized at $B = (50, 0)$, amounting to 250 units, while Y is maximized at either

$$A = (40, 15) \text{ or } D = (\tfrac{500}{17}, \tfrac{300}{17}),$$

producing 200 units.

Given the constraints of resource availability and the sales commitments, the ideal way of solving this problem would be to produce 250 units of X and 200 units of Y. These levels of production are indicated as the ideal point I, in Fig. 8-3.

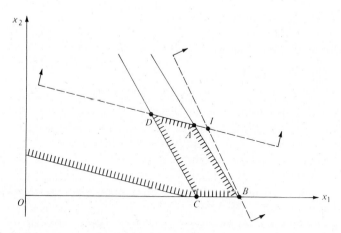

Figure 8-3 An example of the ideal point.

[1] P_1 simply denotes the first priority which carries an infinitely larger weight than priority P_2; P_1 preempts P_2. The summation of terms in the objective function is therefore meaningless. We should have stated: Minimize (d_1^-, d_4^+) in a lexicographic vector sense (see Sec. 9-3). We keep some of this odd notation because it dominates most goal-programming literature the reader is likely to encounter.

Observe that there is no *feasible* pair (x_1, x_2) which would coincide with point I and thus allow 250 units of X and 200 units of Y to be produced simultaneously.

In compromise programming the solution is sought by exploring the points as close as possible to I. The interpretation of "as close as possible" may be, for example, in the form of euclidean distance:

$$\text{Min } \sqrt{(d_1^-)^2 + (d_2^-)^2}$$

subject to

$$5x_1 + 3x_2 + d_1^- = 250$$

$$2x_1 + 8x_2 + d_2^- = 200$$

$$x_1 + 4x_2 \leqq 100$$

$$3x_1 + 2x_2 \leqq 150$$

$$5x_1 + 3x_2 \geqq 200$$

$$2x_1 + 8x_2 \geqq 75$$

$$x_1 \geqq 0$$

$$x_2 \geqq 0$$

Other forms of the objective function could be

$$\text{Min } (d_1^- + d_2^-) \qquad \underset{X}{\text{Min Max }} (d_1^-; d_2^-) \qquad \text{etc.}$$

Also, a weighted version of the objective function is often used, such as $\text{Min } \lambda_1 d_1^- + \lambda_2 d_2^-$.

There are several differences between goal programming and compromise programming. Compromise programming determines its goals internally through computations, it does not use preemptive weighting, and it considers a large variety of distance functions for its objectives.

It is unfortunate that these several methodologies—single-objective optimization, multiobjective programming (via nondominated solutions), goal programming, compromise programming, etc.—are often kept apart instead of synthesized into one flexible methodology. As we have shown, each one arises as an adjustment or generalization of another. Just as it is needlessly self-restricting to ignore anything beyond single-objective optimization, it is self-defeating to draw sharp distinctions among the approaches involving multiple objectives.

The real problems lie elsewhere. Resource constraints, whether in single- or multiobjective programming, are not absolutes or "givens." In most real-life situations they can be relaxed *at cost*. When we want to minimize the use of resources—labor, capital goods, and raw materials—the constraints become goals or objective functions in their own right. Thus, we rarely *maximize* a function subject to given *constraints*, though we frequently optimize or balance a function in *concordance* with a set of other objectives and goals. The crude first model, even though it is possibly a neat approximation of reality, quickly becomes a curse if we forget the provisional nature of its simplified assumptions. The second model is more realistic, providing not the answer but a good starting point for the decision-making process. It is possibly less elegant but more flexible and useful.

We shall deal with the problem of flexible "constraints" in Sec. 10-4. The methodology is referred to as "de novo programming," and it is intended to design optimal systems, not to optimize given systems.

8-3 CONSTRAINTS, GOALS, AND OBJECTIVES

It is useful to discuss the conceptual and technical differences among constraints, goals, and objectives in goal programming, multiobjective programming, and other variants of mathematical programming. The discussion of multiple goals or objectives may have led to some confusion with regard to the traditional notion of a constraint.

A "constraint" is a temporarily fixed requirement which *cannot be violated* in a given problem formulation. That is, upper and lower bounds cannot be exceeded, and strict requirements must be satisfied precisely. For example,

$$3x_1 + 4x_2 \leq 100$$

$$3x_1 + 4x_2 \geq 100$$

$$3x_1 + 4x_2 = 100$$

are the three common versions of a particular constraint. All combinations of values of x_1 and x_2 are feasible as long as the left-side expression does not exceed 100 ($\leq$), or does not dip below 100 ($\geq$), or is equal to 100 ($=$). The right-side expression, 100 in this case, serves no other purpose then to impose a limit. *Constraints divide all possible solutions* (*combinations of variables*) *into two groups*: *feasible and infeasible*. No additional classificatory or ranking cirterion is present: Solutions within each group are not further distinguished. Constraints can of course be changed, e.g., from 100 to 120, but only at cost, over a period of time, or in a new formulation of the problem.

A "goal" is a temporarily fixed requirement which *is to be satisfied as closely as possible* in a given problem formulation. That is, upper and lower bounds as well as fixed requirements are to be approached as closely as possible. An additional criterion has been implicitly stated: It is not sufficient only to satisfy a goal as a constraint. It is necessary to satisfy it in the best way possible. Any constraint can be transformed into a goal by imposing this additional ranking criterion. For example, the following constraint:

$$3x_1 + 4x_2 \leqq 100$$

becomes a goal when a minimization of d^- in

$$3x_1 + 4x_2 + d^- = 100$$

is required. The level of underachievement of 100, deviation d^-, is to be as small as possible. The three constraints discussed above can become goals through the following formulation. Minimize d^- and d^+ subject to

$$3x_1 + 4x_2 + d^- = 100$$

or

$$3x_1 + 4x_2 - d^+ = 100$$

or

$$3x_1 + 4x_2 - d^+ + d^- = 100$$

In these three goals we minimize, respectively, the underachievement, overachievement, and both under- and overachievement of 100. Goals are more flexible than constraints with respect to changes. They are usually set externally and subjectively and can be changed without incurring additional cost, time, or effort.

An "objective" is an unbounded, directionally specified (maximization or minimization) requirement which *is to be followed to the greatest extent possible*. No particular value of the objective is set a priori as a reference point: Only its maximum is sought within the limits of feasibility determined by constraints and goals.

Each optimization problem can be classified into two parts: the set of functions to be optimized (minimized or maximized), i.e., *objectives*; and the set of functions to be satisfied (in terms of their predetermined values), i.e., *constraints*. *Goals* appear among *both* the objectives and constraints. Goals are constraints which are not only to be satisified, but satisfied in the best way. This additional criterion, usually phrased as the minimization of goal deviations, appears among the objectives.

From a purely technical viewpoint, a goal function is characterized by the fact that its slack or surplus variables (i.e., the variables converting inequalities into equalities) appear among the objectives with *nonzero* coefficients. The slack or surplus variables of constraints are assigned *zero* coefficients among the objectives.

As an example, let us introduce a set of simple constraints:

$$3x_1 + 4x_2 \leqq 100$$

$$x_1 + x_2 \geqq 50$$

$$2x_1 + 8x_2 \leqq 80$$

$$2x_1 + x_2 = 100$$

Let us transform these constraints into equalities by appending slack variables (d^-), surplus variables (d^+), or both (in the case of a strict equality constraint):

$$3x_1 + 4x_2 + d_1^- = 100$$

$$x_1 + x_2 - d_2^+ = 50$$

$$2x_1 + 8x_2 + d_3^- = 80$$

$$2x_1 + x_2 + d_4^- - d_4^+ = 100$$

If our objective is to attain the right-hand sides as closely as possible, we could write:

$$\text{Min } d_1^- + d_2^+ + d_4^- + d_4^+$$

Observe that d_3^- does not appear in this objective function (i.e., it has a zero coefficient), and thus the third equality would be classified as a constraint, while the other three are goals.

We should note that a goal might be set from which we would like to be as far as possible, rather than the usual "as close as possible" formulation. Let us take the example:

Suppose that $p_1x_1 + p_2x_2$ is a given profit function (p_1 and p_2 are profit margins per each unit of x_1 and x_2 respectively). The profit goal is set at 50, so we obtain

$$p_1x_1 + p_2x_2 \geqq 50$$

or

$$p_1x_1 + p_2x_2 - d^+ = 50$$

Observe that we do not allow any values below 50. That is, 50 is the lower bound in this formulation. Our goal could be stated as to be as far as possible from 50, that is, we attempt to maximize profits, so long as they are at least 50. Max d^+ would be the correct model. If we chose to Min d^+ under these conditions, we would strive to keep profits over 50, but not much over. For example, excessive profits might look bad in some socioeconomic environments.

In summary, the distinction between goals and constraints is not purely philosophical. While constraints are crude yes or no requirements (which can be either satisfied or not satisfied), goals allow for fine tuning through their control over the *degree of satisfaction*.

In a world of scarce resources we must care about the degrees of utilization of these resources. It is not sufficient to state that an upper limit of fifty workers cannot be exceeded. We either strive to use these fifty workers as fully as possible (i.e., no idle resources), or we attempt to save as many as possible to transfer to another project or to achieve the highest productivity indicators. To formulate that no more than fifty workers can be used, and add no other criterion or qualification, is a sure sign of not merely bad but simple-minded management. Thus, in the real world, we deal with goals and objectives, less so with constraints. Unfortunately, some of our models of the real world still operate in the realm of constraints, paying almost no attention to the utilization of resources.[1]

8-4 MULTICRITERION SIMPLEX METHOD

8-4.1 Graphic Analysis

The main purpose of linear multiobjective programming is to find all nondominated solutions to the types of problems discussed in Sec. 8-2 and shown in Fig. 8-2. The multicriterion simplex method (MSM) is designed to locate all nondominated corner points. Some of its modifications help to identify nondominated segments or faces of a feasible set X.

Consider the following example:

$$\text{Max } f_1(x) = 4x_1 + x_2$$

$$\text{Max } f_2(x) = \qquad x_2$$

subject to
$$X = \begin{cases} 2x_1 + x_2 \leq 20 \\ \frac{5}{6}x_1 + x_2 \leq 10 \\ x_1 + x_2 \geq 5 \end{cases}$$

and the nonnegativity conditions $x_1, x_2, x_3 \geq 0$.

To represent this problem graphically, we first trace out the feasible region X. Each of the inequalities represents a half plane with the strict equality as its boundary. It is therefore sufficient to draw, for example, $2x_1 + x_2 = 20$ and then determine which side of the boundary line consists of feasible points (x_1, x_2).

Any straight line is fully defined by two points. So we find two points which satisfy $2x_1 + x_2 = 20$. First, set $x_1 = 0$, and obviously $x_2 = 20$. Then set $x_2 = 0$ and calculate $x_1 = \frac{20}{2} = 10$. Thus, the two points are $(0, 20)$ and $(10, 0)$. The line $2x_1 + x_2 = 20$ is displayed in Fig. 8-4. Observe that since the line indicates a value of 20 and the inequality $\leq$ designates only values equal to or smaller than 20 as feasible, then the feasible direction is toward 0 on the graph in Fig. 8-4. Because the right-hand sides of constraints are always nonnegative, $\leq$ implies feasibility toward point 0 and $\geq$ implies feasibility away from point 0.

Similarly we draw $\frac{5}{6}x_1 + x_2 = 10$: set $x_1 = 0$ and get $x_2 = 10$; then set $x_2 = 0$ and get $x_1 = \frac{6}{5}(10) = 12$. Then draw the line through points $(0, 10)$ and $(12, 0)$. Shade its feasible side in the direction of 0. Finally, draw $x_1 + x_2 = 5$ through points $(0, 5)$ and $(5, 0)$; its feasible side is in the direction away from 0. The resulting feasible polyhedron of solutions (x_1, x_2) is denoted X.

Next, we have to display the two objective functions $f_1(x)$ and $f_2(x)$. This is usually done by setting the value of a given objective function to some conven-

---

[1]Understanding the distinction between goals and constraints is crucial for following these arguments.

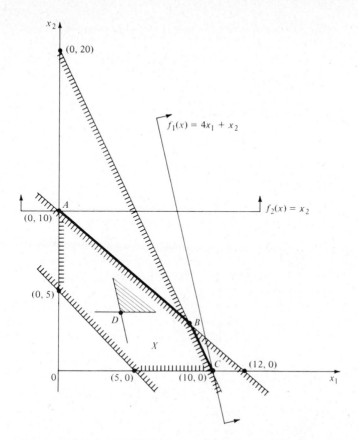

Figure 8-4 Drawing of constraints in two dimensions: the nondominated set.

ient, arbitrary, but positive number, for example, set $f_1(x) = 20$. Then the line $4x_1 + x_2 = 20$ can be drawn as passing through points $(0, 20)$ and $(5, 0)$. Because $f_1(x)$ is to be maximized, the direction of its value increase will be away from 0. Shift the line $4x_1 + x_2 = 20$ in that direction, in a parallel fashion, until it passes through the last feasible point (or points) of X. This happens for $f_1(x)$ at point C; $f_1(x)$ is maximized at C.

The drawing of $f_2(x) = x_2$ is similar: Shift a line parallel with the horizontal axis until it reaches point A. It cannot be moved any further without leaving feasible region X. Thus $f_2(x)$ is maximized at point A.

Take a look at point D in the interior of X. The dashed lines passing through D correspond to the two objective functions $f_1(x)$ and $f_2(x)$. Observe that D is a dominated point: Both functions can be improved in value at any point in the northeast direction from D (the shaded area). All these dominating points are feasible.

The only nondominated points of X are designated by the heavily drawn boundary connecting points A, B, and C. Points A, B, and C are nondominated corner points, and segments AB and BC are the remaining regions of nondominance.

The next example, adjusted from Steuer (1974), is presented as a further exercise for the reader in mastering the graphic analysis.

$$\text{Max } f_1(x) = x_1 + x_2$$
$$\text{Max } f_2(x) = \qquad x_2$$

subject to

$$\begin{aligned}
x_1 + 6x_2 &\leqq 108 \\
x_1 + 2x_2 &\leqq 40 \\
x_1 + x_2 &\leqq 24 \\
3x_1 + x_2 &\leqq 42 \\
4x_1 + x_2 &\leqq 52 \\
x_2 &\leqq 17\tfrac{1}{2} \qquad x_1, x_2 \geqq 0
\end{aligned}$$

In Fig. 8-5 observe that $f_1(x)$ is maximized at points $(8, 16)$ and $(9, 15)$ while $f_2(x)$ is maximized at points $(0, 17\tfrac{1}{2})$ and $(3, 17\tfrac{1}{2})$. But only three corner points are nondominated: $(3, 17\tfrac{1}{2})$, $(6, 17)$, and $(8, 16)$. The entire nondominated set is again indicated as the heavy boundary of X.

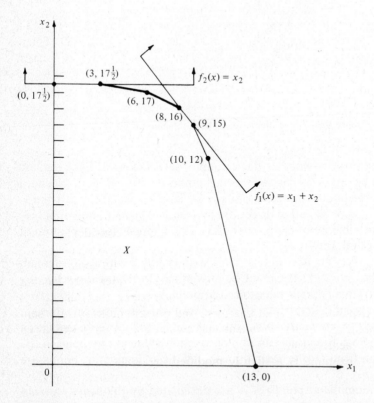

Figure 8-5 Drawing of constraints—an exercise and the nondominated set.

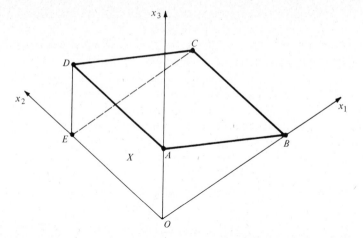

Figure 8-6 Drawing of constraints in three dimensions: the nondominated set.

Drawing three-dimensional figures is much more difficult and less instructive. Let us try at least one case, in Fig. 8-6.

Assume three simple objectives: $f_1(x) = x_1, f_2(x) = x_2$, and $f_3(x) = x_3$. In Fig. 8-6, x_1 is maximized at B and C while x_3 is maximized at A and D. Thus, maximizing $f_1(x)$ and $f_3(x)$ over X would lead to four nondominated corner solutions A, B, C, and D; actually the entire top plane $ABCD$ consists of nondominated solutions and forms the nondominated set. If we maximize all three functions at the same time—note that $f_2(x)$ is maximized at C, D, and E—then the nondominated set is reduced to segment DC only. The reader should check that maximizing $f_2(x)$ and $f_3(x)$ provides only one nondominated solution, point D. Similarly, maximizing $f_1(x)$ and $f_2(x)$ should result in C only.

8-4.2 A Formal Model and an Illustrative Example

To explain the multicriterion simplex method in a short section is not easy. Although computer codes are available and one would never consider solving a large practical problem by hand, some understanding of MSM's conceptual foundations is essential if one is to interpret and evaluate results obtained from using the method. It would, of course, be helpful if the reader were familiar with the conventional simplex method. We cannot assume that familiarity; nonetheless, our exposition will be quite terse and nonredundant. Every sentence, every symbol, and every comment will count. This section should be studied rather than merely read.

Our illustrative example is a slightly modified version of a product-mix problem from Paul Loomba, *Management—A Quantitative Perspective (1978)*. Two products A and B are to be produced by utilizing three different processes (cutting, folding, and packaging). The production of one unit of Product A

requires 10 minutes of processing time in the cutting department, 5 minutes in the folding department, and 7 minutes in the packaging department. (The production-time requirements for both A and B, as well as the total number of minutes available for each production process, are given in Table 8-1.) When sold, product A yields a profit of $23 per unit, while B yields $32. However, producing a unit of A saves 10 minutes of the total company's overall order-processing time, and producing a unit of B saves 20 minutes. Department managers are trying to identify a production program that will maximize profit *and* minimize the department's use of order-processing time. The pressure to maximize time savings comes from top management, as other departments' products are more profitable but can be sold only in conjunction with either A or B. The company's order-processing capacity cannot be expanded at this time.

Table 8-1

Process	Product A	Product B	Minutes available
Cutting	10	6	2500
Folding	5	10	2000
Packaging	7	7	2050
Time savings in minutes per unit	10	20	
Profit per unit	$23	$32	

Let x_1 and x_2 denote the number of units produced of A and B respectively. A feasible product mix $x = (x_1, x_2)$ is such which does not demand resources (minutes available) in excess of those assumed in Table 8-1.

In general, any number of products, or decision variables x_j, and any number of constraints can be assumed. Let $x = (x_1, \ldots, x_n)$ denote a solution consisting of n decision variables x_j, $j = 1, \ldots, n$. In linear multiobjective programming we may consider l linear objective functions defined on x as follows:

$$f_1(x) = c_{11}x_1 + c_{12}x_2 + \cdots + c_{1n}x_n$$
$$\vdots$$
$$f_l(x) = c_{l1}x_1 + c_{l2}x_2 + \cdots + c_{ln}x_n$$

Functions
$$f_i(x) = \sum_{j=1}^{n} c_{ij}x_j,$$

$i = 1, \ldots, l$ are to be maximized subject to a set of m linear constraints:

$$g_1(x) = a_{11}x_1 + a_{12}x_2 + \cdots + a_{1n}x_n = b_1$$
$$\vdots$$
$$g_m(x) = a_{m1}x_1 + a_{m2}x_2 + \cdots + a_{mn}x_n = b_m$$

where $g_r(x) = \sum_{j=1}^{n} a_{rj}x_j = b_r, r = 1, \ldots, m,$

are m linear equations which together with the nonnegativity conditions $x_j \geq 0$ for all j form a feasible set of solutions X.

Coefficients c_{ij} can be positive, negative, or zero; they indicate the amount of gain (or loss) to be realized with respect to the ith objective per each unit of increase in the jth variable. Coefficients a_{rj} are so-called "technological coefficients," indicating how much of the rth resource must be expended per each unit of increase in x_j.

Any linear-programming problem can be transformed into a similar system of linear equations. For example, our production-mix problem can be formulated as follows:

$$\text{Max } 10x_1 + 20x_2$$
and
$$\text{Max } 23x_1 + 32x_2$$

subject to
$$10x_1 + 6x_2 \leq 2500$$
$$5x_1 + 10x_2 \leq 2000$$
$$7x_1 + 7x_2 \leq 2050$$

and the nonnegativity conditions
$$x_1 \geq 0$$
$$x_2 \geq 0$$

First, we shall convert the inequalities into equalities by appending slack variables x_3, x_4, and x_5. These are simply convenient accounting units which help to equalize the left- and right-hand sides of the constraints. The right-hand sides are fixed constants $b_r, r = 1, \ldots m$, indicating the overall availability of the rth resource. All $b_r \geq 0$. After introducing the slack variables we obtain the following system:

$$10x_1 + 6x_2 + x_3 \qquad\qquad = 2500$$
$$5x_1 + 10x_2 \qquad + x_4 \qquad = 2000$$
$$7x_1 + 7x_2 \qquad\qquad + x_5 = 2050$$

Slack variables are not like decision variables, and their changes are not projected into the objective functions. Therefore, x_3, x_4, and x_5 carry zero coefficients in all objective functions. We can write the whole problem as follows:

Maximize functions

$$f_1(x) = 10x_1 + 20x_2 + 0x_3 + 0x_4 + 0x_5$$
$$f_2(x) = 23x_1 + 32x_2 + 0x_3 + 0x_4 + 0x_5$$

subject to

$$10x_1 + 6x_2 + 1x_3 + 0x_4 + 0x_5 = 2500$$
$$5x_1 + 10x_2 + 0x_3 + 1x_4 + 0x_5 = 2000$$
$$7x_1 + 7x_2 + 0x_3 + 0x_4 + 1x_5 = 2050$$

and $x_1, x_2, x_3, x_4, x_5 \geqq 0$.

A feasible solution to this problem is any $x = (x_1, x_2, x_3, x_4, x_5)$ satisfying the constraint conditions. For example, if $x_1 = 200$ and $x_2 = 0$, then $x_3 = 500$, $x_4 = 1000$, and $x_5 = 650$. Observe that we are solving only for the decision variables (x_1, and x_2); the slack variables are implied by the conditions. Take for example the third constraint. Substituting $x_1 = 200$ and $x_2 = 0$ we get:

$$7(200) + 7(0) = 1400 \quad \text{and} \quad 1400 + 650 = 2050$$

Thus x_5 must equal 650 in order to satisfy the third equation.

So, $x^1 = (x_1^1, x_2^1, x_3^1, x_4^1, x_5^1) = (200, 0, 500, 1000, 650)$ is one of the many feasible solutions to our problem. How good is this solution with respect to the objective functions? We simply substitute values of x^1 into $f_1(x)$ and $f_2(x)$. Thus, $f_1(x^1) = 10(200) + 20(0) + 0(0) + 0(0) + 0(650) = 2000$. Similarly, $f_2(x^1) = 4600$. It turns out that solution x^1 is dominated. That is, there exists at least one other feasible solution—say, x^2—such that $f_1(x^2) \geqq f_1(x^1)$ and $f_2(x^2) \geqq f_2(x^1)$.

For example, choose $x^2 = (250, 0, 0, 750, 300)$ and compute $f_1(x^2) = 2500$ and $f_2(x^2) = 5750$. Obviously x^2 dominates x^1. That does not mean that x^2 itself cannot be dominated by yet another feasible solution. The task of MSM is to identify only such feasible solutions as are not dominated by any other feasible solution.

In this example there is only one nondominated solution, $x' = (\frac{1300}{7}, \frac{750}{7}, 0, 0, 0)$, as we shall find out later by applying MSM. Correspondingly, $f_1(x') = 4000$ and $f_2(x') = 7700$. All other solutions in X are dominated. There is one more solution which gives \$4000 for $f_1(x)$, but that one is dominated too. Take $x'' = (0, 200, 1300, 0, 650)$ and check that $f_1(x'') = 4000$ and $f_2(x'') = 6400$; that is, x'' is dominated by x'.

General MSM tableau The next set of symbolic notations and the general simplex tableau format are quite important for understanding the MSM procedure.

All variables, including the slacks, are divided into two groups: m basic variables $x_1, \ldots, x_m$ that are currently forming a solution, and $(n - m)$ nonbasic variables $x_{m+1}, \ldots, x_n$ whose values are, by definition, equal to zero.

Since there are m constraints and n variables, only m variables can be positive, while the remaining $(n - m)$ variables are zero. We do not count the non-negativity conditions as constraints, because they are automatically satisfied through the appropriate simplex method manipulations.

A solution consisting of m basic and $(n - m)$ nonbasic, zero-valued variables is referred to as a "basic" solution. The set of basic variables $x_1, \ldots, x_m$ is often referred to as a "basis." Basic solutions will generally be identified by superscripts, that is, x^0, x^1, x^2, and so on, usually indicating the order in which they were generated. For example, $x^0 = (x_1^0, \ldots, x_n^0)$ or $x^1 = (x_1^1, \ldots, x_n^1)$. Let us now consider a particular feasible basic solution x^0. Its multicriterion simplex tableau is displayed in Table 8-2.

This MSM tableau differs from a conventional simplex tableau only in having multiple-criteria rows instead of a single-criterion row. Before we interpret the entries in the MSM tableau, it is important to note that the tableau corresponds to x^0 only and thus $x_1 = x_1^0, \ldots, x_m = x_m^0$. For better orientation, we have arranged it so that basic variables are identical with the first m variables. Actually, any variable could become basic in the course of computational iterations; the order in Table 8-2 is therefore quite arbitrary. Because the order in which the variables are arranged is not important, we allow ourselves to use this simplification.

Suppose that x^0 is a nondegenerate solution, i.e., all its basic variables are positive. Later on we shall encounter some cases where one or more basic variables are equal to zero, leading to the phenomenon known as "solution degeneracy." Thus, $x^0 = (x_1, \ldots, x_m, 0, \ldots, 0)$, where $x_j = x_j^0 > 0$ for $j = 1, \ldots, m$, and $x_j = 0$ for $j = m+1, \ldots, n$.

Numbers y_{rj}, defined for $r = 1, \ldots, m$ and $j = 1, \ldots, n$, can be interpreted as substitution ratios between variables x_r and x_j. That is, in order to be able to increase x_j by one unit, we must sacrifice y_{rj} units from the current value

Table 8-2

Current basis	Basic variables $x_1 \ldots x_m$	Nonbasic variables $x_{m+1} \ldots x_j \ldots x_n$	Values of basic variables
x_1	$1 \ldots 0$	$y_{1\,(m+1)} \cdots y_{1j} \cdots y_{1n}$	x_1^0
$\cdot$	$\cdot \quad \cdot$	$\cdot \qquad \cdot \qquad \cdot$	$\cdot$
$\cdot$	$\cdot \quad \cdot$	$\cdot \qquad \cdot \qquad \cdot$	$\cdot$
x_m	$0 \ldots 1$	$y_{m\,(m+1)} \cdots y_{mj} \cdots y_{mn}$	x_m^0
Criteria rows	$0 \ldots 0$	$z_{1\,(m+1)} \cdots z_{1j} \cdots z_{1n}$	$f_1(x^0)$
	$\cdot \quad \cdot$	$\cdot \qquad \cdot \qquad \cdot$	$\cdot$
	$\cdot \quad \cdot$	$\cdot \qquad \cdot \qquad \cdot$	$\cdot$
	$0 \ldots 0$	$z_{l(m+1)} \cdots z_{lj} \cdots z_{ln}$	$f_l(x^0)$

of x_r. Observe that for the basic variables, that is, for $j = 1, \ldots, m$, all $y_{rj} = 1$ if $r = j$ and $y_{rj} = 0$ otherwise.

Suppose that we want to increase variable x_j by one unit. What is the total sacrifice in terms of the ith objective? Increasing x_j means that variables $x_1, \ldots, x_m$ will have to be reduced by $y_{1j}, \ldots, y_{mj}$ respectively. But $x_1, \ldots, x_m$ are our current basic variables, and their ith objective function coefficients are $c_{i1}, \ldots, c_{im}$. To evaluate the total value sacrifice we simply multiply all relevant y_{rj}'s by the corresponding c_{ir}'s:

$$\sum_{r=1}^{m} c_{ir} y_{rj}$$

Now, if we actually increase x_j by one unit, how much do we gain by that increase in terms of the ith objective function? Obviously, c_{ij}. The net effect, on the ith objective, of increasing the variable x_j by one unit is:

$$z_{ij} = \sum_{r=1}^{m} c_{ir} y_{rj} - c_{ij}$$

Observe that for the basic variables $j = 1, \ldots, m$, all $z_{ij} = 0$. This is because $y_{rj} = 1$ if $r = j$ and 0 otherwise, implying

$$\sum_{r=1}^{m} c_{ir} y_{rj} = c_{ij} \qquad \text{and} \qquad c_{ij} - c_{ij} = 0$$

Consequently, the basic variables which constitute the current basis cannot improve the value of the ith objective function. But the nonbasic variables can.

Current values of all objectives functions can also be obtained directly from the tableau in Table 8-2. They are

$$f_i(x^0) = \sum_{r=1}^{m} c_{ir} x_r^0 \qquad i = 1, \ldots, l$$

indicating the values of the ith objective function at x^0.

It would be clearly profitable to introduce into the current basis those nonbasic variables for which at least one $z_{ij} < 0$, that is, where the total value sacrifice is smaller than total gain. The value of z_{ij} indicates the amount of increase in $f_i(x^0)$ per each unit of increase in nonbasic x_j. If $z_{ij} \geq 0$ for any nonbasic variable, then the value of $f_i(x^0)$ would actually decrease or stay unchanged per each unit of the increase in x_j.

If, however, $z_{ij} \geq 0$ for *all* nonbasic variables $j = m + 1, \ldots, n$, then the corresponding objective function $f_i(x)$ has reached its maximum and cannot be further improved. If all nonbasic $z_{ij} \geq 0$, but at least one $z_{ij} = 0$, then there is at least one alternative maximum solution. Multiple maxima are quite common in linear programming. They can be found by introducing the x_j corresponding to $z_{ij} = 0$ into the "maximum" basis.

How do we find the initial feasible solution, i.e., how do we form the first simplex tableau? If all constraints are of the type $\leq$, then the task is very simple. Start with the m slack variables by making them all basic variables and thus forming the initial basis. All decision variables then become nonbasic and invariably equal to zero. Also, $y_{rj} = a_{rj}$, that is, substitution ratios are initially equal to the original technological coefficients. Similarly, $x_r^0 = b_r$, that is, slack variables are equal to the full amount of the constraining quantities. Finally, $z_{ij} = -c_{ij}$ because

$$\sum_{r=1}^{m} c_{ir} y_{rj} = 0 \text{ due to } c_{ir} = 0 \text{ for all } r = 1, \ldots, m;$$

recall that coefficients of the slack variables are zero in all objective functions and $z_{ij} = 0$ for $j = 1, \ldots, m$.

An example of MSM iterations We shall now form the initial MSM tableau according to the format displayed in Table 8-2. We simply fill that tableau with the actual numbers corresponding to the product-mix example and then verify their interpretation. Note that the basic variables will not correspond to the first m columns, as in Table 8-2, but will assume arbitrary positions. It would be clumsy to keep renumbering the variables in a course of computational iterations. The results are shown in Table 8-3.

Table 8-3 corresponds to the initial solution $x^0 = (0, 0, 2500, 2000, 2050)$ and $f_1(x^0) = 0, f_2(x^0) = 0; x_1 = 0$ and $x_2 = 0$ express that neither product A nor B is being produced.

In Table 8-3 check that z_{ij}'s are correctly computed. For example, $z_{11} = -10$ has been obtained as follows:

$$z_{11} = c_{13} y_{31} + c_{14} y_{41} + c_{15} y_{51} - c_{11}$$
$$= 0(10) + 0(5) + 0(7) - 10 = -10$$

or

$$z_{22} = c_{23} y_{32} + c_{24} y_{42} + c_{25} y_{52} - c_{22}$$
$$= 0(6) + 0(10) + 0(7) - 32 = -32$$

Table 8-3

Current basis	Nonbasic variables		Basic variables			Values of basic variables
	x_1	x_2	x_3	x_4	x_5	
x_3	10	6	1	0	0	2500
x_4	5	10	0	1	0	2000
x_5	7	7	0	0	1	2050
	-10	-20	0	0	0	0
	-23	-32	0	0	0	0

Recall that $z_{ij} < 0$ implies that if we introduce the corresponding nonbasic variable into the basis, we would improve the value of the ith objective function by z_{ij} per each unit of increase in x_j. In Table 8-3 both x_1 and x_2 would lead to this improvement in both objective functions. The effect of introducing x_2 is slightly more profitable, so we have decided to make x_2 a basic variable: It is currently equal to zero, and we would like to make it as large as possible without violating the constraints. Because there can be only m variables in the basis, the introduction of x_2 will have to force one of the currently basic variables out of the basis.

Recall that $y_{32} = 6$, $y_{42} = 10$, and $y_{52} = 7$ are the substitution ratios, indicating how much of the three basic variables x_3, x_4, x_5 would have to be sacrificed in order to increase x_2 by one additional unit. Currently $x_3 = 2500$, and the maximum increase in x_2 allowed by x_3 is $\frac{2500}{6} = 416\frac{2}{3}$. Similarly the maximum amounts of increase in x_2 allowed by x_4 and x_5 are $\frac{2000}{10} = 200$ and $\frac{2050}{7} = 292.86$, respectively.

Because we cannot sacrifice more than is available, i.e., none of the x_3, x_4, and x_5 can become negative, we have to choose the smallest ratio as the maximum amount of increase in x_2 allowed by *all* basic variables jointly. Thus x_2 will be increased to 200, and x_4 will become zero long before x_3 or x_5 would. This amounts to replacing x_4 with x_2 in the next basis. Thus, x_2 is in and x_4 is out. Such an exchange will affect the two objective functions as follows: $f_1(x^1) = f_1(x^0) + 20(200) = 0 + 4000 = 4000$, and $f_2(x^1) = f_2(x^0) + 32(200) = 0 + 6400 = 6400$.

But how do we actually perform the replacement of x_4 by x_2? How do we transform the tableau for x^0 into that for x^1? Quite simply.

Observe that if x_2 is going to be in the new basis, its corresponding column of coefficients y_{r2} and z_{i2}, $r = 3,4,5$ and $i = 1,2$, should become identical with the column currently corresponding to x_4. In other words, in Table 8-3, "old" x_2:

$$\begin{pmatrix} 6 \\ 10 \\ 7 \\ -20 \\ -32 \end{pmatrix}$$

will be replaced by "old" x_4:

$$\begin{pmatrix} 0 \\ 1 \\ 0 \\ 0 \\ 0 \end{pmatrix}$$

All columns and rows will have to be involved in the transformation. We can summarize all the data from Table 8-3 in the following matrix:

$$
\begin{array}{c}
& x_1 & x_2 & x_3 & x_4 & x_5 & \\
1 & 10 & 6 & 1 & 0 & 0 & 2500 \\
2 & 5 & 10 & 0 & 1 & 0 & 2000 \\
3 & 7 & 7 & 0 & 0 & 1 & 2050 \\
4 & -10 & -20 & 0 & 0 & 0 & 0 \\
5 & -23 & -32 & 0 & 0 & 0 & 0
\end{array}
$$

In the above matrix, the replacement of x_2 by x_4 must be made in such a way that the matrix of coefficient will be fully consistent and precisely related to the original problem. Fortunately, some very simple algebraic operations can be performed on the rows of coefficients while the correct relationships are being preserved. We shall need only two operations:

1. Any row can be multiplied by a positive or negative constant
2. A multiple of one row can be added to another row

Recall that column x_2 should become identical with x_4. If we multiply the second row by $\frac{1}{10}$, a 1 appears in the proper position, i.e., at the intersection of column x_2 and the second row. The resulting new row of coefficients

$$(\tfrac{1}{2}, 1, 0, \tfrac{1}{10}, 0, 200)$$

will be referred to as the *key row*. The key row is always computed first and then used as a reference for computing all the remaining rows. Observe that we need to place zeros in all the remaining positions in column x_2. This can be achieved simply by adding the appropriate multiples (positive or negative) of the key row to the remaining rows. For example, to obtain the new first row, we can multiply the key row by (-6) and add the results to the old first row:

$$
\begin{aligned}
(-6)(\tfrac{1}{2}, 1, 0, \tfrac{1}{10}, 0, 200) &= (-3, -6, 0, -\tfrac{3}{5}, 0, -1200) \\
+ (10, \quad & 6, 1, \quad 0, 0, \quad 2500) \\
\hline
(7, \quad & 0, 1, -\tfrac{3}{5}, 0, \quad 1300)
\end{aligned}
$$

In a similar fashion, the key row is to be multiplied by (-7) and the results added to the third row. In order to replace -10 and -23 in the last two rows with zeros we simply multiply the key row by 10 and 23 and add the results to the fourth and fifth rows respectively.

By performing these operations, we have transformed the tableau of Table 8-3 into that of Table 8-4.

In Table 8-4 we have identified a new basic solution $x^1 = (0, 200, 1300, 0, 650)$. Observe that $z_{1j} \geqq 0$ for all $j = 1, \ldots, 5$; that is, the first criterion row does not contain any negative numbers. Thus, the first objective cannot be further improved, and x^1 represents a maximum solution with respect to the first objective. But notice also that nonbasic variable x_1 has its corresponding $z_{11} = 0$. That means that there is an alternative maximum with respect to the first objective.

Table 8-4

Current basis	x_1	x_2	x_3	x_4	x_5	Values of basic variables
x_3	7	0	1	$-\frac{3}{5}$	0	1300
x_2	$\frac{1}{2}$	1	0	$\frac{1}{10}$	0	200
x_5	$\frac{7}{2}$	0	0	$-\frac{7}{10}$	1	650
	0	0	0	2	0	4000
	-7	0	0	$3\frac{1}{5}$	0	6400

By introducing x_1 into the basis we should not only locate this alternative maximum but actually improve the second objective by 7 per each unit of increase in x_1, while the first objective retains its maximum value of 4000. This also implies that x^1 is a dominated solution. Why?

We next repeat the same procedure, starting with the tableau in Table 8-4. First, the maximum allowed increase in x_1 is dictated by the smallest of the three ratios $1300/7 = 185.71$, $200/\frac{1}{2} = 400$, and $650/\frac{7}{2} = 185.71$. Observe that there are *two* smallest ratios. Therefore, the same value effect would be achieved by replacing either x_3 or x_5 with x_1 in the new basis. In cases like this we simply choose the outgoing variable at random, say, x_3. Both x_3 and x_5 will be driven to zero simultaneously. But only x_3 will become nonbasic, while x_5 will remain in the basis. A solution for which at least one of the basic variables is equal to zero is called a "degenerate" solution. Thus our next solution x^2, will be degenerate.

In order to compute the next tableau, its first column will have to become identical with the third column of the previous tableau. We can multiply the first row of Table 8-4 by $\frac{1}{7}$ and refer to the results as the "key row." Then we multiply the key row by $-\frac{1}{2}$ and by $-\frac{7}{2}$ and add the outcomes to the second and third rows respectively. Observe that the fourth row already contains zero in the proper position. In such cases we can leave the row unchanged. The last row is obtained by multiplying the key row by 7 and by adding the results to the last row. The new tableau appears in Table 8-5.

Table 8-5

Current basis	x_1	x_2	x_3	x_4	x_5	Values of basic variables
x_1	1	0	$\frac{1}{7}$	$-\frac{3}{35}$	0	$\frac{1300}{7}$
x_2	0	1	$-\frac{1}{14}$	$\frac{1}{7}$	0	$\frac{750}{7}$
x_5	0	0	$-\frac{1}{2}$	$-\frac{2}{5}$	1	0
	0	0	0	2	0	4000
	0	0	1	$\frac{13}{5}$	0	7700

Observe that because z_{1j} and z_{2j} are all nonnegative for $j = 1, \ldots, 5, x^2 = (\frac{1300}{7}, \frac{750}{7}, 0, 0, 0)$ maximizes both functions at the same time and is therefore the only nondominated solution for the entire problem. The departmental managers were truly lucky in finding that producing 185.71 units of A and 107.14 units of B would maximize both profits and order-processing time savings at the same time.

Point x^2 provides a unique maximum of $f_2(x)$, while $f_1(x)$ is maximized at both x^2 and x^1. Also, the solution of x^2 is degenerate because basic variable $x_5 = 0$.

Observe that coefficients z_{ij} have not been independently calculated for each tableau. They are being correctly maintained by simply applying the permissible row operations. Let us check their values for column x_4 nevertheless:

$$z_{14} = c_{11}y_{14} + c_{12}y_{24} + c_{15}y_{54} - c_{14}$$
$$= 10(-\tfrac{3}{35}) + 20(\tfrac{1}{7}) + 0(-\tfrac{2}{5}) - 0 = 2$$

and

$$z_{24} = c_{21}y_{14} + c_{22}y_{24} + c_{25}y_{54} - c_{24}$$
$$= 23(-\tfrac{3}{35}) + 32(\tfrac{1}{7}) + 0(-\tfrac{2}{5}) - 0 = \tfrac{13}{5}$$

Looking for nondominance We shall summarize the previously performed numerical computations in terms of their equivalent but more general rules. Observe that each nonbasic variable in Table 8-2 has the following associated column vector in the criteria rows portion of the tableau:

$$z_j = \begin{pmatrix} z_{1j} \\ \cdot \\ \cdot \\ \cdot \\ z_{lj} \end{pmatrix}$$

Also, with each basic solution (and its tableau)—say, x^0—there is associated a corresponding column vector of current values of the objective functions:

$$f^0 = \begin{pmatrix} f_1(x^0) \\ \cdot \\ \cdot \\ \cdot \\ f_l(x^0) \end{pmatrix}$$

Note that this vector f^0 is also maintained and updated automatically by the performance of correct row operations on the individual tableaus.

For any nonbasic variable x_j, such that $y_{rj} > 0$ for at least one $r = 1, \ldots, m$, we define

$$@_j = \mathop{\text{Min}}_{r} \frac{x_r^0}{y_{rj}}$$

Thus $@_j$ is the minimum of the ratios formed for the jth column; the corresponding "minimizing" row r then determines which of the basic variables x_r is going to leave the basis.

The ratios

$$\frac{x_r^0}{y_{rj}}$$

can only be defined for the positive entries y_{rj} of any column x_j, $j = m + 1, \ldots, n$. Suppose that $y_{rj} \leqq 0$ for all $r = 1, \ldots, m$ in the jth column. Then in order to increase x_j, no sacrifice of any of the basic variables is necessary; x_j can be increased indefinitely, and the linear-programming problem has a so-called "unbounded solution." In general, the negative substitution ratios y_{rj} indicate how much x_r would have to be *increased* per each unit of increase in x_j (compare the positive y_{rj}, which indicates the amount of "sacrifice" in x_r). Obviously, if all y_{rj} are nonpositive, we can get something for nothing, and the problem is value-unbounded.

To check one's understanding, one should look at Table 8-4. Column x_1 indicates that if we increase x_1 by one unit, variables x_3, x_2, and x_5 would decrease by 7, $\frac{1}{2}$, and $\frac{7}{2}$ respectively. We have increased x_1 by $\frac{1300}{7}$. That means that the new $x_3 = 1300 - 7(\frac{1300}{7}) = 0$, the new $x_2 = 200 - \frac{1}{2}(\frac{1300}{7}) = \frac{750}{7}$, and the new $x_5 = 650 - \frac{7}{2}(\frac{1300}{7}) = 0$. Check Table 8-5 to see if they are truly so. Next, look at column x_3 in Table 8-5. Per each unit of increase in x_3 we would have to decrease the current value of x_1 by 7 but increase x_2 by $\frac{1}{14}$ and x_5 by $\frac{1}{2}$. It should be clear by now that each unit of increase in x_1 would produce no change in $f_1(x)$ and would reduce the value of $f_2(x)$ by 1. What is the maximum amount by which x_3 can be increased when introduced into the basis? Since there is only one nonnegative y_{r3} in the third column, $y_{13} = \frac{1}{7}$, we can only form the ratio $\frac{1300}{7} / \frac{1}{7}$ and $@_3 = 1300$. That is, x_3 will be increased by 1300. Then the new $x_1 = \frac{1300}{7} - \frac{1}{7}(1300) = 0$, the new $x_2 = \frac{750}{7} + \frac{1}{14}(1300) = 200$, and the new $x_5 = 0 + \frac{1}{2}(1300) = 650$. The new $f_1(x)$ will remain 4000, while the new $f_2(x) = 7700 - 1(1300) = 6400$. The reader should check Table 8-4 and verify these calculations and the resulting basis transformation.

Let us continue with the application of $@_j$. By introducing x_j into the basis of x^0, we obtain a new basic solution—say, x^1—and also its new vector of values f^1, according to the following relation:

$$f^1 = f^0 - @_j z_j$$

Recall that $@_2 = 200$ in Table 8-3. Then $f^1 = f^0 - @_2 z_2$ corresponds to

$$\begin{pmatrix} 4000 \\ 6400 \end{pmatrix} = \begin{pmatrix} 0 \\ 0 \end{pmatrix} - 200 \begin{pmatrix} -20 \\ -32 \end{pmatrix}$$

Similarly, in Table 8-4, $@_1 = 1300/7$ and the $f^2 = f^1 - @_1 z_1$ can be expressed numerically as

$$\begin{pmatrix} 4000 \\ 7700 \end{pmatrix} = \begin{pmatrix} 4000 \\ 6400 \end{pmatrix} - 1300/7 \begin{pmatrix} 0 \\ -7 \end{pmatrix}$$

Given the above relations, one can make some useful statements about whether a given basic solution is dominated or nondominated. Suppose that we are looking at a simplex tableau, say, for x^0. Then,

1. If there is a z_j consisting of only nonpositive components, not all of which are zero, then x^0 must be dominated.
2. If there is a z_j consisting of only nonnegative components, not all of which are zero, then introducing x_j into the basis would result in a dominated solution.
3. Consider two nonbasic variables x_j and x_k. If all the components of $@_j z_j$ are smaller or equal to the components of $@_k z_k$, with at least one $@_j z_{ij} < @_k z_{ik}$, $i = 1, \ldots, l$, then the solution resulting from introducing x_k would be dominated by the solution which would result from introducing x_j.

Such rules greatly accelerate MSM progress toward the first nondominated solution. Once the first nondominated solution has been reached, the iterative procedure can limit itself to generating only nondominated solutions. One can reach the first nondominated solution most efficiently by realizing that at least one of the alternative solutions, maximizing any $f_i(x)$, $i = 1, \ldots, l$, must be nondominated. A unique maximal solution, i.e., when $z_{ij} > 0$ for all nonbasic variables $j = m + 1, \ldots, n$, must be nondominated.

In some cases the issue of nondominance cannot be simply decided by applying one of the three rules given above. An additional feature of MSM, the so-called "nondominance test," helps to determine the status of *any* basic solution beyond doubt.

Suppose that a given basic solution—say, x^*—is to be characterized as either dominated or nondominated. Consider what could be the results of solving the following linear-programming problem:

$$\text{Max} \sum_{i=1}^{l} d_i$$

subject to

$$\sum_{j=1}^{n} a_{rj} x_j = b_r \qquad r = 1, \ldots, m$$

and

$$\sum_{j=1}^{n} c_{ij} x_j - d_i \geq f_i(x^*), \qquad i = 1, \ldots, l$$
$$d_i \geq 0$$
$$x_j = 0$$

We shall use $x^* = (x_1^*, \ldots, x_n^*)$ as the initial basic solution to the above problem. Observe that all $d_i = 0$. This is because

$$\sum_{j=1}^{n} c_{ij} x_j^* = f_i(x^*)$$

Consequently,

$$\sum_{i=1}^{l} d_i = 0$$

This implies that maximizing

$$\sum_{i=1}^{l} d_i$$

would always yield a nonnegative result. Thus, for example,

$$w = \mathrm{Max} \sum_{i=1}^{l} d_i \geq 0$$

The following test is then true:

1. x^* is nondominated if and only if $w = 0$
2. x^* is dominated if and only if $w > 0$

In other words, if x^* itself is the maximum of the nondominance test linear-programming problem, then it is also a nondominated solution.

We shall not discuss further details of the theory of the nondominance test. There are many versions of it, but some useful extensions are available in Zeleny (1973, 1974) and Yu and Zeleny (1975). The test can be best implemented and utilized through a computer, although different codes may employ quite different versions or adaptations of this type of nondominance testing.

A numerical example We shall now analyze a larger, numerically interesting problem in more detail. Its full, step-by-step computational description is also given in App. A. Consider the following problem:

$$
\begin{aligned}
f_1(x) &= x_1 + 2x_2 - x_3 + 3x_4 + 2x_5 && + x_7 \\
f_2(x) &= x_2 + x_3 + 2x_4 + 3x_5 + x_6 \\
f_3(x) &= x_1 + x_3 - x_4 - x_6 - x_7
\end{aligned}
$$

subject to

$$
\begin{aligned}
x_1 + 2x_2 + x_3 + x_4 + 2x_5 + x_6 + 2x_7 &\leq 16 \\
-2x_1 - x_2 + x_4 + 2x_5 + x_7 &\leq 16 \\
-x_1 + x_3 + 2x_5 - 2x_7 &\leq 16 \\
x_2 + 2x_3 - x_4 + x_5 - 2x_6 - x_7 &\leq 16
\end{aligned}
$$

and, of course, $x_j \geq 0$, $j = 1, \ldots, 7$

Table 8-6

Current basis	Nonbasic variables							Basic variables				Values of basic variables
	x_1	x_2	x_3	x_4	x_5	x_6	x_7	x_8	x_9	x_{10}	x_{11}	
x_8	1	2	1	1	2	1	2	1	0	0	0	16
x_9	-2	-1	0	1	2	0	1	0	1	0	0	16
x_{10}	-1	0	1	0	2	0	-2	0	0	1	0	16
x_{11}	0	1	2	-1	1	-2	-1	0	0	0	1	16
	-1	-2	1	-3	-2	0	-1	0	0	0	0	0
	0	-1	-1	-2	-3	-1	0	0	0	0	0	0
	-1	0	-1	1	0	1	1	0	0	0	0	0

This system of inequalities can be converted into equalities by appending the appropriate slack variables x_8, x_9, x_{10}, and x_{11}. The initial simplex tableau is displayed in Table 8-6.

By inspecting the criteria part of the MSM tableau in Table 8-6, we can conclude immediately that $x^0 = (0, 0, 0, 0, 0, 0, 0, 16, 16, 16, 16)$ is dominated. Observe that z_1, z_2, and z_5 consist of nonpositive components; introducing any of the corresponding variables into the basis will lead to a dominating solution, x^1. Let us introduce x_5. Obviously, because $@_5 = 8$ is achieved by three minimal ratios, any of the three variables x_8, x_9, and x_{10} can be selected to leave the basis. We choose x_8 arbitrarily. Observe that the next solution, x^1, will be doubly degenerate. The results of this transformation are displayed in Table 8-7.

The corresponding basic solution is $x^1 = (0, 0, 0, 0, 8, 0, 0, 0, \underline{0}, \underline{0}, \underline{0}, 8)$, that is, $x_5 = 8$ and $x_{11} = 8$ while all other variables are zero. We have underlined

Table 8-7

Current basis	x_1	x_2	x_3	x_4	x_5	x_6	x_7	x_8	x_9	x_{10}	x_{11}	Values of basic variables
x_5	$\frac{1}{2}$	1	$\frac{1}{2}$	$\frac{1}{2}$	1	$\frac{1}{2}$	1	$\frac{1}{2}$	0	0	0	8
x_9	-3	-3	-1	0	0	-1	-1	-1	1	0	0	0
x_{10}	-2	-2	0	-1	0	-1	-4	-1	0	1	0	0
x_{11}	$-\frac{1}{2}$	0	$\frac{3}{2}$	$-\frac{3}{2}$	0	$-\frac{5}{2}$	-2	$-\frac{1}{2}$	0	0	1	8
	0	0	2	-2	0	1	1	1	0	0	0	16
	$\frac{3}{2}$	2	$\frac{1}{2}$	$-\frac{1}{2}$	0	$\frac{1}{2}$	3	$\frac{3}{2}$	0	0	0	24
	-1	0	-1	1	0	1	1	0	0	0	0	0

those zeros which are part of the basis. None of the three objective functions has reached its maximum at x^1. We have to use the nondominance test to establish whether x^1 is nondominated. That is accomplished by maximizing

$$\sum_{i=1}^{l} d_i = d_1 + d_2 + d_3$$

subject to

$$f_1(x) - d_1 \geqq 16$$

$$f_2(x) - d_2 \geqq 24$$

$$f_3(x) - d_3 \geqq 0$$

and the original set of constraints X. We refer the reader to App. A for the computational details.

It turns out that x^1 maximizes the above test problem, that is, $w = 0$. Consequently, x^1 is our first nondominated basic solution, and we can use the three rules introduced earlier for generating the remaining nondominated solutions. For example, in Table 8-7, we cannot introduce x_2, x_6, x_7, or x_8 because they would lead to dominated solutions, that is, z_2, z_6, z_7, and z_8 consist of nonnegative components only. Their impact was discussed in rule 2 on p. 243.

Any of the three remaining eligible variables x_1, x_3, or x_4 could be introduced. But let us first explore the applicability of rule 3. First, compute $@_1 = 16$, $@_3 = \frac{16}{3}$, and $@_4 = 16$, and then form their respective multiples with z_1, z_3, and z_4:

$$16\begin{pmatrix} 0 \\ \frac{3}{2} \\ -1 \end{pmatrix} = \begin{pmatrix} 0 \\ 24 \\ -16 \end{pmatrix} \quad \frac{16}{3}\begin{pmatrix} 2 \\ \frac{1}{2} \\ -1 \end{pmatrix} = \begin{pmatrix} 10.67 \\ 2.67 \\ -5.33 \end{pmatrix} \quad 16\begin{pmatrix} -2 \\ -\frac{1}{2} \\ 1 \end{pmatrix} = \begin{pmatrix} -32 \\ -8 \\ 16 \end{pmatrix}$$

Observe that rule 3 is still indeterminate. Let us extend rule 3 by considering $f^2 = f^1 - @_j z_j$, where $j = 1, 3, 4$ in our case. We get

$$\begin{pmatrix} 16 \\ 24 \\ 0 \end{pmatrix} - \begin{pmatrix} 0 \\ 24 \\ -16 \end{pmatrix} = \begin{pmatrix} 16 \\ 0 \\ 16 \end{pmatrix} \quad \begin{pmatrix} 16 \\ 24 \\ 0 \end{pmatrix} - \begin{pmatrix} 10.67 \\ 2.67 \\ -5.33 \end{pmatrix} = \begin{pmatrix} 5.33 \\ 21.33 \\ 5.33 \end{pmatrix}$$

$$\begin{pmatrix} 16 \\ 24 \\ 0 \end{pmatrix} - \begin{pmatrix} -32 \\ -8 \\ 16 \end{pmatrix} = \begin{pmatrix} 48 \\ 32 \\ -16 \end{pmatrix}$$

Observe that neither of the solutions obtained by introducing x_1, x_3, or x_4 could be declared dominated on the basis of this simple test, because

$$\begin{pmatrix} 48 \\ 32 \\ -16 \end{pmatrix} \quad \begin{pmatrix} 16 \\ 0 \\ 16 \end{pmatrix} \quad \text{and} \quad \begin{pmatrix} 5.33 \\ 21.33 \\ 5.33 \end{pmatrix}$$

are noncomparable vectors. Thus we can introduce any of the eligible columns, either x_1, x_3, or x_4. Let us choose x_4 and replace x_5 in the basis. Table 8-8 shows the results of this transformation.

Table 8-8

Current basis	x_1	x_2	x_3	x_4	x_5	x_6	x_7	x_8	x_9	x_{10}	x_{11}	Values of basic variables
x_4	1	2	1	1	2	1	2	1	0	0	0	16
x_9	-3	-3	-1	0	0	-1	-1	-1	1	0	0	0
x_{10}	-1	0	1	0	2	0	-2	0	0	1	0	16
x_{11}	1	3	3	0	3	-1	1	1	0	0	1	32
	2	4	4	0	4	3	5	3	0	0	0	48
	2	3	1	0	1	1	4	2	0	0	0	32
	-2	-2	-2	0	-2	0	-1	-1	0	0	0	-16

The corresponding solution is $x^2 = (0, 0, 0, 16, 0, 0, 0, 0, 0, 16, 32)$, that is, $x_4 = 16$ and the slack variables x_{10} and x_{11} are 16 and 32 respectively. All other variables are zero. Basic solution x^2 is nondominated. Observe that $z_{1j} > 0$ and $z_{2j} > 0$ for *all* nonbasic variables. That means that *both* $f_1(x)$ and $f_2(x)$ reach their respective *unique* maxima at x^2.

In the next step we would introduce x_1 into the basis. The reader should check that the next basic solution x^3 is also nondominated. Full details are in App. A.

Altogether we find that the stated problem has six different nondominated solutions:

	x_1	x_2	x_3	x_4	x_5	x_6	x_7	x_8	x_9	x_{10}	x_{11}
x^1	0	0	0	0	8	0	0	0	0	0	8
x^2	0	0	0	16	0	0	0	0	0	16	32
x^3	16	0	0	0	0	0	0	0	48	0	16
x^4	8	0	8	0	0	0	0	0	32	16	0
x^5	0	0	$\frac{32}{3}$	$\frac{16}{3}$	0	0	0	0	$\frac{32}{3}$	$\frac{16}{3}$	0
x^6	0	0	$\frac{16}{3}$	0	$\frac{16}{3}$	0	0	0	$\frac{16}{3}$	0	0

These nondominated solutions are characterized by the values of $f_1(x)$, $f_2(x)$, and $f_3(x)$ shown in Table 8-9.

In Table 8-9, notice that two entirely different nondominated solutions, such as x^5 and x^6, can both provide identical values with respect to the corresponding objective functions. We can say that x^5 and x^6 represent a multidimensional version of what we have previously termed "alternative solutions."

Table 8-9

	$f_1(x)$	$f_2(x)$	$f_3(x)$
x^1	16	24	0
x^2	48	32	-16
x^3	16	0	16
x^4	0	8	16
x^5	5.33	21.33	5.33
x^6	5.33	21.33	5.33

8-5 MULTIPARAMETRIC DECOMPOSITION

In this section we introduce a methodology which has important bearings on interactive procedures (Sec. 10-6) and alleviates the problem of a priori weights determination: *multiparametric programming*.

Instead of maximizing objective functions $f_1(x)$, . . . , $f_l(x)$ as separate parallel entities, we may combine them, in linear cases, into the following multiparametric aggregate:

$$f(\lambda, x) = \sum_{i=1}^{l} \lambda_i f_i(x) = \lambda f(x)$$

where $\lambda = (\lambda_1 , . . . , \lambda_l)$ is a vector of parameters or weights such that $\lambda_i \geqq 0$ and $\lambda_1 + . . . + \lambda_l = 1$. In linear cases we can compute the nondominated set of X by maximizing $f(\lambda, x)$ for all possible combinations λ satisfying the above conditions.

If we maximize $f(\lambda, x) = \lambda_1 f_1(x) + . . . + \lambda_l f_l(x)$ over a convex polyhedron X, each nondominated extreme point of X will be associated with a particular subset of λ's such that $f(\lambda, x)$ will reach its maximum at that very point. That is, the set of all parameters can be *decomposed* into subsets associated with individual nondominated solutions.

This option of multiparametric decomposition leads to potentially remarkable benefits. First, we do not have to choose a particular and often arbitrary point λ and maximize the corresponding $f(\lambda, x)$ for each such choice. Instead, we perform all such maximizations at once for all possible λ's. Second, such decompositions are easily computed as byproducts of applying multicriterion simplex method to identifying the nondominated set of X. Third, the impact of considering various combinations of λ's can be readily projected in terms of corresponding nondominated solutions and forms a base for sound decision maker-model interaction. This approach allows the user to formulate the weights λ_i imprecisely, in terms of their ranges or fuzzy linguistic labels.

This usage of $f(\lambda, x)$ should not be confused with formulating $f(\lambda, x)$ as a sort of approximation to decision maker's utility function $U(x)$. It is simply a computational device allowing us to trace out the whole or a part of the non-dominated set.

A simple example of multiparametric sensitivity Consider the following linear multiobjective programming problem:

$$\text{Max } 5x_1 + 20x_2$$

and

$$\text{Max } 23x_1 + 32x_2$$

subject to

$$10x_1 + 6x_2 \leqq 2500$$

$$5x_1 + 10x_2 \leqq 2000$$

where x_1 and x_2 must be nonnegative.

This problem has two nondominated corner solutions: $x^1 = (0, 200)$ and $x^2 = (\frac{1300}{7}, \frac{750}{7})$. Tables 8-10 and 8-11 show their corresponding MSM tableaus.

Table 8-10

Current basis	x_1	x_2	x_3	x_4	Values of basic variables
x_3	7	0	1	$-\frac{3}{5}$	1300
x_2	$\frac{1}{2}$	1	0	$\frac{1}{10}$	200
	5	0	0	2	4000
	-7	0	0	$3\frac{1}{5}$	6400

Table 8-11

Current basis	x_1	x_2	x_3	x_4	Values of basic variables
x_1	1	0	$\frac{1}{7}$	$-\frac{3}{35}$	$\frac{1300}{7}$
x_2	0	1	$-\frac{1}{14}$	$\frac{1}{7}$	$\frac{750}{7}$
	0	0	$-\frac{5}{7}$	$\frac{17}{7}$	$\frac{21500}{7}$
	0	0	1	$\frac{13}{5}$	7700

Let us form the weighted average function of $f_1(x)$ and $f_2(x)$:

$$f(\lambda, x) = \lambda_1 f_1(x) + \lambda_2 f_2(x)$$

where
$$\lambda = (\lambda_1, \lambda_2)$$
$$\lambda_1 + \lambda_2 = 1$$
$$\lambda_1 \geqq 0$$
$$\lambda_2 \geqq 0$$

Table 8-12

Current basis	x_1	x_2	x_3	x_4	Values of basic variables
x_3	10	6	1	0	2500
x_4	5	10	0	1	2000
	$-5\lambda_1 - 23\lambda_2$	$-20\lambda_1 - 32\lambda_2$	0	0	0

For which ranges of values of λ_1 and λ_2 is the maximum of $f(\lambda, x)$ either x^1 or x^2? Observe that if we would venture to maximize $f(\lambda, x)$ directly, the initial simplex tableau shown in Table 8-12 would be formed.

Observe that $f(\lambda, x) = (5\lambda_1 + 23\lambda_2)x_1 + (20\lambda_1 + 32\lambda_2)x_2$. Instead of performing the simplex operations on the parametric tableau in Table 8-12, which would be quite a difficult task, we can use the tableaus of the multicriterion simplex method directly. Form a multicriterion equivalent of Table 8-12, with $z_{11} = -5$, $z_{21} = -23$, $z_{12} = -20$, and $z_{22} = -32$. Check that $z_1(\lambda) = \lambda_1 z_{11} + \lambda_2 z_{21}$ and $z_2(\lambda) = \lambda_1 z_{12} + \lambda_2 z_{22}$ are the criterion indicators in Table 8-12. In general,

$$z_j(\lambda) = \sum_{i=1}^{l} \lambda_i z_{ij} \qquad j = 1, \ldots, n$$

For which ranges of values of λ_1 and λ_2 will x^1 represent the maximal solution to $f(\lambda, x)$? Obviously, as long as $z_1(\lambda)$ and $z_4(\lambda)$ are nonnegative. Observe that $z_1(\lambda) = 5\lambda_1 - 7\lambda_2$ and $z_4(\lambda) = 2\lambda_1 + 3\frac{1}{5}\lambda_2$ can both be obtained directly from Table 8-10. Solution x^1 will stay maximal as long as the following conditions hold:

$$z_1(\lambda) = 5\lambda_1 - 7\lambda_2 \geqq 0$$

and $\qquad\qquad z_4(\lambda) = 2\lambda_1 + 3\tfrac{1}{5}\lambda_2 \geqq 0$

Let us denote this set of conditions as $\Lambda(x^1)$ and represent it graphically in Fig. 8-7. Remember that $\lambda_1 + \lambda_2 = 1$.

Similarly, for which ranges of values of λ_1 and λ_2 will x^2 represent the maximal solution to $f(\lambda, x)$? Obviously as long as the following conditions, directly obtainable from Table 8-11, hold:

$$z_3(\lambda) = -\tfrac{5}{7}\lambda_1 + 1\lambda_2 \geqq 0$$

$$z_4(\lambda) = \tfrac{17}{7}\lambda_1 + \tfrac{13}{5}\lambda_2 \geqq 0$$

The conditions, denoted as $\Lambda(x^2)$, are graphically displayed in Fig. 8-8:

Note Students often have difficulties drawing inequalities with zeros on their right-hand sides. Here's how to do it. In Fig. 8-8, to draw $-\tfrac{5}{7}\lambda_1 + \lambda_2 \geqq 0$, replace 0 with some convenient arbitrary larger number, say, 1. Then

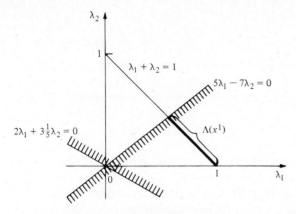

Figure 8-7 Parametric decomposition in two dimensions: $\Lambda(x^1)$.

draw the boundary line of the inequality, that is, $-\frac{5}{7}\lambda_1 + \lambda_2 = 1$. To do that, one has to obtain at least two points of this line. Set $\lambda_1 = 0$, and it follows that $\lambda_2 = 1$. Then set $\lambda_2 = 0$ and compute that $\lambda_1 = -\frac{7}{5}$. Connect the two points, $(0, 1)$ and $(-\frac{7}{5}, 0)$. Draw a parallel line passing through zero and shade it in the direction where the $-\frac{5}{7}\lambda_1 + \lambda_2 = 1$ lies. Similarly for $\frac{17}{7}\lambda_1 + \frac{13}{5}\lambda_2 \geqq 0$: Draw the boundary line $\frac{17}{7}\lambda_1 + \frac{13}{5}\lambda_2 = 1$ by connecting $(0, \frac{5}{13})$ and $(\frac{7}{17}, 0)$. Then draw a parallel line passing through zero and shade it in the appropriate direction.

In Fig. 8-8, combine the above inequalities with $\lambda_1 + \lambda_2 = 1$, and observe that only the heavy line $\Lambda(x^2)$ satisfies all of the conditions.

Note that $\Lambda(x^1)$ and $\Lambda(x^2)$ decompose the line $\lambda_1 + \lambda_2 = 1$ into two complementary regions. If $\lambda = (\lambda_1, \lambda_2)$ is a point in the λ_1, λ_2 plane, then the following is true:

$$\text{Max } f(\lambda, x) = f(\lambda, x^1) = \lambda_1 f_1(x^1) + \lambda_2 f_2(x^1) \qquad \text{for all } \lambda \text{ from } \Lambda(x^1)$$

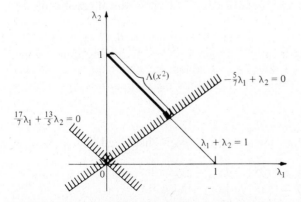

Figure 8-8 Parametric decomposition in two dimensions: $\Lambda(x^2)$.

and

$$\text{Max } f(\lambda, x) = f(\lambda, x^2) = \lambda_1 f_1(x^2) + \lambda_2 f_2(x^2) \qquad \text{for all } \lambda \text{ from } \Lambda(x^2)$$

Essentially, we have found all maximum solutions to $f(\lambda, x) = (5\lambda_1 + 23\lambda_2)x_1 + (20\lambda_1 + 32\lambda_2)x_2$ on X, for all feasible values of λ_1 and λ_2, without computing the problem for each of the infinitely many combinations of λ_1 and λ_2. The power of this methodology becomes apparent when higher dimensional cases are considered. Compare with ZW method on p. 363.

Before we turn our attention to some more complicated numerical examples, let us check another important property of multiparametric decomposition.

In Figs. 8-7 and 8-8, notice that there is at least one point $\lambda = (\lambda_1, \lambda_2)$ common to both $\Lambda(x^1)$ and $\Lambda(x^2)$. This is the point at the intersection of $\lambda_1 + \lambda_2 = 1$ and $5\lambda_1 - 7\lambda_2 = 0$. By solving these two equations we obtain $\lambda_1 = \frac{7}{12}$ and $\lambda_2 = \frac{5}{12}$. That is, $\lambda' = (\frac{7}{12}, \frac{5}{12})$ belongs to both $\Lambda(x^1)$ and $\Lambda(x^2)$. This means that if $\lambda = \lambda' = (\frac{7}{12}, \frac{5}{12})$, then $f(\lambda', x)$ reaches its maximum at both x^1 and x^2.

Recall that $x^1 = (0, 200)$ and $x^2 = (\frac{1300}{7}, \frac{750}{7})$. We shall substitute both x^1 and x^2 in $f(\lambda', x) = (5\lambda'_1 + 23\lambda'_2)x_1 + (20\lambda'_1 + 32\lambda'_2)x_2$:

$$\begin{aligned} f(\lambda', x^1) &= [5(\tfrac{7}{12}) + 23(\tfrac{5}{12})]0 + [20(\tfrac{7}{12}) + 32(\tfrac{5}{12})]200 \\ &= 0 + 5000 = 5000 \end{aligned}$$

$$\begin{aligned} f(\lambda', x^2) &= [5(\tfrac{7}{12}) + 23(\tfrac{5}{12})]\tfrac{1300}{7} + [20(\tfrac{7}{12}) + 32(\tfrac{5}{12})]\tfrac{750}{7} \\ &= 2321.43 + 2678.57 = 5000 \end{aligned}$$

Additional numerical examples We shall analyze the multiparametric decomposition for the problem whose initial MSM tableau is shown in Table 8-6. There are three objective functions, so that $f(\lambda, x) = \lambda_1 f_1(x) + \lambda_2 f_2(x) + \lambda_3 f_3(x)$. Because of the normalization condition $\lambda_1 + \lambda_2 + \lambda_3 = 1$, we can always decrease the dimensionality of our decomposition by 1. That is, we set $\lambda_1 = 1 - \lambda_2 - \lambda_3$ and express all relationships in terms of λ_2 and λ_3 only.

We shall demonstrate the computation of $\Lambda(x^1)$ associated with the basic solution x^1 whose MSM tableau is shown in Table 8-7. Recall that x^1 is the maximum of $f(\lambda, x)$ only if

$$z_j(\lambda) = \lambda_1 z_{1j} + \lambda_2 z_{2j} + \lambda_3 z_{3j} \geqq 0 \qquad \text{for } j = 1, \ldots, n$$

Since this is always true for the basic variables, we shall express $z_j(\lambda)$ only for the nonbasic variables in Table 8-7. The following inequalities characterize the situation:

$$\begin{aligned} z_1(\lambda) &= & 0\lambda_1 + \tfrac{3}{2}\lambda_2 - 1\lambda_3 &\geqq 0 \\ z_2(\lambda) &= & 0\lambda_1 + 2\lambda_2 + 0\lambda_3 &\geqq 0 \\ z_3(\lambda) &= & 2\lambda_1 + \tfrac{1}{2}\lambda_2 - 1\lambda_3 &\geqq 0 \\ z_4(\lambda) &= & -2\lambda_1 - \tfrac{1}{2}\lambda_2 + 1\lambda_3 &\geqq 0 \\ z_6(\lambda) &= & 1\lambda_1 + \tfrac{1}{2}\lambda_2 + 1\lambda_3 &\geqq 0 \\ z_7(\lambda) &= & 1\lambda_1 + 3\lambda_2 + 1\lambda_3 &\geqq 0 \\ z_8(\lambda) &= & 1\lambda_1 + \tfrac{3}{2}\lambda_2 + 0\lambda_3 &\geqq 0 \end{aligned}$$

Using the normalization condition $\lambda_1 = 1 - \lambda_2 - \lambda_3$, we modify the above inequalities as follows:

$$
\begin{aligned}
z_1(\lambda) &= \tfrac{3}{2}\lambda_2 - \lambda_3 \geqq 0 \\
z_2(\lambda) &= 2\lambda_2 \geqq 0 \\
z_3(\lambda) &= \tfrac{3}{2}\lambda_2 + 3\lambda_3 \leqq 2 \\
z_4(\lambda) &= \tfrac{3}{2}\lambda_2 + 3\lambda_3 \geqq 2 \\
z_6(\lambda) &= \tfrac{1}{2}\lambda_2 \leqq 1 \\
z_7(\lambda) &= -2\lambda_2 \leqq 1 \\
z_8(\lambda) &= -\tfrac{1}{2}\lambda_2 + \lambda_3 \leqq 1
\end{aligned}
$$

It turns out that only $z_1(\lambda)$, $z_3(\lambda)$, and $z_4(\lambda)$ are necessary for defining $\Lambda(x^1)$. All other constraints are redundant and do not further reduce $\Lambda(x^1)$ defined below:

$$
\Lambda(x^1) = \begin{cases}
\tfrac{3}{2}\lambda_2 - \lambda_3 \geqq 0 \\
\tfrac{3}{2}\lambda_2 + 3\lambda_3 = 2 \\
\text{and} \\
\lambda_2 + \lambda_3 \leqq 1 \\
\lambda_2 \geqq 0 \\
\lambda_3 \geqq 0
\end{cases}
$$

Note that $z_3(\lambda) \leqq 2$ and $z_4(\lambda) \geqq 2$ imply the equality in $\Lambda(x^1)$. Subregion $\Lambda(x^1)$ is graphically represented in Fig. 8-9.

In Fig. 8-9 observe that $\Lambda(x^1)$ consists of a line segment connecting two points $\lambda = (\lambda_2, \lambda_3)$, namely, $(\tfrac{2}{3}, \tfrac{1}{3})$ and $(\tfrac{1}{3}, \tfrac{1}{2})$. We stress again that $\lambda_2 + \lambda_3 \leqq 1$ and thus the entire triangle to the left of $\lambda_2 + \lambda_3 = 1$ represents feasible pairs λ_2 and λ_3. The value of λ_1 is implied.

One should similarly analyze basic solution x^2 and its tableau in Table 8-8. The multiparametric subregion $\Lambda(x^2)$ is defined as follows:

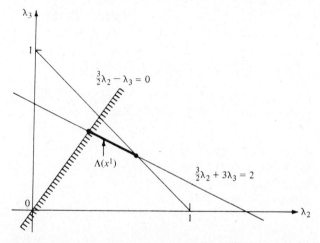

Figure 8-9 Parametric decomposition in two dimensions: $\Lambda(x^1)$.

$$\Lambda(x^2) = \begin{cases} & 4\lambda_3 \leqq 2 \\ & 3\lambda_2 + 6\lambda_3 \leqq 4 \\ & \text{and} \\ & \lambda_2 + \lambda_3 \leqq 1 \\ & \lambda_2 \qquad \geqq 0 \\ & \qquad \lambda_3 \geqq 0 \end{cases}$$

Because x^2 was obtained by a single transformation from x^1, we say that the two basic solutions are "adjacent." Multiparametric subregions of adjacent basic solutions must have some points λ in common. For example, let us substitute the endpoints of $\Lambda(x^1)$, that is, $(\frac{2}{3}, \frac{1}{3})$ and $(\frac{1}{3}, \frac{1}{2})$ into the second constraint of $\Lambda(x^2)$:

$$3(\tfrac{2}{3}) + 6(\tfrac{1}{3}) = 4$$

and

$$3(\tfrac{1}{3}) + 6(\tfrac{1}{2}) = 4$$

Obviously, the boundary line of the second constraint of $\Lambda(x^2)$ contains $\Lambda(x^1)$. The first constraint of $\Lambda(x^2)$ is simply $\lambda_3 \leqq \frac{1}{2}$ and so we can draw $\Lambda(x^2)$ quite easily, as in Fig. 8-10.

Such multiparametric subregions as the ones in Figs. 8-9 and 8-10 can be obtained for all six nondominated solutions summarized in Table 8-9. We shall refrain from any detailed computations and simply list all corresponding subregions. A more precise analysis can be found in App. A. In order to save space, we shall not repeat that $\lambda_2 + \lambda_3 \leqq 1$, $\lambda_2 \geqq 0$, and $\lambda_3 \geqq 0$ in each case:

$$\Lambda(x^1) = \begin{cases} \tfrac{3}{2}\lambda_2 - \lambda_3 \geqq 0 \\ \tfrac{3}{2}\lambda_2 + 3\lambda_3 = 2 \end{cases}$$

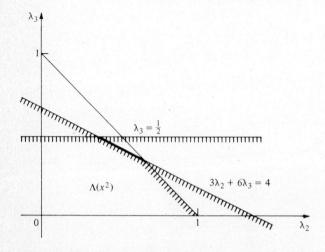

Figure 8-10 Parametric decomposition in two dimensions $\Lambda(x^2)$.

$$\Lambda(x^2) = \left\{ \begin{array}{r} 4\lambda_3 \leq 2 \\ 3\lambda_2 + 6\lambda_3 \leq 4 \end{array} \right.$$

$$\Lambda(x^3) = \left\{ \begin{array}{r} 3\lambda_2 + 2\lambda_3 \leq 2 \\ 4\lambda_3 \geq 2 \end{array} \right.$$

$$\Lambda(x^4) = \left\{ \begin{array}{r} -\tfrac{3}{2}\lambda_2 + 3\lambda_3 \geq 1 \\ \tfrac{3}{2}\lambda_2 + \lambda_3 \geq 1 \end{array} \right.$$

$$\Lambda(x^5) = \left\{ \begin{array}{r} -\lambda_2 + 2\lambda_3 \leq \tfrac{2}{3} \\ \lambda_2 + 2\lambda_3 \geq \tfrac{4}{3} \end{array} \right.$$

$$\Lambda(x^6) = \left\{ \begin{array}{r} -\lambda_2 + 2\lambda_3 \leq \tfrac{2}{3} \\ \lambda_2 + 2\lambda_3 \geq \tfrac{4}{3} \end{array} \right.$$

All the above subregions are represented in Fig. 8-11. They decompose feasible region

$$\Lambda = \left\{ \begin{array}{l} \lambda_2 + \lambda_3 \leq 1 \\ \lambda_2 \qquad \geq 0 \\ \qquad \lambda_3 \geq 0 \end{array} \right.$$

fully, with no holes or gaps.

Fig. 8-11 is to be interpreted as follows: For a given combination of λ_1, λ_2, and λ_3, $f(\lambda, x) = \lambda_1 f_1(x) + \lambda_2 f_2(x) + \lambda_3 f_3(x)$ would reach its maximum at the x^k corresponding to the $\Lambda(x^k)$ satisfied by these λ_1, λ_2, and λ_3.

For example, choose some obvious points in Fig. 8-11, such as $\lambda_2 = 1$,

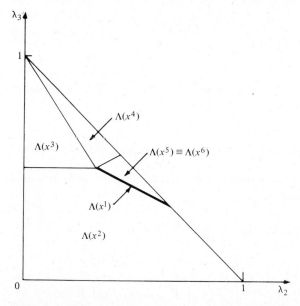

Figure 8-11 Complete parametric decomposition of Λ: linear case.

$\lambda_3 = 0$, and $\lambda_1 = 0$. This point is contained only by $\Lambda(x^2)$, and $f(\lambda, x)$ reduces to $f_2(x)$. Function $f_2(x)$ is maximized at x^2, as can be seen from Table 8-8. Take $\lambda_2 = \lambda_3 = 0$ and $\lambda_1 = 1$; $f(\lambda, x) = f_1(x)$, and it is maximized at x^2 because point 0 in Fig. 8-11 is part of $\Lambda(x^2)$ only. Next, set $\lambda_3 = 1$, that is, $\lambda_2 = \lambda_1 = 0$. Observe that this point belongs to both $\Lambda(x^3)$ and $\Lambda(x^4)$. Consequently, both x^3 and x^4 should maximize $f_3(x)$; check in Table 8-9.

There is one point λ' such that $f(\lambda, x)$ is maximized at all $x^1, \ldots, x^6$ at the same time. This point is $\lambda_1' = \frac{1}{6}$, $\lambda_2' = \frac{1}{3}$, and $\lambda_3' = \frac{1}{2}$; that is, the point $(\frac{1}{3}, \frac{1}{2})$ in Fig. 8-11. For example, let us test x^5:

$$f(\lambda', x) = \tfrac{1}{6}(x_1 + 2x_2 - x_3 + 3x_4 + 2x_5 + x_7) + \tfrac{1}{3}(x_2 + x_3 + 2x_4 + 3x_5 + x_6)$$
$$+ \tfrac{1}{2}(x_1 + x_3 - x_4 - x_6 - x_7)$$

Substituting x^5, that is, $x_3 = \frac{32}{3}$ and $x_4 = \frac{16}{3}$, in the above, we obtain:

$$f(\lambda', x^5) = \tfrac{1}{6}[-\tfrac{32}{3} + 3(\tfrac{16}{3})] + \tfrac{1}{3}[\tfrac{32}{3} + 2(\tfrac{16}{3})] + \tfrac{1}{2}[\tfrac{32}{3} - \tfrac{16}{3}]$$
$$= 0.89 + 7.11 + 2.66 = 10\tfrac{2}{3}$$

Let us test x^2, that is, $x_4 = 16$:

$$f(\lambda', x^2) = \tfrac{1}{6}[3(16)] + \tfrac{1}{3}[2(16)] + \tfrac{1}{2}(-16)$$
$$= 8 + 10\tfrac{2}{3} - 8 = 10\tfrac{2}{3}$$

The reader should check Table 8-9 to assure that the same value $10\frac{2}{3}$ is obtained for all remaining basic solutions.

Also notice that $\Lambda(x^5) \equiv \Lambda(x^6)$, even though x^5 and x^6 are entirely different. Table 8-9 reveals that x^5 and x^6 are alternative solutions with respect to all three objective functions. Similarly, any λ which belongs to the interior of $\Lambda(x^1)$ (endpoints excluded) would maximize $f(\lambda, x)$ at x^1, x^2, x^5, and x^6 at the same time.

Formal summary of multiparametric decomposition First, define Λ as the set of all points $\lambda = (\lambda_1, \ldots, \lambda_l)$ such that $\lambda_i \geqq 0$ and

$$\sum_{i=1}^{l} \lambda_i = 1$$

for all $i = 1, \ldots, l$. The multiparametric linear-programming problem then corresponds to the maximization of $f(\lambda, x)$:

$$\text{Max } f(\lambda, x) = \sum_{i=1}^{l} \lambda_i f_i(x)$$

subject to all $x = (x_1, \ldots, x_n)$ satisfying a given set of constraints X.

If we choose any λ^* from Λ and find that x^k maximizes $f(\lambda^*, x)$ over X, then we can form $\Lambda(x^k)$ as follows: $\Lambda(x^k)$ consists of all points λ which satisfy

$$z_j(\lambda) = \sum_{i=1}^{l} \lambda_i z_{ij} \geqq 0 \qquad \text{for all } j = 1, \ldots, n$$

Then x^k also maximizes $f(\lambda, x)$ for all λ belonging to $\Lambda(x^k)$, including λ^*. For each x^k maximizing $f(\lambda, x)$ there is a nonempty $\Lambda(x^k)$. The union of all $\Lambda(x^k)$ forms a finite decomposition of Λ.

It can be shown that x^k is nondominated if and only if it maximizes $f(\lambda, x)$ for any λ from Λ such that $\lambda_i > 0$ for all $i = 1, \ldots, l$.

Note The requirement $\lambda_i > 0$ should be self-evident. Suppose that $f_1(x) = x_1$ and $f_2(x) = x_2$ are to be maximized over the following feasible set X:

$$x_1 + x_2 \leqq 1$$
$$x_1 \qquad \leqq \tfrac{3}{4}$$
$$x_2 \leqq \tfrac{3}{4}$$
$$x_1 \qquad \geqq 0$$
$$x_2 \geqq 0$$

The situation is depicted in Fig. 8-12.

Observe that nondominated solutions consist of corner points B and C and their connecting segment of X. They can be obtained by maximizing $\lambda_1 x_1 + \lambda_2 x_2$ for all feasible λ_1 and λ_2. But if for example $\lambda_1 = 0$, then maximization of $f(\lambda, x) = f_2(x)$ yields points A and B, which are not *both* nondominated.

Fractional objective functions In many problems of a practical nature, especially in financial planning, one is often concerned about objective functions which are defined as ratios, quotas, proportions, or fractions. This brings an aspect of *nonlinearity* into the analysis. For example, a ratio of two func-

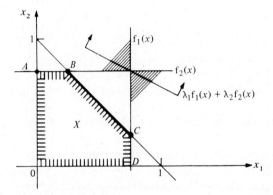

Figure 8-12 Maximization of $f(\lambda, x)$ and the nondominated set.

tions—say, $h(x)$ profits to $g(x)$ sales, $h(x)/g(x)$—is a nonlinear function even though both $h(x)$ and $g(x)$ could be linear.

How are nondominated solutions and the corresponding multiparametric decomposition of Λ affected by considering fractional objective functions in linear multiobjective programming? We shall adapt a simple numerical example from Kornbluth (1979) to demonstrate some relevant issues.

$$\text{Max} f_1 (x) = \frac{x_1 - 4}{-x_2 + 3}$$

and

$$\text{Max} f_2 (x) = \frac{-x_1 + 4}{x_2 + 1}$$

and

$$\text{Max} f_3 (x) = -x_1 + x_2$$

subject to

$$-\tfrac{1}{4}x_1 + x_2 \leqq 1$$

$$\tfrac{1}{3}x_1 - x_2 \leqq \tfrac{2}{3}$$

$$x_1 \qquad \leqq 8$$

$$x_2 \leqq 2\tfrac{1}{2}$$

Observe that the region of feasible solutions X is a convex polyhedron, $f_3(x)$ is a linear, and $f_1(x)$ and $f_2(x)$ are fractions of linear functions.

We shall analyze the problem graphically in order to gain insight into the nature of nondominated solutions under these circumstances.

In Fig. 8-13 observe that, for example, point $(2, 0)$ yields the following values for our objective functions: $f_1 = -\tfrac{2}{3}, f_2 = 2$ and $f_3 = -2$. Similarly, point $(8, 2)$ yields $f_1 = 4, f_2 = -\tfrac{4}{3}$, and $f_3 = -6$. Observe that point $(8, 2\tfrac{1}{2})$, yielding $f_1 = 8, f_2 = -\tfrac{8}{7}$, and $f_3 = -5\tfrac{1}{2}$, dominates point $(8, 2)$ because of the maximization requirement.

It turns out that corner points $(0, 0)$, $(2, 0)$, $(0, 1)$, $(6, 2\tfrac{1}{2})$, and $(8, 2\tfrac{1}{2})$ are nondominated. The nondominated edges are indicated as heavy boundaries of X in Fig. 8-13. Notice the disconnected nature of the nondominated set. In contrast to linear objective functions, fractional functions can lead to discontinuities or jumps: An edge connecting two nondominated corner points is not necessarily nondominated. For example, point $(4, \tfrac{2}{3})$ yields $f_1 = 0, f_2 = 0$, and $f_3 = -3\tfrac{1}{3}$. This is dominated by point $(4, 2)$, which yields $f_1 = 0$, $f_2 = 0$, and $f_3 = -2$. Although the edges connecting points $(2, 0)$ with $(4, \tfrac{2}{3})$ and $(6, 2\tfrac{1}{2})$ with $(2\tfrac{2}{3}, 1\tfrac{2}{3})$ are nondominated, they are open edges; i.e., points $(4, \tfrac{2}{3})$ and $(2\tfrac{2}{3}, 1\tfrac{2}{3})$ are excluded and dominated. [Check that point $(2\tfrac{2}{3}, 1\tfrac{2}{3})$ is dominated by point $(0, 1)$].

How do we establish dominance or nondominance in these types of problems?

Although we do not yet have a direct technique for solution, it is possible to test the nondominance of individual corner points by linear multiobjective programming. Tigan (1975) developed such a test through linearization of fractional functions by taking their derivatives.

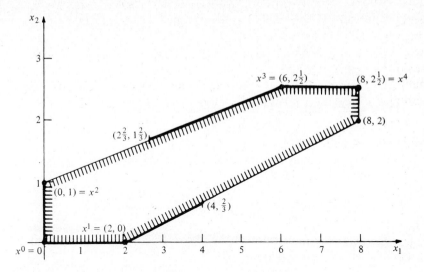

Figure 8-13 Fractional objective functions: the nondominated set.

Tigan's test If we could replace fractional functions $f_i(x)$ by some linear functions $t_i(x)$ so that the nondominance-dominance relationships among the points of X would be preserved, then we could use LMP and MSM for testing the nondominance in fractional linear programming as well.

Recall that the derivative of a function is the slope of the line tangent to the function at a particular point. In the case of a linear function, this tangent coincides with the function itself, and so its derivative is equal to the slope of the function. For example, $f(x) = ax + B$ has its derivative $f'(x) = a$ while the nonlinear $f(x) = ax^2 + bx + C$ has $f'(x) = 2ax + b$. For multivariate functions, such as $f(x, y) = ax + by + C$, we compute a vector of partial derivatives with respect to x and y, that is, $f'(x, y) = (a, b)$. Consequently, if

$$f(x) = \sum_{j=1}^{n} a_j x_j + B$$

we can denote its vector of partial derivatives as $f'(x) = (a_1, a_2, \ldots, a_n)$. We shall use this "gradient," as the vector of partial derivatives is often called, in dealing with our fractionals $f_i(x)$.

From elementary calculus we also learn that the derivative of the ratio of two functions

$$f(x) = \frac{h(x)}{g(x)}$$

is defined as

$$f'(x) = \frac{g(x)h'(x) - h(x)g'(x)}{[g(x)]^2}$$

Consequently, the derivative of

$$f_i(x) = \frac{h_i(x)}{g_i(x)} = \frac{\Sigma\, c_{ij}x_j + C_i}{\Sigma\, d_{ij}x_j + D_i}$$

is equal to

$$\frac{\Sigma\, d_{ij}x_j + D_i\,(c_{i1}, \ldots, c_{in}) - \Sigma\, c_{ij}x_j + C_i\,(d_{i1}, \cdots, d_{in})}{[\Sigma\, d_{ij}x_j + D_i]^2}$$

Notice that all summations Σ run for $j = 1, \ldots, n$.

The above derivative can now be evaluated at any point $x^0 = (x_1^0, \ldots, x_j^0, \ldots, x_n^0)$, yielding:

$$\frac{g_i(x^0)\,(c_{i1}, \ldots, c_{in}) - h_i(x^0)\,(d_{i1}, \ldots, d_{in})}{[g_i(x^0)]^2}$$

Tigan (1975) uses the numerator of the above fraction as a coefficient in forming the following *linear* function:

$$t_i^0(x) = \Sigma\, [g_i(x^0)c_{ij} - h_i(x^0)d_{ij}]\, x_j$$

Tigan has shown that a corner point x^0 of X is nondominated with respect to fractional objectives $f_i(x)$ if and only if it is also nondominated with respect to the linear objectives $t_i^0(x)$. Thus, in order to test x^0 for nondominance we simply replace all fractional $f_i(x)$ by linear $t_i^0(x)$ and use the corresponding linear multiobjective-programming problem. The nondominance test can then be performed as it was described with reference to MSM (see the end of Sec. 8-4.3).

For example, in order to test corner point $x^0 = (2, 0)$, one would replace $f_1(x)$ by $t_1^0(x)$ as follows: Let $h_1(x) = x_1 - 4$ and $g_1(x) = -x_2 + 3$; then $h_1(x^0) = 2 - 4 = -2$ and $g_1(x^0) = 0 + 3 = 3$. Observe that $(c_{11}, c_{12}) = (1, 0)$ and $(d_{11}, d_{12}) = (0, -1)$. Then,

$$t_1^0(x) = [3(1) - (-2)0]x_1 + [3(0) - (-2)(-1)]x_2 = 3x_1 - 2x_2$$

Similarly we obtain

$$t_2^0(x) = -x_1 - 2x_2$$

and

$$t_3^0(x) = -x_1 + x_2$$

Using MSM we can show that corner point $(2, 0)$ is nondominated on X with respect to all three $t_i^0(x)$. It must therefore be nondominated on X with respect to all three $f_i(x)$ as well.

Decomposition of the parametric space Using Tigan's test one can establish that corner points $(0, 0)$, $(2, 0)$, $(0, 1)$, $(6, 2\frac{1}{2})$ and $(8, 2\frac{1}{2})$ are nondominated. Let us summarize the results in Table 8-13.

We now form the weighted linear combination of functions $f_1(x), f_2(x)$, and $f_3(x)$, that is, $f(\lambda, x) = \lambda_1 f_1(x) + \lambda_2 f_2(x) + \lambda_3 f_3(x)$. Again we are interested in finding all subregions $\Lambda(x^0), \ldots, \Lambda(x^4)$ that decompose overall parametric

Table 8-13

Point x	(x_1, x_2)	$f_1(x)$	$f_2(x)$	$f_3(x)$
x^0	$(0, 0)$	$-\frac{4}{3}$	4	0
x^1	$(2, 0)$	$-\frac{2}{3}$	2	-2
x^2	$(0, 1)$	-2	2	1
x^3	$(6, 2\frac{1}{2})$	4	$-\frac{4}{7}$	$-3\frac{1}{2}$
x^4	$(8, 2\frac{1}{2})$	8	$-\frac{8}{7}$	$-5\frac{1}{2}$

space Λ (see p. 256). We set $\lambda_1 = 1 - \lambda_2 - \lambda_3$ and express all results in terms of λ_2 and λ_3 only.

We shall not provide detailed computations of this decomposition, but let us summarize the final results. The reader may consult Kornbluth (1978) for further details.

The space Λ can be decomposed into the following subregions:

$$\Lambda(x^0) = \left\{ \begin{array}{l} 4\lambda_2 + 4\lambda_3 \geqq 1 \\ -32\lambda_2 - 5\lambda_3 \leqq 4 \end{array} \right.$$

$$\Lambda(x^1) = \left\{ \begin{array}{l} 5.78\lambda_2 + 2.78\lambda_3 \geqq 0.78 \\ 4\lambda_2 + 4\lambda_3 \leqq 1 \end{array} \right.$$

$$\Lambda(x^2) = \left\{ \begin{array}{l} \lambda_3 \geqq \frac{1}{2} \\ 4\lambda_2 + 4\lambda_3 \geqq 1 \end{array} \right.$$

$$\Lambda(x^3) = \left\{ \begin{array}{l} 9.143\lambda_2 + 12\lambda_3 \geqq 8 \\ 16.96\lambda_2 + 19\lambda_3 \leqq 16 \end{array} \right.$$

$$\Lambda(x^4) = \left\{ \begin{array}{l} 2.2857\lambda_2 + 3\lambda_3 \leqq 2 \\ 16.3265\lambda_2 + 15\lambda_3 \leqq 16 \end{array} \right.$$

All these subregions of Λ are represented in Fig. 8-14. In order to save space, we have not appended $\lambda_2 + \lambda_3 \leqq 1$ and $\lambda_2 \geqq 0$, $\lambda_3 \geqq 0$, which should accompany each of the subregions above. The reader can compare the different nature of decompositions presented by Fig. 8-11 and 8-14.

In Fig. 8-14, for any given combination of λ_2, λ_3, and consequently λ_1, the corresponding combination $f(\lambda, x)$ would reach its maximum over X at the x^k corresponding to the $\Lambda(x^k)$ containing these λ_1, λ_2, λ_3.

For visual clarity, the subregion $\Lambda(x^0)$ in Fig. 8-14 is simply framed with a heavy boundary. All other subregions are shaded. Note significant overlaps among subregions: $\Lambda(x^0)$, $\Lambda(x^3)$, and $\Lambda(x^2)$ have some interior points in common; as do $\Lambda(x^0)$, $\Lambda(x^4)$, and $\Lambda(x^2)$; and also $\Lambda(x^1)$ and $\Lambda(x^4)$. Subregions $\Lambda(x^0)$ and $\Lambda(x^1)$, as well as $\Lambda(x^3)$ and $\Lambda(x^4)$ are adjacent pairs and have only boundary points in common.

Suppose that the decision maker chooses the weights $\lambda_2 = 0.1$, $\lambda_3 = 0.5$,

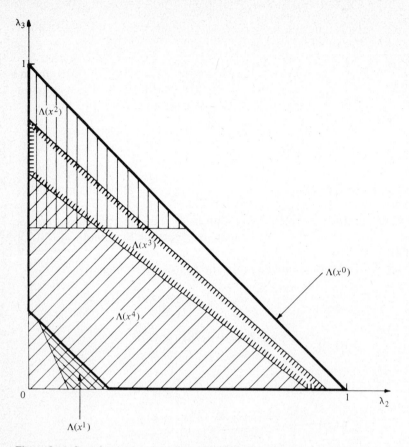

Figure 8-14 Complete parametric decomposition of Λ: fractional case.

and $\lambda_1 = 0.4$; then x^0, x^2, and x^4 would maximize $f(\lambda, x)$. Similarly, $\lambda_2 = 0.25$, $\lambda_3 = 0.5$, and $\lambda_1 = 0.25$ would maximize $f(\lambda, x)$ at x^0, x^2, and x^3.

8-6 THE TRANSPORTATION PROBLEM WITH MULTIPLE OBJECTIVES

One of the most common applications of linear programming is in solving the so-called "*transportation problem*." A homogeneous product is to be transported from each of m sources to any of n destinations. The sources are production facilities, warehouses, or supply points, characterized by available capacities $a_1, \ldots, a_m$. The destinations are consumption facilities, warehouses, or demand points, characterized by required levels of demand $b_1, \ldots, b_n$. Associated with transporting a unit of a given product from the ith source to the jth destination, there is a penalty c_{ij}^k corresponding to the kth decision criterion. The decision criteria could be transportation cost, delivery time, quantity of goods delivered, unfulfilled demand, underused capacity, reliability of delivery, safety of delivery (spoilage), and many others.

One must determine the amounts x_{ij} of the product to be transported from all sources i to all destinations j so that all l criteria are taken into account in a way satisfactory to the decision maker. The problem is of the linear-programming type and can be formally summarized as follows:

$$\text{Minimize } c^1_{11}x_{11} + \ldots + c^1_{mn}x_{mn}$$
$$\cdots\cdots\cdots\cdots\cdots\cdots\cdots\cdots\cdots$$
$$\text{Minimize } c^l_{11}x_{11} + \ldots + c^l_{mn}x_{mn}$$

subject to

$$x_{11} + x_{12} + \ldots + x_{1n} = a_1$$
$$\cdots\cdots\cdots\cdots\cdots\cdots\cdots\cdots$$
$$x_{m1} + x_{m2} + \ldots + x_{mn} = a_m$$

and

$$x_{11} + x_{21} + \ldots + x_{m1} = b_1$$
$$\cdots\cdots\cdots\cdots\cdots\cdots\cdots\cdots$$
$$x_{1n} + x_{2n} + \ldots + x_{mn} = b_n$$

where all
$$x_{ij} \geqq 0$$
$$c^k_{ij} \geqq 0$$
$$a_i > 0$$
$$b_j > 0$$

and
$$\sum_{i=1}^{m} a_i = \sum_{j=1}^{n} b_j$$

is assumed because of the possibility of using fictitious sources or destinations to absorb excess capacity or excess demand.

This transportation problem can be conveniently represented in table form:

Destinations j / Sources i	1	2	$\ldots$	n	Capacity
1	c_{11} x_{11}	c_{12} x_{12}	$\ldots$	c_{1n} x_{1n}	a_1
2	c_{21} x_{21}	c_{22} x_{22}	$\ldots$	c_{2n} x_{2n}	a_2
$\vdots$	$\vdots$	$\vdots$		$\vdots$	$\vdots$
m	c_{m1} x_{m1}	c_{m2} x_{m2}	$\ldots$	c_{mn} x_{mn}	a_m
Demand	b_1	b_2	$\ldots$	b_n	

In the table on p. 263, each route i, j is characterized by a vector of performance criteria $(c_{ij}^1, c_{ij}^2, \ldots, c_{ij}^l) = c_{ij}$.

A general statement of the problem is as follows:

$$\text{Minimize} \qquad \sum_{i=1}^m \sum_{j=1}^n c_{ij}^k x_{ij} \qquad \text{for } k = 1, \ldots, l$$

subject to

$$\sum_{j=1}^n x_{ij} = a_i \qquad \text{for } i = 1, \ldots, m$$

$$\sum_{i=1}^m x_{ij} = b_j \qquad \text{for } j = 1, \ldots, n$$

Observe that c_{ij}^k denotes an element from the kth matrix of criteria coefficients. There are $k = 1, \ldots, l$ matrices. One could solve the transportation problem with respect to each of these l penalty structures, obtain an ideal solution, and then search for a compromise solution which would be as close as possible to the ideal.

By minimizing

$$f_k = \sum_{i=1}^m \sum_{j=1}^n c_{ij}^k x_{ij}$$

we obtain its minimum value f_k^* and the corresponding solution x_{ij}^*. Repeating the procedure for all k we obtain $f^* = (f_1^*, \ldots, f_l^*)$, an ideal solution. In general, there is no feasible x_{ij}^* which would give rise to the above vector f^*. We have to search for a compromise solution as close as possible to f^*. One simple measure of closeness is:

$$d_1 = \sum_{k=1}^l \frac{1}{f_k^*} \sum_{i=1}^m \sum_{j=1}^n c_{ij}^k x_{ij}$$

Another measure is:

$$d_2 = \sum_{k=1}^l \left(\frac{1}{f_k^*} \sum_{i=1}^m \sum_{j=1}^n c_{ij}^k x_{ij} - 1 \right)^2$$

Observe that the minimum possible value of d_1 is l, while the minimum possible value of d_2 is zero. These two measures are variations of the L_p metrics discussed earlier, and were introduced by Díaz (1978). Solutions x_{ij} minimizing d_1 and d_2 are *always nondominated*.

Let us consider a simple numerical example adapted from Díaz. There are four production sources and five destinations; their respective capacities and demands are given in the table below.

Sources i \ Destinations j	1	2	3	4	5	Capacity
1	x_{11}	x_{12}	x_{13}	x_{14}	x_{15}	5
2	x_{21}	x_{22}	x_{23}	x_{24}	x_{25}	4
3	x_{31}	x_{32}	x_{33}	x_{34}	x_{35}	2
4	x_{41}	x_{42}	x_{43}	x_{44}	x_{45}	9
Demand	4	4	6	2	4	

Three criteria guide our search for compromise solutions: transportation costs, delivery times, and the relative safety of a given route i, j. Numerical evaluations of the three criteria are given in the following three matrices of coefficients:

	Cost					Time					Safety				
	1	2	3	4	5	1	2	3	4	5	1	2	3	4	5
1	9	12	9	6	9	2	9	8	1	4	2	4	6	3	6
2	7	3	7	7	5	1	9	9	5	2	4	8	4	9	2
3	6	5	9	11	3	8	1	8	4	5	5	3	5	3	6
4	6	8	11	2	2	2	8	6	9	8	6	9	6	3	1

Observe that the cost values are not necessarily related to the time values, as different means of transportation (trucks, airfreight, freight trains, or ships) might be necessary over different routes. Also road conditions, fees, tolls, and the number of men required to accompany the shipment might vary. The relative safety of each route is determined on a scale from 1 to 10 (1 = the safest, 10 = the least safe), and the company is very much concerned about the overall reliability of particular shipment schedules. For simplicity we shall consider all three criteria to be equally important.

There are many efficient procedures for solving the transportation problem with respect to a single criterion. These procedures can be found in any standard textbook on operations research (see the Bibliographical Note at the end of this chapter).

A digression on solving the transportation problem   For the sake of completeness we shall recapitulate at least some basic features of the methodology for solving the transportation problem. We shall use cost minimization as the criterion. The first step involves finding some good feasible shipping assignment which satisfies all capacity and demand conditions and then testing whether an improvement in overall cost is still possible.

One way of arriving at the initial assignment is the least-cost method:

1. Allocate as much shipment as possible to the lowest-cost route. (Do not exceed the corresponding capacity or demand.)
2. Allocate the remaining capacity or demand to the next lowest cost route.
3. Continue this procedure until all capacities and demands are fully satisfied. If there is a tie among the lowest cost routes, break the tie by selecting one of the routes arbitrarily.

The resulting assignment is given in the table below:

	1	2	3	4	5	Capacity
1	9	12	9 ╲ 5	6	9	5
2	7	3 ╲ 3	7 ╲ 1	7	5 ╲ 4	4
3	6 ╲ 1	5 ╲ 1	9	11	3	2
4	6 ╲ 3	8	11	2 ╲ 2	2 ╲ 4	9
Demand	4	4	6	2	4	

The lowest cost route is either 4, 4 or 4, 5 (a cost of 2). We have chosen 4, 5 arbitrarily and allocated to it as much as possible, that is, min (4,9) = 4. The demand of destination 4 is fully satisfied, and the remaining capacity of source 4 is available for allocation to the next lowest cost route, 4, 4. However, only 2 units can be allocated to 4, 4. The remainder is assigned to the next lowest cost route 4,1. The full capacity of source 9 has been distributed. Demand of destination 1 is still not satisfied; one unit of product can be allocated to the next lowest cost available route 3, 1. The remainder of the capacity at source 2 is then assigned to route 3, 2. Continuing this procedure, we ultimately arrive at the following initial assignment:

$$x_{13} = 5 \quad x_{22} = 3 \quad x_{23} = 1 \quad x_{31} = 1 \quad x_{32} = 1 \quad x_{41} = 3$$
$$x_{44} = 2 \quad x_{45} = 4$$

All remaining $x_{ij} = 0$. All capacities and demands are fully satisfied. The overall cost of this assignment is $9(5) + 3(3) + 7(1) + 6(1) + 5(1) + 6(3) + 2(2) + 2(4) = 102$. The question is, Is this the minimum-cost assignment, or can it be further improved?

The following reasoning can be used to test the optimality of the initial assignment. If there is a better assignment, one with lower overall cost, it would have to be different from the current assignment, i.e., one of the currently unused routes would have to be utilized. Is there such an unused route which would provide further cost savings per unit shipped?

Take for example route 1, 1 with its current $x_{11} = 0$. It costs $9 to send one unit of our product via route 1, 1. But we do not have this additional one unit: All capacities and demands are fully satisfied. In order to send one unit through 1, 1 we would have to adjust the amounts shipped through all other routes in such a way that the conditions would be satisfied again. Set $x_{11} = 1$. This leads to exceeding the demand at destination 1 by 1. We can adjust $x_{31} = 0$. This satisfies destination 1 and we save $6. But the capacity of source 3 is not fully utilized—we have to set $x_{32} = 2$ and incur an additional $5. Then we have to adjust $x_{22} = 2$ with a savings of $3, $x_{23} = 2$ with an additional cost of $7, and finally $x_{13} = 4$ with a savings of $9. To summarize, making $x_{11} = 1$ requires that $x_{31} = 0, x_{32} = 2, x_{22} = 2, x_{23} = 2$, and $x_{13} = 4$, while all other assignments stay unchanged. In terms of costs we are thus facing two alternatives:

1. Send a unit through 1, 1 at a cost of $9 per unit; or
2. Do not send a unit through 1, 1 and incur a cost of $6 − $5 + $3 − $7 + $9 = $6

It is obviously cheaper not to send an additional unit through route 1, 1.

Let us similarly explore the route 3, 3. The direct cost of sending an additional unit through 3, 3 is $9. Making $x_{33} = 1$ requires that $x_{23} = 0$ with a savings of $7, $x_{22} = 4$ with an additional cost of $3, and $x_{32} = 2$ with a savings of $5. This readjustment would again lead to a full satisfaction of all capacities and demands. We have to make the following choice:

1. Send a unit through 3, 3 at a cost of $9 per unit, or
2. Do not send a unit through 3, 3 and incur a cost of $7 − $3 + $5 = $9

Evaluating all unused routes in this manner leads to the conclusion that there is no route which would lead to a further decrease in the overall cost. Our initial allocation is, therefore, a minimum-cost allocation! Of course such evaluations of unused routes for feasible assignment are most efficiently performed by a computer, the user of which does not have to be concerned with performing tedious manual computations. It is good, however, to understand the basic principles behind a particular optimization methodology.

The reader may have noticed that it is equally advantageous to send as not to send an additional unit via route 3, 3. This indicates that there is more than one minimum-cost solution. Sending as many units as possible through 3, 3 will not change the overall costs of $102. The maximum value of $x_{33} = 1$, and the necessary adjustments are $x_{23} = 0, x_{22} = 4$, and $x_{32} = 0$. An alternative optimal solution, then, is

$$x_{13} = 5 \qquad x_{22} = 4 \qquad x_{31} = 1 \qquad x_{33} = 1 \qquad x_{41} = 3 \qquad x_{44} = 2 \qquad x_{45} = 4$$

and its corresponding overall costs of $9(5) + 3(4) + 6(1) + 9(1) + 6(3) + 2(2) + 2(4) = 102$.

Let f_1 denote costs, f_2 time, and f_3 safety. We can now compare the performance of the minimum-cost solutions with respect to the other two criteria:

1. The first minimum-cost solution implies $f_1^* = 102$, as we have asserted earlier; $f_2 = 8(5) + 9(3) + 9(1) + 8(1) + 1(1) + 2(3) + 9(2) + 4(8) = 141$; and $f_3 = 6(5) + 8(3) + 4(1) + 5(1) + 3(1) + 6(3) + 3(2) + 1(4) = 94$.
2. The second minimum-cost solution implies $f_1^* = 102$; $f_2 = 8(5) + 9(4) + 8(1) + 8(1) + 2(3) + 9(2) + 8(4) = 148$; and $f_3 = 6(5) + 8(4) + 5(1) + 5(1) + 6(3) + 3(2) + 1(4) = 100$.

Obviously the second minimum-cost solution is dominated, as $(102, 141, 94) \leqq (102, 148, 100)$.

In order to find f_2^* and f_3^* we have to solve the transportation problem with respect to time and safety coefficients. We obtain:

1. The time-minimizing solution

$$x_{11} = 3 \qquad x_{14} = 2 \qquad x_{25} = 4 \qquad x_{32} = 2 \qquad x_{41} = 1$$
$$x_{42} = 2 \qquad x_{43} = 6$$

and $f_2^* = 2(3) + 1(2) + 2(4) + 1(2) + 2(1) + 8(2) + 6(6) = 72$
The other functions are $f_1 = 157$ and $f_3 = 86$.
2. The safety-maximizing solution:

$$x_{11} = 3 \qquad x_{12} = 2 \qquad x_{23} = 4 \qquad x_{32} = 2 \qquad x_{41} = 1 \qquad x_{43} = 2$$
$$x_{44} = 2 \qquad x_{45} = 4$$

and $f_3^* = 2(3) + 4(2) + 4(4) + 3(2) + 6(1) + 6(2) + 3(2) + 1(4) = 64$

The other functions are $f_1 = 129$ and $f_2 = 126$.

The three nondominated solutions, minimizing each of the three objective functions respectively, are summarized in the table below:

	Cost	Time	Safety
1	ⓐ102	141	94
2	157	ⓐ72	86
3	129	126	ⓐ64

Individual minima are circled, and the ideal solution has been determined: $f^* = (f_1^*, f_2^*, f_3^*) = (102, 72, 64)$. Minimizing measures of closeness d_1 and d_2, we identify the solutions which are as close to the ideal as possible. (Consult Chap. 10 for technical details.)

1. By minimizing d_1 we obtain the following allocation:

$$x_{11} = 3 \qquad x_{14} = 2 \qquad x_{22} = 2 \qquad x_{25} = 2 \qquad x_{32} = 2 \qquad x_{41} = 1$$
$$x_{43} = 6 \qquad x_{45} = 2$$

and its corresponding criteria levels:

$$f_1 = 9(3) + 6(2) + 3(2) + 5(2) + 5(2) + 6(1) + 11(6) + 2(2) = 141$$
$$f_2 = 2(3) + 1(2) + 9(2) + 2(2) + 1(2) + 2(1) + 6(6) + 8(2) = 86$$
$$f_3 = 2(3) + 3(2) + 8(2) + 2(2) + 3(2) + 6(1) + 6(6) + 1(2) = 82$$

Check that the minimum value of $d_1 = \frac{141}{102} + \frac{86}{72} + \frac{82}{64} = 3.858$.

2. By minimizing d_2 the following allocation is obtained:

$$x_{11} = 3 \qquad x_{14} = 2 \qquad x_{22} = 2 \qquad x_{23} = \tfrac{2}{3}, \qquad x_{25} = \tfrac{4}{3} \qquad x_{32} = 2$$
$$x_{41} = 1 \qquad x_{43} = \tfrac{16}{3} \qquad x_{45} = \tfrac{8}{3}$$

Its corresponding criteria levels are:

$$f_1 = 9(3) + 6(2) + 3(2) + 7(\tfrac{2}{3}) + 5(\tfrac{4}{3}) + 5(2) + 6(1) + 11(\tfrac{16}{3}) + 2(\tfrac{8}{3})$$
$$= 136\tfrac{1}{3}$$

$$f_2 = 2(3) + 1(2) + 9(2) + 9(\tfrac{2}{3}) + 2(\tfrac{4}{3}) + 1(2) + 2(1) + 6(\tfrac{16}{3}) + 8(\tfrac{8}{3}) = 92$$

$$f_3 = 2(3) + 3(2) + 8(2) + 4(\tfrac{2}{3}) + 2(\tfrac{4}{3}) + 3(2) + 6(1) + 6(\tfrac{16}{3}) + 1(\tfrac{8}{3}) = 80$$

Check that the minimum value of $d_2 = 0.25296$.

It is interesting to note that the d_2-minimizing compromise solution consists of fractional allocations and corresponds to a nonextreme (nonbasic) solution of the transportation problem.

Note Basic solutions to the transportation problem require exactly $m + n - 1$ nonnegative allocations x_{ij}; such solutions correspond to the corner points of the feasible set X. If there are precisely $m + n - 1$ *positive* x_{ij}, then the solution is also nondegenerate. A degenerate basic solution has fewer than $m + n - 1$ positive assignments x_{ij}. Observe that our second compromise solution has more than $m + n - 1$ positive entries, that is, 9.

The traditional linear-programming problem, because of its particular mathematical structure, generally returns noninteger corner-point solutions. The transportation model returns only integer corner-point solutions. In problems with multiple objective functions—most problems of practical interest—such structural limitations are unwarranted. Linear multiobjective programming techniques can also return nonextreme solutions, and multiobjective transportation methods can return noninteger as well as nonextreme solutions—as we have seen in the above problem.

Let us summarize the first three nondominated solutions and the two latest compromise (also nondominated) solutions in a simple table:

	Cost	Time	Safety
1	⑩②102	141	94
2	157	㉒72	86
3	129	126	㉔64
4	141	86	82
5	$136\frac{1}{3}$	92	80

Nondominated solutions in the transportation problem It is possible to use linear multiobjective programming techniques for finding all nondominated solutions to a multiobjective transportation problem. One can take advantage of the special structure of the transportation problem and adjust the LMP techniques correspondingly; for details of the special algorithms, see Díaz (1979). We shall introduce only a small numerical example, adapted from Díaz, for further analysis and exercise. The problem can be stated as follows:

Sources i \ Destinations j	1	2	3	4	Capacity
1	x_{11}	x_{12}	x_{13}	x_{14}	12
2	x_{21}	x_{22}	x_{23}	x_{24}	8
Demand	7	6	4	3	

The following three matrices characterize the three criteria—cost, time, and safety—used for evaluating any transportation route x_{ij}:

	Cost				Time				Safety			
	1	2	3	4	1	2	3	4	1	2	3	4
1	1	1	3	5	1	1	2	5	1	1	8	1
2	5	1	2	1	1	5	3	1	8	1	1	8

This problem has four nondominated corner-point (i.e., integer) solutions:

(1) $x_{11}=7$ $x_{12}=5$ $x_{13}=0$ $x_{14}=0$ $x_{21}=0$ $x_{22}=1$ $x_{23}=4$ $x_{24}=3$
(2) $x_{11}=7$ $x_{12}=2$ $x_{13}=0$ $x_{14}=3$ $x_{21}=0$ $x_{22}=4$ $x_{23}=4$ $x_{24}=0$

(3) $x_{11} = 6$ $x_{12} = 6$ $x_{13} = 0$ $x_{14} = 0$ $x_{21} = 1$ $x_{22} = 0$ $x_{23} = 4$ $x_{24} = 3$
(4) $x_{11} = 2$ $x_{12} = 6$ $x_{13} = 4$ $x_{14} = 0$ $x_{21} = 5$ $x_{22} = 0$ $x_{23} = 0$ $x_{24} = 3$

The corresponding values of the three criteria are given in the following table:

Nondominated solution	Cost	Time	Safety
1	(24)	32	41
2	36	56	(20)
3	28	28	48
4	48	(24)	104

The minimum values with respect to each criterion are circled. For the sake of completeness, we should note that there are actually many nonextreme nondominated solutions to this problem:

1. All convex combinations of solutions 1 and 2. For example, $\frac{1}{2}$(solution 1) + $\frac{1}{2}$(solution 2) =

$$x_{11} = 7 \quad x_{12} = 3.5 \quad x_{13} = 0 \quad x_{14} = 1.5$$
$$x_{21} = 0 \quad x_{22} = 2.5 \quad x_{23} = 4 \quad x_{24} = 1.5$$

   with cost = 30, time = 44, and safety = 30.5.
2. All convex combinations of solutions 3 and 4. For example $\frac{1}{2}$(solution 3) + $\frac{1}{2}$(solution 4) =

$$x_{11} = 4 \quad x_{12} = 6 \quad x_{13} = 2 \quad x_{14} = 0$$
$$x_{21} = 3 \quad x_{22} = 0 \quad x_{23} = 2 \quad x_{24} = 3$$

   with cost = 38, time = 26, and safety = 76.
3. All convex combinations of solutions 1 and 3. For example, $\frac{1}{2}$(solution 1) + $\frac{1}{2}$(solution 3) =

$$x_{11} = 6.5 \quad x_{12} = 5.5 \quad x_{13} = 0 \quad x_{14} = 0$$
$$x_{21} = 0.5 \quad x_{22} = 0.5 \quad x_{23} = 4 \quad x_{24} = 3$$

   with cost = 27, time = 30, and safety = 44.5

8-7 BIBLIOGRAPHICAL NOTE

Many readers may still desire to study the introductory expositions of traditional single-criterion linear-programming methodology and its applications. Any good textbook on OR/MS would be suitable, such as Wagner (1969) or Loomba (1978). A more advanced classical treatment can be found in Dantzig (1963) or Charnes and Cooper (1961).

Linear multiobjective programming itself is well covered in Cohon (1978). For more advanced formulations, see Zeleny (1974) or Yu and Zeleny (1975). Computational experiences with LMP can be found in Evans and Steuer (1973) and Isermann (1977). Computer programs are well documented and available in Steuer (1974). Steuer also provides a good package of LMP numerical examples for testing. A computer code for the multicriterion simplex method is available in Zeleny (1975). It is of course impossible to comment upon all the relevant literature on LMP, but good surveys are provided by Hwang and Masud (1979) and Cohon and Marks (1975).

Multiparametric decomposition in LMP is further treated by Yu and Zeleny (1976), Zeleny (1973, 1974), and Kornbluth (1977). An interesting interpretation of these decompositions, as probabilities of optima, can be found in Sengupta et al. (1973).

Fractional programming with multiple objectives was advocated by Kornbluth (1973, 1974), developed by Tigan (1975), and further followed by Kornbluth (1979). Integer features are studied by Zionts (1976) and Bitran (1977, 1978).

Transportation problems with multiple objective functions are best researched in the works of Díaz (1978, 1979).

Bitran, G. R.: "Linear Multiple Objective Programs with Zero-One Variables," *Mathematical Programming*, 13, 1977, pp. 121–139.
———: "Theory and Algorithms for Linear Multiple Objective Programs with Zero-One Variables," Operations Research Center Tech. Rep. 150, M.I.T., May 1978.
Charnes, A., and W. W. Cooper: *Management Models and Industrial Applications of Linear Programming*, vols. 1 and 2, Wiley, New York, 1961.
Cohon, J. L.: *Multiobjective Programming and Planning*, Academic, New York, 1978.
——— and D. H. Marks: "A Review and Evaluation of Multiobjective Programming Techniques," *Water Resources Research*, vol. 11, no. 2, 1975, pp. 208–220.
Dantzig, G. B.: *Linear Programming and Extensions*, Princeton, Princeton, N.J., 1963.
Díaz, J. A.: "Finding a Complete Description of All Efficient Solutions to a Multiobjective Transportation Problem," *Ekonomicko-matematický Obzor*, vol. 15, 1979, no. 1, pp. 62–73.
———: "Solving Multiobjective Transportation Problems," *Ekonomicko-matematický Obzor*, vol. 14, no. 3, 1978, pp. 267–274.
Evans, J. P., and R. E. Steuer: "Generating Efficient Extreme Points in Linear Multiple Objective Programming: Two Algorithms and Computing Experience," in J. L. Cochrane and M. Zeleny (eds.), *Multiple Criteria Decision Making*, University of South Carolina Press, Columbia, 1973, pp. 349–365.
Isermann, H.: "The Enumeration of the Set of All Efficient Solutions for Linear Multiple Objective Programs," *Operational Research Quarterly*, vol. 28, no. 3, 1977, pp. 711–725.
Kornbluth, J. S. H.: "Duality, Indifference and Sensitivity Analysis in Multiple Objective Linear Programming," *Operational Research Quarterly*, vol. 25, no. 4, 1974, pp. 599–614.
———: "The Fuzzy Dual: Information for the Multiple Objective Decision Maker," *Computers and Operations Research*, vol. 4, 1977, pp. 65–72.
———: "Indifference Regions and Marginal Utility Weights in Multiple Objective Linear Fractional Programming," Working Pap. 79-02-03, Department of Decision Sciences, The Wharton School, University of Pennsylvania, 1979.
———: "A Survey of Goal Programming," *Omega*, vol. 1, no. 2, 1973, pp. 193–205.
Loomba, P. N.: *Management—A Quantitative Perspective,* Macmillan, New York, 1978.

Sengupta, S. S., M. L. Podrebarac, and T. D. H. Fernando: "Probabilities of Optima in Multi-Objective Linear Programs," in J. L. Cochrane and M. Zeleny (eds.), *Multiple Criteria Decision Making*, University of South Carolina Press, Columbia, 1973, pp. 217–235.

Steuer, R. E.: "ADBASE: An Adjacent Efficient Basis Algorithm for Solving Vector-Maximum and Interval Weighted-Sums Linear Programming Problems," College of Business and Economics, University of Kentucky, Lexington, 1974.

———: "ADEX: An Adjacent Efficient Extreme Point Algorithm for Solving Vector-Maximum and Interval Weighted-Sums Linear Programming Problems," SHARE Program Library Agency, Distribution Code 36OD-15, 2.014, 1974.

———: "Repertoire of Multiple Objective Linear Programming Test Problems for Vector-Maximum and Interval Weighted-Sums Algorithms," College of Business and Economics, University of Kentucky, Lexington, November 1974.

Tigan, S.: "Sur le probleme de la programmation vectorielle fractionnaire," *Mathematica—Revue d'analyse numerique et de theorie de l'approximation*, vol. 4, no. 1, 1975, pp. 99–103.

Wagner, H. M.: *Principles of Operations Research*, Prentice-Hall, Englewood Cliffs, N.J., 1969.

Yu, P. L., and M. Zeleny: "Linear Multiparametric Programming by Multicriteria Simplex Method," *Management Science*, vol. 23, no. 2, 1976, pp. 159–170.

——— and ———: "The Set of All Nondominated Solutions in Linear Cases and a Multicriteria Simplex Method," *Journal of Mathematical Analysis and Applications*, vol. 49, no. 2, 1975, pp. 430–468.

Zeleny, M.: "A Concept of Compromise Solutions and the Method of the Displaced Ideal," *Computers and Operations Research*, vol. 1, no. 4, 1974, pp. 479–496.

———: *Linear Multiobjective Programming*, Springer-Verlag, New York, 1974.

———: "Multicriteria Simplex Method: A Fortran Routine," in M. Zeleny (ed.), *Multiple Criteria Decision Making: Kyoto 1975*, Springer-Verlag, New York, 1976, pp. 323–345.

8-8 PROBLEMS

8-1 Maximize $f_1 = x_1$ and $f_2 = x_2$ subject to the following constraints:

$$0 \leqq x_1 \leqq 2 \qquad 0 \leqq x_2 \leqq 2 \qquad x_1 + x_2 \leqq 3$$

Identify the set of nondominated solutions.

8-2 Consider two functions $f_1 = x$ and $f_2 = 2x - x^2$ defined on a single decision variable x constrained by $x \geqq 0$. Draw a diagram of the situation and assume that both f_1 and f_2 are to be maximized on x. What is the set of nondominated values of x? Is $x = \frac{1}{2}$ nondominated? Is $x = 1$ nondominated? Consider the trade-offs between $x = \frac{1}{2}$ and $x = 1$ and between $x = 1$ and $x = 2$.

8-3 Maximize the following three functions:

$$f_1 = x_1 + 3x_2 - x_3$$

$$f_2 = 4x_1 + x_2 + 2x_3$$

$$f_3 = -x_1 + x_2 + 4x_3$$

subject to the following constraints:

$$x_1 + x_2 + x_3 \leqq 3$$

$$2x_1 + 2x_2 + x_3 \leqq 4$$

$$x_1 - x_2 \leqq 0 \qquad x_1, x_2 \geqq 0$$

by using the multicriterion simplex method (i.e., identify all nondominated extreme points).

8-4 Using Prob. 8-3, consider a linear convex combination of f_1, f_2, and f_3, that is, $(1 - \lambda_1 - \lambda_2)f_3 + \lambda_1 f_1 + \lambda_2 f_2$ for $0 \leq \lambda_1, \lambda_2 \leq 1$ and prepare a complete decomposition of the parametric space of λ_1 and λ_2, $\lambda_1 + \lambda_2 \leq 1$. *Hint*: Arrive at $(-1 + 5\lambda_1 + 2\lambda_2)x_1 + (1 + 2\lambda_2)x_2 + (4 - 2\lambda_1 - 5\lambda_2)x_3$ and maximize this single function with parametric coefficients by using the single-objective simplex method. Display your results graphically.

8-5 Find all nondominated extreme-point solutions to the following problem:

$$\text{Maximize } f_1 = 2x_1 - 3x_2 + 5x_3 - x_4 + x_5$$

and

$$f_2 = 5x_1 - 3x_2 - x_3 + 6x_4 + x_5$$

subject to

$$4x_1 + x_2 + 3x_3 + x_4 \quad\quad = 24$$

$$3x_1 + x_2 + 2x_3 \quad\quad - x_5 = 4$$

All $x_i \geq 0$, for $i = 1, \ldots, 5$.

8-6 Consider the following multiobjective-programming problem in two decision variables:

$$\text{Maximize } f_1 = -120 + 6x_1 + 7x_2$$

and

$$f_2 = 60x_1 + 72x_2 - 3x_1^2 - 4x_1 x_2 - 4x_2^2$$

subject to

$$2x_1 + 5x_2 \leq 60$$

$$4x_1 + 2x_2 \leq 60$$

$$x_1 + x_2 \leq 18 \quad\quad x_1, x_2 \geq 0$$

Construct a graphic representation for this problem. Solve separately for f_1 and f_2 and find their respective maxima. Is $x_1 = 6, x_2 = 6$ nondominated? Is $x_1 = 10, x_2 = 8$ nondominated? Is a linear convex combination of these two points nondominated?

8-7 Using Prob. 8-6, form $\lambda f_1 + (1 - \lambda)f_2$ and maximize with respect to the same constraints for $0 \leq \lambda \leq 1$. Explore specifically the following regions:

$$0 \leq \lambda \leq 0.143$$

$$0.143 \leq \lambda \leq 0.184$$

$$0.184 \leq \lambda \leq 1$$

Identify the corresponding nondominated solutions. It is sufficient to use graphic analysis and numerical substitution.

8-8 Graphically solve the following linear multiobjective problem: Maximize $f_1 = x_1$ and $f_2 = x_2$ with respect to:

$$x_1 + \tfrac{1}{3}x_2 \leq 3.125$$

$$\tfrac{1}{3}x_1 + x_2 \leq 3.125 \quad\quad x_1, x_2 \geq 0$$

Form a linear combination function $\lambda_1 f_1 + \lambda_2 f_2$ and maximize it with respect to the above constraints and the following conditions:

$$(a) \ \tfrac{1}{3}\lambda_2 < \lambda_1 < 3\lambda_2$$

$$(b) \ 2\lambda_2 < \lambda_1 < 3\lambda_2$$

$$(c) \ \tfrac{1}{2}\lambda_2 < \lambda_1 < 2\lambda_2$$

$$(d) \ \tfrac{1}{3}\lambda_2 < \lambda_1 < \tfrac{1}{2}\lambda_2$$

Compare the resulting solutions and comment on the effect of weights. What if the *integer* solution values were required? *Hint*: Use the normalization condition $\lambda_1 + \lambda_2 = 1$ to transform (a) through (d).

8-9 Consider the following multiobjective problem: maximize $f_1 = x_1, f_2 = x_2$, and $f_3 = x_3$ subject to:

$$x_1 - 3x_2 + x_3 + x_4 - x_5 \leq 2$$

$$2x_1 \qquad\qquad - x_4 \qquad \leq 1$$

$$x_2 + x_3 + x_4 + x_5 \leq 10 \qquad x_1, \ldots, x_5 \geq 0$$

Perform a complete multiparametric decomposition of the space $\Lambda = \{\lambda_1 \geq 0, \lambda_2 \geq 0, \lambda_3 \geq 0; \lambda_1 + \lambda_2 + \lambda_3 = 1\}$ by maximizing $\lambda_1 f_1 + \lambda_2 f_2 + (1 - \lambda_1 - \lambda_2) f_3$ with respect to the above constraints. Display the results graphically in the space of λ_1 and λ_2. Interpret the decomposition.

8-10 Consider the following problem:

$$\text{Maximize } f_1 = 4x_1 + x_2 \qquad \text{and} \qquad f_2 = x_2.$$

subject to

$$2x_1 + x_2 \leq 20$$

$$\tfrac{5}{6}x_1 + x_2 \leq 10$$

$$x_1 + x_2 \geq 10 \qquad x_1, x_2 \geq 0$$

(a) Solve graphically.
(b) Support your results by using the multicriterion simplex method.

8-11 Consider the following problem:

$$\text{Maximize } f_1 = 4x_1 + x_2 + 2x_3$$

$$f_2 = x_1 + 3x_2 - x_3$$

$$f_3 = -x_1 + x_2 + 4x_3$$

subject to

$$x_1 + x_2 + x_3 \leq 3$$

$$2x_1 + 2x_2 + x_3 \leq 4$$

$$x_1 - x_2 \qquad \leq 0 \qquad x_1, x_2, x_3 \geq 0$$

Find all nondominated extreme point solutions. Can you identify all nondominated *faces* of the underlying polyhedron? (There are only two.)

8-12 Assume that you have obtained a listing of five extreme point solutions, evaluated with respect to four objective functions. The data are given below:

	f_1	f_2	f_3	f_4
1	6	3	4	8
2	6	8	4	6
3	8	2	6	4
4	7	2	5	6
5	6	7	5	6

(a) Which of the solutions are "obviously" nondominated? (Assume that all individual maxima have been attained.)

(b) Devise a procedure which would help decide nondominance or dominance for any such listing of extreme points.[1] It should take into account the possibility of dominance by a linear convex combination of other points. (For example, form such a combination of rows 1 and 3 by multiplying each by $\frac{1}{2}$ and summing the results; compare this new row with other solutions.)

(c) Write a program for your procedure and test it on larger and higher-dimensional listings. How would you test its correctness?

8-13 In order to have more numerical situations for the procedure required in Prob. 8-12, use the following data:

	f_1	f_2	f_3
1	16.6	3.3	6.6
2	40	0	10.
3	37	2.85	11.4
4	10	10	10

	f_1	f_2	f_3
1	9	8	8
2	8	9	8
3	8	8	9
4	0	8.8	8.8

8-14 Consider the results of the linear-programming problem solved in the chapter:

	f_1	f_2	f_3
x^1	16	24	0
x^2	48	32	-16
x^3	16	0	16
x^4	0	8	16
x^5	5.33	21.33	5.33
x^6	5.33	21.33	5.33

Suppose that x^5 has been selected by the decision maker as a first "tentative" solution. Could you help the decision maker assess the stability of this solution with respect to possibly changing and uncertain weights of importance attributable to f_1, f_2, and f_3? Hint: Verify that the set of weights $\lambda_1, \lambda_2, \lambda_3$ for which the solution remains optimal must satisfy the following:

$$1.33\,\lambda_1 + 0.33\,\lambda_2 - 0.67\,\lambda_3 \leq 0$$

$$-0.67\,\lambda_1 - 1.67\,\lambda_2 + 1.33\,\lambda_3 \leq 0$$

$$\lambda_1 + \lambda_2 + \lambda_3 = 1 \qquad \text{all } \lambda_i \geq 0$$

8-15 Find all nondominated extreme point solutions to the following problem:

$$\text{Maximize } f_1 = -x_1 + x_2 \qquad \text{and} \qquad f_2 = 10x_1$$

$$\text{subject to} \qquad -x_1 + x_2 \leq 2$$

$$x_1 \geq 1$$

$$\text{and} \qquad x_1, x_2 \geq 0$$

Use graphic analysis. Discuss your results.

8-16 It has been shown that if we maximize a convex combination of objective functions—say,

---

[1] See for example S. Zionts and J. Wallenius, "Identifying Efficient Vectors: Some Theory and Computational Results," *Operations Research*, vol. 28, no. 3, pt. 2, 1980, pp. 785–793.

$\lambda_1 f_1 + \lambda_2 f_2 + \cdots + \lambda_l f_l$, over a convex set X and for *all* $\lambda_i > 0$; $\lambda_1 + \lambda_2 + \cdots + \lambda_l = 1$—then the corresponding solutions will be *properly nondominated*.[2]

(a) What would be *improperly nondominated* solutions?

(b) A solution x^0 is said to be properly nondominated if it is nondominated and if there exists a number $M > 0$ such that, for each $i, f_i(x) > f_i(x^0)$ (and x belongs to X) implies

$$\frac{f_i(x) - f_i(x^0)}{f_j(x^0) - f_j(x)} \leq M$$

for some j such that $f_j(x) < f_j(x^0)$.

(c) Reconcile (a) with (b) and comment on the significance of proper nondominance. Construct graphic and numerical examples.

8-17 Consider the following problem:

$$\text{Maximize } f_1 = 2x_1 \quad \text{and} \quad f_2 = 2x_2$$

subject to

$$x_1^2 + x_2^2 \leq 4 \quad \text{and} \quad x_1, x_2 \geq 0$$

(a) Make a graphic sketch of the situation and identify the set of nondominated solutions.

(b) Compare solution $x = (x_1, x_2) = (2,0)$ with $x^0 = (2 - \epsilon, \sqrt{4\epsilon - \epsilon^2})$ where $0 < \epsilon < 2$. Is x properly nondominated? Use the definition stated in Prob. 8-16b. Is the concept of proper nondominance of any significance?

8-18 How many nondominated solutions characterize the following problem?

$$\text{Maximize } f_1 = x_1 \quad \text{and} \quad f_2 = -x_1$$

subject to
$$5x_1 + 4x_2 \leq 20$$
$$x_2 \leq 4$$
$$x_1 + x_2 \geq 2 \qquad x_1, x_2 \geq 0$$

8-19 Consider the following problem:

$$\text{Maximize } f_1 = 3x_1 + x_2 + x_3$$
$$f_2 = x_1 - x_2 + 2x_3$$
$$f_3 = x_1 + x_2$$

subject to
$$4x_1 + 2x_2 + 3x_3 \leq 10$$
$$x_1 + 3x_2 + 2x_3 \leq 8$$
$$x_3 \leq 5 \qquad x_1, x_2, x_3 \geq 0$$

(a) Identify all nondominated extreme points by using the multicriterion simplex method.

(b) The following is one of its possible simplex tableaus:

	x_1	x_2	x_3	x_4	r_5	x_6	
x_1	1	$\frac{1}{2}$	$\frac{3}{4}$	$\frac{1}{4}$	0	0	$\frac{5}{2}$
x_5	0	$\frac{5}{2}$	$\frac{5}{4}$	$-\frac{1}{4}$	1	0	$\frac{11}{2}$
x_6	0	0	0	0	0	1	5
	0	$-\frac{1}{2}$	$-\frac{5}{4}$	$-\frac{3}{4}$	0	0	$\frac{15}{2}$
	0	$-\frac{3}{2}$	$\frac{5}{4}$	$-\frac{1}{4}$	0	0	$\frac{5}{2}$
	0	$\frac{3}{2}$	$-\frac{3}{4}$	$-\frac{1}{4}$	0	0	$\frac{5}{2}$

[2]See for example A. M. Geoffrion, "Proper Efficiency and the Theory of Vector Maximization," *Journal of Mathematical Analysis and Applications*, vol. 22, no. 3, 1968, pp. 618–630.

(x_4 through x_6 are slack variables.) Identify the corresponding nondominated extreme point. For which values of λ_1, λ_2, and λ_3 would $\lambda_1 f_1 + \lambda_2 f_2 + \lambda_3 f_3$ be maximized at that point? Construct the corresponding decomposition polyhedron.

8-20 Find all nondominated extreme point solutions to the following problem:

$$\text{Maximize } f_1 = -x_3 - x_4 \quad \text{and} \quad f_2 = -x_5 - x_6$$

subject to

$$
\begin{aligned}
x_1 + 3x_2 & & & \leq 24 \\
3x_1 + x_2 & & & \leq 24 \\
x_1 + 4x_2 + x_3 - x_4 & & & = 40 \\
4x_1 + x_2 & + x_5 - x_6 & = 40 \quad & x_i \geq 0, \quad i = 1, \dots, 6
\end{aligned}
$$

This problem can be solved by graphic analysis. Why? Interpret the meaning of objective functions with respect to the stated constraints.

8-21 Consider the following multiobjective situation:

$$\text{Maximize } f_1 = 5x_1 - 2x_2 \quad \text{and} \quad f_2 = -x_1 + 4x_2$$

subject to

$$
X = \left\{
\begin{aligned}
-x_1 + x_2 & \leq 3 \\
x_1 + x_2 & \leq 8 \\
x_1 & \leq 4 \\
x_2 & \leq 6 \quad x_1, x_2 \geq 0
\end{aligned}
\right.
$$

(a) Prepare a graphic representation of this problem in the space of objectives f_1 and f_2. *Hint*: Enumerate all extreme points in X and map them in $f(X)$. Identify all nondominated solutions.

(b) What are the advantages and disadvantages of working with X or $f(X)$?

8-22 Show that the following two problems are equivalent for a convex feasible set X:

$$(a) \ \text{Max Min}_{x \quad i} \ \frac{f_i(x) - f_{i*}(x)}{f_i^*(x) - f_{i*}(x)}$$

$$(b) \ \text{Min Max}_{x \quad i} \ \frac{f_i^*(x) - f_i(x)}{f_i^*(x) - f_{i*}(x)}$$

where $f_i^*(x)$ and $f_{i*}(x)$ denote maximum and minimum values of $f_i(x)$ over X.

Show that (a) and (b) are also respectively equivalent to the following:

$$(c) \quad \text{Max } w$$
$$\text{subject to} \quad f_1(x) \geq wf_i^*(x) + (1 - w)f_{i*}(x)$$
$$x \in X$$

$$(d) \quad \text{Min } v$$
$$\text{subject to} \quad f_i(x) \geq vf_{i*}(x) + (1 - v)f_i^*(x)$$
$$x \in X$$

8-23 Consider the following problem:

$$
\begin{aligned}
\text{Maximize } f_1 &= x_1 + 10x_2 + 9x_3 \\
f_2 &= 10x_1 + x_2 + 9x_3
\end{aligned}
$$

subject to

$$x_1 + x_2 + x_3 \leq 2 \quad x_1, x_2, x_3 \geq 0$$

(a) Find the nondominated solutions to this problem.

(b) What are the nondominated extreme points if each variable x_i can only be either 0 or 1 in the solution?

8-24 Consider the following *nonlinear* problem:

$$\text{Maximize } f_1 = x_1 x_2 \quad \text{and} \quad \text{Minimize } f_2 = (x_1 - 4)^2 + x_2^2$$

subject to

$$x_1 + x_2 \leq 25 \quad x_1, x_2 \geq 0$$

(*a*) Identify the set of nondominated solutions through a graphic analysis.

(*b*) Analyze the following solutions: $x_1 = x_2 = 12.5$ and $x_1 = 4$, $x_2 = 0$. What is the ideal solution to this problem?

(*c*) What are the properties of solution $x_1 = 10$, $x_2 = 7.75$?

8-25 Consider the following graphic situation:

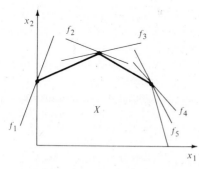

(There are four objective functions maximized over X. Their respective slopes and individual maxima are graphically displayed. The nondominated set is represented by a heavy boundary.)

(*a*) How would the "shape" of the nondominated set change if you would delete functions f_2 and f_3, and f_4 or f_5?

(*b*) With respect to the nondominated set the functions f_2 and f_3 are sometimes called "absolutely nonessential" and functions f_4 and f_5 "relatively nonessential." Functions f_1 and either f_4 or f_5 would then be "essential." How do you understand this classification?

(*c*) Does the above imply that any of the nonessential functions can be deleted? Assume that "nonessential" functions are of primary importance to the decision maker while the "essential" functions are only secondary. Why would you insist on retaining f_2 and f_3?

(*d*) Could it be advantageous to remove nonessential functions *temporarily* in order to speed up the computation of the nondominated set? How would such computationally nonessential functions be identified?

8-26 Enumeration of nondominated extreme point solutions is often inadequate and must be complemented by identifying appropriate *nondominated faces* of a feasible region. Consider the following example:

$$\text{Maximize } f_1 = x_1 \quad \text{and} \quad f_2 = x_2$$

subject to

$$x_1 + x_2 \leq 18$$
$$8x_1 + 6x_2 \geq 112$$
$$5x_1 + 7x_2 \geq 96 \quad x_1, x_2 \geq 0$$

(*a*) Assume that an "unknown" decision maker's preference function is $U = f_1 f_2$. Through a graphic analysis, identify all extreme points of the above problem. Evaluate U at all extreme point solutions, nondominated or dominated. At which point is U the largest? Comment.

(*b*) Find the maximum solution for U. Is this solution an extreme point? Is it nondominated? Comment.

(*c*) How would you present data to the decision maker so that he or she could identify the most preferred solution even though function U remains implicit?

While linear multiobjective programming deals with minimization or maximization of various objective functions, goal programming is concerned with the conditions of achieving prespecified targets or goals.

The setting of goals is a tactical device which often complements the pursuit of objectives. Depending on the situation, for example, an athlete's objective might be to run as fast as possible, or to be the fastest in a given group of runners, or to run 100 meters in no more than 10.2 seconds, or to finish at least third in the field (e.g., in a qualifying heat). The tactics employed will be different in every instance.

It is similar in business decision making. Especially in financial planning, there are many indicators of company performance which should be neither too high nor too low—as strategic or tactical devices, they should be "on target" or as close as possible to it. Typical examples include dividend cover, amount of liquidity, and debt-equity ratio. There are also many legally required target values as well as targets adopted through custom, tradition, and practice.

Once individual goals have been stated, the purpose of goal programming is to achieve the goal portfolio as closely as possible, i.e., to minimize the set of deviations or "distances" from the goals. All goals can be considered simultaneously or they can be taken one by one. Both methods of goal programming are explored in this chapter. Then a third approach, *multigoal programming*, is proposed.

After discussing the simplex method and a partitioning algorithm used in the preemptive-weights version of goal programming, we introduce examples of applications and discuss further extensions of goal programming, such as interactive, nonlinear, integer, and other specialized techniques.

GOAL PROGRAMMING

It is only natural, therefore, that we should never see the picture whole. But the universal goal—the attainment of harmony—is apparent. The very act of perceiving this goal and striving constantly toward it does much in itself to bring us closer and, therefore, becomes an end in itself.

Richard E. Byrd[1]

The setting of goals, targets, or aspiration levels is an old and useful tactic in the the pursuit of human objectives. Setting a concrete target, instead of posing a simple maximization or minimization objective, gives one a clear point of reference and provides a keen sense of direction and a measure of the level of progress one has achieved. Goal setting makes even better sense as part of a multistage approach to an ultimate target. One can evolve a sequence of intermediate goals in order to define a path toward an ultimate objective.

Setting goals is an art. They should be neither too high nor too low. Everybody knows the agony and frustration of failing to achieve a goal set too high; everybody knows the disappointment and dissatisfaction which often sets in after one has "succeeded" in attaining a goal that was set too low.

Given a portfolio of properly established goals, one tries to achieve them as closely as possible. Their actual attainment may not be as important as the *process* of striving toward them. Striving toward a challenging goal can be a worthwhile objective in itself. Attaining a goal is a necessary and sufficient prerequisite for setting a new goal—it is not an end in itself.

Goal programming today is not yet a great goal-setting tool in the sense we have just described. It is still a rather mechanical technique, plagued by insufficient theoretical elaboration, mediocre interpretations, and fast applications. These deficiencies make it controversial. Yet it has potential, and it is a natural complement within the arsenal of MCDM techniques.

There is even some confusion in the literature as to what actually constitutes "goal programming." As originally conceived, it is the attempt to minimize the set of deviations from prespecified multiple goals, which are considered simultaneously but are weighted according to their relative importance. In some cases, however, the name "goal programming" has been

---

[1]From Admiral Richard E. Byrd's account of his struggle to reach the South Pole, *Alone*, Putnam, New York, 1938.

applied to a procedure which is actually a special case of lexicographical screening, as described by Hobbs (1978). That procedure first determines the alternatives that minimize the deviation of the single most important objective from its corresponding goal value. From *those* alternatives are chosen the ones that minimize the deviation of the second most important objective, from its goal, and so on until all objectives and their goals have been considered. This method of lexicographical screening usually goes under the name "preemptive goal programming." We shall deal with it in considerable detail, because every student or practitioner of MCDM can be sure of encountering it sooner or later.

9-1 GOAL-PROGRAMMING FORMULATIONS

Two products are to be produced in a given department of a manufacturer. Quantities of the two products are respectively denoted x_1 and x_2. A production mix (x_1, x_2) is obtained by utilizing two limited resources: labor and raw material.

Each unit of the first product requires 2 hours of labor and 3 units of raw materials; each unit of the second product requires 4 hours of labor and 3 units of raw material. For the next planning period the department has 12 hours of labor and 12 units of raw material available for each working day. The task is to determine the daily production mix of both products over the upcoming planning period.

The department derives $2 profit from each unit of the first product and $4 profit from each unit of the second product. Thus, the total profit function can be written $2x_1 + 4x_2$.

Let us assume that three goals have been established by the department manager:

1. The profit should be at least $8
2. Both products should be produced in amounts as nearly equal as possible
3. The available labor should be utilized as fully as possible

The resource constraints of the problem can be formulated as follows:

$$X \equiv \begin{cases} 2x_1 + 4x_2 \leq 12 & \text{labor constraint} \\ 3x_1 + 3x_2 \leq 12 & \text{raw material constraint} \end{cases}$$

Obviously, $x_1 \geq 0$ and $x_2 \geq 0$, as we do not allow negative production. The situation is represented graphically in Fig. 9-1.

In traditional linear programming we would simply maximize $2x_1 + 4x_2$ with respect to X. The profit line of $8, that is, $2x_1 + 4x_2 = 8$, is drawn as a dashed line in Fig. 9-1. Observe that this line runs parallel with the labor constraint, so that any combination of x_1 and x_2 on the feasible portion of that

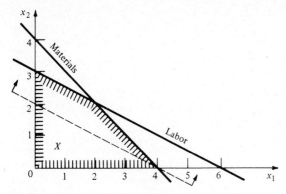

Figure 9-1 Enclosed area X represents feasible combinations of x_1 and x_2. The objective function is parallel to the materials constraint.

constraint boundary would maximize profits. For example, $x_1 = 0$ and $x_2 = 3$ would give us \$12 of profit, i.e., the same as $x_1 = 2$, $x_2 = 2$.

Let us turn now to our three goals:

(a) $2x_1 + 4x_2 \geqq 8$ minimum profits
(b) $x_1 - x_2 = 0$ balanced production mix
(c) $2x_1 + 4x_2 = 12$ fully utilized labor[1]

Introducing these three goals in our graph we obtain a further limited feasible region, shown in Fig. 9-2.

The enclosed area indicates those product mixes which assure \$8 minimum profits and satisfy the constraints of X. Adding a precisely balanced production mix would shrink the feasible region further to the crosshatched portion of the 45° line. The requirement of full employment of labor shrinks the region to a single point x^*. This also represents the solution to the problem as stated, $x^* = (2, 2)$. All constraints and goals are satisfied, and even profit stays at its maximum level of \$12.[2]

Such an ideal conflict resolution is of course extremely rare in most practical problems. Let us change the problem slightly. Let the total-profit function be $4x_1 + 3.2x_2$, maximized at $x_1 = 4$ and $x_2 = 0$, that is, at \$16. Let us also require that the product mix be 3 units of x_1 to 2 units of x_2, that is, $x_1/x_2 = \frac{3}{2}$. Let

---

[1]The goal of minimum profits is an essential survival requirement. Balanced production mix might be dictated by the potential complementarity of the products. Full use of available labor is brought about by union pressure.

[2]Observe how misleading it is to refer to goals and objectives as being a priori "conflicting." In this example, the goals of minimum profits, balanced production mix, and fully utilized labor are not in conflict at all. No objectives or goals should be presumed conflicting until so proved.

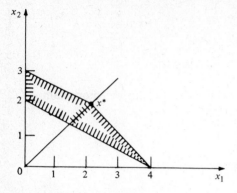

Figure 9-2 Point x^* represents the solution to three simultaneous goals. Enclosed area is a subset of X in Fig. 9-1.

the minimum required profit be \$12. The other constraints and goals will stay unchanged. The new goals are:

(a) $4x_1 + 3.2x_2 \geqq 12$ minimum profits
(b) $x_1 - \frac{3}{2}x_2 = 0$ 3/2 production mix
(c) $2x_1 + 4x_2 = 12$ fully utilized labor

These goals are represented graphically in Fig. 9-3. The enclosed area delimits the production mixes which satisfy the minimum profit requirements. The indicated portion of the labor constraint also satisfies the full utilization of labor, while the enclosed portion of the line through the origin indicates the 3/2 production mixes. Note that the three goals cannot be achieved simultaneously. The second and third goals are in conflict.

Therefore, we must concentrate on the deviations from goals and try to find a solution which minimizes the deviations:

$$(a) \quad 4x_1 + 3.2x_2 - d_1^+ + d_1^- = 12$$

d_1^+ represents the amount of profits *above* \$12, while d_1^- the amount *below* \$12.

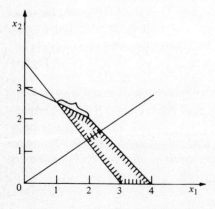

Figure 9-3 Enclosed area is a subset of X in Fig. 9-1. The three goals are now in conflict.

We do not care how big d_1^+ is, but we want d_1^- as small as possible, preferably $d_1^- = 0$.

$$(b)\ x_1 - \tfrac{3}{2}x_2 - d_2^+ + d_2^- = 0$$

In this case we want both d_2^+ and d_2^- to be as small as possible. For example, at $x_1 = 4, x_2 = 0$, we have $d_2^+ = 4$ and $d_2^- = 0$, while at $x_1 = 0, x_2 = 3$, we get $d_2^+ = 0$ and $d_2^- = 4.5$. Also, at $x_1 = 2, x_2 = 1\tfrac{1}{3}$ we have $d_2^+ = d_2^- = 0$.

$$(c)\ 2x_1 + 4x_2 + d_3^- = 12$$

We do not need to consider d_3^+, as it must be equal to zero by definition. Twelve hours of labor is the maximum available. We could similarly omit d_1^- from the first goal if the minimum of \$12 would be so strictly enforced that the goal would become a constraint.

We can summarize the *goal-programming problem* as follows:

$$\text{Minimize } P_1 d_1^- + P_2 (d_2^+ + d_2^-) + P_3 d_3^-$$

subject to
$$4x_1 + 3.2x_2 - d_1^+ + d_1^- = 12$$
$$x_1 + \tfrac{3}{2}x_2 - d_2^+ + d_2^- = 0$$
$$2x_1 + 4x_2 + d_3^- = 12$$
$$3x_1 + 3x_2 + d_4^- = 12$$
$$x_1 \geqq 0,\, x_2 \geqq 0$$

Observe that d_4^- plays the role of the regular slack variable of linear programming. It does not appear in the objective function and serves only as an accounting variable transforming the inequality $\leqq$ into equality. Similarly d_3^- (and all other deviations denoted by d) indicates a slack (or surplus) variable. But because it appears in the objective function with a nonzero coefficient, it transforms the constraint into a goal.

Symbols P_1, P_2, and P_3 in the objective function stand for *preemptive weights*, or priority weights, determining the hierarchy of goals. Goals of higher priority levels are satisfied first, and *only then* may the lower priority goals be considered. Lower priority goals cannot alter the goal attainment at higher priority levels.

Thus, in our case, P_1 forces d_1^- to zero first. Then P_2 takes over and tries to minimize $d_2^+ + d_2^-$, that is, to take this sum, and therefore both of its components, as close to zero as possible while preserving $d_1^- = 0$. Finally, P_3 attempts to minimize d_3^- while sustaining all previous goal achievements. In our example this particular preemptive weighting would lead to a solution point x^*, as shown in Fig. 9-4.

Solution $x^* = (2.4, 1.6)$ implies $d_1^- = 0$ and $d_1^+ = 2.72, d_2^+ = d_2^- = 0, d_3^- = 0.8$,

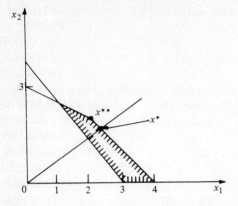

Figure 9-4 Points x^* and x^{**} represent possible conflict resolutions under different goal priorities.

and $d_4^- = 0$. Thus the overall minimum value of the objective function is 0.8, as all other deviations are zero and P_i's indicate simply a priority, not a coefficient.

Suppose we change the priorities in the following way:

$$\text{Minimize } P_1 d_1^- + P_2^+ d_3^- + P_3 (d_2^+ + d_2^-)$$

Now, after securing the minimum profits, we try a full utilization of labor, and only then do we worry about the 3/2 mix. This would lead to solution $x^{**} = (2, 2)$, implying $d_1^- = 0$, $d_1^+ = 2.4$, $d_2^- = 1$, $d_3^- = 0$, and $d_4^- = 0$.

The single-goal model? The goal-programming approach is interesting in that it requires a priori goal setting when there is more than one goal. (When there is only one goal, such an approach is less than sensible.) Suppose that there is only one goal, to attain at least a minimum profit of $12:

$$\text{Minimize } d_1^-$$

subject to

$$4x_1 + 3.2x_2 - d_1^+ + d_1^- = 12 \text{ and feasible set } X$$

Our goal, then, is to minimize underachievement of the target profit, and we don't care if we overachieve; that is, d_1^+ can be as large as possible. Minimizing d_1^- amounts to minimizing $12 - (4x_1 + 3.2x_2)$, which is the same as maximizing $4x_1 + 3.2x_2$. Regardless of whether the goal is set at $12 or $12,000, the same solution would be obtained by maximizing $4x_1 + 3.2x_2$ over X. Similarly, minimization of overachievement can be accomplished by minimizing the objective function itself.

Why is it that when facing multiple goals we tend to abandon a maximization or minimization strategy such as this and start searching for goals and target values that are so difficult to come by? And if we set goals arbitrarily, why bother setting them at all? The goal-programming philosophy is oriented more toward testing the feasibility of predetermined target values than toward searching for the best achievable values. This "satisficing" philosophy is exemplified by Ignizio (1976) in his insistence that "*Every* objective function will, and must, have an associated right-hand side value" (p. 14). In most real-life situations these right-side values are precisely what decision makers want to learn from the analysis.

There are, however, certain goals which should be satisfied as precisely as possible, with minimum underachievement *and* overachievement. In such cases, the goal values must be supplied by an external agent or determined by the decision maker. Budgetary constraints are frequently transformed into goals of this type: Administrators of budget-based institutions strive (or at least should strive) to minimize budget deficits on the one hand and budget surplus on the other. One cannot overachieve the budget, but one does not underachieve it either: In the first case the administrator may get fired; in the second case the administrator may find that next year's budget has been lowered. Certain financial ratios also must be satisfied more or less precisely, rather than simply maximized or minimized. In these cases a goal-programming formulation of objectives is useful and can be handled within the framework of linear multiobjective programming. New developments in *fractional goal programming* (see our short discussion in Sec. 8-5) reflect the need to deal with ratios and fractional goals which must be satisfied with respect to a given target. One-sided, unidirectional goals are best dealt with by restating them as objectives to be minimized or maximized.

9-2 THE SIMPLEX-METHOD APPROACH

Solving goal programming by the simplex method is even simpler than working with the multiple criterion simplex method (MSM). Actually the procedures introduced in Sec. 8-4.2 are entirely sufficient for handling any goal-programming problem.

Let us recapitulate our production-mix example from Sec. 9-1.

$$\text{Minimize } P_1 d_1^- + P_2 (d_2^+ + d_2^-) + P_3 d_3^-$$

subject to

$$4x_1 + 3.2x_2 - d_1^+ \qquad + d_1^- \qquad\qquad = 12$$

$$x_1 - 1.5x_2 \qquad - d_2^+ \qquad + d_2^- \qquad\qquad = 0$$

$$2x_1 + 4x_2 \qquad\qquad\qquad + d_3^- \quad = 12$$

$$3x_1 + 3x_2 \qquad\qquad\qquad\qquad + d_4^- = 12$$

and $x_1, x_2, d_1^+, d_2^+, d_1^-, d_2^-, d_3^-, d_4^- \geqq 0$.

P_1, P_2, and P_3 are *preemptive priorities* or weights. They simply indicate that minimization of d_1^- has the highest priority; minimization of $(d_2^+ + d_2^-)$ is the next highest; and minimization of d_3^- is the lowest priority. This implies that the summation of terms in the above "objective function" is meaningless.

Actually, as in linear multiobjective programming, we are facing multiple objective functions:

$$\text{Min } f_1(d) = d_1^-$$

$$\text{Min } f_2(d) = d_2^+ + d_2^-$$

$$\text{Min } f_3(d) = d_3^-$$

To form the initial tableau we can use the MSM format (see Tables 8-2, 8-3, and 8-6). We obtain the *preemptive goal-programming tableau*, as shown in Table 9-1.

First, recall that $\text{Min } f_i(x) = \text{Max } (-1)f_i(x)$. Thus we have multiplied each objective function by (-1) and used the resulting coefficients, as in maximization cases. Following Table 8-2, observe that

$$z_{ij} = \sum_{r=1}^{m} c_{ir} y_{rj} - c_{ij}$$

still holds, and that $z_{ij} = 0$ for all basic variables.

Take for example the first objective function, now $f_1(d) = -d_1^-$. In Table 9-1,

$$z_{11} = (-1)\, 4 + 0(1) + 0(2) + 0(3) - 0 = -4$$

$$z_{12} = (-1)3.2 + 0(1.5) + 0(4) + 0(3) - 0 = -3.2$$

and so on, in the first criterion row.

In the second criterion row, corresponding to function $f_2(d) = -d_2^+ - d_2^-$,

$$z_{21} = 0(4) + (-1)1 + 0(2) + 0(3) - 0 = -1$$

$$z_{22} = 0(3.2) + (-1)(-1.5) + 0(4) + 0(3) - 0 = 1.5$$

Table 9-1

Current basis	Nonbasic variables				Basic variables				Values of basic variables
	x_1	x_2	d_1^+	d_2^+	d_1^-	d_2^-	d_3^-	d_4^-	
d_1^-	4	3.2	-1	0	1	0	0	0	12
d_2^-	1	-1.5	0	-1	0	1	0	0	0
d_3^-	2	4	0	0	0	0	1	0	12
d_4^-	3	3	0	0	0	0	0	1	12
	-4	-3.2	1	0	0	0	0	0	-12
	-1	1.5	0	2	0	0	0	0	0
	-2	-4	0	0	0	0	0	0	-12

or

$$z_{24} = 0(0) + (-1)(-1) + 0(0) + 0(0) - (-1) = 2$$

and so on for this and other criterion rows.

The main difference from the multicriterion simplex method is that in this type of approach we do not consider all criterion rows at the same time but rather one by one, according to their priority levels P_i. We usually append the criterion rows in the order of their priorities, i.e., the most important is first, the next one is second, etc.

We shall proceed as follows: First, use only the first criterion row to determine which variable should enter the basis. Continue until the first objective is maximized, i.e., until all $z_{1j} \geq 0$. During the transformations from one basic solution to another, extend the computations through all the remaining lower priority criterion rows. Then use the next (second) criterion row as the sole determinant for the incoming variables. Continue until either the next objective is maximized or until the goals attained at higher priority levels would deteriorate through further transformations. Then move to the next lower priority level and continue with the process.

In the first criterion row in Table 9-1, we decide to introduce x_1 because $z_{11} = -4$ promises the largest immediate increase of $f_1(d)$. Observe that $@_1 = 0/1 = 0$ is the lowest ratio; d_2^- will be replaced by x_1 in the next basis. The column of coefficients under x_1 will become identical with the current numbers (zeros and a 1) appearing in the column for d_2^-. (Refresh your understanding of simplex iterations by studying the text following Table 8-3.) A newly computed tableau appears in Table 9-2.

We have introduced x_1 at zero level. Such a transformation might seem at first to be a worthless exercise. But we are getting new y_{ij} and z_{ij} values. The degeneracy will resolve itself, as it usually does, in the next iteration.

Next, replace d_1^- by x_2, shown in Table 9-3.

Observe that the first objective has now reached its maximum level of zero;

Table 9-2

Current basis	x_1	x_2	d_1^+	d_2^+	d_1^-	d_2^-	d_3	d_4^-	Values of basic variables
d_1^-	0	9.2	-1	4	1	-4	0	0	12
x_1	1	-1.5	0	-1	0	1	0	0	0
d_3^-	0	7	0	2	0	-2	1	0	12
d_4^-	0	7.5	0	3	0	-3	0	1	12
	0	-9.2	1	-4	0	4	0	0	-12
	0	0	0	1	0	1	0	0	0
	0	-7	0	-2	0	2	0	0	-12

Table 9-3

Current basis	x_1	x_2	d_1^+	d_2^+	d_1^-	d_2^-	d_3^-	d_4^-	Values of basic variables
x_2	0	1	−0.11	0.43	0.11	−0.43	0	0	1.3
x_1	1	0	−0.165	−0.355	0.165	0.355	0	0	1.95
d_3^-	0	0	0.77	−1	−0.77	1	1	0	2.9
d_4^-	0	0	0.825	−0.225	−0.825	0.225	0	1	2.25
	0	0	0	0	1	0	0	0	0
	0	0	0	1	0	1	0	0	0
	0	0	−0.77	1	0.77	−1	0	0	−2.9

all $z_{1j} \geq 0$. The current solution is $d_3^- = 2.9$ and $d_4^- = 2.25$; all other deviations are equal to zero. This implies that $x_1 = 1.95$ and $x_2 = 1.3$. As we turn our attention to the next priority level P_2, the second criterion row, we discover that we were lucky enough to maximize $f_2(d)$ at the same solution point. The second row has all $z_{2j} \geq 0$ and the right-side value is zero as well.

So we merely look at the last criterion row, our lowest priority level of P_3, and find that there is still some possibility for improvement. Introducing d_2^- is an alternative, but observe that $f_2(d)$ would deteriorate because there is a positive number, 1, right above the −1 in the third row. Because our priorities *are* preemptive, we cannot introduce d_2^-.

However, introducing d_1^+ would improve $f_3(d)$ by 0.77 per each unit of increase in d_1^+ while leaving all higher priority goals unaffected. Notice that there are only zeros directly above the −0.77 in question. Replace d_4^- by d_1^+ in the next basis, Table 9-4.

Examine the last row of Table 9-4. There is only one negative number, −0.79, indicating that introducing d_2^- would further improve the third objective function. Notice, however, that the next higher priority objective would deter-

Table 9-4

Current basis	x_1	x_2	d_1^+	d_2^+	d_1^-	d_2^-	d_3^-	d_4^-	Values of basic variables
x_2	0	1	0	0.4	0	−0.4	0	0.13	1.6
x_1	1	0	0	−0.4	0	0.4	0	0.2	2.4
d_3^-	0	0	0	−0.79	0	0.79	1	−0.93	0.8
d_1^+	0	0	1	−0.273	−1	0.273	0	1.21	2.72
	0	0	0	0	1	0	0	0	0
	0	0	0	1	0	1	0	0	0
	0	0	0	0.79	0	−0.79	0	0.93	−0.8

iorate because of the positive 1 directly above it in the same column. Thus, we have an optimal solution: $x^* = (x_1^*, x_2^*) = (2.4, 1.6)$, and the deviations $d_1^- = 0$, $d_1^+ = 2.72$, $d_2^+ = d_2^- = 0$, $d_3^- = 0.8$, and $d_4^- = 0$. Compare this solution with the graphic analysis in Fig. 9-4.

We can now define the *criterion of optimality* for the preemptive goal programming:

> If all the z_{ij} in the criterion row of priority level P_i are ≥ 0, or the objective function has reached zero, evaluate the next priority criterion row P_{i+1}. Otherwise, select the largest negative z_{ij}, for which there are no *positive* coefficients at higher priority levels, and perform the indicated simplex transformation. If there is no such column j to be found at P_i, move to P_{i+1}. If no transformations can be executed while applying the test for $i = 1, \ldots, l$, *in that order*, the solution is optimal.

Observe that Table 9-3 (column d_1^+) passes the test, while Table 9-4 fails and constitutes an optimal solution.

The highest priority objective should usually reach value zero, and always all $z_{1j} \geq 0$. All lower priority objectives must adjust to the resulting circumstances.

The partitioning algorithm Goal-programming problems with preemptive weights can be solved efficiently by taking advantage of the fact that one is dealing with a series of dependent, ordinally ranked linear-programming problems. Arthur and Ravindran (1978) have devised an efficient "partitioning algorithm" which consists of solving the series of linear-programming subproblems, with the solution to the higher priority problem used as the initial solution to the lower priority problem.

The preemptive priorities apply not only to individual deviational variables in the objective function but also to the corresponding goal constraints. This allows us to consider only those constraints and those variables that are immediately relevant to the subproblem at a given priority level. The best way of presenting the partitioning algorithm is with a comparative example. Consider the goal-programming problem introduced at the beginning of Sec. 9-2. The highest priority is P_1, its corresponding deviational variable is d_1^-, and the relevant goal constraint is the one containing d_1^-. Thus, the "first priority" subproblem can be written as follows:

$$\text{Minimize } d_1^-$$

subject to

$$4x_1 + 3.2x_2 - d_1^+ + d_1^- \qquad = 12$$

$$3x_1 + \quad 3x_2 \qquad\qquad\quad + d_4^- = 12$$

The advantages of this formulation become immediately apparent: fewer constraints, fewer variables,[1] more efficient calculations (compare Tables 9-1

---

[1]What are the reasons for keeping variable d_1^+ in this formulation?

Table 9-5

Current basis	Nonbasic variables			Basic variables		
	x_1	x_2	d_1^+	d_1^-	d_4^-	
d_1^-	4	3.2	−1	1	0	12
d_4^-	3	3	0	0	1	12
	−4	−3.2	1	0	0	−12

through 9-3). We apply the simplex procedure to Table 9-5. We introduce x_1 in the basis and force d_1^- out. The result of the transformation is shown in Table 9-6.

Observe that the present solution, $x_1 = 3$ and $x_2 = 0$, is optimal because it makes $d_1^- = 0$ (check that all $z_{1j} \geqq 0$). When we examine Table 9-6 for alternate optimal solutions, we discover that because of the zeros in the criterion row in nonbasic columns x_2 and d_1^+ there exist at least two alternative optima. They can be reached by introducing either x_2 or d_1^+ in the basis. In order to decide which of these should be entered, we append the next-priority goal constraint and the corresponding objective function variables to the optimal tableau of this subproblem. We can also delete all nonbasic columns with positive criterion coefficients, such as d_1^- in Table 9-6, from further consideration. This in effect deletes the old criterion row. All the indicated adjustments appear in Table 9-7.

In Table 9-7 observe that columns d_2^+ and d_2^- have been appended without any difficulties. (All the previously assumed constraints contained these variables with zero coefficients only.) The next-priority goal constraint, row d_2^-, has been added in such a way that basic column x_1 would have zero in that row: Multiply the first row by (-1) and add the result to the original coefficient of this new goal constraint. The new criterion row is then computed as described earlier. Observe that $d_2^- = -3$ violates one of the requirements of linear programming, namely, that all variables are to be nonnegative; the above solution is therefore infeasible. Normally, we would have to employ the dual simplex method to find a feasible solution; see for example Hartley (1976) or any other OR text. In this case we do not have to do so because d_i^- and d_i^+ can never appear in the solution simultaneously—they are linearly dependent pairs of variables in all goal constraints i. Multiplying the third row of Table 9-7 by (-1) will both replace d_2^- by d_2^+ in the basis and make the corresponding solution

Table 9-6

Current basis	x_1	x_2	d_1^+	d_1^-	d_4^-	
x_1	1	0.8	−0.25	0.25	0	3
d_4^-	0	0.6	0.75	−0.75	1	3
	0	0	0	1	0	0

Table 9-7

Current basis	x_1	x_2	d_1^+	d_2^+	d_2^-	d_4^-	
x_1	1	0.8	−0.25	0	0	0	3
d_4^-	0	0.6	0.75	0	0	1	3
d_2^-	0	−2.3	0.25	−1	1	0	−3
~~0~~	~~0~~	~~0~~	~~0~~	~~0~~	~~0~~	~~0~~	~~0~~ *deleted*
	0	2.3	−0.25	2	0	0	3

feasible. Correspondingly the coefficient of the new criterion row will be changed as well. Because of the special structure of goal programming, we can always add a new goal constraint while preserving the feasibility of a given solution. (Optimality of the solution is never affected by adding new constraints.) Table 9-8 shows the new, correctly adjusted simplex tableau.

Table 9-8

Current basis	x_1	x_2	d_1^+	d_2^+	d_2^-	d_4^-	
x_1	1	0.8	−0.25	0	0	0	3
d_4^-	0	0.6	0.75	0	0	1	3
d_2^+	0	2.3	−0.25	1	−1	0	3
	0	−2.3	0.25	0	2	0	−3

We replace d_2^+ in Table 9-8 with x_2 in the basis and obtain the simplex tableau displayed in Table 9-9.

Table 9-9

Current basis	x_1	x_2	d_1^+	d_2^+	d_2^-	d_4^-	
x_1	1	0	−0.163	−0.348	0.348	0	1.96
d_4^-	0	0	0.815	−0.261	0.261	1	2.22
x_2	0	1	−0.109	0.435	−0.435	0	1.3
	0	0	0	1	1	0	0

The present solution, $x_1 = 1.96$ and $x_2 = 1.3$, is optimal for the current subproblem. Again, there is an alternate optimal solution to be achieved by introducing d_1^+ in the basis. Next, we append the last and the lowest priority goal constraint by adjusting its coefficients to the current optimal tableau. We may delete columns for d_2^+ and d_2^- (and thus also the old criterion row), but we must add a new column corresponding to the objective function variable d_3^-. Adding the last goal constraint is performed in such a way that both basic columns x_1 and x_2 contain zeros in the newly added fourth row instead of the original 2 or 4. This is achieved by multiplying the first row of Table 9-9 by (-2) and adding the results to the new fourth row of coefficients. Then multiply the third row of Table 9-9 by (-4) and add the results to the previously computed coefficients in the fourth row. The criterion row coefficients are then computed in standard fashion, as in Table 9-10.

Table 9-10

Current basis	x_1	x_2	d_1^+	d_3^-	d_4^-	
x_1	1	0	−0.163	0	0	1.96
d_4^-	0	0	0.815	0	1	2.22
x_2	0	1	−0.109	0	0	1.3
d_3^-	0	0	0.762	1	0	2.88
	0	0	−0.762	0	0	−2.88

In Table 9-10 we replace d_4^- by d_1^+ in the basis. The completed transformation appears in Table 9-11.

Table 9-11

Current basis	x_1	x_2	d_1^+	d_3^-	d_4^-	
x_1	1	0	0	0	0.2	2.404
d_1^+	0	0	1	0	1.23	2.724
x_2	0	1	0	0	0.134	1.597
d_3^-	0	0	0	1	−0.937	0.804
	0	0	0	0	0.937	−0.804

The present solution is optimal and unique, and it solves the entire goal-programming problem. Compare these results with the results in Table 9-4. We have achieved the same solution by working generally with a smaller number of constraints, variables, and actual iterations.

We can summarize the partitioning algorithm as follows:

1. Solve the smallest subproblem containing only the goal constraints and the associated variables belonging to the highest priority level.
2. Next, examine the optimal tableau for alternate optimal solutions. If there are none, then the present solution is optimal for the original program, and the algorithm terminates. Otherwise move to step 3.

3. If there is at least one alternate optimal solution, the process moves to the next highest priority level. Goal constraints assigned to the next highest priority are appended to the tableau while preserving its feasibility. Corresponding objective function variables are added while all nonbasic variables with positive criterion coefficients may be dropped. The previous criterion row is replaced by a new criterion row.
4. The new tableau for the next-priority-level subproblem is then optimized, and the process returns to step 2. The algorithm continues until (*a*) there are no alternate optimal solutions to a given priority-level subproblem; (*b*) all priority levels have been included in the optimization.

The advantages of the partitioning algorithm become especially apparent when one is dealing with larger problems. Arthur and Ravindran (1978) report that the partitioning algorithm takes only between 12 and 60 percent of the computer time required by the more traditional approaches proposed by Ignizio and Lee.

9-3 PREEMPTIVE WEIGHTS

In Sec. 9-2 we explored the preemptive-weights version of goal programming, as introduced by Lee (1972) and adopted by Ignizio (1976). In this section we show that this approach is incompatible with utility preferences, can lead to dominated solutions, and might fail to identify an unbounded solution (when an objective function can be made arbitrarily large). Preemptive weights are often referred to as "non-archimedean" weights; we advocate a return to the archimedean-weights (i.e., additive) version of goal programming, as originally proposed by Charnes and Cooper (1961).

Preemptive weighting is based on so-called "lexicographical" ordering of vectors according to the importance of their components. Namely, vector **a** lexicographically dominates vector **b** if and only if the first nonzero component of (**a** − **b**) is positive. For example, (0, 0, 3, 2, −1) lexicographically dominates (0, 0, 2, 3, 0); similarly, (4, 0, 0, 3) lexicographically dominates (3, 0, 4, 6), and so on. It is the order of components which matters: The first component which distinguishes one vector from another determines the dominance. That is, vector components are ordered in terms of their preemptive importance.

As an example, consider the numerical problem in Sec. 9-2. Observe that simplex tableau Tables 9-2 to 9-4 provide a series of goal values characterized by increasing lexicographical dominance. The vector of goal values (−12, 0, −12) is dominated by (0, 0, −2.9) because (0, 0, −2.9) − (−12, 0, −12) = (12, 0, 9.1). Vector (0, 0, −2.9) is in turn dominated by (0, 0, −0.8) because (0, 0, −0.8) − (0, 0, −2.9) = (0, 0, 2.1). The first nonzero component of the compared vectors is always positive.

It can be shown that no utility function *u* can be constructed such that **a** lexicographically dominating **b** would also imply $u(\mathbf{a}) \geqq u(\mathbf{b})$ and vice versa. That is, a decision taken on the basis of preemptive weighting is incompatible with and cannot be substantiated by constructing a scalar preference or utility function u. This is a well-known conclusion derivable from the theory of preferential relations; see for example Maňas (1978) or Debreu (1959).

As a consequence, preemptive-weights goal-programming solutions are not likely to be accepted by decision makers. The preemptive approach would then have to be abandoned in favor of a more sophisticated, multiobjective-programming approach for this reason alone. However, there are other, even more serious difficulties associated with goal programming.

A goal-programming solution can turn out to be dominated, i.e., not the best one with respect to currently available alternatives. This suboptimizing feature of goal programming is implied by the fact that the goals are set a priori, as discussed in Zeleny and Cochrane (1973). These shortcomings of goal programming are demonstrated in Fig. 9-5.

In Fig. 9-5 there are three objective functions f_1, f_2, and f_3 with their minimum satisfactory goal values g_1, g_2, and g_3 defined on a feasible set X.

In preemptive-weights fashion, one might be interested in minimizing d_1^- first, d_2^- second, and d_3^- last, subject to the following set of constraints:

$$f_1(x) - d_1^+ \qquad + d_1^- \qquad = g_1$$
$$f_2(x) \qquad - d_2^+ \qquad + d_2^- \quad = g_2$$
$$f_3(x) \qquad - d_3^+ \qquad + d_3^- = g_3$$

Since we minimize only the slack variables d_1^-, d_2^-, and d_3^-, we want to reach

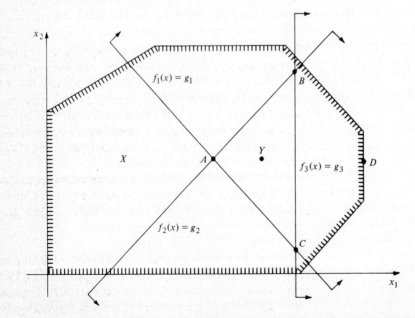

Figure 9-5 A priori setting of goals, such as g_1, g_2, and g_3 levels, leads to suboptimization. Point D dominates point Y.

the goals as closely as possible. The implication is that because surplus variables d_1^+, d_2^+, and d_3^+ are not required to attain their minimum values, the values higher than g_1, g_2, and g_3 would be even more desirable. (If we do not want to exceed the goals, we should also minimize d_1^+, d_2^+, and d_3^+.)

What about maximizing the surplus variables d_i^+ directly? That would amount to maximizing of the objective functions, while maximizing the slack variables directly would amount to minimizing the objective functions. In either case, we are back to linear multiobjective programming. Goal programming is distinct only if the deviations are minimized—and that's where suboptimality is possible.

At point A, in Fig. 9-5, g_1 and g_2 are satisfied fully; $d_1^- = d_2^- = 0$, and g_3 is approached as closely as possible, i.e., d_3^- is minimized on X subject to preserving the zero values of d_1^- and d_2^-. Point A represents the solution to the preemptive goal-programming approach. Observe that point A is dominated by points like B, C, or D—an embarrassing result!

What if, instead of minimizing $P_1 d_1^- + P_2 d_2^- + P_3 d_3^-$, with P_1, P_2, and P_3 indicating preemptive priorities, we would consider the weights to be of the same order of magnitude and minimize a linear combination of deviations, such as $\lambda_1 d_1^- + \lambda_2 d_2^- + \lambda_3 d_3^-$? These λ's would not be preemptive priorities anymore, but rather archimedean weights, as used in Chaps. 6 and 7.

For simplicity, let us assume $\lambda_1 = \lambda_2 = \lambda_3$. Then minimizing $d_1^- + d_2^- + d_3^-$ leads again to point A, a dominated solution. Even taking an analog to the L_∞ metric (see Sec. 6-5.2) and minimizing the maximum of the deviations d_1^-, d_2^-, and d_3^- would lead to a dominated, suboptimal solution, in this case point Y. We have to conclude that the goal-programming approach, using preemptive or any other types of weighting structures, can lead to dominated, suboptimal solutions, because of its heavy reliance on the principle of satisficing. We face a classical example of confusing inputs with outputs: Goals should be the outputs of the analysis, not its inputs. Determining the goals a priori, without being able to explore the limits and the possibilities of the feasible set X first, is one of the main reasons for substandard decision making.[1]

Hannan (1978) gives a few numerical examples of goal-programming difficulties. For example,

$$\text{Minimize } P_1 d_1^- + P_2 d_2^- + P_3 d_3^-$$

subject to

$$
\begin{array}{rcl}
x_2 + x_3 & \leq & 6 \\
x_1 & \leq & 4 \\
2x_2 + x_3 + d_1^- \qquad\quad - d_1^+ & = & 10 \\
x_1 + x_2 + x_3 \qquad + d_2^- \qquad - d_2^+ & = & 12 \\
x_1 + 3x_2 \qquad\qquad + d_3^- \qquad - d_3^+ & = & 16
\end{array}
$$

where all variables are assumed to be nonnegative.

---

[1] Admiral Byrd's goal of reaching the South Pole was set a priori but only after exploring the limits and the possibilities of the globe; thus constituting an output of the analysis. Compare with "goals" of traveling at least 200 miles toward the pole or reaching the halfway mark.

Solving the above goal-programming problem by the preemptive-weights approach described in Sec. 9-2, we obtain an optimal solution of $x_1 = 4$, $x_2 = 4$, and $x_3 = 2$. This implies that the first (highest priority) goal is satisfied fully, that is, $2(4) + 1(2) = 10$; the second goal is satisfied at $1(4) + 1(4) + 1(2) = 10$, that is, $d_2^- = 2$; and the lowest priority goal is satisfied at $1(4) + 3(4) = 16$, that is, $d_3^- = 0$.

This solution is dominated; it is inferior, for example, to $x_1 = 4$, $x_2 = 6$, and $x_3 = 0$. At this feasible solution the first goal reaches $12 - 2(6) + 1(0) = 12$, that is, $d_1^- = 0$ and $d_1^+ = 2$; the second goal attains $10 - 1(4) + 1(6) + 1(0) = 10$; and the third goal is satisfied at the level of $22 - 1(4) + 3(6) = 22$, with $d_3^- = 0$ and $d_3^+ = 6$. A vector of values $(12, 10, 22)$ dominates the previous one, $(10, 10, 16)$.

Dominated solutions are returned by any goal-programming approach, regardless of the weights (preemptive or archimedean) and regardless of the goals (one-sided or two-sided); the reason is that the goals are determined a priori, without the true potentials of a feasible region X being first explored.

Hannan (1978) gives another nice example of an unbounded solution which also can go undetected by goal-programming procedure:

$$\text{Minimize } d_1^- + d_2^-$$

subject to

$$
\begin{aligned}
x_2 - x_3 &\leq 6 \\
x_1 &\leq 4 \\
2x_2 + x_3 + d_1^- - d_1^+ &= 12 \\
x_1 + x_2 + x_3 + d_2^- - d_2^+ &= 10
\end{aligned}
$$

Solving the above goal-programming problem we obtain $x_1 = 4$, $x_2 = 6$, and $x_3 = 0$; that is, $d_1^- = d_2^- = 0$. But observe that both objectives can actually be raised beyond any bounds, because x_3 can be made arbitrarily large. Thus, setting the goals to 12 and 10 respectively is certainly suboptimal in this case. Why shouldn't a decision maker find the nondominated set first and then establish goals? The intelligent setting of goals is one of the main prerequisites of good decision making.

If we want to minimize the underachievement of goals d_i^-, we might as well maximize the corresponding goal function; if we want to minimize the overachievement of goals d_i^+, we can do so by minimizing the corresponding goal functions. Hannan even suggests setting the goals a priori and *then* maximizing or minimizing the corresponding goal functions on a further constrained set X. This amounts to a probably redundant expansion of the number of constraints. Linear multiobjective programming, combined with compromise solutions or filtering (pruning) of a nondominated set, would achieve the same purpose.

Multigoal programming There are three basic approaches to problems characterized by a priori set goals: *preemptive goal programming, archimedean (or nonpreemptive) goal programming,* and *multigoal programming.* We shall briefly summarize their characteristic formulations.

The three approaches differ only in their handling of the objective function(s); they rely on identical formulations of goals and constraints. In general notation, linear goals and constraints can be written as follows:

$$\sum_{j=1}^{n} c_{ij}x_j + d^-_i - d^+_i = b_i \qquad \text{for } i = 1, \ldots, m$$

where x_j are n decision variables, d^-_i denote negative deviations or slack variables, d^+_i denote positive deviations or surplus variables, b_i are m goals or rigid constraining values, and c_{ij} are technological coefficients.

As we discussed in Sec. 8-3, the nature of constants b_i determines whether the corresponding equality is a constraint or a goal. If b_i are rigid limits not to be exceeded, then d^-_i are slack variables and do not appear in the objective function(s). The underlying constraints are of the $\leqq$ type and variables d^+_i can be omitted. If b_i are rigid limits not to be underachieved, then d^+_i are surplus variables and they do not appear in the objective function(s). The underlying constraints are of the $\geqq$ type and variables d^-_i can be omitted (constraints of the $=$ type can be replaced by two $\leqq$ and $\geqq$ constraints).

If b_i are goals (nonrigid, to be achieved as closely as possible) then either d^-_i or d^+_i or both appear in the objective function(s), corresponding to the "at least," "at most," and "precisely" types of goals respectively. All x_j, d^-_i, d^+_i must be nonnegative, and deviations d^-_i, d^+_i are always to be minimized.

It is the way in which we choose to minimize goal deviations which differentiates the three approaches:

1. *Preemptive goal programming.* Minimize $f_i(d^-_i, d^+_i)$ one by one in the order of their (preemptive) priorities. Functions f_i are typically linear functions of deviational variables; for example, $f_i = d^-_i$, $f_i = d^+_i$, $f_i = (d^-_i + d^+_i)$, or $f_i = [w_i d^-_i + (1 - w_i)d^+_i]$, and so on. Additional forms of f_i are conceivable, but the emphasis is on their one-by-one minimization in the lexicographic sense. This approach has been typified by the works of Lee (1972) and Ignizio (1976), and can be found in the voluminous derivative literature.

   The objective function for preemptive goal programming is often written as:

$$\sum_{i=1}^{l} P_i f_i(d^-_i, d^+_i) = P_1 f_1(d^-_1, d^+_1) + \cdots + P_l f_l(d^-_l, d^+_l)$$

   Although we have used this notation in our text, the reader should realize that the summation above is redundant, misleading, and meaningless in this case. It is, however, prevalent in the literature and thus cannot be ignored.

2. *Archimedean goal programming.* Minimize

$$\sum_{i=1}^{l} w_i[f_i(d^-_i, d^+_i)]^p = w_i[f_i(d^-_1, d^+_1)]^p + \cdots + w_l[f_l(d^-_l, d^+_l)]^p$$

Here functions f_i are weighted and their powers p summed up in order to form a measure of the total "distance" from prespecified goals. All objectives f_i are considered at the same time, their weights w_i are not preemptive but reflect relative differential contributions of each function. Powers p could take on any value, but typically $p = 1, 2$, or ∞. This version of goal programming for $p = 2$ has been associated with the work of Charnes and Cooper (1961).

3. *Multigoal programming.* Minimize $[f_1(d_1^-, d_1^+), \ldots, f_l(d_l^-, d_l^+)]$ in a vector sense; that is, identify all nondominated solutions with respect to objective functions $f_i(d_i^-, d_i^+)$, as in multiobjective linear programming. There is no need to specify criterion weights (preemptive or archimedean) and no aggregate preference or distance function. These concepts become useful and more effective only after the set of nondominated solutions has been identified. Multigoal programming has not been dealt with in the goal programming literature.

The three approaches have been presented in the order of their decreasing assumptions about the decision maker's preferences: from one-by-one artifact, through additive aggregate, to no-assumption framework; from preemptive ordering of goal importance, through their relative weighting, to no weighting required; from a uniquely defined solution to a set of nondominated solutions. And if we replace a priori defined goals b_i by the actually achievable ideal values, we enter the area of *compromise programming* (see Chap. 10).

9-4 MACROECONOMIC POLICY MAKING

9-4.1 National Workforce Planning Example[1]

We shall consider a highly simplified situation to demonstrate how multiple goals and objectives may unfold on a national level.

Let us assume that the federal government is planning to launch a vast construction project to complete the interstate highway system. One of its main goals is to alleviate unemployment among various labor groups. A budget of $120 million has been assigned to cover the cost of labor. It has been estimated that at least 20 million skilled worker-hours will be necessary for the project. Three sources of skilled labor are being considered:

1. Local skilled labor. Available at an average rate of $5.50 per hour, x_1 denotes the total number of worker-hours of local skilled labor engaged.
2. Foreign skilled labor. Available at an average rate of $4 per hour, x_2 denotes the total number of worker-hours of foreign skilled labor put on the project.

[1]Based on S. S. Sengupta, M. L. Podrebarac, and T. D. H. Fernando, "Probabilities of Optima in Multi-Objective Linear Programmes," in J. L. Cochrane and M. Zeleny (eds.), *Multiple Criteria Decision Making*, University of South Carolina Press, Columbia, 1973, pp. 217–235.

3. Local skilled labor, retrained at government expense. This retrained labor is available at the average hourly wage of $6, which includes the total cost of retraining. Only 2 million worker-hours can be obtained through the retraining program. The total number of worker-hours in this category is denoted by x_3.

The total budget disbursement and workforce constraints can be formulated as follows:

$$5.50x_1 + 4.00x_2 + 6.00x_3 \leq 12,000,000$$
$$x_1 + x_2 + x_3 \geq 20,000,000$$
$$x_3 \leq 2,000,000$$

Unionized local workers have achieved an agreement that the amount budgeted for foreign workers must be at least $20 million less than the amount ultimately budgeted for themselves; that is,

$$5.50x_1 - 4.00x_2 \geq 20,000,000$$

A number of additional objectives must be considered:

(a) Min $5.50x_1 + 4.00x_2 + 6.00x_3$

That is, government spending must be limited in order to combat inflation.

(b) Max $x_1 + x_2 + x_3$ or   Max $x_1 + x_3$

That is, planners must strive for the highest employment rate, either total or domestic.

(c) Min $x_1 + x_2 + x_3$

That is, planners must try to satisfy all requirements with the least number of total worker-hours in order to boost the productivity of labor.

Furthermore, there might be additional pressures from labor unions, social welfare groups, and the Department of Immigration. For example, a union might wish to maximize the earnings of the workers from whom it derives its dues:

$$\text{Max } 5.50x_1 + 6.00x_3$$

(The above is based on the assumption that foreign labor will not become unionized.)

A social welfare group could press for Max $6.00x_3$ (maximizing the earnings of the retrained group), or for Min d_1^- subject to $x_3 + d_1^- = 2,000,000$ (maximizing the size of the retrained group).

The Department of Immigration might favor Min x_2, while the Internal Revenue Service might push for Min $4.00x_2$.

Each of the above objectives or goals might be viewed as "legitimate" by the federal government. Weights of importance could be attached to each of the partial objectives, and a variety of alternative solutions could be assessed in terms of each involved party's satisfaction. The methodologies of goal programming, multiobjective programming, or compromise programming could be applied.

9-4.2 The Case of Finnish Industries[1]

Macroeconomic policy problems are almost exclusively characterized by multiple goals and objectives. Existing econometric models concentrate on identifying the complex interrelationships among different variables and sectors of the economy. They are not generally helpful in finding the best policy decisions, especially when multiple objectives are present. This deficiency might be accountable for the general failure of econometric models as macroeconomic decision-making aids.

A multicriterion approach was applied toward policy assessment of the Finnish economy in February 1976. Four macroeconomic criteria were considered: (1) gross domestic product (GDP) increase (percent), (2) inflation rate (percent), (3) unemployment rate (percent), and (4) trade deficit (billions of Fmk). Three high-level decision makers participated in evaluating alternative policies with respect to the given criteria: (1) chief of the Bank Inspectorate, (2) deputy managing director of the Confederation of Finnish Industries, and (3) director of the Bank of Finland.

The underlying linearized econometric model, incorporating the feasible region of the decision variables (such as public consumption, investments and expenditures, indirect and direct taxes, income transfers, and devaluation) was used to compute different simulated variants evaluated with respect to the four main criteria. Optimization of each criterion separately led to elucidation of ideal values which were not attainable all at the same time. This ideal solution was useful for "calibrating" decision makers' responses and preferences. The most preferred solutions of each decision maker are summarized in Table 9-12.

The reader should study Table 9-12 in order to appreciate the implied tradeoffs and preferences of individual decision makers, the implied importance of individual criteria, and the deviations from ideal values. For example, although GDP growth of 7.18 percent appears attainable, the decision makers are opting for much lower rates and one is even content with a decrease in its value. Inflation is considered much more important, as all decision makers are pushing quite close to the ideal. The third decision maker (director of the Bank of Finland) is obviously trading growth for lower trade deficit. One can also see that the criterion weight of importance is directly related to some sort of "distance" of preferred or acceptable levels from the ideal levels of criteria.

[1]Adapted from H. Wallenius, J. Wallenius, and P. Vartia, "An Approach to Solving Multiple Criteria Macroeconomic Policy Problems and an Application," *Management Science*, vol. 24, no. 10, June 1978, pp. 1021–1029.

Table 9-12

	GDP increase %	Inflation %	Unemployment %	Trade deficit Billions Fmk
Ideal solution	7.18	8.16	1.88	1.21
First decision maker	1.81	8.88	2.64	6.54
Second decision maker	0.17	8.29	2.88	5.08
Third decision maker	−1.39	8.69	3.06	3.46

The MCDM approaches can also be used as aids for generating the most preferred solutions. One can start with a basic solution as a reference point and suggest a set of tradeoffs to the decision maker. If the tradeoffs are acceptable, the reference solution is transformed into a new solution. The process is continued until no acceptable set of tradeoffs can be found. For example, a vector of initial criterion values could be (2.73, 10.24, 4.75, 1.46), characterizing GDP, inflation, unemployment, and deficit respectively. The decision maker is then asked whether he or she would accept an increase in GDP of 0.0728 percent, a decrease in inflation of 0.2202 percent, a decrease in unemployment of 0.0109 percent, and an increase in trade deficit of Fmk 0.0388 billion, corresponding to a tradeoff vector (0.0728, −0.2202, −0.0109, 0.0388). If acceptable, the new reference solution would be (2.8, 10.02, 4.74, 1.5). This vector indicates the directions of acceptable improvement and can be replaced by a feasible solution which dominates this vector in all dimensions, for example (3.9, 9.18, 4.57, 2.48). The procedure is then repeated. We shall discuss such interactive procedures in Sec. 10-6 in more detail. Similarly the conflict among multiple decision makers will be addressed in Sec. 10-5.1. More explicit utilization of the ideal solution is further elaborated in Chap. 10. The question of tradeoffs and their assessment reappears in Chap. 12.

9-5 BIBLIOGRAPHICAL NOTE

There is much additional reading available on *goal programming*: It is an "ancient" technique within MCDM—first described in 1961 by Charnes and Cooper. In their 1975 paper, these authors actually trace goal programming's origins back into the early fifties. Goal programming was originally based on archimedean weights, but the concept of preemptive weights, explored in Ijiri (1965) and Charnes et al. (1967), is the source of its subsequent metamorphosis into a lexicographical screening tool.

The preemptive version of goal programming found its full realization in Lee (1972). This book contains a large number of examples and real-life applications, and it includes a listing of a working goal-programming computer routine. It is still one of the major references within the area. A subsequent book by Ignizio (1976) mostly reinforces the original preemptive version of Lee. The Lee book also triggered a large number of goal-programming applications. Lin (1980) lists at least seventy since 1972. The first published application of goal programming is probably Charnes et al. (1963), dealing with break-even analysis.

To sample a few typical applications of goal programming one can consult Charnes et al. (1976) on workforce planning, Lee and Lerro (1973, 1974) on portfolio selection and capital budgeting, Goodman (1974) on aggregate production planning, and McKenna (1980) on labor planning.

The best reviews of goal programming, in addition to Lin (1980), are those by Kornbluth (1973), Hwang and Masud (1979), and Ignizio (1978).

There are also some interesting methodological extensions: into integer goal programming by Lee and Morris (1977), computational algorithmic advances by Arthur and Ravindran (1978) and Dauer and Kruger (1977), interactive and nonlinear goal programming by Monarchi et al. (1976), another interactive version by Nijkamp and Spronk (1978), and some fractional goal considerations summarized by Soyster and Lev (1978). Contini (1968) explores goal programming under the conditions of risk and uncertainty.

Critiques of the underlying theoretical principles of goal programming appear in Zeleny and Cochrane (1973), Hannan (1978), Harrald et al. (1977), and Karwan and Wallace (1978).

Arthur, J. L., and A. Ravindran: "An Efficient Goal Programming Algorithm Using Constraint Partitioning and Variable Elimination," *Management Science*, vol. 24, no. 8, 1978, pp. 867–868.

Awerbuch, S., J. G. Ecker, and W. A. Wallace: "A Note: Hidden Nonlinearities in the Application of Goal Programming," *Management Science*, vol. 22, no. 8, 1976, pp. 918–920.

Charnes, A., and W. W. Cooper: "Goal Programming and Constrained Regression—A Comment," *Omega*, vol. 3, no. 4, 1975, pp. 403–409.

——and ——: *Management Models and Industrial Applications of Linear Programming*, vol. 1, Wiley, New York, 1961, Chap. 6 and App. B.

——, R. W. Clower, and K. O. Kortanek: "Effective Control Through Coherent Decentralization with Preemptive Goals," *Econometrica*, vol. 35, no. 2, 1967, pp. 294–320.

——, W. W. Cooper, and Y. Ijiri: "Break-Even Budgeting and Programming to Goals," *Journal of Accounting Research*, vol. 1, no. 1, 1963, pp. 16–43.

——, ——, K. A. Lewis, and R. J. Niehaus: "A Multi-Objective Model for Planning Equal Employment Opportunities," in M. Zeleny (ed.), *Multiple Criteria Decision Making: Kyoto 1975*, Springer-Verlag, New York, 1976, pp. 111–134.

Contini, B.: "A Stochastic Approach to Goal Programming," *Operations Research*, vol. 16, no. 3, 1968, pp. 576–586.

Dauer, J. P., and R. J. Krueger: "An Iterative Approach to Goal Programming," *Operational Research Quarterly*, vol. 28, no. 3, 1977, pp. 671–681.

Debreu, G.: *Theory of Value—An Axiomatic Analysis of Economic Equilibrium*, Cowles Foundation Monograph, Yale, New Haven, Conn., 1959, pp. 72–73.

Goodman, D. A.: "A Goal Programming Approach to Aggregate Planning of Production and Workforce," *Management Science*, vol. 20, no. 12, 1974, pp. 1569–1575.

Hannan, E. L.: "Effects of Substituting a Linear Goal for a Fractional Goal in the Goal Programming Problem," *Management Science*, vol. 24, no. 1, 1977, pp. 105–107.

——: "Efficiency in Goal Programming," Working Pap. AES-7809, Union College, Schenectady, N.Y., 1978.

Harrald, J., J. Leotta, W. A. Wallace, and R. E. Wendell: "A Note on the Limitations of Goal Programming as Observed in Resource Allocation for Marine Environmental Protection," *Naval Research Logistics Quarterly*, vol. 25, no. 4, 1978, pp. 733–739.

Hartley, R. V.: *Operations Research: A Managerial Emphasis*, Goodyear Publishing, Pacific Palisades, Calif., 1976, Chaps. 8 and 14.

Hobbs, B. F.: "Analytical Multiobjective Decision Methods for Power Plant Siting: A Review of Theory and Applications," Policy Analysis Div., Brookhaven National Lab., Upton, N.Y., 1978, pp. 147–156.

Hwang, C. L., and A. Masud: *Multiple Objective Decision Making—Methods and Applications*, Springer-Verlag, New York, 1979, pp. 56–101.

Ignizio, J. P.: *Goal Programming and Extensions*, Lexington Books, Heath, Lexington, Mass., 1976.

——: "A Review of Goal Programming: A Tool for Multiobjective Analysis," *Journal of the Operational Research Society*, vol. 29, no. 11, 1978, pp. 1109–1119.

Ijiri, Y.: *Management Goals and Accounting for Control*, North-Holland Publishing, Amsterdam, 1965.

Karwan, K. R., and W. A. Wallace: "A Comparative Evaluation of Conjoint Measurement and Goal Programming as Aids in Decision Making for Marine Environmental Protection," in G. Fandel and T. Gal (eds.), *Multiple Criteria Decision Making Theory and Application*, Springer-Verlag, New York, 1980, pp. 135–149.

Kornbluth, J. S. H.: "A Survey of Goal Programming," *Omega*, vol. 1, no. 2, 1973, pp. 193–205.

Lee, S. M.: *Goal Programming for Decision Analysis*, Auerbach Publishers, Philadelphia, 1972.

—— and A. J. Lerro: "Capital Budgeting for Multiple Objectives," *Financial Management*, vol. 3, no. 1, 1974, pp. 58–66.

—— and ——: "Optimizing the Portfolio Selection for Mutual Funds," *Journal of Finance*, vol. 28, no. 5, 1973, pp. 1067–1101.

—— and R. L. Morris: "Integer Goal Programming Methods," in M. K. Starr and M. Zeleny (eds.), *Multiple Criteria Decision Making*, TIMS Studies in the Management Sciences, vol. 6, North-Holland Publishing, Amsterdam, 1977, pp. 273–289.

Lin, W. T.: "A Survey of Goal Programming Applications," *Omega*, vol. 8, no. 1, 1980, pp. 115–117.

Maňas, M.: "Úlohy Vektorové Maximalizace," *Ekonomicko-matematický Obzor*, vol. 14, no. 3, 1978, pp. 251–266.

McKenna, C. K.: *Quantitative Methods for Public Decision Making*, McGraw-Hill, New York, 1980, pp. 265–269.

Monarchi, D. E., J. E. Weber, and L. Duckstein: "An Interactive Multiple Objective Decision-Making Aid Using Nonlinear Goal Programming," in M. Zeleny (ed.), *Multiple Criteria Decision Making: Kyoto 1975*, Springer-Verlag, New York, 1976, pp. 235–253.

Nijkamp, P., and J. Spronk: "Interactive Multiple Goal Programming," Centre for Research in Business Economics Rep. 7803/A, Erasmus University, Rotterdam, 1978.

Soyster, A. L., and B. Lev: "An Interpretation of Fractional Objectives in Goal Programming as Related to Papers by Awerbuch, et al., and Hannan," *Management Science*, vol. 24, no. 14, 1978, pp. 1546–1549.

Zeleny, M., and J. L. Cochrane: "A Priori and A Posteriori Goals in Macroeconomic Policy Making," in J. L. Cochrane and M. Zeleny (eds.), *Multiple Criteria Decision Making*, University of South Carolina Press, Columbia, 1973, pp. 373–391.

9-6 PROBLEMS

9-1 "In situations characterized by multiple objectives, postulating a utility function over the objectives is theoretically inconsistent with the pre-emptive goal programming approach of specifying a goal for each of the objectives and partitioning the goals into different priority classes." How do you understand this statement? Can a "consistency" be achieved?

9-2 Solve the following preemptive goal-programming problem:

$$\text{Minimize } P_1 d_1^- + P_2(d_2^- + d_2^+) + P_3 d_3^-$$

subject to

$$
\begin{aligned}
x_2 + x_3 &\le 6 \\
x_1 &\le 4 \\
2x_2 + x_3 + d_1^- - d_1^+ &= 10 \\
x_1 + 3x_2 \quad\quad + d_2^- - d_2^+ &= 16 \\
2x_1 + 2x_2 - 5x_3 \quad\quad + d_3^- - d_3^+ &= 6
\end{aligned}
$$

where all variables are assumed nonnegative. Compare the resulting solution with $x_1 = 0$, $x_2 = \frac{16}{3}$, $x_3 = \frac{2}{3}$.

9-3 Compare the results of the above problem with the following solutions:

$$x_1 = 1 \quad\quad x_2 = 5 \quad\quad x_3 = 0$$

and

$$x_1 = 0 \quad\quad x_2 = \frac{16}{3} \quad\quad x_3 = 0$$

What are the properties and relationships of all four solutions?

9-4 Whenever a goal-programming solution yields zero deviations, i.e., all postulated goals have been met, the analyst should suspect that the underlying solution could be dominated. Explain and comment.

9-5 Consider the following preemptive goal-programming formulation:

$$\text{Minimize } P_1 d_1^- + P_2 d_{21}^+ + 2P_3 d_2^- + P_3 d_3^- + P_4 d_2^+ + 3P_4 d_3^+$$

subject to

$$
\begin{aligned}
5x_1 + 2x_2 + d_1^- - d_1^+ &= 5500 \\
x_1 \quad\quad + d_2^- - d_2^+ &= 800 \\
x_2 + d_3^- - d_3^+ &= 320 \\
d_{21}^- + d_2^+ - d_{21}^+ &= 100
\end{aligned}
$$

where all variables are nonnegative.

(a) Variables x_1 and x_2 respectively denote total full-time salesperson hours and total part-time salesperson hours worked in a month. Prepare a written statement analyzing all remaining variables and all constraints in the above problem formulation. What can you say about the implied goal structure and priorities of the firm using the above model? Prepare a detailed verbal analysis of all implied goals.

(b) Solve by using preemptive goal programming.

(c) Prepare a report evaluating the impact of the following solution:

$$x_1 = 900 \text{ and } x_2 = 500$$

What are the overtime hours allocated to full-time and part-time salespeople?

9-6 Consider the following goal-programming problem:

$$\text{Minimize } f_1 = d_1^+ + d_2^+$$
$$f_2 = d_3^-$$

subject to
$$x_1 + \quad x_2 + d_1^- - d_1^+ = 400$$
$$2x_1 + \quad x_2 + d_2^- - d_2^+ = 500$$
$$0.4x_1 + 0.3x_2 + d_3^- - d_3^+ = 240$$

(a) Solve graphically if f_1 has a preemptive priority over f_2.

(b) Solve by treating the above as a linear multiobjective-programming problem, i.e., find the set of nondominated solutions.

(c) Solve by nonpreemptive goal programming, i.e., minimize the distance from the goals (assume L_1 measure of distance and equal weights).

(d) Discuss the results and provide a comparison of methods used.

9-7 Let us reverse our usual reasoning. Instead of formulating a problem, let us attempt to provide an interpretation for a given formulation:[1]

Minimize
$$f_1 = 0.225x_1 + 2.2x_2 + 0.8x_3 + 0.1x_4 + 0.05x_5 + 0.26x_6$$

$$f_2 = 10x_1 + 20x_2 + 120x_3$$

$$f_3 = 24x_1 + 27x_2 + 15x_4 + 1.1x_5 + 52x_6$$

subject to
$$720x_1 + 107x_2 + 7080x_3 + 134x_5 + 1000x_6 \geqq 5000$$

$$0.2x_1 + 10.1x_2 + 13.2x_3 + 0.75x_4 + 0.15x_5 + 1.2x_6 \geqq 12.5$$

$$344x_1 + 460x_2 + 1040x_3 + 75x_4 + 17.4x_5 + 240x_6 = 2500$$

$$18x_1 + 151x_2 + 78x_3 + 2.5x_4 + 0.2x_5 + 4x_6 = 63$$

$$x_1 \leqq 6$$

$$x_2 \leqq 1$$

$$x_3 \leqq 0.25$$

$$x_4 \leqq 10$$

$$x_5 \leqq 10$$

$$x_6 \leqq 4 \qquad \text{all } x_i \geqq 0, i = 1, \ldots, 6$$

The variables denote minimum daily diet requirements for pints of milk (x_1), pounds of beef (x_2), dozens of eggs (x_3), ounces of bread (x_4), ounces of lettuce (x_5), and pints of orange juice (x_6). Functions f_1, f_2, and f_3 refer to dollar costs, units of cholesterol, and grams of carbohydrates respectively. The first four constraints refer to units of vitamin A, milligrams of iron, calories, and grams of protein respectively.

(a) Interpret this problem in terms of its objectives, constraints, and goals. Prepare a verbal description of the problem.

(b) Interpret the following solution in terms of the problem:

$$x_1 = 4.15 \qquad x_2 = 0.32 \qquad x_3 = 0.2 \qquad x_4 = 6 \qquad x_5 = 6.03 \qquad x_6 = 0.71$$

(c) What are the main characteristics of the above diet? Prepare a comparative analysis of some well-publicized diets by trying to identify their objectives and constraints.

---

[1]Adapted from C. L. Hwang and A. S. M. Masud, *Multiple Objective Decision Making*, Springer-Verlag, New York, 1979, pp. 111–113.

(d) How would the formulation and interpretation of this problem change if, instead of minimizing f_1, f_2, and f_3, you specified their respective goal values as 2.2, 17, and 150 and minimized their underachievement?

(e) Interpret the following solution:

$$x_1 = 5.12 \qquad x_2 = 0.66 \qquad x_3 = 0.25 \qquad x_4 = 0 \qquad x_5 = 10 \qquad x_6 = 0$$

for both the original and (d) formulation. Compare with the solution in (b). How would the results be affected by considering the ideal values in (d)?

9-8 Consider the following nonpreemptive goal-programming problem:

$$\text{Minimize} \sum_{i=1}^{4} w_i \, (d^+_i + d^-_i)$$

subject to
$$6x_1 + 10x_2 + 2x_3 \leq 100$$
$$4x_1 + 7x_2 + 14x_3 \leq 30$$
$$12x_1 + 5x_2 + 3x_3 \leq 40$$

and
$$12x_1 + 4x_2 + 8x_3 - d^+_1 + d^-_1 = 35$$
$$13x_1 + 6x_2 + 8x_3 - d^+_2 + d^-_2 = 78$$
$$x_1 + 8x_2 + 2x_3 - d^+_3 + d^-_3 = 60$$
$$14x_1 + 6x_2 + 8x_3 - d^+_4 + d^-_4 = 70$$

(a) It was found that the solution $x_1 = 2.03$, $x_2 = 3.13$, and $x_3 = 0$ is optimal for the following set of weights: $w_1 = 0.5$, $w_2 = 0.4$, $w_3 = 0.1$, $w_4 = 0.0$. It was also found[1] that this solution remains optimal for the following sets of weights:

w_1	w_2	w_3	w_4
0.2	0.1	0.4	0.3
0.1	0.2	0.4	0.3
0.1	0.3	0.4	0.2
0.1	0.15	0.4	0.35
0.2	0.15	0.3	0.35
0.2	0.15	0.2	0.45
0.25	0.1	0.2	0.45
0.0	0.4	0.6	0.0

If these results are true (check), why should it be important to spend efforts on identifying a decision maker's a priori weights of importance assigned to individual objectives?

(b) A set of weights such that the higher weight always corresponds to a more important objective is referred to as "naive weights" by Morse. If our four goals are listed in descending order of importance, then some of the above combinations of weights are naive and some are "nonnaive." How important is it that *both* types of weights could lead to the same solution?

(c) Although the listing of goals according to their decreasing importance has been accepted and preserved, a "crazy" analyst has suggested that the following weights be used: $w_1 = 0.2$, $w_2 = 0.4$, $w_3 = 0.1$, and $w_4 = 0.3$ [Compare with the "correct" naive set of weights $w_1 = 0.5$, $w_2 = 0.4$, $w_3 = 0.1$, and $w_4 = 0$ used in (a)]. The following solution was obtained: $x_1 = 3.01$, $x_2 = 0$, and $x_3 = 1.28$. Analyze this solution in terms of the originally stated relations of importance.

(d) Could it ever happen that naive weights would lead to a solution inferior to that obtained by using nonnaive weights? Under what conditions?

[1]See J. N. Morse, "A Theory of Naive Weights," in S. Zionts (ed.), *Multiple Criteria Problem Solving*, Springer-Verlag, New York, 1978, pp. 384–401.

9-9 Analyze the following nonpreemptive goal-programming problem:

$$\text{Minimize} \sum_{i=1}^{4} w_i(d^+_i + d^-_i)$$

subject to

$$4x_1 + 6x_2 + 8x_3 \leq 50$$

$$7x_1 + 12x_2 + 34x_3 \leq 100$$

$$16x_1 + 2x_2 + 19x_3 \leq 89$$

$$5x_1 + 20x_2 + 10x_3 \leq 120$$

and

$$12x_1 + 4x_2 + 8x_3 - d^+_1 + d^-_1 = 32$$

$$2x_1 - 4x_2 + 9x_3 - d^+_2 + d^-_2 = 30$$

$$x_1 + 8x_2 + 2x_3 - d^+_3 + d^-_3 = 60$$

$$14x_1 + 6x_2 + 8x_3 - d^+_4 + d^-_4 = 45$$

Consider the following weights of importance:

(a)

w_1	w_2	w_3	w_4
0.4	0.35	0.15	0.1
0	0.2	0	0.8
0	1	0	0

(b)

w_1	w_2	w_3	w_4
0.1	0.35	0.45	0.1
0	0.35	0.55	0.1

(c)

w_1	w_2	w_3	w_4
0	0	0.9	0.1
0	0	0.7	0.3
0	0	0.6	0.4
0	0	0.5	0.5
0	0	0.4	0.6
0	0	0.3	0.7
0	0	0.2	0.8

(d) Consider also $w_1 = 0$, $w_2 = 0$, $w_3 = 1$, $w_4 = 0$. Perform an analysis of the impacts of differential weighting similar to that in Prob. 9-8.

(e) Somebody has said that a decision maker might wastefully "burn up" his or her weights on goals which do not need such emphasis, as they will be satisfied for any set of weights. From analyzing these problems, what is your understanding of this statement?

9-10 The objective which received the highest *preemptive* weight in building the Aswân Dam on the Nile was to increase the electricity supply. The dam caused the Nile to deposit its fertilizing sediments in Lake Nasser, where it is unavailable to farmers. Egyptian fields must now be artificially fertilized, and fertilizer plants have been built to meet this new need. These plants require enormous amounts of electricity, consuming most of the dam's electrical output. What were the neglected objectives? How might such considerations have affected the project design? Do you know of similar real-life examples of "optimization."

9-11[1] Mr. H. J. Oakes is the production manager in a rather old-fashioned plywood plant with a complex and intricate production process. He is responsible for both operations and the short- and long-range planning tasks of the production process. As the competition is very keen and the market has reached a state of zero growth, Mr. Oakes wishes to base his production plans on the principle that *all* incoming orders should be accepted, though some exceptions will be allowed for products of special dimensions.

Mr. Oakes's immediate task is to develop a tactical production plan for the coming 2-week period. In this period, he is to produce and deliver plywood sheets of 7 standard dimensions. Mr. Oakes easily obtains the data needed to develop the production plan:

Product	Specification, in	Production costs, Fmk/sheet	Demand, sheets/2 weeks
1	50 x 50	25.2	1320
2	50 x 100	41.2	550
3	64 x 64	31.3	1285
4	64 x 128	75.4	730
5	64 x 50	32.3	433
6	64 x 100	58.8	225
7	75 x 150	118.3	113

All relevant cost factors, meaning all activities and resources needed to produce a sheet of plywood, are included in the production costs.

The production capacity available is limited to a 2-week period. The shop is organized in 4 production lines, which are scheduled to operate in 1, 2, 2, and 3 shifts respectively. Mr. Oakes has easy access to normal production times (hours/sheet of plywood); not all dimensions, however, go through all production lines:

Line \ Product	1	2	3	4	5	6	7	Capacity, hours/2 weeks
1	0.22	0.30		0.28	0.15		0.045	80
2	0.039		0.041	0.043		0.045	0.052	160
3	0.041	0.044	0.037		0.042		0.062	160
4	0.062		0.059	0.070		0.082	0.095	240

Mr. Oakes thinks he can do much better in his production plans than just fulfill the (minimum) requirements of his leading customer. As he is also fond of teasing his fellow managers with his knowledge of mathematics, he puts his intentions in the following form:

Besides delivering according to the demand, he also intends to minimize total production costs and create a buffer stock as an insurance against last-minute increases in demand, poor quality, etc.:

[1]This case from Prof. Carlsson of Åbo Akademi, Finland.

(1) Min $25.2x_1 + 41.2x_2 + 31.3x_3 + 75.4x_4 + 32.5x_5 + 58.8x_6 + 118.3x_7$

s.t. $x_1 - d_1^+ + d_1^- \geq 1320$ $28 \leq d_2^+ \leq 55$

$x_2 - d_2^+ + d_2^- \geq 550$ $37 \leq d_4^+ \leq 73$

$x_3 - d_3^+ + d_3^- \geq 1285$ $11 \leq d_6^+ \leq 23$

$x_4 - d_4^+ + d_4^- \geq 730$ $7 \leq d_7^+ \leq 11$

$x_5 - d_5^+ + d_5^- \geq 433$

$x_6 - d_6^+ + d_6^- \geq 225$ $(d_1^+ = d_3^+ = d_5^+ = 0)$

$x_7 - d_7^+ + d_7^- \geq 113$

where x_i is the number of sheets of product i produced, d_i^+ is the number of sheets in the buffer stock, and d_i^- represents a shortage of product i. The buffer stock should be created by 5 to 10 percent surplus production of products 2, 4, 6, and 7.

There are, however, certain costs associated with both the buffer stock and shortages, and Mr. Oakes intends to minimize them both:

(2) Min $45.3\,d_2^+ + 82.9\,d_4^+ + 64.7d_6^+ + 130.1d_7^+$

(3) Min $27.7d_1^- + 61.8d_2^- + 32.9d_3^- + 125.2d_4^- + 37.1d_5^- + 76.4d_6^- + 147.9d_7^-$

A production plan should normally utilize existing capacity to the full. Mr. Oakes likes to minimize both under- and overutilization of capacity, though the former is considerably more important than the latter:

(4) Min $e_1^+ + e_1^- + e_2^+ + e_2^- + e_3^+ + e_3^- + e_4^+ + e_4^-$

$.022x_1 + .030x_2 + .028x_4 + .015x_5 + .045x_7 - e_1^+ + e_1^- \leq 80$

$.039x_1 + .041x_3 + .043x_4 + .045x_6 + .052x_7 - e_2^+ + e_2^- \leq 160$

$.041x_1 + .044x_2 + .037x_3 + .042x_5 + .060x_7 - e_3^+ + e_3^- \leq 160$

$.062x_1 + .059x_3 + .070x_4 + .082x_6 + .095x_7 - e_4^+ + e_4^- \leq 240$

where e_j^+ is overutilization and e_j^- is underutilization of producton line j.

Finally, there is a trimming problem in the process, which Mr. Oakes would like to solve in the production plan—if it is at all possible. In one phase of the process the products are cut from two larger sheets of plywood (dimensions: 154 × 310 inches and 132 × 204 inches), and as the facilities are a bit old-fashioned, only one product can be cut at a time. He would, however, like to minimize the waste from the cutting process. The number of sheets and the wastes generated for different alternatives are as follows:

Product	A = 154 × 310 inches		B = 132 × 204 inches	
	Sheets/A	Percent	Sheets/B	Percent
1	18	5.74	8	25.73
2	9	5.74	4	25.73
3	8	31.36	6	8.73
4	4	31.36	2	39.16
5	12	19.56	8	4.93
6	6	19.56	4	4.93
7	4	5.74	1	72.15

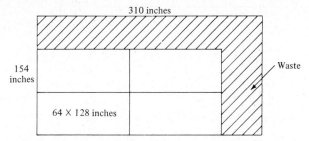

Figure 9-6 Sheet *A* and the cutting pattern for 64 × 128 inches.

These are the only technically feasible cutting alternatives due to the structure of a sheet of plywood; see also Fig. 9-6. For the 2-week period there are 310 sheets of 154 × 310 inches, and 370 sheets of 132 × 204 inches available.

Mr. Oakes would like to have a production plan that enables simultaneous attainment of all his objectives in the planning period and is operational as well.

The methodologies of linear multiobjective programming and goal programming bring the concepts of nondominance and satisficing into the framework of problems with an infinite number of decision alternatives—i.e., the problems of mathematical programming. Is there a mathematical programming method equivalent to the concept of the displaced ideal introduced in Chaps. 5 and 6? Yes, and it goes under the name "compromise programming."

Compromise programming is a relatively recent methodology. Though not yet as developed or applied as its older counterparts, it is much more flexible. It combines the best and most useful features of both LMP and GP. It is not limited to linear cases; it can be used for identifying nondominated solutions under the most general conditions; it allows prespecified goals; and most importantly, it provides an excellent base for interactive programming.

Compromise programming is based on the notion of distance from an ideal solution. Therefore, in this chapter, the reader is first introduced to some rudimentary properties of the most common distance measures.

Graphic analysis of compromise solutions in two-dimensional linear cases follows, then numerical analysis and applications. We also introduce interactive versions of compromise programming.

Chapter 10 also contains a new and hitherto unpublished version of mathematical programming for designing "the best" system (as opposed to "optimizing a given system")—so-called "de novo programming." This relatively complex methodology is introduced through a simple managerial story highlighting its major conceptual advantages as compared to traditional mathematical programming.

Finally, we introduce an example of the interrelatedness of individual and collective decision making—for there are not only multiple objectives but also multiple decision makers. Some sort of compromise or consensus then becomes mandatory. We use as our example the realistic problem of choosing among several combustion engines for development. This also gives us an opportunity to review the so-called "assignment problem" of classical operations research.

A maximal desired ultimate consequence is an ideal which is the only kind of any end that can have purely intrinsic value. Therefore, the instrumental value of any end that is less than an ideal lies in the amount of progress towards one or more ideals that its attainment represents.

To the extent that OR's concept of optimality fails to take extrinsic value of ends, progress toward ideals, into account, it is seriously deficient.

Russell L. Ackoff[1]

What is compromise? Ludwig Erhard once remarked that compromise is the art of cutting the cake so that everyone *thinks* he or she got the largest piece. We might further exploit this analogy and describe a good compromise as everybody getting a little bit more than each one *expected* to get. Compromise is based on the assumption that the cake is always smaller than the sum of claims on it.

Compromise naturally arises as a factor in collective decision making. But it is also an important tool in individual decision making with multiple objectives. One can imagine that behind each of our objectives is a little person screaming for a larger piece of cake.

In our current context we shall view *compromise* as *an effort to approach or emulate the ideal solution as closely as possible.* Observe that the ideal solution is the situation where everybody *does* get the largest possible piece.

In a technical sense, we measure the "goodness" of any compromise by its closeness to the ideal or, as we shall see, by its remoteness from the anti-ideal. Thus, we cannot avoid the notion of distance and its measurement in decision making.

10-1 BASIC PROPERTIES OF DISTANCE MEASURES

One of the best-known concepts of distance is the pythagorean theorem, for measuring the distance between two points whose coordinates are known. That

---

[1]Russell L. Ackoff, "The Future of Operational Research is Past," *Journal of the Operational Research Society,* vol. 30, no. 2, 1979, p. 99.

is, given points $x^1 = (x^1_1, x^1_2)$ and $x^2 = (x^2_1, x^2_2)$ in a plane, distance d between them is found to be

$$d = \sqrt{(x^1_1 - x^2_1)^2 + (x^1_2 - x^2_2)^2}$$

For example, the distance between points $(8, 6)$ and $(4, 3)$ is computed as follows:

$$d = \sqrt{(8 - 4)^2 + (6 - 3)^2} = \sqrt{4^2 + 3^2} = \sqrt{16 + 9} = \sqrt{25} = 5$$

The pythagorean concept of distance is displayed geometrically in Fig. 10-1.

But instead of measuring the distance between any two points, we are interested in comparing the distances of various points from one point of reference, the ideal point. That is, various points x^k are compared in terms of their distance from point x^*. In a two-dimensional case,

$$d = \sqrt{(x^*_1 - x^k_1)^2 + (x^*_2 - x^k_2)^2}$$

Observe that the geometric concept of distance here is very simple: Differences between the coordinates of the ideal point and the corresponding coordinates of a given point are computed and raised to the second power. These second powers are then added, and the square root of the total is taken. The concept is readily generalizable to higher dimensions. If there are n attributes (measured along n coordinates) characterizing the points being compared, the distance formula becomes

$$d = \left(\sum_{i=1}^{n} (x^*_i - x^k_i)^2 \right)^{1/2} \qquad \text{for } k = 1, \ldots, m$$

Recall that taking the square root of a given expression is equivalent to raising it to the power of ½. In the above formula, the deviations $(x^*_i - x^k_i)$ are raised to the power $p = 2$; in general, they could be raised to any power $p = 1, \ldots, \infty$ before being summed. Also, different deviations, corresponding to different attributes i, can be weighted by differential levels of their contribu-

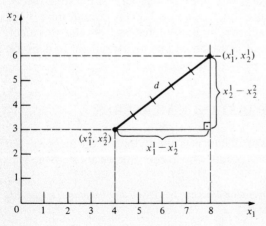

Figure 10-1 The distance d between two points: euclidean measure.

tion to the total sum, weights λ_i. A generalized family of distance measures, dependent on power p, can be expressed as follows:

$$d_p = \left(\sum_{i=1}^{n} \lambda_i^p (x_i^* - x_i^k)^p \right)^{1/p}$$

where $\lambda_i > 0$ and p ranges from 1 to ∞.[1] For $p = \infty$, the above expression is reduced to

$$d_\infty = \text{Max}_i \{ \lambda_i (x_i^* - x_i^k) \} \qquad i = 1, \ldots, n$$
$$k = 1, \ldots, m$$

Let us consider points (8, 6) and (4, 3) again. We can compare their distance numerically for different levels of p; we shall assume λ_i to be equal to 1 for all i, that is, they can be ignored.

In Table 10-1 observe the effect of the increasing p on the relative contribution of individual deviations: The larger the p, the greater the emphasis given to the largest of the deviations in forming the total. Ultimately, for $p = \infty$, the largest of the deviations completely dominates the distance determination. One can also see why the values $p = 1$, 2, and ∞ are strategically important: $p = 1$ implies the "longest" distance between the two points in a geometric sense—one has to traverse the full extent of all deviations. This measure d_1 is therefore often referred to as a "city block" or "Manhattan block" measure of distance. The shortest distance between any two points is a straight line, and this is achieved for $p = 2$. For $p > 2$ we consider distances that are based on even "shorter" measures of distance than a straight line. How do we interpret them and why are we interested in them?

Recall that we employ distance as a proxy measure for human preference and not as a purely geometric concept only. We use distance as a measure of

Table 10-1

p	$(x_1^1 - x_1^2)^p$	$(x_2^1 - x_2^2)^p$	Total sum	d_p
1	4	3	7	7
1.5	8	5.2	13.2	5.584
2	16	9	25	5
3	64	27	91	4.498
5	1024	243	1267	4.174
.	.	.	.	.
.	.	.	.	.
.	.	.	.	.
.	.	.	.	.
∞	4^∞	3^∞	∞	4^*

*Maximum of the two deviations.

[1] We have simplified our notation of distance measures: symbol d_p describes the same family of measure as does $L_p(\lambda, x)$, used in Chap. 6.

resemblance, similarity, or proximity with respect to individual coordinates, dimensions, and attributes. Thus we cannot narrow our attention to only one p or even to the interval of geometrically intuitive measures of $1 \leq p \leq 2$. Consider the example shown in Fig. 10-2.

Assuming that x_1 and x_2 are equally important attributes, observe that in Fig. 10-2 the decision maker could as easily consider point B to be closer than point C to point A as vice versa. Let us compare the effect of $p = 1, 2,$ and ∞; the distances of A to B and A to C are given in Table 10-2.

Observe that C is farther from A with respect to d_1 and d_2 but closer to A with respect to d_∞. What about values $0 \leq p < 1$ or even $p < 0$? For $p = 1$ the deviations were amplified and their differences further increased (until for $p = \infty$ only the maximum deviation mattered). But for $0 \leq p < 1$ the differences between deviations are deemphasized; the larger deviations are reduced more and the smaller ones less until, for $p = 0$, all deviations are equal to 1, regardless of the actual coordinate values. For negative values of p the behavior of d_{-p} represents a mirror image of that of d_p: Smaller deviations make a larger contribution for $-1 > p \geq -\infty$, until for $p = -\infty$ the smallest of the deviations completely dominates, that is, $d_{-\infty} = \underset{i}{\text{Min}} \{\lambda_i(x^*_i - x^k_i)\}$.

We studied the concept of the ideal solution and that of a set of compromise solutions in Chap. 6. These concepts are fully applicable to the problems of mathematical programming, where a feasible set X is described indirectly through a set of functions serving as constraints.

Given a set of decision variables $x = (x_1, \ldots, x_n)$ and a set of constraint functions $g_r(x) \leq b_r, r = 1, \ldots, m$, a feasible set X is the set of decision variables x which satisfies the constraints, $X = \{x | g_r(x) \leq b_r, r = 1, \ldots, m\}$. Let $f_1, f_2, \ldots, f_l$ denote the objective functions defined on X; that is, $f_i(x)$ is the value achieved at x from X with respect to the ith objective function

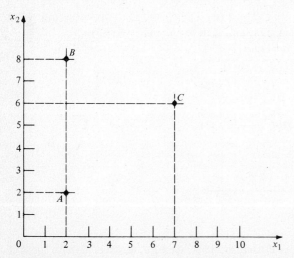

Figure 10-2 Comparison of distance AB with distance AC (see Table 10-2).

Table 10-2

	Deviation along x_1	Deviation along x_2	d_1	d_2	d_∞
Distance AB	0	6	6	6	6
Distance AC	5	4	9	6.4	5

$i = 1, \ldots, l$. Observe that $f = (f_1 \ldots, f_l)$ maps the n-dimensional set X into its l-dimensional image $f(X) = Y$. It is often useful to explain some concepts in terms of the value space Y rather than the decision space X.

Let us demonstrate the mapping from X to Y on a simple numerical-geometric example of linear multiobjective programming:

Maximize
$$f_1(x) = 3x_1 + x_2$$
$$f_2(x) = x_1 + 2x_2$$

subject to
$$X = \begin{cases} x_1 + x_2 \leq 7 \\ x_1 \quad\quad \leq 5 \\ \quad\quad x_2 \leq 5 \\ x_1, x_2 \geq 0 \end{cases}$$

In Fig. 10-3 observe that f_2 is maximized at point $B = (2, 5)$, achieving value $f_2(B) = 12$; function f_1 reaches its maximum at point $C = (5, 2)$, and the value $f_1(C) = 17$. The heavy boundary N of X denotes the set of nondominated solutions, including both corner points B and C. All other solutions in X are inferior to those in N.

The ideal solution, although infeasible, is $x^* = (4.4, 3.8)$; it provides maxima for both objective functions. Check that $f_1(x^*) = 17$ and $f_2(x^*) = 12$.

Next, we translate points $0, A, B, C, D$, and x^* into the corresponding value space $Y = f(X)$, consisting of points $y = f(x)$ based on all x from X.

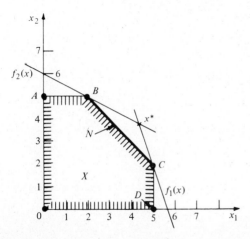

Figure 10-3 Set of nondominated solutions N and the ideal x^* in the decision space.

In Fig. 10-4, $y^* = f(x^*)$, that is, $f(4.4, 3.8) = (17, 12)$. All other points of the polyhedron X are similarly translated. Observe that a point $\bar{y}$ from Y is non-dominated if there is no other y in Y such that $y \geq \bar{y}$ and $y \neq \bar{y}$.

Any point $\bar{y}$ from Y is a compromise solution if it minimizes

$$d_p = \left[\sum_{i=1}^{l} \lambda_i^p (y_i^* - y_i)^p \right]^{1/p}$$

for some choice of weights $\lambda_i > 0$, $\sum_{i=1}^{l} \lambda_i = 1$, and $1 \leq p < \infty$. It can be shown that each compromise solution satisfying these conditions is nondominated. For $1 < p < \infty$ these compromise solutions are also unique.

> **Note** In some situations, distances could be influenced by the chosen unit of measurement along a given attribute. But we try to eliminate any undesirable effects of the units of measurement on the modeling of preferences. There is no difference between 2 kilograms and 2000 grams of meat, and whether one walks 5 kilometers or 5000 meters should not make any difference either. But clearly units of measurement do affect our preferences. One would not be fully indifferent about receiving $100 versus 10,000 pennies, just as one is likely to buy 800 inches of tape more readily than 22.22 yards of it.

Figure 10-5 demonstrates the problem of measurement scale. Three alternatives A, B, and C are positioned according to their attained levels of weight and length. In Fig. 10-5a observe that A and x^* are closer to one another than C

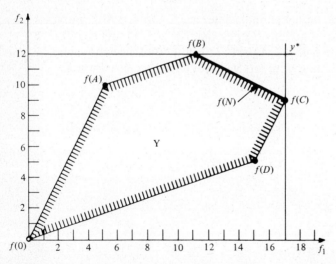

Figure 10-4 Set of nondominated solutions $f(N)$ and the ideal y^* in the value space: mapping from Fig. 10-3.

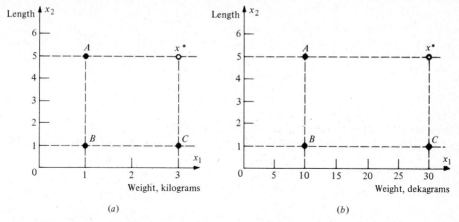

Figure 10-5 Effect of the chosen scale on distance measurement.

and x^*. But if we measure the weight in dekagrams instead of kilograms, as in Fig. 10-5b, points C and x^* are now closer to one another, A and x^* more distant. In Fig. 10-5a we compute the distance between A and x^* as $d(A) = ((5 - 5)^2 + (3 - 1)^2)^{1/2} = (4)^{1/2} = 2$. Similarly, $d(C) = 4$, and finally $d(B) = 4.472$. After rescaling weight in terms of dekagrams, we would still obtain $d(C) = 4$, but $d(A) = ((5 - 5)^2 + (30 - 10)^2)^{1/2} = 20$ and $d(B) = 20.396$.

It would certainly be inappropriate to conclude that A has become less desirable than C, in the sense of being more distant from x^*, just because we have decided to measure weight in dekagrams instead of kilograms. We are facing the issue of commensurability of individual attributes. Is it necessary to make all dimensions commensurable, i.e., express them in terms of dollars, utilities, or another common denominator? No.

We can still "add apples and oranges" in a composite measure of distance. This is achieved by using relative rather than absolute deviations:

$$d = \left[\sum_{i=1}^{n} \left(\frac{x^*_i - x^k_i}{x^*_i} \right)^2 \right]^{1/2} \qquad \text{for } k = 1, \ldots, m$$

Computing the distances by using the above formula, we obtain

$$d(A) = \left[\left(\frac{3 - 1}{3} \right)^2 + \left(\frac{5 - 5}{5} \right)^2 \right]^{1/2} = (\tfrac{4}{9})^{1/2} = \tfrac{2}{3}$$

and similarly $d(C) = \tfrac{4}{5}$ for the situation in Fig. 10-5a. After rescaling, as in Fig. 10-5b, we obtain:

$$d(A) = \left[\left(\frac{30 - 10}{30} \right)^2 + \left(\frac{5 - 5}{5} \right)^2 \right]^{1/2} = (\tfrac{4}{9})^{1/2} = \tfrac{2}{3}$$

and similarly $d(C) = \frac{4}{5}$. The relative distances of A and C from x^* stayed unaffected by the rescaling of x_1 (weight).

The relative measure of distance can be generalized into

$$d_p = \left[\sum_{i=1}^{n} \left(\frac{x^*_i - x^k_i}{x^*_i} \right)^p \right]^{1/p}$$

Fuzzy sets and distance measures[1] We introduced the essentials of fuzzy-sets theory in Sec. 6-4.1. The reader should briefly review the concepts presented there. In Sec. 6-5.2 we let d^k_i represent the degrees of closeness of the kth alternative x^k_i from the ideal alternative x^*_i with respect to the ith attribute or objective. Individual d^k_i are numbers between 0 and 1 indicating the degree of compatibility of a given alternative with the ideal preferred value according to the ith criterion. In other words, d^k_i is a measure of the satisfaction which the kth alternative attains with respect to the ith criterion.

We have also introduced a composite distance measure, capturing the compatibility of any x^k with x^* with respect to all criteria $i = 1, \ldots, n$. Recall that this measure d_p can be expressed as

$$d_p(k) = \left[\sum_{i=1}^{n} (1 - d^k_i)^p \right]^{1/p}$$

where $d^*_i = 1$, all criteria are assumed to be equally important (i.e., weights λ_i can be omitted), and p indicates a power (not to be confused with superscript k).

Yager (1978) introduces the notions of compensatory versus noncompensatory and competitive versus noncompetitive criteria. Two or more objectives are *compensatory* if, for a given alternative, a low value in one objective can be offset by a higher value in one or more other objectives. Two or more objectives are *competitive* if each of them is to be optimized per se, so that they restrain each other and "bargain" with each other over a limited set of alternatives. *Noncompetitive* objectives are only the means for optimizing an overall utility function; their individual satisfaction levels are subservient to the overall global optimization of function u. We deal with the utilitarian handling of noncompetitive criteria in Chaps. 12 and 13.

In the noncompetitive or utilitarian case, one can choose or interchange criteria in any way which provides the highest overall satisfaction (or utility), regardless of how this satisfaction is actually distributed among individual criteria.

In the competitive case, the individual criteria and their satisfaction levels are of paramount importance; they compete with each other for the available alternatives, and compromise is a typical form of conflict resolution.

---

[1]This subsection can be omitted on the first reading.

Noncompetitive criteria, objectives, and attributes can never be in conflict: Actual attainment levels do not matter so long as the overall u is maximized. *Thus, we cannot talk about conflicting objectives on the one hand and invoke the principle of global utility maximization on the other.* Individual criteria can be brought into or dropped from the analysis as long as u attains its maximum. Noncompetitive criteria serve only as inputs to and components in the construction of the overall u.

Competitive criteria are in apparent direct conflict: Each of them is to be maximized or satisfied—their individual attainment levels cannot be ignored or sacrificed for the collective good of utility maximization. The conflict among them can be dissolved only if the ideal solution, maximizing all of them at the same time, can be achieved. Otherwise, a compromise must be reached among the individual criteria.

We have used $d_p(k)$ and its minimization as one suitable model of compromise formation. Next, we introduce another model. Each alternative $k = 1, \ldots, m$ is evaluated by a vector $d^k = (d_1^k, d_2^k, \ldots, d_n^k)$. The ideal alternative is $d^* = (1, 1, \ldots, 1)$ as explained in Sec. 6-5.2. We have also, in Sec. 6-6.2, defined an anti-ideal, characterized by the worst achievable values, and postulated that under certain conditions the decision maker might prefer to be as far away as possible from such an undesirable alternative. An anti-ideal can be characterized by $d_* = (0, 0, \ldots, 0)$ if we compute individual d_i^k according to the transformation

$$d_i^k = \frac{x_i^k - x_{i*}}{x_i^* - x_{i*}}$$

as it was discussed in Sec. 6-4.2 Recall that x_{1*} denotes the minimum achievable value with respect to the ith criterion.

To identify the alternatives which are as far as possible from the anti-ideal we simply *maximize* the following measure of distance:

$$d_p'(k) = \left[\sum_{i=1}^{n} (d_i^k)^p \right]^{1/p}$$

Next, we can show that minimizing $d_p(k)$ or maximizing $d_p'(k)$ for certain values of power p would provide precisely the same solutions as the composite decision functions derived from the theory of fuzzy sets. Yager (1978) explores the properties of $d_1(k)$ and $d_1'(k)$ as well as those of $d_\infty(k)$ and $d_\infty'(k)$ and demonstrates that extreme cases of both competitiveness and compensation among criteria are simply special cases of $d_p(k)$ and $d_p'(k)$.

Let us look at the four extreme cases: competitive and noncompensatory, competitive and compensatory, noncompetitive and noncompensatory, and noncompetitive and compensatory. The interchangeability of criteria in the noncompetitive case implies that an overall decision function should satisfy criterion 1 or 2 or . . . or n, while in the competitive case a decision function should satisfy criteria 1 and 2 and . . . and n.

1. *Competitive and noncompensatory criteria.* The only way to define "and" in fuzzy sets, so that the condition of noncompensation is preserved, is as follows: Maximize function $d(k)$, defined as

$$d(k) = \underset{i}{\text{Min}}\{d^k_i\} = \underset{i}{\text{Min}}\{d^k_1, d^k_2, \ldots, d^k_n\} \quad i = 1, \ldots, n$$

But minimization of $d_p(k)$ for $p = \infty$ provides the same solution as applying the fuzzy-sets-based $d(k)$. That is, the solution to $\underset{k}{\text{Max}} \underset{i}{\text{Min}} \{d^k_i\}$ is the same as the solution to

$$\underset{k}{\text{Min}} \, d_\infty(k) = \underset{k}{\text{Min}} \underset{i}{\text{Max}} \{(1 - d^k_i)\}$$

2. *Competitive and compensatory criteria.* The so-called "Nash solution" is partially compensatory as well as competitive: Maximize

$$d(k) = d^k_1 \cdot d^k_2 \cdot \cdots \cdot d^k_n$$

Another compensatory "and" is obtained as follows: Let $d^k_i * d^k_j = \text{Max}\{0; d^k_i + d^k_j - 1\}$. Then maximize

$$d(k) = d^k_1 * d^k_2 * \cdots * d^k_n$$

But minimization of $d_p(k)$ for $p = 1$ provides the same solution as the above fuzzy-sets-based decision functions. For example, taking the logarithm of $d(k)$ does not change its maximum, because ln is a monotonic transformation. It can be shown that

$$\ln d(k) = - \sum_{p=1}^{\infty} \sum_{i=1}^{n} \frac{1}{p} (1 - d^k_i)^p$$

according to the MacLaurin expansion of $\ln d(k)$ around the point $\ln d(k) = 1$. Using $p = 1$ as a first-order approximation, we find that

$$\ln d(k) = - \sum_{i=1}^{n} (1 - d^k_i)$$

reaches its maximum solution when $d_p(k)$ reaches its minimum for $p = 1$.

3. *Noncompetitive and noncompensatory criteria.* The fuzzy-sets-based decision function is

$$d(k) = \underset{i}{\text{Max}}\{d^k_i\} = \text{Max}\{d^k_1, d^k_2, \ldots, d^k_n\}$$

which is to be maximized. However, maximizing $d'_p(k)$ for $p = \infty$ has the same effect. Recall that $d'_\infty(k) = \underset{i}{\text{Max}} \{d^k_i\}$.

4. *Noncompetitive and compensatory criteria.* The fuzzy-sets-based decision function is either

$$d(k) = \sum_{i=1}^{n} d^k_i - \sum_{j=i+1}^{n} \sum_{i=1}^{n} d^k_i d^k_j + \sum_{r=j+1}^{n} \sum_{j=i+1}^{n} \sum_{i=1}^{n} d^k_i d^k_j d^k_r + \cdots$$

or

$$d(k) = d_1^k * d_2^k * \cdots * d_n^k \qquad \text{where } d_i^k * d_j^k = \text{Min } \{1; d_i^k + d_j^k\}$$

The maximization of both functions leads to the same solution as the maximization of $d_p'(k)$ for $p = 1$.

Observe that $p = 1$ corresponds to the cases of absolute compensation among the criteria, while $p = \infty$ indicates no compensation among the criteria. Similarly, competitive objectives are related to the minimization of $d_p(k)$, while the noncompetitive objectives are related to the maximization of $d_p'(k)$. The advantage of using the distance measures $d_p(k)$ and $d_p'(k)$ for all p's in the range $1 \leqq p \leqq \infty$ is that more realistic situations of criteria which are neither purely competitive nor purely cooperative can be included.

So far we have considered all criteria to be of equal importance. In most practical problems the criteria, objectives, and attributes are not equivalent in terms of their "bargaining strength" or contribution. In competitive cases we associate each criterion with a number α_i indicative of its importance. As α_i increases, the $(d_i^k)^{\alpha_i}$ decreases, and the ith criterion becomes more important in its effects on the overall decision function.

In the cooperative or utilitarian case the criteria do not compete, and their importance does not derive from some externally assessed "bargaining strength." Rather, the importance of a criterion is measured in terms of its contribution to an overall utility function u. The structure of u favors or "prefers" some criteria more than others in terms of their contribution. The more a criterion is preferred, the smaller is its required contribution. As α_i increases, the $(d_i^k)^{1/\alpha_i}$ increases, and the ith criterion becomes more important in its effects on the overall decision function.

Thus, we can introduce a weighted distance measure $d_p(k, \alpha)$ for the competitive case, as

$$d_p(k, \alpha) = \left\{ \sum_{i=1}^{n} \lfloor 1 - (d_i^k)^{\alpha_i} \rfloor \right\}^{1/p}$$

and for the cooperative case, as

$$d_p'(k, \alpha) = \left[\sum_{i=1}^{n} (d_i^k)^{1/\alpha_i} \right]^{1/p}$$

The effect of these weighting procedures is discussed in more detail in Sec. 7-1.4.

10-2 GRAPHIC EXAMPLES

We shall adapt a few of Nykowski's numerical examples from his helpful overview of compromise programming (1977).

First, two objective functions are to be maximized:

$$\text{Max} \begin{cases} f_1(x) = -4x_1 + 3x_2 \\ f_2(x) = 7x_1 + 5x_2 \end{cases}$$

subject to

$$x_1 + x_2 \geqq 3$$
$$-2x_1 + 3x_2 \leqq 12$$
$$6x_1 + x_2 \leqq 42$$
$$x_2 \leqq 6$$
$$x_1 \geqq 0, x_2 \geqq 0$$

In Fig. 10-6, the set of all nondominated solutions is denoted by N, a heavily traced boundary of the feasible set X.

The set of nondominated solutions does not necessarily coincide with the boundary of X; in fact, in some situations $N \equiv X$, as shown in Fig. 10-7:

$$\text{Max} \begin{cases} f_1(x) = x_1 + 3x_2 \\ f_2(x) = 2.5x_1 \\ f_3(x) = -3x_1 - 2x_2 \end{cases}$$

subject to

$$x_1 + x_2 \leqq 10$$
$$-x_1 + x_2 \leqq 2$$
$$4x_1 - x_2 \leqq 20$$
$$2x_1 + 3x_2 \geqq 6$$
$$x_1 \geqq 0, x_2 \geqq 0$$

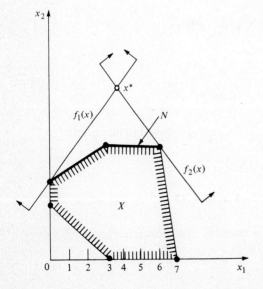

Figure 10-6 Example of compromise programming situation and the nondominated set N.

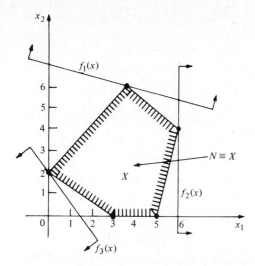

Figure 10-7 All feasible solutions are non-dominated: $N \equiv X$.

Note that in the first example $x^* = (x_1^*, \ldots, x_n^*)$ is the ideal solution at which *all* objective functions $f_i(x)$, $i = 1, \ldots, l$, would attain their maxima. That is,

$$\underset{x}{\text{Max}}\, f_i(x) = f_i(x^*) = f_i^*$$

where Max indicates maximization over feasible set X.
x

In some cases, as in the second example, x^* is not available, i.e., there is no x^* in the two-dimensional space at which all three objectives would attain their maxima.

To accommodate all possible situations, including the two discussed above, we shall use f^* as the ideal point. That is,

$$f^* = (f_1^*, \ldots, f_l^*)$$

where $\qquad f_i^* = \underset{x}{\text{Max}}\, f_i(x), i = 1, \ldots, l.$

In this sense the ideal point f^* is simply a vector of all respective maximal values of $f_i(x)$ individually attainable on X.

In Fig. 10-7, observe that

$$\underset{x}{\text{Max}}\, f_1(x) = f_1(4, 6) = 4 + (3 \times 6) = 22 = f_1^*$$

$$\underset{x}{\text{Max}}\, f_2(x) = f_2(6, 4) = 2.5 \times 6 = 15 = f_2^*$$

$$\underset{x}{\text{Max}}\, f_3(x) = f_3(0, 2) = (-3 \times 0) - (2 \times 2) = -4 = f_3^*$$

Note Maximization of $f_3(x) = -3x_1 - 2x_2$ is graphically portrayed as minimization of $3x_1 + 2x_2$. This is because Max $f(x)$ can be replaced by

Min $[-f(x)]$, and the same solution applies in both situations. We can transpose a minimizing objective function into a maximizing one by multiplying the function to be minimized by -1. Therefore, $\text{Max}(-3x_1 - 2x_2)$ is achieved at the same point as $\text{Min}(3x_1 + 2x_2)$ is attained, i.e., at $x_1 = 0$, $x_2 = 2$.

We have thus established $f^* = (22, 15, -4)$ as the ideal point for our second example. For the first example we have

$$\text{Max}_x f_1(x) = f_1(0, 4) = (-4 \times 0) + (3 \times 4) = 12 = f^*_1$$

and

$$\text{Max}_x f_2(x) = f_2(6, 6) = (7 \times 6) + (5 \times 6) = 72 = f^*_2$$

That is, $f^* = (12, 72)$. Also $x^* = (3.805, 9.073)$, because

$$f_1(x^*) = 12 \quad \text{and} \quad f_2(x^*) = 72$$

To determine the solutions which are the closest to the ideal, we shall employ the following measure of distance:

$$L_p(x) = \left\{ \sum_{i=1}^{l} \left[\frac{f^*_i - f_i(x)}{f^*_i} \right]^p \right\}^{1/p} \qquad p = 1, 2, \ldots, \infty$$

But we could also use

$$L_p(x) = \left[\sum_{i=1}^{l} \left(\frac{f^*_i - f_i(x)}{f^*_i - f_{i*}} \right)^p \right]^{1/p} \qquad p = 1, 2, \ldots, \infty$$

where $f_{i*} = \text{Min}_x f_i(x)$ and the distances would all be between 0 and 1. We do not introduce this second measure in our example. Also, we omit all explicit weights of importance λ_i; thus all objective functions are assumed to be of equal importance.

We shall not calculate the complete set of compromise solutions. Rather, we shall approximate it by minimizing L_p for $p = 1, 2,$ and ∞. The corresponding solutions, members of the compromise set, are denoted x^p, that is, x^1, x^2, and x^∞ in our case.

Let us consider the first example. To achieve further insight and to avoid frequent numerical errors, we shall map some of the nondominated points from Fig. 10-6 into their proper images in the corresponding value space (f_1, f_2) in Fig. 10-8.

For instance, point $(x_1, x_2) = (6, 6)$ can be transformed through functions

$$f_1 = -4x_1 + 3x_2 \quad \text{and} \quad f_2 = 7x_1 + 5x_2$$

as follows:

$$f_1(6, 6) = (-4 \times 6) + (3 \times 6) = -6$$
$$f_2(6, 6) = (7 \times 6) + (5 \times 6) = 72$$

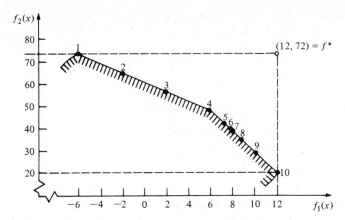

Figure 10-8 Mapping of N from Fig. 10-6 into the value space: numerical values of ten selected points are in Table 10-3. Points 6, 7, and 10 are typical compromise solutions.

That is, point (6, 6) is transformed into $(-6, 72)$ in the value space. Similarly we can translate additional points, such as (5, 6), (4, 6), (3, 6), and so on, as they are summarized in Table 10-3.

Thus, for $p = 1$ the corresponding compromise is $x^1 = (0, 4)$, that is, solution 10 in the table, because

$$\underset{x}{\text{Min }} L_1(x) = L_1(0, 4) = [0 + 0.722] = 0.722$$

is the minimum possible value.

Table 10-3

	x_1	x_2	f_1	f_2	$\dfrac{f_1^* - f_1}{f_1^*}$	$\dfrac{f_2^* - f_2}{f_2^*}$
1	6	6	-6	⑦72	1.5	0
2	5	6	-2	65	1.167	0.097
3	4	6	2	58	0.833	0.194
4	3	6	6	51	0.5	0.292
5	2.5	5.667	7	44.833	0.416	0.377
6	2.33	5.553	7.34	44.075	0.3883	0.3878
7	2.15	5.433	7.7	42.216	0.358	0.413
8	2	5.333	8	40.666	0.333	0.435
9	1	4.666	10	30.333	0.166	0.578
10	0	4	⑫	20	0	0.722

For $p = 2$, we get $x^2 = (2.15, 5.433)$, which is solution 7 in the table. This point provides the minimum of

$$\underset{X}{\text{Min}}\; L_2(x) = L_2(2.15, 5.433) = [(0.358)^2 + (0.413)^2]^{1/2} = 0.546$$

Finally, x^∞ is approximately solution 6, where $x^\infty = (2.33, 5.553)$, because the larger of the two deviations is minimized at that point:

$$\underset{X}{\text{Min}}\; L_\infty(x) = \underset{X}{\text{Min}}\; \underset{i}{\text{Max}}\; \left[\frac{f^*_i - f_i}{f^*_i} \right]$$

$$= \underset{X}{\text{Min}}\; L_\infty\, (2.33, 5.553)$$

$$= \text{Max}[0.3883, 0.3878]$$

$$= 0.38$$

Compromise from the anti-ideal We have already encountered the concept of the *anti-ideal*, i.e., the worst possible outcome, in Sec. 6-6.2. We have seen that being as close as possible to the ideal constitutes a different proposition from being as far as possible from the anti-ideal.

Let us consider the following example:

Maximize

$$f_1(x) = x_1$$

$$f_2(x) = x_2$$

subject to

$$X = \begin{cases} 3x_1 + 6x_2 \geq 15 \\[4pt] 2x_1 + 4x_2 \leq 16 \\[4pt] x_1 \qquad\quad \leq 5 \\[4pt] \qquad\quad x_2 \leq 2\tfrac{1}{2} \\[4pt] x_1 \qquad\quad \geq 2 \\[4pt] \qquad\quad x_2 \geq 1 \end{cases}$$

This problem is graphed in Fig. 10-9.

Let us first consider a purely geometric interpretation of Fig. 10-9. Observe that the ideal point is $x^* = (5, 2\tfrac{1}{2})$, while the anti-ideal is $x_* = (2, 1)$. Point x^s is the closest to x^* in the sense that the largest of deviations $(x^*_i - x_i)$ is minimized at $(4\tfrac{1}{3}, \tfrac{11}{6})$. Similarly, point x^r is the farthest away from x_* in the sense that the smallest of deviations $(x_i - x_{i*})$ is maximized at $(3\tfrac{1}{3}, 2\tfrac{1}{3})$. Observe that $x^s \neq x^r$.

It is possible to use Fig. 10-9 for direct geometric interpretation because $f_1(x) = x_1$ and $f_2(x) = x_2$. For more general cases, let us use $y = f(x)$, $y^* = f(x^*)$, etc. Then $y_i = f_i(x)$, and we can set the following definition of deviations:

$$d_i = \frac{y_i - y_{i*}}{y^*_i - y_{i*}}$$

Observe that $(1 - d_i)$ is well defined as $(y^*_i - y_i)/(y^*_i - y_{i*})$ because the following holds true:

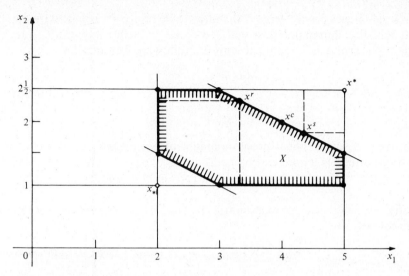

Figure 10-9 Compromise from the anti-ideal x_*.

$$\frac{y^*_i - y_i}{y^*_i - y_{i*}} + \frac{y_i - y_{i*}}{y^*_i - y_{i*}} = 1$$

Using the family of distance measures $d_p(x)$ and $d'_p(x)$, let us choose $p = \infty$ for simplicity. That is, we either *minimize* the largest of the deviations from the ideal $d_\infty(x)$ or *maximize* the smallest of the deviations from the anti-ideal $d'_\infty(x)$.

Recall that

$$d_\infty(x) = \underset{i}{\text{Max}} \ \{(1 - d_i)\}$$

and

$$d'_\infty(x) = \underset{i}{\text{Min}} \ \{(d_i)\} = \underset{i}{\text{Max}} \ \{(1 - d_i)\}$$

In Fig. 10-9 observe that point $x^c = (4, 2)$ both minimizes the largest deviation from the ideal *and* maximizes the smallest deviation from the anti-ideal.

How do we identify the point x in X at which the smallest of deviations d_i is the largest over the entire X? Consider the following mathematical programming problem:

$$\text{Max } w$$

subject to

$$d_i - w \geqq 0 \quad i = 1, \ldots, l$$

$$x \in X\dagger$$

---

†The symbol ϵ used in this section simply means belongs to.

Observe that at any point x from X the magnitude of w is determined by the smallest d_i for all i. Maximizing w will therefore yield the required result. Observe that this problem is identical with the following formulation:

$$\text{Max } w$$

subject to
$$y_i - (y^*_i - y_{i*}) w \geq y_{i*} \qquad i = 1, \ldots, l \tag{1}$$

$$x \in X$$

The above is a simple linear-programming problem because $y_i = f_i(x)$ are linear functions and X is a convex polyhedron. All y^*_i and y_{i*} are known constants, and so the appropriate $x = (x_1, \ldots, x_n)$ can be found by the simplex method.

Similarly, we could attempt to minimize the largest of deviations $(1 - d_i)$ by solving the following:

$$\text{Min } z$$

subject to
$$z - (1 - d_i) \geq 0 \qquad i = 1, \ldots, l$$

$$x \in X$$

The reader should check that the above problem is equivalent to

$$\text{Min } z$$

subject to
$$y_i + (y^*_i - y_{i*}) z \geq y^*_i \qquad i = 1, \ldots, l \tag{2}$$

$$x \in X$$

In Eqs. (1) and (2), observe that $w \leq (y_i - y_{i*})/(y^*_i - y_{i*})$ and $z \geq (y^*_i - y_i)/(y^*_i - y_{i*})$ must hold respectively for all feasible solutions. For the maximum value of w there is *at least one* inequality that is satisfied as an equality; similarly for the minimum value of z. Suppose that w^c and x^c solve Eq. (1); then x^c also solves Eq. (2) with $z^c = 1 - w^c$. (See Fig. 10-9 for a graphic interpretation.)

Solution y^c is not necessarily unique; there may be multiple solutions to Eqs. (1) and (2), giving identical values of w^c and z^c, depending on how many inequalities can be satisfied as equalities. It can be shown that at least one solution is to be found on the straight line connecting the ideal point with the anti-ideal, at its intersection with the outer boundary of X. It can also be shown that at least one solution is nondominated. The two solutions are necessarily identical.

Let us use a simple example introduced by Negoita (1979):

Maximize $f_1(x) = x_1$

and $f_2(x) = x_2$

subject to $x_1 + x_2 \leq 1$ $x_1 \leq 1$ $x_2 \leq 1$ $x_3 \leq 1$

and the usual nonnegativity conditions $x_1, x_2, x_3 \geq 0$. (Readers should provide their own graphic interpretation.)

Observe that the ideal $x^* = (1, 1, 1)$ and the anti-ideal $x_* = (0, 0, 0)$. The solution lying on the connecting straight line is $x^{c1} = (\frac{1}{2}, \frac{1}{2}, \frac{1}{2})$. The nondominated solution is $x^{c2} = (\frac{1}{2}, \frac{1}{2}, 1)$. All solutions connecting the points x^{c1} and x^{c2} (that is, their convex combinations) solve Eqs. (1) and (2); but only one of them, x^{c2}, is nondominated. Negoita provides a procedure for finding the nondominated solution to Eqs. (1) and (2) in a finite number of steps.

10-3 APPLICATIONS OF COMPROMISE PROGRAMMING

Before discussing some real-life applications of compromise programming, let us analyze a simple numerical exercise adapted from Saska (1968).

Four products x_1, x_2, x_3, and x_4 are to be produced at three different plants with capacities (in workers per planning period) of 3780, 4410, and 350 respectively. The capacity constraints for the three plants are written as follows:

$$45x_1 + 20x_2 + 20x_3 + 9x_4 \leqq 3780$$
$$45x_1 + 25x_2 + 25x_3 \qquad\ \leqq 4410$$
$$5x_2 \qquad\qquad\qquad \leqq\ 350$$

Subject to the above constraints, the management is interested in maximizing the overall sales realized from a given production. This objective is characterized by function $f_1(x)$:

$$f_1(x) = 1260x_1 + 1960x_2 + 700x_3 + 1000x_4$$

Maximizing $f_1(x)$ subject to the above constraints is a regular linear-programming problem which can be solved by the simplex method. The optimal solution is x^1:

$$x^1 = (0, 0, 0, 420)$$

That is, $x_4 = 420$ units, and none of the other products is produced. Moreover, product 4 can be produced only at the first plant—none of the remaining plants would participate in such production mix!

Plant managers argue that the profitability of product 4 at \$50 per unit is not high enough and that overall profitability of the operations would suffer in the long run. Maximization of profits, characterized by function $f_2(x)$, has been suggested:

$$f_2(x) = 120x_1 + 180x_2 + 140x_3 + 50x_4$$

Maximizing $f_2(x)$ with respect to the capacity constraints yields the solution x^2:

$$x^2 = (0, 70, 106, 28)$$

This solution provides a larger variety of production, but still no x_1 would be produced.

Results of the two production mixes with respect to the two criteria of optimality are given in the following table:

Production mix	Sales (\$) $f_1(x)$	Profits (\$) $f_2(x)$
x^1	420,000	21,000
x^2	239,400	28,840

The existing large demand for product 4 and its major contribution to overall sales is important over the long term for the company's market penetration and image building. Producing $x_4 = 28$ instead of $x_4 = 420$ is deemed unsatisfactory in spite of the increased profits generated by the second mix. Therefore, management begins a search for a compromise which is as close as possible to the ideal set of objective values $f^* = (420,000, 28,840)$. Because of the nature of the conflict between the two objectives, the resulting compromise solution must reflect the fact that there can be no compensation among the criteria. That is, a low value in one objective cannot be offset by a higher value in another objective. This is achieved by minimizing d_p for $p = \infty$; that is,

$$\underset{X}{\text{Min}} \ \underset{i}{\text{Max}} \left\{ \frac{f^*_i - f_i(x)}{f^*_i} \right\}$$

It can be shown that in the case of two objective functions, the maximum deviation reaches its minimum at the point where both deviations are equal to one another, that is, when

$$\frac{f^*_i - f_1(x)}{f^*_1} = \frac{f^*_2 - f_2(x)}{f^*_2}$$

$x^\infty = (0, 70, 13, 234)$ is such a compromise solution, yielding the following values with respect to the two objectives: $f_1(x^\infty) = 380,300$ and $f_2(x^\infty) = 26,120$. This solution has become acceptable to top management as well as to plant managers. Both parties end up within 90.6 percent of their objective's maximum attainable level: $\frac{380300}{420000} = 90.6$ percent $= \frac{26120}{28840}$.

Observe also that $\frac{26120}{380300} = \frac{28840}{420000}$; that is, at the compromise solution x^∞ the ratio of attained objective function values is equal to the ratio of their respective maxima.

10-3.1 Interactive Water Resources Planning

One application of the ideal-point-type methodology, the STEM (*Step Method*) of Benayoun et al. (1971), is reported by Loucks (1977) in connection with a water-resources planning project in northern Africa.

Loucks describes how a single best preliminary water-resources plan can be derived through the use of interactive multiobjective methods. The government's preferences, not only the planners', establish the relative importance of various objectives. The process enables government officials to choose what they consider the best compromise among three conflicting objectives:

1. Maximum water yield
2. Maximum yield reliability
3. Minimum total cost

There are many "potentially best" plans depending on the relative importance given to water yield, reliability, and cost by different government decision makers, planners, and officials at different stages of the interaction process.

First, generating a set of nondominated solutions is rejected because of the relatively large number of alternatives involved—almost all alternatives are nondominated, and evaluating them would be time-consuming and costly for both the planners and the government.

Starting from a given nondominated solution (a feasible combination of water yield, cost, and reliability not dominated by any other combination in all three dimensions), the government officials are asked to indicate how much of the achieved levels could be given up (i.e., how much the yield could be reduced, the reliability reduced, or the cost increased) in order to obtain improved values for the objectives at currently unacceptable levels.

The purpose of this interaction is to avoid an exhaustive examination of all the possible trade-offs. The technique "teaches" the officials to understand what they like and what they do not like at any particular time. The situation is dynamic, characterized by changing preferences and planning environments, difficult to capture with a single, petrified super function of aggregate preference.

During the interaction process one is likely to identify new objectives and new constraints, and so changing parameters and preferences enter the model. Changes are continually being made in the relative importance of each of the three objectives. No fixed and stable "normalization constants" would do in this type of multiobjective problem.

The STEM approach minimizes the maximum weighted deviation between each attainable attribute value and its ideal value. Let the ideal point be

$$\text{Ideal} = (\max Y, \min C, \max R),$$

where Y is the water yield, C is the total costs, and R is the reliability of a particular water source.

We want to minimize deviation d in such a way that:

$$d \geq w_1 (\max Y - Y)$$

$$d \geq w_2 (\min C - C)$$

$$d \geq w_3 (\max R - R)$$

where w's represent relative weights of importance, scaled between 0 and 1 and adding to unity. This set of constraints assures that the maximum deviation d will not be smaller than each weighted difference between the ideal and the considered value of each objective.

For each solution, i.e., a particular nondominated combination of Y, C, and R, the officials determine the set of objective values which they consider unsatisfactory at a given iteration t. For each objective $i = 1, 2, \ldots, l$ (in this case $l = 3$), the corresponding weight $w_{i,t+1}$ for the next iteration $t + 1$ is determined as follows:

$$w_{i,t+1} = \begin{cases} \left[\underset{i}{\text{Max}} \; x_i \; \left(\sum_i \dfrac{1}{\text{Max}_i x_i} \right) \right]^{-1} & \text{if value of objective } i \\ & \text{is unsatisfactory} \\[2ex] 0 & \text{if value of objective } i \\ & \text{is satisfactory} \end{cases}$$

Observe that relative weights of satisfactory objectives are automatically set to zero. Let us assume that at one particular solution the value of Y is satisfactory while the values of R and C are unsatisfactory; maximum achievable values of R and C are 85 percent and 20 percent above zero respectively. Then

$$w_Y = 0$$

$$w_R = [85(\tfrac{1}{85} + \tfrac{1}{20})]^{-1} = 0.19$$

$$w_C = [20(\tfrac{1}{85} + \tfrac{1}{20})]^{-1} = 0.81$$

After each iteration the bounds of Y, R, and C can be adjusted to yield different maximum values, and thus to lead to a new set of relative weights. The process continues until the government is satisfied with a particular solution or until it is obvious that there is no satisfactory solution.

One obvious shortcoming of this methodology is its tendency toward the satisficing philosophy: The process stops whenever a satisfactory solution has been located. Nobody asks whether any better or possibly more satisfying solution could be found. Such an attitude might not be "good enough" in the long run.

10-3.2 Regional Planning

Nijkamp and van Delft (1977) presented a regional planning application of interactive compromise programming: Selecting an optimum combination of industrial activities for the newly reclaimed "Maasvlakte" area in the Rhine-delta region in the Netherlands.[1]

The Maasvlakte area (some 1,300 usable hectares) poses an unusual challenge to regional-industrialization policy makers. A great variety of industrial activities and their combinations can be considered: blast furnaces and steel-

---

[1] P. Nijkamp and A. van Delft, *Multi-criteria Analysis and Regional Decision-making*, Studies in Applied Regional Science, vol. 8, Martinus Nijhoff, Leiden, 1977, pp. 71-95, 115-126.

works, ore slurries, coal mill, pelleting plant, petrochemical industries, tank storage plant, tanker cleaning plant, oil refinery, container terminal, and so on. Different *variants* (see Sec. 4-1.2) of industrialization can be generated by combining individual alternatives. For example, one variant could consist of blast furnaces and steelworks, ores transshipment plant (ore slurry and pelleting), coal transshipment plant (integrated with liquified gas plant), tank storage plant, and ship repair yard and tanker cleaning plant. A number of such integrated variants was generated and evaluated with respect to eight selected criteria:

1. *Economic importance and regional welfare* is calculated as the total value added (the sum of wages, returns on investments and returns on infrastructure) and measured in millions Dfl (Dutch florins) per hectare.
2. *Land-use index* is the total area occupied by the activities of a given variant, divided by the total area available. It can be measured directly in hectares of land used.
3. *Total demand for labor* is calculated in worker-years per hectare of land use.
4. *Structural balance of labor demand* consists of relative shares of three labor categories (low, medium, and high-skilled) amalgamated into a so-called discrepancy index between the labor demand of each variant and the labor supply in the broader Rhine-delta region. The index ranges from 0 to 100.
5. *Environmental impact* is measured by total emission of pollutants (particulates, SO_2, etc.) in tons per hectare per year.
6. *Impact on the differentiation of the industrial structure,* measured by the specialization index, as the sum of the absolute differences between the employment shares of the industrial sectors of a given variant and the employment shares of the same sectors present in the greater Rhine-delta region before location of that industrial complex. The index ranges from 0 to 100.
7. *Demand for foreign labor* as a percentage of foreign workers required for a given variant, is to be minimized.
8. *Efficient utilization of the adjacent harbor* (Europoort) is measured by estimated port charges in millions Dfl.

Criteria 1, 2, 3, 6, and 8 are interpreted as maximizing objectives, while criteria 4, 5, and 7 are objectives to be minimized.

A set of alternative plans can be generated which covers all feasible combinations of all industrial activities. Nijkamp and van Delft started with only 8 component industrial activities so that 258 (2^8) represents the theoretical maximum of their combinations. After introducing some obvious geographical and technological constraints, the number of feasible candidate plans was reduced to 151 and evaluated with respect to the eight criteria described above.

The ideal solution was computed as the following 8-dimensional vector:

$$x^* = (1389.9, \ 100, \ 15520, \ 6.9, \ 0, \ 100, \ 0, \ 90)$$

Calculating the points closest to x^* with respect to distance measures based on $1 \leqq p \leqq \infty$, one would obtain the sensitivity of recommended choice with regard to the metric distance used. For example, the compromise solution with respect to $p = \infty$ is:

$$x^{1(\infty)} = (787.3, \ 98.9, \ 7740, \ 13.2, \ 43.6, \ 56.7, \ 7.1, \ 77.5)$$

The decision maker rejected this compromise because of the low level of the employment criterion. Employment level of 7741 was taken as the minimum level acceptable to the decision maker, and all alternatives which do not satisfy this new explicit constraint were eliminated. Only 41 alternatives were retained.

A new ideal solution x^* was calculated and a new compromise $x^{2(\infty)}$ computed:

$$x^{2(\infty)} = (879.3, \ 94.4, \ 8220, \ 12.6, \ 131.1, \ 52.1, \ 7.1, \ 62.5)$$

This compromise is again proposed to the decison maker, his preferences for criteria improvement incorporated, and the whole process is repeated. After 7 iterations the decison maker arrived at the following compromise:

$$x^{7(\infty)} = (1077.4, \ 93.3, \ 12820, \ 13.1, \ 55.8, \ 85.4, \ 9.5, \ 55)$$

No a priori determination of criteria importance is needed: decision maker's priorities unfold through the learning and self-corrective process of partial decision making. The problem of trade-offs among marginal shifts in the value of decision criteria has been avoided and is implicit in the interaction. More detailed discussion of interactive procedures can be found in Sec. 10-6.

Compromise solution $x^{7(\infty)}$ corresponds to the variant consisting of steelworks, tank storage, integrated transshipment plant, ship repair yard, and tanker cleaning plant. Observe that no container terminal is included although Maasvlakte is adjacent to an excellent shipping port. Having a terminal could be a goal in itself (perhaps political) and would have to be included among the criteria. These studies show how dangerous it could be to base decisions on criterion values only (the ends) and neglect the underlying instrumental variables (the means). The reader should recall our discussion in Sec. 5-3.1.

Another neglected approach to solving the Maasvlakte problem is the generation of new alternatives (Sec. 4-1). Why should we not consider a nuclear power plant instead of the traditional steelworks? What about using Maasvlakte as a freight and passenger aircraft landing and storage area for Europe?

10-4 DE NOVO PROGRAMMING

We have already discussed a widely used precept of conventional decision theory: the assumption that decision alternatives are "given." In problems of mathematical programming the alternatives are defined indirectly, through a set of constraints. These constraints are also considered to be given. That is, the orderly arrangement of resources and their availability or capacity are assumed to be known and determined by some means other than operations research analysis. The availabilities of resources are regarded as inputs into mathematical programming computations.

We shall demonstrate the "problem of the givens" with the following simplified linear-programming case. A small company has been producing a highly profitable decorative material for the last several Christmas seasons. This decorative material came in two versions, x and y. Five components are needed: golden thread, silk, velvet, silver thread, and nylon. The prices of these inputs and their technological contribution to both x and y are given in Table 10-4.

Note that in order to produce one unit of x, one needs 4 units of golden thread, 2 units of silk, 12 units of velvet, and 4 units of nylon; silver thread is not used in x. The technological conditions for the production of y are to be interpreted similarly.

Specialized machinery and skilled operators are available for the production run, but no plans for expanding the activity are being considered by top management. The profit margins are $400 per unit of x and $300 per unit of y. In order to maintain these margins the company does not allow more than $2600 to be spent on the purchase of components. Although prices have been stable over the past several seasons and the company has always managed to sell all it produced, overall profits have fluctuated as different managers organized the production in different ways.

1. Manager A, who introduced the whole operation, used inventory-cost analysis to establish that 20 units of golden thread, 24 units of silk, 60 units of velvet, 10.5 units of silver thread, and 26 units of nylon should be purchased. That exhausted the budget, $20(\$30) + 24(\$40) + 60(\$9.50) + 10.5(\$20) + 26(\$10) = \$2600$, and established the available resources for the season. Manager A then proposed a simple strategy: Produce as much x as possible. This meant producing 5 units of x, that is, $x = 5$, and producing no y. This would bring in profits of $2000 but also leave $560 worth of unused silk. There were some raised eyebrows about spending all this money on silk and then not using it, and Manager A decided to change the strategy: Produce as much x as possible while utilizing all the silk. Manager A finally

Table 10-4

Resource	x	y	Price: $ per unit
Golden thread	4	0	30
Silk	2	6	40
Velvet	12	4	9.5
Silver thread	0	3	20
Nylon	4	4	10

figured out that $x = 3.75$ and $y = 2.75$ would not waste any of the "precious" silk and could be produced within all available constraints. Surprisingly, the realized profits were $400(3.75) + $300(2.75) = 2325. While Manager A was trying to figure out why profits increased when the company produced less of a more profitable product and more of a less profitable product, her performance was noticed, and she was advanced to a higher executive position.

2. Next, Manager B took over the operations. This was a young MBA with good training in linear programming. Manager B soon got tired of listening to the stories about how the previous manager increased profits, utilized all the silk, etc. Manager B decided to check the optimality of the ongoing system by formulating it as a linear-programming problem and by solving it mathematically. The problem was stated as follows:

$$\text{Max} \quad 400x + 300y$$

$$\text{subject to} \qquad\qquad 4x \qquad\quad \leq 20$$

$$2x + 6y \leq 24$$

$$12x + 4y \leq 60$$

$$3y \leq 10.5$$

$$4x + 4y \leq 26$$

By solving this problem by the simplex method, Manager B obtained $x = 4.25$ and $y = 2.25$. The profits were even higher than previously: $400(4.25) + $300(2.25) = 2375. There were some comments about the unused silk from the previous manager, but the new one countered: "If you want to maximize profits, don't worry about the underutilization of resources; this is a maximizing solution, and we can't do any better unless they give us more budget money." Manager B was also promoted; his high profits and high confidence impressed even Manager A.

3. Manager B hired Manager C for the next season. Manager B wanted somebody who would continue in his footsteps, and manager C was a true expert in linear programming. The newest manager immediately found that the *shadow prices* of velvet and nylon were 12.5 and 62.5 respectively. That is, C explained, if we increase our stock of nylon by one unit, ceteris paribus, our profits will increase by $62.50. Similarly, by increasing the availability of velvet by one unit, the profits will increase by $12.50. Therefore, Managers B and C asked for an increased budget. They argued that by raising the amount of nylon to 27 they could increase profits to $2437.50 and, since a unit of nylon was only $10, realize a net gain of $52.50. But top management did not want to increase the budget, and Manager A argued higher profit levels should be attained within current budget limits. Manager A did increase the nylon to 27 but then tried to rearrange the availability of the remaining resources and arrived at the following system:

$$\text{Max} \quad 400x + 300y$$

subject to

$$4x \qquad \leq 16.5$$
$$2x + 6y \leq 24$$
$$12x + 4y \leq 60$$
$$3y \leq 7.875$$
$$4x + 4y \leq 27$$

Manager A solved the problem on the computer (having become familiar with linear programming by now) and found that it was possible to produce $x = 4.125$ and $y = 2.625$ and realize a profit of $400(4.125) + \$300(2.625) = \$2437.50$. This was the same as the two young managers had proposed to achieve. Manager A then checked the budget: $16.5(\$30) + 24(\$40) + 60(\$9.50) + 7.875(\$20) + 27(\$10) = \$2452.50$! That is, not only was no budget increase needed, but the higher profits were attainable by actually saving \$147.50 from the current budget. Managers B and C were both fired, and the days of linear programming at the company seemed to be numbered. Manager A had to look for a replacement, but she had to prepare production for the upcoming season herself. She ended up with:

$$\text{Max} \quad 400x + 300y$$

subject to

$$4x \qquad \leq 16.25$$
$$2x + 6y \leq 25$$
$$12x + 4y \leq 60$$
$$3y \leq 8.4375$$
$$4x + 4y \leq 27.5$$

That is, a production of $x = 4.0625$ and $y = 2.8125$ realized profits of $400(4.0625) + \$300(2.8125) = \$2468.75$—the highest profits ever, and with a budget of only $16.25(\$30) + 25(\$40) + 60(\$9.50) + 8.4375(\$20) + 27.5(\$10) = \$2501.25$! Everybody was saying, "Manager A did it again!"

4. Manager A was further promoted, but they asked A to find one suitable replacement for Managers B and C. This time they tried to avoid MBA's and do without their shadow prices and requests for higher budgets. Manager A finally came across a young Ph.D. in systems, or something like that. The young Ph.D. complained of difficulties: There are no systems courses in most business schools, and the industry does not want Ph.D.'s because they are "overeducated" and want to make changes all the time. Manager A decided to try the Ph.D. and briefed the new Manager D about their experience with the production of the decorative material. The young Ph.D. said, "If you want to maximize profits, then your system is no good. It is actually a very bad, suboptimal system. You should produce version x

only. Forget about y and silver thread. Get 29.4 units of golden thread, 14.7 units of silk, 88 units of velvet, and 29.4 units of nylon.'' Manager A was not ready for that kind of talk. Manager D was fired the next day.

5. Over the weekend, on a personal minicomputer, A tried Manager D's suggestion. Its linear-programming expression was as follows:

$$\text{Max} \quad 400x + 300y$$

subject to

$$4x \qquad \leqq 29.4$$
$$2x + 6y \leqq 14.7$$
$$12x + 4y \leqq 88$$
$$4x + 4y \leqq 29.4$$

And, as the young Ph.D. said, forget the silver thread! Well, first the budget was checked: 29.4($30) + 14.7($40) + 88($9.50) + 29.4($10) = $2600. ''At least the budget constraint is respected by this new generation!'' Manager A thought to herself. ''Let us then solve the problem: $x = 7.34$ and $y = 0$; the profits $400(7.34) = \$2936$! That is $467.25 more than my best solution! I still remember my promotion when I squeezed $2325 of profits out of this budget!''

Our story will end here, although it could go on for many pages. There is only one thing the reader should remember from the story: *There is a difference between "optimizing" a given system and designing an optimal system.*

Very little methodology and effort are devoted to the design of systems de novo. Most operations research methodology concentrates on the redesign and improved functioning of *existing* systems. Often we might take a given system which is suboptimal and badly conceived and attempt to ''optimize'' it. Although some might call the results ''optimal solutions,'' there is probably nothing optimal about them. Optimization means designing an optimal system, not optimizing a given system.

As our managerial fairy tale demonstrated, we may ask two kinds of questions:

1. Given a set of constraints that include available work force, machine capacities, warehouse limitations, raw materials, market potentials, etc., what choice of variables (production mix) will satisfy these constraints while optimizing a given figure of merit (profit)?
2. Given a figure of merit (profit), how much and what kinds of resources should be acquired, within affordable limits, to design an optimal system of constraints?

In the world of limited resources one should not leave the specification of the ''givens'' to the experiential, capricious, traditional approach, as it is often exemplified by OR/MS modeling efforts. If one has a bad system to start with, no amount of optimization, sensitivity analysis, or parameterization will remove the inadequacies of its inferior design. If an optimal system is designed, providing the largest return per unit of committed resources, no further optimization is needed.

As we have seen in the previous example, the level of utilization of resources is potentially significant. The underutilization of resources does matter: It decreases the *productivity* of the system. If the same level of profits can be achieved with smaller amounts of resources, such "higher productivity" systems will be preferable.[1] Let us assume that two systems can provide the same value of an objective function while consuming different amounts of resources. Then the system using the smaller level of a particular resource (measured in either physical or monetary units) attains higher productivity with respect to that resource. If we measure the total value of resources used, for example in current or future market prices, then the system requiring the smaller total investment attains the higher total productivity. For each value of an objective function, the system yielding the highest productivity is the one achieving that value with the lowest total investment in necessary resources.

If we denote the available amounts of resources b_i, $i = 1, \ldots, m$ and their prices p_i, then $p_1b_1 + \cdots + p_mb_m$ represents the total valuation of resources. Individual b_i's are not "given" constants but rather decision variables affecting the value of the objective functions involved.

Suppose that W indicates the amount of money available (budget) for the purchase of the resources. We want to maximize profits $c_1x_1 + \cdots + c_nx_n$ by solving the following problem:

$$\text{Maximize} \quad c_1x_1 + \cdots + c_nx_n$$

$$\text{subject to} \quad a_{11}x_1 + \cdots + a_{1n}x_n - b_1 \qquad\qquad\qquad = 0$$

$$a_{21}x_1 + \cdots + a_{2n}x_n \qquad - b_2 \qquad\qquad = 0$$

$$\vdots \qquad\qquad \vdots \qquad\qquad\qquad \vdots$$

$$a_{m1}x_1 + \cdots + a_{mn}x_n \qquad\qquad\qquad - b_m = 0$$

$$p_1b_1 + p_2b_2 + \cdots + p_mb_m = W$$

Observe that we have added m variables and only one constraint. Only $m + 1$ variables could constitute the solution, even if the constraints would be satisfied as inequalities ($\leq$) rather than equalities ($=$).

Thus, the final solution to our case of the production of seasonal decorative material came from solving the following problem:

[1]See also M. Zeleny, "Multiobjective Design of High-Productivity Systems," *Proceedings of Joint Automatic Control Conference*, July 27–30, 1976, Purdue University, Pap. APPL9-4, ASME, New York, 1976, pp. 297–300.

$$\text{Max } 400x + 300y$$

subject to

$$4x \quad - b_1 \qquad\qquad\qquad = 0$$

$$2x + 6y \quad - b_2 \qquad\qquad\quad = 0$$

$$12x + 4y \qquad\quad - b_3 \qquad\qquad = 0$$

$$3y \qquad\qquad\quad - b_4 \quad\quad = 0$$

$$4x + 4y \qquad\qquad\qquad - b_5 = 0$$

$$30b_1 + 40b_2 + 9.5b_3 + 20b_4 + 10b_5 = 2600$$

Our solution to the above problem was $x = 7.34, y = 0, b_1 = 29.4, b_2 = 14.7,$ $b_3 = 88, b_4 = 0,$ and $b_5 = 29.4.$ We would need to add more constraints if a larger variety of $x_1, \ldots, x_n$ were required.

Our formulation produces a "tight" system design with no or minimum slack resources. It is recognized that operating a system under such conditions is quite risky and that some "safety" levels of spare or additional resources are desirable. These safety "buffers" should be added a posteriori to the optimally designed system; they should not be a capricious outcome of the mathematical properties of a system's model. Safety reserves can be determined either as experimental percentages of the actual usage or as distinct managerial policy operators. Observe that the budget limitation W can be relaxed, and the system analyzed for a series of alternative budgets $W_1, W_2, \ldots,$ or parametrically for $\lambda W,$ where $\lambda \geqq 0.$

10-5 GROUP DECISION MAKING

10-5.1 Search for Collective Compromise

To show that individual and collective decision making are interrelated and can be approached from the same methodological viewpoint, we shall analyze a simplified problem of evaluating and ranking automobile engines, in terms of their individual and collective desirability.

Engine selection problem A large automobile manufacturer is evolving a new research and development (R&D) strategy for combustion engines. Obvious problems with fuel consumption, pollution control, and performance can be foreseen in the near future.

A committee of ten departmental experts has been charged with the following task: Provide an overall ranking of the five most promising, currently available engine concepts, in terms of their strategic R&D desirability. Company executives understand that this task involves a large number of subjective, qualitative, and uncertain judgments, but an R&D strategy is to be formed quite soon, and the ranking is to provide essential support in the deliberations.

Committee members must agree on which alternative engine concepts to evaluate, and with respect to which criteria. Then individual group members, representing different departments, are to provide their rankings. In the next stage, these individual rankings will be compared, discussed, and possibly revised. The committee, as a whole, must then reach a consensus and submit the overall committee ranking to the top management.

Note What is the difference between "consensus" and "compromise"? A compromise is a solution, or a settlement of differences, in which each side makes some concessions. A consensus is a collective opinion or accord. There can be many compromise solutions but only one consensus. A group can define different compromise solutions; one of them will emerge as a consensus. (See Secs. 6-5.3 and 10-2.)

The following alternatives are those ultimately considered by the committee:

Otto engine. Internal combustion; spark plug ignition system; mixture of fuel and air; piston to output shaft mechanical transmission; catalytic converter reduces exhaust emissions.

Diesel engine. Internal combustion; compression ignition system (fuel is ignited solely by the heat of highly compressed air within its cylinders); glow plug for starting; relatively small quantities of pollutants.

Rankine engine. External combustion; vapor-cycle system (heat is transferred from fuel combustion to a condensable fluid within a closed system; the fluid—water, in the case of a steam engine—is vaporized and superheated in a boiler; its expansion produces energy to drive a piston or turbine; gases are condensed again for reuse); complicated heat exchanger needed.

Stirling engine. External combustion; heat-recapture system (gases are alternately heated and cooled; the heat of combustion is continually absorbed by hydrogen or helium in a sealed system; the regenerator captures the entering heat during the interval between power strokes); noiseless; few moving parts; heat exchanger needed.

Brayton engine. Internal combustion; driven by expansion of hot gases through a turbine (or vaned wheel) which turns a drive shaft; a portion of the output is used to compress the inlet air that is fed into the combustor; two versions, open cycle (also called "gas turbine") and closed cycle, the latter requiring a heat exchanger.

Considering the two versions of the Brayton engine, the committee has decided to evaluate six different alternatives.

Note There is of course also the Wankel or *rotary* internal combustion engine, in which one or more three-sided rotors perform all the functions of a four-stroke piston engine with each revolution. Subsumed under the first alternative, this engine concept forms the Otto-Wankel option. The *electric motor* has not been considered explicitly because most of its characteristics are still only theoretical and difficult to assess. Also, its air-pollution level (produced not directly by the engine itself but by power-generating stations in charging the engine's batteries) is currently unacceptable. *Hydrogen-burning* engines were not considered.

Four basic criteria, derived from the most important and measurable technical attributes of the engines, were finally agreed upon:

1. *Temperature ratio.* The ratio of heat addition to heat rejection. It measures the maximum achievable (ideal) thermodynamic efficiency (MTE).
2. *Components efficiency.* The efficiency with which the released energy is converted into mechanical work.
3. *Relative efficiency.* Components efficiency relative to maximum thermodynamic efficiency; more efficient engine components come closer to the MTE ideal.
4. *Heat rejection device.* A heat exchanger. Closed-cycle engines require more or less sophisticated ones. They add to an engine's bulkiness and reduce its efficiency.

Each of the six alternatives is now evaluated with respect to these four technical criteria. Since these criteria are based on some objectively measurable characteristics, the committee members are able to agree on the verbal designations summarized in Table 10-5.

Table 10-5

Criterion: Alternative	1 Temperature ratio	2 Components efficiency	3 Relative efficiency	4 Heat-rejection device
1. Otto-Wankel	High*	Fair	Poor	None*
2. Diesel	High*	Fair	Poor	None*
3. Brayton (closed cycle)	Moderate	Very good*	Good	Moderate
4. Stirling	Moderate	Good	Very good*	Moderate
5. Brayton (gas turbine)	Potentially high	Very good*	Good	None*
6. Rankine	Low	Good	Fair	Large

*Most desirable verbal designations

As can be seen from inspecting Table 10-5, the Rankine engine is dominated with respect to all four criteria by the Stirling as well as by both versions
of the Brayton (closed cycle and gas turbine). As a matter of fact, the Brayton
gas turbine also dominates the closed cycle version. All committee members
agree to drop the Rankine alternative from further consideration but retain both
Brayton versions. They feel that closed-cycle engines should be well represented and that these engines are better typified by Brayton than by Rankine.

The remaining five alternatives are now ranked on an ordinal scale from
1 to 5. (See the discussion of ordinal and cardinal ranking in Sec. 5-1.) Members' perceptions of company objectives, as well as some additional, less
measurable criteria, enter into this *individual ranking*. Although using the four
technical criteria discussed above, members may modify their individual rankings by considering safety, comfort, adaptability to computerization and advanced electronics, maintainability, the potential for modularization, etc. They
must also assess the impact of future scenarios, such as solar energy development, various traffic-congestion patterns, public transportation trends, hydrogen fuel, automated dual-mode highway systems, and new tire designs.

Such considerations are highly qualitative, imprecise, and even speculative. Not enough information is available for anything more than subjective
ordinal ranking of preferences, and committee members perceive and weight
such factors differently. Top management hopes that if a large number of expert
rankings, arrived at in a careful and systematic way, can be secured, then for
strategic purposes some aggregate representative ranking can be obtained as
well.

Each of the ten experts on this team first independently prepares a ranking
of the five alternatives. These individual rankings then serve as inputs into the
committee's collective deliberations and decision making.

The highest rank is 1; the lowest is 5. To induce committee members to use
as many relevant criteria as possible, *no ties* in the rankings with respect to any
one criterion are allowed. Members are free to support their individual analyses
with any MCDM techniques they find appealing and helpful. The rankings of
the ten individual committee members are shown in Table 10-6.

In Table 10-6 we read, for example, that committee member no. 5 ranks the

Table 10-6

Alternative	Committee member: 1	2	3	4	5	6	7	8	9	10
1. Otto-Wankel	2	3	4	1	3	1	3	1	4	1
2. Diesel	5	2	1	4	1	4	4	4	3	3
3. Brayton (closed cycle)	4	5	5	3	5	2	2	3	1	4
4. Stirling	1	4	3	5	4	5	1	2	5	2
5. Brayton (gas turbine)	3	1	2	2	2	3	5	5	2	5

engines in the following order: (1) diesel, (2) Brayton gas turbine, (3) Otto-Wankel, (4) Stirling, and (5) Brayton closed cycle; while member no. 1 ranks them (1) Stirling, (2) Otto-Wankel, (3) Brayton gas turbine, (4) Brayton closed cycle, and (5) diesel.

In trying to generate compromise rankings which all committee members can agree upon, and thus reach a consensus, it is decided that each alternative (as it is ranked by *all* members, i.e., individual horizontal rows in Table 10-6) will be evaluated in terms of its resemblance to, or distance from, the *ideal alternative*.

Obviously, there would be no conflict among the members and no consensus would have to be reached if such an ideal engine were available. The ideal engine would receive rank 1 from all members.

Which of the existing five sets of all members' rankings would come closest to the ideal ranking? For example, how close is vector (2, 3, 4, 1, 3, 1, 3, 1, 4, 1), the Otto-Wankel alternative as ranked by the ten committee members, to the vector of rankings (1, 1, 1, 1, 1, 1, 1, 1, 1, 1), which would be given to the ideal engine?

Although we could use a large number of different measures (see Secs. 6-5.2 and 10-1), we shall measure this distance by using

$$d_j = \sum_{i=1}^{10} (r_{ij} - r^*_i)$$

where r_{ij} denotes the rank given to engine alternative j by individual i, r^*_i designates the rank given to the ideal by the ith individual ($r^*_i = 1$ for all $i = 1, \ldots, l$), and d_j captures the overall compatibility of engine j with the ideal in terms of a geometric distance (essentially we use a version of L_1 measure, discussed in Sec. 6-5.2).

Because all $r^*_i = 1$, we simply collect individual differences ($r_{ij} - 1$) in Table 10-7.

Of course, given the special structure of the problem, we could simply add the rankings for a given j in Table 10-6, then subtract 10 from each sum, and we would get the same d_j's as in Table 10-7. For example, for the Otto-Wankel

Table 10-7

Alternative	Committee member: 1	2	3	4	5	6	7	8	9	10	d_j
1. Otto-Wankel	1	2	3	0	2	0	2	0	3	0	13
2. Diesel	4	1	0	3	0	3	3	3	2	2	21
3. Brayton (closed cycle)	3	4	4	2	4	1	1	2	0	3	24
4. Stirling	0	3	2	4	3	4	0	1	4	1	22
5. Brayton (gas turbine)	2	0	1	1	1	2	4	4	1	4	20

alternative the sum of r_{ij} is $2 + 3 + 4 + 1 + 3 + 1 + 3 + 1 + 4 + 1 = 23 - 10 = 13$, the same as d_1 in Table 10-6.

The five engines would then be ranked to reflect the increasing d_j: (1) Otto-Wankel, (2) Brayton gas turbine, (3) diesel, (4) Stirling, and (5) Brayton closed cycle. Observe that this particular ranking, which would correspond to a column

$$
\begin{vmatrix} 1 \\ 3 \\ 5 \\ 4 \\ 2 \end{vmatrix}
$$

in Table 10-7, has not been proposed by any of the committee members individually. This fact should *increase* its chances for acceptance as the consensus; no member has to accept another member's personal rankings directly.

Another way of suggesting a consensus would be the following: Do not consider an "ideal engine" but instead assume a "mediocre engine," one whose ranking would differ from all currently available individual rankings as little as possible. In other words, we have to create a ranking which would be the closest to all ten rankings in Table 10-6.

We shall formulate the above problem as follows: Find a ranking $r^m = (r_1^m, \ldots, r_5^m)$ of the five engines listed in Table 10-6 and measure its distance from the ith member's ranking. That is, compute

$$
d_i = \sum_{j=1}^{5} |r_{ij} - r_j^m| \qquad i = 1, \ldots, 10
$$

then form

$$
d = \sum_{i=1}^{10} d_i = \sum_{i=1}^{10} \sum_{j=1}^{5} |r_{ij} - r_j^m|
$$

There is always a ranking r^m such that the overall measure of distance d reaches its minimum value. Such a solution r^m is called "median ranking" by Cook and Seiford (1978).

How would we go about finding median ranking r^m? Observe that in order to form r^m we have to *assign* to each of the five engines $j = 1, \ldots, 5$ one and only one of the five rank-indicating numbers $k = 1, \ldots, 5$. We should perform this assignment so that d reaches its minimum.

It is convenient to rewrite the expression for d as follows:

$$
d = \sum_{j=1}^{5} \sum_{i=1}^{10} |r_{ij} - r_j^m|
$$

Note that r_j^m can be equal to only one of the $k = 1, \ldots, 5$. Consequently, if $r_j^m = k$, we can define

$$d_{jk} = \sum_{i=1}^{10} |r_{ij} - k|$$

and compute $d = \sum_{j=1}^{5} d_{jk}$ for all $k = 1, \ldots, 5$.

For example, take the first row of Table 10-7 again—that is, $j = 1$—and set $k = 1$ and $r_j^m = 1$ for all j. Now we can compute

$$d_{11} = \sum_{i=1}^{10} |r_{i1} - 1| = |2 - 1| + |3 - 1| + |4 - 1| + |1 - 1| + |3 - 1| + |1 - 1|$$
$$|3 - 1| + |1 - 1| + |4 - 1| + |1 - 1|$$
$$= 1 + 2 + 3 + 0 + 2 + 0 + 2 + 0 + 3 + 0 = 13$$

Similarly, keeping $k = 1$ and $r_j^m = 1$, but for $j = 2$, we obtain:

$$d_{21} = \sum_{i=1}^{10} |r_{i2} - 1| = |5 - 1| + |2 - 1| + |1 - 1| + |4 - 1| + |1 - 1| + |4 - 1|$$
$$|4 - 1| + |4 - 1| + |3 - 1| + |3 - 1|$$
$$= 4 + 1 + 0 + 3 + 0 + 3 + 3 + 3 + 2 + 2 = 21$$

These calculations can be repeated for the remaining $j = 3, 4$, and 5. Next, change to $k = 2$ and keep $r_j^m = 2$ for all j. Then perform the same calculations for $j = 1, \ldots, 5$. For example, setting $k = 2$ and $r_j^m = 2$, for $j = 1$ we obtain:

$$d_{12} = \sum_{i=1}^{10} |r_{i1} - 2| = |2 - 2| + |3 - 2| + |4 - 2| + |1 - 2| + |3 - 2| + |1 - 2|$$
$$|3 - 2| + |1 - 2| + |4 - 2| + |1 - 2|$$
$$= 0 + 1 + 2 + 1 + 1 + 1 + 1 + 1 + 2 + 1 = 11$$

Thus, r_j^m can assume five different values k for each of the five engines j, that is, twenty-five distance coefficients

$$d_{jk} = \sum_{i=1}^{10} |r_{ij} - k|$$

can be computed. Table 10-8 summarizes these d_{jk}.

Table 10-8

Rank k Engine j	1	2	3	4	5
1	13	11	11	17	27
2	21	15	11	11	19
3	24	16	12	12	16
4	22	16	14	14	18
5	20	12	12	16	20

In Table 10-8 we want to match engines j with rank numbers k so that the sum of the corresponding assigned distances d_{jk} is the smallest possible. This task can be achieved by solving the so-called "assignment problem" of linear programming:

$$\text{Min} \sum_{j=1}^{5} \sum_{k=1}^{5} d_{jk} x_{jk}$$

subject to

$$\sum_{j=1}^{5} x_{jk} = 1 \qquad k = 1, \ldots, 5$$

and

$$\sum_{k=1}^{5} x_{jk} = 1 \qquad j = 1, \ldots, 5$$

where $x_{jk} = 1$ if k has been assigned to j and $x_{jk} = 0$ otherwise.

The computational details for solving an assignment problem can be found in almost any introductory OR/MS text. We shall review some of the basic ideas because our problem can be solved quickly by hand.

First, because we are dealing with minimization, we can regard individual d_{jk} as costs and simply minimize the total cost of assigning j to k. We shall transform Table 10-8 into its opportunity cost equivalent:

j \ k	1	2	3	4	5
1	13	11	11	17	27
2	21	15	11	11	19
3	24	16	12	12	16
4	22	16	14	14	18
5	20	12	12	16	20

Subtract the smallest number from each *column*

j \ k	1	2	3	4	5
1	0	0	0	6	11
2	8	4	0	0	3
3	11	5	1	1	0
4	9	5	3	3	2
5	7	1	1	5	4

which is displayed in Table 10-9:

Table 10-9 Opportunity cost

Subtract the smallest number from each *row*.

j \ k	1	2	3	4	5
1	⓪	0	0	6	11
2	8	4	⓪	0	3
3	11	5	1	1	⓪
4	7	3	1	①	0
5	7	⓪	0	4	3

We shall now attempt to find an assignment which would minimize the cost displayed in the opportunity cost table. This can be accomplished by assigning those js to those ks where the associated opportunity cost value is 0. If a complete assignment can be made, consisting of 0s only, such a result also represents a solution to the problem. Otherwise, some further coefficient matrix adjustment is necessary, and several more algorithmic steps are needed; consult for example Loomba (1978).

In our particular case we are quite lucky. Although we cannot form an all-zero assignment, we can form a complete assignment by taking up one assignment pair (j, k) with the *next lowest* opportunity cost, which is 1. There cannot be any assignment cheaper than that; the circled positions represent the minimal solution, consisting of the following assignment pairs:

$$(1, 1) \quad (2, 3) \quad (3, 5) \quad (4, 4) \quad (5, 2)$$

with the corresponding minimum distance $d = 13 + 11 + 16 + 14 + 12 = 66$.

Note It appears that some other feasible assignments would not exceed $d = 66$. These are *alternative solutions* to the assignment problem. We shall indicate these additional alternative solutions by circles in the opportunity cost table. There are three:

Table 10-10

	1	2	3	4	5
1	(0)	0	0	6	11
2	8	4	(0)	0	3
3	11	5	1	(1)	0
4	7	3	1	1	(0)
5	7	0	0	4	3

	1	2	3	4	5
1	(0)	0	0	6	11
2	8	4	0	0	3
3	11	5	(1)	1	0
4	7	3	1	1	0
5	7	(0)	0	4	3

	1	2	3	4	5
1	(0)	0	0	6	11
2	8	4	0	(0)	3
3	11	5	1	1	0
4	7	3	(1)	1	0
5	7	(0)	0	4	3

Thus, we are able to identify *four* different median solutions:

1. $(1, 1), (2, 3), (3, 5), (4, 4), (5, 2)$ with $d = 13 + 11 + 16 + 14 + 12 = 66$
2. $(1, 1), (2, 3), (3, 4), (4, 5), (5, 2)$ with $d = 13 + 11 + 12 + 18 + 12 = 66$
3. $(1, 1), (2, 4), (3, 3), (4, 5), (5, 2)$ with $d = 13 + 11 + 12 + 18 + 12 = 66$
4. $(1, 1), (2, 4), (3, 5), (4, 3), (5, 2)$ with $d = 13 + 11 + 16 + 14 + 12 = 66$

It is interesting to note that the "ideal engine" solution, derived earlier, would be characterized as

$$(1, 1), (2, 3), (3, 5), (4, 4), (5, 2) \quad \text{with } d = 13 + 11 + 16 + 14 + 12 = 66$$

That is, it is identical with the first median ranking.

We may conclude that there are four different rankings suggested by the two techniques:

1. (1) Otto-Wankel, (2) Brayton (gas turbine), (3) diesel, (4) Stirling, (5) Brayton (closed cycle)
2. (1) Otto-Wankel, (2) Brayton (gas turbine), (3) diesel, (4) Brayton (closed cycle), (5) Stirling
3. (1) Otto-Wankel, (2) Brayton (gas turbine), (3) Brayton (closed cycle), (4) diesel, (5) Stirling
4. (1) Otto-Wankel, (2) Brayton (gas turbine), (3) Stirling, (4) diesel, (5) Brayton (closed cycle)

In the columns of Table 10-6, these rankings would appear as follows:

(1)	(2)	(3)*	(4)
1	1	1	1
3	3	4	4
5	4	3	5
4	5	5	3
2	2	2	2

Note that the third ranking, designated with an asterisk, is identical with committee member 4's in Table 10-6. Consequently, the third ranking does not represent a compromise for this member of the committee. The other three rankings, not having been postulated by any of the ten members, have a greater chance of being chosen as the consensus of the committee.

10-5.2 Game-Theoretical Approach

Resolution of conflict among multiple decision makers is often approached from the viewpoint of *game theory*. In this section we present game-theoretical formulations characterized by *multiple payoffs*.

Classical game theory, as developed by Von Neumann and Morgenstern,[1] is mathematically complex and challenging, but its underlying assumptions are simplistic and its results are difficult to apply in real-life decision problems.

Among the many types of games studied is the so-called finite, two-person, zero-sum game with imperfect information. That is, each of the two players has only a finite number of alternatives to consider at each turn (compare with the infinite number of alternatives in mathematical programming), one player's gain is another player's loss (i.e., the sum of winnings and losses is always zero, hence "zero-sum"), and the players do not know each other's moves in advance.

In Table 10-11 we show a simple *payoff matrix* for the type of game described above. Player X can choose between alternatives x^1 and x^2, while Player Y can choose between alternatives y^1 and y^2. The numbers indicate what Player Y pays Player X.

[1] J. von Neumann and O. Morgenstern, *Theory of Games and Economic Behavior*, Princeton University Press, Princeton, N.J., 1944.

Table 10-11

		Player Y	
		y^1	y^2
Player X	x^1	-1	5
	x^2	3	-5

For example, if Player X chooses x^1 and Player Y chooses y^1, Player X loses 1 unit (point, dollar, marble, chip, etc.). If, however, Player Y matches x^1 with y^2, then Player X gains 5 units.

In order to play the game of Table 10-11, one adopts a *strategy*, a description of how one will behave under every conceivable circumstance of the opponent's moves. The so-called "minimax theorem" guarantees that all games of this type have a unique *value* (an average amount of payoff), and either player can achieve this value by selecting the appropriate minimax strategy. In this case, Player X can play x^1 $\frac{4}{7}$ of the time and x^2 $\frac{3}{7}$ of the time, Player Y can play y^1 $\frac{5}{7}$ of the time and y^2 $\frac{2}{7}$ of the time—their respective minimax strategies—and Player X will realize an average win of $\frac{5}{7}$ {value of the game; check $\frac{5}{7}[\frac{4}{7}(-1) + \frac{3}{7}(3)] + \frac{2}{7}[\frac{4}{7}(5) + \frac{3}{7}(-5)] = \frac{5}{7}$}.

Given the value of the game and the existence of minimax strategies, Player X will not settle for anything less than $\frac{5}{7}$ and Player Y is guaranteed not to lose more than $\frac{5}{7}$. The minimax theorem is often considered the maxim of rational behavior: A player who deviates from his or her minimax strategy *alone* is likely to be disadvantaged. But what if *both* players deviate from their minimax strategies? That is, what if they play a real game and gamble to win rather than strive to limit their opponent's average win? Can they both lose in a zero-sum game? What if the game is played only once or in a small number of moves: Does it still pay to stick to the minimax strategy?

The minimax strategies offer security of mediocre gains. One can gamble for higher gains by deviating from the minimax strategy but only at the expense of security. This is the trade-off which many people are willing to take. In fact, that is why they engage in game playing; only rarely are minimax strategies followed.

Mathematical programming and zero-sum games All two-person, zero-sum games can be represented by the payoff matrix displayed in Table 10-12. Observe that Players X and Y have k and l strategies, respectively, at their disposal. If Player X chooses x^1 and Player Y chooses y^j, then the payoff to Player X is a_{ij} and the payoff to Player Y is $(-a_{ij})$ because of the zero-sum assumption. Each player can select either *pure strategies* (x^1 or x^2 or $\cdots x^k$, and y^1 or y^2 or $\cdots y^l$) or *mixed strategies* by attaching a probability p_i to each pure strategy x^i (and q_j to each y^j) to maximize the expected payoff. We can also interpret p_i and q_j as weights and invoke maximization of weighted average payoff.

Table 10-12

		Player Y			
		y^1	y^2	$\cdots$	y^l
Player X	x^1	a_{11}	a_{12}	$\cdots$	a_{1l}
	x^2	a_{21}	a_{22}	$\cdots$	a_{2l}
	.	.	.	.	.
	.	.	.		.
	.	.	.		.
	x^k	a_{k1}	a_{k2}	$\cdots$	a_{kl}

According to the minimax theorem, Player X should choose p_i to maximize the minimum expected payoff, and Player Y should choose q_j to minimize the maximum expected payoff. (Recall that payoffs a_{ij} in Table 10-12 relate to Player X.) Let us denote the minimum expected payoff as u and the maximum expected payoff as v. The players then face the following problems:

Player X Maximize u

subject to

$$\sum_{i=1}^{k} p_i a_{ij} \geqq u \quad j = 1, \ldots, l$$

$$\sum_{i=1}^{k} p_i = 1 \quad p_i \geqq 0$$

Player Y Minimize v

subject to

$$\sum_{j=1}^{l} a_{ij} q_j \leqq v \quad i = 1, \ldots, k$$

$$\sum_{j=1}^{l} q_j = 1 \quad q_j \geqq 0$$

These two problems are intimately related: Y's problem is the *dual* of X's problem and vice versa. From the duality theory we learn that the maximum value of u will be equal to the minimum value of v.[1] That is, there is only one value of the game. Moreover, solving the primal problem automatically reveals the corresponding dual solution: it is sufficient to concentrate on only one of the above problems.

Let us solve Y's problem. We are asked to find $q_1, \ldots, q_l$ and v such that all constraints are satisfied and v reaches its minimum value. Observe that if $q_j = 1$ for some j we obtain a pure strategy; otherwise we obtain a mixed

[1] For a good introduction to duality theory, the reader is advised to consult, for example, Y. Hillier and G. Lieberman, *Introduction to Operations Research*, Holden-Day, San Francisco, Calif., 1967, chap. 15.

strategy. Y's problem can be further simplified by dividing both sides of all constraints by v. We obtain the following:

$$\sum_{j=1}^{l} a_{ij} q_j' \leqq 1 \qquad i = 1, \ldots, k$$

$$\sum_{j=1}^{l} q_j' = 1/v \qquad q_j' \geqq 0$$

(We can leave a_{ij} unchanged because the solution is not affected if they are all multiplied by the same number.) Our new variables are $q_j' = q_j/v$. Observe, from the last constraint, that minimum v is achieved by maximizing $q_1' + \ldots + q_l'$. After solving this problem we only have to convert q_j' back to q_j through $q_j = v q_j'$. The maximum of the objective function is $1/v$, i.e., the reciprocal value of v (the value of the game).

Let us demonstrate this approach on a simple numerical example. Consider a game characterized by a payoff matrix in Table 10-13.

Table 10-13

		Player Y		
		y^1	y^2	y^3
Player X	x^1	32	0	32
	x^2	8	0	32
	x^3	16	32	0

Y's problem can be formulated as follows:

$$\text{Maximize } q_1' + q_2' + q_3'$$

subject to
$$32q_1' \qquad\quad + 32q_3' \leqq 1$$
$$8q_1' \qquad\quad + 32q_3' \leqq 1$$
$$16q_1' + 32q_2' \qquad\quad \leqq 1$$
$$q_1', q_2', q_3' \geqq 0$$

After two simplex iterations we obtain the optimum tableau displayed in Table 10-14.

Table 10-14

	q_1'	q_2'	q_3'	q_4'	q_5'	q_6'	
q_3'	1	0	1	$\frac{1}{32}$	0	0	$\frac{1}{32}$
q_5'	-24	0	0	-1	1	0	0
q_2'	$\frac{1}{2}$	1	0	0	0	$\frac{1}{32}$	$\frac{1}{32}$
	$\frac{1}{2}$	0	0	$\frac{1}{32}$	0	$\frac{1}{32}$	$\frac{2}{32}$

In Table 10-14 observe that q'_4, q'_5, and q'_6 are the slack variables. The primal solution is $q'_1 = 0$, and $q'_2 = \frac{1}{32}$, and $q'_3 = \frac{1}{32}$. The corresponding dual solution is to be found in the criterion row in slack-variable columns: $p'_1 = \frac{1}{32}, p'_2 = 0, p'_3 = \frac{1}{32}$. The maximum of the objective function is $\frac{2}{32} = 1/v$. The value of the game is $\frac{32}{2} = 16$. Player Y can assure not losing more than 16 by playing y^1, y^2, and y^3 with probabilities $(q_1, q_2, q_3) = \frac{32}{2}(0, \frac{1}{32}, \frac{1}{32}) = (0, \frac{1}{2}, \frac{1}{2})$. Player X can assure winning at least 16 by playing x^1, x^2, and x^3 with probabilities $(p_1, p_2, p_3) = \frac{32}{2}(\frac{1}{32}, 0, \frac{1}{32}) = (\frac{1}{2}, 0, \frac{1}{2})$. The reader should verify this equilibrium solution by applying the probabilities to the payoffs in Table 10-13.

We cannot dwell any further on this particular version of game theory. The reader is advised to consult any of the available game theory literature.[1] Although extended to non-zero-sum situations, n players, and infinite number of alternatives, game theory still remains more of a "parlor game theory" than a theory of economic behavior. Any theory based on the strict opposition of the two players' interests, that is, on the zero-sum assumption, is not valid and is irrelevant and misleading for studying real-life economic conflict situations.[2] Zero-sum games are an approximation to reality where the interests of the players are opposed in some respects and complementary in others. The non-zero-sum element is best exemplified in a kind of game that has been labeled the *prisoners' dilemma*.

Prisoners' Dilemma Two men suspected of committing a crime together are awaiting trial in separate cells. Each suspect may either confess or remain silent. The possible consequences of their actions are given in the payoff matrix in Table 10-15.

The prisoners' dilemma shown in Table 10-15 is a typical non-zero-sum game: Wins of one do not cancel the losses of the other. Being rational, according to game theory, Suspect 1 determines his strategy by taking into account all possible actions of Suspect 2. If Suspect 1 confesses, then he can either get 5 years or go free depending on his partner's two options; if he

Table 10-15

		Suspect 2	
		Confess	Remain silent
Suspect 1	Confess	5 years, 5 years	Go free, 20 years
	Remain silent	20 years, go free	1 year, 1 year

---

[1]Stimulating discussions of game-theoretical approach can be found in M. D. Davis, *Game Theory*, Basic Books, New York, 1973; S. J. Brams, *Paradoxes in Politics*, The Free Press, New York, 1976; and N. Howard, *Paradoxes of Rationality*, MIT Press, Cambridge, Mass., 1971.

[2]An extreme manifestation of noncritical application of zero-sum assumption can be found in L. C. Thurow, *The Zero-Sum Society*, Basic Books, New York, 1980.

remains silent he can get either 20 years or 1 year in jail. In either case, Suspect 1 is better off confessing. Symmetrically, Suspect 2 finds out that he too is better off if he confesses. However, the prisoners have a dilemma: If they heed the very best game-theory advice and confess, they will both end up in jail for 5 years; but if they are too ignorant, naive, or irrational to follow such a compelling argument, they will remain silent and get only 1 year in jail. Traditional game theory fails right here, at the very first contact with more realistic conflict situations.

Games with multiple payoffs The main purpose of this section is to alleviate another and equally damaging assumption of game theory: that each player is assumed to employ only a single criterion (or payoff) to be maximized or minimized. In real-life games, players are usually facing multiple and incommensurate objectives that may vary in time in both form and number. In socioeconomic settings, not only is the result of the players' respective moves likely to exhibit a non-zero sum, but the payoff is a vector rather than a single number. Real games are more likely to result in both players winning some blue chips, losing some red chips, and maintaining green chips, after *each* move.

Games with multiple payoffs have been studied by Blackwell (1956), Shapley (1959), and Contini (1966). Here we introduce only a simple numerical example adapted from the recent article of this author.[1] The reader will recognize its relationship to multiobjective programming, compromise programming, and multiparametric decomposition. Problems 10-3, 10-4, 10-5, and 10-6 of Sec. 10-8 present additional examples of game-theoretical situations.

Consider a simple two-person, zero-sum game with two-dimensional payoffs, given in Table 10-16. Observe that each player faces three alternatives to choose from and a *vector* of payoffs as a consequence of choice. If, for example, both players choose to play their second strategy, Player X gains 3 units along the first dimension *and* two units along the second dimension; Player Y loses the same amounts.

The game of Table 10-16 can be formulated as a mathematical multiparametric programming problem. We shall employ the zero-sum format introduced earlier in this section.

Table 10-16

		Player Y		
		y^1	y^2	y^3
Player X	x^1	(3, 2)	(3, 4)	(1, 5)
	x^2	(2, 1)	(3, 2)	(2, 2)
	x^3	(4, 1)	(1, 3)	(3, 1)

[1] M. Zeleny, "Games with Multiple Payoffs," *International Journal of Game Theory*, vol. 4, no. 4, 1976, pp. 179–191.

Each vector payoff $a_{ij} = (a^1_{ij}, a^2_{ij})$ is to be replaced by a convex combination of both components (see Sec. 8-5): $\lambda a^1_{ij} + (1 - \lambda)a^2_{ij}$. For example, $a_{11} = 3\lambda + (1 - \lambda)2 = \lambda + 2$, and so on. We are ready to formulate the problem:

$$\text{Maximize } q'_1 + q'_2 + q'_3$$

$$
\begin{aligned}
\text{subject to } (\lambda + 2)q'_1 + (4 - \lambda)q'_2 + (5 - 4\lambda)\ q'_3 &\leq 1 \\
(\lambda + 1)q'_1 + (\lambda + 2)q'_2 + 2q'_3 &\leq 1 \\
(3\lambda + 1)q'_1 + (3 - 2\lambda)q'_2 + (2\lambda + 1)\ q'_3 &\leq 1
\end{aligned}
$$

The initial simplex tableau to the above problem is given in Table 10-17. Observe that q'_4, q'_5, and q'_6 denote slack variables. Set $\lambda = 0$ and solve by simplex method. Then explore the optimality for parameter λ changing from 0 to 1, as in Sec. 8-5. We leave the actual computations as an exercise for the reader. The results are summarized below:

For $0 \leq \lambda \leq \frac{3}{5}$ the optimal solution is

$$q'_1 = \frac{1}{2 + \lambda}, q'_2 = 0, q'_3 = 0$$

and the dual solution is

$$p'_1 = \frac{1}{2 + \lambda}, p'_2 = 0, p'_3 = 0$$

while the objective function reaches $\dfrac{1}{2 + \lambda}$.

For $\frac{3}{5} \leq \lambda \leq 1$ the optimal solution is

$$q'_1 = 0, q'_2 = 0, q'_3 = \frac{1}{5 - 4\lambda}$$

and the dual solution is

$$p'_1 = \frac{1}{5 - 4\lambda}, p'_2 = 0, p'_3 = 0$$

while the objective function reaches $\dfrac{1}{5 - 4\lambda}$.

Table 10-17

	q'_1	q'_2	q'_3	q'_4	q'_5	q'_6	
q'_4	$\lambda + 2$	$4 - \lambda$	$5 - 4\lambda$	1	0	0	1
q'_5	$\lambda + 1$	$\lambda + 2$	2	0	1	0	1
q'_6	$3\lambda + 1$	$3 - 2\lambda$	$2\lambda + 1$	0	0	1	1
	-1	-1	-1	0	0	0	0

It appears that there are *two nondominated pairs of pure strategies*: (1) If λ is between 0 and $\frac{3}{5}$,

$$(q_1, q_2, q_3) = (2 + \lambda) \left(\frac{1}{2 + \lambda}, 0, 0 \right) = (1, 0, 0)$$

and

$$(p_1, p_2, p_3) = (2 + \lambda) \left(\frac{1}{2 + \lambda}, 0, 0 \right) = (1, 0, 0)$$

(2) If λ is between $\frac{3}{5}$ and 1, then

$$(q_1, q_2, q_3) = (5 - 4\lambda) \left(0, 0, \frac{1}{5 - 4\lambda} \right) = (0, 0, 1)$$

and

$$(p_1, p_2, p_3) = (5 - 4\lambda) \left(\frac{1}{5 - 4\lambda}, 0, 0 \right) = (1, 0, 0)$$

In order to secure the value of the game $(2 + \lambda)$ for $0 \le \lambda \le \frac{3}{5}$, Player X plays strategy x^1 and Player Y plays strategy y^1. In order to secure the value of the game $(5 - 4\lambda)$ for $\frac{3}{5} \le \lambda \le 1$, Player X plays x^1 and Player Y plays y^3. The respective payoffs are $(3, 2)$ and $(1, 5)$.

Depending on λ (the importance of a^1_{ij} relative to a^2_{ij}), an average payoff can be calculated. Observe that for $\lambda = \frac{3}{5}$ both strategies lead to the same average return: $\frac{3}{5}(3) + \frac{2}{5}(2) = \frac{3}{5}(1) + \frac{2}{5}(5)$. The reader should further check the nondominance of suggested solutions, parameter-dependent multiple values of the game, and the numerical correctness of presented results.

Games with multiple payoffs are one of the least explored areas of MCDM. Considerable research effort is still needed to find better solution concepts, more accurate interpretations of parameters, more efficient computational algorithms, and new applications.

10-6 INTERACTIVE PROCEDURES

Interactive MCDM procedures are often referred to as methods for *progressive articulation of preferences*. An underlying assumption is that the decision maker's preferences form and evolve only in connection with a particular problem. That is, there are no fixed or given human preferences per se, but only situation-dependent, circumstance-shaped, evolving, changing preference patterns. This evolution of preferences is an important *learning process* to be taken into account.

In contrast, some MCDM approaches concentrate on *a priori articulation of preferences*; i.e., they assume that all necessary information about a decision maker's preferences can be extracted prior to the actual problem solving, independently of a given decision situation. In this view, human preferences are relatively fixed and consistent; There is no significant learning process. These are the assumptions underlying multiattribute utility theory and all its derivative methodologies.

Still other approaches do not attempt any substantial articulation of preferences before or during the problem-solving process. Preferences remain implicit; the choice is arrived at by some other means. After the final decision or solution has been arrived at, the preference structure can be made explicit. Hence, these are methods for *a posteriori articulation of preferences*. These approaches include linear multiobjective programming, multiparametric decomposition, stochastic dominance, and compromise programming.

All three basic approaches are covered in this text. But in this section we concentrate on the interactive approach, the articulation of preferences via some sort of man-machine dialogue.

An interactive conversational system, possibly incorporating computer graphics, provides an opportunity for real-time interaction between analysts and the decision maker. Such a system can guide decision makers to what *they* consider the best compromise, without forcing them into an exhaustive examination of all the trade-offs.

Computer-graphics capabilities lessen the time and effort required for the preparation of input data, and they become a means for graphic, tabular, or even pictorial feedback. Any changes, reconsiderations, or alternative scenarios can be readily incorporated to enhance the communication and interpretation of results.

Overview of some earlier interactive methods One of the earlier interactive approaches is the method of Geoffrion, Dyer, and Feinberg (1972), designated as the "GDF method." An overall preference (or utility) function u is assumed to be unknown (but differentiable and with positive marginal utility), while its arguments, i.e., individual objective functions $f_i(x)$, are well defined and the feasible set X is convex.

It is assumed that function $u[f(x)]$ can be approximated by a linear function $w_1 f_1(x) + \cdots + w_l f_l(x)$ at any point x^k from X. The algorithm determines the best direction of improvement from the current point x^k. The direction of improvement of each $f_i(x)$ at any x^k is determined by its gradient $\nabla f_i(x^k)$,

$$\nabla f_i(x^k) = \left(\frac{\partial f_i}{\partial x_1^k}, \ldots, \frac{\partial f_i}{\partial x_n^k} \right)$$

The direction of improvement of the linear approximation is given by the weighted combination of individual gradients:

$$\sum_{i=1}^{l} w_i^k \nabla f_i(x^k)$$

The weights w_i assessed at a particular solution point x^k are denoted w_i^k. Weights w_i^k are the marginal substitution rates between each f_i, $i = 1, \ldots, l$, and f_1. (That is, one function, in this case f_1, is chosen as an arbitrary reference criterion.) One way to determine w_i^k is to ask the decision maker the question, With all other criteria held constant at the solution point x^k, how much would you be willing to decrease the value of $f_i(x^k)$ in order to compensate for a designated (infinitesimal) change in f_1, $\Delta f_1(x^k)$? The decision maker could answer, By $\Delta f_i(x^k)$. This response would allow us to approximate w_i^k as follows:

$$w_i^k = \frac{\Delta f_1(x^k)}{\Delta f_i(x^k)}$$

After we determine $l - 1$ trade-offs w_i^k, the following linear approximation function can be formed: $w_1^k f_1(x) + \cdots + w_l^k f_l(x)$. In order to determine the best direction of its improvement we solve the following problem:

$$\text{Maximize} \sum_{i=1}^{l} w_i^k \nabla f_i(x^k) \cdot y \qquad \text{for } y \in X$$

which for linear functions $f_i(x)$ reduces to

$$\text{Find } y^k \in X$$

such that $w_1^k f_1(y^k) + \cdots + w_l^k f_l(y^k)$ reaches its maximum value on X. The best direction is then given by $z^k = y^k - x^k$.

The next question is how far one should move in the designated direction z^k in order to determine the next solution x^{k+1}. In other words, what is the value α in $x^{k+1} = x^k + \alpha z^k$?

A proper value of α must be selected directly by the decision maker. One has to evaluate values $f_i(x^k + \alpha z^k)$ for a selected grid of points α between 0 and 1, display them in a tabular or graphic way, and let the decision maker determine a value of α for which the most preferred values of objectives are attained, say, α^k.

Next, one calculates $x^{k+1} = x^k + \alpha^k z^k$. The whole procedure is then repeated at the solution point x^{k+1}. The process terminates when any two subsequent solutions are equal, i.e., when $x^{k+1} = x^k$, for some $k = 1, 2, \ldots$.

We spend so much time explaining this method, which so greatly burdens the information-processing capability of the decision maker, in order to show how early interactive procedures were designed. Rather than these methods helping the decision maker, in some sense the decision maker was "helping" the methods.

There are many variations on the GDF method. For example, the interactive goal programming of Dyer (1972) is almost identical with it. Dyer (1973) and Wehrung (1973) attempted to relieve some of the difficulties of information gathering, but unsuccessfully.

Another approach was proposed by Haimes, Hall, and Freedman (1975), the *surrogate worth trade-off (SWT) method*. This is a rather complex procedure: First, a representative set of nondominated solutions is computed. Each nondominated solution is then characterized by the corresponding trade-off ratios between any *two* objective functions, say $\lambda_{ij} = -\partial f_i(x)/\partial f_j(x)$, at a given nondominated point x. All the remaining objectives are kept at their given levels of attainment. The decision maker is then asked to assess how much (on an ordinal scale, say from -10 to $+10$ with 0 indicating indifference) he or she prefers trading λ_{ij} marginal units of the ith objective $f_i(x)$ for one marginal unit of the jth objective $f_j(x)$, given that all other objectives remain at their current values. The decision maker's response constitutes the so-called "surrogate worth function" w_{ij}. That is, if $w_{ij} > 0$ then the decision maker prefers the above trade, if $w_{ij} = 0$ the decision maker is indifferent, and if $w_{ij} < 0$ then he or she does not prefer λ_{ij} marginal units of $f_i(x)$ over one marginal unit of $f_j(x)$, other things being equal. Each trade-off ratio λ_{ij} is similarly evaluated for all i, $j = 1, \ldots, 1, i \neq j$. The most preferred solution is found at the nondominated point where all trade-off ratios λ_{ij} make the corresponding surrogate worth functions w_{ij} simultaneously equal to zero.

The SWT method is also described in Haimes and Hall (1974) and Hall and Haimes (1976). Two larger numerical examples of SWT are demonstrated by Hwang and Masud (1979).

The *Zionts and Wallenius (ZW) method* (1976) is one of the simplest interactive procedures of this type. It assumes, however, that the decision maker's implicit utility function is linear, namely, $u(x) = f(\lambda, x) = \lambda_1 f_1(x) + \cdots + \lambda_l f_l(x)$. Through the interaction, one attempts to identify the set of weights λ at which this function is maximized. First, an arbitrary set of weights, normalized between 0 and 1, is selected. This weighted combination of functions is then maximized over X, and a nondominated solution is obtained. In the corresponding simplex tableau one can identify those nonbasic variables which, when introduced into the basis, cannot increase one objective without decreasing at least one other objective. These nonbasic variables indicate the trade-offs involved in moving from a given nondominated solution to all its adjacent nondominated solutions. (Because of linearity, only corner-point solutions are considered.)

Let us denote as w_{ij} the amount of decrease in $f_i(x)$ due to the introduction of one unit of nonbasic variable x_j into the solution. The decision maker is then asked, Are you willing to accept a decrease w_{1j} in $f_1(x)$, a decrease of w_{2j} in $f_2(x)$, $\ldots$, and a decrease w_{lj} in $f_l(x)$? The decision maker must respond "yes," "no," or "indifferent" to this trade. The question is repeated for all nonbasic variables x_j which would lead to adjacent nondominated solutions.

If the responses are negative for all such variables x_j, the procedure can be terminated, and the corresponding set of weights declared the best. Otherwise, a new set of weights is generated and the procedure repeated.

Essentially, the ZW method allows the decision maker, for any given nondominated corner-point solution, to explore whether a move to one of the adjacent nondominated solutions would be desirable. If yes, the move is made to a new solution, and the procedure is repeated. Observe that the use of weights would become redundant if either the multicriterion simplex method or the multiparametric decomposition method were used.

The decision maker is required to make full pairwise comparisons among multidimensional solutions. If the number of objectives or attributes is large— say, more than six—then these holistic comparisons could be difficult and unreliable.

The pattern followed by earlier interactive procedures, such as GDF, SWT, and ZW methods, is:

1. Generate a solution, preferably nondominated, and characterize the trade-offs which would have to be made to allow movement from its immediate neighborhood
2. Let the decision maker evaluate the trade-offs, either directly or in connection with the solution that implies each trade-off
3. Generate a new solution by moving in the direction of the most preferred trade-off
4. Repeat the first three steps until no further "preferable" move can be elicited from the decision maker's information

Reducing the size of the nondominated set In linear multiobjective programming, the number of computed nondominated solutions is often too large for a decision maker to make an intelligent identification of the most preferable one. Approaches are being developed which would allow one to "prune," "filter," or simply "reduce" the size of the nondominated set to manageable size.

Steuer (1977, 1979) and Steuer and Schuler (1978) have developed a battery of reducing approaches, based on the maximization of $\lambda_1 f_1(x) + \cdots + \lambda_l f_l(x)$. As we know from our discussion of multiparametric decomposition (Sec. 8-5), maximizing such weighted function for all weights

$$\lambda_i \geqq 0, \sum_{i=1}^{l} \lambda_i = 1$$

generates all nondominated solutions to the LMP problem. Obviously, if the decision maker specifies some lower and upper bounds L_i and U_i for each weight λ_i, then the resulting set of nondominated solutions will be correspondingly smaller. The tighter are the bounds $L_i \leqq \lambda_i \leqq U_i$, the smaller will be the nondominated set, as shown in Sec. 8-5.

The decision maker receives only the cluster of nondominated solutions corresponding to the prespecified bounds on weights. The decision maker is then asked to select the most preferred solution. New intervals of weights (L_i, U_i) are computed so that they generate the most preferred point but through a proportionally smaller subspace of weight combinations. Thus, one gradually contracts the subspace of eligible weights while simultaneously shifting the subspace in the direction of the most preferred choices. This process continues until a small portion of the nondominated set is located which contains the most preferred solution for the overall problem.

In order to avoid presenting the decision maker with large clusters of nondominated solutions corresponding to a particular set of prespecified bounds, only representative solutions, adequately characterizing a given portion of the nondominated set, are computed. This is achieved by filtering.

The idea is that some solutions could be quite "close" to each other, not sufficiently "dissimilar." Therefore, they would be redundant and overburden the decision maker in the solution-focusing task. This dissimilarity is measured via a general distance function of the kind discussed earlier in this chapter. The following rule constitutes a "filter":

$$\left\{ \sum_{i=1}^{l} r_i \mid f_i(x^k) - f_i(x^{k-1}) \mid^p \right\}^{1/p} \leq d$$

where l indicates the number of objectives; r_i is the normalized reciprocal of the range of values associated with the ith objective, that is,

$$r_i = 1/(f^*_i - f_{i*}) \div \sum_{i=1}^{l} 1/(f^*_i - f_{i*})$$

x^k is the nondominated point currently tested by the filter; and x^{k-1} represents (sequentially) all nondominated solutions previously retained by the filter. This filter assures a minimum "spacing" between retained solutions according to parameter d.

Another method for portraying the nondominated set by a representative subset has been developed by Morse (1979). Morse is motivated by the observation that there is a threshold of resolution beyond which the decision maker cannot perceive the difference between two similar multidimensional solutions; there is little point in making the decision maker waste time by processing redundant information. The statistical technique of cluster analysis is used to "prune" the nondominated set, in Morse's terminology.

In statistics, clusters are composed of objects, e.g., nondominated solutions, that are qualitatively or quantitatively similar. Clusters are dense areas, where the objects are close to each other, surrounded by areas where they are more sparse.

To avoid the pitfalls of specifying a particular distance function, e.g., parameter p in the filter introduced above, one can resort to block clustering which does not require the explicit specification of a distance function. (It is specified only implicitly by the choice of the number of intervals.) Block clustering works as follows: Each dimension (criterion, attribute) is partitioned into intervals spanning the range between the lowest and the highest attained value on the particular nondominated set of solutions. Each value $f_i(x)$ is then replaced by a rank number 1, 2, 3, etc., depending on which interval occurs (counted from the lowest value). If one lists the solutions vertically and the criteria horizontally, one obtains a matrix of "classified" data. By switching the rows and columns until similar values are positioned near each other (which can be done efficiently by a computer routine), one obtains clusters of objectives and solutions specified along the margins of the matrix. Each cluster can then be represented by an arbitrarily selected nondominated point.

The clustering of criteria is very useful: One can discover that some criteria are correlated to the extent that they provide a similar ranking of the alternatives. Such criteria are thus redundant and can be either discarded or replaced.

Another clustering technique is the so-called "hierarchical clustering." At first, each object is a cluster in its own right. The distance of each object to the centroid of its parent cluster is measured. For each cluster these distances are then squared and added. The next two clusters to be joined are those for which the increase in this sum of squares of distances is minimized. (In block clustering, interval splits are performed which maximize the decrease in the sum of squares.)

Both filtering and pruning (clustering) yield a representative set of nondominated solutions, while redundant solutions are temporarily discarded. If the decision maker shows a particular interest in one solution, some of the previously discarded neighboring solutions may be filtered back (reverse filtered) into consideration. Similarly, some nonextreme point solutions, especially those on "long" edges connecting adjacent corner points, and their convex combinations, can be brought to a decision maker's attention (intraset point generation).

Filtering and intraset point generation can also be used in single-objective LP for sifting through alternative solutions, if they exist. (Alternative solutions to a linear-programming problem are not equally desirable to the decision maker.)

Törn (1979) completes our pruning-filtering troika by combining the methods of Morse and Steuer. All three approaches are referenced in the Bibliography on MCDM.

Goal-programming interactions In Sec. 9-3 we discussed the inadequacy of goal programming with respect to the a priori setting of goals (e.g., setting them too low) and the possibility of ending up with dominated solutions. Another problem is that goal programming generates too few solutions, and they tend either to be unrelated or only poorly to represent the nondominated set.

There have been frequent efforts to enrich GP methodology by incorporating interactive features. Monarchi et al. (1973, 1976) distinguish between goals and aspiration levels: *Goals*, i.e., required values of objectives, are difficult to change because they are imposed on the decision maker by external circumstances; *aspiration levels*, i.e., desired values of objective functions, may change due to learning, improved understanding, or shifts in a preference pattern.

The *Monarchi technique* assumes that aspiration levels a_i and goals g_i are defined for each of the objective functions $f_i(x)$. Each objective is further characterized by a relevant range of values f^U_i and f_{iL}, that is, upper and lower limits imposed externally. Note that these limits do not necessarily coincide with f^*_i and f_{i*}, that is, with the attainable maxima and minima of $f_i(x)$. The following transformation translates values of $f_i(x)$ into a unit interval $\langle 0, 1 \rangle$:

$$y_i(x) = \frac{f_i(x) - f_{iL}}{f^U_i - f_{iL}}$$

Similarly, the aspiration levels a_i and goals g_i should be also transformed, to assure comparability:

$$A_i = \frac{a_i - f_{iL}}{f^U_i - f_{iL}} \quad \text{and} \quad G_i = \frac{g_i - f_{iL}}{f^U_i - f_{iL}}$$

Observe that $f^U_i - f_{iL}$ must be larger than zero. If $f^U_i - f_{iL} = 0$, replace zero by an arbitrarily small number to avoid the division by zero.

One can see that the combination of goals g_i and ranges $f^U_i - f_{iL}$ is redundant. If goals g_i are truly mandatory, then they constrain the feasible region directly. That is, if it is required that $f_i(x) \geq g_i$, then $f_{iL} = g_i$; for $f_i(x) \leq g_i$ we set $f^U_i = g_i$, and for $f_i(x) = g_i$ we obtain $f^U_i = f_{iL} = g_i$. Thus we dispose of goals g_i by translating them directly into f^U_i and f_{iL}. The original feasible set X of constraints is appended by $f_{iL} \leq f_i(x) \leq f^U_i$ constraints.

It is sufficient to concentrate on aspiration levels a_i and their transformed values A_i. If the set of values a_i does not satisfy the (extended) set X, then the problem has no solution. The set of aspiration levels must satisfy X if the problem is to have a solution.

Our task is to find a solution which approximates the aspiration levels as closely as possible. To that end we introduce deviations d_i which indicate the extent of "disagreement." The following types of aspiration levels can be used:

(a) $f_i(x) \leq a_i$; $\quad d_i = \dfrac{y_i(x)}{A_i}$

(b) $f_i(x) \geq a_i$; $\quad d_i = \dfrac{A_i}{y_i(x)}$

(c) $f_i(x) = a_i$; $\quad d_i = \frac{1}{2} \left[\dfrac{A_i}{y_i(x)} + \dfrac{y_i(x)}{A_i} \right]$

(d) $a_i \leq f_i(x) \leq \bar{a}_i$; $\quad d_i = \left(\dfrac{\bar{A}_i}{A_i + \bar{A}_i} \right) \left[\dfrac{A_i}{y_i(x)} + \dfrac{y_i(x)}{\bar{A}_i} \right]$

(e) $f_i(x) \leq a_i \quad \text{or} \quad f_i(x) \geq \bar{a}_i$; $\quad d_i = \left(\dfrac{A_i + \bar{A}_i}{\bar{A}_i} \right) \left[\dfrac{1}{\dfrac{A_i}{y_i(x)} + \dfrac{y_i(x)}{\bar{A}_i}} \right]$

Note that $a_i \leq \bar{a}_i$ and $\bar{A}_i = (\bar{a}_i - f_{iL})/(f^U_i - f_{iL})$.

Monarchi suggests minimizing objective function f:

$$f = w_1 d_1 + w_2 d_2 + \cdots + w_l d_l$$

All $d_i \leq 1$ indicate that the corresponding aspiration levels have been satisfied; $d_i > 1$ indicate unsatisfied aspiration levels.

The interaction with the decision maker enters in the following way. Initial weights w_i and aspiration levels a_i (and $\bar{a}_i$) are established, and the problem is solved. If the solution achieved is satisfactory, terminate. If not, the decision maker can put larger weights on unsatisfied aspiration levels or change the aspiration levels. One then recomputes the problem, and the result is again subjected to the decision maker's assessment. The weights can also be used as preemptive priorities.

Another *interactive multiple goal programming* (IMGP) technique has been developed by Nijkamp and Spronk (1978). This approach tries to avoid setting aspiration levels and priority weights a priori.

One can compute, separately for each objective function, the minimum and the maximum achievable values with respect to X. These two vectors of values determine the potential for change with respect to each objective; they could be called "pessimistic" and "optimistic" vectors respectively. The current trial solution is computed so that it returns the minimum achievable values. If there is no potential for improvement of any of the objectives, stop. Otherwise, the decision maker evaluates the current solution and indicates which of the minimum values should be raised. The decision maker does not have to specify by how much. Nor do weighting factors have to be specified, because by selecting a particular objective the decision maker has implicitly indicated that it is the most important one in the current situation. Observe that it is advantageous to set the initial pessimistic vector as the anti-ideal and the optimistic vector as the ideal with respect to the nondominated set of solutions (see Secs. 6-6.2 and 5-3.4). The situation is depicted in Fig. 10-10.

The minimum values of the current solution are now imposed as constraints and the size of X correspondingly reduced. The minimum value of the selected objective is raised to the midpoint of its potential, and the IMGP algorithm returns a new trial solution. A new optimistic vector is calculated. The decision maker evaluates whether the solution is satisfactory. If not, the decision maker indicates which of the objectives should be raised further.

This procedure converges to a solution as long as the decision maker is able to declare at least one solution to be satisfactory. If there are several satisfactory solutions and the decision maker is unable to state a preference among

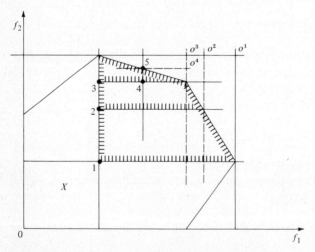

Figure 10-10 An example of IMGP algorithmic progression.

them, one solution would have to be chosen arbitrarily. If a preference is always expressed, a unique satisfactory solution will ultimately be found. A problem arises when the decision maker is unable to declare *any* solution satisfactory. Two conclusions could be drawn: (1) There is no satisfactory solution, and the problem must be restated (changing constraints, objectives, etc.); (2) there is a satisfactory solution, but the decision maker cannot recognize it (too many objectives, fatigue, etc.). In the latter case the analysis must provide practical guidance based on a theory which is acceptable to the decision maker.

In Fig. 10-10 observe how the IMGP algorithm progresses from trial solution 1, through 2, 3, and 4, until it reaches satisfactory solution 5. Point 1 is the initial pessimistic solution. The set of feasible solutions X is thus reduced to the overall shaded area. The corresponding optimistic solution consists of the maxima of functions f_1 and f_2 over X. Solution 1 is not acceptable. The decision maker indicates that f_2 should be raised. IMGP sets its new value at the midpoint of its potential, that is, at point 2. The feasible region has been further reduced and the corresponding optimistic solution (with respect to a new constraint) computed (point o^2). Point 2 is unsatisfactory, because the decision maker desires a further rise in f_2. A new solution is proposed at the midpoint of the remaining potential, that is, at point 3, and the corresponding optimistic solution is o^3. Assume that the bound of point 3 is accepted, and the decision maker identifies f_1 to be raised. The new proposed value of f_1 is set at the midpoint of its potential (halfway between values of 3 and o^3); point 4 is reached. Point 4 is acceptable, and f_2 is raised to its maximum under current constraints, reaching point 5 (which should be acceptable, since point 4 was acceptable).

In summary, the IMGP algorithm can be based on preemptive prioritization of objectives—the decision maker would be expected to raise each of the objectives to its acceptable value in the order of their importance. This would be a drawback, however, and the IMGP should allow shifts in the priorities of objectives. For example, at point 4 of Fig. 10-10 the decision maker should be able to declare the level of f_2 unacceptable in spite of his or her statement at point 3. As it is now, IMGP assumes a rather high level of consistency in the decision maker's expression of preferences. Also, reversals of the previously set bounds (returning them to the previous or at least lower levels) should be allowed. One can also ask whether the decision maker should not explore only nondominated solutions rather than progressing from dominated ones, as in Fig. 10-10. In its current form, the IMGP algorithm implicitly assumes that there is a stable preference function in the mind of the decision maker. Thus, the solution is assumed to exist.

Interactive decision evolution aid (IDEA) In the quest for the simplest, most effective, and theoretically sound interactive procedure, we provide a general framework of requirements and assumptions on which such methodology should be based. The IDEA approach is a graphic interactive tool for aiding the decision maker in the search for a solution. The following assumptions should be emphasized:

- The decision maker's preference function is unknown and evolving throughout the decision process. It is situation-dependent, subject to learning and "changes of mind."
- The set of alternatives can be specified (through constraints or through listing). The most preferred values with respect to each objective (maxima, minima, or mandatory goals) can be specified. That is, the ideal solution can be identified.
- The decision maker prefers a nondominated solution to a dominated one and would accept the ideal if it were made available.
- No weights of criteria importance are to be specified. They are implicit in the attention levels accorded to individual criteria during the decision process. No goals or "satisfactory" values (except the mandatory constraints) are to be specified a priori.
- The decision maker is expected to characterize each solution as acceptable or unacceptable with respect to the ideal. An inability to make such a declaration is interpreted as indicating that the solution is unacceptable.
- The decision maker must be allowed to introduce new alternatives, to add or drop some criteria, and to be inconsistent in the expression of criteria importance.

This set of requirements and assumptions should perhaps be relaxed further, but we shall consider them reasonable for the time being.

The IDEA approach proceeds as follows:

1. The set of all nondominated solutions or nondominated extreme-point solutions is identified but not displayed to the decision maker. It is to be used for internal purposes only. (For nonlinear objectives and constraints a set of representative nondominated solutions is identified.)
2. The ideal and anti-ideal solutions are computed. These two reference points identify the ranges or potentials for change for each criterion. Criteria potentials are displayed as a bar diagram. The direction of improvement proceeds from the bottom to the top of each bar. (In cases where the most preferred value can be approached from both directions the dividing point of the bar is clearly marked.)
3. The bars could be either presented in their original incommensurate scales (commensurate scales pose no problem, and the bar length directly reflects the potential) or scaled between 0 and 1 (or 0 and 100) in terms of percentage values of the ideal.
4. The decision maker starts at the anti-ideal. The decision maker generally attempts to exploit available potentials, either fully or by predetermined

steps. Feasible increments or decrements are predetermined because of the finite listing of nondominated solutions.

5. Any change in any potential is translated into all remaining criteria potentials, and a new bar diagram is displayed. Used-up portions are clearly identified, and the remaining permissible changes are displayed.

6. In a few preliminary steps the decision maker is encouraged to reach for the ideal. Its unavailability is quickly realized, and the notion of necessary trade-offs is quickly learned. The purpose is to make all potentials as small as possible so that the ideal will be approximated as closely as possible. If all potentials could be reduced to zero, the ideal would be perfectly matched. In reality, there will be combinations of potential residuals which the decision maker must judge in terms of their closeness to the ideal.

7. The decision maker is allowed to retrace, follow different paths, or use trial and error. It is desirable that multiple decision makers (if any) first use the technique separately, later joining in a committee for group negotiations. Ultimately, the decision maker enters a subset of points which are cyclically entered again and again. A compromise set has been identified.

8. One tests whether none of the compromise solutions is truly acceptable. Their mathematical distances from the ideal are computed (for different p in L_p metric), and the results are made available to the decision maker for comparison. Some of the less important criteria can be temporarily removed in order to decrease the dimensionality of the problem.

9. If none of the compromise solutions has been found acceptable, the problem must be redefined. New constraints and new alternatives must be brought into the picture, different criteria considered, or the decision recommended for postponement. New alternatives should be generated as closely as possible to the ideal. Then the entire IDEA process should be repeated.

We shall demonstrate the process of IDEA with a simplified example. Consider three objective functions which can be expressed in a commensurate scale (for example, in dollars, physical units, or score points). The set of nondominated solutions has been identified and is given in Table 10-18.

The decision maker is not shown the data in Table 10-18, as they can be too voluminous, many-dimensional, and difficult to absorb. Instead a bar diagram

Table 10-18

	f_1	f_2	f_3
1	10	5	7
2	6	7	3
3	3	8	2
4	7	4	9
5	1	5	8

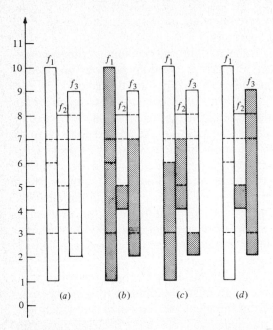

Figure 10-11 An example of applying IDEA interactive approach to decision making.

is produced, as in Figure 10-11. Observe that the ideal has been identified as (10, 8, 9), the anti-ideal as (1, 4, 2). These two vectors determine individual potentials for the problem.

The initial situation is summarized in Fig. 10-11a. The decision maker first attempts to learn the limits and trade-off behavior of the problem at hand. The large potential of function f_1 is fully exploited; that is, the value of f_1 is moved from 1 to 10. The remaining potentials for f_2 and f_3 are automatically displayed, and the overall impact of this move is summarized in Fig. 10-11b. The shaded areas indicate used-up potentials; white sections are potentials that are still available.

Obviously f_1 cannot be increased any further. The decision maker becomes interested in f_2 which has the lowest value and highest available potential. Instead of exploiting the f_2 potential in full, the decision maker takes the next recommended step (raise f_2 from 5 to 7) in order to learn the impact of such a move on f_1. The situation is displayed in Fig. 10-11c.

Observe that the current level of f_2 can only be achieved by dropping f_1 from 10 to 6 and f_3 from 7 to 3. The analyst can point out that there is an alternative way of securing f_2 at 5. This alternative is displayed in Fig. 10-11d. Comparing situations b and d leads to a preference for b because of the unacceptably low level of f_1 in d. Being unsatisfactory, situation d can be temporarily removed from consideration. Thus, situation c represents a starting point for further interaction. One can reverse f_2 from 7 to 5 and come back to situation b. The trade-offs are now clear: To increase f_2 from 5 to 7 is "paid for" by decreasing f_1 from 10 to 6 and f_3 from 7 to 3. Though not willing to pay such a "price," the decision maker is willing to settle for f_2 minimally at 5 and reverses back to situation b. The decision maker indicates a willingness to forego some of f_1, relaxing it from 10 to 7. The analysis shows that available alternatives do not allow that: Changing f_1 from 10 to 7 would drop f_2 to 4 while increasing f_3 from 7 to 9. If f_2 at 5 is truly the minimum acceptable value, the only available decision is situation b. The only way out of this decision would be to reformulate the problem. A new alternative characterized by f_1 at 7, f_2 at 4, and f_3 at either 8 or 9 would have to be invented.

Thus, situation b—that is, points $f_1 = 10$, $f_2 = 5$, and $f_3 = 7$—represents the current most preferable solution. A number of actions can be recommended at this point: search for new alternative(s), add or drop some criteria, delay the decision and try a new interaction run after group consultation and gathering of more information, or accept the decision.

The conflict among objectives is dictated by the lack of alternatives, not by an inherently conflicting nature of the objectives. Realizing this is crucial to the decision-making task. The trade-offs arc situation-dependent, and evaluating them in terms of the objectives per se would be futile. It would not lead to conflict resolution. Only some, not all, trade-offs are possible and relevant to the task.

The use of computer graphics in interactive decision making is only beginning. Endless columns of numbers can be translated into colorful charts, graphs, and maps, helping managers to make decisions quickly and efficiently. It is often claimed that about three times as much information can be absorbed through graphic as through numerical means. Business graphics is becoming the vital core of modern decision support systems. A vivid display of trade-offs overcomes the difficulty of explicating them from rows and columns of figures. Different phases of graphic interaction can be "frozen," that is, put on 35-mm slides and used as a base for discussions or record.

Existing graphics terminals already offer better resolution than do television sets, they can generate graphs in up to eight colors and produce prints with photographic quality, and their costs are decreasing rapidly. In this case at least, the theory of interactive decision support systems is falling behind the technology.

The proliferation of personal computer graphics terminals, the ability to play and replay a number of "what if" scenarios, the possibility of direct interaction via light-sensitive pens, and the steadily dropping prices of terminals and printers represent a technological potential which MCDM methodologies should exploit to the fullest degree. The full potential of MCDM theory is only beginning to be realized.

10-7 BIBLIOGRAPHICAL NOTE

Unlike that of goal programming, the literature of compromise programming is still rather scarce. It evolved with the notion of the displaced ideal; the reader is advised to refer to Sec. 6-1, "Historical Note."

Compromise programming became of mathematical, empirical, and practical interest after Zeleny's introduction of the concept of *compromise solutions* (1973). Entitled "Compromise Programming," this paper contains most of the seminal ideas and presents a good starting point for further research. It spawned a series of follow-up publications by the author (1974, 1975, 1976, 1977, 1981).

Yu (1973) extended the concept of compromise solutions to group decision making. This work also confirms the broad potential of the approach.

There is considerable mathematical interest in compromise programming, especially with reference to its obvious efficiency in tracing out nondominated solutions, even in the most generally defined sets of feasible alternatives. Bowman (1975), Gearhart (1979), and Ecker and Shoemaker (1980) are good representatives of this new trend.

We can recommend few other follow-up readings on compromise programming at this time. But there is a good review by Nykowski (1977), in Polish, and a recent overview by Hwang and Masud (1979).

Benayoun, R., J. de Montgolfier, J. Tergny, and O. I. Larichev: "Linear Programming with Multiple Objective Functions: Step Method (STEM)," *Mathematical Programming,* vol. 1, no. 3, 1971, pp. 366–375.

Bowman, V. J.: "On the Relationship of the Tchebycheff Norm and the Efficient Frontier of Multiple-Criteria Objectives," in H. Thiriez and S. Zionts (eds.), *Multiple Criteria Decision Making, Jouy-en-Josas, France 1975*, Springer-Verlag, New York, 1976, pp. 76–85.

Cook, W. D., and L. M. Seiford: "Priority Ranking and Consensus Formation," *Management Science*, vol. 24, no. 16, 1978, pp. 1721–1732.

Ecker, J. G., and N. E. Shoemaker: "Multiple Objective Linear Programming and the Tradeoff-Compromise Set," in G. Fandel and T. Gal (eds.), *Multiple Criteria Decision Making Theory and Application*, Springer-Verlag, New York, 1980, pp. 60–73.

Gearhart, W. B.: "Compromise Solutions and Estimation of the Noninferior Set," *Journal of Optimization Theory and Applications*, vol. 28, 1979, pp. 29–47.

Hwang, C. L., and A. S. M. Masud: *Multiple Objective Decision Making—Methods and Applications*, Springer-Verlag, New York, 1979, pp. 169–242.

Loomba, P. N.: *Management—A Quantitative Perspective*, Macmillan, New York, 1978.

Loucks, D. P.: "An Application of Interactive Multiobjective Water Resources Planning," *Interfaces*, vol. 8, no. 1, November 1977, pp. 70–75.

Negoita, C. V.: *Management Applications of System Theory*, Birkhäuser Verlag, Basel, 1979, pp. 136–143.

Nykowski, I.: "Rozwiazania kompromisowe w wielokryteriowym programowaniu liniowym," *Przeglad Statystyczny*, vol. 24, no. 1, 1977, pp. 3–19.

Saska, J.: "Lineární Multiprogramování," *Ekonomicko-matematický Obzor,* vol. 4, no. 3, 1968, pp. 359–373.

Yager, R. R.: "Competitiveness and Compensation in Decision Making: A Fuzzy Set Based Interpretation," Iona College Tech. Rep. RRY 78-14, New Rochelle, N. Y., 1978.

Yu, P. L.: "A Class of Solutions for Group Decision Problems," *Management Science,* vol. 19, no. 8, 1973, pp. 936–946.

Zeleny, M.: "Adaptive Displacement of Preferences in Decision Making," in M. K. Starr and M. Zeleny (eds.), *Multiple Criteria Decision Making*, TIMS Studies in the Management Sciences, vol. 6, North-Holland Publishing, Amsterdam, 1977, pp. 147–158.

———: "The Attribute-Dynamic Attitude Model (ADAM)," *Management Science*, vol. 23, no. 1, 1976, pp. 12–26.

———: "Compromise Programming," in J. L. Cochrane and M. Zeleny (eds.), *Multiple Criteria Decision Making,* University of South Carolina Press, Columbia, 1973, pp. 262–301.

————: "A Concept of Compromise Solutions and the Method of the Displaced Ideal," *Computers and Operations Research*, vol. 1, no. 4, 1974, pp. 479-496.

————: "Descriptive Decision Making and Its Applications," in R. L. Schultz (ed.), *Applications of Management Science,* vol. 1, JAI Press, Greenwich, Conn., 1981, pp. 327-388.

————: "The Theory of the Displaced Ideal," in M. Zeleny (ed.), *Multiple Criteria Decision Making: Kyoto 1975*, Springer-Verlag, New York, 1976, pp. 151-205.

10-8 PROBLEMS

10-1 Prepare a graphic representation of the following problem: Maximize $f_1 = 2x_1 + x_2$ and $f_2 = -4x_1 + x_2$ with respect to the following constraints:

$$X = \begin{cases} -2x_1 + x_2 \leq 1 \\ -x_1 + 2x_2 \leq 8 \\ x_1 - 2x_2 \leq 16 \\ x_1 + x_2 \leq 10 \\ 2x_1 - x_2 \leq 8 \\ 4x_1 + 3x_2 \geq 8 \quad \text{and } x_1, x_2 \geq 0 \end{cases}$$

(a) Outline the set of nondominated solutions in X.

(b) Prepare a graphic representation of the same problem in the value space of objective functions f_1 and f_2. That is, transform X into $f[X]$ where $f = (f_1, f_2)$. *Hint*: Map each extreme point of X into the corresponding extreme point of $f[X]$. For example, point $x_1 = 6, x_2 = 4$ is mapped into point $f_1 = 2(6) + 4 = 16, f_2 = -4(6) + 4 = -20$ in $f[X]$.
Identify the nondominated set in $f[X]$.

(c) In the space of $f[X]$ designate the ideal point. Identify graphically the points closest to the ideal with respect to L_1, L_2, and L_∞ with equally weighted f_1 and f_2.

(d) Transform the compromise set of solutions, identified in (c), back to the space of X.

10-2 How are the results of Prob. 10-1 affected by maximizing a third objective function $f_3 = -x_1 + x_2$?

10-3 Two groups of settlers compete to acquire beaver pelts and gold from the Indians in a given area. Each group of settlers can adopt one of two strategies: trade or steal. Two hundred pelts and 100 pounds of gold are attainable by trade. Stealing is more effective in the sense that 60 percent of the available quantities could be acquired at the expense of the trading party, which would then be left with only 40 percent of the total. If both parties adopt the same strategy, trading or stealing, they will split the proceeds 50/50. Stealing has a cost attached to it: The Indians are able to hide or destroy 10 percent of both commodities before encountering the thieving settlers. Thus, if both parties engage in the raid, 20 percent of the commodities become unavailable. Under these conditions, the following is the matrix of potential payoffs available to "our" group:

		Other group	
		Trade	Steal
Our group	Trade	100, 50*	72, 36
	Steal	108, 54	80, 40

*The first number of each entry corresponds to pelts, the second to gold. The "other" group is facing exactly the same matrix of payoffs.

(Please check the entries so that you understand how they are derived.) Both parties adopt the dominant stealing strategy, as they appear always better off no matter what the other side decides to do. But they each end up with 20 percent less of both commodities than would have been available to them from trade! (Observe that this is a non-zero-sum "game"—the gains of one are not the losses of the other; the gains of one only limit the gains of the other.)

(a) Relate this situation to the games with multiple payoffs described in the text.

(b) Suppose that only pelts (or only gold) are of interest to both (or to one) groups. How is the situation and its outcome affected?

(c) It is often said that the above dilemma shows that voluntary agreements to cooperate are bound to be unstable. Assume that both parties, after assessing the individual advantages of stealing, decide to steal together, to form one efficient raiding party and split the loot. Such a joint and voluntary cooperative action would allow the Indians to withdraw only 15 percent of the commodities. Would such a collusion be unstable?

(d) What would be the conditions under which both parties could *voluntarily* engage in trade?

10-4 It is often said that real business games are of the non-zero-sum variety, where the sum of total proceeds is not fixed, where the number of payoffs is large, and where the number of "players" is larger than two. Which of these factors would, in your opinion, have a determining effect on the occurrences in Prob. 10-3? Can you construct a zero-sum game exhibiting the same dilemma?

10-5 Consider the following payoff matrix:

		Other group B	
		Trade	Steal
Our group A	Trade	A: 100, 90* B: 80, 60	A: 60, 50 B: 100, 90
	Steal	A: 100, 100 B: 50, 30	A: 70, 50 B: 70, 50

*Each entry contains the proceeds to both A and B resulting from the adoption of a particular strategy; the first number are pelts, the second gold.

Determine the strategies which are likely to be adopted by both A and B.

10-6 Why is the prisoners' dilemma situation in non-zero-sum games called a "dilemma"? Zero-sum games are very special cases of the broader class of games exhibiting a dilemma. Can a general situation produce a dilemma with respect to its special case? If a strategy which works in a special case is found not to be applicable in a more general case, is it a dilemma? This is a very important issue.

10-7 Consider the following problem:

$$\text{Maximize } f_1 = -x_1 + 2x_2 \quad \text{and} \quad f_2 = 2x_1 + x_2$$

$$\text{subject to} \quad -x_1 + 3x_2 \leq 21$$

$$x_1 + 3x_2 \leq 27$$

$$4x_1 + 3x_2 \leq 45$$

$$3x_1 + x_2 \leq 30 \qquad x_1, x_2 \geq 0$$

(a) Find the set of all nondominated solutions graphically.

(b) Find the ranges of values attainable by f_1 and f_2 over the nondominated set.

(c) On each range decision makers can express the intensity of their preferences by assigning numbers between 0 and 1 (corresponding to unacceptable, so-so, good, very good, excellent, etc.). Obviously the lowest values of the ranges identified in (b) could be assigned 0 and the highest 1. Using $(f_1 + 3)/17$ and $(f_2 - 7)/14$ as "membership functions" for the intermediate values,

(1) Evaluate all nondominated extreme points with respect to their "degree of desirability."

(2) Which points give (1, 1) and (0, 0) assessments of "desirability"?

(3) Select a single point by (i) multiplying the corresponding degrees of desirability and by (ii) choosing always the minimum of the two. Which points give the highest values computed through (i) and (ii)?

(4) Are the types of solutions derived in (3) always nondominated? Can you show why?

10-8[1] The Hardee Toy Company makes two kinds of toy dolls: A produces \$0.40 in profits per doll and B produces \$0.30. Each A requires twice as much time to make as each B. The company has the capacity to make 400 dolls of both types per day or 500 dolls of type B per day. All dolls produced can be sold. A preferred customer always buys all A's produced by Hardee. The company has adopted two objectives: Maximize total profits, and maximize the production of A.

(a) Formulate the Hardee problem as a multiobjective linear-programming problem.

(b) A young MBA argues that maximizing the production of A is sufficient: It is the most profitable product and the preferred customer takes the whole production anyway; no B should be produced. Comment on the suggestion.

(c) Find the set of all nondominated solutions. Find the ideal solution. Find the solutions minimizing the distances L_1 and L_2 from the ideal [use $(f_i^* - f_i)/f_i^*$ for individual deviations].

(d) The following overall utility function was derived by using MAUT:

$$u(f_1, f_2) = -0.2708 (1 - e^{-0.0048f_1}) - 0.1237 (1 - e^{-0.0072f_2})$$

$$+ 3.1725 (1 - e^{-0.0048f_1})(1 - e^{-0.0072f_2})$$

Plot the individual utility transformations of f_1 and f_2 [exponential functions of the form $a(1 - e^{-bf_i})$]. How would one maximize $u(f_1, f_2)$ over the given set of constraints?

(e) Function $u(f_1, f_2)$ in (d) is maximized at 223 of A and 53 of B. Compare this solution with those derived in (c).

10-9 Modify Prob. 10-8 as follows: The preferred customer orders 300 dolls, and the company decides to honor this request as closely as possible within its current capacity restrictions (that is, no overtime, no additional resources).

(a) Formulate the new problem as a *preemptive* goal-programming problem where the highest priority is given to respecting the current capacity constraints, the second priority to approaching the 300 of A goal as closely as possible, and the lowest priority to profit maximization. What is the solution?

(b) The young MBA suggests that the priorities of the last two goals should be reversed. How would this reversal affect the solution found in (a)?

(c) Solve this problem by considering all three goals equally important and using the *non-preemptive version* of goal programming.

10-10 Modify Prob. 6-5b by considering only the numerators of the deviations, ceteris paribus. How are the solutions to both problems related?

(a) Apply the above to the following numerical situation: Maximize $f_1 = x_1, f_2 = x_2$, and $f_3 = x_3$ with respect to $x_1 + x_2 \leq 1, 0 \leq x_1, x_2, x_3 \leq 1$.

(b) Apply the above to the following problem:

---

[1]Adapted from C. L. Hwang and A. S. M. Masud, *Multiple Objective Decision Making—Methods and Applications*, Spring-Verlag, New York, 1979, p. 59.

Maximize $f_1 = -x_1 + 3x_2$

$\qquad f_2 = 2x_1 + x_2$

and $\qquad f_3 = -2x_1 + x_2$

subject to $\qquad -x_1 + x_2 \leqq 1$

$\qquad\qquad\quad x_1 + x_2 \leqq 7$

$\qquad\qquad\quad x_1 \qquad \leqq 5$

$\qquad\qquad\qquad x_2 \leqq 3 \qquad x_1, x_2 \geqq 0$

Consider the weights of f_1, f_2, f_3, to be $w_1 = 0.1$, $w_2 = 0.3$, and $w_3 = 0.6$ respectively. Solve both numerically and graphically.

10-11 Consider the following problem:

Minimize $f = 10w_1 + 8w_2 + 5w_3$

subject to $\qquad 4w_1 + w_2 \qquad\quad \geqq 3, 1, 1$

$\qquad\qquad\quad 2w_1 + 3w_2 \qquad\quad \geqq 1, -1, 2$

$\qquad\qquad\quad 3w_1 + 2w_2 + w_3 \geqq 1, 2, 0$

$\qquad\qquad\quad w_i \geqq 0, i = 1, \ldots, 3$

(a) How is this problem related to Prob. 10-10? Is it its dual?

(b) One of the simplex tableaus corresponding to the above problem is:

	w_1	w_2	w_3	w_4	w_5	w_6			
w_1	1	$\frac{1}{4}$	0	$-\frac{1}{4}$	0	0	$\frac{3}{4}$	$\frac{1}{4}$	$\frac{1}{4}$
w_5	0	$-\frac{5}{2}$	0	$-\frac{1}{2}$	1	0	$\frac{1}{2}$	$\frac{3}{2}$	$-\frac{3}{2}$
w_6	0	$-\frac{5}{4}$	0	$-\frac{3}{4}$	0	1	$\frac{5}{4}$	$-\frac{5}{4}$	$\frac{3}{4}$
	0	$-\frac{11}{2}$	-5	$-\frac{5}{2}$	0	0	$\frac{15}{2}$	$\frac{5}{2}$	$\frac{5}{2}$

where w_4 through w_6 are surplus variables. How do you interpret that $w_1 = (\frac{3}{4}, \frac{1}{4}, \frac{1}{4})$—that is, is it a vector? Substitute the solution indicated by this tableau in the initial problem formulation.

(c) Suppose that we replace the right-hand sides of the initial formulation by:

$$3\lambda_1 + \lambda_2 + \lambda_3$$

$$\lambda_1 - \lambda_2 + 2\lambda_3$$

$$\lambda_1 + 2\lambda_2$$

For any particular combination of λ_1, λ_2, and λ_3 we obtain unique fixed values for the right-hand sides. How could this property be used for the design problem of de novo programming?

10-12 Solve the following multiobjective-programming problem on a computer:[1]

---

[1] Adapted from H. Isermann, "Relevance of Duality in Multiple Objective Linear Programming," in M. K. Starr and M. Zeleny (eds.), *Multiple Criterion Decision Making*, TIMS studies in the Management Sciences, vol. 6, North-Holland Publishing, 1977, pp. 241–262.

$$\text{Maximize} \quad f_1 = 800x_1 + 700x_2 + 1100x_3$$
$$f_2 = 200x_1 + 260x_2 + 190x_3$$
$$f_3 = \quad x_1 + \quad x_2 + \quad 1\tfrac{1}{4}x_3$$
$$\text{subject to} \quad x_1 + \quad x_2 + \quad 1\tfrac{1}{4}x_3 \leq 1000$$
$$x_1 + \quad 1\tfrac{1}{4}x_2 + \quad x_3 \leq 1000$$
$$x_1 \qquad\qquad \leq 800$$
$$x_2 + \quad x_3 \leq 600 \qquad x_1, x_2, x_3, \geq 0$$

(*a*) Find all nondominated extreme point solutions.

(*b*) Let the decision maker specify the following goals to be attained as closely as possible; that is, their underachievement is to be minimized: $f_1 = 900{,}000, f_2 = 200{,}000,$ and $f_3 = 900$. Do not use any "goal-programming" procedure, but consider the following: A solution is *goal-nondominated* (or nondominated with respect to given goals) if there is *no* other solution such that its goal underachievement values would be lower or equal for *all* objective functions respectively.

(*c*) From the nondominated solutions computed in (*a*) select those which are goal-nondominated with respect to (*b*).

(*d*) Can a goal-nondominated solution be dominated? For which set of goal values? Is every nondominated solution necessarily goal-nondominated?

(*e*) Suppose that the goals were fixed as follows:

$$f_1 = 860{,}000 \qquad f_2 = 206{,}000 \qquad f_3 = 1000$$

Which of the solutions in (*a*) is the closest to these goals? Which of the solutions in (*b*) is the closest to these goals? Use $L_1, L_2,$ and L_∞ as the measures of "closeness"; make appropriate assumptions.

10-13 The following constitutes a *dual* formulation of the multiobjective problem in Prob. 10-12.

$$\text{Minimize} \ 1000w_1 + 1000w_2 + 800w_3 + 600w_4$$

$$\text{subject to} \quad w_1 + \quad w_2 + \quad w_3 \qquad\qquad \geq 800, 200, 1$$
$$w_1 + \quad 1\tfrac{1}{4}w_2 + \qquad\qquad w_4 \geq 700, 260, 1$$
$$1\tfrac{1}{4}w_1 + \quad w_2 + \qquad\qquad w_4 \geq 1100, 190, 1\tfrac{1}{4}$$

where

1. Dual variables $w_1 = (w_{i1}, w_{i2}, w_{i3})$ are three-dimensional vectors (corresponding to three objectives in the primal), there are four of them (four constraints in the primal), and they are unrestricted in sign.

2. The inequality signs $\geq$ must be interpreted as follows: There is at least one set of *nonnegative* numbers (weights) $\lambda_1, \lambda_2,$ and λ_3, which makes the linear combination of left-side components equal to or greater than the linear combination of right side components.

    Example $w_2 = (800, 200, 1), w_4 = (-300, 10, -\tfrac{1}{4})$ constitutes a feasible solution to this problem (w_1 and w_3 are zero vectors). Obviously, the first two constraints are satisfied as equalities. Substituting in the last constraint we obtain $(800, 200, 1) + (-300, 10, -\tfrac{1}{4}) = (500, 210, \tfrac{3}{4})$ on the left-hand side. Observe that $500\lambda_1 + 210\lambda_2 + \tfrac{3}{4}\lambda_3 \geq 1100\lambda_1 + 190\lambda_2 + 1\tfrac{1}{4}\lambda_3$ for $\lambda_1 = 0, \lambda_2 = 1,$ and $\lambda_3 = 0$.

(*a*) Compare a primal solution $x_1 = 250, x_2 = 600$ with the dual solution (stated in the Example) in terms of the objectives.

10-14 Consider the following multicriterion simplex tableau, which refers to Prob. 10-12.

	x_1	x_2	x_3	x_4	x_5	x_6	x_7	
x_1	1	0	$-\frac{1}{4}$	0	1	0	$-1\frac{1}{4}$	250
x_2	0	1	1	0	0	0	1	600
x_4	0	0	$\frac{1}{2}$	1	-1	0	$\frac{1}{4}$	150
x_6	0	0	$\frac{1}{4}$	0	-1	1	$1\frac{1}{4}$	550
	0	0	-600	0	800	0	-300	620,000
	0	0	20	0	200	0	10	206,000
	0	0	$-\frac{1}{2}$	0	1	0	$-\frac{1}{4}$	850

(a) Identify the corresponding primal solution. Is this solution nondominated?

(b) The corresponding dual solution, solving Prob. 10-13, can be identified directly in this tableau. How?

(c) Both primal and dual solutions identified above provide identical values for their respective objective function. Thus, they are both nondominated in their respective formulations. Verify.

(d) In the above tableau, consider introducing x_3 into the basis. What is the trade-off vector (gains and losses with respect to all objectives) characterizing such a move?

10-15 Consider the following listing of six nondominated solutions obtained by solving Prob. 10-12:

	f_1	f_2	f_3
x^1	620,000	206,000	850
x^2	752,000	201,600	960
x^3	800,000	200,000	1000
x^4	800,000	200,000	1000*
x^5	816,000	190,400	1000
x^6	860,000	164,000	1000
Goals	900,000	200,000	900

*Solutions x^3 and x^4 are different in terms of decision variables $x_1, x_2,$ and x_3. Verify.

Observe that the goals—say, at x^4—are *under*achieved by 100,000, 0, and 0 and *over*achieved by 0, 0, and 100 respectively. [Verify that x^1 is dominated by x^4 with respect to the (stated) goals.]

(a) Which solutions are goal-nondominated in terms of their underachievement?

(b) Which solutions are goal-nondominated in terms of their overachievement?

10-16 Seiford and Yu (1979) introduced the concept of the *potential solution*. Consider the following problem:

Maximize: $f_1 = x_1 - x_2 + x_3$

$f_2 = 2x_1 + x_2 + 2x_3$

$f_3 = x_1 + x_2 - x_3$

subject to $x_2 + x_3 \leq 1, -1, 2$

$2x_1 + 3x_2 - x_3 \leq -1, 3, 0$

$2x_1 - x_2 \leq 0, 1, -3 \quad x_1, x_2, x_3 \geq 0$

(Observe that the right-hand sides of the constraints are vectors rather than scalars.) A solution to this problem is a potential solution if it is *optimal* for:

Maximize $\lambda_1 f_1 + \lambda_2 f_2 + \lambda_3 f_3$

subject to

$$x_2 + x_3 \leq \gamma_1 - \gamma_2 + 2\gamma_3$$
$$2x_1 + 3x_2 - x_3 \leq -\gamma_1 + 3\gamma_2$$
$$2x_1 - x_2 \leq \gamma_2 - 3\gamma_3 \qquad x_1, x_2, x_3 \geq 0$$

for *positive* values of $\lambda_1, \lambda_2, \lambda_3$ and $\gamma_1, \gamma_2, \gamma_3$.

(a) How does the concept of the potential solution generalize that of the nondominated solution?

(b) The potential solution is a function of γ. Explain.

(c) Verify that $x_1 = (0, \frac{1}{2}, -\frac{3}{2})$, $x_2 = (0, 0, 0)$, and $x_3 = (1, -1, 2)$ constitutes a potential solution. Choose $\gamma = (5, 5, 1)$ and $\lambda = (5, 1, 1)$.

(d) Verify that for the above weights γ we obtain $x_1 = 1$, $x_2 = 0$, $x_3 = 2$.

(e) What is the potential significance of potential solutions?

10-17 Consider the following problem:

Maximize $f_1 = 5x_1 - 2x_2$

$$f_2 = -x_1 + 4x_2$$

subject to $-x_1 + x_2 \leq 3$

$$x_1 + x_2 \leq 8$$
$$x_1 \leq 6$$
$$x_2 \leq 4 \qquad x_1, x_2 \geq 0$$

(a) Draw a graphic representation of this problem.

(b) Compute the points that are closest to the ideal solution with respect to d_1, d_2, and d_∞, the distance measures defined in Sec. 10-1.

(c) Identify the set of nondominated solutions and the compromise set. Discuss the relationship of these two sets.

(d) Perform the same analysis as above in the space of f_1 and f_2 rather than in x_1 and x_2.

10-18 Consider the following problem:

Maximize $f_1 = 10x_1 + 30x_2 + 50x_3 + 100x_4$

$$f_2 = x_1 + x_2$$
$$f_3 = x_1 + 4x_2 + 6x_3 + 2x_4$$

subject to $5x_1 + 3x_2 + 2x_3 \leq 240$

$$3x_3 + 8x_4 \leq 320$$
$$2x_1 + 3x_2 + 4x_3 + 6x_4 \leq 180 \qquad \text{all } x_i \geq 0, i = 1, \ldots, 4$$

(a) Find all nondominated extreme solutions.

(b) Identify the ideal solution.

(c) Compare the following solution $x_1 = 0$, $x_2 = 60$, $x_3 = 0$, $x_4 = 0$ with the ideal with respect to L_1, L_2, and L_∞. (Assume that all objectives are of equal importance.)

10-19 Consider the following simple problem.

Maximize $f_1 = 3x_1 + 5x_2$

$$f_2 = 8x_1 + 4x_2$$

subject to $x_1 + x_2 \leq 10,000$

$$6x_1 + 4x_2 \leq 50,000 \qquad x_1, x_2 \geq 0$$

(a) Verify that $x_1 = -\frac{1}{28}(4f_1 - 5f_2)$. What is x_2 similarly expressed in terms of f_1 and f_2?

(b) In the original constraints, substitute the expressions for x_1 and x_2 found in (a). You should obtain:

$$2f_1 + f_2 \leq 140{,}000$$
$$4f_1 + 9f_2 \leq 700{,}000$$
$$4f_1 - 5f_2 \leq 0$$
$$-8f_1 + 3f_2 \leq 0$$

(c) Prepare graphic representations of both sets of contraints, i.e., the original one in x_1, x_2 space and the one in f_1, f_2 space identified in (b). How are these two sets related? Identify the set of nondominated solutions for both.

10-20 Analyze the following nonlinear problem graphically:

Maximize $f_1 = (x_1 - 4)^2 + (x_2 - 2)^2$

$\qquad\qquad f_2 = (x_1 - 1)^2 + (x_2 - 8)^2$

subject to $x_1^2 - x_2 \leq 0$

$\qquad\qquad x_1^2 + 2x_2 \leq 12 \qquad x_1, x_2 \geq 0$

(a) Identify all nondominated solutions.

(b) Identify the ideal solution. What is the "absolute" ideal?

(c) Interpret solutions $(\frac{4}{3}, \frac{22}{9})$ and $(2, 4)$.

(d) Form $\lambda_1 f_1 + \lambda_2 f_2$ and maximize it with respect to the same constraints. (Use for example $\lambda_1 = \frac{3}{5}$ and $\lambda_2 = \frac{2}{5}$.)

(e) Consider the following problem:

$\qquad$ Max $\quad 1 - |\lambda_1 - \lambda_2|$

subject to $\quad 4\lambda_1 - 2\lambda_2 - 4w_1 - 4w_2 + w_3 \qquad\qquad = 0$

$\qquad\qquad -4\lambda_1 + 8\lambda_2 + w_1 - 2w_2 + \qquad\qquad w_4 = 0$

$\qquad\qquad\qquad\qquad\qquad\qquad\qquad - 2w_3 - 4w_4 = 0$

$\qquad\qquad \lambda_1 + \lambda_2 \qquad\qquad\qquad\qquad\qquad\qquad = 1$

where all variables are nonnegative. What is the optimum solution? Compare the results with (d). What is their relationship?

Most decisions, of course, are made under conditions of risk and uncertainty. Traditionally, the amount of risk inherent in a given project or endeavor is quantified by measuring the dispersion of potential outcomes around the mean, or expected value, of a given probability distribution of returns. The measure of dispersion most favored by statisticians is the *variance* (or its square root, the standard deviation). A small variance implies that the distribution is closely grouped around the mean value, and consequently one can predict the final outcome with a fair degree of accuracy. A large variance implies a high degree of uncertainty as to what the actual outcome is likely to be. In other words, risk is identified with the degree of dispersion of potential outcomes.

One problem with equating risk and dispersion is that high variance implies not only high risk but also the potential for realizing returns well above the mean. Low variance implies high predictability of actual return but with little chance for exceptional outcomes. That is, investing in a low-variance project protects oneself against extremely low returns, but one is also running a "risk" of *not* realizing potentially high returns.

In this chapter we review the current, dispersion-based concepts of risk measurement and show their practical inadequacy as well as their theoretical inaccuracy. Next, we review the concept of *stochastic dominance*, a theoretically sound framework for risk analysis which is, however, plagued by unrealistic requirements for empirical data and other hard-to-obtain information.

MCDM theory allows us to treat risk as one of the attributes or criteria of choice. We introduce the *prospect ranking vector* as a new and multidimensional measure of risk. We use the example of portfolio selection to demonstrate its use. The reader will find again that the concept of an ideal solution plays a central role.

Prospect ranking vector requires the availability of only *partial information*. This allows us to conduct an analysis without explicit knowledge of the probability distributions of returns.

This chapter is probably the most demanding on the reader: It contains rather formal mathematical analysis, and it presumes at least a rudimentary knowledge of probability distributions. Yet the reader should attempt to grasp its major precepts—the analysis of risk is vital in most business endeavors, and the current state of the art is worse than disappointing.

MULTIDIMENSIONAL MEASURE OF RISK

Some financial writers, unfortunately, have come to look upon the standard deviation of the distribution of returns as a measure not only of the variability (which it is) but of the risk inherent in a project (which it is not).

In everyday usage, risk means the probability of a loss or the probability that a return will be lower than some target level.

E. Lerner[1]

A decision maker usually does not know the exact consequences which would eventually result from a choice among several available alternatives. The various possible consequences pertaining to a given alternative can be described only probabilistically; that is, each possible outcome is associated with a (somehow) estimated probability of its occurrence.

In this sense we can speak of risky alternatives. The problem of comparing, ranking, and selecting them can be characterized as the problem of risky choice.

What is risk? How can riskiness be measured? How do decision makers perceive and deal with risk? Can the degree of riskiness be described by a single-dimensional index, or is the risk inherently multidimensional? These and similar questions must be asked and answered before any practical guidance can be offered to decision makers.

Each risky alternative is characterized by a probability distribution defined over its possible (or conceivable) outcomes. According to the nature of the outcomes, such distributions can be continuous or discrete, bounded or unbounded, fully or partially known, subjectively estimated or objectively measured. It is obvious that the riskiness of a given situation is directly related to the position and shape of the probability distribution associated with the outcomes. If only one outcome can occur with a probability of 1—that is, if the "distribution" of probabilities is degenerate, with a single mass point—then no riskiness is perceived or measured.

[1]E. Lerner, *Managerial Finance*, Harcourt Brace Jovanovich, New York, 1971, p. 328.

As we shall see, however, the distribution alone is not sufficient for declaring a situation to be risky or nonrisky. We must ask, Risky with respect to what? Thus, we should speak only of potentially risky alternatives before answering this question.

The major task is as follows: How do we ascertain that one distribution describes a situation which is perceived as being more (or less) risky than a situation described by another distribution? That is, how can we derive a measure of risk on the basis of the attributes of a given distribution?

We shall briefly discuss three basic approaches to the above question: The expected-utility approach, the mean-variance approach, and stochastic dominance.

Expected-utility approach The expected-utility approach does not attempt to measure the riskiness of a given situation as perceived by the decision maker, but rather tries to describe the decision maker's *attitude* toward risk per se, without reference to any particular situation. This is done through structured and subjective interrogation of the decision maker about a battery of hypothetical (and artificial) situations. We shall describe this interrogation process in Chap. 12 in some detail.

Suppose there are n consequences $X_1, X_2, \ldots, X_n$ associated with a given alternative or prospect x. Let the worst consequence be X_1 and the best consequence X_n, and let the corresponding distribution of probabilities of occurrence be $p_1, p_2, \ldots, p_n$. The decision maker is being asked: Consider (1) an option X_i which you could obtain for sure, and (2) a risky option (a lottery, a gamble) characterized by X_n with probability π_i and X_1 with probability $1 - \pi_i$. At what value of π_i would you be indifferent between receiving X_i for sure and engaging in the risky gamble?

The question is repeated for all possible X_i, $i = 1, 2, \ldots, n$. A set of probabilities $\pi_1, \pi_2, \ldots, \pi_n$ is derived. The procedure is further simplified by assigning $\pi_1 = 0$ and $\pi_n = 1$.

The fundamental result of utility theory is that each X_i can be replaced by the corresponding risky option characterized by X_1, X_n, and π_i. Observe that each consequence X_i occurs with probability p_i. The decision maker said that he or she was indifferent between X_i and a π_i chance for X_n and a $(1 - \pi_i)$ chance for X_1. Consequently, π_i and their positive linear transformations can be taken as representing the utilities of individual consequences X_i, that is, u_i (ranging from 0 to 1). The expected utility index is

$$\sum_i p_i u_i = \sum_i p_i(a + b\pi_i) = a + b \sum_i p_i \pi_i$$

The assessment of $u_i = a + b\pi_i$ results in assigning utility indexes u_i to consequences X_i. That is, a utility function u has been constructed so that it assigns a utility $u(X)$ to any possible consequence X over a continuous or discrete range of values.

Depending on the shape of u, the function can be said to reflect a decision maker's risk aversion (u is concave), risk preference (u is convex), or risk neutrality (u is linear); see Fig. 12-1.

This type of risk measure does say something about the decision maker's attitude toward the risky gambles formulated by the analyst. It does not say much about the actual risk content perceived by the decision maker in a real situation.

Mean-variance approach This approach is based on the assumption that a larger mean (or expected value) of a given distribution is preferred to a smaller one, and a smaller variance (dispersion) is preferred to a larger one. The most common risk measure is the variance σ^2 or its square root, standard deviation σ of a distribution characterized by mean $\bar{x}$. A rational decision maker is expected to maximize $\bar{x}$ and to minimize σ^2.

It has become obvious that variance per se does not measure risk. Many researchers have turned to semivariance as an alternative. While variance measures the total dispersion of possible outcomes around the mean, semivariance measures the dispersion of outcomes below some predetermined target value. Business executives' emphasis on "downside risk" indicates that semivariance may be a better approximation of their perception of risk than variance.

However, most executives perceive risk as a *probability* of not achieving a minimum target return. Neither variance nor semivariance seems to be an adequate measure of risk. The same holds true for all proposed combinations of mean and variance, for example, $K\sigma - \bar{x}$, $K > 0$, or a $\sigma^2 - (1 - a)\bar{x}$ with $0 < a < 1$. These are all unidimensional aggregates or indexes, often one-sided and difficult to justify.

Neither approach addresses the fundamental question of risk assessment: Can the risk associated with a given alternative be characterized and measured by a single number? Or is the concept of risk and its perception essentially multidimensional, that is, comprised of a number of incommensurable and therefore irreducible components?

We shall review, in Sec. 11-1, a family of unidimensional measures of risk and show how most current risk concepts are simply special cases of a general unidimensional risk function.

Stochastic dominance approach Because of the problems associated with expected-utility theory, that is, the difficulty of accurately assessing the decision maker's utility function, and because of the inadequacy of single-dimensional indexes in the mean-variance (or semivariance) approaches, much attention has recently been accorded to stochastic dominance.

This approach is based on the assumption that only limited information is available about a decision maker's utility function u. It is assumed that all we can say about u is that it belongs to a broad family of real valued functions U. We shall discuss stochastic dominance in some detail in Sec. 11-2.

What is a portfolio The most common application of risk concepts appears in problems of portfolio selection and management. We have already provided a brief introduction to these problems in Sec. 2-1.1. But what is a portfolio?

We can use the term "portfolio" synonymously with the expression "collection of assets" or, even more generally, "collection of prospects." A portfolio could consist of both financial and real assets: savings deposits, bonds, treasury bills, debentures, equity shares, etc., as well as real estate, antique Persian rugs, jewelry, paintings, antique coins, wines, or other collectibles. Portfolios also may include such prospects as investment ventures—both projected and going concerns.

Portfolio management, then, is the process of defining, evaluating, selecting, maintaining, adjusting, and dismantling an investment portfolio.

We are concerned only with portfolios which are held for the purposes of realizing a return on investment, either monetary or in kind. But there are other portfolios, especially individually held ones, which are solely for the purpose of consumption (that is, some wine cellars) or for purely aesthetic satisfaction. We do not have much to say about the "risk" involved in these important activities.

The large institutional portfolios of insurance companies, banks, corporations, universities, pension funds, building societies, union trusts, etc., are maintained mostly for investment purposes, although they might be subject to stricter and more explicit constraints than individual portfolios.

There is no investment without risk. Risk is one of the major criteria used in assessing a portfolio. It is therefore essential that we know how the risk involved should be measured.

11-1 CURRENT CONCEPTS OF RISK

We say that a prospect return x_i is risky if it is characterized by a probability distribution $F_i(x)$. Let $\bar{x}_i$ and σ_i^2 respectively denote the mean and variance of F_i. The most common risk measures discussed in the literature are all *single-dimensional*. Fishburn (1978) provides a rather complete review of the variety of such risk measures.

Some authors simply use σ_i^2 or σ_i directly, with little regard for the actual investors' risk perceptions and behavior. The risk associated with x_i—say, R_i—can then be measured by

$$R_i = \sigma_i^2 = \int_{-\infty}^{\infty} (\bar{x}_i - x_i)^2 dF_i(x)$$

in the continuous, and

$$R_i = \sigma_i^2 = \sum_{j=-\infty}^{\infty} (\bar{x}_i - x_{ij})^2 p(x_{ij})$$

in the discrete case, where $p(x_{ij})$ designates probability of the jth level of return to the ith prospect, or x_{ij}. Standard deviation $\sigma_i = \sqrt{\sigma_i^2}$ is frequently used in both cases. This measure is often further modified as follows:

$$R_i = \alpha\sigma_i^2 - (1 - \alpha)\bar{x}_i \qquad 0 < \alpha < 1$$

or

$$R_i = k\sigma_i - \bar{x}_i$$

or

$$R_i = \frac{\sigma_i^2}{\bar{x}_i}$$

etc. There is a whole family of risk measures based on *semivariance*

$$R_i = \int_{-\infty}^{t_i} (t_i - x_i)^\alpha \, dF_i(x) \qquad \alpha > 0 \qquad \left(R_i = \sum_{j=-\infty}^{t_i} (t_i - x_{ij})^\alpha p(x_{ij}) \right)$$

One can substitute various parameters for t_i: a desired target level return, the break-even point, or even $\bar{x}_i$. Most writers also prefer to set $\alpha = 2$.

A different type of measure was proposed by Philippatos and Wilson (1972). This one is based on entropy (see Sec. 7-1.2) and it reaches its maximum value for uniform distributions:

$$R_i = -\int_{-\infty}^{\infty} \ln[f_i(x)] \, dF_i(x) \qquad \left(R_i = -\sum_{j=-\infty}^{\infty} [\ln p(x_{ij})]p(x_{ij}) \right)$$

Stone (1973) shows that almost all commonly used risk measures can be viewed as special cases of the family of three-parameter risk measures. This rich and fairly general group of functions provides the research with an infinite variety of "risk measures" through different combinations of appropriate parameter values of c, α, and λ:

$$R_i = \int_{-\infty}^{\lambda} |c - x_i|^\alpha \, dF_i(x) \qquad \left(R_i = \sum_{j=-\infty}^{\lambda} |c - x_{ij}|^\alpha p(x_{ij}) \right)$$

In this general formula, c is a reference level of wealth from which deviations are measured. For example, c could represent $\bar{x}_i$, zero, the initial wealth level, the mode, the median, etc. Parameter α is the power to which deviations are raised, and thus α reflects the relative importance of large and small deviations. For $\alpha = 1$ all deviations are weighted equally, for $0 < \alpha < 1$ small deviations become relatively more important than large deviations. Values $1 < \alpha \leq \infty$ induce the opposite effect, with $\alpha = \infty$ taking only the largest deviation into consideration.

If $\alpha = 0$, we get an important special case, independent of c:

$$R_i = \int_{-\infty}^{\lambda} dF_i(x) = P(x \leq \lambda) \qquad \left(R_i = \sum_{j=-\infty}^{\lambda} p(x_{ij}) \right)$$

that is, the probability of an outcome being smaller than some predetermined level λ.

Parameter λ specifies what deviations are to be included in the risk measure if $\alpha > 0$. Possible choices of the parameter λ include ∞, c, t_i, and some others.

Of course, one can introduce the "root mean deviation power" to obtain a more homogeneous family of measures:

$$R_i = \left[\int_{-\infty}^{\lambda} |c - x_i|^\alpha \, dF_i(x) \right]^{1/\alpha} \qquad \alpha > 0$$

These measures are now entirely analogous with so-called "L_p metrics," common measures of distance discussed in Sec. 6-5. All the measures of risk introduced so far *are* single-dimensional. Most of them have been shown to be theoretically and empirically incompatible with risk-related human behavior. There now exists a body of rapidly expanding literature which attempts to remove the conceptual difficulties of the traditional variance-based measures of risk. Most of this literature simply argues for different values of c, α, and λ without paying sufficient attention to the concept of risk itself. What are the dimensions of risk? How are they perceived by different individuals under different environmental conditions? Why is simplicity often confused with correctness?

It is characteristic of the problem that many researchers seem willing to recommend incorrect or even nonsensical measures for the time being. Typical is this statement by Porter:

> The EV [mean-variance] rule implies violations of the assumptions of rational behavior and leads to decisions that are empirically unjustified. The use of semivariance around the mean as a measure of risk *also leads to incorrect choices* [italics mine], but with less frequency. (Porter 1974, p. 204)

11-2 STOCHASTIC DOMINANCE

If we know cumulative distribution functions $F_i(x)$, then prospect x_1 *stochastically dominates* prospect x_2 if and only if either

$$F_1(x) \leq F_2(x) \qquad \text{for all } x$$

(first-degree stochastic dominance [FSD]) or

$$\int_{-\infty}^{x} F_1(y)dy \leq \int_{-\infty}^{x} F_2(y)dy \qquad \text{for all } x$$

(second-degree stochastic dominance [SSD]).

Third and higher degrees of stochastic dominance are straightforward generalizations of the same concept; see for example Whitmore and Findlay (1977).

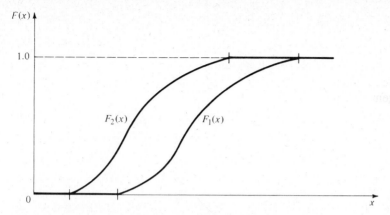

Figure 11-1 Prospect x_1 stochastically dominates prospect x_2.

Figure 11-1 represents first-degree stochastic dominance graphically. If x_1 dominates x_2, as in Fig. 11-1, then x_1 will be preferred by any rational investor. That is, x_1 is less risky than x_2—regardless of their variances.

In Fig. 11-2 we look at the problem of risk through the densities of stochastic returns. Any determined risk averter would choose x_1 even though it has the largest variance. Prospects x_2 and x_3 would not be chosen. Observe that the largest-variance distribution *stochastically dominates* the other two.

In Fig. 11-3 we have concentrated all the relevant information, $\bar{x}_i$ and σ_i^2, on the horizontal axis of the traditional mean-variance space. Assuming normal distributions let us compare two prospects by drawing their densities and cumulative curves so that they correspond to the relative magnitudes of $\bar{x}_i$ and σ_i^2. Both prospects, that is, points $(\bar{x}_1, \sigma_1^2)$, and $(\bar{x}_2, \sigma_2^2)$, are on the efficiency frontier (see Secs. 2-1.1 and 2-4). But any investor would always choose $(\bar{x}_2, \sigma_2^2)$, which assures that the probability of getting less than a fixed return would always be smaller than if $(\bar{x}_1, \sigma_1^2)$ were chosen. Therefore, among the two

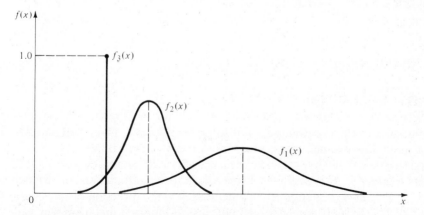

Figure 11-2 Prospects x_2 and x_3 are stochastically dominated by prospect x_1.

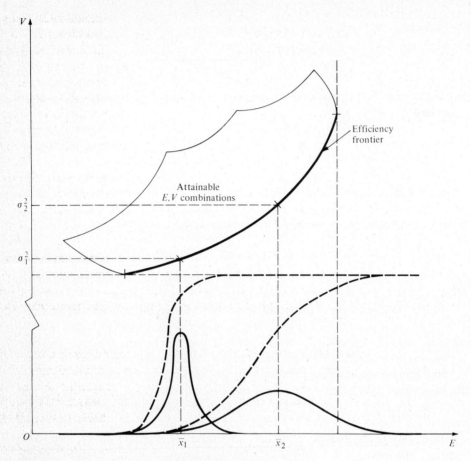

Figure 11-3 "Efficient portfolios" and stochastic dominance.

"efficient" prospects the one with larger variance is infinitely less risky. Why, then, should we measure risk by variance?

11-3 THE PROSPECT RANKING VECTOR

11-3.1 Sketch of the Model

From the previous discussion it follows that "riskiness" is related to the *relative* positioning of the distributions, not to their variances. (We shall actually design a three-dimensional vector measure of risk in Sec. 11-3.2)

Let us assume that a hypothetical measure of risk R_i decreases with smaller σ_i^2 *and* with larger x_i. It is useful to display R_i in the traditional mean-variance space, as in Fig. 11-4. Function R_i now decreases in the direction of the southeast corner. This reflects our previously discussed intuition that a smaller variance indicates less riskiness *only* if coupled with a larger return. In Fig. 11-4 the heavily drawn boundary represents a traditional mean-variance efficiency frontier. Its shaded portion represents a new nondominated set.

Note the point I in Fig. 11-4. This is another version of the well-known *ideal prospect*. It is characterized by the lowest achievable risk as well as the highest achievable expected return. It is, in general, nonattainable. Regardless of the form of a decision maker's utility function, the ideal prospect I would always be preferred by all investors who base their decisions on expected return and risk only.

The current universe of available stocks and other investment possibilities determines the set of feasible prospects. The shape and location of this region defines the position of I. Each decision maker would prefer I to all other prospects or would like to move *as close as possible* to it.

In Fig. 11-4 on the x axis are a few hypothetical density functions reflecting the relative magnitudes of variances taken from the σ^2 axis. Our next goal is actually to design R_i in such a way that all prospects in the nondominated (shaded) set would satisfy the concept of stochastic dominance and also provide some protection against very low returns.

Let us now assume that R_i replaces σ_i^2 so that a proper picture can be drawn, as in Fig. 11-5. Since we do not know the utility function, we have to use I as the point of reference. If both the expected return and the risk are

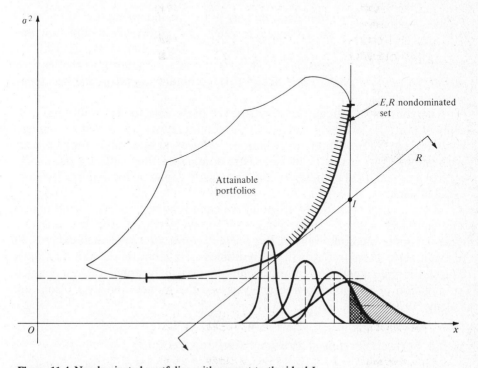

Figure 11-4 Nondominated portfolios with respect to the ideal I.

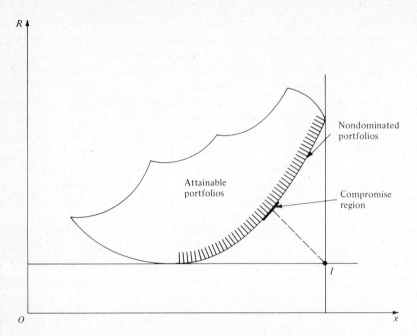

Figure 11-5 Compromise region of nondominated portfolios.

equally important, then the small, heavily drawn boundary section in Fig. 11-5 is the closest to the ideal. Changes in weights of importance would shift this *compromise region* along the nondominated set. Depending on the actual measure R_i, there is also a possibility of reaching inside the interior of the feasible set, in the *solution pocket* (see Sec. 6-6.1), to obtain *stochastically nondominated* prospects.

The concept of stochastic dominance is preferable to the traditional concepts of portfolio selection. Its main shortcoming, however, is that a *complete* knowledge of the probability distribution is a necessary condition for its proper application. Current theory of stochastic dominance thus suffers from an excessive mathematical complexity and unrealistic demands for empirically inaccessible data.

From a purely practical veiwpoint we cannot hope to measure and obtain anything more sophisticated than $\bar{x}$ and σ^2. We shall develop the new risk measure under the conditions of this *partial information*. We shall express all relevant parameters in terms of the multiples of σ_i from the $\bar{x}_i$, and thus most distribution-free inequalities of probability theory can be applied. For a detailed examination of distribution-free analysis see the monograph by Colson and Zeleny (1979).

11-3.2 Formal Version of Prospect Ranking Vector

Consider a set of independent uncertain *returns* x_i associated with investment prospects $i, i = 1, \ldots, n$.

Each x_i can be defined on a given interval, say,

$$x_i \epsilon [a_i, b_i] \subseteq [a, b]$$

where $[a, b]$ may extend over the entire line of real numbers x.

Let $f_i(x)$, $F_i(x)$, $\bar{x}_i$, and σ_i denote the density function, the cumulative distribution function, the mean, and the standard deviation of the ith uncertain return, respectively.

Given two random prospects 1 and 2, the *first stochastic dominance rule* can be summarized as follows (see also Fig. 11-1):

$$1 \succ 2 \Leftrightarrow \begin{cases} F_2(x) \geqq F_1(x) & \text{for all } x \epsilon [a, b] \\ \text{and} \\ F_2(x) > F_1(x) & \text{for some } x \epsilon [a, b] \end{cases} \tag{1}$$

That is, prospect 1 stochastically dominates prospect 2 if and only if the above conditions are true. We can also state that:

$$1 \succ 2 \Leftrightarrow \begin{cases} \bar{u}(f_1) \geqq \bar{u}(f_2) & \text{for all } u \epsilon U \\ \text{and} \\ \bar{u}(f_1) > \bar{u}(f_2) & \text{for some } u \epsilon U \end{cases} \tag{2}$$

where U denotes a class of nondecreasing utility functions, continuous and with a first derivative, and $\bar{u}(f_i)$ denotes the expected value of a utility function defined on f_i. Symbol $\succ$ means "stochastically dominates," and symbol $\Leftrightarrow$ means "if and only if." Thus, any investor not wishing a decrease in wealth would prefer prospect 1 to prospect 2.

Porter and Gaumnitz (1972) have observed that the FSD rule is very sensitive to low returns. Indeed, even a single intersection of the distribution functions F_i can be responsible for rejecting a prospect. Moreover, the lowest possible return, even if it has a very low probability of occurrence, can induce a prospect's rejection. Although protection against very low returns is generally desired, this safety requirement may vary from one individual to another and be situation-dependent as well. Taking this into account we propose a reasonable hypothesis of rational behavior, forming the first decision rule:

1. Prospect 1 will be preferred to prospect 2 if, ceteris paribus, the minimal return a_1 attainable by prospect 1 is greater than the minimal return a_2 attainable by prospect 2:

$$a_1 > a_2 \Rightarrow 1 \succ 2 \tag{3}$$

We would consider it unwise if an investor, all other things being equal, would not choose the prospect yielding *the highest possible minimal return*.

Investors often set a threshold on their required return: *a minimal acceptable return* r_m. Observe that r_m can be interpreted as a minimum threshold or as an a priori investment goal or aspiration level determined by the mth investor.

We may write the first objective function to be minimized as follows:

$$R_{im}^{(1)} = P_i(x < t_m) = P_i(x < \max\{L; r_m\})$$

$$= P_i(x < \max_i\{\max_i a_i; r_m\}) \qquad (4)$$

Thus, in Eq. (4) we have defined the *first component of risk* $R^{(1)}$. The least risky choice among all available investments is the one minimizing the probability P_i of realizing an outcome below the *individual effective threshold return* t_m. Observe that t_m is either the largest of all the smallest realizable returns (L) or the individually determined minimum acceptable return (r_m), whichever is larger.

Equation (4) can be viewed in terms of opportunity costs. Similarly, we can define opportunity costs with respect to high returns. We state our second hypothesis of rational behavior, the second decision rule, as follows:

2. Prospect 1 will be preferred to prospect 2 if, ceteris paribus, the maximum attainable return b_1 of prospect 1 is greater than the maximum return b_2 attainable by prospect 2:

$$b_1 > b_2 \Rightarrow 1 \succ 2 \qquad (5)$$

It would be unwise if an investor seeking maximum returns, would not, all other things being equal, choose the prospect yielding *the highest possible maximum return*.

We can write the second objective function as follows:

$$1 - R_i^{(2)} = P_i(x \geq S) \qquad \text{where } S = \max_i b_i \qquad (6)$$

and $(1 - R_i^{(2)})$ is to be maximized; or, minimize $R_i^{(2)}$, the complement to P_i.

$R_i^{(2)}$ represents the *second component of risk*: The least risky choice among all available investments is the one that minimizes the probability of not realizing the best outcome attainable.

As it is defined here, risk is *not* a single-dimensional concept, but it consists of *at least two* components $R_i^{(1)}$ and $R_i^{(2)}$. Thus, $R_i = [R_{im}^{(1)}, R_i^{(2)}]$ is a risk vector describing the riskiness of the ith prospect. Observe that the first component is more subjective, that is, more closely associated with an individual investor m and the specificity of that investor's position. Their simultaneous consideration is necessary to avoid a pessimistic view, $R_{im}^{(1)}$ alone, or an optimistic view, $R_i^{(2)}$ alone. These two components are consistent with both the habits of the practitioners[1] and the FSD rule.

The consistency of R_i with the FSD rule implies that an investor applying stochastic dominance is not allowed to make any choice which would be contradictory to the one implied by R_i.

Next we present a third hypothesis of rational behavior, that which is based

---

[1] Practitioners scrutinize both the "upside potential" and the "downside risk" of an investment, in the language of Wall Street.

on the knowledge of the first moment (the expected value) of the probability distribution of returns:

3. Prospect 1 will be preferred to prospect 2 if, ceteris paribus, the expected return $\bar{x}_1$ of 1 is greater than the expected return $\bar{x}_2$ of 2:

$$\bar{x}_1 > \bar{x}_2 \Rightarrow 1 \succ 2 \tag{7}$$

Thus, under conditions of risk indifference, when we face linear utility functions, a reliance on expected returns is sufficient.

We shall compose a vector of the three objective functions, the *prospect* (or portfolio) *ranking vector* (PRV). We adjust the components of PRV_{im}, so that the increases in their numerical values correspond to the increases in their desirability, namely:

$$PRV_{im} = (1 - R_{im}^{(1)}, \bar{x}_i, 1 - R_i^{(2)}) \tag{8}$$

We then define a *nondominated prospect* as follows:

Definition A *nondominated prospect* is an attainable prospect for which an increase in value of any one component of PRV_{im} can only be achieved at the expense of a decrease in value of at least one other component.

The set of all such prospects constitutes the *nondominated set*. If we know the first two moments of the distributions (expected value E and variance V), then the nondominated set would replace the traditional E-V efficiency frontier, except under two conditions:

1. When only E and V are known, and they are sufficient to describe the distribution completely—as is the case for the *normal distribution*; or
2. When the utility function is assumed to belong to the class of *quadratic functions*

We define the ideal prospect as the one which *simultaneously* maximizes all three components of the PRV vector. The ideal is thus the best with respect to the three stated hypotheses concerning rational behavior. Following the pessimistic hypothesis, one would choose the prospect which maximizes the first component. Following the risk-indifference hypothesis, one would choose the prospect which maximizes the second component. The prospect which maximizes the third component would be the choice of those following the optimistic hypothesis.

If this ideal prospect is unattainable—the usual case—the decision maker will attempt to move *as close as possible* to it. Only those nondominated prospects which are the closest to the ideal would then be recommended. A discussion of how to measure "closeness" is found in Sec. 6-5.2

Risk components in Eqs. (4) and (6) are only sufficient for comparisons between any two individual prospects. The ranking of *all* prospects, however, requires the knowledge of probabilities that the maximin L and the maximax S

will be reached.[1] Observe that according to Eq. (6) the probability of reaching S would be zero for all prospects. Also, the search for the actual maximin and maximax might not be trivial from a practical viewpoint, and it is actually meaningless for unbounded distributions. We shall redefine L, S, and t_m in terms of available information.

If the first two moments are known for all distributions, one may compute the distance from the mean and express it as a multiple k of the standard deviation. The threshold L in Eq. (4) will thus be determined as

$$L = \max_i(\bar{x}_i - k'\sigma_i) \tag{9}$$

and the threshold S in Eq. (6) will be expressed as

$$S = \max_i(\bar{x}_i + k\sigma_i) \tag{10}$$

Observe that both k' and k may be set equal to zero. In principle, however, they could assume any positive value.

Thus we can summarize:

$$S = \max_i(\bar{x}_i + k\sigma_i)$$

$$L = \max_i(\bar{x}_i - k'\sigma_i) \tag{11}$$

and

$$t_m = \max(L; r_m)$$

11-3.3 PRV under Partial Information

Under conditions of partial information, such as the knowledge of means and variances, an investor does not know the required probabilities. For the two components of risk one must estimate the probabilities $P(x_i \geq K)$ without the benefit of knowing the distribution function $F_i(x)$. Symbol K stands for t_m, L, or S, depending on the consideration of r_m and the PRV components.

We shall use the generalized forms of *Chebyshev inequality* to provide a solution to the problem, although there is a loss of reliability associated with it. We express K in terms of the multiples of σ_i from $\bar{x}_i$, according to Eqs. (9) and (10), and define k_i and k'_{im}:

$$k_i = \frac{S - \bar{x}_i}{\sigma_i} \quad \text{where } S = \max_i(\bar{x}_i + k\sigma_i) \tag{12}$$

and

$$k'_{im} = \frac{t_m - \bar{x}_i}{\sigma_i} \quad \begin{array}{l} L = \max_i(\bar{x}_i - k'\sigma_i) \\ t_m = \max(L; r_m) \end{array} \tag{13}$$

Both Eqs. (12) and (13) imply

$$\bar{x}_i + k_i\sigma_i = S \quad \text{and} \quad \bar{x}_i + k'_{im}\sigma_i = t_m$$

---

[1]L stands for the maximum of all minimal returns a_i—hence "maximin." S stands for the maximum of all maximal returns b_i—hence "maximax." Compare maximin here with the *minimax theorem* discussed in Sec. 10-5.2.

Since we are interested in the probability of deviations from the mean in only one direction, we can use the *Cramér inequality* of probability theory

$$1 - R_i^{(2)} = P(x_i \geq S) = P(x_i \geq \bar{x}_i + k_i \sigma_i) \leq \frac{1}{k_i^2 + 1} \qquad (14)$$

for the third PRV component, and

$$R_{im}^{(1)} = P(x_i \leq \bar{x}_i + k'_{im} \sigma_i) \geq 1 - \frac{1}{k'^2_{im} + 1} \qquad (15)$$

for the first component of risk. We can also express Eq. (15) as follows:

$$1 - R_{im}^{(1)} = P(x_i \geq \bar{x}_i + k'_{im} \sigma_i) \leq \frac{1}{k'^2_{im} + 1} \qquad (16)$$

To summarize, for the *i*th prospect and the *m*th investor we obtain the *prospect ranking vector*, by taking the right-side limits from Eqs. (14) and (16), thus obtaining[1]

$$\text{PRV}_{im} \overset{P}{\Leftrightarrow} \left(\frac{1}{k'^2_{im} + 1}, \bar{x}_i, \frac{1}{k_i^2 + 1} \right)^{\dagger} \qquad (17)$$

Observe that Eqs. (12) to (17) can be used for the general class of probability distributions (discrete, mixed or continuous, unimodal and multimodal, skewed, symmetric, etc.).

We can now define, in analogy with stochastic dominance, decision rules designated as *PRV dominance* and based on partial information: Prospect *j* dominates prospect *l* in the PRV sense, $j \underset{PRV}{\succ} l$, if and only if

$$(a) \quad j \underset{PRV_1}{\succ} l \Leftrightarrow \frac{1}{k'^2_{jm} + 1} \geq \frac{1}{k'^2_{lm} + 1}^{\ddagger}$$

$$(b) \quad j \underset{PRV_2}{\succ} l \Leftrightarrow \bar{x}_j \geq \bar{x}_l$$

$$(c) \quad j \underset{PRV_3}{\succ} l \overset{P}{\Leftrightarrow} \frac{1}{k_j^2 + 1} \geq \frac{1}{k_l^2 + 1}$$

with at least one strict inequality holding.

The majority of theorems and corollaries presented in Colson and Zeleny (1979) contain the probable implications $\overset{P}{\Leftrightarrow}$. Strictly speaking, we should not call them necessary and/or sufficient conditions of partial information. Thus, the inequalities of the above definition are the best guide in cases of imperfect knowledge, but they would often supply misleading conclusions if perfect information about the distributions were available.

Observe that PRV dominance depends on the investor through coefficients r_m, k, and k'. We have already interpreted r_m on p. 395.

---

[1] $\overset{P}{\Leftrightarrow}$ denotes a probable implication.
†This formula is for $k'_{im} > 0$; how would PRV$_{im}$ change for $k'_{im} < 0$? What about $k'_{im} = 0$?
‡For k'_{jm} and $k'_{lm} > 0$; explore implication (a) for k'_{jm} and $k'_{lm} < 0$, $k'_{im} < 0$ and $k'_{lm} > 0$, and $1 + k'_{im} k'_{lm} \leqq 0$.

The assessment of k and k' depends on the investor's confidence in the occurrence of extreme values among different available prospects. The farther the extreme values are from the means, the larger are k and k'. Also, the more optimistic the investor, the larger will be the values for k and $1/k'$. The more pessimistic the investor, the larger will be the values of $1/k$ and k'. Hyperoptimistic is the investor who chooses $k = \infty$ and $k' = 0$, and hyperpessimistic the one who chooses $k' = \infty$ and $k = 0$. Thus, we can represent the whole spectrum of attitudes ranging from a great fear of low returns (k' high) to a speculative liking for high returns (k high).

11-4 CONCLUDING REMARKS

In this chapter we have mostly dealt with financial risk as it relates to problems of portfolio analysis. The reader should be aware that not all risks are financial in nature (although they can usually be expressed in dollar amounts): there are physical risks; technological risks; biological, psychological, and political risks; and so on. There are public risks, individual risks, and average risks as well. Some risks are characterized by very small probabilities of potentially catastrophic loses (or gains), while others involve relatively large probabilities of only mediocre gains or losses. Even the multidimensional concept of risk presented here cannot be presumed to apply to all of this vast area of risk management; all single-dimensional measures of risk, however, can be *safely* ignored.

We are lacking an acceptable and reasonably general definition of risk. Although most humans can intuitively distinguish between risky and nonrisky situations, as they can between life and nonlife, the definition and measurement of risk is equally difficult and elusive. Identical risky situations are often perceived differently by different individuals and human perception of risk is frequently in conflict with its analytical assessment. The risk levels acceptable to some are not acceptable to others. Within the framework of this book we address problems of perception through the perceived ideal point and its displacements, and the problems of acceptability through introducing the minimum acceptable threshold level r_m of a given individual. But our approach is still predominantly analytical.

One conclusion at least, rooted firmly in the PRV approach, is the fact that the acceptability of risk has been found to increase with increasing potential returns and benefits. This is why even so called "zero-risk" programs might not be acceptable if associated with minimal benefits. Risks and benefits are inseparable, jointly perceived and evaluated. Thus the expected level of return is an important component of PRV risk vector.[1]

---

[1]A good overview of the vexing problems of risk assessment, evaluation, and management is C. Starr and C. Whipple, "Risks of Risk Decisions," *Science*, vol. 208, June 6, 1980, pp. 1114–1119.

It appears that the issue of *individual control* over the risk situation is a more important determinant of risk acceptability than the actual risk level involved. In situations characterized by little individual control (air travel, recombinant DNA–research) the acceptable risk levels are much lower than in situations characterized by more substantial individual control (automobile travel, cigarette smoking). People are more adamant about lowering the risks of public programs that are beyond their control, and resist risk regulation in situations perceived to be under their control through free choice. Increasing the possibility of choice among specific-risk level options, rather than striving for all-encompassing zero-risk policy, could be a way toward alleviating many risk-based social conflicts.

There are three basic philosophies pertaining to public risk and its distribution among individuals:

1. Minimize the overall single measure of risk (average risk per person, expected number of fatalities) and accept its differential impacts on specific groups and individuals. Even a very inequitable distribution of risk among individuals could produce the minimum level of risk in the aggregate.
2. Strive for an equitable distribution of risk: an equal amount of risk to each individual. One assumes that a more equitable distribution of risk is preferred to a less equitable distribution. In this approach the aggregate level of risk is only secondary, one does not strive for its minimization. It also assumes that all individuals have nearly equal preferences for risk-benefit trade-offs.
3. Strive for an ideal distribution of risk by creating enough options so that each individual can choose (as closely as possible) his or her preferred risk–benefit combination. Minimization of risk is now dependent on different circumstances and value preferences of groups and individuals.

The first approach, based on optimizing a single aggregate superobjective, is inherently unfair as it leads to inequitable and haphazard treatment of components. The second approach promotes equity by treating all individuals as "equal."[1] They are not equal in the sense of being able to pursue their own objectives and preferences freely, but are assumed to have identical objectives and preferences. The third approach is the MCDM approach: pursuing multiple and incommensurate objectives of individuals and groups.

In public domain there is generally only one measure, program, or option which would minimize the aggregate superobjective, and only one which would result in an equitable distribution. But there would have to be, theoretically, N options available in the marketplace in order to achieve the ideal distribution of

[1]See R.L. Keeney, "Equity and Public Risk," *Operations Research,* vol. 28, no. 3, part 1, May-June 1980, pp. 527–533.

risk among N individuals. Public decision making, too, can proceed either by selecting one from a *given* number of alternatives, or through expanding the set of feasible options by creating *new* alternatives.

The reader is invited to explore the "superobjective" approach in more detail in the next chapter.

11-5 BIBLIOGRAPHICAL NOTE

Although a lot has been written about risky choices, risk attitudes, and risky environments, precious little is available on the actual nature of risk and its measurement. Commonly, decision makers are classified as risk-averse, risk-prone, or risk-neutral types according to their measured attitudes toward "what if" lotteries or "gambles." The reader will find all this nicely summarized in Keeney and Raiffa (1976).

Of course, any decision maker can display all three risk attitudes in different situations and at different times. Colson (1979) attempts to move beyond simple-minded classifications by asserting that every person possesses both speculative and conservative sides.

A common measure of risk is *variance* (or standard deviation) of a given probability distribution of returns. This identification of risk with variance is due to Markowitz (1952, 1959), and it still has its defenders, for example, Samuelson (1970). There are, of course, many critics of the risk-variance approach. It is obvious that a large variance is *both* desirable and undesirable: It points to larger potential losses, but it also implies larger potential gains. Lerner (1971), Baumol (1963), and even Porter (1974) are among its earlier critics.

The concept of stochastic dominance is the strongest "critic" of variance because of its theoretical superiority. Its original exposition can be found in a classic paper by Quirk and Saposnik (1962) and in Hadar and Russell (1969). There is an excellent synthesis of stochastic dominance concepts in Brumelle and Vickson (1975). The book by Whitmore and Findlay (1977) is also recommended. The application of stochastic dominance to portfolio selection is skillfully presented by Bawa (1977).

Fishburn (1978) is a good technical review of common theories of risk measurement. Stone (1973) provides an original insight into the concept that all variance-based measures come from one mathematical family.

The multidimensional approach to risk, as it is sketched in this chapter, can be studied in full detail in an extensive monograph by Colson and Zeleny (1979). Shorter and less detailed expositions are available in Colson and Zeleny (1980) and Zeleny (1978). A similar type of risk measure was also introduced by Heimann and Lusk (1976). Wallin (1978) reports significant computational and empirical experience with this type of risk measure.

Baumol, W. J.: "An Expected Gain-Confidence Limit Criterion for Portfolio Selection," *Management Science*, vol. 10, 1963, pp. 175–182.

Bawa, V. S.: "Mathematical Programming of Admissible Portfolios," *Management Science*, vol. 23, no. 7, 1977, pp. 779–785.

Brumelle, S. L., and R. G. Vickson: "A Unified Approach to Stochastic Dominance," in W. T. Ziemba and R. G. Vickson (eds.), *Stochastic Optimization Models in Finance*, Academic, New York, 1975, pp. 101–113.

Colson, G.: "Towards a Bipolar Theory of Risk," paper presented at TIMS/ORSA National Meeting, New Orleans, April 1979 (to appear in *European Journal of Operational Research*).

—— and M. Zeleny: "Multicriterion Concept of Risk under Incomplete Information," *Computers & Operations Research*, vol. 7, no. 1-2, 1980, pp. 125–143.

—— and ——: *Uncertain Prospects Ranking and Portfolio Analysis under the Conditions of Partial Information,* Mathematical Systems in Economics, no. 44, Verlag Anton Hain, Meisenheim, 1979.

Fishburn, P. C.: "A Survey of Multiattribute/Multicriterion Evaluation Theories," in S. Zionts (ed.), *Multiple Criteria Problem Solving*, Springer-Verlag, New York, 1978, pp. 181–224.

Hadar, J., and W. R. Russell: "Rules for Ordering Uncertain Prospects," *American Economic Review*, vol. 59, 1969, pp. 25–34.

Hanoch, G., and H. Levy: "The Efficiency Analysis of Choices Involving Risk," *Review of Economic Studies*, vol. 36, 1969, pp. 335–346.

Heimann, S. R., and E. J. Lusk: "Decision Flexibility: An Alternative Evaluation Criterion," *Accounting Review*, vol. 51, January 1976, pp. 51–64.

Keeney, R. L., and H. Raiffa: *Decisions with Multiple Objectives*, Wiley, New York, 1976.

Lerner, E.: *Managerial Finance*, Harcourt Brace Jovanovich, New York, 1971.

Markowitz, H.: "Portfolio Selection," *Journal of Finance*, vol. 7, no. 1, 1952, pp. 77–91.

——: *Portfolio Selection: Efficient Diversification of Investments*, Wiley, New York, 1959.

Philippatos, G. C., and C. J. Wilson: "Entropy, Market Risk, and the Selection of Efficient Portfolios," *Applied Economics*, vol. 4, 1972, pp. 209–220.

Porter, R. B.: "Semivariance and Stochastic Dominance: A Comparison," *American Economic Review*, vol. 64, 1974, pp. 200–204.

—— and J. E. Gaumnitz: "Stochastic Dominance vs. Mean-Variance Portfolio Analysis: An Empirical Evaluation," *American Economic Review*, vol. 62, 1972, pp. 438–446.

Quirk, J. P., and R. Saposnik: "Admissibility and Measurable Utility Functions," *Review of Economic Studies*, vol. 29, 1962, pp. 140–146.

Samuelson, P. A.: "The Fundamental Approximation Theorem of Portfolio Analysis in Terms of Means, Variances and Higher Moments," *Review of Economic Studies*, vol. 37, October 1970, pp. 537–542.

Stone, B. K.: "A General Class of Three-Parameter Risk Measures," *Journal of Finance*, vol. 28, June 1973, pp. 675–685.

Wallin, J.: *Computer-Aided Multiattribute Profit Planning*, Skriftserie Utgiven av Handelshögskolan vid Åbo Akademi, Åbo, Finland, 1978.

Whitmore, G. A., and M. C. Findlay (eds.): *Stochastic Dominance: An Approach to Decision Making Under Risk*, Heath, Lexington, Mass., 1977.

Zeleny, M.: "Multidimensional Measure of Risk: Prospect Rating Vector (PRV)," in S. Zionts (ed.), *Multiple Criteria Problem Solving*, Springer-Verlag, New York, 1978, pp. 529–548.

11-6 PROBLEMS

11-1 "Every man's attitude toward risk is characterized by both the speculative and the conservative pole. The same person could be risk-prone when gambling or in the face of bankruptcy, while assuming a risk-averse attitude when facing an investment decision. The fundamental human attitude toward risk is situation-dependent." Explain and comment.

11-2 An "efficient portfolio" is defined by Markowitz as one for which "it is impossible to obtain a greater average return without incurring greater standard deviation; it is impossible to obtain smaller standard deviation without giving up return on the average." (Markowitz, 1952)

(a) Can there be an efficient portfolio which all investors would reject out of hand?

(b) Consider two portfolios A and B, evaluated with respect to their average return and standard deviation (assume they are both efficient):

	Average return	Standard deviation
A	8	2
B	15	4

The most likely outcomes for A lie between $8 - 2 = 6$ and $8 + 2 = 10$; for B they lie between $15 - 4 = 11$ and $15 + 4 = 19$. Other things being equal, under what conditions would an investor prefer A to B? That is, why should the investor be interested in standard deviation per se?

11-3 Consider two competing investment alternatives where the gains achievable by each are dependent on five uncertain events characterized by the probabilities of their occurrence:

Event	1	2	3	4	5
Probability	.3	.25	.2	.2	.05
A_1	100	8	7	10	1
A_2	5	3	4	2	1000

(a) Confirm that if one maximized expected gain, A_2 would be preferred to A_1.

(b) If, however, one wanted to maximize the probability of achieving the better of the two possible outcomes under uncertain conditions, the probability would be .95 for A_1 and .05 for A_2. Verify. Is this a reasonable criterion of choice?

11-4 Investment prospects 1 and 2 are characterized by cumulative distribution functions $F_1(x)$ and $F_2(x)$, defined as follows:

$$F_1(x) = \begin{cases} 0 & \text{for } x < 0 \\ .1 & \text{for } 0 \leq x < 1 \\ 1 & \text{for } x \geq 1 \end{cases}$$

and

$$F_2(x) = \begin{cases} 0 & \text{for } x < 0.1 \\ 1 & \text{for } x \geq 0.1 \end{cases}$$

(a) Compare prospects 1 and 2 in terms of first- and second-degree stochastic dominance. Recall that $F_i(x) = P_i(x_i \leq x)$.

(b) What are the underlying density functions $f_1(x)$ and $f_2(x)$? Are they discrete or continuous? Calculate the following probabilities: $P_1(x_1 = 0)$, $P_1(x_1 = 1)$, and $P_2(x_2 = 0.1)$.

(c) What is the probability that x_1 outperforms x_2, that is, $P(x_1 > x_2)$? Is it larger than .5?

(d) Based on the above analysis, why would you expect prospect 1 to be preferable to prospect 2?

11-5 Prospects 1 and 2 are characterized by discrete outcomes with the following probabilities: $P_1(x_1 = 0) = .4$, $P_1(x_1 = 100) = .6$, and $P_2(x_2 = 99) = 1$. Display graphically their respective $F_1(x)$ and $F_2(x)$.

(a) Compare prospects 1 and 2 in terms of their means and variances, first- and second-degree stochastic dominance, and $P(x_1 > x_2)$.

(b) Why would you expect prospect 2 to be preferable to prospect 1?

(c) Discuss the relative merits of the four criteria used in Probs. 11-4 and 11-5: first- and second-degree stochastic dominance, mean-variance, and the probability of outperformance. Can one rely on any of these criteria exclusively? How would you devise a strategy for their joint use?

11-6 The following problem is due to Blyth.[1] You are to bet on the winner of a foot race among three runners (prospects). Their running times are random variables characterized by the following probabilities:

Minutes		1	2	3	4	5	6
	x_1	0	0	0	1	0	0
Runners	x_2	.22	0	.22	0	.56	0
	x_3	0	.49	0	0	0	.51

Observe, for example, that the probability of the first runner winning is $P(x_1 < x_2 < x_3) + P(x_1 < x_3 < x_2) = .2856 + 0 = .2856$.

(a) Which runner has the highest probability of winning?

(b) Calculate $P(x_1 < x_2)$ and $P(x_1 < x_3)$. How do you reconcile these probabilities with the results obtained in (a)?

11-7 Consider nine mutually exclusive investment prospects with returns defined on [0, 100] and characterized by the following probabilities:

Return	0	1	10	50	78.83	81	99	100
Prospect 1	0	0	1	0	0	0	0	0
2	0	.5	0	0	0	.5	0	0
3	0	.1	0	.8	0	0	.1	0
4	0	0	.1	.4	0	.4	.1	0
5	0	0	.1	.3	.6	0	0	0
6	0	0	.1	.3	.1	.4	.1	0
7	1	0	0	0	0	0	0	0
8	e	0	$.1 - e$	.3	.1	.4	.1	0
9	$1 - e$	0	0	0	0	0	0	e†

†Symbol e represents an extremely small number

[1] C. R. Blyth, "Some Probability Paradoxes in Choice from among Random Alternatives," *Journal of the American Statistical Association*, vol. 67, 1972, pp. 366–373.

(a) Interpret individual prospects with respect to the nature of their returns. For example, prospect 7 could represent hoarding of cash at home, prospect 1 the bank deposit, and so on.

(b) Evaluate the prospects with respect to the following ranking characteristics: σ_i^2, $R_{gm}^{(1)}$, $\bar{x}_i$, $R_i^{(2)}$, $(\sigma_i^2, \bar{x}_i)$, FSD, SSD, and PRV$_{im}$. Interpret these eight criteria, decide on their minimization, maximization, or nondominance screening.

(c) Explore the impact of different levels of r_m on the rankings obtained in (b). Consider $r_m \leqq$ 10, $10 < r_m \leqq 50$, $50 < r_m \leqq 78.83$, $78.83 < r_m \leqq 81$, $81 < r_m \leqq 99$, $99 < r_m \leqq 100$.

(d) Summarize your observations and discuss relative merits of individual criteria. Prepare a short paper justifying your recommendation of a particular prospect for investment (they are mutually exclusive). Pay special attention to prospect 6.

(e) According to PRV analysis, the ideal prospect is characterized by the following vector: $(1, 66.18, e)$. Compare all prospects with the ideal.

11-8 Governments are spending large amounts of money in order to alleviate innumerable risks and hazards faced by individuals in a high-technology society. Transportation risks especially are increasingly regulated. Many programs are politically appealing as they obviously decrease the average number of fatalities or the average probability of a fatality per person. Because the value of human life is so difficult to assess, many governmental programs are acceptable to the public. Consider comparison of programs in terms of added life expectancy per dollar spent:

a. Reducing the carbon monoxide in auto emissions from 15 grams/mile to 3.4 grams/mile costs $500 million per life saved or $25 million for one person to live a year longer.
b. Introducing a specialized ambulance service to treat victims of heart attacks would cost $500 for one person to live a year longer.

Why are governments spending more on programs of type a than on programs of type b? Should the criterion of change in life expectancy per dollar spent be considered?

11-9 Let us define risk as the probability p_i that individual i will become a fatality. Let the number of individuals at risk be N. Observe that the average risk per person is $\bar{p} = (1/N) \sum p_i$ and the expected number of fatalities is $\bar{x} = \sum_i p_i = N\bar{p}$. Evaluate the following programs characterized by vectors $(p_1, p_2, \ldots, p_N)$:

1. $(1/N, 1/N, \ldots, 1/N)$
2. $(1, 1, \ldots, 1)$ with probability $1/N$ and $(0, 0, \ldots, 0)$ with probability $(1 - 1/N)$
3. $(1/N + e, 1/N - e, 1/N, \ldots, 1/N)$
4. $(.01, .01, \ldots, .01)$ for $N = 100$
5. $(.4, .4, 0, \ldots, 0)$ for $N = 100$
6. $(.5, .5, 0, \ldots, 0)$ for $N = 100$
7. $(1, 0, \ldots, 0), (0, 1, 0, \ldots, 0), \ldots, (0, \ldots, 0, 1)$ each with probability $1/N$

Compare specifically the following pairs: 1 and 2, 1 and 3, 4 and 5, 6 and 7.

11-10 Many analysts are prone to measure the value of human life in terms of the expected value of the stream of dollar income over the expected number of remaining years of life. Discuss the implications of this criterion for those who are handicapped and unable to work, persons permanently dependent on expensive life-support machinery, lifelong work volunteers, self-reliant farmers, star talk-show hosts, 90-year-old geniuses, and 1-year-old imbeciles.

11-11 Many people who intuitively fear travel by airplane are all too willing to travel by automobile even though aviation is statistically safer. Discuss in terms of *risk perception* and the degree of individual *control over risk*.

TWELVE

In this chapter we summarize one of the oldest theories of decision analysis, utility theory, and a more recent version of it, multiattribute utility theory. The reader might ask why MAUT, a *single*-criterion approach to maximization of utility (or expected utility), is included in a text on *multiple* objectives or criteria? The answer is simple: It provides a point of reference, a measure of our progress, the point of our departure.

First, we elaborate the concept of trade-off, using a simple example of automobile selection. Then we provide a rather detailed description of the steps involved in assessing a utility function. The decomposition of global utility into its constituent components is summarized in its different forms in Table 12-1. Section 12-4.5, dealing with the alternate handling of risk via lottery evaluations, is particularly important. After completing the five basic steps of utility assessment, we turn to a more promising and livelier extension of this theory—*interactive evaluation procedures*.

Interactive procedures do not aim at identifying a decision maker's utility function but are concerned with solving the decision problem itself. No artificial lotteries are evaluated; no indifference judgments are required. Situation-dependent preferences, expressed only in terms of their lower and upper bounds, are all that is needed. It is in this interactive approach that MAUT interfaces with MCDM—another good reason for including this chapter in our book. Again we use a practical case of automobile selection to demonstrate the main features of interaction.

MAUT has often been applied to problems involving multiple decision makers. We have already dealt with this problem in Sec. 10-5.1, and now we return to it by providing an account of one particular application: The trajectory selection problem in a space exploration project.

MULTIATTRIBUTE UTILITY MEASUREMENT

Without the precision and formalism of rationalist theory, we would almost certainly have made less progress in developing descriptive insights; it has provided axioms to be challenged, hypotheses to be opposed by counterexamples, and a vocabulary that we need to use even to disagree with it. For example, the concept of consistent, absolute utility functions has been invaluable in all theories of decisionmaking, especially those that argue such functions are nonexistent.

Peter G. W. Keen and
Michael S. Scott Morton[1]

Multiattribute utility theory evaluates utility functions intended to accurately express a decision maker's outcome preferences in terms of multiple attributes. MAUT grew out of the unidimensional utility theory and its central dogma of "rational" behavior: If an appropriate utility is assigned to each possible outcome and the expected utility of each alternative is calculated, then the best course of action for *any* decision maker is the alternative with the highest expected utility.

MAUT tends not to replace unidimensional utility functions defined over single attributes. Rather, it reduces the complex problem of assessing a multiattribute utility function into one of assessing a series of unidimensional utility functions. Such individually estimated "component" functions are then glued together again; the "glue" is known as "value trade-offs."

Determining the trade-off often requires the subjective judgment of the decision maker, who must reflect deeply on the question, How much achievement in terms of a given objective am I willing to give up in return for improved, specific achievement in another objective?

Because answering (and asking) such questions is essential in MAUT, we shall start this chapter with intuitive examples of decision situations, questioning, trade-offs, and explicit formalization of a decision maker's value structures.

[1]*Decision Support Systems: An Organizational Perspective*, Addison-Wesley, Reading, Mass., 1978. p. 65.

12-1 OVERVIEW AND INTRODUCTORY EXAMPLES

We shall illustrate several key concepts of MAUT by using a simple and intuitively appealing decision situation. When deciding which automobile to purchase we often face the dilemma of multiple conflicting objectives, for example:

1. Minimize cost (cash or financed price in dollars)
2. Maximize performance (in horsepower)
3. Maximize economy (in miles per gallon)
4. Minimize value depreciation (percent of the purchase price recoverable 5 years from now)
5. Minimize maintenance and insurance costs (in dollars per year)
6. Maximize overall appeal (on a scale from 1 to 5, where 1 is ugly and 5 is beautiful)

Of course, these are not the only criteria which could have a bearing on the final decision. Different decision makers would consider different criteria, for example, safety features, exhaust emissions, size, weight, the feel of the ride, noise, interior appointments, styling, manufacturer's reputation, dealer's reputation, or financing available.

The main purpose of MAUT is to establish a superobjective, to *maximize the overall utility*, as the criterion for selecting an automobile. Objectives, such as the six listed above, would be the *attributes* of the available alternatives, and a utility function would be constructed on their basis.

Each available automobile, or alternative of choice, could then be conveniently represented as an ordered sextet of attribute levels of cost, horsepower, economy, depreciation, maintenance, and appeal. For example, cars A, B, and C could be described as follows:

$$A = (\$3000, 120 \text{ hp}, 30 \text{ mi/gal}, 40\%, \$1600, 3)$$

$$B = (\$3500, 140 \text{ hp}, 21 \text{ mi/gal}, 30\%, \$2000, 4)$$

$$C = (\$3600, 130 \text{ hp}, 25 \text{ mi/gal}, 50\%, \$1800, 5)$$

How should one go about making a choice of this type? We all make these decisions sometimes, somehow. But how can we make them more correctly, more precisely, and on a larger scale?

One approach is based on direct estimation of the decision maker's tradeoffs. Dyer (1973) and Geoffrion, Dyer, and Feinberg (1972) have developed interactive computerized procedures that assist the decision maker in determining the necessary trade-off information and arriving at a final choice (Sec. 10-6).

The trade-off process can be illustrated by examples of its procedural stages. Suppose we choose one particular alternative, say, $A = (\$3000, 120 \text{ hp}, 30 \text{ mi/gal}, 40 \text{ percent}, \$1600, 3)$, as a point of reference. Then we might interrogate the decision maker as follows: "Consider automobile A, but suppose that we shall reduce its gas mileage from 30 to 20. How much cheaper would A have to be before you would be *indifferent* between buying A and its new version, $A_1 = (?, 120$ hp, 20 mi/gal, 40 percent, \$1600, 3)?''

The decision maker could derive the answer as follows: Estimate the number of years before trading the present car A_1 in, then multiply by the number of miles driven in a year to get the total mileage. Divide the result by the gas mileage to figure the amount of gas to be used, and multiply by the price of gas. The total outlay for gas for car A_1, based on 10,000 miles per year, trade-in after 5 years, and an average price of \$0.60 per gallon, is \$300 per year as compared with \$200 per year based on a mileage of 30 mi/gal for car A. The decision maker might even figure that this \$100 of additional cost, that is, \$500 over the 5-year period, represents something like \$380 today, considering a discount rate of 10 percent. (The net present value of \$500 savings over the next 5 years, \$100 per year, is about \$380 at a 10 percent discount rate.) That is, the decision maker would have to be given \$380 now in order to consider spending an extra \$500 over the next 5 years.

After pondering some intangibles and additional nonquantifiable criteria, the decision maker might agree that it would probably take a \$400 cut in price to make the choice indifferent between car A and the proposed alternative A_1. That is, the decision maker would be indifferent between

$$A = (\$3000, 120 \text{ hp}, 30 \text{ mi/gal}, 40\%, \$1600, 3)$$

and
$$A_1 = (\$2600, 120 \text{ hp}, 20 \text{ mi/gal}, 40\%, \$1600, 3)$$

being willing to give up 10 mi/gal for a price reduction of \$400. The trade-off value of 1 mi/gal is then about \$40.

Through similar questioning we would determine the decision maker's trade-off values between price and horsepower, price and depreciated (resale) value, price and maintenance costs, and price and appeal. Note that all trade-offs are expressed in terms of price and that other relevant comparisons, such as horsepower versus miles per gallon, miles per gallon versus other maintenance, or depreciation versus appeal are not considered in this approach.

Suppose that the decision maker would pay \$100 for an additional 10 horsepower, \$200 for upgrading the appeal from 3 to 4, \$250 for each 10 percent of lower depreciation, and \$50 for each \$100 of lower maintenance costs. Alternative A could then be characterized in terms of its relevant trade-off values *only*: $A = (\$100, \$40, \$250, \$50, \$200)$, representing the horsepower, miles per gallon, depreciation, maintenance, and appeal trade-offs in that order.

The interactive assessment of trade-offs must be repeated also for automobiles B, C, and any other alternatives considered. All the alternatives are then expressed in terms of commensurable dollar trade-off values, and the decision maker may attempt to compare them directly at this point.

It must be assumed that expressions of indifference are fully *transitive*, that is, a decision maker who is indifferent between A and A_1 and between A_1 and A_2 is also indifferent between A and A_2. This assumption is extremely important;

otherwise, many more questions would have to be asked, and multiple trade-off values could characterize a pair of attributes compared for the same alternative of choice. (See Sec. 5-3.3 for a more detailed discussion of transitivity.)

Estimated trade-offs should also be reliable, constant over a reasonable period of time, easy to obtain, not too numerous, and intuitively clear. Large numbers of attributes, large numbers of alternatives, inconsistent or impatient decision makers, incompetent interviewers, changing preference structures, and the vagueness of some comparisons (appeal versus price) would tend to make the trade-off process clumsy, difficult to use, and ultimately ineffective. Even though the described trade-off process does not require an explicit evaluation of a decision maker's preferences as a function of the attributes and their levels (utility function), it is time-consuming and applicable only to simple problems of very low dimensionality.

If there is a large number of alternatives (but still relatively few criteria), it is preferable to attempt an explicit assessment of the overall utility function, u(price, horsepower, miles per gallon, depreciation percent, maintenance costs, appeal), of the applicable multiple attributes. Then it is no longer sufficient to rely on simply interviewing the decision maker; additional assumptions must be introduced.

One of the most common assumptions is that function u is *additive*. This means that it can be written as follows:

u(price, hp, mi/gal, depreciation percent, maintenance costs, appeal)
$= \lambda_1 u_1(\text{price}) + \lambda_2 u_2 (\text{hp}) + \lambda_3 u_3 (\text{mi/gal}) + \lambda_4 u_4 (\text{depreciation percent})$
$\qquad\qquad\qquad + \lambda_5 u_5 (\text{maintenance costs}) + \lambda_6 u_6 (\text{appeal})$

where $u_1, \ldots, u_6$ are unidimensional utility functions defined over single attributes, and $\lambda_1, \ldots, \lambda_6$ are scaling constants or "weights."

Additivity and the determination of individual u's and λ's require *independence* of attributes. For example, a decision maker's preferences regarding the price of a car should not be affected by changes in its gas mileage. Even though the buyer would be willing to trade off money against mileage, a price of $3000 should be considered equally desirable (or undesirable) whether the car delivers 30 or 20 mi/gal. That is, u_1 ($3000) can be assessed by a single number—say, u_1 ($3000) = 0.6 on the utility scale from 0 to 1—for both 30-mi/gal and 20-mi/gal levels. Obviously, without such an assumption of independence the individual utility functions could not be assessed. For $3000 is $3000 is $3000—or is it?

For most decision makers the "value" of lower price is simply worth less if gas mileage is very low, 10 mi/gal, for example, than if it is something like 30 mi/gal. The two attributes, price and mileage, are *not* independent. Especially in view of the steadily increasing cost of gasoline, both could be related to a more specific objective of the decision maker: minimize overall automobile-related expenses over the next 5 years. Cash price and gas mileage do not have intrinsic values of their own. It is their *relationship* that matters; they are hardly independent. The use of an additive utility function would be difficult to substantiate over the given set of attributes.

One has to *redefine the objectives*, i.e., combine purchase price and gas mileage into an overall automobile cost over the 5-year period. This could be achieved by adding purchase price, gasoline costs, and maintenance costs, all properly discounted over 5 years. One could then subtract the expected resale or trade-in value and use total cost as a criterion. A typical automobile would then be characterized by the triplet of total cost, horsepower, and appeal.

We must test, of course, whether total cost, horsepower, and appeal are mutually independent attributes. If they are not, we have to resort to additional combinations of attributes.

What if one cannot find a truly independent set of attributes and objectives? We might ultimately discover that the overall utility function u is not decomposable into its components, that it must be assessed holistically, as an irreducible unity.

Consequently, one of the most important tasks of MAUT is to *verify* the independence of attributes. It is generally quite difficult for humans to say whether attributes are independent. Analysts usually try to help by confronting the decision maker with a battery of *lottery* questions.

For example, choose any arbitrary values of attributes, say, ($3000, 120 hp, 30 mi/gal 40 percent, $1600, 3) and ($3500, 140 hp, 21 mi/gal, 30 percent, $2000, 4). Offer these two alternatives to the decision maker as a lottery with a 50/50 chance of getting either one. Then *switch* the values of horsepower between the two alternatives, leaving all other attribute levels unchanged. Offer the decision maker a new 50/50 lottery between ($3000, 140 hp, 30 mi/gal, 40 percent, $1600, 3) and ($3500, 120 hp, 21 mi/gal, 30 percent, $2000, 4). If the decision maker feels that the attributes of horsepower and price are independent, the choice between the two lotteries (*not* alternatives) should be indifferent. Several such lottery comparisons should be used to verify the independence reliably.

After independent attributes suitable for analysis have been established, all individual single-attribute utility functions must be constructed. Again, the lottery approach is used (see Sec. 12-4.5).

Similarly, the scaling factors λ_i must be determined. These "weights," unfortunately, do not measure the relative importance of each attribute. Their intuitive interpretation, and thus the intuitive appeal of the additive utility decomposition, is not among the strongest aspects of MAUT. These constants *do* reflect the relative importance of each attribute as it changes from its worst available to its best available value. They indicate the relative importance of, say, total cost changing from $8000 to $3500, as compared to horsepower changing from 50 hp to 250 hp or appeal from 1 to 5. Again, the lottery approach can be used to answer such questions, and we provide the details in Sec. 12-4.6.

After ascertaining that the sum of the "weights" is equal to 1, as it must be for the additive decomposition of u, we shall finally be able to explicate the estimated utility function. For example, we could derive something like

u(total cost, hp, appeal) $= 0.75u_1$(total cost) $+ 0.05u_2$(hp) $+ 0.2u_3$(appeal)

where u_1, u_2, and u_3 would be estimated and available as specific functions.

This overall utility function u is then used for evaluating *all* available alternatives by simply substituting their appropriate attribute levels in the formula and searching for the highest value of u.

It is apparent that this approach places very high demands on a decision maker's judgments in terms of their complexity as well as numbers. We shall, nevertheless, develop MAUT in more detail in the next sections because its techniques are well known, often applied, and invaluable in describing the logic of optimal choice.

Because of the heavy information burden generated by the conventional approach to MAUT by Keeney and Raiffa (1976), there have been attempts to design interactive procedures which would significantly reduce the amount of information required. This research has been spearheaded by Sarin (1977). We shall discuss its basic ideas in Sec. 12-5. Sarin's evaluation and bound procedure can be fully computerized, its works even with imprecise data, and it represents an important step toward more human-oriented decision support systems. But first let us study the traditional MAUT in more detail.

12-2 ON NOTATION AND PURPOSE

Each alternative of choice is characterized by a set of attributes, criteria, or objectives.

We shall denote the alternatives of choice in two ways. If only two or three are being compared, we shall simply use the letters x, y, and z. If we need to list a larger number of them or for generalization purposes, we shall use a *superscript* numbering system $k = 1, 2, \ldots, m$. For example, $x^1, x^2, \ldots, x^m$, with the general symbol x^k, represent a listing of m alternatives of choice. But here we shall usually use only the first letter x.

Similarly, we shall denote attributes in two ways, either with capital letters X, Y, and Z (usually for definitions or qualitative statements) or, more frequently, with a *subscript* numbering system, $i = 1, 2, \ldots, n$. For example, x_1, $x_2, \ldots, x_n$ with the general symbol x_i, represent a set of attribute levels characterizing alternative x.

This notation allows numerous combinations. Two alternatives x and y can be evaluated with respect to n attributes, that is, each is characterized by a vector of n numbers:

$$x = (x_1, \ldots, x_n) \quad \text{and} \quad y = (y_1, \ldots, y_n)$$

Or, if we use the superscript numbering system, two alternatives x^1 and x^2 are expressed in the following way:

$$x^1 = (x_1^1, \ldots, x_n^1) \quad \text{and} \quad x^2 = (x_1^2, \ldots, x_n^2)$$

Thus, the general symbol x_i^k designates the level of attribute i achieved by alternative k. For example, if k denotes two different automobiles, 1 signifies price, and 2 signifies horsepower, then x_1^1 is the price of the first car, x_1^2 is the price of the second, x_2^2 is the horsepower of the second car, etc. The following table shows m alternatives evaluated with respect to n attributes:

Attributes i \ Alternatives k	Car 1	Car 2	$\cdots$	Car m
1 (price)	x_1^1	x_1^2	$\cdots$	x_1^m
2 (horsepower)	x_2^1	x_2^2	$\cdots$	x_2^m
$\vdots$	$\vdots$	$\vdots$	$\vdots$	$\vdots$
n (styling)	x_n^1	x_n^2	$\cdots$	x_n^m

Let us consider two alternatives of choice, $x = (x_1, \ldots, x_n)$ and $y = (y_1, \ldots, y_n)$ characterized by n-dimensional vectors of attribute scores or objectives. The decision maker must choose between them, and we are to create a model capable of predicting the choice.

Utility theory states that it is adequate to specify a scalar-valued function u which assigns a number called the "utility index" that "measures" the preferability or worthiness of each alternative. The decision maker then chooses the alternative with the highest utility index. If there is a function u such that

$$u(x_1, \ldots, x_n) \geqq u(y_1, \ldots, y_n)$$

whenever the decision maker either prefers x to y or is indifferent between the two, then the function u is a utility function. If the decision maker's actual choices and the mathematically implied choices imposed by u agree over a large range of situations, then we say that u "captures" the preference structure of the decision maker.

There is nothing in human experience to indicate that humans actually employ such global utility measures. Yet, people do exhibit *some* consistency in their preferences, tastes, and choices. Therefore, it is theoretically possible to construct models (utility functions) that predict decision-making behavior over certain classes of situations. These models are not explanatory and do not reveal any causal mechanisms, despite their potential predictive power. Utility function assessment, that is, the complete formalization of the preference structure, is not directed toward revealing how people actually go about making their decisions.

Although this issue brings us to the edges of philosophy, it is worthwhile to explore its implications. Explanation and prediction, exemplified by descriptive and prescriptive models, are interdependent concepts, "conflicting" objectives in most scientific inquiry. Yet increased predictive power can be viewed as a by-product of advancing coherent explanations or better descriptive models. Nor is there anything inherently contradictory in this approach. The best prescriptive (or normative) model is a sound descriptive model. Moreover, it is possible to single out the predictive capacity of a model as the main objective of inquiry, regardless of its explanatory powers. This is the road taken by modern utility theory and by multiattribute utility theory in particular.

Unfortunately, prediction and explanation are not concepts of equal significance. Following Harvey Leibenstein (1976), it can be argued that the purpose of scientific theories should be to obtain explanations of phenomena and events. Predictive capacity without explanatory capacity is secondary. Only predictive capacity that arises from coherent and communicable explanations has scientific standing. Explanation without prediction is sufficient, but prediction without explanation is of doubtful scientific consequence—it belongs to the category of ESP, clairvoyance, and intuition.

12-3 UTILITY DECOMPOSITION MODELS

It is a major effort of multiattribute utility theory to avoid the problem of direct assessment of $u(x_1, \ldots, x_n)$. Deriving $u_i(x_i)$, that is, utility functions for a single numerically scaled attribute x_i, is difficult enough. Why should we attempt to deal with higher-dimensional cases before succeeding completely in one-dimensional space? One method of dealing with the problem is to decompose a multiattribute utility assessment into a series of single-attribute assessments.

More formally, one may ask, Can we find a decomposition function f such that

$$u(x_1, \ldots, x_n) = f[u_1(x_1), \ldots, u_n(x_n)]$$

where u_i designates a utility function over a single attribute x_i? Depending on the exact form of f it is then necessary to obtain at least n individual component assessments. For example, one of the simplest decomposition functions is a simple additive function, a linear combination of individual component functions:

$$u(x_1, \ldots, x_n) = \lambda_1 u_1(x_1) + \cdots + \lambda_n u_n(x_n)$$

where x_i is a measure of the extent to which a given alternative possesses the ith attribute, u_i is the unidimensional utility function of the ith attribute, and λ_i represents relative weights of importance, indicating how much of one attribute the decision maker is willing to sacrifice in order to gain a particular amount of another attribute.

The assessment of the compound utility function can be broken down into its component parts in a large variety of ways. The decomposition is usually based on a number of assumptions (independence axioms) which must be verified before any particular decomposition model can be applied. Most important of these assumptions are the concepts of preferential and utility independence of attributes. We shall discuss these assumptions in Sec. 12-4.2, providing only a simple summary of various decompositions here.

Because rather cumbersome expressions are obtained for higher-dimensional cases, we shall limit our comparative review to three attributes only. The most common utility decomposition models are presented in Table 12-1.

The decision maker is expected to choose the decomposition model which best fits a given decision situation. Certain assumptions of attribute independence must be tested. Then one has to determine the unidimensional utility functions $u_i(x_i)$ or $f_i(x_i)$. In some decompositions, for example quasipyramid, semicube, etc., one has to evaluate nonseparable interactions, that is, utility functions containing several attributes, $u_{ij}(x_i, x_j)$ for example. Next, one has to assess the necessary number of weights and scaling factors λ_i, λ_{ij}, λ_{ijk}, and k.

Scaling factors or weights can be determined in many different ways. For example, the multiplicative form involves weights λ_i and a scaling factor k. Utility functions u_i are scaled from 0 to 1, and the role of k is to assure that the compound utility function u will also assume values in the interval 0 to 1. Thus, k is deduced from the λ_i's. If we assume that $\lambda_1 + \lambda_2 + \cdots + \lambda_n = 1$, then $k = 0$, and we can see that the multiplicative decomposition reduces to the weighted additive decomposition. Only when the sum of relative weights is not equal to 1,

$$\sum_{i=1}^{n} \lambda_i \neq 1$$

does $k \neq 0$, and the multiplicative form is of interest.

Observe that the multiplicative form is a special case of the quasiadditive form ("additive model with interaction terms," as it is often called), as it requires only n parameters to be estimated and not $2^n - 1$ as is required for the latter form. Why is it called a "multiplicative" form? We can rewrite it as

$$ku(x_1, x_2, x_3) + 1 = [k\lambda_1 u_1(x_1) + 1][k\lambda_2 u_2(x_2) + 1][k\lambda_3 u_3(x_3) + 1]$$

Similarly observe that both the additive and multiplicative functions are special cases of the multilinear decomposition.[1]

---

[1]Note that as the number of attributes increases beyond three, we find the decomposition formulas rather complex and unappealing. For example, the multilinear decomposition for n attributes yields the following expression:

$$u(x) = \sum_{i=1}^{n} \lambda_i u_i(x_i) + \sum_{i=1}^{n} \sum_{j>i} \lambda_{ij} u_i(x_i) u_j(x_j)$$

$$+ \sum_{i=1}^{n} \sum_{j>i} \sum_{k>j} \lambda_{ijk} u_i(x_i) u_j(x_j) u_k(x_k)$$

$$+ \cdots + \lambda_{123\cdots n} u_1(x_1) u_2(x_2) \cdots u_n(x_n)$$

Table 12-1 Common utility decompositions

Model	Three-attribute representation
Additive	$u(x_1, x_2, x_3) = u_1(x_1) + u_2(x_2) + u_3(x_3)$
Weighted additive	$u(x_1, x_2, x_3) = \lambda_1 u_1(x_1) + \lambda_2 u_2(x_2) + \lambda_3 u_3(x_3)$
Multiplicative or log additive	$u(x_1, x_2, x_3) = \lambda_1 u_1(x_1) + \lambda_2 u_2(x_2) + \lambda_3 u_3(x_3) + k\lambda_1\lambda_2 u_1(x_1)u_2(x_2)$ $\qquad + k\,\lambda_1\lambda_3 u_1(x_1)u_3(x_3) + k\lambda_2\lambda_3 u_2(x_2)u_3(x_3)$ $\qquad + k^2\,\lambda_1\lambda_2\lambda_3 u_1(x_1)u_2(x_2)u_3(x_3)$
Quasiadditive	$u(x_1, x_2, x_3) = \lambda_1 u_1(x_1) + \lambda_2 u_2(x_2) + \lambda_3 u_3(x_3) + \lambda_{12} u_1(x_1)u_2(x_2)$ $\qquad + \lambda_{13} u_1(x_1)u_3(x_3) + \lambda_{23} u_2(x_2)u_3(x_3)$ $\qquad + \lambda_{123} u_1(x_1)u_2(x_2)u_3(x_3)$
Bilateral†	$u(x_1, x_2, x_3) = \lambda_1 u_1(x_1) + \lambda_2 u_2(x_2) + \lambda_3 u_3(x_3) + \lambda_{12} f_1(x_1)f_2(x_2)$ $\qquad + \lambda_{13} f_1(x_1)f_3(x_3) + \lambda_{23} f_2(x_2)f_3(x_3)$ $\qquad + \lambda_{123} f_1(x_1)f_2(x_2)f_3(x_3)$
Hybrid (a special example for particular independence conditions)	$u(x_1, x_2, x_3) = \lambda_1 u_1(x_1) + \lambda_2 u_2(x_2) + \lambda_3 u_3(x_3) + \lambda_{12} u_1(x_1)f_2(x_2)$ $\qquad + \lambda_{13} u_1(x_1)f_3(x_3) + \lambda_{23} f_2(x_2)f_3(x_3)$ $\qquad + \lambda_{123} u_1(x_1)f_2(x_2)f_3(x_3)$
Quasipyramid	$u(x_1, x_2, x_3) = \lambda_1 u_1(x_1) + \lambda_2 u_2(x_2) + \lambda_3 u_3(x_3) + \lambda_{12} u_{12}(x_1, x_2)$ $\qquad + \lambda_{13} u_{13}(x_1, x_3) + \lambda_{23} u_{23}(x_2, x_3)$ $\qquad + \lambda_{123} u_1(x_1)u_2(x_2)u_3(x_3)$
Semicube	$u(x_1, x_2, x_3) = \lambda_1 u_1(x_1) + \lambda_2 u_2(x_2) + \lambda_3 u_3(x_3) + \lambda_{12} u_{12}(x_1, x_2)$ $\qquad + \lambda_{13} u_{13}(x_1, x_3) + \lambda_{23} u_{23}(x_2, x_3)$ $\qquad + \lambda_{123} f_1(x_1)f_2(x_2)f_3(x_3)$
Interdependent variable	$u(x_1, x_2, x_3) = \lambda_1 u_1(x_1) + \lambda_2 u_2(x_2) + \lambda_3 u_3(x_3)$ $\qquad + \lambda_{12} u_{12}(x_1, x_2) + \lambda_{13} u_{13}(x_1, x_3) + \lambda_{23} u_{23}(x_2, x_3)$
Multilinear	$u(x_1, x_2, x_3) = \lambda_1 u_1(x_1) + \lambda_2 u_2(x_2) + \lambda_3 u_3(x_3)$ $\qquad + \lambda_{12}\lambda_1\lambda_2 u_1(x_1)u_2(x_2) + \lambda_{13}\lambda_1\lambda_3 u_1(x_1)u_3(x_3)$ $\qquad + \lambda_{23}\lambda_2\lambda_3 u_2(x_2)u_3(x_3)$ $\qquad + \lambda_{123}\lambda_1\lambda_2\lambda_3 u_1(x_1)u_2(x_2)u_3(x_3)$

†Functions $f_i(x_i)$ are normalized utility *difference* functions. See Farquhar (1977) for more details.

12-4 UTILITY ASSESSMENT

12-4.1 Five Basic Steps

The purpose of dealing with different utility-decomposition forms is to replace the assessment of an n-attribute utility function with the assessment of n one-attribute utility functions, plus the necessary weights and scaling factors. In general, the process of assessment can be reduced to five basic steps:

1. Introducing the decision maker to the terminology, concepts, and techniques which are necessary for conducting meaningful assessment interviews.
2. Verifying relevant independence conditions to identify the appropriate utility-decomposition form. (Because this step is extremely difficult to perform in practice, many analysts simply *assume* that a particular utility decomposition is correct for a given situation.)
3. Assessing the component utility functions, usually through probabilistic interrogation of the decision maker.
4. Determining the parameters, weights, and scaling constants by which the individual utilities will be amalgamated into one number.
5. Testing the consistency of the compound utility function against the decision maker's actual rankings and preferences.

Before discussing the process of assessment, we shall give some idea of the dimensions of the problem. Both additive and multiplicative decompositions require the assessment of n individual utility functions and n scaling constants. The quasiadditive decomposition requires the assessment of n individual utility functions and $2^n - 1$ scaling constants. Thus, for example, if $n = 10$, that is, 10 attributes characterize the problem, the decision maker will be asked to assist in estimating 10 utility functions and 1023 constants.

The bilateral utility model requires $2n$ one-attribute utility functions and $2^n - 1$ scaling constants. The quasipyramid model, with nonseparable interactions, requires the assessment of $n(n - 1)/2$ individual utility functions. For $n = 10$ there are 45 functions to be estimated plus the scaling constants! The multilinear utility function can be assessed from n one-attribute utility functions and $2^n - 2$ scaling constants—1022 for $n = 10$.

There is no need to explore the dimensionality of assessment any further. Obviously, it presents a problem for practical implementation. It also assures that the first step of the assessment process, convincing the decision maker that all this work will be worth it, becomes a crucial element in implementing multiattribute utility theory. We shall discuss this step only after all the remaining steps are adequately explained. Thus we start with step 2 of the assessment process.

12-4.2 Verifying Independence Conditions

Two fundamental concepts of multiattribute utility theory, *preferential independence* and *utility independence*, are usually tested at this stage. Preferential independence concerns ordinal preferences among attributes, while utility independence concerns the cardinal preferences of the decision maker.

We have already explained what is meant by value trade-offs—measures of how much of one attribute one has to sacrifice in order to gain a fixed amount of another attribute. Such trade-offs may be dependent or independent of the achieved levels of remaining attributes. For example, in buying a car we might judge performance, price, and comfort to be the three major attributes affecting our decision. Now, the value trade-offs between performance and price *may not* depend on the level of comfort achievable across a variety of cars, especially if extreme levels of discomfort and cases of outright luxury are excluded. Also, given a particular level of performance, the preference structure describing the trade-off between price and comfort may be independent of it. That is, price and performance may be preferentially independent of comfort. Similarly, price and comfort may be preferentially independent of performance.

All or any of these conditions are dependent on a number of circumstances:

1. Who or what is the decision-making "agent"? A person? A representative of a group? A machine? Etc.
2. What is the available set of choice alternatives? (For example, how many and what kinds of cars are being considered?) What are the extreme achievable levels of attributes?
3. How many and what kinds of attributes are being considered? For example, would aesthetic considerations affect the independency conditions among performance, price, and comfort?
4. Are the currently established independency conditions stable over time, or are they highly volatile?

> **Definition** The pair of attributes X and Y is *preferentially independent* of attribute Z if the value trade-off between X and Y is not affected by a given level of Z.

This definition can be extended to more than three attributes: The set of attributes may be preferentially independent of the set of complementary attributes. For example, there may be several benefit attributes and several payment plans available from an insurance company. It may be that the preferences among various benefit packages are independent of the payment plans. But here we are stretching the point too far. Considering the four circumstances listed above, we should limit the preferential independence to pairs of attributes only.

Utility independence refers to one attribute at a time. It can be viewed as the risky or probabilistic analog of preferential independence. An attribute X is said to be utility-independent of attribute Y if the decision maker's preferences among lotteries (gambles, bets, probabilistic equivalents, etc.) involving only X, with Y fixed at a particular level, do not depend on the level of Y.

For example, let X represent the rate of return on an investment associated with a series of risky outcomes. Let Y represent the amount of initial capital needed. Suppose that there are two values of X, $X_1 = 35$ percent and $X_2 = 10$ percent, each having a 50 percent chance of attainment. If Y is fixed at $Y_1 = 100,000$, we may ask the decision maker, What is the *certain* rate of return you would accept as an equivalent for the 50/50 gamble yielding 10 percent and 35 percent respectively?

The answer might be, for example, 15 percent. That is, 15 percent is a decision maker's certainty equivalent for having a 50/50 chance of earning either 10 percent or 35 percent with a 100,000 investment.

Let us assume that the same situation is explored with a changed initial investment level, say $Y_2 = 200,000$. Would a decision maker's certainty equivalent be affected by the shift from Y_1 to Y_2? We do not know. If it does not, i.e., if the certainty equivalent would depend *solely* on the X_1 and X_2 values and not on any fixed value Y_1 or Y_2, then attribute X would be utility-independent of attribute Y.

Definition Attribute X is *utility-independent* of attribute Y when conditional preferences for lotteries on X, given Y, do not depend on the particular level of Y.

What if Y changes to $Y_3 = 1$ billion or $Y_4 = 10$? Although some utility independence may be observed for a limited range of Y, it is unlikely that it would be an absolute property of a given set of attributes.

Observe also that since risky alternatives include nonrisky alternatives as a special case (a nonrisky alternative assigns probability 1 to a particular outcome), preferential independence holds whenever utility independence is satisfied. The converse is not necessarily true.

Utility independence is one of the most important concepts in utility theory. Without it, speaking about even a single utility function over one of the attributes is meaningless. Only when X is utility-independent of Y, can a single utility function over X be defined. Unfortunately, the concept of utility independence is directional; X being utility-independent of Y does not imply that the reverse is true as well.

Thus, in order to decompose $u(X, Y)$ into its unidimensional components

$$u(X, Y) = u_X(X) + u_Y(Y)$$

we have to establish that X is utility-independent of Y *and* that Y is utility-independent of X. If, say, X is not utility-independent of Y, then the conditional utility functions are not "strategically" equivalent and $u(X, Y_1), u(X, Y_2), u(X, Y_3), \ldots$, etc., must *all* be assessed separately and completely!

12-4.3 Example of the Swedish Air Force

Bertil Tell (1976) has discussed the difficulties of multiattribute utility assessment. One of the real-life problems he studied concerned the evaluation of squadron capability in the Swedish Air Force. Three relevant criteria are the pilots' ability to use bombs, missiles, and guns, expressed by x_1, x_2, and x_3 respectively.[1]

In order to assess any compound utility function on the three attributes $u(x_1, x_2, x_3)$, one has to check whether x_1 and x_2 are preferentially independent of x_3. The decision maker is asked to consider two squadrons. The first has 2 pilots with acceptable tests on x_1 and 14 pilots who tested well on x_2. The other squadron consists of 3 pilots who tested well on x_2 and an undetermined number of pilots who were successful on x_1. Both squadrons have 13 pilots who were acceptable on x_3. The decision maker is then asked how many pilots from the second squadron would have to test well on x_1 for the choice between the two squadrons to be indifferent. Assume the decision maker answers, ''12 pilots.'' The questions must then be repeated for all other levels of x_3, the number of pilots able to do well with guns. If the decision maker provides about the same answer at any level of x_3, we conclude that x_1 and x_2 are preferentially independent of x_3. This procedure should be followed for all pairwise combinations of the attributes.

The next requirement is to test the assumption of utility independence. Is x_1 utility-independent of x_2 and x_3? Again, two hypothetical squadrons must be considered. The first has an undetermined number of pilots who are proficient in x_1, while in the second there is a 50/50 lottery—either 0 or 15 pilots are able to do well on x_1. Both squadrons have 15 pilots who are able to do well on x_2 and x_3. The evaluator answers, ''9 pilots.'' Then the question must be repeated for all other values of x_2 and x_3. If the evaluator gives the answer nine for all combinations of x_2 and x_3, then we may say that x_1 is utility-independent of x_2 and x_3. This procedure is then repeated for all remaining criteria.

12-4.4 Determining the Decomposition Form

If one finds all attributes preferentially independent as well as utility-independent of the others, then the one-attribute utility function can be assessed for a given decomposition form. For example, preferential independence among attributes is required for all simple additive decompositions, while utility independence is necessary for multiplicative and quasiadditive utility models. The multiplicative form assumes that the attributes are *jointly* (or mutually) utility-independent, while the quasiadditive utility model assumes only that *individual* attributes are utility-independent. It is worth mentioning that a multiplicative decomposition produces *the same* ranking of outcomes as a nonrisky

---

[1]Note that we use again the subscript notation as defined in Sec. 12-2.

additive utility function, because the multiplicative model can be transformed into an additive function by taking logarithms.

There are many other decomposition forms to choose from, but they all require verifying additional specialized independence conditions: generalized utility independence, diagonal independence, bilateral independence, fractional independence, and so on. From a purely practical viewpoint, the additive and multiplicative utility functions are both simple and robust approximations, and they are the only practical options for cases with more than four attributes.

12-4.5 Assessing the Component Utility Functions

The assessment of unidimensional utility functions is essential to the assessment of a multiattribute utility function. Although there are no unidimensional "decision" problems as such, there are many situations where one is searching for the alternative which maximizes or minimizes a single measure of merit: net monetary profit, response time of an emergency vehicle, price, cost, etc. It is around situations of this type that unidimensional utility theory has evolved.

One notices that the examples of one-attribute problems come across as being a bit forced. It is quite rare, and therefore difficult to imagine, that a comparison of decision alternatives proceeds in so simple-minded a fashion. Nearly always, there are multiple criteria to be taken into account.

Let us return to a single attribute X—say, net monetary profit—and let $x_1, \ldots, x_n$ represent n levels of profit achievable through a particular decision alternative x. An example of five such monetary consequences might be $(-\$1000, \$0, \$1000, \$2000, \$3000)$. The least preferred is $-\$1000$, and the most preferred is $\$3000$. The relative utility scale can be arbitrarily anchored as follows:

$$u(-\$1000) = 0 \quad \text{and} \quad u(\$3000) = 1$$

Next, we have to assess utilities for the remaining intermediate values $\$0$, $\$1000$, and $\$2000$. An imaginary lottery is established, yielding $-\$1000$ with probability $(1 - p)$ and $\$3000$ with probability p. Thus, the expected utility of the lottery is equal to

$$(1 - p)\, u(-\$1000) + pu(\$3000) = p$$

We must find the value of p such that the decision maker would become indifferent between a given consequence and the offered lottery. This, by definition, is assumed to happen if and only if the utility of a consequence is precisely equal to the expected utility of the lottery; that is,

$$u(X) = (1 - p)\, u(-\$1000) + pu(\$3000) = p$$

The decision maker can directly assess p by answering the following question: You can choose between (1) getting $\$0$ for sure and (2) playing a lottery in which you may win $\$3000$ with probability p or lose $\$1000$ with probability

$(1 - p)$. What would be the value of p which would make you indifferent between the two options?

This is not an easy question to answer. Most people do not think in terms of lotteries, and they are quite unaccustomed to this kind of comparison. The lottery itself is only imaginary, and taking or not taking the gamble might not reflect the actual attitude of the decision maker toward risk.[1] Moreover, assessment of indifference is much more difficult than assessment of preference. It would be relatively easy to find a value of p for which either the certain consequence or the lottery would be preferred, but finding the unique p which implies indifference is a demanding task.

Assume that $p = \frac{1}{2}$ would make the decision maker indifferent between receiving \$0 and playing the lottery with the expected gain $\frac{1}{2}(-\$1000) + \frac{1}{2}(\$3000)$ = \$1000. Then of course $u(\$0) = \frac{1}{2}$. In a similar vein we could, for example, arrive at $u(\$1000) = \frac{3}{4}$ and $u(\$2000) = \frac{8}{9}$. Figure 12-1 displays the utility curve thus obtained.

By fitting a curve through the individually assessed points we can gain some idea about the shape and a possible functional form of the utility function. If such a curve lies above the straight line connecting the endpoints of a given interval of values, it is said to be concave over that interval. Concave utility functions reflect a decision maker's *aversion to risk*; straight lines, i.e., linear utility functions, define *risk neutrality* or indifference; while convex utility functions (everywhere below the straight line) define *risk propensity*, or risk preference.

The utility function in Fig. 12-1 is that of a risk-averse decision maker. Risk neutrality and risk preference, both hypothetical, are indicated by dashed

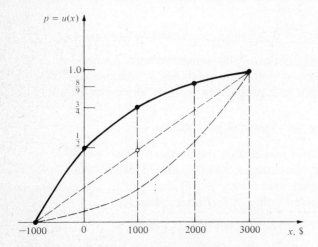

Figure 12-1 A unidimensional utility function.

[1] It has been established that decision makers' verbally expressed preferences are not consistent with those revealed in their behavior. See Sec. 13-5 for more details.

curves. Most functions should display all three basic attitudes toward risk over certain nonoverlapping subregions of possible attribute levels. The human attitude toward risk is a relative or conditional one; it depends on the circumstances of a given situation: What are the alternatives? What are their basic characteristics? What are the minimum and maximum attribute levels achievable? What are the past experience, current status, future outlook of the decision maker, etc.?

In Fig. 12-1 we note that the utility of $1000 is $\frac{3}{4}$ while the utility of the lottery, with an expected win of $1000, is only $\frac{1}{2}$. A decision maker who prefers the sure return to the lottery with the same expected return is risk-averse. One can see that this is true over the entire range of returns in Fig. 12-1. Similar definitions can be offered for risk neutrality and risk preference.

An alert observer has already noticed that this procedure for assessing utility functions will not be very reliable. Despite its rather mathematical treatment in the literature and the outward appearance of precision and scientific logic, the methodology is highly subjective, counterintuitive for a practitioner, and frustrating for the analyst. Whether the thing being assessed is actually a decision maker's utility function or something quite different is one of the most challenging questions for any analyst to answer. One must exercise caution for several reasons:

1. The assessment must be performed over a definite interval of possible attribute levels because one needs to anchor the scale by assigning $u(X) = 1$ and $u(X) = 0$ to the appropriate endpoints of the evaluation space. The assessed function $u(X)$ is thus affected by a given situation and should be applied to that one situation only. Ideally the assessment procedure should be repeated for every new decision situation.
2. The lotteries are chosen in an ad hoc, arbitrary way, while the questioning is carried out in a highly intuitive fashion, through a combination of wishful thinking and realism. Thus, in an iterative manner, decision makers can investigate their preferences or near preferences by considering a set of lotteries. When the consistency checks reveal inconsistent preferences, a decision maker is taken through the mill again until reaching the limits of patience or until the decision maker no longer perceives the expected value of such assessment procedure to be worth the effort in terms of time and cost of analysis.
3. Descriptions of the risk character of the decision maker are made without any reference to the actual risk or uncertainty associated with the problem at hand. That is, instead of responding to probabilities of the actual states of nature, the decision maker is probing his or her inner attitudes toward an analyst's 50/50 lotteries.
4. Utility-assessment questions are usually formulated in an unfamiliar manner and out of context. For example, "Is the expected consequence of $400 always preferred to a 50/50 lottery between $1000 and $0?" How does one interpret that innocent word "always"? And if not always, then what are the

conditions of change? How does one compare the $500 expected from the lottery with the certain $400 without having a firm grasp of what is meant by the expected value of the lottery and by the expected utility of that value?[1]

Note Consider a simple linear utility function, assigning 0, $\frac{1}{2}$, and 1 to potential earnings of $0, $500, and $1000 as their respective utilities. Under two different environmental conditions, each occurring with probability $\frac{1}{2}$, one is to compare the following decision alternatives:

1. Earn either $0 or $1000
2. Earn $500 under both conditions

Notice that for each of the alternatives, the expected utility is equal to $\frac{1}{2}$:

$$1.\ \tfrac{1}{2}u(\$0) + \tfrac{1}{2}u(\$1000) = \tfrac{1}{2}(0) + \tfrac{1}{2}(1) = \tfrac{1}{2}$$
$$2.\ \tfrac{1}{2}u(\$500) + \tfrac{1}{2}u(\$500) = \tfrac{1}{2}(\tfrac{1}{2}) + \tfrac{1}{2}(\tfrac{1}{2}) = \tfrac{1}{2}$$

If one is to maximize expected utility, one is expected to be indifferent between the two options above. But the two situations *are not alike*. Many decision makers would not be indifferent about which alternative is chosen.

Identical expected utilities are analogous to the problem of Buridan's ass,[2] standing exactly midway between two bales of hay. Buridan reasoned that the ass must starve to death because it could not reach a decision about which way to turn.

Like the hypothetical ass, the decision maker is not asked to take any action or to invoke *another rule or criterion*—for example, toss a coin. Indeed, after hundreds of years of development, decision analysis still struggles with philosophical problems similar to that of Buridan's ass.

Observe that although we have assumed a risk-neutral decision maker (linear utility function), the description of the risk character of the decision maker was made without any reference to the actual risk factors in the problem. The utilities u are determined without considering the probabilities describing the riskiness of a given situation (in our example, $\frac{1}{2}$ and $\frac{1}{2}$).

The two alternatives are equivalent only for a person who is willing to lose (0) some of the time and win (1) some of the time in order to average out with the same expected utility $\frac{1}{2}$. But what if the decision is to be made only once? There will be no opportunity to average out.

Even if the decision is repeated a number of times, a run of bad luck could force the decision maker to face consequences (e.g., ruin) that were not included in the formulation of utilities. Thus, the risk averter would prefer the

---

[1] Decision analysts assess their clients' preferences by assuming a priori that clients evaluate lotteries in an expected utility-maximizing fashion! Observe that $u(X) = p$ (utility equals probability) is not valid unless p's were assessed under such assumption.

[2] A parable attributed to Jean Buridan, Rector of the University of Paris in 1340, who believed that the will had no liberty to make decisions.

second alternative, whether the decision was made once or many times. On the other hand, a risk taker might prefer the first alternative, which provides the opportunity for a run of wins (1) or even just one win. Consequently, a decision maker would be justified in stating that the use of the standard lottery interview has simply preserved the problem and moved it along to the next step in the decision analysis.

Various investigations have indicated that decision makers do have a preference between (1) and (2). Therefore, no single criterion, such as expected utility maximization, can correctly represent their preferences. Yet some authors still advocate that if an appropriate utility is assigned to each possible decision consequence and the expected utility of each alternative is calculated, then the best course of action is the alternative with *the highest expected utility*.

This conviction, although supported by various sets of ex post facto axioms, is usually defended on strictly subjective grounds. Keeney and Raiffa, for example, address the decision makers in the following well-argued and empirically grounded way:

> There have been endless debates of this kind in the literature and suffice it to say, here, that *we* become more and more committed to the principle of maximization of expected utility, the younger we get and *the more arguments we hear*. Of course, this in itself should not be a compelling argument to you, but we are reporting what we feel is a relevant empirical fact [emphasis added]. (Keeney and Raiffa 1976, pp. 136–137)

12-4.6 Determination of Scaling Constants

Consider the weighted additive utility function for three attributes:

$$u(x_1, x_2, x_3) = \lambda_1 u_1(x_1) + \lambda_2 u_2(x_2) + \lambda_3 u_3(x_3)$$

Assuming that we successfully tested for preferential independence among attributes x_1, x_2, and x_3, we have then assessed individual one-attribute utility functions $u_1(x_1)$, $u_2(x_2)$, and $u_3(x_3)$ according to the procedure outlined in the previous section. Each of the u_i has been assessed independently, and all three have been scaled from 0 to 1 through their assessment.

The next step is the evaluation of the three *scaling constants* λ_1, λ_2, and λ_3. The role of the scaling constants is to insure internal consistency of the overall multiattribute function u. That is, if both x and y are equally preferred, then of course $u(x) = u(y)$.

Since we need three scaling constants, it is necessary to obtain a set of three independent equations with three unknowns and solve them for the λ's. This is of course no easy task, and for a large number of attributes it could become impossible.

We have to generate those three equations in any way we can. Let us assume that

$$\lambda_1 + \lambda_2 + \lambda_3 = 1$$

Now only two more equations are needed. But how do we get them? The remaining two equations must be assessed empirically, i.e., we have to question the decision maker some more. If, for example, we can obtain the decision maker's assurance of indifference between $x = (x_1, x_2, x_3)$ and $y = (y_1, y_2, y_3)$, then

$$\lambda_1 u_1(x_1) + \lambda_2 u_2(x_2) + \lambda_3 u_3(x_3) = \lambda_1 u_1(y_1) + \lambda_2 u_2(y_2) + \lambda_3 u_3(y_3)$$

constitutes another equation, because $u_i(x_i)$ and $u_i(y_i)$ are simply numbers at this stage.

There is a danger that the generated equations might not be independent or even consistent. To guide ourselves against inconsistency we should try some other procedure for the next equation. For example, given three alternatives x, y, and z, we may try to find the probability p which will make the decision maker indifferent between x and the lottery $py + (1 - p)z$. Finding such a p would lead to another equation:

$$u(x) = pu(y) + (1 - p)\, u(z)$$

that is,

$$\lambda_1 u_1(x_1) + \lambda_2 u_2(x_2) + \lambda_3 u_3(x_3) = p[\lambda_1 u_1(y_1) + \lambda_2 u_2(y_2) + \lambda_3 u_3(y_3)]$$
$$+ (1 - p)[\lambda_1 u_1(z_1) + \lambda_2 u_2(z_2) + \lambda_3 u_3(z_3)]$$

In this equation both p and all $u_i(x_i)$, $u_i(y_i)$, and $u_i(z_i)$ are numbers.

Now we have to solve the system of three equations for the λ's. In general, manually solving a system of n equations with n unknowns is not simple, and some computer interaction must enter into the analysis.

The described procedure is still rather unstructured. In practice we often use the extreme levels of the attributes as reference points for the assessment. The maximum and minimum levels of attributes are the most and least preferred respectively.

First, we select the highest level of attribute i among m alternatives:

$$x_i^* = \max_k x_i^k \qquad k = 1, \ldots, m$$

Or, we select the largest number from $(x_i^1, \ldots, x_i^m)$.

Recall that $u_i(x_i^*) = 1$, $i = 1, \ldots, n$, and that $u_i(x_i^0) = 0$, $i = 1, \ldots, n$. Observe that we can form two distinct reference points:

$$x^* = (x_1^*, \ldots, x_n^*)$$

similar to the *ideal*, and

$$x^0 = (x_1^0, \ldots, x_n^0)$$

similar to the *anti-ideal* discussed in Secs. 6-3 and 6-6.2. It follows that u should be scaled so that

$$u(x^*) = u(x_1^*, \ldots, x_n^*) = 1$$

and
$$u(x^0) = u(x_1^0, \ldots, x_n^0) = 0$$

In the current context both these points serve only as references for determining scaling constants. It is important to note, however, that each particular set of k alternatives is characterized by different x^* and x^0. That is, the two points are relative and subject to displacement.

Given the above, Keeney and Raiffa recommend some guidelines as to what types of questions should lead to independent and consistent equations for computing the scaling constants. Their prescription is as follows:

1. Find probability p which would make you indifferent between the lottery $px^* + (1 - p)x^0$ and the outcome $(x_1^0, \ldots, x_i^*, \ldots, x_n^0)$, a point obtained by substituting x_i^* for x_i^0 in the anti-ideal point. Let's say the answer is p_i. Then

$$p_i u(x^*) + (1 - p_i)u(x^0) = u(x_1^0, \ldots, x_i^*, \ldots, x_n^0)$$

Because $u(x^*) = 1$ and $u(x^0) = 0$, it follows that

$$p_i = \lambda_i u_i(x_i^*) = \lambda_i$$

since $u_i(x_i^0) = 0$ and $u_i(x_i^*) = 1$ for all i. Continue with this type of interrogation until all λ_i are generated.

2. For two attributes i and j select their particular levels x_i' and x_j' so that, for any fixed levels of all other attributes, you become indifferent between

$$(x_1, \ldots, x_i', \ldots, x_j^0, \ldots, x_n)$$

and

$$(x_1, \ldots, x_i^0, \ldots, x_j', \ldots, x_n)$$

Such indifference would imply that $\lambda_i u_i(x_i') = \lambda_j u_j(x_j')$, another useful equation.

The above are hard questions to ask.

How do we interpret the scaling constants λ_i's? Do they have any meaning? Can the decision maker relate to them in any way and thus facilitate their assessment? Each scaling constant λ_i is directly dependent on the range from x_i^0 to x_i^*, $[x_i^0, x_i^*]$. If $[x_i^0, x_i^*]$ is relatively small, then λ_i is going to be relatively small, becoming zero when $x_i^0 = x_i^*$. Changing the range x_i^0 to x_i^* will necessarily change the value of λ_i. The larger the distance between x_i^0 and x_i^*, the larger the λ_i. It can be argued that since scaling constants do not indicate the relative importance of attributes, using them as indicators of importance promotes misinterpretation. If, for example, attribute x_i refers to monetary rewards, and all jobs under consideration pay almost the same amount—that is, x_i^0 and x_i^* are very close together—then λ_i may approach zero, but this does not mean that money is unimportant to the decision maker. Right? Wrong.

Although we may not conclude that money as such is unimportant to the decision maker, it is unimportant *in the given situation* as an attribute on which a decision is to be based. If $x_i^0 = x_i^*$, then the ith attribute does not allow the individual to make a decision, because it transmits *no information* to the decision maker. There is no sense in claiming that the attribute is important if it is actually useless as a decision-making tool in a given situation. Obviously the concept of attribute importance is relative, not absolute, and it is dependent on the particular set of alternatives being considered at any one time. We have discussed this important issue in Chap. 7.

Thus, scaling constants λ_i's reflect the relative importance of attributes in a given situation. In this sense they should be determined objectively, by analyzing the situation at hand, and not subjectively through an interview. Such misinterpretation and confusion between objective and subjective concepts of attribute importance is, however, more than common. The decision maker is forced to respond to questions that are much more difficult to evaluate than is theoretically necessary.

Asking questions is an art in itself. Through one set of questions an analyst may conclude that λ_1 is larger than λ_2, while another analyst or a different battery of questions may yield λ_2 larger than λ_1. The results are inconsistent— and that is not allowed. The decision maker will just have to think harder about the issues and modify some of the assumptions or evaluations in order to attain consistency. But what if the decision maker responds to different analysts or to different batteries of questions differently, but in a consistent way? Is the artificial "consistency" of preferences really a part of rational behavior? Must all learning, differential perception, information reprocessing, change of mind, and preference reversals be eliminated, discouraged, or allowed to move in one direction only? Checking for consistency is another step in the long process of utility assessment.

12-4.7 Testing for Consistency

After we finally nail down the scaling constants, we arrive at our final product $u(x)$. For example,

$$u(x_1, x_2, x_3) = 0.6u_1(x_1) + 0.28u_2(x_2) + 0.12u_3(x_3)$$

But what if this function does not represent the decision maker's preferences over attributes x_1, x_2, x_3 at a time when it is to be applied? What if it represents nothing at all? Such questions are, of course, always lurking (or should be lurking) somewhere within the right hemisphere (or is it the left one?) of the decision analyst's brain.[1] Such questions lead to the need for this testing stage of the utility assessment process.

There are many possible causes of final discrepancies when the assessed

---

[1] Scientific observations of brain functions suggest that those functions we think of as rational occur mainly in the left hemisphere and those we consider intuitive, occur mainly in the right. Right-hemisphere intuitive thinking may perceive patterns and connections too difficult for the left hemisphere, but it may also detect patterns where none exists. See, for example, C. Sagan, *The Dragons of Eden*, Random House, New York, 1977.

utility function, tested by hypothetical examples, does not confirm the decision maker's preferences:

1. The *analyst* made an error in testing the independency conditions, assessing the component utility functions, determining the scaling constants, or testing the consistency of all these. The chosen form of utility function may not be appropriate; the interviews and questionnaries may be inconsistent or irrelevant; the number and types of attributes considered may be incorrect.
2. The *decision maker* made an error in expressing his or her indifference, preference, attitude toward risk, or perception of attribute independency or dependency. There could be a misunderstanding of some concepts, such as lottery, trade-off, indifference, or probability, or of questions as formulated by the analyst.
3. The decision maker's *attitudes* have changed, having learned more about his or her preferences, processed more information, sharpened personal views, or softened convictions. The decision maker has switched from being risk-prone to risk-averse, or sees what was unseen before. The decision maker has been tired by the interrogation, has become careless, or is unable to relate to hypothetical situations. Or tired before, now the decision maker is fresh and ready for the problem.
4. The *situation* has changed. Some alternatives have been added; some have been dropped. Many measurements and estimates have been found faulty and must be corrected and reevaluated. Attributes have been added and dismissed. Since their importance is now perceived differently, previously unimportant issues have become very relevant.

The first two causes are annoying but theoretically removable. The last two causes are serious and cannot be corrected within the realm of a given paradigm. They are not usually taken into account, are dismissed as insignificant or irrational, or defined out of the set of "interesting" cases. A painfully derived and expensive global utility function must exhibit at least some degree of stability and consistency. Therefore, the preferences of decision makers are forbidden to fluctuate; they must stay stable over a given time horizon—any other state of affairs would render $u(x)$ a historical monument or a religious antique.

12-5 INTERACTIVE EVALUATION PROCEDURES

The *evaluation-and-bound procedure* of Sarin (1977) elicits information from the decision maker through a sequential interactive process. The evaluation process consists of two phases:

1. *The analyst* (or the computer) calculates lower and upper bounds on the

utilities of available alternatives; some obviously poor alternatives can be identified and excluded at this stage.

2. *The decision maker* selects a particular score x_i^k, evaluates its utility, and supplies the evaluation to the analyst. A new set of bounds is computed, and the sequence returns to phase 1.

The procedure is terminated when a preferred alternative is identified. No more information is required than is minimally sufficient for making such an identification.

Let us consider the additive utility function again and summarize some of its basic properties:

$$u(x) = \lambda_1 u_1(x_1) + \cdots + \lambda_n u_n(x_n) = \sum_{i=1}^{n} \lambda_i u_i(x_i)$$

where

$$u(x^*) = 1 \qquad u(x^0) = 0$$

$$u_i(x_i^*) = 1 \qquad u_i(x_i^0) = 0$$

and

$$\sum_{i=1}^{n} \lambda_i = 1 \qquad \lambda_i \geq 0$$

as in Sec. 12-4.6.

To evaluate the above function, the decision maker would have to provide at least n judgments to estimate the λ_i, and at least $n(m + 2)$ judgments to estimate $u_i(x_i^k)$ for $k = 1, \ldots, m$ and $i = 1, \ldots, n$. Recall that x_i^k designates the level or *score* of attribute i achieved by alternative k.

The evaluation-and-bound procedure requires estimating only the *ranges* of probabilities for determining λ_i and $u_i(x_i)$. This implies that only expressions of *preference* are required, not the indifference judgments of conventional MAUT.

First, lower and upper bounds on the utilities of each alternative $k = 1, \ldots, m$ are established. Let $\underline{u}_i(x_i^k)$ and $\bar{u}_i(x_i^k)$ denote the lower and upper bounds on the utility of the kth alternative's score with respect to the ith attribute.

Initially, we set

$$\underline{u}_i(x_i^k) = 1 \qquad \text{if } x_i^k = x_i^*$$
$$= 0 \qquad \text{otherwise}$$

and

$$\bar{u}_i(x_i^k) = 0 \qquad \text{if } x_i^k = x_i^0$$
$$= 1 \qquad \text{otherwise}$$

that is, if x_i^k is the best available score with respect to a given attribute, then its lowest possible utility, its lower bound, is 1. If a score is the worst score on a given attribute, then its highest possible utility, its upper bound, is 0.

Overall lower and upper bounds on the utility of the kth alternative are

$$\underline{B}^k = \sum_{i=1}^{n} \lambda_i \underline{u}_i(x_i^k)$$

and
$$\overline{B}^k = \sum_{i=1}^{n} \lambda_i \overline{u}_i(x_i^k)$$

where $\underline{u}_i(x_i^k) \leq u_i(x_i^k) \leq \overline{u}_i(x_i^k)$. Bounds $\underline{B}^k$ and $\overline{B}^k$ are computed for all alternatives $k = 1, \ldots, m$. If $\underline{B}^k \geq \overline{B}_l$, then alternative k is either preferred or indifferent with respect to alternative l. Individual λ_i can be estimated as illustrated in Sec. 12-4.6, but Sarin (1977) shows that exact estimates of the λ_i are not actually required.

Let us now consider a simple numerical example. As in Sec. 12-1, we shall evaluate three automobiles A, B, and C in terms of six attributes. The performance x_i^k, or score, of each of the automobiles on each of the attributes is given in Table 12-2.

Table 12-2

Attributes	Automobile		
	A	B	C
1. Price ($)	⟨3000⟩	3500	3600
2. Performance (hp)	120	⟨140⟩	130
3. Economy (mi/gal)	⟨30⟩	21	25
4. Depreciation (%)	40	30	⟨50⟩
5. Maintenance ($)	⟨1600⟩	2000	1800
6. Appeal (grades 1–5)	3	4	⟨5⟩

The best value of each attribute is circled, while the worst values are underlined. We shall assume that the constants λ_i have been determined as follows: $\lambda_1 = 0.4$, $\lambda_2 = 0.1$, $\lambda_3 = 0.2$, $\lambda_4 = 0.05$, $\lambda_5 = 0.05$, and $\lambda_6 = 0.2$

It is now possible to determine all the necessary lower and upper bounds. The results are summarized in Table 12-3. To obtain its column values $\underline{u}_i$, replace all circled numbers in Table 12-2 with 1 and replace the rest with 0s; for columns $\overline{u}_i$ replace all underlined numbers with 0 and replace the rest with 1s.

Table 12-3

Attributes	λ_i	Car A		Car B		Car C	
		$\underline{u}_i$	$\overline{u}_i$	$\underline{u}_i$	$\overline{u}_i$	$\underline{u}_i$	$\overline{u}_i$
1	0.4	1	1	0	1	0	0
2	0.1	0	0	1	1	0	1
3	0.2	1	1	0	0	0	1
4	0.05	0	1	0	0	1	1
5	0.05	1	1	0	0	0	1
6	0.2	0	0	0	1	1	1
		$\underline{B}^A = 0.65$	$\overline{B}^A = 0.7$	$\underline{B}^B = 0.1$	$\overline{B}^B = 0.7$	$\underline{B}^C = 0.25$	$\overline{B}^C = 0.6$

Also computed are the overall utility bounds $\underline{B}^k$ and $\bar{B}^k$ for the three alternatives. Recall that if any lower bound is greater than any upper bound, then the alternative corresponding to this *dominated* upper bound can be excluded from further consideration. Observe that in our case $\underline{B}^A$ is greater than $\bar{B}^C$ ($\underline{B}^A = 0.65 > \bar{B}^C = 0.6$), so we can eliminate car C.

Next, the decision maker evaluates a selected score; for example, one still unevaluated x_i^k of the attribute with the highest λ_i. We select a price of \$3500, that is, x_1^B for the utility assessment. Through the decision maker's judgments we may determine that

$$u_i(x_i^k) = u_1(x_1^B) = u_1(\$3500) = 0.4$$

The bounds are then revised so that

$$\underline{u}_i(x_i^k) = u_i(x_i^k) = \bar{u}_i(x_i^k)$$

and then, in our case, $\underline{u}_1(x_1^B) = \bar{u}_1(x_1^B) = 0.4$.

The newly calculated bounds are entered in Table 12-4. All other numbers are kept unchanged. Observe in Table 12-4 that the lower bound on the utility of car A is greater than the upper bound on the utility of car B, ($\underline{B}^A = 0.65 > \bar{B}^B = 0.46$). Thus, car B can be eliminated, and car A becomes the preferred alternative of our obviously economy-conscious, money-saving hypothetical individual.

It is encouraging to see that the decision maker is required to supply only information that is absolutely necessary for reaching a decision. Conventional MAUT is based on the principle that the more information the better, and thus it attempts to gather almost all the information there is to gather before eliminating even one of the available alternatives (see also Sec. 14-4).

There have been some attempts to apply conventional MAUT to complex decision problems involving multiple decision makers. We shall explore that possibility and recapitulate the main concepts with the following example from the space exploration industry.

Table 12-4

Attributes	λ_i	Car A		Car B	
		$\underline{u}_i$	$\bar{u}_i$	$\underline{u}_i$	$\bar{u}_i$
1	0.4	1	1	0.4	0.4
2	0.1	0	0	1	1
3	0.2	1	1	0	0
4	0.05	0	1	0	0
5	0.05	1	1	0	0
6	0.2	0	0	0	1
		$\underline{B}^A = 0.65$	$\bar{B}^A = 0.7$	$\underline{B}^B = 0.26$	$\bar{B}^B = 0.46$

12-6 SELECTION OF FLIGHT TRAJECTORIES FOR SPACE MISSIONS

Dyer and Miles (1977) describe an interesting trajectory selection problem in the Mariner Jupiter/Saturn project.

A collective-choice analysis was performed, based on the principles of collective-choice theory, which is designed to determine what alternatives a group should prefer, given the preferences of the individuals within the group. One approach was to treat the problem as a single-decision-maker problem with multiple attributes, i.e., by invoking multiattribute utility theory.

Ten scientific teams evaluated and ranked possible trajectories with respect to their individual viewpoints on the mission. Consequently, ten basic "attributes" of each trajectory were entered into the MAUT analysis:

1. Radio science (RS)
2. Infrared radiation (IR)
3. Imagining science (IS)
4. Photopolarimetry (PP)
5. Ultraviolet spectroscopy (UVS)
6. Cosmic ray particles (CR)
7. Low-energy-charged particles (LE)
8. Magnetic fields (MAG)
9. Plasma particles (PLS)
10. Planetary radio astronomy (PRA)

A simple, weighted additive utility form

$$u(x) = \lambda_1 u_1(x) + \cdots + \lambda_{10} u_{10}(x)$$

was selected because of its operational simplicity.

A total of 105 single trajectories was developed. All were designed to comply with the major constraints of the mission: launch-vehicle capability, total flight time, Jupiter closest encounter, and navigation capability.

From these 105 single trajectories were assembled candidate trajectories and candidate trajectory *pairs* (two spacecraft were launched). A total of 2624 trajectory pairs were created. Adding two other constraints, the Jupiter encounter dates of the two trajectories to be separated by more than 1 month and the Saturn encounter dates to be separated by fewer than 5 months, reduced the possible number of trajectory pairs to 32 candidates.

In order to measure the strength of preference between trajectory pairs, the Von Neumann–Morgenstern expected utility theory was used because of its theoretical consistency, wide acceptance, and ease of implementation.

First, the science teams were asked to ordinally rank all 32 candidate trajectory pairs. That is, each science team determined its most preferred and least preferred trajectory pair. These preferences were ranked cardinally through Von Neumann–Morgenstern *lotteries*. Each trajectory pair was compared to a lottery between the most preferred and least preferred trajectory pairs. Each science team was then requested to assign a probability number p such that it became indifferent between a given trajectory pair for sure, or the lottery which yielded the most preferred trajectory pair with probability p, or the least preferred trajectory pair with probability $1 - p$. This procedure is demonstrated in Sec. 12-4.5.

Each of the 10 science teams generated 32 probability numbers p, one for each of the 32 trajectory pairs. The scientists were then requested to calculate utility function values based on their p's and the utility scaling requirements, $u = 1$ for the most preferred and $u = 0$ for the least preferred trajectory pair. Such normalized scaling of utilities was not, however, achieved. The final values assigned by the science teams to the least preferred trajectory pairs ranged from 0.101 to 0.800. Such utility values might indicate that the teams lacked the gambling nature required by the theory: "The utilities serve more as a group Rorschach test than as a useful gauge to scientific judgments" (Dyer and Miles 1977, p. 18). Also, by spreading the utility function values for the candidate trajectory pairs over the entire range 0 to 1 rather than, say, 0.8 to 1, a science team would obviously increase its influence on a collective-choice rule. Dyer and Miles admit that, "in retrospect, it probably was not appropriate to request the science teams to evaluate the normalization lottery, thus in effect handicapping themselves" (p. 19).

The utility function values of each science team were then arbitrarily normalized into the range 0 to 1. Another issue was the choice of the weighting factors λ_i for each science team i in the aggregate collective-choice rule. Two weighting policies were used: (1) equal weights for all science teams, and (2) $\lambda_i = 2$ for the encounter-oriented science teams (RS, IR, IS, PP, UVS, PRA) and $\lambda_i = 1$ for the other science teams (CR, LE, MAG, PLS).

Various collective-choice rules were applied (rank-sum, additive with different weightings, Nash bargaining rule, etc.), nine rules altogether, and substantial agreement was found among *all* of them. Three trajectory pairs were ranked in the top three by all the collective-choice rules. After a discussion with all scientific teams, one trajectory was tentatively selected as the science-preferred trajectory pair.

In evaluating this process, Dyer and Miles found that there was almost unanimous agreement that the ordinal ranking process had increased the science teams' understanding of the relationship between their science objectives and the characteristics of the trajectory pairs. The assignment of a utility function value to the least preferred trajectory pair based on a lottery was not considered a useful exercise. The science teams generally believed that the same trajectory pair would have been selected without the development of ordinal rankings and utility function values. The science teams expressed no unanimity as to whether the collective-choice rules were a useful way to express group preferences, or were an accurate measure of the "science value" of the mission as flown on each trajectory pair.

The "lotteries" were considered an artifact of the collective-choice analysis. Trajectory selection was not generally perceived as risky, and the extreme risk aversion of some science teams only exacerbated this problem. Dyer and Miles conclude that one contemporary problem of collective-choice theory is how to obtain cardinalization.

Among other, nontraditional conclusions of Dyer and Miles is that the *generation* of the candidate trajectory pairs was an essential part of the trajectory-pair *selection* process. In more general terms, the generation of decision alternatives plays an essential role in the decision-making process itself. Yet the issue of alternative generation is almost totally absent from modern decision analysis. We have dealt with these important aspects of the decision process in Chap. 4.

12-7 FINAL COMMENT ON MAUT

Multiattribute utility theory arises from the classical precepts of perfect rationality, utility or profit maximization, and predictability of aggregate phenomena. MAUT is prescriptive, concerned with the choice among prespecified alternatives according to the principle of maximization of subjective expected utility. It draws from statistical decision theory, game theory, mathematical economics, and econometrics. It is often classified as part of "decision analysis"; in fact, MAUT is now becoming identical with the term.[1]

The axiomatization of utility and probability theory and the development of bayesian statistics allow direct empirical testing to determine whether people choose in order to maximize subjective expected utility. The experiments of

---

[1]"Decision analysis" refers to normative approaches to decision making using judgmental probabilities and/or subjectively assessed utility functions (C. W. Kirkwood, *Operations Research*, vol. 28, no. 1, 1980, p. 1). This narrow definition of decision analysis compels some authors to use "multiobjective decision analysis" or "decisions with multiple objectives" in order to stress its relevancy to MCDM. It appears that the MAUT label is often avoided even by its very inventors.

Kahneman and Tversky (1973) provide dramatic and convincing empirical refutations of the theory. They report large and striking departures from the behavior predicted by the maximization of expected utility. Similar results have been obtained by Kunreuther and his coworkers (1978).

Herbert A. Simon, in his 1978 Nobel Memorial lecture, takes note of these developments:

> On the basis of these and other pieces of evidence, the conclusion seems unavoidable that the SEU [subjective expected utility] theory does not provide a good prediction—not even a good approximation—of actual behavior.
>
> Notice that the refutation of the theory has to do with the *substance* of the decisions, and not just the process by which they are reached. It is not that people do not go through the calculations that would be required to reach the SEU decision—neoclassical thought has never claimed that they did. What has been shown is that they do not even behave *as if* they had carried out those calculations, and that result is a direct refutation of the neoclassical assumptions. (Simon 1978, p. 32)

12-8 BIBLIOGRAPHICAL NOTE

An excellent, detailed, and complete overview of traditional MAUT can be found in Keeney and Raiffa, *Decisions with Multiple Objectives*. When awarded the 1977 Lanchester prize by the Operations Research Society of America, it was described as the best book written on the topic of operations research so far. It is a difficult work, uneven in its exposition and sometimes discouragingly complicated by mathematical formalism. But it is precise and complete, and it contains a wealth of carefully documented examples of practical applications. It is especially suitable for doctoral seminars and research projects.

Simpler overviews of MAUT are also available—for example, Huber (1974), MacCrimmon (1973), and chap. 4 in Buffa and Dyer, *Management Science/Operations Research* (1977). These sources might provide an entry to the more difficult Keeney and Raiffa book.

Farquhar's important technical survey of MAUT (1977) pays particular attention to attribute interdependency and more complex decompositions based on fractional hypercubes. A similar survey, more formal and less complete, but including a concise discussion of risk measurement and stochastic dominance, can be found in Fishburn (1978). Parametrically dependent attributes were introduced by Kirkwood (1976). Parametric dependency of attributes can be thought of as an approximation of the lack of utility independence, discussed in Sec. 12-4.2.

For simpler and more practical utility assessment procedures, one should turn to Sarin's interactive evaluation-and-bound technique (1977), or to Oppenheimer (1978) for his proxy approach. For the simplest and probably most effective method of all, the reader should refer back to Benjamin Franklin's letter to Joseph Priestley on page 13.

Some good practical applications can be found in Drake, Keeney, and Morse, *Analysis of Public Systems*. Other specific examples of practical methodologies are described in Geoffrion, Dyer, and Feinberg (1972), Klee (1971), and Keeney (1972). In addition, Krischer (1976) evaluates medical corrective procedures for a cleft palate; Keeney (1973a) considers policies for expanding the Mexico City airport facilities; Grochow (1972) evaluates time-sharing computer systems; Keeney (1973b) examines response times to fires, and Green and Wind (1973) explore marketing applications of multiattribute decision models.

Buffa, E. S., and J. S. Dyer: *Management Science/Operations Research*, Wiley, New York, 1977, chap. 4.

Drake, A. W., R. L. Keeney, and P. M. Morse: *Analysis of Public Systems*, M.I.T., Cambridge, Mass., 1972.

Dyer, J. S.: "A Time-Sharing Computer Program for the Solution of the Multiple Criteria Problem," *Management Science*, vol. 19, no. 12, 1973, pp. 1379–1383.

―――― and R. S. Miles, Jr.: "A Critique and Application of Collective Choice Theory; Trajectory

Selection for the Mariner Jupiter/Saturn 1977 Project," Jet Propulsion Lab. Internal Document 900-777, Pasadena, Cal., February 1977.

Farquhar, P. H.: "A Survey of Multiattribute Utility Theory and Applications," in M. K. Starr and M. Zeleny (eds.), *Multiple Criteria Decision Making*, TIMS Studies in the Management Sciences, vol. 6, North-Holland Publishing, Amsterdam, 1977, pp. 59–89.

Fishburn, P. C.: "A Survey of Multiattribute/Multicriterion Evaluation Theories," in S. Zionts (ed.), *Multiple Criteria Problem Solving*, Springer-Verlag, New York, 1978, pp. 181–224.

Franklin, B.: "Letter to Joseph Priestley (1772)," *The Benjamin Franklin Sampler*, Fawcett, New York, 1956.

Geoffrion, A. M., J. S. Dyer, and A. Feinberg: "An Interactive Approach for Multi-Criterion Optimization with an Application to the Operation of an Academic Department," *Management Science*, vol. 19, no. 4, 1972, pp. 357–368.

Green, P. E., and Y. Wind: *Multiattribute Decisions in Marketing*, Dryden Press, Hinsdale, Ill., 1973.

Grochow, J. M.: "A Utility Theoretic Approach to Evaluation of a Time-Sharing System," in W. Freiberger (ed.), *Statistical Computer Performance Evaluation*, Academic, New York, 1972.

Huber, G. P.: "Multi-Attribute Utility Models: A Review of Field and Field-Like Studies," *Management Science*, vol. 20, no. 10, 1974, pp. 430–458.

Kahneman, D., and A. Tversky: "On the Psychology of Prediction," *Psychological Review*, vol. 80, 1973, pp. 237–251.

Keen, P. G. W., and M. S. Scott Morton: *Decision Support Systems: An Organizational Perspective*, Addison-Wesley, Reading, Mass., 1978.

Keeney, R. L.: "A Decision Analysis with Multiple Objectives: The Mexico City Airport," *Bell Journal of Economics and Management*, vol. 4, 1973a, pp. 101–117.

———: "An Illustrated Procedure for Assessing Multiattributed Utility Functions," *Sloan Management Review*, vol. 14, 1972.

———: "A Utility Function for the Response Times of Engines and Ladders to Fires," *Urban Analysis*, vol. 1, no. 1, 1973b, pp. 37–50.

——— and H. Raiffa: *Decision Analysis with Multiple Objectives*, Wiley, New York, 1976.

Kirkwood, C. W.: "Parametrically Dependent Preferences for Multiattributed Consequences," *Operations Research*, vol. 24, 1976, pp. 92–103.

Klee, A.: "The Role of Decision Models in the Evaluation of Competing Environmental Health Alternatives," *Management Science*, vol. 18, no. 2, 1971.

Krischer, J. P.: "Utility Structure of a Medical Decision-Making Problem," *Operations Research*, vol. 24, 1976.

Kunreuther, H., et al.: *Disaster Insurance Protection: Public Policy Lessons*, Wiley, New York, 1978.

Leibenstein, H.: *Beyond Economic Man*, Harvard, Cambridge, Mass., 1976.

MacCrimmon, K. R.: "An Overview of Multiple Objective Decision Making," in J. L. Cochrane and M. Zeleny (eds.), *Multiple Criteria Decision Making*, University of South Carolina Press, Columbia, 1973, pp. 18–44.

Oppenheimer, K. R.: "A Proxy Approach to Multi-Attribute Decision Making," *Management Science*, vol. 24, no. 6, 1978, pp. 675–689.

Sagan, C.: *The Dragons of Eden*, Random House, New York, 1977.

Sarin, R. K.: "Interactive Evaluation and Bound Procedure for Selecting Multi-Attributed Alternatives," in M. K. Starr and M. Zeleny, *Multiple Criteria Decision Making*, TIMS Studies in the Management Sciences, vol. 6, North-Holland Publishing, Amsterdam, 1977, pp. 211–224.

Simon, H.A.: "Rational Decision-Making in Business Organizations," Nobel Foundation, Dec. 8, 1978.

Starr, M. K., and I. Stein: *The Practice of Management Science*, Prentice-Hall, Englewood Cliffs, 1976, unit 5.

Tell, B.: *A Comparative Study of Some Multiple-Criteria Methods*, Economics Research Institute, Stockholm School of Economics, Stockholm, 1976.

12-9 PROBLEMS

12-1 The following objection has been raised to MAUT: People are not machines calculating values according to simple arithmetic rules. Therefore, the models (e.g. expected utility model) must be wrong. Proponents of MAUT often answer that MAUT models do not claim to represent the psychological processes that produce human value judgments; it is the important end product of these processes that is reflected by MAUT models. Comment on the relative merits of both arguments. Can they be reconciled?

12-2 It has been found that people tend to prefer bets with equal probabilities to those with disparate probabilities even though the expected return is the same. That is, a bet promising $150 with a probability $\frac{1}{2}$ and $100 with $\frac{1}{2}$ is often preferred to the one characterized by $200 with $\frac{1}{4}$ and $100 with $\frac{3}{4}$. What can be said about the utility function underlying such preferences?

12-3 Kenneth Arrow once stated that one-dimensional answers are no answers. What does this mean? How does Arrow's statement relate to optimization in terms of a single supercriterion?

12-4 Consider the following statement: "Certainly, it would be foolish to incur data-collection and analysis costs on perfecting measures that will not change the problem's solution." (Starr and Stein, 1976, unit 5)

 (*a*) Discuss this statement as it relates to the MAUT approach.

 (*b*) Is there any way to determine whether the solution might be affected before one "perfects" the measures?

12-5 It is often said that multiple objectives do not pose a serious problem when they can all be evaluated on the same scale—dollars, for example. Consider the following situation: Machines *A* and *B* have to be replaced. Two producers offer both types. Because producer 1's machines are technologically incompatible with producer 2's, we can buy from only one of the producers. Each machine's profitability has been assessed as follows:

	Profitability		Total profitability
	Machine *A*	Machine *B*	
Producer 1	$3500	$3500	$7000
Producer 2	$6000	$1000	$7000

 (*a*) Both offers are obviously equally profitable. Does this imply that the decision maker should be indifferent between them? Are $3500 from *A* and $3500 from *B* really the same as $6000 from *A* and $1000 from *B*? Can we base our decisions simply on dollar totals?

 (*b*) You need $10,000. You can get $9000 from your mother and $1000 from the government, or $1000 from your mother and $9000 from the government. You are not expected to pay back either source. Are you indifferent between the two options? Try not to involve any criteria other than money.

 (*c*) One cannot "add apples and oranges." Can one add dollars originating from different sources or intended for different purposes?

12-6 Government "analysts" sometimes attempt to place a value (often in dollars) on individual human life. An alternative would be to maximize *lives saved* or to minimize *lives lost*. Discuss the merits and disadvantages of both approaches.

12-7 In choosing between two products we must consider their weight, size, and cost—all to be minimized:

	Weight in kg	Size in cm³	Cost in $
A	40	70	15
B	20	100	13

(a) A young MBA assigns the following attribute weights of importance: weight—0.4, size—0.2, and cost—0.4. The MBA then simply calculates the weighted average of the attribute scores for A and B, i.e., 36 and 33.2 respectively. Which alternative is preferred?

(b) In one application of this model, the size was expressed in mm³ rather than cm³. Using the same set of weights, the decision maker calculated the averages as 14,022 for A and 20,013.2 for B. The preferences of B to A was thus reversed. Should such a thing be allowed to happen?

(c) Starr and Stein (1976) suggest transforming a set of evaluations into logarithms, i.e.,

$$\log A = 0.4 \log 32 + 0.2 \log 70 + 0.4 \log 15$$
$$\log B = 0.4 \log 20 + 0.2 \log 100 + 0.4 \log 13$$

Is this transformation invariant to the unit of measurement, such as the change from cm³ to mm³?

(d) Compare the transformation in (c) with the following:

For A: $(40)^{0.4}(70)^{0.2}(15)^{0.4}$

For B: $(20)^{0.4}(100)^{0.2}(13)^{0.4}$

How is this *multiplicative* evaluation to be interpreted?

(e) Is the logarithmic transformation in (c) a correct method of proceeding when no single scale can be found? What are its shortcomings?

(f) Can a concept of an "ideal" product be used? How does it compare with the calculations performed in (a) through (d)?

12-8 The following assumption is often introduced: Individual utilities are functions only of the individual's own consumption; that is, I am no less satisfied with my bundle of goods when you are starving than when you have plenty. What is your attitude toward this assumption?

12-9 A social welfare function U is to be derived from the utility functions of l individuals, $u_i(x)$, defined over n commodities $x = (x_1, \ldots, x_n)$. Compare the following hypotheses for expressing social welfare [function $U(x)$ is to be maximized]:

(a) $U(x) = u_1(x) + \cdots + u_l(x)$

(b) $U(x) = \lambda_1 u_1(x) + \cdots + \lambda_1 u_l(x)$

(c) $U(x) = [u_1(x), \ldots, u_l(x)]$

(d) $U(x) = \min[u_1(x), \ldots, u_l(x)]$

What are the assumptions behind each hypothesis? [Consider case (c) in the MCDM sense, i.e., leading to nondominated solutions.]

12-10 Individuals 1 and 2 are trying to select between investment alternatives A and B. The selection is influenced by the uncertain future event E. The individual utilities of the outcomes are as follows:

		E occurs	E does not occur
Individual 1	A	10	5
	B	7	9
Individual 2	A	4	8
	B	8	6

(a) Individual 1 estimates the probabilities of occurrence and nonoccurrence of E as 0.8 and 0.2 respectively; individual 2's estimates are 0.2 and 0.8. Under the rule of expected-utility maximization, which investments would be selected by each individual?

(b) Before the outcomes of (a) are known, an analyst suggests a group decision-making rule as follows: Take the average of individual utilities as the group utility and the average of the two probability estimates as the group estimate; then use the expected-utility rule. Show that this *must* be unacceptable to both decision makers.

12-11 In most decision situations, attributes are *interdependent*; they interact. The level achieved by one attribute will be interpreted differently by the same decision maker, depending upon the levels achieved by other attributes.

(a) Given the above, the additive MAUT models which assume independence of attributes will be inadequate. True or false?

(b) Give some real-life examples of attribute interdependence (food additives, pollutants, etc.).

(c) Diamonds are typically appraised in terms of clarity, color, and size. When a diamond has excellent clarity, then color matters. If clarity is only fair, then color is unimportant compared to size. Are the attributes interdependent?

12-12 With both steak and chicken, suppose you prefer potato to salad, salad to corn, and corn to peas. Would these preferences necessarily be preserved with lobster? What kind of interdependence of attributes is involved? What about your preferences for wines (red, white, rosé) in combination with entrées (red meats, poultry, seafood)?

12-13 Assume that the utility of saving no lives through a given decision alternative is zero, that is, $u(0) = 0$. One program has a 50/50 chance of saving 100 lives or none and another could save 45 lives with complete certainty. The majority of people prefer the certainty alternative.

(a) Verify that this preference implies a relationship between utilities of $2u(45) > u(100)$.

(b) In comparing a program that has 1 chance in 10 to save 45 lives and 9 chances in 10 to save none, and a program that has 1 chance in 20 to save 100 lives and 19 in 20 to save none, the majority of people would select the latter option. Verify that this preference implies $2u(45) < u(100)$.

(c) What can you say about the utility function of lives saved derived from the above expressions of preferences?

(d) Replace the number of lives saved with dollar equivalents, that is, $0, $45, and $100. Is it likely that the same preferences could be maintained over the corresponding monetary gambles?

(e) On the basis of the above results, Tversky concluded, "Utility theory does not permit attitudes towards risk *per se*, only attitudes towards money."[1] How do you understand his statement?

[1]D. E. Bell et al. (eds.), *Conflicting Objectives in Decisions*, Wiley, New York, 1977, p. 212.
[2]Ibid, p. 435.

12-14 Professor Raiffa has stated:[2] "I somehow have a feeling—perhaps I'm so biased because my conversion took many, many years and involved very painful decisions, and I tried desperately to find some substitute instead—that maximization of expected utility is going to be around for another 50 years, because there isn't anything that comes close." This poignant personal statement says much about the human side of science. However, should one's sympathy with an analyst be a rationale for accepting a conclusion?

12-15 One crucial assumption of the multiattribute utility approach is the independence of attributes. Independence assumptions must be tested because ignoring attribute dependencies could lead to disastrous results. Consider the following numerical example of three alternatives and three attributes:

	x_1	x_2	x_3
A	30	20	50
B	20	50	30
C	40	40	40

(a) In terms of MAUT, for example, attributes x_1 and x_2 would be independent if $u_1(30)$, that is, the desirability of $x_1 = 30$ would be unaffected by the level achieved with respect to x_2. Obviously, the preference functions u_1 can only be assessed if x_1 is independent of other attributes. Otherwise we would have to assess *conditional utility functions*: $u_1(x_1 \mid$ given $x_2 = 20$ and $x_3 = 50)$, $u_1(x_1 \mid$ given $x_2 = 50$ and $x_3 = 30)$, $u_1(x_1 \mid$ given $x_2 = 40$ and $x_3 = 40)$, etc. The vastness of this task becomes apparent if a large number of values in all possible combinations would have to be considered. Provide some real-life examples of dependent attributes and estimate the number of conditional functions to be assessed.

(b) The above problem arises in MAUT because its purpose is to estimate a decision maker's preferences over the *attributes*, independently of the alternatives. A function must be applicable to different and changing feasible sets—deriving a new utility function for any new or even slightly changed set of alternatives would be impractical. Can the assessment of conditional functions be avoided?

(c) Consider the above table again: It is obvious that $x_1 = 30$ is associated with and only with $x_2 = 20$ and $x_3 = 50$. For this set of alternatives it is irrelevant what $u_1(30 \mid$ given $x_2 = 50$ and $x_3 = 30)$ would be. Attempting to assess such information is wasteful of a decision maker's time and money. True or false?

12-16 Consider two investment alternatives evaluated in terms of their future impact on *ecological improvement*, evaluated in monetary units. Both alternatives are based on the same initial investment outlay. Only one of the alternatives can be chosen, as they are mutually exclusive.

	Benefits achieved in years from now				
	5	10	15	20	25
Alternative A	50	40	20	10	0
Alternative B	0	10	40	60	60

(1) A 65-year-old analyst considers this a rather simple problem. The analyst proposes to compute the net present value of each investment alternative with a discounting factor of, say, 10 percent, and select the better one.

(2) A 35-year-old country teacher with six children strongly disagrees with the analyst's discounting procedure. After some reflection the teacher is not willing to settle for *any* discounting factor and rejects the very idea of discounting because it ignores the long-run future. "We are selling future generations short," says the teacher.

(3) The analyst answers that simple discounting has a lot going for it: It is so transparent that everybody sees what you are doing. The teacher responds, "That is precisely why I oppose it. I see clearly what you are doing."

Analyze the points expressed in (1) to (3) and attempt to clarify your own attitude. How can the conflicts arising from intertemporal and intergenerational trade-offs be resolved?

12-17 To act rationally means to choose the course of action which promises maximum expected value over the long run. Analyze the following reactions to this assertion.

(*a*) People don't maximize utility because they are rational; their preferences are observed first, and *then* the utility function is established.

(*b*) "Over the long run" has nothing to do with it. Utilities are assigned to one-shot gambles.

12-18 Consider the following statement: It should be understood that in the process of establishing utility function, *nothing* new was added; the grand final ordering is implicit in the simple choices made earlier. But the practical advantage of having a concise utility function rather than a great many preferences is enormous. True or false? Could anything possibly be *lost* through the process of establishing a utility function?

12-19 An interesting utility function is the *S-branch utility tree*. Suppose that n commodities are grouped into S subsets with n_s components in each. Let x_{si} denote the consumed quantity of the ith commodity of the sth type; $s = 1, \ldots, S$ and $i = 1, \ldots, n_s$. Let y_{si} denote the *minimal* consumption of the ith commodity of the sth type. The utility function U is

$$U = \left\{ \sum_{s=1}^{S} w_s \left[\sum_{i=1}^{n_s} b_{si}(x_{si} - y_{si})^{es} \right]^{e/e_s} \right\}^{1/e}$$

where $y_{si} \geq 0$ and $b_{si}, w_s > 0$. Constants e_s and e indicate intragroup and intergroup elasticities of substitution respectively.

(*a*) Compare U with the anti-ideal (Sec. 6-6.2) hypothesis of preference. Is there any similarity? What are the differences?

(*b*) How would the function be changed if we replaced y_{si} with y^*_{si}, that is, the minimum by the maximum?

(*c*) What are the difficulties of assessing U?

THIRTEEN

As the reader might suspect, management scientists, operations researchers, and decision analysts are not the only ones concerned with human decision making; psychologists are also becoming more and more involved in studying this fascinating subject. Using extremely simple tools (mostly linear regression models), they have produced a wealth of applications, decision maker–analyst interactions, and some skillful uses of computers.

The formal aspects of *social judgment theory* (SJT) are quite similar to those of MAUT. Actually they differ only in the way the input data are obtained. The underlying assumption of a linear decomposition model, that is, a weighted average of relevant components, remains the same.

We summarize several different forms of regression-based decomposition, ranging from linear to exponential. But as the introductory quotation indicates, it is mostly the linear model which stimulates SJT research, because of its simplicity.

Although the formalism involved in this chapter is quite simple, the reader is expected to have at least a rudimentary knowledge of linear regression analysis—a basic concept taught in college statistics.

The main purpose of applied SJT is to obtain an explicit, quantitative description of the decision maker's cognitive system (the *policy*), by which information is integrated into an expression of preference. This is quite similar to MAUT's efforts to unravel a decision maker's utility function. We provide a comparative analysis of the two approaches in Sec. 13-3.

This chapter concludes with critical comments on the properties and uses of linear regression models in decision theory. These comments are intended to stimulate thought about the concepts and methods presented in this book. It is from the synthesis of all the pros and cons that a useful personal model can emerge.

REGRESSION ANALYSIS
OF HUMAN JUDGMENT

Could it be that bootstrapping worked because linear models *in general* are superior to human judges? And that it does not matter that the weights of the linear model were derived from an expert judge? What would happen if I selected weights at random—although in the appropriate direction—and constructed linear models based on these weights?

The results surprised hell out of me. In the examples discussed in this paper, linear models whose weights were randomly selected in the manner just described *on the average* outperformed the linear models whose weights were selected on the basis of the experts' judgments.

Robyn M. Dawes[1]

We use *judgment* in the title of this chapter only to reflect the accepted terminology as it evolved in psychological literature. Social judgment theory or behavioral decision theory also deal with decisions and choice, only their methodology is different: it reflects psychologists' almost exclusive reliance on regression analysis.

Regression analysis (See Prob. 13-4) starts with collecting data about a series of decisions (real or experimental) performed by an individual or group. A set of relevant variables (attributes, *cues*) is identified as determinants of a decision. Outcomes of decisions (choice of the most preferred alternative, ranking, etc.) are also noted and recorded. One then attempts to build a regression model (usually a linear function) which "fits" the data by assigning weights to cues so that the outcomes can be reliably recovered through the regression equation. Such equation correctly captures the relationships between decision outcomes and the underlying independent variables (cues): it "captures" decision maker's "policy". If the decision maker is consistent in applying his "policy" over a broad range of situations, then the regression equation can be used to *predict* outcomes derivable from new and previously unencountered sets of cues.

The reader should not confuse the ability to predict with the ability to explain: regression analysis can often predict but it cannot establish causal relationships, it cannot explain. Through regression, one can successfully es-

[1]Robyn M. Dawes, "Objective Optimization Under Multiple Subjective Functions," in J. L. Cochrane and M. Zeleny (eds.), *Multiple Criteria Decision Making,* University of South Carolina Press, Columbia, 1973, p. 14.

tablish that darkness falls when streetlights are lit or that the incidence of common colds rises as larger number of leaves fall from trees. One can use these insights for a successful prediction of phenomena. Underlying causal links, however, must be established through other tools of science.

Although judgment is often assumed to be synonymous with choice or decision, they are not equivalent. Judgment refers to evaluation of alternatives per se, it does not have to result in actual choice. One can choose in conflict with one's better judgment. There is a difference between judging the alternative *as if* one is to choose one, and ranking of alternatives for the purpose of actual choice. Judgment is neither necessary nor sufficient for choice; it is an aid to choice, often a crucial one, in some decision situations.

After these words of caution, we are ready to explore the principles of SJT in more detail. We rely on its analogy with MAUT and assume that the reader is familiar with the contents of Chap. 12.

13-1 REGRESSION DECOMPOSITION MODELS

Let us consider a basic additive utility–decomposition model from MAUT theory, say,

$$u(x_1, x_2, x_3) = \lambda_1 u_1(x_1) + \lambda_2 u_2(x_2) + \lambda_3 u_3(x_3)$$

Next, let us introduce one particular utility transformation of individual attribute variables, namely, $u_i(x_i) = x_i, i = 1, 2, 3$. We obtain

$$u(x_1, x_2, x_3) = \lambda_1 x_1 + \lambda_2 x_2 + \lambda_3 x_3$$

a basic regression type of utility-decomposition model. We have simply assumed that all individual attribute utility functions are linear. We could, of course, use $u_i(x_1) = x_i^2$ or $u_i(x_i) = \log x_i$, as is sometimes suggested, but we shall save our energies and reserve judgment on these matters for the time being (see Sec. 13-4 for further discussion).

What has actually been achieved? By setting $u_i(x_i) = x_i$ arbitrarily for all attributes, we have avoided the need for the often tedious and elaborate assessment of component utility functions. Only the assessment of weights or scaling constants λ_i remains.

In MAUT, these weights are estimated through a *direct interrogation* of the decision maker. A set of independent and consistent equations is derived, and the weights—the scaling constants in MAUT—are computed (see Sec. 12-4.6).

In the regression-based SJT, weights are estimated by analyzing the decision maker's *past choices* and behavior or, if such data are not available, the decision maker's evaluations of a battery of experimentally generated alternative scenarios or combinations of objects. This procedure amounts to an *indirect interrogation* of the subject.

The differences between MAUT and SJT are found in the methodologies for obtaining $u_i(x_i)$ and λ_i. The underlying decomposition forms are often common and shared equally. Methodological combinations of the two approaches are of course possible, although such hybrid methods have not yet been fully explored. For example, direct interrogation could be used to establish $u_i(x_i)$, and regression analysis to obtain λ_i, or vice versa. However, efforts to preserve the "theoretical purity" of each approach seem to have prevented researchers from establishing a common ground.

13-1.1   Analysis of the Judgment Process

An interactive computer program, POLICY, has been designed by Hammond and his associates[1] to help decision makers learn about their own and each other's judgment processes by providing a quantitative, pictorial representation of the characteristics of the processes.

POLICY is one of the best developed of this family of regression-based approaches. It provides graphic-quantitative displays of (1) the relative weights of importance λ_i that the decision makers place on the factors under consideration, (2) the functional form of the relations between the decision makers' judgments and the values of each attribute, and (3) the measure of consistency with which decision makers' judgments can be "captured" by that particular functional form.

The typical person-machine interaction includes the following steps:

1. *Judgment*.   The decision maker is asked to make a series of preference judgments based on displays presented by the POLICY program. Each display represents an alternative combination of specific values of goals, objectives, or attributes. A large number of such scenarios must be evaluated to assure that the possibly extreme impacts of individual scenarios are smoothed out.
2. *Computer analysis*.   Next, a multiple regression analysis is performed, and a polynomial curve is fitted through the data. (In other approaches, discriminant analysis or an analysis of variance is also applied).

   The fitted function form that approximates (or "captures") the data best is said to describe the decision maker's policy in terms of the weights placed on each attribute and the consistency with which the judgments were made.
3. *Graphic displays*.   The decision maker's policy is then externalized with pictorial and quantitative displays. Relative weights are displayed with bar graphs, while linear or nonlinear function forms are displayed on plotted curves. Consistency is measured by the multiple correlation coefficient.

Table 13-1 lists the common function forms which are most often suggested and used for fitting through the data. As mentioned before, the scenarios can

---

[1] K. R. Hammond et al.: "POLICY: An Aid for Decision Making and International Communication," *Columbia Journal of World Business*, vol. 12, no. 3, 1977, pp. 79–93.

Table 13-1 Preference regression models

Model	Three-attribute representation
Linear	$u(x_1, x_2, x_3) = \lambda_1 x_1 + \lambda_2 x_2 + \lambda_3 x_3$
Conjunctive	$u(x_1, x_2, x_3) = x_1^{\lambda_1} \cdot x_2^{\lambda_2} \cdot x_3^{\lambda_3}$
Disjunctive*	$u(x_1, x_2, x_3) = \left(\dfrac{1}{c_1 - x_1}\right)^{\lambda_1} \left(\dfrac{1}{c_2 - x_2}\right)^{\lambda_2} \left(\dfrac{1}{c_3 - x_3}\right)^{\lambda_3}$
Distance*	$u(x_1, x_2, x_3) = \sqrt{\lambda_1^2 (c_1 - x_1)^2 + \lambda_2^2 (c_2 - x_2)^2 + \lambda_3 (c_3 - x_3)^2}$
Logarithmic	$u(x_1, x_2, x_3) = \lambda_1 \log x_1 + \lambda_2 \log x_2 + \lambda_3 \log x_3$
Exponential	$u(x_1, x_2, x_3) = e^{\lambda_1 x_1} \cdot e^{\lambda_2 x_2} \cdot e^{\lambda_3 x_3}$
Linear with interactions	$u(x_1, x_2, x_3) = \lambda_1 x_1 + \lambda_2 x_2 + \lambda_3 x_3 + \lambda_{12} x_1 x_2 + \lambda_{13} x_1 x_3 + \lambda_{23} x_2 x_3$ $+ \lambda_{123} x_1 x_2 x_3$

*We define $c_i \geqq \max_i \{x_i\}$; that is, c_i is a parameter which is equal to or larger than the maximum achievable value of each individual attribute. We assume that $\lambda_i \geqq 0$ for all $i = 1, \ldots, n$.

be represented as combinations of values of attributes, say x_1 and x_2, as in Fig. 13-1.

These combinations, represented by points (x_1, x_2) in Fig. 13-1, are then *ranked*, according to the decision maker's preferences from the most to the least preferred. In Fig. 13-1 the first seven alternatives are numbered 1 to 7 in terms of their decreasing attractiveness. Other scenarios are ranked in the same manner. The process yields a series of rankings. All the first-ranked alternatives can then be summarized in the same (x_1, x_2) space, as for example in Figure 13-2.

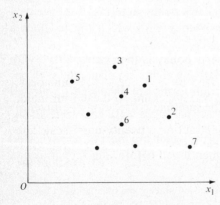

Figure 13-1 Ranking of alternatives—a typical scenario. Alternative 1 is transferred to Fig. 13-2.

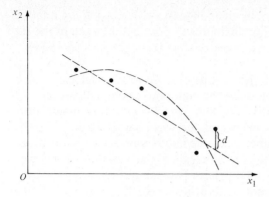

Figure 13-2 Fitting a set of decision outcomes with "as close as possible" line or curve.

A line (or curve) which approximates these points most closely is then fitted. It captures the decision maker's "most consistent" policy hypothesis. Any of the function forms in Table 13-1 could be tested in this way. In practice, analysts usually limit themselves to the linear model. The coefficients of the fitted line or curve are determined so that the sum of squares of deviations d (see Fig. 13-2) is minimized.

13-1.2 A Study of Labor-Management Negotiations

Balke, Hammond, and Meyer (1973) report an application of judgment analysis in a labor-management negotiation. After experiencing a long and bitter conflict at a major chemical company, six negotiators (three from labor and three from management) agreed to reenact the negotiation in order to determine whether cognitive and judgment aspects had contributed to the dispute. The reenactment recreated the situation as it stood 1 week prior to the settlement.

Four major attributes (issues) characterized each alternative of choice (contract package):

1. Contract duration (in years)
2. Wage increases (in percentage)
3. Number and use of special workers (in percentage)
4. Number of strikers to be recalled (in percentage)

Each contract package was then characterized by a vector of four numbers, such as (2.5, 7, 30, 40) or (2.5, 11, 70, 60), corresponding to these four major attributes. Twenty-five representative contract packages were analyzed. Each negotiator rated the acceptability of each contract on a twenty-point scale and indicated the relative weights that he thought he had placed on the four attributes. Negotiators were also invited to predict the ratings given to each of the twenty-five contracts by their counterparts.

Four negotiators received a graphic online feedback displaying the relative weights and function forms of the four attributes as provided by each of the six negotiators. One pair of negotiators did not receive feedback and served as a "control."

After analyzing the ratings of the twenty-five contract packages, each negotiator's judgment policy was derived through regression analysis. It was then described in terms of the relative weights placed on the four major attributes. For example, one management negotiator was characterized by (0.05, 0.74, 0.19, 0.02), reflecting the weights associated with contract duration, wage increases, special workers, and strikers to be recalled; one labor negotiator was characterized by (0.05, 0.02, 0.10, 0.83). These two sample vectors indicate a possible reason for the disagreement: There is a large disparity in relative importance between the second and fourth issues as judged by two negotiators. One considered wages to be the most important aspect of the negotiation; the other, the recall of strikers.

The negotiators were then asked to evaluate the contracts a second time under conditions approximating the final hours of the negotiation. It was found that the pairs of negotiators who had received judgment information feedback were able to achieve agreement in the final phase, while the control pair was not.

Both sides tended to be inaccurate in predicting the judgments of their counterparts. The researchers observe: "This finding illustrates one of the more important contributions of externalization. The negotiators were confident that they understood their counterparts' policies, a belief based on years of association and negotiation. Yet they were wrong" (Balke, Hammond, and Meyer, 1973, p. 320).

The negotiators' self-knowledge was also poor. All negotiators had a tendency to underestimate the attribute weight they each placed on the particular issue most important to them and to overestimate the weight they placed on the issue least important to them. This deficiency in self-knowledge was shown when the subjective weights specified by the negotiators did not agree with the relative weights computed by the program.

All negotiators felt the negotiation would have proceeded differently had this analytic tool of judgment analysis been available to them during the real negotiation.

13-2 POLICY DESCRIPTION:
METHODOLOGY AND APPLICATIONS

Judgment analysts, especially the group around Kenneth R. Hammond at the Institute of Behavioral Science in Boulder, Colorado, concluded a long time ago that most complex social problems are beyond the *unaided* cognitive capacities of human decision and policy makers.

Decision aids, decision support systems, and decision-making models are being developed by psychologists, behavioral scientists, and policy analysts. Studies of decision making have long since ceased to be the exclusive domain of economists, management scientists, operations researchers, and systems analysts.

Judgment analysts strive to discover and *externalize* the policy maker's judgment *policy* (often referred to as a "policy capturing" task) and apply it with respect to the objectives and goals of the decision maker and the means by which the decision maker would like to achieve them.

A typical model used in judgment-analysis studies is of the simple linear-regression type, for example,

$$J = f(x_1, \ldots, x_n) = \lambda_1 x_1 + \lambda_2 x_2 + \cdots + \lambda_n x_n$$

where J represents judgment, expressed as a function (in this case a linear function) of n policy variables x_i and their associated measures of relative importance, weights λ_i.

For example, a hypothetical policy maker wishes to satisfy certain future energy goals—gasoline consumption, household heating, tons of steel produced, etc. The policy maker considers a variety of means by which these goals may be achieved. Among typical means for producing energy would be included:

- Conventional oil and gas supplies, x_1
- Synthetic oil and gas supplies, x_2
- Oil and gas imports, x_3
- Nuclear power, x_4
- Coal, x_5

The preferences of individual policy makers will of course differ. The main purpose of applied social judgment theory is to obtain an explicit, quantitative description of the policy maker's cognitive system (i.e., the variables, their weights, and the aggregate functions) by which information is integrated into an expression of preference. The quantitative description of the policy maker's cognitive system is referred to as his or her "policy." Thus, for example, one policy maker could be characterized by policy J_1;

$$J_1 = 0.1x_1 + 0.1x_2 + 0.5x_3 + 0.1x_4 + 0.2x_5$$

another by policy J_2:

$$J_2 = 0.38x_1 + 0.06x_2 + 0.31x_3 + 0.19x_4 + 0.06x_5$$

etc.

Once constructed, if such cognitive models truly represent a policy, then they permit prediction of the policy maker's preference judgments in response to variations (real or hypothetical) in both the future goals and the current means.

How are the quantitative forms derived? First, the necessary constraints must be determined. In this case, the policy maker would be required to indicate the acceptable limits in the range or share of each energy source in the total energy supply.

Next, a large number of variations (within the established ranges) in both future goals and current means would be randomly generated. The purpose is to generate a sufficiently large and unbiased sample of possible variants or scenarios tying the current means with future goals. No significant subset of combinations should be omitted; hence, the generation is random.

The policy maker then judges each combination of goals and means, indicating preferences among the "packages" by ranking them on a twenty-point rating scale. A weighted average regression model is fitted through the observations, and the weights λ_i are calculated.

The policy maker's judgment policy is then displayed via computer graphics. The policy maker observes the weights and function form and is advised about the consistency with which his or her judgment was exercised. By "consistency" we mean the level of correspondence between the policy maker's judgments and the fitted model, i.e., the predictability of the judgments from the model.

Such quantitative descriptions are supposed to make the judgment process explicit and understood. However, the following question remains: Does the weighted linear function, despite its possible predictability, have anything to do with the way people actually go about forming their judgments?

It is always possible to fit a set of observed past data with a simple or complex function in such a way that a best possible fit (or consistency) is achieved. But such a function could be entirely alien to the actual mechanism by which human beings process information and form preferences. Then, of course, its predictive value would be unreliable and spurious, and its explanatory value would be negligible. We shall discuss some of these important issues in Sec. 13-4.

13-3 COMPARATIVE ANALYSIS OF MAUT AND SJT

Bertil Tell (1976) tested some representative methods using both the *direct*-interrogation (MAUT) and the *indirect*-interrogation (SJT) approach. A real-life problem of evaluating the overall capability of air force squadrons was used as a basis for the comparisons.

The capability of a squadron is determined by tests of interception technique. These tests measure three basic attributes: the pilot's ability to use bombs, missiles, and guns. (For more details refer to Sec. 12-4.3.)

Tell tested six regression models: linear, conjunctive, disjunctive, logarithmic, exponential, and linear with interactions (see Table 13-1). These were compared with four models based on the direct interrogation of decision makers: a multiplicative model, two versions of weighted additive models, and a simple version of a quasi-additive form with interaction terms (see Tabe 12-1 for their three-dimensional representations).

The MAUT techniques differed from the SJT mainly in the strategy used for estimating the component utility functions $u_i(x_i)$ and the parameters λ_i. For example, the standard lottery technique, advocated by Keeney and Raiffa (1976), was applied for estimating $u_i(x_i)$ and λ_i in connection with the multiplicative form. The direct graphic assessment of unidimensional utility function shape, developed by Miller (1970), was another approach. The least complicated procedure was to assume that the unidimensional utility functions were simply linear.

Tell has developed an interesting set of criteria for judging the comparative advantages of the individual approaches. We shall expand them into more general terms:

1. *Precision of the model.* The accuracy of a model can be established by comparing the predictions of the model with real data. But in many cases, like the one studied by Tell, no real data are available. The accuracy can then be derived from various notions of how closely the model approximates the independent and unaided judgments of the decision maker. That is, alternatives are evaluated both by the decision maker and by the "model of the decision maker," and the resulting level of concordance is measured, usually by correlation coefficients.

2. *Ease of use.* How difficult is it to understand the questions being asked? How difficult is it to answer these questions? Some methodologies are easy to understand but difficult to use; others seem to have precisely the opposite characteristics. Some are judged difficult on both counts. Easy to understand and easy to use—this is obviously a winning combination.

3. *Decision maker's belief in the precision of the model.* This might well turn out to be the most important criterion. Is the model "trustworthy"? Does it enhance the decision maker's confidence? Are the results perceived as reliable? Such characteristics will determine the "implementability" of a model, its acceptance and subsequent development. Decision makers may prefer using a simple model that they understand to a more realistic but also more complex model.

4. *Time and cost requirements.* Many decisions are made under significant time constraints, and the time required for complete analysis could become a crucial factor. The expected impacts of other decisions might be incompatible with the cost of adopting a given model. The time-and-cost criterion will exhibit some dependency on the ease-of-use criterion.

There are other factors to be considered: level of generality, record of previous applications, etc. The relative importance of all criteria will also change with the nature and specific characteristics of each decision-making project. For example, a problem with a large variety of possible decision outcomes and a broad range of attainable values would require a different type of methodology than would a relatively "decision-insensitive" problem. The *decision sensitivity* of a given problem can be measured; it is dependent on the expected variety and variability of possible outcomes. To the degree that all available alternatives are comparable along all significant dimensions, the need for sophisticated decision-making technique is diminished.

Let us return to Tell's comparative study. He explored the correlations between the utility indexes produced in an intuitive and unaided manner and those generated by formal models. All MAUT-type models produced rather high correlation coefficients, but their value differences were insignificant. Bias, variance, and mean square error were the additional measures of precision used in the study. The model based on standard lottery estimation produced significantly higher variances in the estimates of the parameters. Also, the lottery-based estimation of unidimensional utilities showed inconsistencies to a degree not present in other approaches. The low precision found in the multiplicative model can perhaps be attributed to the idiosyncratic method of estimation rather than to the decomposition form itself.

Among the indirect, regression-based methods, the linear model was found to be the best and the disjunctive model the worst. The conjunctive, exponential, and logarithmic models were found to be indistinguishable in this study.

The comparison between the precision of the two types of models, direct and indirect, was inconclusive.

With respect to the remaining criteria—ease of use, belief in the model's precision, etc.—the lottery-based technique consistently scored the lowest. This technique was found to be hard to explain, and its questions judged unrealistic and very difficult or impossible to answer.

Overall, Tell concluded, simple additive models seemed to be preferred to more complex models with respect to most criteria of desirability. The Von Neumann–Morgenstern standard lottery technique was shown to be hard both to understand and to use; it required substantially more time, and it produced a greater variance in the outcomes than the other methods. Its accuracy was generally lower. The simpler models, such as the linear and the additive, based on regression analysis or direct and easy-to-follow interrogation, seemed both to attract users and to be at least as accurate as the more complex models.

13-4 DIFFICULTIES WITH LINEAR REGRESSION MODELS

We have already noted that the weights λ_i in $J = \lambda_1 x_1 + \lambda_2 x_2 + \cdots + \lambda_n x_n$, measuring the relative importance of individual attributes x_i, can be obtained in essentially two ways:

1. *Directly*, i.e., "subjective" weights obtained through direct interrogation of the decision maker; or
2. *Indirectly*, i.e., "objective" weights obtained through indirect interrogation of the decision maker.

Regardless of the way of obtaining λ_i, the linear model can be summarized as follows: The variables $x_1, x_2, \ldots, x_n$ are information sources (attributes, variables, cues) upon which the judgment is based and which are to be combined and weighted in order to arrive at the subject's final response or prediction. The assumption is that the decision maker's predictions can be characterized as a linear combination of available variables or achieved attribute levels.

The basic linear model

$$J = \sum_{i=1}^{n} \lambda_i x_i$$

appears in a large variety of analytical approaches. For example, the *analysis of variance* (ANOVA) model would add terms like $\lambda_{ij} x_i x_j$ to this linear function. For example, if $n = 2$, we can write

$$J = \lambda_1 x_1 + \lambda_2 x_2 + \lambda_{12} x_1 x_2$$

which, through simple changes in notation, say, $\lambda_3 \equiv \lambda_{12}$ and $x_3 = x_1 x_2$, would then become

$$J = \sum_{i=1}^{3} \lambda_i x_i = \lambda_1 x_1 + \lambda_2 x_2 + \lambda_3 x_3$$

where x_3 represents a new "interactive" attribute weighted by λ_3. Although J contains a multiplicative function of x_1 and x_2 and thus its linearity is removed in a two-dimensional space of x_1 and x_2, the model *stays linear* in three dimensions (that is, x_1, x_2, and $x_3 = x_1 x_2$). Similarly, introducing exponential terms, like x_i^2, x_i^3, or x_i^q, would not affect the underlying linearity of this model. For example,

$$J = \lambda_1 x_1 + \lambda_2 x_2^2 + \lambda_3 x_3^3$$

is still linear if the transformations $x_i' = x_i^q$ are performed. That is,

$$J = \lambda_1 x_1' + \lambda_2 x_2' + \lambda_3 x_3'$$

where $x_1' = x_1$, $x_2' = x_2^2$, and $x_3' = x_3^3$. The linearity has been preserved in the space of x_1', x_2', and x_3'.

We see that the linear model is the underlying core of most of the approaches in question. The nonlinear rescaling of attributes affects only the ways in which the attributes enter the basic model. Most main approaches thus differ only in the ways by which inputs into

$$J = \sum_{i=1}^{n} \lambda_i x_i$$

that is, λ_i's and x_i's, are obtained or measured. But they are all identical with respect to the basic linearity of the underlying model.

The very fact that a choice is being made by human decision makers implies that some kind of a *preference function* (trade-off function, ordering function, utility function, etc.), ordering the available alternatives, can be applied to model the decision maker's preferences. The particular form of the preference ordering determines the manner in which a decision maker's usage of attributes is represented.

Let us denote an imaginary preference function as U, defined on a set of available attributes, as follows:

$$U = f(x_1, x_2, \ldots, x_n)$$

Such a complex, nonlinear, explicitly unknown, and possibly even indeterminable preference structure U can be used to induce the necessary ordering of the available alternative choices. This is not meant to imply that people *actually* make their choices on the basis of complex and nonlinear preference-ordering principles. It simply means that human choices can be so described or modeled. Ward Edwards cautions that not much should be read into any particular form of U:

> This notion of maximization is mathematically useful, since it makes it possible for a theory to specify a unique point or a unique subset of points among those available to the decider. It seems to me psychologically unobjectionable. *So many different kinds of functions can be maximized that almost any point actually available in an experimental situation can be regarded as a maximum of some sort* [emphasis added]. (Edwards 1954, p. 382)

The linear function

$$J = \sum_{i=1}^{n} \lambda_i x_i$$

represents the simplest and the most widely used approximation of U. There are many attractive reasons why such an approximation should be used. First, humans do understand and employ the concept of weighting attribute importance. Second, if the weights λ_i could be determined in such a way that they would fully capture the essentials of the underlying U, then the maximization of J should lead to the same choices as the maximization of U. Third, linear regression analysis, a highly developed and widely known analytical tool, can be applied. The main purpose of so-called "policy capturing" methodology is to estimate λ_i's in such a way that the predictions, judgments, or choices based on J would at least statistically coincide with the predictions of a decision maker based on U.

13-4.1 The Linearity Trap

However, the linear regression paradigm cannot usually achieve objectives such as those just cited. We shall now show why. We shall use graphs to develop our argument and avoid obscuring its impact with excessive mathematical formalism.

Assume that only two attributes x_1 and x_2 are relevant to the choice, so that simple two-dimensional geometry may be employed. In Fig. 13-3, a set of

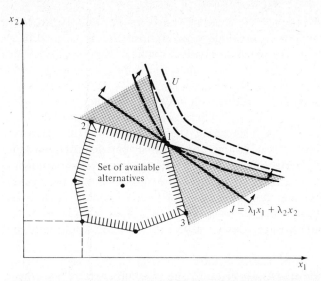

Figure 13-3 Indeterminacy of weights in linear approximation model.

points in the (x_1, x_2) space represents the currently available alternatives characterized by their particular levels of attributes x_1 and x_2. The desirability of
alternatives is indicated by the contours of the utility function U (indifference
curves). U increases in the northeast direction (in the direction of the arrows)
and reaches its maximum at alternative 1. The decision maker's preferences are
assumed to be represented or "modeled" by this particular form of U, and
alternative 1 is the decision maker's choice.

We do not know U. The best we can hope for is its approximation, in this
case $J = \lambda_1 x_1 + \lambda_2 x_2$. This is an equation of a family of straight lines with J
increasing in the direction of the arrows. Each particular combination of
weights λ_1 and λ_2 characterizes the slope of these straight lines with respect to
the origin. In Fig. 13-3, we have determined λ_1 and λ_2 so that J also reaches its
maximum at point 1. In this sense, J is a good approximation of U because it
correctly predicts the decision maker's choice. If we achieve such good correspondence between the decision maker's choice and its prediction by the model
in a large number of decision situations, the model is said to "capture" the
decision maker's preferences through the corresponding uniquely estimated set
of weights λ_1 and λ_2. What is the significance of this insight into the weighting
policy of a decision maker?

In Fig. 13-3 observe that a large number (actually an infinite number) of
different straight lines (indicated by the shaded area), expressing a large
number of possible weighting combinations, would lead to exactly the same
prediction: They reach their maximum at point 1 and, therefore, also "capture"
the decision maker's policy and approximate U. Which set of weights then
represents the "true" combination of weights characterizing the decision
maker's judgment?

This is *the first inadequacy* of the linear model: It may be indeterminate to the extent that other combinations of weights, even those chosen arbitrarily or through a random process, may predict equally as well as the weights which were painfully extracted through regression analysis, if they happen to fall in the same shaded area as in Fig. 13-3.

The ability of linear models to predict well under a large variety of weighting combinations is called "robustness." There are many studies which claim the superiority of linear models because of their robustness, for example, Dawes and Corrigan (1974). It is of course conceivable that this robustness is only situation-dependent, reflecting a particularly favorable positioning of available alternatives. For example, in Fig. 13-3, the "prominence" of alternative 1 practically assures that almost any set of weights would lead to its prediction. But what if the situation changed? What if alternative 1 were removed or displaced? Would the previously "captured" weighting policy still be applicable?

In Fig. 13-4 we have displaced alternative 1 closer to the origin. Such a displacement could occur due to an error in the measurement of its corresponding attribute levels. Let us continue with the same decision maker, represented by the unchanged function U.

Observe that U is maximized again at point 1. The decision maker still prefers alternative 1, which carries the highest utility. But now, if we try to predict the same choice through linear approximation—we fail in all cases! There is *no* set of weights available which could lead to the prediction of alternative 1. For all possible combinations of weights we always end up at point 2, point 3, or both. This is *the second inadequacy* of the linear model: There are cases where the model is never capable of reaching a correct prediction. In our example, while point 1 is the most preferred, the model always predicts incorrectly.

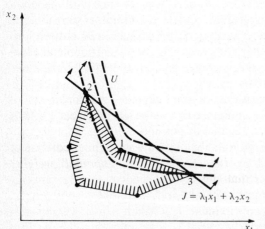

Figure 13-4 No set of weights allows predicting point 1 as the best outcome.

The implications of this flaw are potentially very significant. Let us re-capitulate. In Fig. 13-3, the policy corresponding to the heavily traced straight line was captured through a series of experiments and regression analysis. If U is applied consistently, then the choice would be matched by the model in most comparable situations. The analyst and the decision maker may become convinced that the policy has been captured.

But in Fig. 13-4 we present the same person with a slightly changed situation, namely, point 1 is displaced closer to the origin, behind points 2 and 3 in the southwest direction, possibly due to a simple rescaling of attribute levels corresponding to 1. The decision maker remains consistent, applying the same U and correctly identifying 1 as the most preferred alternative. But the model stubbornly predicts either 2 or 3. Something is wrong. Either the weights are not yet correctly captured, or the decision maker has made an error. The analyst may start changing the previously captured weights or try to recapture them through a new battery of tests. But it is to no effect. The decision maker insists on 1; the model keeps predicting 2 or 3. The question of the decision maker's consistency and rationality is finally raised. Maybe the decision maker is tired and prone to error. Maybe we should help, correct, rid the decision maker of the inconsistency. We show the decision maker that using the previously captured weights, which led to correct prediction in hundreds of cases, indicates that he or she *actually* prefers 2 or 3. If we are skillful enough in our persuasive abilities, possibly backed by some correlation coefficients, computer displays, and a solid record of achievement, we may persuade the decision maker to accept our recommendation (2 or 3) and abandon the true preferred choice (1). Then the decision maker will ultimately derive lower utility at 2 or 3 instead of opting for the highest utility at 1. He or she may continue to wonder why all this happened: Intuition keeps attracting the decision maker (correctly) to 1, yet the rationally argued and professionally recommended "captured" policy points to 2 or 3—the choices the decision maker neither wanted, liked, nor preferred.

There is also *a third inadequacy* of the linear model. Let us assume that the same decision maker (with the same underlying U) is facing two entirely different sets of alternatives. In Fig. 13-5 there are two sets of available alternatives, denoted I and II. The same decision maker, applying identical U, chooses point 1 in I and point 2 in II.

The same solutions can be predicted by specifying a particular set of weights in $J = \lambda_1 x_1 + \lambda_2 x_2$ and by maximizing J over feasible sets I and II respectively. The differently shaded regions of possible weights, applying to I and II, indicate all combinations of weights that would lead to the prediction of point 1 in I and point 2 in II. *Observe that the two regions of "optimal" weights are not even similar.* The point is that the decision maker, by consistently applying U, would imply (or reveal) that two entirely different sets of weights were used in arriving at the respective choices. As a matter of fact, the two sets of weights do not have a single combination of weights in common!

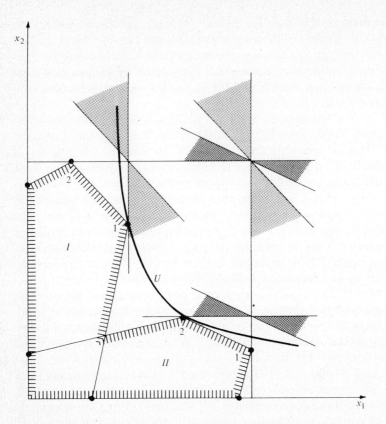

Figure 13-5 Two nonintersecting sets of weights approximate the same preference function U.

Which set of weights "captures" the decision maker's preferences, the first one or the second one? Observe that by applying only one set of weights to both I and II we would go wrong in at least one case. About the only way the decision maker can have consistent choice behavior is to change the attribute weights substantially when transferring attention from I to II. Observe also that situations I and II do not differ significantly: The same decision maker judges an identical set of attributes (x_1, x_2); only the positioning of alternatives in the attribute space is different.

This experience implies that the oversimplified concept of *consistency* needs to be expanded. In social judgment theory, "consistency" implies that the decision maker employs a nonfluctuating, stable combination of attribute weights. If such stability of weights would not be postulated for at least a reasonably useful period of time, any methodology designed to capture such weights would be doomed to failure.

However, in Fig. 13-5, any "consistent" application of a "captured" weighting combination would lead to an inconsistency of preferences (with respect to the decision maker's U). If we assume a stable U, then we have to let the weights change. Having stability in both U and the λ_i's is inadequate. Allowing changes in both U and the λ_i's leads to the theory of the displaced ideal.

The only way to achieve consistency in a dynamic, ever-changing, and flexible environment is to be inconsistent, i.e., to be dynamic, ever-changing, and flexible.

13-4.2 Multicriterion Regression Analysis

The purpose of regression analysis is to approximate a set of observed data as closely as possible by a function. The reader should consult Prob. 13-4 where the problem of regression analysis is briefly summarized. The question is: How is the "closeness" measured and what is the regression criterion?[1]

Traditionally, the regression line is fitted so that the sum of squared deviations is minimized. In Prob. 13-4 we ask the reader to consider also minimization of the sum of absolute deviations and minimization of the maximum absolute deviation, among others. Using different regression criteria implies that different regression lines will be "as close as possible" to the data. Why should we rely exclusively on minimizing the sum of squares of deviations?

There are different conditions and assumptions under which one or another criterion is more suitable for regression. The following should be noted:

1. Sum of squared deviations is appropriate only if deviations are independent, normally distributed with mean zero and common (although unknown) variance. Applying this criterion implies that quadratic loss function is tacitly assumed. Extreme, untypical observations (outliers) are given too much weight and there is often a tendency to "clean up" the data by removing them.
2. Sum of absolute deviations requires independent deviations which follow a Laplace or Cauchy probability distribution. The results are more robust, outliers are correctly handled, and a goal-programming formulation is possible. One can weight individual deviations differentially and independently in order to perform sensitivity analysis of a fitted regression line.
3. Maximum deviation is appropriate if deviations are uniformly distributed with wide ranges, or with high-probability, sharply defined outliers. The problem can be formulated as a goal-programming problem and deviations can be differentially weighted.

Other regression criteria are also noted in Prob. 13-4. We are not suggesting that the sum of squared deviations should be replaced or that any single criterion should be used. We recommend *multicriterion regression analysis,* based

---

[1] A good discussion of multiple regression criteria can be found in S. C. Narula and J. F. Wellington, "Linear Regression Using Multiple Criteria," in G. Fandel and T. Gal (eds.), *Multiple Criteria Decision Making Theory and Application,* Springer-Verlag, New York, 1980, pp. 266–277.

on exploring the impact of multiple regression criteria. The reasons for multi-criterion analysis can be summarized as follows:

1. The nature of the probability distribution of deviations is not known.
2. The choice of an implicit loss function would have to be justified and the theory is ambiguous at the moment.
3. Different sets of deviations might be characterized by different probability distributions.
4. Extreme observations (outliers) occur often and are potentially significant; they are hard to detect.

Goal-programming and multiobjective programming methodologies make it possible to approach regression analysis problems through mathematical programming. See Prob. 13-5 for possible formulations. More flexibility, more powerful computational algorithms, and more opportunity for sensitivity analysis are implied by such methodological reorientation.

13-5 BIASES OF HUMAN JUDGMENT

Both MAUT and SJT are normative theories which attempt to prescribe what a decision maker *should* do in order to make rational choices. The maxims of rational choice (consistency, transitivity of preferences, independence of irrelevant alternatives, maximization of expected utility, and so on) are often violated consistently by sophisticated as well as naive decision makers. The violations are often large and highly persistent (Tversky, 1977). Some psychologists declared man "an intellectual cripple" (Slovic, 1976) because intuitive judgments and decisions violate many of the principles of optimal behavior. They insist that human judgmental biases should be eliminated and offer *debiasing* procedures as a remedy (Lichtenstein et al., 1978).

We face the following dilemma: the axioms of rational choice are in conflict with the actual choice behavior of humans. Should the humans try to adhere to such axioms or should the axioms be rejected?

When humans deviate from the principles of rationality, the violations are often treated as random errors, carelessness, or momentary changes of heart. Those who persist in such deviations are labeled as "irrational." It is believed that once the axioms are carefully explained, any reasonably intelligent person would want to change his behavior to be in accord with the axioms. Yet people are persistent: They do not *wish* to accept Savage's independence axiom (Slovic and Tversky, 1974); they want their judgments to be intransitive (Tversky, 1969); they do not wish to be consistent in their attitudes toward risk (Wright and Phillips, 1980); their verbally expressed preferences are not consistent with those revealed in their behavior (Schuman and Johnson, 1976), and so on.

Even the economists have noticed this body of psychologists' data and theories:

> The inconsistency is deeper than the mere lack of transitivity or even stochastic transitivity. It suggests that no optimization principles of any sort lie behind even the simplest of human choices and that the uniformities in human choice behavior which lie behind market behavior may result from principles which are of completely different sort from those generally accepted. (Grether and Plott, 1979, p. 623)

Consider the following example. Lottery *A* offers $4 with probability .99 and $0 with .01. Lottery *B* offers $16 with probability .33 and $0 with .66. Which lottery do you prefer? Correct; a large proportion of people will indicate a preference for lottery *A*. You can either play a lottery or sell it at a price; for which lottery would you ask higher minimum price? Most people place a higher monetary value on *B* (Grether and Plott, 1979).

The above behavior violates expected utility hypothesis; but why is the preference measured one way the reverse of preference measured another way? *Why should an individual place a lower price on the object he prefers?*[1]

The preference reversal phenomenon is inconsistent with the traditional statement of preference theory, both in economics and psychology. According to Grether and Plott there is only one theory which would be capable of explaining the phenomenon: People look for an anchor or reference point against which the preferences are measured; an anchor itself is a function of the context in which a decision is being made. That is, individual choice depends upon *the context* in which the choices are made! The reader is invited to refer to Chaps. 5 and 6 and Sec. 13-4.1 in order to appreciate this point.

So it is not that humans are necessarily irrational, biased, or in error. They have evolved a set of principles of decision making under constantly changing circumstances and contexts, high multidimensionality and uncertainty, and adaptively evolving preferences. It is self-evident that a theory based on assumptions of given circumstances and fixed preferences, singleness of a criterion of choice, and maximization of expected utility, will be at variance with reality.

There are of course simple circumstances under which axioms of rational behavior may be followed by humans. If there is one and only one criterion of choice, unchanging situations, inability to learn, and inflexible drive for satiation (maximization), then, in the simplest decision tasks, even humans might adhere to the axioms. It has already been established that lower animals generally follow optimizing principles suggested by normative theories of rational

---

[1]How should one view cost-benefit analysis if the sign of the benefit-minus-cost figure can be reversed by simply measuring preference in terms of "most preferred" options rather than in dollar amounts?

behavior. The reader is invited to consult the experiments of Kagel and Battalio (1975), Killeen (1978), Rachlin and Burkhard (1978), and Staddon and Motherall (1978).[1] The question is, can the existing theory of rational behavior be successfully extended to explain also nontrivial choices of human decision makers? Can any single-criterion or single-goal principle of optimality, which guides animal behavior, be generalized to encompass the multiple goals and criteria of humans?

13-6 BIBLIOGRAPHICAL NOTE

The literature dealing with "human judgment" (the term psychologists use for choice or decision making) is voluminous, and one simply cannot do justice to it in a bibliographical note. Nevertheless, we shall make some inroads into it and leave the matter of "doing justice" to the reader.[2]

The subject of this chapter, social judgment theory, measures human performance in judgment tasks, including interpersonal learning and interpersonal conflict. Usually, SJT relies on the statistical tool of regression analysis for measurement. One of the best books covering this approach is Kaplan and Schwartz (1975). A simple and short introduction to judgment analysis, and especially to the interactive computer program POLICY, can be found in Hammond et al. (1977). A more detailed overview of SJT is provided by Hammond et al. (1975b). An interesting application of SJT can be found in Hammond et al. (1975a).

Another "psychological" approach, not covered in this text, is *information integration theory* (IIT). The principal aim of IIT is to discover the precise metric form of "cognitive algebra" human beings employ in various cognitive activities. IIT is best exemplified in the works of Anderson (1970, 1974). In providing a theoretical foundation for the concept of attribute weight as amount of intrinsic information, IIT moves beyond the arbitrariness of SJT.

Attribution theory (AT) derives its concerns from gestalt psychology: It deals with naive, intuitive, holistic, commonsense judgments per se—no models, no weights or component "functions," and no prescriptions are ever aimed for. People grapple to make sense out of the environment; AT attempts to explicate this process. The major readings are Jones and Davis (1965) and Jones and McGillis (1976).

[1]J. H. Kagel and R. C. Battalio: "Experimental Studies of Consumer Demand Behavior Using Laboratory Animals," *Economic Inquiry,* vol. 13, March 1975, pp. 22–38; P. R. Killeen: "Superstition: A Matter of Bias, Not Detectability," *Science,* vol. 199, 1978, pp. 88–90; H. Rachlin and B. Burkhard: "The Temporal Triangle: Response Substitution in Instrumental Conditioning," *Psychological Review,* vol. 85, 1978, pp. 22–47; J. E. R. Staddon and S. Motherall: "On Matching and Maximizing in Operant Choice Experiments," *Psychological Review,* vol. 85, 1978, pp. 436–444; also J. H. Kagel and R. C. Battalio: "Demand Curves for Animal Consumers," mimeo., Washington University, St. Louis, 1976.

[2]The interested reader can consult "The List" of researchers active in SJT and related areas, maintained by Sarah Lichtenstein, Decision Research, 1201 Oak Street, Eugene, Oregon 97401.

In another approach, *psychological decision theory* (PDT), psychologists attempt to make decision makers aware of their own errors and biases. PDT is mostly the work of Kahneman and Tversky. We refer to their pursuits quite often, especially in Chaps. 5, 12, and 14, but their experiments are so important that even more reading cannot hurt: See Kahneman and Tversky (1973), Tversky and Kahneman (1973, 1977), and Tversky (1977).

Behavioral decision theory (BDI), deriving from Edwards (1954, 1961), is based on the *subjective expected utility* concept. It has now been transformed into a "poor person's" MAUT: See for example the description of the SMART approach in Gardiner and Edwards (1975).

There are some classic papers on the use of linear models in decision making, e.g., Dawes (1973), Dawes and Corrigan (1974), and Dawes and Eagle (1976). Slovic and Lichtenstein (1971) provide an extensive review of the regression-based approaches.

Last but not least is the heroic effort of Hammond et al. (1980) to integrate all these psychological approaches—SJT, IIT, AT, and BDT—together with MAUT!

A critique of the linearity assumption in judgment modeling was offered by Zeleny (1976).

Anderson, N. H.: "Cognitive Algebra," in L. Berkowitz (ed.), *Advances in Experimental Social Psychology*, vol. 7, Academic, New York, 1974.

———: "Functional Measurement and Psychophysical Judgment," *Psychological Review*, vol. 77, no. 3, 1970, pp. 153–170.

Balke, W. M., K. R. Hammond, and G. D. Meyer: "An Alternative Approach to Labor-Management Relations," *Administrative Science Quarterly*, vol. 18, 1973, pp. 311–327.

Dawes, R. M.: "Objective Optimization Under Multiple Subjective Functions," in J. L. Cochrane and M. Zeleny (eds.), *Multiple Criteria Decision Making*, University of South Carolina Press, Columbia, 1973, pp. 9–17.

——— and B. Corrigan: "Linear Models in Decision Making," *Psychological Bulletin*, vol. 81, 1974, pp. 95–106.

——— and J. Eagle: "Multivariate Selection of Students in a Racist Society: A Systematically Unfair Approach," in M. Zeleny (ed.), *Multiple Criteria Decision Making: Kyoto 1975*, Springer-Verlag, New York, 1976, pp. 97–110.

Edwards, W.: "The Theory of Decision Making," *Psychological Bulletin*, vol. 51, no. 4, 1954, pp. 380–417.

Gardiner, P. C., and W. Edwards: "Public Values: Multiattribute Utility Measurement for Social Decision Making," in M. F. Kaplan and S. Schwartz (eds.), *Human Judgment and Decision Processes*, Academic, New York, 1975.

Grether, D. M., and C. R. Plott: "Economic Theory of Choice and the Preference Reversal Phenomenon," *American Economic Review*, vol. 69, no. 4, 1979, pp. 623–638.

Hammond, K. R.: "Externalizing the Parameters of Quasirational Thought," in M. Zeleny (ed.), *Multiple Criteria Decision Making: Kyoto 1975*, Springer-Verlag, New York, 1976, pp. 75–96.

——— et al. (eds.): *Human Judgment and Decision Making*, Praeger, New York, 1980.

———, R. L. Cook, and L. Adelman: "POLICY: An Aid for Decision Making and International Communication," *Columbia Journal of World Business*, vol. 12, no. 3, Fall 1977, pp. 79–93.

———, J. K. Klitz, and R. L. Cook: "How Systems Analysts Can Provide More Effective Assistance to the Policy Maker," IIASA Res. Memorandum RM-77-55, Schloss Laxenburg, Austria, October 1977.

————, G. H. McClelland, and J. Mumpower: "The Colorado Report on the Integration of Approaches to Judgment and Decision Making," Center for Research on Judgment and Policy Rep. 213, Institute of Behavioral Science, University of Colorado, Boulder, October 1978.

————, T. R. Stewart, L. Adelman, and N. E. Wascoe: "Report to the Denver City Council and Mayor Regarding the Choice of Handgun Ammunition for the Denver Police Department", Center for Research on Judgment and Policy Rep. 179, Institute of Behavioral Science, University of Colorado, Boulder, 1975a.

————, ————, B. Brehmer, and D. Steinmann: "Social Judgment Theory," in M. F. Kaplan and S. Schwartz (eds.), *Human Judgment and Decision Processes*, Academic, New York, 1975b.

Jones, E. E., and D. McGillis: "New Directions in Attribution Theory Research," in J. H. Harvey, W. J. Ickes, and R. F. Kidd (eds.), *New Directions in Attribution Research*, Erlbaum Associates, Hillsdale, N.J., 1976.

———— and K. E. Davis: "From Acts to Dispositions: The Attribution Process in Person Perception," in L. Berkowitz (ed.), *Advances in Experimental Social Psychology,* vol. 2, Academic, New York, 1965.

Kahneman, D., and A. Tversky: "Prospect Theory: An Analysis of Decision under Risk," *Econometrica,* vol. 47, no. 2, 1979, pp. 263–291.

———— and ————: "On the Psychology of Prediction," *Psychological Review*, vol. 80, no. 4, 1973, pp. 237–251.

————, P. Slovic, and A. Tversky (eds.): *Judgment under Uncertainty: Heuristics and Biases,* Cambridge University Press, New York, 1980.

Kaplan, M. F., and S. Schwartz (eds.): *Human Judgment and Decision Processes*, Academic, New York, 1975.

Keeney, R. L., and H. Raiffa: *Decisions with Multiple Objectives: Preferences and Value Tradeoffs*, Wiley, New York, 1976.

Lichtenstein, S., et al.: "Perceived Frequency of Lethal Events," Decision Research Report 76-2, Decision Research, Eugene, Ore., 1978.

Miller, J. R.: *Professional Decision Making: A Procedure for Evaluating Complex Alternatives*, Praeger, New York, 1970.

Rappoport, L., and D. A. Summer (eds.): *Human Judgment and Social Interaction*, Holt, New York, 1973.

Schuman, H., and M. P. Johnson: "Attitudes and Behavior," *Annual Review of Sociology,* vol. 40, 1976, pp. 161–207.

Slovic, P.: "Choice Between Equally Valued Alternatives," *Journal of Experimental Psychology: Human Perception and Performance,* vol. 1, Aug. 1975, pp. 280–287.

————: "Towards Understanding and Improving Decisions," in E. I. Salkovitz (ed.), *Science, Technology, and the Modern Navy: Thirtieth Anniversary 1946–1976,* Dept. of Navy, Office of Naval Research, Arlington, Va., 1976.

———— and S. Lichtenstein: "Comparison of Bayesian and Regression Approaches to the Study of Information Processing Judgment," *Organizational Behavior and Human Performance*, vol. 6, 1971, pp. 649–774.

———— and A. Tversky: "Who Accepts Savage's Axiom?" *Behavioral Science,* vol. 19, 1974, pp. 368–373.

Tell, B.: *A Comparative Study of Some Multiple-Criteria Methods*, Economic Research Institute, Stockholm School of Economics, Stockholm, 1976.

Tversky, A.: "On the Elicitation of Preferences: Descriptive and Prescriptive Considerations," in D. E. Bell, R. L. Keeney, and H. Raiffa (eds.), *Conflicting Objectives in Decisions*, Wiley, New York, 1977, pp. 209–222.

————: "Intransitivity of Preferences," *Psychological Review,* vol. 76, Jan. 1969, pp. 31–48.

———— and D. Kahneman: "Availability: A Heuristic for Judging Frequency and Probability," *Cognitive Psychology*, vol. 5, 1973, pp. 207–232.

———— and ————: "Causal Schemata in Judgments Under Certainty," in M. Fishbein (ed.), *Progress in Social Psychology*, Erlbaum Associates, Hillsdale, N.J., 1977.

Wright, G. N., and L. D. Phillips: "Personality and Probabilistic Thinking," *British Journal of Psychology,* in press.

Zeleny, M.: "On the Inadequacy of the Regression Paradigm Used in the Study of Human Judgment," *Theory and Decision*, vol. 7, 1976, pp. 57–65.

———: "Intuition, Its Failures and Merits," in B. Persson (ed.), *Surviving Failures,* Humanities, Atlantic Highlands, N.J., 1979, pp. 172–183.

———: "Intuition and Probability," *Wharton Magazine,* vol. 1, no. 4, 1977, pp. 63–68.

13-7 PROBLEMS

13-1 Is there a need to differentiate among "judgment," "choice," and "decision making"? In most of the literature these terms are used interchangeably. Yet judgment does not always imply choice. Consider: "The probability of A is p," or "the utility of A is higher than that of B." These are judgmental statements showing no explicit intention of choice. Compare "I select A because of its p" or "I'll invest in both A and B," statements indicating the intention of choice. I suggest the following definition: *Decision making is a process of transforming the acts of judgment into the acts of choice.* What is your understanding of this statement? Why would maintaining the distinction between judgment and choice be significant?

13-2 Are assessments of utilities, evaluation of lotteries, measurement of preferences, etc., decision making, choice, or judgment? When a deputy fire chief expresses indifference between (1) a 50/50 chance that the first ladder will arrive in either 1 or 5 minutes and (2) its definite arrival in 3.4 minutes, is that a decision, a choice, or a judgment?

13-3 Humans are more able to recall someone else's face by recognizing its holistic pattern than by concentrating on individual traits or attributes and reconstructing the whole through some procedure of aggregation. How does this relate to the problem of explicating an essentially implicit preference function defined over a multitude of attributes?

13-4 Recall the problem of regression analysis. Given a set of m observational measurements on n independent variables x_{ij}, $i = 1, \ldots, n, j = 1, \ldots, m$, and one dependent variable y_j, we can plot a scatter diagram of the corresponding points $(y_j, x_{1j}, \ldots, x_{nj})$. Our task is to "fit" the data with a linear function

$$y_j = a + b_1 x_{1j} + b_2 x_{2j} + \cdots + b_n x_{nj} + \epsilon_j$$

as closely as possible. If we consider a special case with only one independent variable—say, x_1—we might obtain the following scatter diagram of ten observation points $(y_j, x_{1j}), j = 1, \ldots, 10$ fitted with a straight line $y = a + b_1 x_1$:

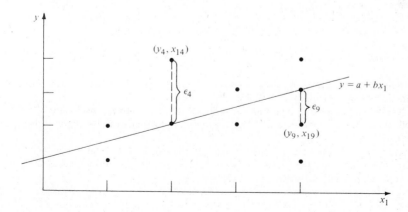

ϵ_4 indicates the deviation (or "distance") of the fourth observation point from the fitted line; ϵ_9 is the deviation for the ninth point, etc. Note that y_j and x_{ij} are *known* numbers (observations), while $a, b_1, \ldots, b_n$ are (still) unknown *regression coefficients*. We want to find a set of regression coefficients so that the deviations ϵ_j will be as small as possible (a perfect fit would be obtained if all $\epsilon_j = 0$). Each deviation can be expressed as

$$\epsilon_j = y_j - \left(a + \sum_{i=1}^{n} b_i x_{ij}\right)$$

and all deviations are unrestricted in sign.

(a) Classical regression analysis finds such a set of regression coefficients so that

$$\sum_{j=1}^{m} \epsilon_j^2$$

that is, the sum of squares of deviations, is minimized. Interpret and discuss also the minimization of the following functions of deviations:

$$\sum_{j=1}^{m} |\epsilon_j| \qquad \sum_{j=1}^{m} |\epsilon_j|^3 \qquad \sum_{j=1}^{m} \epsilon_j^4 \qquad \underset{j}{\text{Max}} \, |\epsilon_j|$$

Why should the minimization of the sum of squares be preferred to any of the above?

(b) Observe that ϵ_j can be expressed as $\epsilon_{1j} + \epsilon_{2j}$, that is, the sum of "above" and "below" deviations. Then the second problem of (a) can be written as

$$\text{Minimize} \sum_{j=1}^{m} (\epsilon_{1j} + \epsilon_{2j})$$

subject to

$$a + \sum_{i=1}^{n} b_i x_{ij} + \epsilon_{1j} - \epsilon_{2j} = y_j$$

where $\epsilon_{1j}, \epsilon_{2j} \geq 0$, and b_i are unrestricted in sign. Interpret this linear-programming problem. How does it relate to the goal-programming formulation?

(c) The last problem of (a) can be similarly expressed in a linear-programming form:

$$\text{Minimize} \, \epsilon$$

subject to

$$a + \sum_{i=1}^{n} b_i x_{ij} - \epsilon \leq y_j$$

Is this a correct formulation? See also Prob. 13-5b.

(d) On a set of numerical data perform a comparative study of the approaches discussed in (a) through (c).

13-5 Interpret the following goal-programming formulations of regression analysis problem:

(a)

$$\text{Minimize} \sum_{j=1}^{m} w_j (\epsilon_j^+ + \epsilon_j^-)$$

subject to

$$a^+ - a^- + \sum_{i=1}^{n} x_{ij} (b_i^+ - b_i^-) + \epsilon_j^+ - \epsilon_j^- = y_j$$

$$\epsilon_j^+, \epsilon_j^- \geq 0, b_i^+, b_i^- \geq 0$$

where

$$w_j = 1 \text{ or } \left|\frac{1}{y_j}\right|, y_j \neq 0$$

(b)

$$\text{Maximize} \sum_{j=1}^{m} w_j (d_j^+ - d_j^-) y_j$$

subject to
$$\sum_{j=1}^{m} w_j (d_j^+ - d_j^-) = 0$$

$$\sum_{j=1}^{m} w_j (d_j^+ - d_j^-) x_{ij} = 0 \qquad i = 1, \ldots, n$$

$$\sum_{j=1}^{m} (d_j^+ + d_j^-) \leq 1$$

$$d_j^+, d_j^- \geq 0, w_j > 0$$

where
$$w_j = 1 \text{ or } \left|\frac{1}{y_j}\right|, y_j \neq 0.$$

Hint: Observe that only w_j, x_{ij}, and y_j are constant coefficients and that the solution vector is $(a, b_1, \ldots, b_m)$. Consult Chap. 9 on goal-programming formulations. Interpret the results in connection with Prob. 13-4. Supply numerical and graphic examples.

13-6 Prepare a term project intended to predict sale price y_j of house j to be sold in your area. Assume that the price can be predicted on the basis of 11 variables listed below. Obtain sufficiently large sample of real estate data on houses already sold, in terms of the 11 attributes and the selling price:

x_1 local, school, and county taxes
x_2 number of bathrooms
x_3 lot size
x_4 living space
x_5 number of garages
x_6 number of rooms
x_7 number of bedrooms
x_8 age of the house
x_9 construction type: brick (1), brick and frame (2), aluminum and frame (3), frame (4)
x_{10} style: two-story (1), one-and-one-half story (2), ranch (3)[1]
x_{11} number of fireplaces
y sale price

Explore the following regression equation:

$$y_j = b_1 x_{1j} + b_2 x_{2j} + \cdots + b_{11} x_{11j} + \epsilon_j$$

Observe that $a = 0$ because $x_1 = x_2 = \cdots = x_{11} = 0$ implies $y = 0$.

13-7 It is often claimed, as in the quote by Dawes introducing Chap. 13, that optimal linear regression models can be designed to overcome intuitive shortcomings of human judgment. Yet the "correctness" of results and underlying assumptions can only be established by relying on the judgment of the analyst. If we claim that human judgment is deficient, can we rely on human judgment in substantiating such a claim? Discuss the dilemma involved.

13-8 Analytical techniques of MAUT and SJT are intended to promote rational behavior of human decision makers. Is it rational to attain a goal of committing a crime through meticulous and consistent planning, analysis, and calculations? Is it irrational to attain a goal of helping needy persons through suboptimal and inefficient efforts? Are decision analysts justified in their efforts to recommend the best means of attaining *given* goals of their clients?

---

[1]Numbers in parentheses represent the values of corresponding variables x_9 and x_{10} in regression.

Even though this is the last chapter of this book, it could very well be the first chapter of the next book; it might even have been the first chapter in this book—in short, if the reader is looking for the end to our guided tour through MCDM, the end has already occurred. Don't ask the author where—anywhere *you* put it.

Chapter 14 deals with some aspects of the postdecision phase of decision making—for example, how are the decisions to be implemented, what is the political process involved, how does one use information for building up confidence about decisions, and where do we go from here?

First, we try to explain where MCDM fits in the following chain of acronyms: OR/MS, EDP, MIS, DSS, HSM. How are these related to the notions of *data*, *information*, *knowledge*, and *wisdom* in decision making? And we ask even more: How are these related to the concepts of *efficiency*, *effectiveness*, and *explicability* in decision making? And what are the roles of *operational*, *tactical*, and *strategic* decision making? Although we cannot provide satisfactory answers to all these vexing questions, we hope to set the reader to thinking about them.

Section 14-5 is devoted to *decision support systems* (DSS). MCDM and especially its interactive versions find their most fruitful interface with DSS. A DSS-MCDM marriage is already upon us—the two participants provide a glimpse of decision making in the eighties and beyond.

DECISION MAKING IS A VERY HUMAN BUSINESS

> *Computer software will have to be designed with people in mind, not to replace them, but to let people relate to machines in ways that more nearly resemble the ways people relate to one another. All this involves a new personal relationship with the computer, but humans, being intellectually inefficient creatures, may be unprepared for this new interactive role. But I think it is important to distinguish between a powerful servant, which the computer is, and a powerful god, which the computer, for all our hyperbole, is not.*
>
> *Lewis M. Branscomb*[1]

We have already discussed some typical MCDM interactive procedures in Sec. 10-6. These computer-aided decision-making procedures offer the distinct advantages of a user-machine symbiosis and partnership. The machine is able to process *data* through complex models of the decision problem and translate them into relevant *information* for the decision maker's use. Judgmental processing of information for the purpose of acquiring *knowledge* about the problem is rooted in a decision maker's subjective evaluations, experiences, and values. Knowledge of different problems can then be interrelated on a comparative basis, and thus decision-making *wisdom* evolves. These four stages of progression—data, information, knowledge, wisdom—are different from each other in nature but interlocked in purpose.

Let us attempt to use the following analogy: Data are like starch molecules, H_2O, yeast bacteria, and other separate elements. Information is like flour, sugar, water, and spices—it has to be processed, then blended together to produce good bread. The difference between a successful loaf of bread and bland mush or black cinder is the difference between knowledge and ignorance. Wisdom then is knowing the difference between good bread and a superb morning croissant or knowing the compatibility of bread with smoked sausage and beer.

Continuing our analogy, data have no particular meaning per se; they are too remote from a given purpose and decision maker's intentions. Molecules of

---

[1]Lewis M. Branscomb, "Information: The Ultimate Frontier," *Science,* vol. 203, Jan. 12, 1979, pp. 143–147.

H_2O could as well be elements of bread as of an atom bomb. But flour, salt, water, yeast, and spices already carry implicit information about the bread to come. We should add that not just any random or intuitive processing of the necessary information will yield bread. A procedure, a formula, a recipe is needed. But the list of ingredients and a set of directions represent only knowledge acquired earlier, tested, and recorded for future use. Some recipes are complete and reliable, always yielding the same expected end product. Some recipes are meant to provide only the essential framework; they are to be accompanied by judgment, experimentation, and imagination. If followed slavishly and mechanically, they yield only unexceptional results. In many cases knowledge has to be evolved for the first time. To evolve a new formula or a new receipe requires human interaction with the data and information. Knowledge can be specialized: One can know how to bake bread but not croissants, or analogously, one can know all about corporate bonds but not much about money or real estate. To be able to judge why and when certain information and data should be used to produce bread rather than bombs requires wisdom. Wisdom refers to the comparative, integrative processing of knowledge about both bread and bombs. Knowledge of one *or* the other is not sufficient to make a wise decision between them. Wisdom is interdisciplinary, nonspecialized, holistic in its very nature.

We shall now translate this rather lengthy analogy back into the terms describing the evolving role of the computer in the management decision-making process.

Operations research/management science has been mostly concerned with developing *new* "recipes" for structured and well-defined problems. It has provided detailed *recommendations* for handling complex data and information. OR/MS is not generically dependent on computers; in fact, most of its methodologies and algorithms have been developed without the explicit assistance of computers. OR/MS is, however, much too remote both from the elemental data and information and from the judgmental integration of the decision maker. It does not provide bread nor does it claim any experience with producing it; it attempts to convey to *others* what might be the best ways of making it.

Electronic data processing (EDP) has gone from "recipes" to "ingredients." EDP has concentrated on the data part, which has been so blatantly neglected by OR/MS. But it has neglected the "recipe" part and, therefore, management decision making entirely. The "paper-pushing" operations of payroll, invoicing, inventory, record keeping, etc., have become fully automated. No information for decision making, corporate planning, or strategic intelligence has been produced—only data. The total integrated data base has emerged; enormous data banks, maintaining huge sets of files with no particular purpose, have been the tangible outcomes of the "dinosaur age" of computer-aided decision making.

Management information systems (MIS) finally bunched the "ingredients" into purposeful groupings and packages. Where OR/MS and EDP had little or no impact on managerial decision making, MIS has attempted to translate data into information and supplement it with standard operating procedures, decision rules, and predefined information flows. But what MIS ultimately amounts to is the dictum that better data and better information can be expected to improve the quality of decisions. As we shall see in Sec. 14-4, this is not so obvious a consequence. Human judgment, imagination, and experimentation with the basic "recipes" are missing—and needed for exceptional results.

Decision support systems (DSS) provide the integration of nonstandard and new "recipes" of OR/MS with the information base of MIS. DSS does not attempt to automate the decision process, predefine objectives, or impose solutions, as does OR/MS. It does not aim to improve efficiency by reducing costs and turnaround time and by replacing clerical personnel, as does MIS. Rather, DSS provides a flexible *supportive* tool under full control of the decision makers, which helps to improve their effectiveness in the decision-making process. It is a technology which addresses, for the first time, unstructured managerial problems. We shall deal with DSS in more detail in Sec. 14-5.

Human systems management (HSM) intends to go beyond knowledge toward wisdom in decision making. Decision-making knowledge, produced and aided by DSS through OR/MS and MIS integration, must be further interrelated across individual projects as well as decision makers. That is how the essence, the understanding of human beings and their experiences within organizations, can be distilled. Decisions must be *efficient* (MIS and OR/MS), they must be *effective* (DSS and MCDM), but more and more they should be *explicable* (HSM). These three requirements correspond to the interdependence of know-how, know-what, and know-why.

We have introduced a new term, "explicability." Let us reflect on the above three requirements once more. Efficiency is performing a given task as well as possible with respect to a given performance criterion, usually economic. Effectiveness involves identifying what should be done and the desired effect or purpose upon which the selection of tasks is based. Explicability is related to the fact that proposed goals and purposes, even if effective, must be capable of explanation. Whose purpose is to prevail and why? Today's decisions involve, at an increasing rate, interests of a large number of individuals, groups, and constituencies. To be able to explain and convince others about the desirability of a given purpose is a necessary condition for a successful decision implementation. Implementation simply refers to the process of carrying a given decision into effect.

Obviously, one can pursue an ineffective goal efficiently. On the other hand, one may attain future effectiveness of a given decision in spite of carrying out its related tasks inefficiently. But even effective goals could be inexplicable and, therefore, unacceptable to other agents participating in the decision process.

Efficiency involves the minimization of the time, cost, and effort required to carry out a given activity. This is fine in a stable and predictable environment. But environmental instability and uncertainty call for the adaptation and redefinition of existing activities; effectiveness then becomes vital and the pursuit of efficiency secondary. In an environment of conflicting demands—for example, from market, shareholders, government, consumers, employees, and different interest groups—the explicability of various courses of action becomes necessary.

During the fifties and early sixties a relatively favorable and stable business environment made the concurrent preoccupation with efficiency very appropriate. Under the turbulent and uncertain economic conditions of the seventies top executives found themselves increasingly concerned with effectiveness while delegating the problems of efficiency to lower echelons. Concerns with corporate planning, strategic management, and analysis of alternative future scenarios are natural outcomes of such a shift in managerial focus. Well into the eighties, we shall probably witness increases in the regulatory activities of government, public debate, union bargaining, and interest-group pressuring. Top management will have become preoccupied with the issues of explicability, accountability, and conflict management. Advocacy advertising, the concern with corporate image, the realization and balancing of multiple, conflicting objectives among individuals and groups, an increased sensitivity to the natural environment—these are a few signs of an ongoing shift in decision-making emphasis.

In summary, let us illustrate these distinctions with a simple hypothetical example. The harnessing of nuclear fission so that it becomes not only feasible but also economical and time-efficient represents necessary know-how which can be exploited for different purposes and effects. Effective goals might be the construction of a power plant of targeted capacity or the development of an atom bomb of desired potency. These goals, effective in their underlying purposes, represent the necessary know-what with respect to a given technology. But why should the purpose of effective destruction or defense be pursued at the expense of other effects or purposes, like production of usable energy? Explicability of purpose provides the know-why necessary for the successful implementation of a given decision. Observe that the availability of know-how is a necessary prerequisite for pursuing effective goals, but it does not guarantee their effectiveness, only the efficiency of their pursuit. Similarly, the effectiveness of a given goal does not automatically imply its explicability and, therefore, its subsequent implementability.[1]

Classification of management problems   Our discussion of *efficiency, effectiveness,* and *explicability* in decision problems is directly related to a more traditional classification of management problems into the categories of *operational management, tactical management,* and *strategic management.*

---

[1]In the late sixties, Edward Teller advocated that the moon be blown up through a huge nuclear explosion. This is an effective goal which could be pursued quite efficiently, but it seems inexplicable under the circumstances. See also E. Teller's *The Pursuit of Simplicity,* Pepperdine University Press, Malibu, Calif., 1980.

Operational, tactical, and strategic management tasks are not independent of the business or managerial environment. The environment can be relatively stable and predictable, unstable and fluctuating, or influenced and "molded" by managerial action. Management can be characterized, respectively, as either *steering and control, adaptation*, or *development*.

These classifications can be conveniently captured in the *task matrix* of Table 14-1.

The diversity of tasks captured in Table 14-1, which is far from complete, should demonstrate why the extensive gathering of data à la EDP or MIS and the setting of rules and prescriptions à la OR/MS are insufficient in their separation. Different decision tasks, operational, tactical, or strategic, performed in different environments and by different decision agents, must be matched by different data and information derived from them. User-machine and manager-analyst interactions become essential. The transitions from decision analysis to decision support systems and from external to participative consultancy become very desirable trends. The task matrix of Table 14-1, developed originally at the Management Science Research Group of the Copenhagen School of Economics [see Johnsen (1978)], can aid in specifying a manager's needs for appropriate information. While EDP, MIS, and OR/MS seem to be

Table 14-1

	Stable environment (steering and control)	Unstable environment (adaptation)	Influencing the environment (development)
Strategic management (explicability)	Improvement of products and services, employee reward systems, new forms of satisfying current needs, setting of goals	Search for new adaptive organizational structures, shape a new internal policy, new information sources	Search for new external policy, political solutions, image and advocacy advertising (public relations), development of future scenarios
Tactical management (effectiveness)	Attaining objectives, satisficing, resource coordination and allocation, specifying resource requirements	Redesign of work relations, conflict resolution, consultation, negotiation and implementation	Close interaction between the organization and its circumstances, information management
Operational management (efficiency)	Optimization of current processes, management according to given rules, administration in accordance with agreed norms	Changing the work conditions, tools, technological and group climate, individual adaptation, and participation	Dialogue; self-determination; create conditions for creativity, responsibility, and risk taking; experimentation

related to the lower-left corner of Table 14-1, MCDM and DSS occupy its middle and upper-right sections, and HSM evolves as a synthetic view of the task matrix as a whole.[1]

14-1 DECISION IMPLEMENTATION

The question of implementation has received considerable attention in recent OR/MS literature. Decisions recommended by normative decision analysis have proved difficult to implement, experience showing that most chosen alternatives tend to change significantly during implementation. Their initial attributes, including those which played a major role in their selection in the first place, may become perceptibly transformed and distorted in the process. The alternative which is finally implemented may be far from optimal.

Are the failures of OR/MS models due to inadequate implementation efforts? According to R. F. Barton (1977), blaming implementation protects the cherished conceptualizations of our models and analyses. But what if our models are themselves deficient? What if important goals, attributes, and qualitative aspects have been left out? If we do not have the right product, then no amount of advertising, promotion, or persuasion will make it better.

There are many reasons for implementation failures: lack of communication, changes in the problem situation subsequent to the analysis, insufficient commitment. But the most important reason, the one which is least explored and only rarely admitted, is the inadequacy of single-objective, simplistic, mathematically "overcharged" models.

One difficulty is that decision making and implementation tend to be viewed as two separate processes. The problem of implementation is then reduced to the problem of accepting and selling the previously derived independent solution. Attempts to focus on implementation as an issue separate from design and technique only further aggravate the difficulties. Whenever implementation becomes synonymous with persuasion and selling, we probably do not have the right product in the first place.

Peter F. Drucker (1973) states that the only people who have developed a systematic and standardized approach to decision making are the Japanese.

Instead of decision *making*, we should probably talk about *unfolding* a decision in the Japanese sense, with emphasis on the process rather than on the act of making a decision. The process revolves around formulating the alternatives, reassessing the goals and objectives, "tuning up" the evaluations, and making partial decisions. The people who actually implement the final decision are involved throughout the whole decision-unfolding process.

In this process, after some time a decision emerges. One prominent alternative is tossed around, scrutinized, discussed, and finally agreed upon by most of the people involved. In some sense a decision has been made, although

---

[1]HSM integrative efforts are being pursued in an international journal, *Human Systems Management*, published quarterly by North-Holland Publishing Company.

pinpointing the actual time when it "happened" would be quite difficult and rather unimportant. The process of "implementation" has already been under way for some time. Many different decisions require similar implementation efforts and ground preparation; there is no need to wait until after the decision has been made.

Decision consensus is usually arrived at through this process. There is no doubt about implementing such a decision. All the selling, accommodation, negotiation, persuasion, politicking, organizational changes, and power adjustments have already been undertaken through the process of arriving at the decision. Actually, "making" the decision simply means reaching the action stage of the whole process. Although such a process is certainly time-consuming, it produces very effective, fully supported, and smoothly implementable decisions.

The Japanese do not view the tasks of implementation, selling, and advocacy as separate from the decision-making process. All these features are already built in. What is the advantage of making fast, efficient, optimal decisions if you then have to spend all your efforts and available time in explaining and "selling" them? They could become obsolete, suboptimal, and even wrong well before they finally get implemented.

Truly effective decisions tend to be "self-made," unfolded through the decision process. Though they are the result of human action, they often have not been created deliberately or designed according to a preconceived plan. Rather, they represent the spontaneous outcome of actions by many individuals without their intending explicitly to create any particular decision. Motivations, purposes, and needs for a decision may be clear enough, but the process of its actual unfolding is complex. After a large number of opinions, preconceived ideas, conflicts, dissents, influences, pieces of information, and other useful components have been repeatedly combined and recombined in a given organizational framework, a decision unfolds that reflects the organization, its management, and its environmental context.

Can multiple-criteria decision making offer any hope for the "implementation problem"? MCDM models can include a larger variety of the decision maker's objectives and criteria, especially those criteria which are so important that they can overrule many analytical conclusions that ignore them. Since values and weights are instrumental in resolving conflicts posed by multi-criterion models, one hopes that analysts will learn to incorporate the values of their decision-making constituents into their analyses. But as R. F. Barton cautions the OR/MS profession,

> Hope diminishes relative to the "implementation problem" when one sees the many articles in the multicriteria literature that appear to repeat the "sins" of single-criterion theory of the past: too much emphasis on elegance of models, a dedication to optimization in terms of a single supercriterion, and failure to deal with uncertainty other than by expected value. (Barton 1977, p. 73)

Where no supercriterion is applicable (as in most practical decisions), there is no measure of trade-off among the many goals. The basis for selecting an alternative is less straightforward, more complex, and rather judgmental. One important aspect of MCDM is that its models rely heavily on the decision maker's judgment in the selection of alternatives. Relying more on the decision maker's rationality means relying less on the rationality built into the model.

Barton draws our attention to the fact that action programs are usually extremely complex, and the evaluation of a total action program can be so mind-boggling as to be impossible. Under these circumstances, the idea of mutually exclusive alternatives that are evaluated against one another under a conflict-resolving single supercriterion (the fundamental idea of optimization) is nonoperational. The implication for OR/MS models is that they should become more alternative-creating and less exclusively alternative-evaluating; more information-seeking, less information-processing. As this book witnesses, the author could not agree more.

14-2 THE DECISION MAKER'S INVOLVEMENT

The decision-making process has evolved through the painful and unforgiving tests of social and individual history. Its dynamics, adaptability, and flexibility have persisted and demonstrated a high degree of survival value. Approximate reasoning, fuzziness, and dynamic readjustment characterize this process. In dealing with complex reality, the human being as a decision maker is *irreplaceable*. Human capabilities have not even been approached by the most dizzying superstructures of mathematical analysis.

The decision-making paradigm that has evolved in modern society must be amplified rather than retarded, understood rather than ignored, respected rather than degraded. Normative models cannot be constructed without genuine understanding of the most advanced decision-making "model" evolved so far: the *human decision-making process*.

Much remains to be done. Interactive decision aiding, decision support systems, multicriterion conflict management, information-processing patterns, the adaptability of preferences—these are only some of the decision-making aspects we are just beginning to explore.

We have yet to design a computer-based decision support system which could be "driven" like an automobile. To try to replace the driver before we have the car may only mean that we will never travel.

14-3 DECISON MAKING AS A POLITICAL PROCESS

Formulating an effective decision and designing policies to pursue it efficiently are necessary but not sufficient conditions for its successful implementation. The policy must be explicable, convincing, and easily communicated. Why? Different people—decision makers, managers, analysts, and policy makers— are likely to favor different criteria and purposes. They might all exhibit sufficient degrees of effectiveness or efficiency. There is an internal *political dimension* in most organizations which cannot be ignored, as it represents one of the most significant factors of implementation.

Efficiency and effectiveness are not enough. The politics of a decision maker's organizational environment is different from that of an analyst or from that perceived by the analyst. Political ramifications for a top executive are different from those for a floor manager. In a political environment, OR/MS methods cannot be successful so long as they ignore the underlying need for the ideas of cognitive psychology, sociology, economics, and political science. Complementing the basic quantitative rational-analytic content of OR/MS in this way can only extend its implementational capabilities.

A decision which has not been implemented amounts to failure, even if its objectivity, rationality, and scientific value are undisputed. As long as a decision remains inexplicable in terms of the value systems, criteria, and purposes of some of the participants in the decision-making process, its implementation is not assured.

As an example, socioeconomic reforms in a given country can have full scientific and evolutionary validity, their pursuit might be desired by most of the population, and yet they might fail when overruled by crude and "unscientific" military action. A significant "participant" in the decision process was, perhaps, ignored. The rationality and potential effectiveness of a given decision have remained inexplicable to certain parties. Simply accusing them of ignorance will not be sufficient for a successful implementation of the decision.

Similarly, blaming changing circumstances is not sufficient for explaining a failure of implementation. We hear too often that a given forecasting model would have worked if only the oil embargo or the union strike could have been envisaged. But if unforeseen events did not happen, one would not need forecasts. It was precisely the embargo or strike which needed to be predicted. The model simply ignored certain nonquantitative factors, political trends, and ahistorical, newly emerging social phenomena.

As we have argued throughout this book, there is no "objective" reality or rationality; these categories are context-dependent, observer-dependent, and subject to individual interpretation under given circumstances. The subject is inseparable from the circumstances of its deliberation, judgment, and decision making. José Ortega y Gasset condensed this simple, important, and often forgotten truth into a single sentence: I am myself plus my circumstance."

The decision maker and the decision maker's circumstance, i.e., his or her problem and ultimate responsibility for its solution, cannot be fully communicated to or comprehended by the analyst. The analyst's circumstances are quite different and the personal consequences of approval and implementation of a given alternative are very different from those of the decision maker. Thus, the acceptability and explicability of proposed solutions must be very important dimensions in the decision maker's objectives. They are actually more important than the optimality or objective rationality of the proposal. A suboptimal solution, successfully implemented, may often be more desirable than an optimal solution which is actively resisted, sabotaged during implementation, or rejected altogether.

There is a difference between a solution "pulled in" by the user and a solution imposed by the analyst. A good product does not have to be "pushed"; it sells itself. Bad or undistinguished products must be continually pushed, advertised, and oversold. Where this tactic might work with beer, it is inadequate for the implementation of management-science models.

A management-science model must be a good product first—"good" in the sense of desired by the user, sought by the user, recognized by the user as satisfying his or her needs. It must take into account the user's official and political power base. This is why decision support systems come closer than mathematical optimization models to approximating a decision maker's circumstance. They provide the decision maker with the facility to conduct a dialogue with a model. The decision maker can explore potential intervention strategies and their impacts in terms of the data, information, knowledge, and wisdom of his or her particular circumstances.

Why are the "objectively" derived, scientific policies recommended by analysts often not accepted and implemented by decision makers? Harris (1975) concludes that many analysts want to be the professional servants of objective knowledge and rationality rather than of a decision maker who is a *human being*, whose policies are formulated and implemented in and around an organization of human beings. Complex social relationships of human systems involve power, influence, negotiation, persuasion, and a large dose of organizational politics. The rationality and desirability of most decisions are not self-evident outside the circumstances of a particular individual and organization. An analysis of political feasibility must be a part of the analyst–decision maker interaction.

14-4 INFORMATION AND CONFIDENCE

It is not true that the more information there is, the better. More information does not necessarily imply better decisions: The quality, the relevance, and the *timing* (at which stage of the decision process it is considered) of information are much more important aspects of successful decision making.

Tversky and Kahneman (1975) exposed two groups of subjects to brief personality descriptions of several individuals supposedly selected from among 100 engineers and lawyers. The subjects were asked to assess, for each personality description, the probability that it belonged to an engineer rather than to a lawyer. One group was told that the descriptions covered 30 engineers and 70 lawyers, while the other group was told the reverse ratio. The descriptions contained absolutely *no information* that would reveal whether the unknown individual was in fact an engineer or lawyer.

Prior to reading the descriptions, the subjects correctly judged the probability of an individual being an engineer or lawyer as .3 or .7, depending on the group they were in. However, after they read the descriptions both groups of subjects disregarded the prior probabilities. They also were sufficiently influenced by the worthless descriptions that, as a group, they made essentially identical probability judgments about each statement (typically .5).

People tend to utilize whatever information is available—even though it might be erroneous or unrelated to the task at hand. Consequently, people may actually be hindered from penetrating to the core of a decision problem when they are overloaded with extraneous information. Without specific information people tend to use whatever knowledge of logical analysis, statistical laws, and rational evaluation they can muster. When worthless information is given, they tend to use it and ignore the laws and rules! It is no wonder that the age of the information explosion is accompanied by incompetent, sloppy, and sometimes disastrous decision making—as were, of course, earlier ages.

The relationship between *information* and *predictive accuracy* is still more complicated. Correlated data often lead people to make *less* accurate predictions than uncorrelated or independent data. If you are told that a job candidate is *meticulous*, a certain stereotype may emerge in your mind. If you are then told that the candidate is *punctual*, your stereotype may be reinforced by the information, but you have not learned much since punctuality and meticulousness usually go together. This is called "redundant" information. If you then learn that the candidate is *a baseball fan*, you might tend to discount the information because it does not fit the developing stereotype—but, in fact, this uncorrelated data is *new* information and could lead you to a better, if less confident, judgment about the person's prospects.

Next, consider the study by S. Oskamp (1965), in which thirty-two psychologists, including eight professional clinicians, were given background information about a patient. The information was presented to them in four stages. After reading each section of the case they made a diagnosis. (The correct diagnosis—adolescent maladjustment—was known only to the researcher.) Oskamp found that as the amount of information grew, the psychologists' confidence in their diagnoses increased dramatically. Their accuracy, however, remained at about the same level!

Oskamp's findings can be tentatively generalized as three interrelated hypotheses:

1. Beyond some early point in the information-gathering process, predictive accuracy reaches a threshold
2. Nevertheless, confidence in one's decisions continues to climb steadily as more information is obtained
3. Thus, toward the end of the information-gathering process, most people are overconfident about their judgments

In short, decision makers face an important dilemma. They are most likely to be confident about predictions which are based on excessive, redundant data that are highly interrelated in a pattern that appears consistent. However, the correlation among elements of data does not necessarily make the information more useful. Less correlated data are more likely to yield accurate predictions. Unfortunately, people trust such data the least!

An excessive craving for *more*, but not better, information, manifested in the current boom in management information systems, is not uniformly beneficial. Although additional information boosts a manager's confidence and helps the manager to implement decisions more forcefully, it does not necessarily improve the quality of the decisions.

This might explain why managers often reject analytical models of management science, intended to improve the accuracy of their predictions and decisions, but accept management information systems which tend to support and increase their confidence. Although the decisions themselves may continue to be inferior, they are at least more forcefully and confidently implemented.

14-4.1 A Mind Snapping Shut

After obtaining the minimum amount of information necessary for reaching a decision, expert decision makers tend to use any additional information to increase their confidence rather than the quality of their decisions. This finding should not be interpreted to mean that additional information could not lead to improved decision making under proper circumstances (if it were correctly processed, nonredundant, independent, etc.). But it does imply that human judgment and information processing are loaded with potentially significant biases.

An extreme manifestation of the information threshold is the situation where additional information is not even redirected for confidence-building purposes but is rejected altogether.

Expert decision makers, after some years of "practice," tend to discover that more information rarely causes them to reverse previous conclusions. Their confidence does not have to be boosted, as was necessary in their early years. There is a growing tendency to disregard and reject such additional information as extraneous and redundant, often before the information threshold is reached: A mind "snaps shut."

Perrin and Goodman (1978) explore the effects of the mind snapping shut by evaluating the telephone management of five common acute pediatric problems. A "programmed mother" made unidentified calls to 5 pediatric nurse practitioners, 28 pediatric house officers, and 23 pediatricians in practice. Calls were tape-recorded and scored for history-taking, disposition, and interviewing skills.

Their results demonstrate that nurse practitioners perform at least as well as, or better than, pediatricians in all measured aspects of telephone care. Practicing pediatricians seem to perform better in prescribing than in obtaining pertinent information. Their attitude is likely to cause them occasionally to miss seriously ill children because of incomplete information.

Perrin and Goodman found a transition phenomenon occurring at that point in the interview when the professional has made up his or her mind about the nature of the problem and is ready to prescribe therapy. The professional then communicates clearly to the mother that she is to stop talking and allow the professional to talk. There were a number of cases in which this phenomenon of the mind snapping shut occurred quite early in the interview, sometimes before any history had been obtained beyond the chief complaint.

This eagerness to provide standard "textbook" advice and the inability to listen sympathetically and thus to guide an interview efficiently toward a conclusion, are not exclusive attributes of practicing pediatricians. A large variety of expert decision makers, stockbrokers, corporate headhunters, interviewers, consultants, etc., are susceptible to similar information-processing biases.

14-4.2 Notes on Intuition

Intuition or inspiration refers to the act or faculty of decision making without the explicit use of rational processes. There is a continuing debate about the proper roles of rational and logical analyses versus human intuition and judgment in the decision-making process.[1] Relying solely on one or the other extreme mode of problem solving is usually effective in only one of the stages of the overall decision process. The analytical approach, possibly computerized and mathematically argued, can be useful in avoiding the errors and imprecisions of evaluating and selecting desirable alternatives. Yet, it does not guarantee that the right problem is being solved or that the premises and assumptions were correctly identified. Similarly, the subsequent implementation stage can rarely be executed through neat calculations or a logical sequence of directives.

Experience, intuition, and judgment have their rightful places in decision making; often they present the only legitimate and available recourse. However, relying exclusively on experience, professional "feel," and intuitional "hunches" does not guarantee that a "best" course of action will be chosen. We may solve the right problem and implement the solution skillfully, but the solution itself may be inferior, habitual, or poorly informed.

We have developed a rather impressive battery of analytical tools: mathematics and computers allow us to perform fast and mostly error-free calculations; quantitative models of econometrics, operations research, and management science assist in untangling complicated cause-effect structures and interdependencies. Yet, in terms of the underlying assumptions, input specification, output interpretation, and other "uses" of these tools, we rely on

---

[1] Recall our discussions in Secs. 2-3, 12-7, and 13-5. See also this author's "Intuition, Its Failures and Merits," in B. Persson (ed.), *Surviving Failures*, Humanities Press, Atlantic Highlands, N.J., 1979, pp. 172–183; and "Intuition and Probability," *Wharton Magazine*, vol. 1, no. 4, 1977, pp. 63–68.

mostly unaided, ill-understood, and subconscious "mysteries" of human intuition and judgment. To use a metaphor, a complex machine is being driven by an ignorant driver.

It is quite natural that an ignorant driver will resist driving a complex machine and prefer to move on foot or in a horse-drawn carriage. So OR/MS proponents attempt to avoid inexpert usage of a complex tool by evolving self-driven machines that eliminate any need for a driver. Decision maker's experience and intuition are largely ignored, the models prescribe what should be done, in every situation, at every step. The machine drives itself and human interference is viewed as a necessary nuisance.

One approach (OR/MS) provides the decision maker with an efficient and reliable tool while it takes control away from him; the other lets the decision maker retain control, but only over a slow, unreliable, and often capricious tool of human intuition. Our approach has been to educate the driver so that his confidence can be increased and to redesign the machine so that it actually can be driven by humans.

Our aim is to improve the whole *human system,* that is the human being *and* the machine in their intimate interrelationship, not just one or the other of its components. OR/MS and MIS are becoming DSS, and DSS are becoming *personal* DSS, ultimately leading to HSM, as discussed in the introduction to this chapter.

The reader has probably noticed that the fallibility and biases of human judgment have only been demonstrated with respect to simple, well-defined, and quantitatively flavored problems. Take, for example, the following simple task: estimating intuitively the product of the first 1000 integers. This is a well-defined problem, unambiguous, and with a single correct answer. Yet, human intuition is bound to fail and all its biases and imprecisions will come to a full bloom in trying to guess the answer. Rationality, mathematics, and computers are obviously superior here.

Take a more complex task: crossing a busy intersection in New York City. Imagine a computerized machine employing a mathematical model, a set of rules, attempting to deal with this task. Its sensors must register the masses and velocities of all moving objects in the relevant vicinity. Probability distributions of their responses must be evaluated. Possibilities of unexpected moves must be assessed. Changes in rates of motion must be constantly monitored and reevaluated by the model. An optimal strategy of action must be computed, put into execution, and probably recomputed somewhere in the middle of the crossing. Still, the machine is likely to get hit. Any old lady or small child is capable of solving this complex problem with a certain elegance and relative ease—intuitively.

Both analysis and intuition are useful—when applied to the right problem. We have enhanced human analytical powers enormously, even to the point of suggesting that they may suitably replace human intuitive powers. Yet we have not considered enhancing human intuition to the same extent. Why not take advantage of this marvel of parallel processing and approximate reasoning?

Why should we strive for the elimination of judgmental biases? They might be too precious and useful as aids in coping with complexity. They have been evolved over millenia and have demonstrated high survival value to the human race. Decision makers should learn how to make their "biases" work for them, turning weakness to strength somewhat as in judo where one tries to use an opponent's strength against him and to one's own advantage. Instead of removing the biases, let us enhance them; let us build our decision support systems upon them; let us adjust our theories of rational behavior to them.

Such a strategy calls for descriptive rather than normative models of decision making. We know next to nothing about how and why people make decisions; yet we feel entitled to advise them how and why they *should* make them. If atoms and molecules failed to adhere to the laws supposedly describing their behavior, we would not call such behavior irrational or suboptimal. Yet, when people fail to follow the axioms of rationality invented by other people, their behavior is considered suboptimal and irrational: It is the people who should conform to the "laws," not the other way around! The irrationality of such an attitude to human beings is staggering in its implications: social engineering, human manipulation and debiasing, slavish following of the rules of optimality, demise of free will.

James G. March[1] insists that,

> . . . goal ambiguity like limited rationality, is not necessarily a fault in human choice to be corrected but often a form of intelligence to be refined by the technology of choice rather than ignored by it.

It is now evident that we need new theories of human choice rather than a more technical elaboration and refinement of the old ones. These theories must take into account multiple criteria, ambiguity and approximate reasoning, context-dependent adaptation of preferences, reliance on reference points and ideals, and a continuous redefinition of concepts like satisfactory, attainable, and ideal.

Let us conclude this section with the words of Eugene O'Neill, the American playwright who inspired millions the world over:

> The people who succeed and do not push on to a greater failure are the spiritual middle classers. Their stopping at success is the proof of their compromising insignificance. How pretty their dreams must have been! The man who pursues the mere attainable should be sentenced to get it—and keep it. Let him rest on his laurels and enthrone him in a Morris chair, in which laurels and hero may wither together. Only through the unattainable does man achieve a hope worth living and dying for—and so attain himself. He with the spiritual guerdon of a hope in hopelessness, is nearest to the stars and the rainbow's foot. (*New York Tribune*, February, 1921)

---

[1] J. G. March, "Bounded Rationality, Ambiguity, and the Engineering of Choice," *Bell Journal of Economics*, vol. 9, 1978, p. 598.

14-5 TOWARD DECISION SUPPORT SYSTEMS

Decision support systems (DSS) are computer-based systems designed to mesh with managers' existing activities and needs while also extending human capabilities. Their role is not to suggest a solution that would be better than the decision maker's; rather, they attempt to extend the decision maker's capabilities so that *his* or *her* solution becomes better.

The first comprehensive overview of the evolving technology of DSS is contained in Keen and Morton, *Decision Support Systems: An Organizational Perspective* (1978). The authors define a strategy for meshing the analytic power and data-processing capabilities of the computer with a manager's problem-solving processes and needs. The emphasis is on the decision *process* and its descriptive understanding rather than on a solution and its structured attainment and justification.

A typical DSS described by Keen and Morton is the portfolio management system designed to support investment managers in their day-to-day decisions administering clients' portfolios. The investment process is characterized by a complex mix of marketing, analysis, judgment, and experience. Such a process cannot be captured by a set of formal rules, ready for algorithmization and computerization. It is an unstructured or ill-structured process. Imposing a structure artificially, as through econometric forecasting, mean-variance analysis, etc., leads only to a very simplified, partial, and insufficient picture of the decision maker's reality.

The portfolio management system was built with explicit attention to the following four points:

1. Each manager requires varying types of information, in varying formats and detail. Individual information-processing abilities, needs, and behavior are primary; increasing the amount of information, supplying more timely information, and gathering more precise information are only secondary issues.
2. The system does not provide answers, solutions, or rules. Managers retain full control of their decision-making process; *they* provide their own answers and solutions. A system that would improve an artificial structure or model on a complex, ill-structured, and human-centered process would not be accepted and used by the managers.
3. DSS enhances managers' specialized abilities by providing analytic support and facilities for testing new concepts, exploring new alternatives, and playing out different decision scenarios. It helps to provide the decision maker with more insight into the problem situation. Assumptions, constraints, objectives, and expectations can be scrutinized, evolved, and tested with respect to data and information on one side of the decision process and values and judgments on the other.
4. DSS must mesh with the wider organizational constraints. Managers are part of their circumstance; they are embedded within a complex political,

power, and personal structure. Ignoring such ramifications would render the system ineffectual. It would be viewed as a "foreign body" and could not become an initiator of organizational change—it would be either removed or ignored.

These are the identifying marks of most DSS compared to OR/MS and MIS or EDP. OR/MS insists on working with formal structures even when there are none. MIS ignores the decision maker entirely and recognizes only the obvious, "objective," routine structures.

We have attempted to describe the decision *process* in Chaps. 3 to 6. It is an ill-structured, flexible, and dynamic process, evolving and adapting itself to different decision circumstances. We have not imposed any permanent mathematical structure on it—but we could have. The OR/MS basic paradigm for decision making simply divides the complex decision process into its components, i.e., states, acts, and outcomes, and considers them together in a two-dimensional table or a neat decision tree. But such a structure is not found within the process itself; it is imposed from without.

The inadequacy of the OR/MS approach is demonstrated with the well-known example given originally by Savage and later recalled by Vazsonyi (1978). There are five good eggs broken in the bowl, and you are supposed to finish the omelet. A sixth egg, which must either be used for the omelet or wasted altogether, lies unbroken beside the bowl. It can be good or rotten. You must decide what to do with this unbroken egg. This problem is said to have two states (the egg is good or rotten), three acts (break into the bowl, break into a cup, or throw away), and six outcomes (the reader is invited to enumerate them).

The above is a highly structured situation. One has to evaluate the desirability of each of the six outcomes (measurement) and then select the outcome characterized by the highest desirability index (search). Nothing more is involved. Most real managerial problems are either ill-structured or unstructured altogether. That is, in the terms of Savage's example, an egg is typically neither rotten nor good; rather, it can be characterized by a large number of degrees of quality or even by a continuous transition function from good to rotten. Acts are not readily enumerable; usually a large number of alternative acts can be invented and analyzed (save the egg for future use, check it by light before breaking, crack it and smell it, paint it and use it for decoration regardless of its state, etc.). In real life, one does not necessarily have to produce an *omelet* from five eggs. The eggs can be scrambled, added to soup, or mixed with rice or salad. Even more, one cannot often determine whether an egg is good or rotten; it is a matter of subjective judgment. In terms of the outcome, you might prefer a six-egg omelet, your housekeeper might prefer a five-egg omelet and no cup to wash, while your child may not want any omelet but prefer to save the extra egg for painting if it is good or for some "beautiful" mischief if it is rotten. Multiple criteria and multiple decision agents (or participants) are often present.

Suppose you invite an analyst to solve the problem for you. The analyst structures the problem according to Savage. After extensive claculations the analyst concludes that the highest expected return is to be realized from breaking the egg into the bowl because the probability of the egg being rotten is very small. But the egg turns out to be rotten, or if it is good, you aren't able to finish eating the six-egg omelet anyway, in spite of your optimistic expectations. Your original inclination to avoid this "decision" problem now seems justified—the problem was improperly structured anyway, and the probabilities were estimated incorrectly. You might feel that if *you* had been allowed to make this decision, instead of the analyst, you would have chosen one of the "other" acts. Your confidence in the analytic tool is further shaken.

DSS allows the decision maker to stay in control through the entire decision process: exploration and alternative generation, structuring and modeling, solution seeking, interpretation of results, implementation. The formal optimization procedure is only one part of the solution-seeking stage of the whole process. Yet OR/MS research has devoted most of its effort to improving and refining formal optimization procedures.

14-6 THE CHALLENGES OF THE NEXT TWENTY YEARS

We are entering a long period of turbulent transformations. The idea of maximization, "more is better," is losing ground. But "less" is the alternative to "more" only in the simple, single-objective framework of past thinking. In a multiobjective view of the world, achieving less with respect to one objective means that more can be attained with respect to other objectives. It is the balance achieved with respect to all objectives, rather than the linear pursuit of the quantitative maximum of a single objective, which leads to an enhanced sense of prosperity, well-being, and quality of life.

Traditional economics and contemporary economic theory, in their exclusive concentration on maximization of profits or growth, fail to grasp and explain the way the real, multiobjective universe works. Economic theory treats "other" objectives or criteria as externalities. The criteria of equity and fairness, employment and education, energy and the environment, personal privacy and self-reliance, ethics and beauty, individual safety and security—all are becoming the inner core of the new way of thinking about life; they are not an aggregate externality.

Economists can only offer minimum costs or maximum growth or zero growth or maximum profits or minimum losses or. . . . It is the sense of balance which is missing, the sense of the vast multiplicity of human purposes. Economic man, the tragic caricature of a maximizing automaton, is dead.

The challenges to MCDM are enormous. Economic theory being unable or unwilling to incorporate the multiplicity of objectives, MCDM and related fields must substitute for it. MCDM thinking must undertake the challenges of the next twenty years.

Professor Daly characterizes singleness of purpose in areas other than religion as fanaticism.[1] Any attempt to be efficient with respect to only a single specific goal, or without any concept of a highest ideal by which objectives are ranked, is an enterprise suitable for economists. It has nothing to do with the emerging challenge of a new reality.

One example would be the use of so-called "cost-benefit analyses" (crude, single-purpose dollar aggregations of a variety of criteria) in judging bio-energy (solar and its renewable conversions) versus fossil fuels and nuclear fission. One should not make the comparison on the basis of purely economic criteria, for much more important criteria are at stake: decentralization versus centralization, self-reliance versus dependency, living off income versus living off capital, safety and stability versus danger and turbulence, a democratic versus a totalitarian state. *All* criteria, even ethical ones, must be taken into account.

Objectives that are genuinely qualitative cannot be replaced by quantitative objectives any longer. Decision makers of the next 20 years will not be exonerated from making difficult judgments and assuming responsibility. Quantification, counting, and arithmetics impose no responsibility—arithmetical decisions are by their nature implicit, and so everybody should reach the same ones. Conflicting judgments of quality, although incomparably more difficult than conflict-free counts of quantity, represent the growing core of responsible decision making.

The precepts of expected values, probabilities, and averages will decline in importance. These concepts are value-free, remove responsibility from decision making, and justify suffering in the name of random selection. But it cannot be acceptable to recommend policies killing or endangering thousands of unidentified, "randomly selected" persons, when saving a specific number of particular individuals commands all available resources and appeals to criteria of ethics. All individuals are particular, whether specifically identified or hidden behind the paravane of expected values! The decision to kill or harm can never be justified on the basis of economic criteria or fiddling with expected values—it must be made on a different level, on the basis of ethical criteria; and the decision maker must bear the responsibility for the ethics employed.

I do not mean to imply that risk and uncertainty can be driven down to zero, or that absolute, perfect equality can be achieved, or that there should be no economic growth, or that unemployment and inflation can reach zero levels—far from it. But when making decisions involving such categories, purely economic criteria are not enough. They would propel us, efficiently, where we did not want to be in the first place. There are no "externalities"; all criteria and all purposes must be considered. Only then can their shifting importance be understood and a selection of the most relevant ones justified.

MCDM will become a major policy-supporting tool in the remaining years of this century. Interaction and interactive decision support systems will be-

[1]H. E. Daly, "Economics, Ethics, and Cost-Benefit Analysis," *Human Systems Management*, vol. 2, no. 1, 1981, in press.

come effective tools in conjunction with the advances in electronics and computers. Interactive graphics, interconnected global computer networks, and powerful mathematical algorithms will allow decision makers to cope with complexity. MCDM will provide the base for a new economic theory—a theory dedicated to balancing human objectives, reconciling or dissolving conflicts, striving for harmony and human dignity, searching for ideals.

MCDM is still limited and bounded by the roots from which it sprang. It is too mathematical, too formal, still groping for its own independent expression. Thus, the material presented in this book is only the tip of the iceberg; it is only a beginning and perhaps not even a very good one. But it is all we have for now. Let us hope that it is sufficiently flexible and malleable to be capable of assuming new directions and new extensions.

Many colleagues urged me to conclude the book with some "powerful" insight, some idea that would connect the present state of MCDM with the future. This is, of course, a quite unrewarding and almost unfair task. To distill any sort of experience and study into a single insight, after subjecting the reader to so many pages of hopeful directions, dead ends, controversies, and plain ignorance, could easily result in an anticlimax. But every book must have an ending.

So, dear reader, the end already was. I hope you did not miss it. If you did, let me try to make another one.

There are no conflicting objectives per se. No human objectives are in conflict by definition, that is, inherently conflicting. Everything depends on the given situation, the historical state of affairs, the reigning paradigm, or the lack of imagination.

We often hear that one cannot minimize unemployment and inflation at the same time. We are used to the notion that maximizing quality precludes minimizing costs, that safety conflicts with profits, Arabs with Jews, and industry with the environment. Although these generalizations may be true, they are only conditionally true. Usually inadequate means or technology, insufficient exploration of new alternatives, lack of innovation—not the objectives or criteria themselves—are the causes of apparent conflict.

For example, Japanese semiconductor and integrated-circuit companies are achieving higher quality and lower costs for their products at the same time. How? In the United States, the term "quality control" is often synonymous with increased screening and inspections: This assumes that better quality is to be achieved by more frequent and stricter inspection procedures, that is, by raising the costs substantially. The Japanese, in contrast, use production designs and technology which do not generate failures and rejects in the first place. Quality is "built in"—often there is no need for inspection at all. Costs come down and quality yield goes up because the technological bounds and rigid ways of thinking have been overcome, and the set of available alternatives has been enriched and extended. Multiple criteria have lost their conflicting nature.

It is my conviction that proper management of conflicting objectives comes not from the application of politics, negotiation, persuasion, or argumentation to decision making. That view denies the reality of the conflict. Rather, one *dissolves* the conflict by inventing new decision alternatives, by innovation, and by breaking inflexible habits of thought. Therein lies the challenge for MCDM in the next twenty years.

14-7 BIBLIOGRAPHICAL NOTE

Chapter 14 deals with a large number of topics which could have been written up as separate chapters. They are all related to MCDM, they are all important, but their full elaboration is simply not possible within the framework of this text. So a listing of some additional readings will have to suffice.

As MCDM evolves in the direction of interactive programming, its methodology will become embedded in decision support systems and/or decision aiding systems. Keen and Scott Morton (1978) provide a good overview of this "framework for MCDM embedding." This reading should be supplemented by Edelman (1977) and Vazsonyi (1978). One of the best collections of interactive programming papers appears in the special issue of *Computers and Operations Research* (1980) on mathematical programming with multiple objectives.

Implementation and the political aspects of decision making are discussed by Barton (1977) and Harris (1975). An even more general framework for MCDM is provided by the continuing work of Johnsen (1976, 1978). Johnsen is one of the pioneers of MCDM, and his current insights are particularly valuable.

Discussions of OR/MS philosophy and its current paradigmatic transformation are well documented and present a challenging set of views on the future of OR/MS. For example, Axelrod (1978) is a collection of essays by charter members and presidents of the Institute of Management Sciences. Some of the more insightful contributions are those by Barankin, Cyert, Geisler, Magee, and Norden. The two articles by Ackoff (1979) contain a merciless challenge to OR/MS by one of its founding fathers.

A new way of thinking about OR/MS comes from the writings of Tocher (1977), Radford (1978), and Zeleny (1975, 1979), among others.

Ackoff, R. L.: "The Future of Operational Research is Past," *Journal of the Operational Research Society*, vol. 30, no. 2, 1979, pp. 93–104.
———: "Resurrecting the Future of Operational Research," *Journal of the Operational Research Society*, vol. 30, no. 3, 1979, pp. 189–199.
Axelrod, C. Warren (ed.): *TIMS at 25*, TIMS/ORSA Bulletin: New York Meeting, no. 5, May 1–3, 1978, pp. 8–32.
Barton, R. F.: "Models with More than One Criterion—Or Why Not Build Implementation Into the Model," *Interfaces*, vol. 7, no. 4, August 1977, pp. 71–75.

Drucker, P. F.: *Management: Tasks, Responsibilities, Practices*, Harper & Row, New York, 1974.

Edelman, F.: "They Went Thataway," *Interfaces*, vol. 7, no. 3, May 1977, pp. 39–43.

Harris B.: "Model Building and Rationality," in R. Baxter, M. Echenique, and J. Owers (eds.), *Urban Development Models*, LUBSS Conference no. 3, Longman, Construction Press, Lancaster, U.K., 1975.

Johnsen, E.: "Experiences in Multiobjective Management Processes," in M. Zeleny (ed.), *Multiple Criteria Decision Making: Kyoto 1975*, Springer-Verlag, New York, 1976, pp. 135–152.

——: "Multiobjective Management of the Small Firm," in S. Zionts (ed.), *Multiple Criteria Problem Solving*, Springer-Verlag, New York, 1978, pp. 286–298.

Kahneman, D., and A. Tversky: "The Framing of Decisions and the Psychology of Choice," *Science*, vol. 211, 1981, pp. 453–458.

Keen, P. G. K., and M. S. Scott Morton: *Decision Support Systems: An Organizational Perspective*, Addison-Wesley, Reading, Mass., 1978.

Oskamp, S.: "Overconfidence in Case-Study Judgments," *Journal of Consulting Psychology*, vol. 29, 1965, pp. 261–265.

Perrin, E. C., and H. C. Goodman: "Telephone Management of Acute Pediatric Illnesses," *The New England Journal of Medicine*, vol. 298, no. 3, Jan. 19, 1978, pp. 130–135.

Radford, K. J.: "Decision-Making in a Turbulent Environment," *Journal of the Operational Research Society*, vol. 29, 1978, pp. 677–682.

Tocher, K. D.: "Systems Planning," *Philosophical Transactions of the Royal Society of London*, vol. A287, 1977, pp. 425–441.

Tversky, A.: "On the Elicitation of Preferences: Descriptive and Prescriptive Considerations," in D. E. Bell, R. L. Keeney, and H. Raiffa (eds.), *Conflicting Objectives in Decisions*, Wiley Interscience Publishers, New York, 1977, pp. 209–222.

—— and D. Kahneman: "Judgment Under Uncertainty: Heuristics and Biases," *Science*, vol. 185, 1974, pp. 1124–1131.

Vazsonyi, A.: "Decision Support Systems: The New Technology of Decision Making," *Interfaces*, vol. 9, no. 1, November 1978, pp. 72–77.

Zeleny, M. (ed.): *Computers and Operations Research*, special issue on mathematical programming with multiple objectives, vol. 7, no. 1–2, 1980.

——: "The Last Mohicans of OR: Or, It Might Be in the 'Genes'," *Interfaces*, vol. 9, no. 5, 1979, pp. 135–141.

——: "Managers Without Management Science?" *Interfaces*, vol. 5, no. 4, 1975, pp. 35–42.

——: "New Vistas of Management Science," *Computers and Operations Research*, vol. 2, no. 2, 1975, pp. 121–125.

14-8 PROBLEMS

14-1 Compare the following conceptual triads:

1. Profitability, competition, efficiency
2. Profitability potential, entrepreneurship, effectiveness

Do you discern the linkages within the triads? How are the two modes of business characterized by (1) and (2) related to the single- versus multiple-criteria question? How are they related to one another? In a short essay, unravel the philosophies implicit in (1) and (2).

14-2 Ackoff, in *A Concept of Corporate Planning*, suggests the following reasoning with respect to employee relations (or morale):

1. The greater the *attrition rate* of employees, the lower their morale. Attrition involves the *costs* of hiring, training, breaking in, and separation.

2. The greater the *absenteeism* of employees, the lower their morale. Absenteeism involves the *costs* of lost production and substitution of personnel.
3. The lower the *productivity* of employees, the lower their morale. Productivity involves the *cost* of direct labor per unit of output of acceptable quality.

Consequently, the minimization of *total operating costs* will result in improved employee morale! Should this "corporate strategy" work? What if you reverse the causality of the three assertions—e.g., what if you assert that the lower the morale, the greater the attrition rate?

14-3 Some interactive procedures define the "best" solution as the one about which a decision maker expresses satisfaction. If there is no such expression of satisfaction, the decision maker is asked to identify the objectives whose levels can be "sacrificed" in order to achieve higher levels of other objectives. The interactive process thus moves to a new solution. Often the decision maker is neither satisfied with a given solution nor willing to sacrifice *any* objective. Some analysts suggest that there is no solution under such circumstances. Cohon makes the following statement concerning this:

> Such a conclusion to the planning process conveys a mental picture of sulking analysts walking off into the sunset while the decision maker gazes after them with a stunned look. The conclusion that a solution does not exist when some course of action will be taken in any event is a silly and totally useless observation.[1]

(*a*) Should any decision support method be allowed to end up with the statement, "There is no solution"? What could be the possible merits of reaching such a conclusion?

(*b*) Does some course of action always have to be taken? Discuss the following options:

(1) Delay the decision
(2) Reformulate the problem
(3) Gather more data
(4) Look for new alternative courses of action
(5) Reexamine preferences
(6) Use another method (or another analyst)
(7) Invite a new decision maker

Would any of the above processes ever be triggered if the decision method always guaranteed convergence to a solution? How important are these seven options in decision making?

14-4 "A problem in many multiple-criteria studies is that the model should express the preferences of an organization and not those of a single decision maker."[2]

(*a*) Can an organization have preferences? Can it have objectives, goals, etc.?

(*b*) Compare the above statement with the following: "Individuals pursue their objectives and express their preferences within organizations. An independent observer could describe the behavior of the overall organization *as if* a particular set of objectives was followed by it." Is there any difference between the two views?

(*c*) With reference to the statement in (*b*), ponder the idea that different observers might ascribe different sets of objectives to an organization. How meaningful is it to search for organizational objectives? Who should be the observer?

[1] J. L. Cohon, *Multiobjective Programming and Planning,* Academic, New York, 1978, p. 203.

[2] S. Zionts makes a similar statement: "In many instances, groups, not individuals, make decisions," in G. Fandel and T. Gal (eds.) *Multiple Criteria Decision Making Theory and Application,* Springer-Verlag, New York, 1980, p. 542.

14-5 Kornai once remarked: "People may not be classified as 'peripheral equipment' of the computer, as a data input or result-evaluating device."[1] How do you understand this statement? What is Kornai advocating? Do you know any mathematical models which do classify people in the way described by Kornai?

14-6 "Human sensitivity to changes decreases as one moves away from the reference point. A given cost that appears exorbitant by itself often becomes insignificant when placed in the context of a much larger expense. This phenomenon implies that people's utility function for losses is risk-seeking and not risk-averse. People are *both* risk-seeking and risk-averse in dependency on a given situation." (Tversky, 1977, p. 217) Perhaps on the basis of your own experience, what position do you take with respect to this statement?

14-7 How do you explain the fact that many people are serious about getting a $1 discount on a $10 item but remain unmoved when offered such a discount on a $1000 item? Isn't a dollar a dollar?

14-8 Suppose you are asked to evaluate two programs characterized as follows:

1. An even chance of losing 500 lives or none
2. A even chance of losing 100 lives or 400 lives

(*a*) Which of the two would you prefer?

(*b*) Suppose that the current yearly death toll is 500 lives. How does this information affect your answer to (*a*)?

(*c*) Most people reverse their preferences in answering (*b*). Why should they? What is the role of a reference point in determining a utility?

(*d*) Analyze the following statement: "The marginal utility of an attribute usually decreases with the *absolute* distance from the reference point (status quo, aspiration level, ideal, anti-ideal, etc.). Accordingly, the shape of the utility function depends critically on the location of the reference point. Human perceptual apparatus is attuned to the evaluation of changes, distances, or differences rather than to the evaluation of absolute magnitudes." (Tversky, 1977, pp. 216–217)

14-9 Test your intuition. There are two glasses holding equal amounts of red wine and water respectively. You take a tablespoon from the glass of wine and transfer it to the glass of water. You thoroughly stir the mixture. You then transfer a tablespoon of the mixture back to the wine glass. Is there more water in the wine or more wine in the water?

(*a*) Answer on the basis of your immediate intuition.

(*b*) Answer after mathematically analyzing the situation.

(*c*) Why is it that the respective amounts must be the same?

14-10 Test your intuition. A man rides a bicycle to a point 1 mile away at 2 mi/h. He returns over the same distance at 6 mi/h. His average speed is therefore

1. 4 mi/h
2. 3 mi/h
3. $3\frac{1}{2}$ mi/h
4. Cannot determine

(*a*) Answer intuitively.

(*b*) Answer after carefully analyzing the problem.

14-11 Major "philosophical" differences between the multicriterion approach (MCDM) and the supercriterion approach (MAUT) can be demonstrated by the following examples. Consider four objectives or criteria f_1, f_2, f_3, and f_4 guiding a choice over a set of available alternatives. We can view the problem in two essentially different frameworks:

(1) MAUT super-function: Maximize $U(f_1, \ldots, f_4)$ where function U can assume different forms, that is $U = u_1(f_1) + \cdots + u_4(f_4)$ or any of its weighted versions. Observe that the

---

[1]J. Kornai, *Mathematical Planning of Structural Decisions*, North-Holland Publishing, Amsterdam, 1975, p. 516.

maximum of U is the main guiding principle; the actual values of $f_1, \ldots, f_4$ achieved are of only secondary importance.

For example, consider that two alternatives provide the following results with respect to each criterion and compute the overall value of U for each:

$$U(A) = 50 + 50 + 50 + 50 = 200$$
$$U(B) = 110 + 30 + 30 + 30 = 200$$

With respect to U, both A and B are equally attractive. Actually should we change 110 to 111, alternative B might be recommended. Yet, there is an *essential* difference between A and B in terms of relative values achieved with respect to all criteria. A is more equitable; each criterion has a "good" value. B is unbalanced; one criterion achieves an excellent score, the remaining ones are only "mediocre." Actually, *any* combination of values for $f_1, \ldots, f_4$ would do as long as U is maximized.

(2) MCDM multicriterion approach: Maximize f_1, f_2, f_3, and f_4 all at the same time. Observe that the individual criterion values achieved now are of primary importance; their total performance with respect to some U is only secondary. The conflict among them is resolved through some "bargaining" or "negotiating" procedure or compromise, not through a supercriterion. Thus, A could be preferred to B even though

$$U(A) = 50 + 50 + 50 + 50 = 200$$
$$U(B) = 111 + 30 + 30 + 30 = 201$$

(*a*) Analyze the above distinction by assuming that f_1, f_2, f_3, and f_4 represent objectives of four *human* participants in the decision-making process. Assume that they consider themselves equally important and their objectives equally legitimate and worthy. Is the above distinction strengthened or weakened in this situation?

(*b*) Show that the possibility of differential weighting of importance does not affect the main argument, as it is equally applicable in both cases. (Or is it?)

(*c*) Why would you expect MAUT to be more popular and applicable in socialistic economies, with MCDM more suitable in capitalistic ones? Or is it the other way around?

(*d*) How do the above considerations relate to concepts of cooperation and competition, dictatorship and democracy, compensatoriness and noncompensatoriness of criteria?

(*e*) Some objectives are externally imposed and some are self-generated. How would their differential treatment fit in the above frameworks (1) and (2)?

14-12 An expert on managerial efficiency suggested: "Efficiency in operations results from arranging conditions of work in such a way that *human elements interfere to a minimum degree*." What is your view of this concept of efficiency?

CODA

After completing this book one cannot escape the feeling that it contains as much criticism, implicit or explicit, as "positive" or "objective" treatment of different theoretical and practical approaches. I am well aware of this fact, as it was the most common and recurring criticism of the earlier drafts of the book. Although extensive changes were made to "tone down" the criticism, this feeling still remains.

A major concern is whether such critical material belongs in textbooks or whether it distracts the student's attention, thus interfering with learning. That is, textbooks should present material simply, objectively, and without unnecessary commentaries; discussion and criticism belong in professional journals.

This represents conventional wisdom. Unfortunately I have never been able to find enough support for it in my own teaching experience. One should not protect students from the arguments, ambiguities, personal biases, and even errors of our profession. To do so denies students the ability to make their own judgments, denies them comprehension of the material, and discourages them from thinking. Even worse, we deny the human side of science, making it inaccessible, remote and untrue.

In short, I consider criticism an essential tool for achieving understanding. I like to criticize and I like being criticized. We would be deeply unhappy in a world where criticism was not allowed or where our students were shielded from our own critical attitude. To criticize does not mean to disagree. Criticism is a reflection of an effort to comprehend—it is the highest honor that can be bestowed on an originator of an idea. To withstand criticism is one of the greatest achievements; to elicit *no* criticism is a sure sign of mediocrity; to fail to criticize is a reflection of indifference.

Another common criticism was that I used too many direct quotes which might distract from the material of the text. We know, of course, many textbooks with no direct quotes at all. But aren't the original words of authors at least as good as those of a mere interpreter? I think they are *much* better. Judge for yourself:

> Whatever we read we must first comprehend and, when we have comprehended, criticize. Criticizing is only another aspect of the effort to comprehend.
>
> We should be given the habit of critical attention so that our first contact with anything worth the effort will give us as keen an impression as we are capable of. Criticism, when we read, think or feel in that way, is sure to be what it should always be, viz., the balance of what we should bow to with what we feel doubtful of. We do not insult great writers or great thinkers by submitting them to this test, but the reverse.
>
> Comprehension is criticism, and criticism or judgment is a mere synonym for THOUGHT.

The above comes from Abbé Ernest Dimnet's *The Art of Thinking* (Simon and Schuster, New York, 1928).

So, dear reader, criticize.

MULTICRITERION SIMPLEX METHOD: COMPUTATIONAL DETAILS

To demonstrate the procedure, we shall analyze a large numerical example step by step:

$$\text{Max} \begin{cases} f_1(x) = & x_1 + 2x_2 - \ x_3 + 3x_4 + 2x_5 \quad\quad + \ x_7 \\ f_2(x) = & x_2 + \ x_3 + 2x_4 + 3x_5 + \ x_6 \\ f_3(x) = & x_1 \quad\quad + \ x_3 - \ x_4 \quad\quad - \ x_6 - \ x_7 \end{cases}$$

subject to

$$x_1 + 2x_2 + \ x_3 + \ x_4 + 2x_5 + \ x_6 + 2x_7 \leqq 16$$
$$-2x_1 - \ x_2 \quad\quad + \ x_4 + 2x_5 \quad\quad + \ x_7 \leqq 16$$
$$- \ x_1 \quad\quad + \ x_3 \quad\quad + 2x_5 \quad\quad - 2x_7 \leqq 16$$
$$x_2 + 2x_3 - \ x_4 + \ x_5 - 2x_6 - \ x_7 \leqq 16$$

where

$$x_j \geqq 0 \quad\quad j = 1, 2, \ldots, 7$$

The composite function denoted Σf_i is calculated as the sum of $f_1(x), f_2(x)$, and $f_3(x)$:

$$\Sigma f_i = 2x_1 + 3x_2 + x_3 + 4x_4 + 5x_5$$

Now we may construct the initial simplex tableau for $x^1 = (0, 0, 0, 0, 0, 0, 0)$:

← y_1	1	2	1	1	②	1	2	1	0	0	0	16
y_2	−2	−1	0	1	2	0	1	0	1	0	0	16
y_3	−1	0	1	0	2	0	−2	0	0	1	0	16
y_4	0	1	2	−1	1	−2	−1	0	0	0	1	16
	−1	−2	1	−3	−2	0	−1	0	0	0	0	0
	0	−1	−1	−2	−3	−1	0	0	0	0	0	0
	−1	0	−1	1	0	1	1	0	0	0	0	0
Σ	−2	−3	−1	−4	−5	0	0	0	0	0	0	0

We can see that x^1 is dominated by looking at the fifth column and recalling rules 1 and 3 on p. 243. Replace y_1 by x_5:

← x_5	½	1	½	(½)	1	½	1	½	0	0	0	8
y_2	-3	-3	-1	0	0	-1	-1	-1	1	0	0	0
y_3	-2	-2	0	-1	0	-1	-4	-1	0	1	0	0
y_4	-½	0	¾	-⅜	0	-⅝	-2	-½	0	0	1	8
	0	0	2	-2	0	1	1	1	0	0	0	16
	3/2	2	½	-½	0	½	3	3/2	0	0	0	24
	-1	0	-1	1	0	1	1	0	0	0	0	0
Σ	½	2	3/2	-3/2	0	5/2	5	5/2	0	0	0	40

No objective is at its maximum at $x^2 = (0, 0, 0, 0, 8, 0, 0)$; compare with Tables 8-6 to 8-8. Use the subroutine to establish nondominance:

0	0	2	-2	1	1	1	1	0	0	0
3/2	2	½	-½	½	3	3/2	0	1	0	0
-1	0	-1	(1)	1	1	0	0	0	1	0
½	2	3/2	-3/2	5/2	5	5/2	0	0	0	0

-2	0	0	0	3	3	1	1	0	2	0
(1)	2	0	0	1	7/2	3/2	0	1	½	0
-1	0	-1	1	1	1	0	0	0	1	0
-1	2	0	0	4	13/2	5/2	0	0	3/2	0

0	4	0	0	5	10	4	1	2	3	0
1	2	0	0	1	7/2	3/2	0	1	½	0
0	2	-1	1	2	9/2	3/2	0	1	3/2	0
0	4	0	0	5	10	4	0	1	2	0

Note: x^2 is nondominated because Max $w = 0$ (see p. 244).

In the next step, replace x_5 by x_4:

← x_4	(1)	2	1	1	2	1	2	1	0	0	0	16
y_2	-3	-3	-1	0	0	-1	-1	-1	1	0	0	0
y_3	-1	0	1	0	2	0	-2	0	0	1	0	16
y_4	1	3	3	0	3	-1	1	1	0	0	1	32
	2	4	4	0	4	3	5	3	0	0	0	48
	2	3	1	0	1	1	4	2	0	0	0	32
	-2	-2	-2	0	-2	0	-1	-1	0	0	0	-16
Σ	2	5	3	0	3	4	8	4	0	0	0	64

This point $x^3 = (0, 0, 0, 16, 0, 0, 0)$ is nondominated because, for example, the first and the second objective functions are at their *unique maxima* at this point. (Similarly, the composite objective function is at its unique maximum.)

Next introduce the first column. (An alternative choice might be the third column.)

	1	2	1	1	2	1	2	1	0	0	0	16
x_1	1	2	1	1	2	1	2	1	0	0	0	16
y_2	0	3	2	3	6	2	5	2	1	0	0	48
y_3	0	2	2	1	4	1	0	1	0	1	0	32
← y_4	0	1	②	−1	1	−2	−1	0	0	0	1	16
	0	0	2	−2	0	1	1	1	0	0	0	16
	0	−1	−1	−2	−3	−1	0	0	0	0	0	0
	0	2	0	2	2	2	3	1	0	0	0	16
Σ	0	1	1	−2	−1	2	4	2	0	0	0	32

↑

Again, $x^4 = (16, 0, 0, 0, 0, 0, 0)$ is nondominated since the third objective function is at its maximum. The alternate solution resulting from introducing the third column would give us the following vector of values of objective functions:

$$\begin{pmatrix} 0 \\ 8 \\ 16 \\ \text{----} \\ 24 \end{pmatrix} \text{ as compared with } \begin{pmatrix} 16 \\ 0 \\ 16 \\ \text{----} \\ 32 \end{pmatrix}$$

of the above tableau for x^4.

Introduce the third column to get the following tableau:

	1	$\frac{3}{2}$	0	$\frac{3}{2}$	$\frac{3}{2}$	2	$\frac{5}{2}$	1	0	0	$-\frac{1}{2}$	8
← x_1	1	$\frac{3}{2}$	0	$\frac{3}{2}$	$\frac{3}{2}$	2	$\frac{5}{2}$	1	0	0	$-\frac{1}{2}$	8
y_2	0	2	0	4	5	4	6	2	1	0	−1	32
y_3	0	1	0	2	3	3	1	1	0	1	−1	16
x_3	0	$\frac{1}{2}$	1	$-\frac{1}{2}$	$\frac{1}{2}$	−1	$-\frac{1}{2}$	0	0	0	$\frac{1}{2}$	8
	0	−1	0	−1	−1	3	2	1	0	0	−1	0
	0	$-\frac{1}{2}$	0	$-\frac{5}{2}$	$-\frac{5}{2}$	−2	$-\frac{1}{2}$	0	0	0	$\frac{1}{2}$	8
	0	2	0	2	2	2	3	1	0	0	0	16
Σ	0	$\frac{1}{2}$	0	$-\frac{3}{2}$	$-\frac{3}{2}$	3	$\frac{9}{2}$	2	0	0	$-\frac{1}{2}$	24

↑

Also $x^5 = (8, 0, 8, 0, 0, 0, 0)$ is nondominated since the third objective function is at its maximum and the two alternate solutions x^4 and x^5 are noncomparable with respect to dominance.

Introduce the fourth column:

← x_4	$\frac{2}{3}$	1	0	1	①	$\frac{4}{3}$	$\frac{5}{3}$	$\frac{2}{3}$	0	0	$-\frac{1}{3}$	$\frac{16}{3}$
y_2	$-\frac{8}{3}$	-2	0	0	1	$-\frac{1}{3}$	$-\frac{2}{3}$	$-\frac{2}{3}$	1	0	$\frac{1}{3}$	$\frac{32}{3}$
y_3	$-\frac{4}{3}$	-1	0	0	1	$\frac{1}{3}$	$-\frac{7}{3}$	$-\frac{1}{3}$	0	1	$-\frac{1}{3}$	$\frac{16}{3}$
x_3	$\frac{1}{3}$	1	1	0	1	$-\frac{1}{3}$	$\frac{1}{3}$	$\frac{1}{3}$	0	0	$\frac{1}{3}$	$\frac{32}{3}$
	$\frac{2}{3}$	0	0	0	0	$\frac{13}{3}$	$\frac{11}{3}$	$\frac{5}{3}$	0	0	$-\frac{4}{3}$	$\frac{16}{3}$
	$\frac{5}{3}$	2	0	0	0	$\frac{4}{3}$	$\frac{11}{3}$	$\frac{5}{3}$	0	0	$-\frac{4}{3}$	$\frac{64}{3}$
	$-\frac{4}{3}$	0	0	0	0	$-\frac{2}{3}$	$-\frac{1}{3}$	$-\frac{1}{3}$	0	0	$\frac{2}{3}$	$\frac{16}{3}$
Σ	1	2	0	0	0	5	7	3	0	0	-1	32

Thus, $x^6 = (0, 0, \frac{32}{3}, \frac{16}{3}, 0, 0, 0)$, and since no objective function is at its maximum, we have to use the subroutine to test for nondominance:

$\frac{2}{3}$	0	$\frac{13}{3}$	$\frac{11}{3}$	$\frac{5}{3}$	$-\frac{4}{3}$	1	0	0	0
$\frac{5}{3}$	2	$\frac{4}{3}$	$\frac{11}{3}$	$\frac{5}{3}$	$-\frac{1}{3}$	0	1	0	0
$-\frac{4}{3}$	0	$-\frac{2}{3}$	$-\frac{1}{3}$	$-\frac{1}{3}$	$\left(\frac{2}{3}\right)$	0	0	1	0
1	2	5	7	3	-1	0	0	0	0

-2	0	3	3	1	0	1	0	2	0
①	2	1	$\frac{21}{6}$	$\frac{3}{2}$	0	0	1	$\frac{1}{2}$	0
-2	0	-1	$-\frac{1}{2}$	$-\frac{1}{2}$	1	0	0	$\frac{2}{3}$	0
-1	2	4	$\frac{13}{2}$	$\frac{5}{2}$	0	0	0	$\frac{3}{2}$	0

0	4	5	10	4	0	1	2	3	0
1	2	1	$\frac{21}{6}$	$\frac{3}{2}$	0	0	1	$\frac{1}{2}$	0
0	4	1	$\frac{13}{2}$	$\frac{5}{2}$	1	0	2	$\frac{5}{2}$	0
0	4	5	10	4	0	0	1	2	0

Observe that x^6 is nondominated. Next introduce the fifth column in the simplex tableau for x^6—it will give us the same values for all objective functions, i.e., we can declare x^7 nondominated without further analysis (x^6 and x^7, though different, both have identical images in the value space). We get:

← x_5	$\frac{2}{3}$	1	0	1	1	$\left(\frac{1}{3}\right)$	$\frac{5}{3}$	$\frac{2}{3}$	0	0	$-\frac{1}{3}$	$\frac{16}{3}$
y_2	$-\frac{10}{3}$	-3	0	-1	0	$-\frac{8}{3}$	$-\frac{7}{3}$	$-\frac{4}{3}$	1	0	$\frac{2}{3}$	$\frac{16}{3}$
y_3	-2	-2	0	-1	0	-1	-4	-1	0	1	0	0
x_3	$-\frac{1}{3}$	0	1	-1	0	$-\frac{5}{3}$	$-\frac{4}{3}$	$-\frac{1}{3}$	0	0	$\frac{2}{3}$	$\frac{16}{3}$
	$\frac{2}{3}$	0	0	0	0	$\frac{13}{3}$	$\frac{11}{3}$	$\frac{5}{3}$	0	0	$-\frac{4}{3}$	$\frac{16}{3}$
	$\frac{5}{3}$	2	0	0	0	$\frac{4}{3}$	$\frac{11}{3}$	$\frac{5}{3}$	0	0	$-\frac{4}{3}$	$\frac{64}{3}$
	$-\frac{4}{3}$	0	0	0	0	$-\frac{2}{3}$	$-\frac{1}{3}$	$-\frac{1}{3}$	0	0	$\frac{2}{3}$	$\frac{16}{3}$
Σ	1	2	0	0	0	5	7	3	0	0	-1	32

We get $x^7 = (0, 0, \frac{16}{3}, 0, \frac{16}{3}, 0, 0)$. We may introduce the sixth or seventh column. Introducing the sixth column, we get the following:

← x_6	$\frac{1}{2}$	$\frac{3}{4}$	0	$\frac{3}{4}$	$\frac{3}{4}$	1	$\boxed{\frac{5}{4}}$	$\frac{1}{2}$	0	0	$-\frac{1}{4}$	4
y_2	-2	2	0	1	2	0	1	0	1	0	0	16
y_3	$-\frac{3}{2}$	$-\frac{5}{4}$	0	$-\frac{1}{4}$	$\frac{3}{4}$	0	$\frac{11}{4}$	$-\frac{1}{2}$	0	1	$-\frac{1}{4}$	4
x_3	$\frac{1}{2}$	$\frac{5}{4}$	1	$\frac{1}{4}$	$\frac{5}{4}$	0	$\frac{3}{4}$	$\frac{1}{2}$	0	0	$\frac{1}{4}$	12
	$-\frac{3}{2}$	$-\frac{13}{4}$	0	$-\frac{13}{4}$	$-\frac{13}{4}$	0	$-\frac{7}{4}$	$-\frac{1}{2}$	0	0	$-\frac{1}{4}$	-12
	1	1	0	-1	-1	0	2	1	0	0	0	16
	-1	$\frac{1}{2}$	0	$\frac{1}{2}$	$\frac{1}{2}$	0	$\frac{1}{2}$	0	0	0	$\frac{1}{2}$	8
Σ	$-\frac{3}{2}$	$-\frac{7}{4}$	0	$-\frac{15}{4}$	$-\frac{15}{4}$	0	$\frac{3}{4}$	$\frac{1}{2}$	0	0	$\frac{1}{4}$	12

↑

So, $x^8 = (0, 0, 12, 0, 0, 4, 0)$. To check the nondominance of x^8, we must use the subroutine again:

$-\frac{3}{2}$	$-\frac{13}{4}$	$-\frac{13}{4}$	$-\frac{13}{4}$	$-\frac{7}{4}$	$-\frac{1}{2}$	$-\frac{1}{4}$	1	0	0	0
1	1	-1	-1	2	1	0	0	1	0	0
-1	$\frac{1}{2}$	$\boxed{\frac{1}{2}}$	$\frac{1}{2}$	$\frac{1}{2}$	0	$\frac{1}{2}$	0	0	1	0
$-\frac{3}{2}$	$-\frac{7}{4}$	$-\frac{15}{4}$	$-\frac{15}{4}$	$\frac{3}{4}$	$\frac{1}{2}$	$\frac{1}{4}$	0	0	0	0

-8	0	0	0	$\frac{3}{2}$	$-\frac{1}{2}$	3	1	0	$\frac{13}{2}$	0
-1	2	0	0	3	1	1	0	1	2	0
-2	1	1	1	1	0	1	0	0	2	0
-9	2	0	0	$\frac{9}{2}$	$\frac{1}{2}$	4	0	0	$\frac{15}{2}$	0

Because of the first column and $@_1 > 0$, x^8 is dominated. We now introduce the seventh column in the tableau for x^8 and get

x_7	$\frac{9}{5}$	$\frac{9}{5}$	0	$\frac{3}{5}$	$\frac{3}{5}$	$\frac{4}{5}$	1	$\frac{2}{5}$	0	0	$-\frac{1}{5}$	$\frac{16}{5}$
y_2	$-\frac{12}{5}$	$\frac{7}{5}$	0	$\frac{2}{5}$	$\frac{7}{5}$	$-\frac{4}{5}$	0	$-\frac{4}{5}$	1	0	$\frac{1}{5}$	$\frac{64}{5}$
y_3	$-\frac{2}{5}$	$\frac{2}{5}$	0	$\frac{7}{5}$	$\frac{12}{5}$	$\frac{11}{5}$	0	$\frac{3}{5}$	0	1	$\frac{4}{5}$	$\frac{64}{5}$
x_3	$\frac{1}{5}$	$\frac{1}{5}$	1	$-\frac{1}{5}$	$\frac{4}{5}$	$-\frac{3}{5}$	0	$\frac{1}{5}$	0	0	$\frac{2}{5}$	$\frac{48}{5}$
	$-\frac{4}{5}$	$-\frac{11}{5}$	0	$-\frac{11}{5}$	$-\frac{11}{5}$	$\frac{7}{5}$	0	$\frac{1}{5}$	0	0	$-\frac{3}{5}$	$-\frac{32}{5}$
	$\frac{1}{5}$	$-\frac{1}{5}$	0	$-\frac{11}{5}$	$-\frac{11}{5}$	$-\frac{8}{5}$	0	$\frac{1}{5}$	0	0	$\frac{2}{5}$	$\frac{48}{5}$
	$-\frac{6}{5}$	$\frac{1}{5}$	0	$\frac{1}{5}$	$\frac{1}{5}$	$-\frac{2}{5}$	0	$-\frac{1}{5}$	0	0	$\frac{3}{5}$	$\frac{32}{5}$
Σ	$-\frac{9}{5}$	$-\frac{11}{5}$	0	$-\frac{21}{5}$	$-\frac{21}{5}$	$-\frac{3}{5}$	0	$\frac{1}{5}$	0	0	$\frac{3}{5}$	$\frac{48}{5}$

So, $x^9 = (0, 0, \frac{48}{5}, 0, 0, 0, \frac{16}{5})$. To check the nondominance, use the subroutine:

$-\frac{4}{5}$	$-\frac{11}{5}$	$-\frac{11}{5}$	$-\frac{11}{5}$	$\frac{7}{5}$	$\frac{1}{5}$	$-\frac{3}{5}$	1	0	0	0
$\frac{1}{5}$	$-\frac{1}{5}$	$-\frac{11}{5}$	$-\frac{11}{5}$	$-\frac{8}{5}$	$\frac{1}{5}$	$\frac{2}{5}$	0	1	0	0
$-\frac{8}{5}$	$\frac{1}{5}$	$\boxed{\frac{1}{5}}$	$\frac{1}{5}$	$-\frac{8}{5}$	$-\frac{1}{5}$	$\frac{3}{5}$	0	0	1	0
$-\frac{9}{5}$	$-\frac{11}{5}$	$-\frac{21}{5}$	$-\frac{21}{5}$	$-\frac{3}{5}$	$\frac{1}{5}$	$\frac{2}{5}$	0	0	0	0

-14	0	0	0	-3	-2	6	1	0	11	0
-13	2	0	0	-6	-2	7	0	1	11	0
-6	1	1	1	-2	-1	3	0	0	5	0
-27	2	0	0	-9	-4	13	0	0	$\frac{107}{5}$	0

$\uparrow$

We see that x^9 is obviously dominated because of the first column and $@_1 > 0$.

To summarize the results, we have explored the following noncomparable extreme points and established their dominance D or nondominance N:

	x^2	x^3	x^4	x^5	x^6	x^7	x^8	x^9
$f_1(x)$	16	48	16	0	5.33	5.33	-12	-6.4
$f_2(x)$	24	32	0	8	21.33	21.33	16	9.6
$f_3(x)$	0	-16	16	16	5.33	5.33	8	6.4
	N	N	N	N	N	N	D	D

Notice that though all the extreme points are noncomparable with each other, x^8 and x^9 *are* dominated. We can see that, for example, x^8 is dominated by $\frac{1}{2}x^2 + \frac{1}{2}x^5$. That is,

$$\frac{1}{2}\begin{pmatrix} 16 \\ 24 \\ 0 \end{pmatrix} + \frac{1}{2}\begin{pmatrix} 0 \\ 8 \\ 16 \end{pmatrix} = \begin{pmatrix} 8 \\ 16 \\ 8 \end{pmatrix} \geqq \begin{pmatrix} -12 \\ 16 \\ 8 \end{pmatrix}$$

Also, x^9 is dominated by the same point. That is,

$$\begin{pmatrix} 8 \\ 16 \\ 8 \end{pmatrix} \geqq \begin{pmatrix} -6.4 \\ 9.6 \\ 6.4 \end{pmatrix}$$

COMPUTER PROGRAMS

Note on computer programs There are, of course, many computer programs available for solving problems of goal programming, multiobjective programming, compromise programming, and the like. Some of them have been published; some are available for the asking; and some are available on a commercial basis.

Instead of giving one or two such programs in full here, taking up much valuable space and running the risk of inadequate choice, we provide a short guide to publications and places where such programs can be readily acquired. Instructors and students should then be able to make the appropriate choice on the basis of their real needs, interests, and available funds.

Multiobjective Linear Programming Package (MLPP®)[1]

This is a commercially available self-contained software package for multiobjective linear programming based on the original multicriterion simplex method. The package replaces most standard linear-programming software supplied by the majority of hardware vendors. It contains the single-objective linear programming package as a special case.

Also programmed in Fortran, it is machine-independent; it is thoroughly tested on such systems as CDC-6400, IBM 360/75, IBM 370/155, B-7700, DEC 20, and Itel AS/6; it is flexible in storage requirements; and the degree of interaction is adjusted to specific needs during the installation.

MLPP® operates on a simple control, task, procedure and option input system, and its terminology is very much akin to SPSS input/output control. It allows for data manipulation, recoding, computation, variable editing, and logic control prior to the actual application of the multicriterion simplex method. Output is well structured and is user controlled for optional degrees of detail; variables are named and an English language summary is provided.

The basic version of MLPP® consists of all control and options for multiobjective linear programming. As a form of solution, the nondominated extreme points are printed and the final tableau is presented, all output being

---

[1]MLPP® is a registered trademark of Computing and Systems Consultants, Inc. (C&SC, Inc.). Software lease and purchase plans are available upon request from Computing and Systems Consultants, Inc., P.O. Box 836, 5600 AV Eindhoven, Holland, which developed, distributes, and fully supports MLPP®. Quick-Reference Guides at $2.00 and User Manuals at $9.50 can be ordered separately.

within A4 format limits. Although the basic version is suitable for instructional and medium-size applications, MLPP® is also available in extended versions, ready to suit the needs of more advanced research and larger applications.

Particular extensions include Goal Programming (preemptive and non-preemptive weights versions), Multiparametric Decomposition, Compromise Programming (available in an interactive mode), De Novo Programming with "flexible constraints," as well as some integer and large-scale features. Repetitive and/or sequential application of the basic as well as the supplemental tasks is user controlled.

MLPP® thus allows comparative analysis of problems with respect to different multicriterion methodologies and algorithmic approaches.

Multiple Objective Linear Programming (MOLP)

Ralph E. Steuer of the University of Kentucky developed MOLP. This program generates nondominated extreme points for linear-programming problems with multiple objectives. It consists of three basic packages all written in Fortran:

ADEX: Generates only nondominated extreme points and allows usage of interval weights for objective functions.

ADBASE: Generates nondominated bases; that is, all basic solutions characterizing a given extreme point are computed; includes the option of interval weights.

ADBASE/FILTER: Generates all nondominated basic solutions and allows interactive reduction of their number through interval weights and specification of "filtering" distance function. Only a characteristic set of nondominated solutions, reflecting user's specifications, is generated.

The Steuer MOLP package is available from the following sources:

Steuer, R. E.: "ADEX: An Adjacent Efficient Extreme Point Algorithm for Solving Vector-Maximum and Interval Weighted-Sums Linear Programming Problems," SHARE Program Library Agency, Distribution Code 360D-15.2.014, 1974.

Steuer, R. E.: "ADBASE: An Adjacent Efficient Basis Algorithm for Solving Vector-Maximum and Interval Weighted-Sums Linear Programming Problems," College of Business and Economics, University of Kentucky, 1974.

Steuer, R. E.: "Operating Manual for the ADBASE/FILTER Computer Package for Solving Multiple Objective Linear Programming Problems," (Release: 5/78), College of Business and Economics, University of Kentucky, no. BA7, 1977.

Isermann's Linear Multiple Objective Program (LMOP)

Isermann developed a program in Algol 60 which computes all nondominated basic solutions and all nondominated faces of the polyhedron of feasible solutions. Thus, in fact, this program allows all nondominated solutions (not only the extreme points) to be generated. The program also accepts external specification of differential weights of objective functions.

A description of the Isermann procedure is available in:

Isermann, H.: "The Enumeration of the Set of All Efficient Solutions for a Linear Multiple Objective Program," Discussion Paper B 7601, Department of Economics, University of Saarland, March 1976. This report was published in *Operational Research Quarterly*, vol. 28, no. 3, 1977, pp. 711–725.

The code of LMOP is available from its author, Prof. H. Isermann, Fakultät für Wirtschaftswissenschaften, Universität Bielefeld, Postfach 8640, 48 Bielefeld 1, West Germany.

Zeleny's Multicriterion Simplex Method (MSM)

This is a program version of the technique, Multicriterion Simplex Method (MSM), which is presented in this book. This technique generates all nondominated extreme points for a linear-programming problem. The code is written in Fortran IV and its alternate listings are available in:

Zeleny, M.: *Linear Multiobjective Programming*, Springer-Verlag, New York, 1974, pp. 197–220.
Zeleny, M. (ed.): *Multiple Criteria Decision Making: Kyoto 1975*, Springer-Verlag, New York, 1976, pp. 332–345.

The above versions of MSM are only research codes limited to smaller-size problems. The full version of MSM forms the core of MLPP® described earlier.

Lee's Linear Goal Programming Program

This goal-programming program is available in Fortran and is based on preemptive weighting of goals. Ranking of goals in terms of their priorities is required and the total sum of deviations from goals is minimized.

Full listing of Lee's program is available in:

Lee, S. M.: *Goal Programming for Decision Analysis*, Auerbach Publishers, Philadelphia, 1972, pp. 126–157.

Ignizio's Goal Programming Package

All Ignizio's codes are written in Fortran and apply to the preemptive weights version of goal programming. The linear goal-programming part includes an option for integer solutions. So-called "Modified Pattern Search Code" solves nonlinear goal-programming problems, that is the individual goal functions do not have to be linear. Listing of both codes is available in:

Ignizio, J.P.: *Goal Programming and Extensions*, Lexington Books, Lexington, Mass. 1976, pp. 227–247.

Goal programming codes by Lee and Ignizio are fully listed but are based on the unmodified simplex method. This affects the efficiency of these codes for larger problems. There are more efficient codes reported in the literature, based on useful modifications of the underlying simplex method, but their listing is not readily available. Their algorithmic descriptions are published, but the codes should be requested from the authors. Below we provide the sources of these more efficient modifications.

Assorted Goal Programming Modifications

Arthur, J. L., and A. Ravindran: "An Efficient Goal Programming Algorithm Using Constraint Partitioning and Variable Elimination," *Management Science*, vol. 24, no. 8, 1978, pp. 867–868.

Dauer, J. P., and R. J. Krueger: "An Iterative Approach to Goal Programming," *Operational Research Quarterly,* vol. 28, no. 3, 1977, pp. 671–681.

Despontin, M., J. Moscarola, and J. Spronk: "A User-Oriented Listing of Multiple Criteria Decision Methods," Report CSOOTW/152, Vrije Universiteit Brussel, December 1980.

Ignizio, J. P., and J. H. Perlis: "Sequential Linear Goal Programming: Implementation via MPSX," *Computers and Operations Research,* vol. 6, no. 3, 1979, pp. 141–145.

Kornbluth, J. S. H.: "A Manual for the Multiple Objective Linear Fractional Programming Algorithms," Decision Sciences Working Paper 80-08-03, Wharton School, University of Pennsylvania, 1980.

Nijkamp, P., and J. Spronk: "Interactive Multiple Goal Programming: An Evaluation and Some Results," in G. Fandel and T. Gal (eds.), *Multiple Criteria Decision Making: Theory and Application,* Springer-Verlag, Berlin, 1980, pp. 278–293.

Ouwerkverk, C., and J. Spronk: "A PL/1 Computer Program for I.M.G.P. Using the MPSX Package," Center for Research in Business Economics Rep. 7823/A, Erasmus University, Rotterdam, 1977.

ELLIPSOID ALGORITHM FOR
LINEAR PROGRAMMING

In Chap. 9, we have exposed the reader to the simplex method for solving linear-programming problems. It is important to realize that the simplex method is not the only possible approach, especially when dealing with complex, multiobjective, large-scale, and interactive mathematical programming problems. One exceptionally promising approach is the *ellipsoid algorithm* (EA).

EA was developed by N. Z. Shor (1977), L. G. Khachiyan (1979), and other mathematicians (D. B. Yudin, A. S. Nemirovskii). Its main characteristic is that it does not proceed from one corner point of a convex polyhedron (feasible set) to another but zeroes in on a final solution from the outside—by successively tightening an ellipsoid which contains at least a single point of the feasible region.

One of the most attractive features of EA is that it converges to a solution in a polynomial time. (The simplex method does so in exponential time only.) For example, imagine that the number of computations (and thus the computer time) is dependent on parameter L of the problem. A polynomial-time algorithm would require perhaps L^2 steps at the most. For $L = 100$ it would take only a fraction of a second of computer time. On the other hand, an exponential-time algorithm like the simplex method would require 2^L steps and could take theoretically millions of years for the same problem.

We present the reader with a short description of the underlying theory, the algorithm itself, and its graphic interpretation, together with some hints with regard to its relevance to multiobjective and goal-programming problems. Exploring EA's numerical and graphic properties on a programmable calculator or computer and carrying out a comparative analysis with the simplex method could be a very useful educational task. It may even lead to significant research projects in MCDM. A short bibliography of EA is appended in order to facilitate such endeavors.

Formal summary of the Shor-Khachiyan approach Consider a feasible set X defined by a system of $m \geq 2$ linear *inequalities* (constraints) in $n \geq 2$ real variables and integer coefficients a_{ij}, b_j:

$$a_{i1}x_1 + \cdots + a_{in}x_n \leq b_i \qquad i = 1, 2, \ldots, m$$

Note that $x^T = (x_1, \ldots, x_n)$, $b^T = (b_1, \ldots, b_m)$, so that,[1] in matrix nota-

---

[1] x^T is a transpose of x; that is, if x is a row vector, x^T is a column vector, and vice versa.

tion, $X = \{x | Ax \leq b\}$ where $A = [a_{ij}]$ is an m-by-n matrix. Let $a_i = (a_{i1}, \ldots, a_{in})$ denote the ith row of A so that the ith inequality can also be written as

$$a_i x \leq b_i \qquad i = 1, 2, \ldots, m$$

Some writers insist that the above inequalities should be strict inequalities. This is to assure that the volume of X will be nonzero. The algorithm works with nonstrict inequalities as well—as long as the volume of X is nonzero (not a point or line).

EA is designed to determine whether the system of inequalities X is consistent (has a feasible solution) or not. Nothing more. Observe that no objective function(s) is present, and thus no directed optimization takes place. In order to apply EA successfully to a linear-programming problem one would have to transform such a problem into a feasible-point problem. We shall return to this question later.

The algorithm proceeds as follows:

1. A large hypersphere containing the feasible region X is constructed. An a priori positive lower bound on the volume of X is determined.
2. A sequence of ellipsoids with progressively smaller volumes is recursively generated. If the center of any ellipsoid is feasible (falls in X), the algorithm terminates.
3. As the algorithm proceeds, the volume of some ellipsoid will eventually become smaller than the lower bound on the volume of X. Thus, an upper bound on the number of iterations exists; an ellipsoid must be generated whose center is contained in X, or there is no solution. (Note that if X has zero volume, e.g., it is a point, then the property of finite termination is lost.)

The major parameter of the system of inequalities X is defined as follows:

$$L = \left[\sum_{i,j} \log_2 \left(|a_{ij}| + 1 \right) + \sum_i \log_2 \left(|b_i| + 1 \right) + \log_2 nm \right] + 1$$

where L characterizes the input of the system and indicates the number of symbols 0 and 1 that are necessary to write the inequalities in the binary number system. The EA computational bounds are polynomially dependent on L.

Because the consistency or inconsistency of X is to be determined, one has to establish a measure of inconsistency characterizing the steps before reaching a solution. The so-called "residual" of the system at point x in R^n is defined:

$$\Theta(x) = \max_i \{a_{i1}x_1 + \cdots + a_{in}x_n - b_i\} \qquad i = 1, 2, \ldots, m$$

Observe that the residual simply identifies the constraint which is violated by the largest amount at point x. One would like to minimize such a maximum deviation remaining in the system. It is obvious that if $x = x^k$ is a solution, then $\Theta(x^k) \leq 0$. Actually, if the overall minimum residual has been driven to zero or less, the algorithm terminates; the corresponding point x must be a solution. If the minimum residual still remains positive after $N = 16n^2L$ iterations, the system is inconsistent.

Khachiyan showed that if system X with input L is consistent, then a solution x^k can be found in the euclidean hypersphere S, $S = \{x \,|\, (x_1^2 + \cdots + x_n^2)^{1/2} \leq 2^L\}$. Thus, S is the initial "ellipsoid." Further, if the system X with input L is inconsistent, then for any x in R^n the residual $\Theta(x) \leq 2 \cdot 2^{-L}$. In order to decide whether the system is consistent or not, it suffices to find a point x in R^n such that $\Theta(x) \leq \Theta_S + 2^{-L}$. Scalar Θ_S is the minimum residual over the entire initial hypersphere S. Either $\Theta(x) \leq 2^{-L}$ (that is, Θ_S is zero or less) and the system is consistent, or $\Theta(x) \geq 2 \cdot 2^{-L}$ and the system is inconsistent.

The algorithm, which also constitutes the proof of the above assertions, is constructed to find the required point x.

Define a sequence of points x^k (ellipsoid centers) and of matrices A_k, $k = 0$, $1, \ldots, N$, recursively as follows:

1. Set $x^0 = 0$ and $A_0 = 2^L I$ (A_0 is an n-by-n diagonal matrix with components 2^L, I is a unitary matrix). This defines the initial ellipsoid $E_0 \sim (x^0, A_0)$. Observe that E_0 coincides with the initial hypersphere S with center x^0. Compute $\Theta_0 = \max \{-b_i\}$, the magnitude of the residual at the center of the hypersphere.

2. Assume that ellipsoid $E_k \sim (x^k, A_k)$ is defined. Evaluate the residual $\Theta(x^k)$ at the center of E_k. Keep track of the minimum residual achieved so far by setting $\Theta_{k+1} = \min [\Theta_k, \Theta(x^k)]$. That is, Θ_{k+1} is the smallest minimal value of the residual over the already obtained approximations $x^0, \ldots, x^k$. (Although the center of the preceding ellipsoid could be arbitrarily close to a feasible point, the next center could be still farther away.)

3. If x^k solves the inequalities, stop. If not, select the most violated inequality according to $\Theta(x^k)$, say the ith,

$$a_i x^k > b_i$$

and construct a new ellipsoid $E_{k+1} \sim (x^{k+1}, A_{k+1})$. The new ellipsoid fully contains the half-ellipsoid $\frac{1}{2}E_k$ in which the residual $\Theta(x)$ is certainly smaller than $\Theta(x^k)$. That is, one defines a hyperplane $a_i x = d$, $d < a_i x^k$, which is tangent to E_k, and a parallel hyperplane $a_i x = a_i x^k$ which intersects E_k. Then E_{k+1} is obtained by computing

$$x^{k+1} = x^k - \frac{1}{n+1} \frac{A_k a_i^T}{(a_i A_k a_i^T)^{1/2}}$$

and

$$A_{k+1} = \frac{n^2}{n^2 - 1} \left[A_k - \frac{2}{n+1} \frac{(A_k a_i^T) \cdot (a_i A_k)}{a_i A_k a_i^T} \right]$$

4. Repeat steps 3 and 4 as long as $k < 16n^2L$; if $k = 16n^2L$, stop. The smallest minimal residual Θ_{N+1} is the output.

Khachiyan also showed that $\Theta_{N+1} \leqq \Theta_S + 2^{-L}$. It follows that either

$$\Theta_{N+1} \leqq 2^{-L} \text{ (system is consistent)}$$

or

$$\Theta_{N+1} \geqq 2 \cdot 2^{-L} \text{ (system is inconsistent)}$$

Consult the References for technical details and mathematical proofs.

Graphic interpretation It is desirable to provide some graphic examples of the procedure. Figure C-1 shows a small convex polyhedron X. Our task is to find at least one feasible point. We start by enclosing the polyhedron in a large hypersphere centered at $x^0 = 0$. Evaluate the residual at the center and identify the most violated constraint. Draw a parallel hyperplane through the center and mark its points of intersection with the hypersphere A and B. Cut off the halfsphere containing only the larger residuals. Another parallel hyperplane is tangential to the remaining halfsphere and identifies point C. Fix the center of the new ellipsoid so that it passes through points A, B, and C. Its volume is the minimum possible. Construct the new ellipsoid.

In Fig. C-2 the procedure is continued. Once the center of a new ellipsoid falls within the polyhedron, stop. The center is the solution.

Murray (1979) proposes a useful modification of EA. The most violated

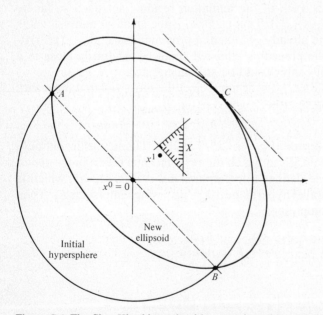

Figure C-1 The Shor-Khachiyan algorithm, starting with a large initial hypersphere centered at $x^0 = 0$. The volume ratio of successive ellipsoids is initially large. (The initial hypersphere is not drawn to scale.)

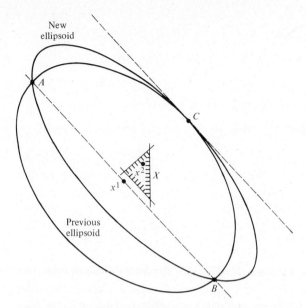

Figure C-2 Continuation from Fig. C-1. Observe that x^2, center of the third ellipsoid, falls within X; x^2 represents the solution and the algorithm stops.

constraint is identified, and the hyperplane $a_i x = b_i$ intersects the current ellipsoid at points A and B. A tangential parallel hyperplane identifies point C. Only the excerpted subsection of the ellipsoid is now enclosed by the ellipsoid of the smallest volume, passing through A, B, and C. This approach is demonstrated in Fig. C-3.

The advantage of Murray's modification is that the ratio of the volume of the new ellipsoid to that of the old one has been significantly improved. The performance of EA represents a lower bound with respect to this modification. Further, the center x^{k+1} is always feasible with respect to the violated constraint chosen at the kth step. Also, the worse the initial choice, the more the initial reduction in the volume of the ellipsoid. Obviously, there are many possible further modifications. The flexibility and open-endedness of ellipsoid methods assure that a lively interest in research and application will continue.[1]

Discussion We mentioned that EA cannot be applied to linear programming without transformation into a feasible-point problem. The following approach is based on the well-known results of the duality theory; see Gács and Lovász (1979).

---

[1]Philip Wolfe (1980) has compiled a bibliography for the ellipsoid algorithm containing references to 46 technical papers dealing with the Shor-Khachiyan approach. Also, no less than 32 popular writings are listed as well as 18 "pre-Khachiyan" papers related to EA.

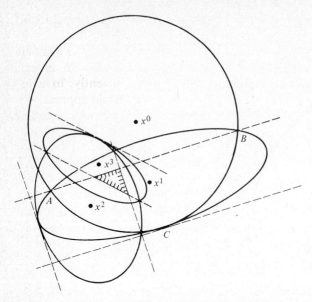

Figure C-3 Murray's modification. Observe the relatively rapid and tight enclosure of X. The ratios of the volumes of successive ellipsoids are much smaller. The solution is obtained in the next step by computing x^4.

Consider the following linear-programming problem:

$$\text{Maximize } c^T x$$

subject to
$$Ax \leqq b$$
$$x \geqq 0$$

where $c^T = (c_1, \ldots, c_n)$.

This problem is identical to that of finding a feasible solution to the following system of inequalities:

$$c^T x = b^T y$$
$$Ax \leqq b$$
$$x \geqq 0$$
$$A^T y \geqq c$$
$$y \geqq 0$$

where $y^T = (y_1, \ldots, y_m)$. Recall that for any solution (x, y) of this system, x constitutes an optimal solution of the original maximization problem.

Unfortunately, EA cannot be simply applied to the transformed problem. As noted by Murray (1979), any transformation of a linear program into a single feasible-point problem will inevitably yield a feasible region of zero volume. The simplex method still performs much better on this type of formulation. One possible approach would be to formulate a feasible-point problem in which the feasible region is a hypersphere of chosen, arbitrarily small volume, enclosing the solution point. But such a minute volume of a feasible region would still cause the expected number of iterations to be very large.

Further research is certainly desirable. EA does not depend on the number of constraints but on the number of variables. Even problems with an extremely large number of constraints could be solved very efficiently. In addition, nonlinear inequalities could also be handled by the ellipsoid approach.

There is a class of important linear-programming problems in which a solution is characterized by a feasible set of nonzero volume. Recall that in goal programming one predetermines the values which are considered to be satisfactory with respect to all objective functions. In fact, one transforms all such objectives into additional constraints and defines a satisfactory feasible region of solutions. If a feasible solution is found, the region could be further reduced by readjusting the goals to their more preferred levels. The algorithm is then applied again. If the system is inconsistent, that is, if the satisfactory region is empty, the goals could be lowered until a feasible region of nonzero volume is found. An interactive version of EA could be used to guide such a process of search.

Even for single- or multiple-objective linear-programming problems, one does not have to resort to the transformed problem described earlier. Consider Fig. C-4.

First, we consider the polyhedron of feasible solutions defined by constraints only. The objective functions are not yet brought into the picture. A feasible solution, if it exists, is found by applying EA. In Fig. C-4, the center x^1

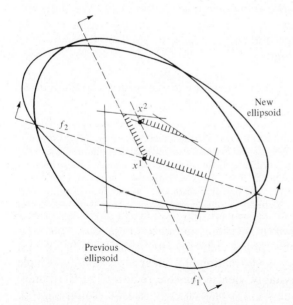

Figure C-4 Application of EA to linear multiobjective programming. Observe that the iterative improvement of both objectives f_1 and f_2 is assured.

identifies the first feasible solution. The levels of both objective functions f_1 and f_2 are established at point x^1. The new feasible region, identifying all feasible solutions where both objectives are improved, is identified (a shaded subsection of the original polyhedron). One of the objectives, in this case f_2, is chosen as the most violated constraint, and EA is applied. A new solution to the reduced feasible region is found. In Fig. C-4 this is achieved in the very next step, by computing the new center x^2. The advantage of this approach is that we already know that there is a feasible solution to the previous problem. The next feasible solution either exists and both functions must be improved, or it does not exist and the achieved levels of f_1 and f_2 must be maximal.

In Fig. C-4, values of f_1 and f_2 are newly established at x^2, identifying an even smaller feasible region (smaller shaded subsection of the initial polyhedron), and EA is applied again. The decision maker could interact by identifying the objective which needs improvement in the next step.

McClain (1980) provides helpful intuitive imagery for students comparing the simplex and ellipsoid algorithms. The simplex method employs tiny, blind bugs wandering the multifaceted surface of a cut diamond (convex polyhedron of feasible solutions). A bug that travels from corner to corner, following only uphill edges, is certain to find the top. The EA approach embeds the diamond in a shrinking watermelon. As it shrinks, the motion of the exact center of the melon is observed. If the center of the melon is not within the diamond, the melon is sliced through its center and the half containing the diamond is saved. Because the melon shrinks after each slice, the central point will eventually slip into the diamond. The next slice chops through both melon and diamond, cutting off only the lower part of the diamond. Ultimately, the shrinking watermelon collapses into a single point, identical with the pinnacle of the diamond. If the gem has a large number of edges, the melon-chopping robot beats blind diamond-crawling bugs.

REFERENCES

Aspvall, B., and R. E. Stone: "Khachiyan's Linear Programming Algorithm," Department of Computer Science Tech. Rep. STAN-CS-79-776, Stanford University, Stanford, Calif., 1979.

Gács, P., and L. Lovász: "Khachiyan's Algorithm for Linear Programming," Department of Computer Science Tech. Rep. STAN-CS-79-750, Stanford University, Stanford, Calif., 1979.

Goldfarb, D., and M. J. Todd: "Modifications and Implementation of the Shor-Khachiyan Algorithm for Linear Programming," Department of Computer Science Tech. Rep. 446, Cornell University, Ithaca, N.Y., 1980.

Khachiyan, L. G.: "A Polynomial Algorithm in Linear Programming," *Dokl. Akad. Nauk SSSR*, vol. 224, no. 5, 1979, pp. 1093–1096; English translation in *Soviet Math. Dokl.*, vol. 20, no. 1, 1979, pp. 191–194.

McClain, J. O.: "Linear Programming Is a Shrinking Watermelon and Optimality Is a Black Hole," *Interfaces,* vol. 10, no. 3, June 1980, pp. 106–107.

Murray, W.: "Ellipsoidal Algorithms for Linear Programming," Systems Optimization Lab. Working Pap. 79-1, Stanford University, Stanford, Calif., November 1979.

Shor, N. Z.: "Cut-Off Method with Space Extension in Convex Programming Problems," *Kibernetika*, vol. 13, 1977, pp. 94–95; English translation in *Cybernetics*, vol. 13, 1977, pp. 94–96.

Wolfe, P.: "A Bibliography for the Ellipsoid Algorithm," IBM Research Center, RC 8237, Yorktown Heights, N.Y., April 1980.

Zeleny, M.: "Ellipsoid Algorithms in Mathematical Programming," *Human Systems Management*, vol. 1, no. 2, 1980, pp.173–178.

BIBLIOGRAPHY ON MCDM

It is today virtually impossible to produce a complete bibliography of works dealing with multiple criteria decision making. But it is at the same time essential for researchers, students, and managers to have within their reach a quick and reliable reference to *most* of the MCDM literature. In this compilation we attempt to list the books, monographs, proceedings, and papers on MCDM appearing up to 1980. We confine this listing only to *published* works written *in English*. This is not to imply that there are no institutional reports, working papers, and unpublished Ph.D. dissertations of great value and usefulness, but they are usually produced in very limited editions and are reliably obtainable only within a severely restricted period of time. Similarly, there is a large number of important and often seminal works written in other languages, but these are mostly directed to local rather than international audiences. We can only hope that at least some of these works will ultimately appear in English and thus become accessible to the worldwide community of scholars. Consequently, in compiling this bibliography, the important criterion of *accessibility* was taken squarely into account.

For the sake of completeness, a representative sample of studies on multiattribute utility theory and social judgment theory has been included in this MCDM listing. On the other hand, many of the items referred to earlier in this text are not listed here: Several do not relate directly to MCDM; others are not readily accessible. Bibliographical Notes at the ends of chapters represent self-contained units serving a different purpose from the compilation which follows.

One of the most complete bibliographies on MCDM (1138 entries), also containing works in other languages than English (for example over 100 references in Russian), is available in:

Achilles, A., K.-H. Elster, and R. Nehse: "Bibliographie zur Vektoroptimierung (Theorie und Anwendungen)," *Mathematische Operationsforschung und Statistik*, vol. 10, no. 2, 1979, pp. 277–321.

Books, monographs, and collective works

1. Barrett, J. H.: *Individual Goals and Organizational Objectives: A Study of Integration Mechanisms*, University of Michigan Press, Ann Arbor, 1970.
2. Bell, D. E., R. L. Keeney, and H. Raiffa (eds.): *Conflicting Objectives in Decisions*, Wiley, New York, 1977.
3. Blair, P. D.: *Multiobjective Regional Energy Planning: Applications to the Energy Park Concept*, Martinus Nijhoff, Boston, 1979.
4. Cochrane, J. L., and M. Zeleny (eds.): *Multiple Criteria Decision Making*, University of South Carolina Press, Columbia, 1973.
5. Cohon, J. L.: *Multiobjective Programming and Planning*, Academic, New York, 1978.
6. Easton, A: *Complex Managerial Decisions Involving Multiple Objectives*, Wiley, New York, 1973.
7. Fandel, G., and T. Gal (eds.): *Multiple Criteria Decision Making Theory and Application*, Springer-Verlag, New York, 1980.
8. Green, P. E., and Y. Wind: *Multiattribute Decisions in Marketing: A Measurement Approach*, Dryden Press, Hinsdale, Ill., 1973.
9. Haimes, Y. Y., W. A. Hall, and H. T. Freedman: *Multiobjective Optimization in Water Resources Systems, The Surrogate Worth Trade-Off Method*, Elsevier, New York, 1975.
10. Hemming, T.: *Multiobjective Decision Making under Certainty*, Economic Research Institute, Stockholm School of Economics, Stockholm, 1978.
11. Hwang, C. L., A. S. M. Masud, S. R. Paidy, and K. Yoon: *Multiple Objective Decision Making–Methods and Applications: A State-of-the-Art Survey*, Springer-Verlag, New York, 1979.

12. Ignizio, J. P.: *Goal Programming and Extensions*, D. C. Heath, Lexington, Mass., 1976.
13. Ijiri, Y.: *Management Goals and Accounting for Control*, North-Holland Publishing, Amsterdam, 1965.
14. Johnsen, E.: *Studies in Multiobjective Decision Models*, Monograph 1, Economic Research Center, Lund, Sweden, 1968.
15. Keeney, R. L., and H. Raiffa: *Decisions with Multiple Objectives: Preferences and Value Tradeoffs*, Wiley, New York, 1976.
16. Lahdenpää, M.: *Multiple Criteria Decision Making: With Empirical Study on Choice of Marketing Strategies*, Acta Helsingiensis, ser. A:22, Helsinki School of Economics, Helsinki, 1977.
17. Lee, S. M.: *Goal Programming for Decision Analysis*, Auerbach Publishers, Philadelphia, 1972.
18. Leitmann, G. (ed.): *Multicriteria Decision Making and Differential Games*, Plenum, New York, 1976.
19. ———, and A. Marzollo (eds.): *Multicriteria Decision Making*, Springer-Verlag, New York, 1975.
19a. Major, D. C., and R. Lenton: *Multiobjective, Multi-Model River Basin Planning: The MIT-Argentina Project*, Prentice-Hall, Englewood Cliffs, N.J., 1978.
19b. Michalson, E., E. Engelbert, and W. Andrews (eds.): *Multiple Objectives Planning Water Resources*, vol. 1, Idaho Research Foundation, Moscow, Idaho, 1974.
20. Miller, J. R.: *Professional Decision Making: A Procedure for Evaluating Complex Alternatives*, Praeger, New York, 1970.
21. Nijkamp, P., and J. Spronk (eds.): *Multiple Criteria Analysis: Operational Methods*, Gower Press, London, 1981.
22. ——— and A. van Delft: *Multi-Criteria Analysis and Regional Decision-Making*, Martinus Nijhoff, Leiden, 1977.
23. Olve, Nils-Göran: *Multiobjective Budgetary Planning*, Economic Research Institute, Stockholm School of Economics, Stockholm, 1977.
23a. Rietveld, P.: *Multiple Objective Decision Methods and Regional Planning*, Studies in Regional Science and Urban Economics, vol. 7, North-Holland Publishing, Amsterdam, 1980.
23b. Salukvadze, M. E.: *Vector-Valued Optimization Problems in Control Theory*, translated from Russian by J. L. Casti, Academic, New York, 1979.
24. Sfeir-Younis, A., and D. W. Bromley: *Decision Making in Developing Countries–Multiobjective Formulation and Evaluation Methods*, Praeger, New York, 1977.
25. Starr, M. K., and M. Zeleny (eds.): *Multiple Criteria Decision Making*, TIMS Studies in the Management Sciences, vol. 6, North-Holland Publishing, Amsterdam, 1977.
26. Tell, B.: *A Comparative Study of Some Multiple-Criteria Methods*, Economics Research Institute, Stockholm School of Economics, Stockholm, 1976.
27. Thiriez, H., and S. Zionts (eds.): *Multiple Criteria Decision Making: Jouy-en-Josas, France*, Springer-Verlag, New York, 1976.
28. Wallenius, J.: *Interactive Multiple Criteria Decision Methods: An Investigation and an Approach*, Acta Helsingiensis, ser. A:14, Helsinki School of Economics, Helsinki, 1975.
29. Wallin, J.: *Computer-Aided Multiattribute Profit Planning*, Skriftserie utgiven av Handelshögskolan vid Åbo akademi, ser. A, no. 19, Åbo, Finland, 1978.
30. Wilhelm, J.: *Objectives and Multi-Objective Decision Making under Uncertainty*, Springer-Verlag, New York, 1975.
31. Zeleny, M. (ed.): *Computers and Operations Research: Special Issue on Mathematical Programming with Multiple Objectives*, vol. 7, no. 1–2, 1980.
32. ———: *Linear Multiobjective Programming*, Springer-Verlag, New York, 1974.
33. ———(ed.): *Multiple Criteria Decision Making: Kyoto 1975*, Springer-Verlag, New York, 1976.
34. Zionts, S. (ed.): *Multiple Criteria Problem Solving: Proceedings, Buffalo, N. Y. (U.S.A.), 1977*, Springer-Verlag, New York, 1978.

Published articles, papers and sections of books

Abad, P., and D. J. Sweeney: "An Interactive Algorithm for Optimal Control of a System with Multiple Criteria," *International Journal of Systems Science*, vol. 8, no. 2, 1977, pp. 221–229.

Adams, E. W., and R. Fagot: "A Model of Riskless Choice," *Behavioral Science*, vol. 4, 1959, pp. 1–10.

Adulbhan, P., and M. T. Tabucanon: "Bicriterion Linear Programming," *Computers and Operations Research*, vol. 4, no. 2, 1977, pp. 147–153.

Albers, S.: "An Extended Algorithm for Optimal Product Positioning," *European Journal of Operational Research*, vol. 3, 1979, pp. 222–231.

Allesio, F. J.: "Multiple Criteria in Environmental Control: Use of Economic Maximization Rules to Determine Relative Standards," in [4], pp. 544–549.

Aneja, Y. P., and K. P. K. Nair: "Bicriteria Transportation Problem," *Management Science*, vol. 25, no. 1, 1979, pp. 73–78.

———, V. Aggarwal, and K. P. K. Nair: "Maximization of the Vector-Flow in Multicommodity Networks," *INFOR*, vol. 17, no. 3, 1979, pp. 276–286.

Armstrong, R. D., and W. D. Cook: "Goal Programming Models for Assigning Search and Rescue Aircraft to Bases," *Journal of the Operational Research Society*, vol. 30, no. 6, 1979, pp. 555–562.

Arrow, K., E. Barankin, and D. Blackwell: "Admissible Points of Convex Sets," in H. W. Kuhn and A. W. Tucker (eds.), *Contributions to the Theory of Games*, Princeton University Press, Princeton, N. J.,1953, pp. 87–91.

Arthur, J. L., and K. D. Lawrence: "A Multiple Goal Blending Problem," *Computers and Operations Research*, vol. 7, no. 3, 1980, p. 125.

——— and A. Ravindran: "A Branch and Bound Algorithm with Constraint Partitioning for Integer Goal Programming Problems," *European Journal of Operational Research*, vol. 4, no. 6, 1980, pp. 421–425.

——— and A. Ravindran: "An Efficient Goal Programming Algorithm Using Constraint Partitioning and Variable Elimination," *Management Science*, vol. 24, no. 8, 1978, pp. 867–868.

——— and ———: "*PAGP*: A Partitioning Algorithm for (Linear) Goal Programming Problems," *ACM Transactions on Mathematical Software*, in press.

Ashour, S.: "Measures of Performance," *Sequencing Theory*, Springer-Verlag, New York, 1972, chap. 3.

Ashton, D. J., and D. R. Atkins: "Multicriteria Programming for Financial Planning," *Journal of Operational Research Society*, vol. 30, no. 3, March 1979, pp. 259–270.

——— and ———: "Multicriteria Programming for Financial Planning: Some Second Thoughts," in [21].

Athans, M., and H. P. Geering: "Necessary and Sufficient Conditions for Differentiable Non-scalar-Valued Functions to Attain Extrema," *IEEE Transactions on Automatic Control*, vol. AC-18, no. 2, 1973, pp. 132–139.

Aubin, J. P.: "Multi-Games and Decentralization in Management," in [4], pp. 313–326.

———: "A Pareto Minimum Principle," in H. W. Kuhn and G. P. Szegö (eds.), *Differential Games and Related Topics*, North-Holland Publishing, Amsterdam, 1971, pp. 147–175.

Awerbuch, S., and W. Wallace: "A Goal-Setting and Evaluation Model for Community Development," *IEEE Transactions on Systems, Man, and Cybernetics*, vol. SMC-7, no. 8, 1977, pp. 589–597.

———, J. G. Ecker, and W. A. Wallace: "A Note: Hidden Nonlinearities in the Application of Goal Programming," *Management Science*, vol. 22, no. 8, 1976, pp. 918–920.

Baas, J. M., and H. Kwakernaak: "Rating and Ranking of Multi-Aspect Alternatives Using Fuzzy Sets," *Automatica*, vol. 13, 1977, pp. 47–58.

Bacopoulos, A., and I. Singer: "On Convex Vectorial Optimization in Linear Spaces," *Journal of Optimization Theory and Applications*, vol. 21, 1977, pp. 175–188.

———, G. Godini, and I. Singer: "Infima of Sets in the Plane and Applications to Vectorial Optimization," *Revue Roumaine de mathématiques pures et appliquées*, vol. 23, 1978, pp. 343–360.

Bailey, A. D., and W. J. Boe, "Goal and Resource Transfers in the Multigoal Organization," *Accounting Review*, July 1976, pp. 559–573.

Bajgier, S. M., et al.: "Multiattribute Risk/Benefit Analysis of Citizen Attitudes Towards Societal Issues Involving Technology," in [34], pp. 424–448.

Bamba, E.: "Constrained Optimization under Vector-Valued Performance Index," *Systems and Control*, vol. 16, no. 5, 1972, pp. 405–418.

Bammi, De., and Da. Bammi: "Development of a Comprehensive Land Use Plan by Means of a Multiple Objective Mathematical Programming Model," *Interfaces*, vol. 9, no. 2, 1979, pp. 50–63.

—— and ——: "Land Use Planning: An Optimizing Model," *Omega*, vol. 3, no. 5, 1975, pp. 583–594.

Banker, R. L., and S. K. Gupta: "A Process for Hierarchical Decision Making with Multiple Objectives," *Omega*, vol. 8, no. 2, 1980, pp. 137–149.

Baptistella, L. F. B., and A. Ollero: "Fuzzy Methodologies for Interactive Multicriteria Optimization," *IEEE Transactions on Systems, Man and Cybernetics*, vol. SMC-10, no. 7, July 1980, pp. 355–365.

Barber, G.: "Land-Use Plan Design via Interactive Multiple-Objective Programming," *Environment and Planning*, vol. 8, 1976, pp. 625–636.

Baron, D. P.: "Stochastic Programming and Risk Aversion," in [4], pp. 124–138.

Barron, F. H., and H. B. Person: "Assessment of Multiplicative Utility Functions via Holistic Judgments," *Organizational Behavior and Human Performance*, vol. 24, no. 2, 1979, pp. 147–166.

Barton, R. F.: "Models with More than One Criterion—Or Why Not Build Implementation into the Model," *Interfaces*, vol. 7, no. 4, August 1977, pp. 71–75.

Basar, T.: "Decentralized Multicriteria Optimization of Linear Stochastic Systems," *IEEE Transactions on Automatic Control*, vol. 23, 1978, pp. 233–243.

Bassler, J. F., et.al.: "Multiple Criteria Dominance Models: An Empirical Study of Investment Preferences," in [34], pp. 494–508.

Bauer, V., and M. Wegener: "A Community Information Feedback System with Multiattribute Utilities," in [2], pp. 323–357.

Baum, S., and R. C. Carlson: "Multigoal Optimization in Managerial Science," *Omega*, vol. 2, no. 5, 1974, pp. 607–623.

Baumgartner, T., T. R. Burns, P. DeVille, and L. D. Meeker: "A Systems Model of Conflict and Change in Planning Systems with Multi-Level, Multiple-Objective Evaluation and Decision Making," *General Systems Yearbook*, 1975, pp.167–183.

Bedelbaev, A. A., J. A. Dubov, and B. L. Shmulyan: "Adaptive Decision Procedures in Multicriterion Problems," *Automation and Remote Control*, vol. 37, no. 1, 1976, pp. 76–85.

Beedles, W. L.: "A Micro-Econometric Investigation of Multiobjective Firms," *Journal of Finance*, vol. 32, 1977, pp. 1217–1234.

Beeson, R. M., and W. S. Meisel: "The Optimization of Complex Systems with Respect to Multiple Criteria," *IEEE Systems, Man and Cybernetics Group Annual Symposium Record, IEEE*, 1971, pp. 144–149.

Behringer, F. A.: "Lexicographic Quasiconcave Multiobjective Programming," *Zeitschrift für Operations Research*, vol. 21, no. 3, 1977, pp. 103–116.

Belenson, S. M., and K. C. Kapur: "An Algorithm for Solving Multicriterion Programming Problems with Examples," *Operational Research Quarterly*, vol. 24, no. 1, 1973, pp. 65–77.

Bell, D. E.: "A Decision Analysis of Objectives for a Forest Pest Problem," in [2], pp. 389–421.

——: "Interpolation Independence," in [34], pp. 1–7.

——: "Multiattribute Utility Functions: Decompositions Using Interpolation," *Management Science*, vol. 25, no. 8, 1979, pp. 744–753.

Benayoun, R., J. Tergny, and D. Keuneman: "Mathematical Programming with Multi-Objective Functions: A Solution by P.O.P. (Progressive Orientation Procedure)," *Metra*, vol. 9, no. 2, 1970, pp. 279–299.

——, O. Larichev, J. De Montgolfier, and J. Tergny: "Linear Programming with Multiple Objective Functions: The Method of Constraints," *Automation and Remote Control*, vol. 32, no. 8, 1971, pp. 1257–1264.

——, J. De Montgolfier, J. Tergny, and O. Larichev: "Linear Programming with Multiple Objective Functions: Step Method (STEM)," *Mathematical Programming*, vol. 1, no. 3, 1971, pp. 366–375.

Ben-Israel, A., A. Ben-Tal, and A. Charnes: "Necessary and Sufficient Conditions for a Pareto-Optimum in Convex Programming," *Econometrica*, vol. 45, no. 4, 1977, pp. 811–822.

Benson, H. P., and T. L. Morin: "The Vector Maximization Problem: Proper Efficiency and Stability," *SIAM Journal of Applied Mathematics*, vol. 32, 1977, pp. 64–72.

Ben-Tal, A.: "Characterization of Pareto and Lexicographic Optimal Solutions," in [7], pp. 1–11.

——, and S. Zlobec: "Convex Programming and the Lexicographic Multicriteria Problem," *Mathematische Operationsforschung und Statistik*, ser. Optimization, vol. 8, no. 1, 1977, pp. 61–73.

Benveniste, M.: "Testing for Complete Efficiency in a Vector Maximization Problem," *Mathematical Programming*, vol. 12, no. 2, 1977, pp. 285–288.

Bereanu, B.: "Large Group Decision Making with Multiple Criteria," in [27], pp. 87–102.

Bergstresser, K., and P. L. Yu: "Domination Structures and Multicriteria Problems in N-Person Games," *Theory and Decision*, vol. 8, no. 1, 1977, pp. 5–48.

——, A. Charnes, and P. L. Yu: "Generalization of Domination Structures and Nondominated Solutions in Multicriteria Decision Making," *Journal of Optimization Theory and Applications*, vol. 18, no. 1, 1976, pp. 3–13.

Berhold, M.: "Multiple Criteria Decision Making in Consumer Behavior," in [4], pp. 570–576.

Bernardo, J. J.: "A Linear Assignment Formulation of the Multi-Attributed Purchase Decision," *Journal of Business Administration*, vol. 7, no. 2, May 1976, pp. 23–44.

—— and H. Lanser, "A Capital Budgeting Decision Model with Subjective Criteria," *Journal of Financial and Quantitative Analysis*, vol. 12, no. 2, 1977, pp. 261–275.

Bernstein, S., and W. Mellon: "Multidimensional Considerations in the Evaluation of Urban Policy," in [4], pp. 530–543.

Bertier, P., and J. De Montgolfier: "On Multicriteria Analysis: An Application to a Forest Management Problem," *Metra*, vol. 13, no. 1, 1974, pp. 33–45.

Bilkey, W. J.: "Empirical Evidence Regarding Business Goals," in [4], pp. 613–634.

Birkin, S. J., and J. S. Ford: "The Quantity/Quality Dilemma: The Impact of a Zero Defects Program," in [4], pp. 517–529.

Bitran, G. R.: "Linear Multiple Objective Programs with Zero-One Variables," *Mathematical Programming*, vol. 13, no. 2, 1977, pp. 121–139.

——: "Theory and Algorithms for Linear Multiple Objective Programs with Zero-One Variables," *Mathematical Programming*, vol. 17, no. 3, 1979, pp. 362–390.

—— and K. D. Lawrence: "Locating Service Facilities: A Multicriteria Approach," *Omega*, vol. 8, no. 2, 1980, pp. 201–206.

—— and T. L. Magnanti: "Duality Based Characterizations of Efficient Facets," in [7], pp. 13–23.

—— and ——: "The Structure of Admissible Points with Respect to Cone Dominance," *Journal of Optimization Theory and Applications*, vol. 29, no. 4, 1979, pp. 573–614.

Blackwell, D.: "An Analog of the Minimax Theorem for Vector Payoffs," *Pacific Journal of Mathematics*, vol. 6, no. 1, 1956, pp. 1–8.

Blaquiere, A.: "Vector Valued Optimization in Multi-Player Quantitative Games," in [19], pp. 33–54.

Blin, J. M.: "Fuzzy Sets in Multiple Criteria Decision-Making," in [25], pp. 129–146.

——: "The General Concept of Multidimensional Consistency: Some Algebraic Aspects of the Aggregation Problem," in [4], pp. 164–178.

——: "A Linear Assignment Formulation of the Multi-Attribute Decision Problem," *Revue Française d'automatique, d'informatique et de recherche operationelle*, vol. 6, no. 2, 1976, pp. 21–32.

——— and J. A. Dodson: "A Multiple Criteria Decision Model for Repeated Choice Situations," in [34], pp. 8–22.

Bodily, S. E.: "Evaluating Joint Life-Saving Activities Under Uncertainty," in [34], pp. 23–41.

Boebion, J., and L. Pun: "A Series-Parallel Multiple-Criteria Model for a Scheduling Problem in the Dress-Making Industry," in [27], pp. 305–318.

Bona, B., D. Merighi, and A. Ostanello-Borreani: "Financial Resource Allocation in a Decentralized Urban System," in [21].

Borreani-Ostanello, A., and P. Capellaro: "Efficient Solutions of a Multiple-Objective Programming Model for a Problem of School Allocation and Dimensioning," in M. Roubens (ed.), *Advances in Operations Research*, North-Holland Publishing, Amsterdam, 1977, pp. 55–60.

Borwein, J.: "Proper Efficient Points for Maximizations with Respect to Cones," *SIAM Journal on Control and Optimization*, vol. 15, 1977, pp. 57–63.

Bowen, K. C.: "Personal and Organizational Value Systems: How Should We Treat These in O.R. Studies?" *Omega*, in press.

Bowling, A. L., and J. F. Hair: "Optimal Decisions on Multiple Objectives Through Canonical Analysis," in [4], pp. 729–731.

Bowman, V. J.: "On the Relationship of the Tchebycheff Norm and the Efficient Frontier of Multiple-Criteria Objectives," in [27], pp. 76–86.

Boychuk, L. M., and V. O. Ovchinnikov: "Principal Methods of Solution of Multicriterial Optimization Problems (Survey)," *Soviet Automatic Control*, vol. 6, no. 3, 1973, pp. 1–4.

Bracken, J., and J. Y. McGill: "Production and Marketing Decisions with Multiple Objectives in a Competitive Environment," *Journal of Optimization Theory and Applications*, vol. 24, 1978, pp. 449–458.

Brauers, W. K.: "Multiple-Criteria Decision Making with a Special Application on Defense Problems," in [27], pp. 199–200.

Brill, E. D.: "The Use of Optimization Models in Public-Sector Planning," *Management Science*, vol. 25, no. 5, May 1979, pp. 413–422.

Briskin, L. E.: "Establishing a Generalized Multi-Attribute Utility Function," in [4], pp. 236–245.

———: "A Method of Unifying Multiple Objective Functions," *Management Science*, vol. 12, no. 10, 1966, pp. B406–B416.

Brucker, P.: "Discrete Parameter Optimisation Problem and Essential Efficient Points," *Zeitschrift für Operations Research*, vol. 16, no. 5, 1972, pp. 189–197.

Buffa, E. S., and J. S. Dyer: *Management Science/Operations Research*, Wiley, New York, 1977, Chap. 4.

Buffa, F. P.: "A Goal Programming Approach for Simultaneous Determination of Safety Stock Levels," *Production and Inventory Management*, vol. 17, no. 1, 1976, pp. 94–104.

Burns, T., and L. D. Meeker: "A Mathematical Model of Multi-Dimensional Evaluation, Decision-Making and Social Interaction," in [4], pp. 141–163.

Bussey, L. E.: *The Economic Analysis of Industrial Projects*, Prentice-Hall, Englewood Cliffs, N. J., 1978, Chap. 9.

Buyanov, B. B., and V. M. Ozernoy: "A Decision Method Using Vector Criterion," *Engineering Cybernetics*, vol. 12, no. 3, 1974, pp. 49–54.

Callahan, J. R.: "An Introduction to Financial Planning through Goal Programming," *Cost and Management*, vol. 47, no. 1, January-February 1973, pp. 7–12.

Candler, W.: "Linear Programming in Capital Budgeting with Multiple Goals," in [4], pp. 416–428.

——— and M. Boehlje: "Use of Linear Programming in Capital Budgeting with Multiple Goals," *American Journal of Agricultural Economics*, vol. 53, no. 2, 1971, pp. 325–330.

Cantley, M. F.: "The Choice of Corporate Objectives," *Long Range Planning*, vol. 3, no. 1, 1970, pp. 36–41.

Caplan, D. A., and J. S. H. Kornbluth: "Multiobjective Investment Planning Under Uncertainty," *Omega*, vol. 3, no. 4, 1975, pp. 423–441.

Carlson, R. C., and H. H. Thorp: "A Multicriteria Approach to Strategic Planning: An Application in Inventory Control," in M. Roubens (ed.), *Advances in Operations Research*, North

Holland Publishing, Amsterdam, 1977, pp. 75–83; also in *Omega*, vol. 5, no. 1, 1977, pp. 57–65.

Carlsson, C.: "An Approach to Adaptive Multigoal Control Using Fuzzy Automata," in M. Roubens (ed.), *Advances in Operations Research*, North-Holland Publishing, Amsterdam, 1977, pp. 85–93.

———: "Linking MP Models in a Systems Framework," *IEEE Transaction on Systems, Man, and Cybernetics*, vol. SMC-9, no. 12, Dec. 1979.

———: "Solving Complex and Ill-Structured Problems: An MCDM-Approach," in [21].

Castellani, G.: "Explicit Solution for a Class of Allocation Problems," in [19], pp. 351–386.

Cenzor, Y.: "Pareto-Optimality in Multiobjective Problems," *Applied Mathematics and Optimization*, vol. 4, 1977, pp. 41–59.

Chaiken, J. M., and P. Dormont: "A Patrol Car Allocation Model: Background, Capabilities and Algorithms," *Management Science*, vol. 24, no. 12, 1978, pp. 1280–1300.

Chang, S. S. L.: "General Theory of Optimal Processes," *SIAM Journal of Control*, vol. 4, no. 1, 1966, pp. 46–55.

Chankong, V., and Y. Y. Haimes: "The Interactive Surrogate Worth Trade-Off (ISWT) Method for Multiobjective Decision Making," in [34], pp. 42–67.

Charnes, A., et al: "A Goal Interval Programming Model for Resource Allocation in a Marine Environmental Protection Program," *Journal of Environmental Economics and Management*, vol. 3, no. 4, December 1976, pp. 347–362.

——— and B. Collomb: "Optimal Economic Stabilization Policy: Linear Goal-Interval Programming Models," *Socio-Economic Planning Sciences*, vol. 6, 1972, pp. 431–435.

——— and W. W. Cooper: "Constrained Extremization Models and Their Use in Developing Systems Measures," in M. D. Mesarović (ed.), *Views on General System Theory*, Wiley, New York, 1964, pp. 61–88.

——— and ———: "Deterministic Equivalents for Optimizing and Satisficing under Chance Constraints," *Operations Research*, vol. 11, no. 1, 1963, pp. 18–39.

——— and ———: "Goal Programming and Constrained Regression—A Comment," *Omega*, vol. 3, no. 4, 1975, pp. 403–409.

——— and ———: "Goal Programming and Multiple Objective Optimization—Part 1," *European Journal of Operational Research*, vol. 1, no. 1, 1977, pp. 39–54.

——— and ———: "Management Models and Industrial Applications of Linear Programming," *Management Science*, vol. 4, no. 1, 1957, pp. 81–87.

——— and ———: *Management Models and Industrial Applications of Linear Programming*, vol. 1, Wiley, New York, 1961, chap. 6, app. B.

——— and ———: "Some Network Characterizations for Mathematical Programming and Accounting Approaches to Planning and Control," *Accounting Review*, vol. 42, no. 1, 1967, pp. 24–52.

——— and A. Stedry: "Investigations in the Theory of Multiple Budgeted Goals," in C. P. Bonini, R. K. Jaedicke, and H. M. Wagner (eds.), *Management Controls*, McGraw-Hill, New York, 1964.

——— and ———: "Search-Theoretic Models of Organization Control by Budgeted Multiple Goals," *Management Science*, vol. 12, no. 5, 1966, pp. 457–482.

——— and J. Storbeck: "A Goal Programming Model for the Siting of Multilevel EMS Systems," *Socio-Economic Planning Sciences*, vol. 14, no. 4, 1980, pp. 155–161.

———, R. W. Clower, and K. O. Kortanek: "Effective Control Through Coherent Decentralization with Preemptive Goals," *Econometrica*, vol. 35, no. 2, 1967, pp. 294–320.

———, W. W. Cooper, and Y. Ijiri: "Break-Even Budgeting and Programming to Goals," *Journal of Accounting Research*, vol. 1, no. 1, 1963, pp. 16–43.

———, ———, and R. J. Niehaus: "Dynamic Multiattribute Models for Mixed Manpower Systems," *Naval Research Logistics Quarterly*, vol. 22, no. 2, 1975, pp. 205–220.

———, ———, D. Klingman, and R. J. Niehaus: "Explicit Solutions in Convex Goal Programming," *Management Science*, vol. 22, no. 4, 1975, pp. 438–448.

———, ———, D. B. Learner, and E. F. Snow: "Note on an Application of a Goal Programming Model for Media Planning," *Management Science*, vol. 14, no. 8, 1968, pp. B431–B436.

———, ———, K. A. Lewis, and R. J. Niehaus: "A Multi-Objective Model for Planning Equal Employment Opportunities," in [33], pp. 111–134.

———, ———, R. J. Niehaus, and A. Stedry: "Static and Dynamic Assignment Models with Multiple Objectives and Some Remarks on Organizational Design," *Management Science*, vol. 15, no. 8, 1969, pp. B365–375.

———, K. E. Haynes, J. E. Hazleton, and M. J. Ryan: "A Hierarchical Goal Programming Approach to Environmental Land Use Management," *Geographical Analysis*, April 1975, pp. 122–130.

———, W. W. Cooper, J. K. DeVoe, D. B. Learner, and W. Reinecke: "A Goal Programming Model for Media Planning," *Management Science*, vol. 14, no. 8, 1968, pp. B423–B430.

Charnetski, J. R.: "Linear Programming with Partial Information," *European Journal of Operational Research*, vol. 5, no. 4, October 1980, pp. 254–261.

———: "Multiple Criteria Decision Making with Partial Information: A Site Selection Problem," in M. Chatterji (ed.), *Space Location and Regional Development*, Pion, London, 1976, pp. 51–62.

——— and R. M. Soland: "Multiple-Attribute Decision Making with Partial Information: The Comparative Hypervolume Criterion," *Naval Research Logistics Quarterly*, vol. 25, no. 2, 1978, pp. 279–288.

——— and ———: "Multiple-Attribute Decision Making with Partial Information: The Expected-Value Criterion," *Naval Research Logistics Quarterly*, vol. 26, no. 2, 1979, pp. 249–256.

Chateau, J. P. D.: "The Capital Budgeting Problem under Conflicting Financial Policies," *Journal of Business Finance and Accounting*, vol. 2, no. 1, 1975, pp. 83–103.

Chisman, J. A., and D. Rippy: "Optimal Operation of a Multipurpose Reservoir Using Goal Programming,"*Review of Industrial Management and Textile Science*, Fall 1977, pp. 69–82.

Choo, E. U., and D. R. Atkins: "An Interactive Algorithm for Multicriteria Programming," in [31], pp. 81–87.

Chu, K. C.: "On the Noninferior Set for the Systems with Vector-Valued Objective Function," *IEEE Transactions on Automatic Control*, vol. AC-15, no. 5, 1970, pp. 591–593.

Churchman, C. W.: "Morality as a Value Criterion," in [4], pp. 3–8.

——— and R. L. Ackoff: "An Approximate Measure of Value," *Operations Research*, vol. 2, no. 2, 1954, pp. 172–187.

Chyung, D. H.: "Optimal Systems with Multiple Cost Functionals," *SIAM Journal of Control*, vol. 5, no. 3, 1967, pp. 345–351.

Clarke, D., and B. H. P. Rivett: "A Structural Mapping Approach to Complex Decision-Making," *Journal of Operational Research Society*, vol. 29, no. 2, 1978, pp. 113–128.

Clayton, E. R., and L. J. Moore: "Goal vs. Linear Programming," *Journal of Systems Management*, November 1972, pp. 26–31.

Cohon, J. L.: "Applications of Multiple Objectives to Water Resources Problems," in [33], pp. 255–270.

——— et al.: "Application of a Multiobjective Facility Location Model to Power Plant Siting in a Six-State Region of the U.S.," in [31], pp. 107–123.

——— and D. H. Marks: "Multiobjective Analysis in Water Resources Planning," in R. De Neufville and D. Marks (eds.), *Systems Planning and Design*, Prentice-Hall, Englewood Cliffs, N. J., 1974, pp. 304–321.

——— and ———: "Multiobjective Screening Models and Water Resource Investment," *Water Resources Research*, vol. 9, no. 4, 1973, pp. 826–836.

——— and ———: "A Review and Evaluation of Multiobjective Programming Techniques," *Water Resources Research*, vol. 11, no. 2, 1975, pp. 208–220.

———, R. Church, and D. Sheer: "Generating Multiobjective Tradeoffs: An Algorithm for Bicriterion Problems," *Water Resources Research*, vol. 15, 1979.

Collins, D. C: "Applications of Multiple Criteria Evaluation to Decision Aiding," in [4], pp. 477–505.

Colson, G., and M. Zeleny: "Multicriterion Concept of Risk under Incomplete Information," in [31], pp. 125–141.
────── and ──────: *Uncertain Prospects Ranking and Portfolio Analysis under the Conditions of Partial Information*, Mathematical Systems in Economics, Verlag Anton Hain, Meisenheim am Glan, 1979/80.
Contini, B.: "A Decision Model under Uncertainty with Multiple Payoffs," in A. Mensch (ed.), *Theory of Games: Techniques and Applications*, English Universities Press Ltd., London, 1966, pp. 50–63.
──────: "A Stochastic Approach to Goal Programming," *Operations Research*, vol. 16, no. 3, 1968, pp. 576–586.
────── and S. Zionts: "Restricted Bargaining for Organizations with Multiple Objectives," *Econometrica*, vol. 36, no. 2, 1968, pp. 397–414.
Cook, W. D.: "Zero-Sum Games with Multiple Goals," *Naval Research Logistics Quarterly*, vol. 23, no. 4, 1976, pp. 615–621.
────── and L. M. Seiford: "Priority Ranking and Consensus Formation," *Management Science*, vol. 24, no. 16, 1978, pp. 1721–1732.
────── and W. S. Shields: "Assignment of Military Officers to Groups: A New Multiattribute Team Balancing Problem," *INFOR*, vol. 17, no. 2, 1979, pp. 114–123.
Courtney, J. F., T. D. Klastorin, and T. W. Ruefli: "A Goal Programming Approach to Urban-Suburban Location Preferences," *Management Science*, vol. 18, no. 6, 1972, pp. B258–B268.
Crawford, A. B.: "Impact Analysis Using Differentially Weighted Evaluative Criteria," in [4], pp. 732–735.
Crawford, D. M., B. C. Huntzinger, and C. W. Kirkwood: "Multiobjective Decision Analysis for Transmission Conductor Selection," *Management Science*, vol. 24, no. 16, 1978, pp. 1700–1709.
Crowston, W. B., and P. R. Kleindorfer: "Coordinating Multi-Project Networks," in [4], pp. 668–685.
Da Cunha, N. O., and E. Polak: "Constrained Minimization under Vector-Valued Criteria in Finite Dimensional Spaces," *Journal of Math. Anal. and Appl.*, vol. 19, no. 1, 1967, pp. 103–124.
────── and ──────: "Constrained Minimization under Vector-Valued Criteria in Linear Topological Spaces," in A. V. Balakrishnan and L. W. Neustadt (eds.), *Mathematical Theory of Control*, Academic, New York, 1967, pp. 96–108.
Daellenbach, H. G., and C. A. De Kluyver: "Note on Multiple Objective Dynamic Programming," *Journal of Operational Research Society*, vol. 31, no. 7, 1980, pp. 591–594.
Dalkey, N. C.: "Group Decision Analysis," in [33], pp. 45–74.
Das. P., and Y. Y. Haimes: "Multiobjective Optimization in Water Quality and Land Management," *Water Resources Research*, vol. 15, no. 4, 1979.
Dauer, J. P.: "An Equivalence Result for Solutions of Multiobjective Linear Programs," in [31], pp. 33–39.
────── and R. J. Krueger: "An Iterative Approach to Goal Programming," *Operational Research Quarterly*, vol. 28, no. 3, 1977, pp. 671–681.
────── and ──────: "A Multiobjective Optimization Model for Water Resources Planning," *Applied Mathematical Modeling*, vol. 4, no. 3, 1980, pp. 171–175.
David, L., and L. Duckstein: "Multicriterion Ranking of Alternative Long-Range Water Resources Systems," *Water Resources Bulletin*, vol. 12, no. 4, 1976, pp. 731–754.
Dawes, R. M.: "A Case Study of Graduate Admissions: Applications of Three Principles of Human Decision Making," *American Psychologist*, vol. 26, no. 2, 1971, pp. 180–188.
──────: "Objective Optimization Under Multiple Subjective Functions," in [4], pp. 9–17.
────── and B. Corrigan: "Linear Models in Decision Making," *Psychological Bulletin*, vol. 81, 1974, pp. 95–106.
────── and J. Eagle: "Multivariate Selection of Students in a Racist Society: A Systematically Unfair Approach," in [33], pp. 97–110.
Day, R. H., and S. M. Robinson: "Economic Decisions with L** Utility," in [4], pp. 84–92.

Dean, J. H., and C. S. Shih: "Multiattribute Water Resources Decision Making," *AIIE Transactions*, vol. 7, no. 4, 1975, pp. 408–413.

Deckro, R. F.: "Multiple Objective Districting: A General Heuristic Approach Using Multiple Criteria," *Operational Research Quarterly*, vol. 28, no. 4, 1977, pp. 953–961.

De Kluyver, C. A.: "An Exploration of Various Goal Programming Formulations—With Application to Advertising Media Scheduling," *Journal of the Operational Research Society*, vol. 30, no. 2, 1979, pp. 167–172.

Delft, A. van, and P. Nijkamp: "A Multi-Objective Decision Model for Regional Development, Environmental Quality Control and Industrial Land Use," *Papers of the Regional Science Association*, vol. 36, 1976, pp. 15–37.

De Neufville, R., and R. L. Keeney: "Multiattribute Preference Analysis for Transportation Systems Evaluation," *Transportation Research*, vol. 7, no. 1, 1973, pp. 63–76.

—— and ——: "Use of Decision Analysis in Airport Development for Mexico City," in A. W. Drake, R. L. Keeney, and P. M. Morse (eds.), *Analysis of Public Systems*, M.I.T., Cambridge, Mass., 1972, pp. 497–519.

Deshpande, D. V., and S. Zionts: "Sensitivity Analysis in Multiple Objective Linear Programming: Changes in the Objective Function Matrix," in [7], pp. 26–39.

Despontin, M., and P. Vincke: "Multiple Criteria Economic Policy," in M. Roubens (ed.), *Advances in Operations Research*, North-Holland Publishing, Amsterdam, 1977, pp. 119–128.

Díaz, J. A.: "Finding a Complete Description of All Efficient Solutions to a Multiobjective Transportation Problem," *Ekonomicko-matematický Obzor*, vol. 15, no. 1, 1979, pp. 62–73.

——: "Solving Multiobjective Transportation Problems," *Ekonomicko-matematicky Obzor*, vol. 14, no. 3, 1978, pp. 267–274.

DiGuglielmo, F.: "Nonconvex Duality in Multiobjective Optimization," *Mathematics of Operations Research*, vol. 2, no. 3, 1977, pp. 285–291.

Dinkel, J. J., and J. E. Erickson: "Multiple Objectives in Environmental Protection Programs," *Policy Sciences*, vol. 9, 1978, pp. 87–96.

Dinkelbach, W.: "Multicriteria Decision Models with Specified Goal Levels," in [7], pp. 52–59.

—— and H. Isermann: "On Decision Making under Multiple Criteria and under Incomplete Information," in [4], pp. 302–312.

—— and ——: "Resource Allocation of an Academic Department in the Presence of Multiple Criteria: Some Experience with a Modified STEM Method," in [31], pp. 99–106.

DiRoccaferrera, G. M. F.: "Behavioral Aspects of Decision Making under Multiple Goals," in [4], pp. 635–656.

Doležal, J.: "Necessary Optimality Conditions for Discrete Systems with State-Dependent Control Region and Vector-Valued Objective Function," *Systems Science*, vol. 3, no. 2, 1977, pp. 171–184.

Donckels, R.: "Regional Multiobjective Planning under Uncertainty: A Stochastic Goal Programming Approach," *Journal of Regional Science*, vol. 17, no. 2, 1977, pp. 207–216.

Dubois, T.: "A Teaching System Using Fuzzy Subsets and Multicriteria Analysis," *International Journal of Mathematical Education in Science and Technology*, vol. 8, no. 2, 1977, pp. 203–217.

Dubov, Y. A.: "Resource Allocation Under Multiple Criteria," *Automation and Remote Control*, vol. 38, 1977, pp. 1807–1814.

—— and B. L. Shmulyan: "Improvement of the Solution of Discrete Multicriterion Problem," *Automation and Remote Control*, vol. 34, no. 12, 1973, pp. 1953–1959.

Duckstein, L., and J. Kempf: "Multicriteria Q-Analysis for Plan Evaluation," in [21].

Dyer, J. S.: "The Effect of Errors in the Estimation of the Gradient in the Frank-Wolfe Algorithm, with Implications for Interactive Programming," *Operations Research*, vol. 22, no. 1, 1974, pp. 160–1704.

——: "An Empirical Investigation of a Man-Machine Interactive Approach to the Solution of Multiple Criteria Problem," in [4], pp. 202–216.

——: "Interactive Goal Programming," *Management Science*, vol. 19, no. 1, 1972, pp. 62–70.

————: "A Time-Sharing Computer Program for the Solution of the Multiple Criteria Problem," *Management Science*, vol. 19, no. 12, 1973, pp. 1379–1383.

———— and R. F. Miles: "Alternative Formulations for a Trajectory Selection Problem: The Mariner Jupiter/Saturn 1977 Project," in [2], pp. 367–388.

———— and R. K. Sarin: "Cardinal Preference Aggregation Rules for the Case of Certainty," in [34], pp. 68–86.

———— and ————: "Measurable Multiattribute Value Functions," *Operations Research*, vol. 27, no. 4, 1979, pp. 810–821.

———— and ————: "Multicriteria Decision Making," in *Encyclopedia of Computer Science and Technology*, vol. 11, Marcel Dekker, New York, 1979, pp. 511–576.

Dyson, R. G.: "Maximin Programming, Fuzzy Linear Programming, and Multi-Criteria Decision Making," *Journal of the Operational Research Society*, vol. 31, no. 3, 1980, pp. 263–267.

Easton, A.: "One-of-a-Kind Decisions Involving Weighted Multiple Objectives and Disparate Alternatives," in [4], pp. 657–667.

Eatman, J. L., and C. W. Sealey: "A Multiobjective Linear Programming Model for Commercial Bank Balance Sheet Management," *Journal of Bank Research*, vol. 9, Winter 1979, pp. 227–236.

Eckenrode, R. T.: "Weighing Multiple Criteria," *Management Science*, vol. 12, no. 3, 1965, pp. 180–192.

Ecker, J. G., and N. S. Hegner: "On Computing an Initial Efficient Extreme Point," *Journal of the Operational Research Society*, vol. 29, no. 10, 1978, pp. 1005–1007.

———— and I. A. Kouada: "Finding All Efficient Extreme Points for Multiple Objective Linear Programs," *Mathematical Programming*, vol. 14, no. 2, 1978, pp. 249–261.

———— and ————: "Finding Efficient Points for Linear Multiple Objective Programs," *Mathematical Programming*, vol. 8, no. 3, 1975, pp. 375–377.

———— and N. E. Shoemaker: "Multiple Objective Linear Programming and the Tradeoff-Compromise Set," in [7], pp. 60–73.

———— and ————: "Selecting Subsets from the Set of Efficient Vectors," *SIAM Journal of Control and Optimization*, in press.

————, N. S. Hegner, and I. A. Kouada: "Generating All Maximal Efficient Faces for Multiple Objective Linear Programs," *Journal of Optimization Theory and Applications*, vol. 30, no. 3, 1980, pp. 353–381.

Edwards, W.: "Use of Multiattribute Utility Measurement for Social Decision Making," in [2], pp. 247–276.

————: "How to Use Multiattribute Utility Measurement for Social Decisionmaking," *IEEE Transactions on Systems, Man, and Cybernetics*, vol. SMC-7, no. 5, 1977, pp. 326-340.

Efstathiou, J., and V. Rajkovič: "Multi-Attribute Decision-Making Using A Fuzzy, Heuristic Approach," *IEEE Transactions on Systems, Man, and Cybernetics*, vol. SMC-9, no. 6, 1979, pp. 326–333.

Eilon, S.: "Goals and Constraints in Decision-Making," *Operational Research Quarterly*, vol. 23, no. 1, 1972, pp. 3–15.

Einhorn, H. J.: "The Use of Nonlinear, Noncompensatory Models in Decision Making," *Psychological Bulletin*, vol. 73, no. 3, 1970, pp. 221–230.

———— and R. M. Hogarth: "Unit Weighting Schemes for Decision Making," *Organizational Behavior and Human Performance*, vol. 13, 1975, pp. 171–192.

———— and W. McCoach: "A Simple Multiattribute Utility Procedure for Evaluation," *Behavioral Science*, vol. 22, no. 4, 1977, pp. 270–282.

———— and ————: "A Simple Multiattribute Utility Procedure for Evaluation," in [34], pp. 87–115.

Ellis, H. M., and R. L. Keeney: "A Rational Approach for Government Decisions Concerning Air Pollution," in A. W. Drake, R. L. Keeney, and P. M. Morse (eds.), *Analysis of Public Systems*, M.I.T., Cambridge, Mass., 1972, chap. 18.

El-Sheshai, K. M., G. B. Harwood, and R. H. Hermanson: "Cost-Volume-Profit Analysis with Integer Goal Programming," *Management Accounting*, October 1977, pp. 43–47.

Elster, K. -H., and R. Nehse: "Necessary and Sufficient Conditions for the Order-Completeness of Partially Ordered Vector Spaces," *Mathematische Nachrichten*, vol. 81, 1978, pp. 301-311.

Emelyanov, S. V., V. M. Ozernoi, and M. G. Gaft: "Formulation of Decision Rules in Multicriterial Problems," *Soviet Physics Doklady*, vol. 21, 1976, pp. 249-250.

——, V. I. Borisov, A. A. Malevic, and A. M. Cercasin: "Models and Methods of Vector Optimization," *Engineering Cybernetics*, vol. 11, no. 5, 1973, pp. 386-448.

Evans, J. P., and R. E. Steuer: "Generating Efficient Extreme Points in Linear Multiple Objective Programming: Two Algorithms and Computing Experience," in [4], pp. 349-365.

—— and ——: "A Revised Simplex Method for Linear Multiple Objective Programs," *Mathematical Programming*, vol. 5, no. 1, 1973, pp. 54-72.

Fabozzi, F. J., and A. W. Bachner: "Mathematical Programming Models to Determine Civil Service Salaries," *European Journal of Operational Research*, vol. 3, no. 3, 1979, pp. 190-198.

Falkson, L. M.: "Discussion: 'Approaches to Multi-Objective Planning in Water Resource Projects,' by B. W. Taylor III, R. Davis, and R. M. North," *Water Resources Bulletin*, vol. 12, no. 5, 1976, pp. 1071-1077.

Fandel, G.: "A Multiple-Objective Programming Algorithm for the Distribution of Resources among Teaching and Research," in H. Albach and G. Bergendahl (eds.), *Production Theory and Its Application*, Springer-Verlag, New York, 1977, pp. 146-175.

——: "Perspectives of the Development in Multiple Criteria Decision Making," in [7], pp. ix-xvi.

——: "Public Investment Decision Making with Multiple Criteria; An Example of University Planning," in [34], pp. 116-130.

—— and J. Wilhelm: "Rational Solution Principles and Information Requirements as Elements of a Theory of Multiple Criteria Decision Making," in [27], pp. 215-231.

Farquhar, P. H.: "A Fractional Hypercube Decomposition Theorem for Multiattribute Utility Functions," *Operations Research*, vol. 23, 1975, pp. 941-967.

——: "Interdependent Criteria in Utility Analysis," in [34], pp. 132-180.

——: "Pyramid and Semicube Decompositions of Multiattribute Utility Functions," *Operations Research*, vol. 24, 1976, pp. 256-271.

——: "A Survey of Multiattribute Utility Theory and Applications," in [25], pp. 59-90.

—— and V. R. Rao: "A Balance Model for Evaluating Subsets of Multiattributed Items," *Management Science*, vol. 22, no. 5, 1976, pp. 528-539.

Fayette, J. R.: "Appraisal of Non-Independent Projects," in [21].

Ferguson, C. E.: "The Theory of Multidimensional Utility Analysis in Relation to Multiple-Goal Business Behavior: A Synthesis," *Southern Economic Journal*, vol. 32, no. 2, 1965, pp. 169-175.

—— and R. Blair: "Inferior Factors, Externalities and Pareto Optimality," *Quarterly Review of Economics and Business*, vol. 11, no. 3, 1971, pp. 17-25.

Fichefet, J.: "GPSTEM: An Interactive Multiobjective Optimization Method," in A. Prékopa (ed.), *Progress in Operations Research*, vol. 1, North Holland Publishing, Amsterdam, 1976, pp. 317-332.

Field, D. B.: "Goal Programming for Forest Management," *Forest Services*, vol. 19, no. 2, 1973, pp. 125-135.

Firstman, S. I., and D. S. Stoller: "Establishing Objectives, Measures, and Criteria for Multi-Phase Complementary Activities," *Operations Research*, vol. 14, no. 1, 1966, pp. 84-99.

Fischer, G. W.: "Convergent Validation of Decomposed Multiattribute Utility Assessment Procedures for Risky and Riskless Decisions," *Organizational Behavior and Human Performance*, vol. 18, 1977, pp. 295-315.

——: "Experimental Applications of Multi-Attribute Utility Models," in D. Wendt and C. A. J. Vlek (eds.), *Utility, Probability, and Human Decision Making*, D. Reidel Publishing, Boston, 1975, pp. 7-45.

——: "Multidimensional Utility Models for Risky and Riskless Choice," *Organizational Behavior and Human Performance*, vol. 17, 1976, pp. 127-146.

————: "Utility Models for Multiple Objective Decisions: Do They Accurately Represent Human Preferences?" *Decision Sciences*, vol. 10, no. 3, 1979, pp. 451–479.

Fishburn, P. C.: "Additive Utilities with Finite Sets: Applications in the Management Sciences," *Naval Research Logistics Quarterly*, vol. 14, no. 1, 1967, pp. 1–10.

————: "Approximations of Two-Attribute Utility Functions," *Mathematics of Operations Research*, vol. 2, 1977, pp. 30–44.

————: "Bernoullian Utilities for Multiple-Factor Situations," in [4], pp. 47–61.

————: "Independence in Utility Theory with Whole Product Sets," *Operations Research*, vol. 13, 1965, pp. 28–45.

————: "Lexicographic Orders, Utilities and Decision Rules: A Survey," *Management Science*, vol. 20, no. 11, 1974, pp. 1442–1471.

————: "Multiattribute Utilities in Expected Utility Theory," in [2], pp. 172–196.

————: "Multicriteria Choice Functions Based on Binary Relations," *Operations Research*, vol. 25, 1977, pp. 989–1012.

————: "A Survey of Multiattribute/Multicriterion Evaluation Theories," in [34], pp. 181–224.

———— and R. L. Keeney: "Seven Independence Concepts and Continuous Multiattribute Utility Functions," *Journal of Mathematical Psychology*, vol. 11, no. 3, 1974, pp. 294–327.

Fisk, J. C.: "A Goal Programming Model for Output Planning," *Decision Sciences*, vol. 10, no. 4, 1979, pp. 593–603.

Flavell, R. B., and G. R. Salkin: "Resource Allocation in a Decentralised Organisation," in M. Roubens (ed.), *Advances in Operations Research*, North-Holland Publishing, Amsterdam, 1977, pp. 169–175.

Focke, J.: "The Vector Maximum Problem and Parametric Optimization," *Mathematische Operationsforschung und Statistik*, vol. 4, 1973, pp. 365–369.

Ford, C. K., R. L. Keeney, and C. W. Kirkwood: "Evaluating Methodologies: A Procedure and Application to Nuclear Power Plant Siting Methodologies," *Management Science*, vol. 25, no. 1, January 1979, pp. 1–10.

Forsyth, J. D.: "Utilization and Goal Programming in Production and Capital Expenditure Planning," *CORS Journal*, vol. 7, no. 2, 1969, pp. 136–140.

———— and D. J. Laughhunn: "Capital Rationing in the Face of Multiple Organizational Objectives," in [4], pp. 439–446.

Frederick, D. G.: "Multiple Objectives in Bayesian Analysis: An Applied Case," in [4], pp. 736–737.

Freeland, J. R.: "A Note on Goal Decomposition in a Decentralized Organization," *Management Science*, vol. 23, September 1976, pp. 100–102.

———— and N. R. Baker: "Goal Partitioning in a Hierarchical Organization," *Omega*, vol. 3, no. 6, 1975, pp. 673–688.

Freeman, A. M., and R. H. Haveman: "Benefit-Cost Analysis and Multiple Objectives: Current Issues in Water Resources Planning," *Water Resources Research*, vol. 6, no. 6, 1970, pp. 1533–1539.

Freimer, M., and P. L. Yu: "The Applications of Compromise Solutions to Reporting Games," in A. Rapoport (ed.), *Games Theory as a Theory of Conflict Resolution*, D. Reidel Publishing, Boston, 1974, pp. 235–260.

———— and ————: "Some New Results on Compromise Solutions for Group Decision Problems," *Management Science*, vol. 22, no. 6, 1976, pp. 688–693.

Gaft, M. G., and V. M. Ozernoi: "Isolation of a Set of Noninferior Solutions and Their Estimates in Decision-Making Problems with a Vector-Valued Criterion," *Automation and Remote Control*, vol. 34, no. 11, 1973, pp. 1787–1795.

Gal, T.: "A General Method for Determining the Set of All Efficient Solutions to a Linear Vector Maximum Problem," *European Journal of Operational Research*, vol. 1, no. 5, 1977, pp. 307–322.

————: "A Note on Size Reduction of the Objective Functions Matrix in Vector Maximum Problems," in [7], pp. 74–84.

————: "An Overview on Recent Results in MCP As Developed in Aachen, Germany," in [34], pp. 225-248.

————: "Postefficient Sensitivity Analysis in Linear Vectormaximum Problems," in [21].

———— and H. Leberling: "Redundant Objective Functions in Linear Vector Maximum Problems and Their Determination," *European Journal of Operational Research*, vol. 1, no. 3, 1977, pp. 176-184.

———— and ————: "Relaxation Analysis in Multi-Criteria Linear Programming: An Introduction," in M. Roubens (ed.), *Advances in Operations Research*, North-Holland Publishing, Amsterdam, 1977, pp. 177-180.

———— and J. Nedoma: "Multiparametric Linear Programming," *Management Science*, vol. 18, no. 7, 1972, pp. 406-421.

Gardiner, P. C., and W. Edwards: "Public Values: Multiattribute Utility Measurement for Social Decision Making," in M. F. Kaplan and S. Schwartz (eds.), *Human Judgment and Decision Processes*, Academic, New York, 1975, pp. 1-37.

Garrod, N. W., and B. Moores: "An Implicit Enumeration Algorithm for Solving Zero-One Goal Programming Problems," *Omega*, vol. 6, no. 4, 1978, pp. 374-377.

Gearhart, W. B.: "On the Characterization of Pareto-Optimal Solutions in Bicriterion Optimization," *Journal of Optimization Theory and Applications*, vol. 27, no. 2, 1979, pp. 301-307.

————: "Compromise Solutions and Estimation of the Noninferior Set," *Journal of Optimization Theory and Applications*, vol. 28, no. 1, 1979, pp. 29-47.

————: "On Vectorial Approximation," *Journal of Approximation Theory*, vol. 10, 1974, pp. 49-63.

Gembicki, F. W., and Y. Y. Haimes: "Approach to Performance and Sensitivity Multiobjective Optimization—Goal Attainment Method," *IEEE Transactions on Automatic Control*, vol. 20, no. 6, 1975, pp. 769-771.

Geoffrion, A. M.: "Proper Efficiency and the Theory of Vector Maximization," *Journal of Mathematical Analysis and Applications*, vol. 22, no. 3, 1968, pp. 618-630.

————: "Solving Bicriterion Mathematical Programs," *Operations Research*, vol. 15, no. 1, 1967, pp. 39-54.

————: "Strictly Concave Parametric Programming, Part I: Basic Theory," *Management Science*, vol. 13, no. 3, 1966, pp. 244-253.

————: "Strictly Concave Parametric Programming, Part II: Additional Theory and Computational Considerations," *Management Science*, vol. 13, no. 5, 1967, pp. 359-370.

———— and W. Hogan: "Coordination of Two-level Organizations with Multiple Objectives," in A. Balakrishnan (ed.), *Techniques of Optimization*, Academic, New York, 1972, pp. 455-466.

————, J. S. Dyer, and A. Feinberg: "An Interactive Approach for Multi-Criterion Optimization, with an Application to the Operation of an Academic Department," *Management Science*, vol. 19, no. 4, part 1, 1972, pp. 357-368.

Georgescu-Roegen, N.: "Choice, Expectations and Measurability," *Quarterly Journal of Economics*, vol. 68, no. 4, 1954, pp. 503-541.

Giauque, W. C., and T. C. Peebles: "Application of Multidimensional Utility Theory in Determining Optimal Test-Treatment Strategies for Streptococcal Sore Throat and Rheumatic Fever," *Operations Research*, vol. 24, no. 5, 1976, pp. 933-950.

Gibbs, T. E.: "Goal Programming," *Journal of Systems Management*, vol. 24, no. 5, May 1973, pp. 38-41.

Giesy, D. P.: "Calculation of Pareto-Optimal Solutions to Multiple-Objective Problems Using Threshold-of-Acceptability Constraints," *IEEE Transactions on Automatic Control*, vol. 23, 1978, pp. 1114-1115.

Giordano, J. L., and J. C. Suquet: "On Multicriteria Decision Making: An Application to a Work-Shop Organization Problem," in M. Roubens (ed.), *Advances in Operations Research*, North-Holland Publishing, Amsterdam, 1977, pp. 181-192.

Gittins, J. C.: "A Generalization of a Result in Linear Programming," *Journal of the Institute of Mathematics and Its Applications*, 1967, pp. 193-201.

Gleason, J. M., and C. C. Lilly: "A Goal Programming Model for Insurance Agency Management," *Decision Sciences*, vol. 8, January 1977, pp. 180–190.

Goffin, J.-L., and A. Haurie: "Necessary Conditions and Sufficient Conditions for Pareto Optimality in a Multicriterion Perturbed System," in B. Contini and A. Ruberti (eds.), *Fifth Conference on Optimization Techniques, Part I*, Springer-Verlag, New York, 1973, pp. 184–193.

—— and ——: "Pareto Optimality with Nondifferentiable Cost Functions," in [27], pp. 232–246.

Goodman, D. A.: "A Goal Programming Approach to Aggregate Planning of Production and Work Force," *Management Science*, vol. 20, no. 12, 1974, pp. 1569–1575.

Goodwin, G. C., P. V. Kabaila, and T. S. Ng: "On the Optimization of Vector-Valued Performance Criteria," *IEEE Transactions on Automatic Control*, vol. AC-20, no. 6, 1975, pp. 803–804.

Gorokhovik, V. V.: "On the Problem of Vector Optimization," *Engineering Cybernetics*, vol. 10, no. 6, 1972, pp. 995–1002.

Gray, D. F., and W. R. S. Sutherland: "Inverse Programming and the Linear Vector Maximization Problem," *Journal of Optimization Theory and Applications*, vol. 30, no. 4, 1980, pp. 523–534.

Green, P. E.: "Multidimensional Scaling and Conjoint Measurement in the Study of Choice among Multiattribute Alternatives," in [4], pp. 577–609.

Gum, R. L., T. G. Roefs, and D. B. Kimball: "Quantifying Societal Goals: Development of a Weighting Methodology," *Water Resources Research*, vol. 12, no. 4, 1976, pp. 612–622.

Gusev, M. J.: "Vector Optimization of Linear Systems," *Soviet Mathematics Doklady*, vol. 13, 1972, pp. 1440–1444.

Habenicht, W.: "Efficiency in General Vector Maximum Problems," *Ricerca Operativa*, vol. 8, no. 5, 1978, pp. 89–101.

Haimes, Y. Y.: "Coordination of Hierarchical Models via a Multiobjective Optimization Method," *Transactions of American Geophysical Union*, vol. 55, 1974, p. 248.

——: "The Surrogate Worth Trade-Off (SWT) Method and its Extensions," in [7], pp. 85–108.

—— and V. Chankong: "Kuhn-Tucker Multipliers as Trade-Offs in Multiobjective Decision-Making Analysis," *Automatica*, vol. 15, no. 1, 1979, pp. 59–72.

—— and W. A. Hall: "Analysis of Multiple Objectives in Water Quality," *ASCE Journal-Hydraulics Division*, vol. 101, no. 4, 1975, pp. 387–400.

—— and ——: "Multiobjectives in Water Resources Systems Analysis: The Surrogate Worth Trade-Off Method," *Water Resources Research*, vol. 10, no. 4, 1974, pp. 615–623.

—— and ——: "Sensitivity, Responsivity, Stability and Irreversibility as Multiple Objectives in Civil Systems," *Advances in Water Resources*, vol. 1, no. 2, 1977.

—— and K. Tarvainen: "Hierarchical Multiobjective Framework for Large-Scale Systems," in [21].

——, L. S. Lasdon, and D. A. Wismer: "On the Bicriterion Formulation of Integrated System Identification and Systems Optimization," *IEEE Transactions on Systems, Man, and Cybernetics*, vol. SMC-1, no. 3, 1971, pp. 296–297.

Haith, D. A., and D. P. Loucks: "Multiobjective Water-Resources Planning," in A. K. Biswas (ed.), *Systems Approach to Water Management*, McGraw-Hill, New York, 1976.

Halbritter, G.: "Multiobjective Programming and Siting of Industrial Plants," in A. V. Balakrishnan and M. Thoma (eds.), *Optimization Techniques*, Springer-Verlag, Berlin, 1978, pp. 454–466.

Hall, W. A., and Y. Y. Haimes: "The Surrogate Worth Trade-Off Method with Multiple Decision-makers," in [33], pp. 207–234.

Hammond, K. R.: "Externalizing the Parameters of Quasirational Thought," in [33], pp. 75–96.

——, R. L. Cook, and L. Adelman: "POLICY: An Aid for Decision Making and International Communication," *Columbia Journal of World Business*, vol. 12, no. 3, Fall 1977, pp. 79–93.

——, T. R. Stewart, B. Brehmer, and D. Steinmann: "Social Judgment Theory," in M. F. Kaplan and S. Schwartz (eds.), *Human Judgment and Decision Processes*, Academic, New York, 1975.

Hanieski, J. F.: "Technological Change as the Optimization of a Multidimensional Product," in [4], pp. 550-569.

Hannan, E. L.: "Allocation of Library Funds for Books and Standing Orders—A Multiple Objective Formulation," *Computers and Operations Research*, vol. 5, no. 2, 1978, pp. 109-114.

————: "The Application of Goal Programming Techniques to the CPM Problem," *Socio-Economic Planning Sciences*, vol. 12, no. 5, 1978, pp. 267-270.

————: "Effects of Substituting a Linear Goal for a Fractional Goal in the Goal Programming Problem," *Management Science*, vol. 24, no. 1, 1977, pp. 105-107.

————: "Using Duality Theory for Identification of Primal Efficient Points and for Sensitivity Analysis of MOLP: Reply," *Journal of the Operational Research Society*, vol. 30, no. 3, 1979, pp. 287-288.

————: "Using Duality Theory for Identification of Primal Efficient Points and for Sensitivity Analysis in Multiple Objective Linear Programming," *Journal of the Operational Research Society*, vol. 29, no. 7, 1978, pp. 643-649.

Hansen, P.: 'Bicriterion Path Problems," in [7], pp. 109-127.

———— and M. Delattre: "Bicriterion Cluster Analysis as an Exploration Tool," in [34], pp. 249-273.

————, M. Anciaux-Mundeleer, and P. Vincke: "Quasi-Kernels of Outranking Relations," in [27], pp. 53-63.

Hanssmann, F.: *Operations Research in Production and Inventory Control*, Wiley, New York, 1962.

Harnett, R. M., and J. P. Ignizio: "A Heuristic Program for the Covering Problem with Multiple Objectives," in [4], pp. 738-740.

Harrald, J., et al.: "A Note on the Limitations of Goal Programming as Observed in Resource Allocation for Marine Environmental Protection," *Naval Research Logistics Quarterly*, vol. 25, no. 4, 1978, pp. 733-739.

Harrington, T. C., and W. A. Fischer: "Portfolio Modeling in Multiple-Criteria Situations under Uncertainty: Comment," *Decision Sciences*, vol. 11, no. 1, 1980, pp. 171-177.

Hartley, R.: "On Cone-Efficiency, Cone-Convexity and Cone-Compactness," *SIAM Journal of Applied Mathematics*, vol. 34, 1978, pp. 211-222.

Hartley, R. V.: *Operations Research: A Managerial Emphasis*, Goodyear Publishing, Pacific Palisades, Calif., 1976, chaps. 8 and 14.

Harwood, G. B., and R. W. Lawless: "Optimizing Organization Goals in Assigning Faculty Teaching Schedules," *Decision Sciences*, vol. 6, no. 3, 1975, pp. 513-524.

Hasenauer, R.: "Theoretical Analysis and Empirical Application of Goal Programming with Preemptive Priority Structures," in [27], pp. 120-135.

Hatry, H. P.: "Measuring the Effectiveness of Non-Defense Public Programs," *Operations Research*, vol. 18, no. 5, 1970, pp. 772-784.

Haurie, A.: "On Pareto Optimal Decisions for a Coalition of a Subset of Players," *IEEE Transactions on Automatic Control*, vol. AC-18, no. 2, 1973, pp. 144-149.

———— and M. C. Delfour: "Individual and Collective Rationality in a Dynamic Pareto Equilibrium," in [18], pp. 149-162.

Hawkins, C. A., and R. A. Adams: "A Goal Programming Model for Capital Budgeting," *Financial Management*, vol. 3, no. 1, 1974, pp. 52-57.

Heenan, D. A., and R. B. Addleman: "Quantitative Techniques for Today's Decision Makers," *Harvard Business Review*, vol. 54, no. 3, 1976, pp. 32-62.

Hemming, T.: "A New Method for Interactive Multiobjective Optimization: A Boundary Point Ranking Method," in [27], pp. 333-340.

Hendrix, G. G., and A. C. Stedry: "The Elementary Redundancy-Optimization Problem: A Case Study in Probabilistic Multiple Goal Programming," *Operations Research*, vol. 22, no. 3, 1974, pp. 610-621.

Herner, S., and K. J. Snapper: "Application of Multiple-Criteria Utility Model to Evaluation of

Information Systems," *Journal of the American Society for Information Science*, vol. 29, 1978, pp. 289–296.

Hill, M.: "Goals-Achievement Matrix for Evaluating Alternative Plans," *Journal of the American Institute of Planners*, vol. 34, no. 1, 1968, pp. 19–28.

———: *Planning for Multiple Objectives*, Monograph 5, Regional Science Research Institute, Philadelphia, 1973.

——— and Y. Tzamir: "Multidimensional Evaluation of Regional Plans Serving Multiple Objectives," *Papers of the Regional Science Association*, vol. 29, 1972, pp. 139–165.

Hindelang, T. J.: "QC Optimization through Goal Programming," *Quality Progress*, vol. 6, no. 12, 1973, pp. 20–22.

Hirsch, G.: "The Notion of Characteristic Set and Its Implication for the Analysis and Development of Multicriterion Methods," in [27], pp. 247–262.

Hitch, C. J.: "On the Choice of Objectives in Systems Studies," in D. P. Eckman (ed.), *Systems, Research and Design*, Wiley, New York, 1961.

———: "Sub-Optimization in Operations Research," *Operations Research*, vol. 1, no. 3, 1953, pp. 87–99.

Hoag, W. M.: "The Relevance of Cost in Operations Research," *Operations Research*, vol. 4, 1956, pp. 448–459.

Holl, S. T., and J. P. Young: "Planning for Education in the Health Services: A Multicriterion Approach," *Socio-Economic Planning Sciences*, vol. 14, no. 2, 1980, pp. 79–84.

Hopkins, D. S. P., J.-C. Larréché, and W. F. Massy: "Multiattribute Reference Functions of University Administrators," in [33], pp. 287–290.

House, P. W.: "How Do You Know Where You're Going?," in [4], pp. 741–744.

Huang, S. C.: "Note on the Mean-Square Strategy of Vector Valued Objective Functions," *Journal of Optimization Theory and Applications*, vol. 9, no. 5, 1972, pp. 364–366.

Huber, G. P.: "Methods for Quantifying Subjective Probabilities and Multiattribute Utilities," *Decision Sciences*, vol. 5, July 1974, pp. 430–458.

———: "Multi-Attribute Utility Models: A Review of Field and Field-Like Studies," *Management Science*, vol. 20, no. 10, 1974, pp. 1393–1402.

Huber, O.: "Nontransitive Multidimensional Preferences: Theoretical Analysis of a Model," *Theory and Decision*, vol. 10, 1979, pp. 147–165.

Huckert, K., et al.: "On the Interactive Solution to a Multicriteria Scheduling Problem," *Zeitschrift für Operations Research*, vol. 24, no. 1, 1980, pp. 47–60.

Hughes, A., and D. Grawoig: *Linear Programming: An Emphasis on Decision Making*, Addison-Wesley, Reading, Mass., 1973, chap. 15.

Humphreys, P.: "Applications of Multiattribute Utility Theory," in H. Jungermann and G. De Zeeuw (eds.), *Decision Making and Change in Human Affairs*, D. Reidel, Dordrecht, 1977.

——— and A. Humphreys: "An Investigation of Subjective Preference Orderings for Multiattributed Alternatives," in D. Wendt and C. Vlek (eds.), *Utility, Probability, and Human Decision Making*, D. Reidel, Boston, 1975, pp. 119–133.

Hwang, C. L., A. S. M. Masud, S. R. Paidy, and K. Yoon: "Mathematical Programming with Multiple Objectives: A Tutorial," in [31], pp. 5–31.

Ignizio, J. P.: "Antenna Array Beam Pattern Synthesis via Goal Programming," *European Journal of Operational Research*, vol. 5, 1980, pp. 406–410.

———: "An Approach to the Capital Budgeting Problem with Multiple Objectives," *Engineering Economist*, vol. 21, no. 4, Summer 1976, pp. 259–272.

———: "A Review of Goal Programming: A Tool for Multiobjective Analysis," *Journal of the Operational Research Society*, vol. 29, no. 11, 1978, pp. 1109–1119.

——— and J. H. Perlis: "Sequential Linear Goal Programming: Implementation via MPSX," *Computers and Operations Research*, vol. 6, no. 3, 1979, pp. 141–145.

Ijiri, Y.: "A Historical Cost Approach to Aggregation of Multiple Goals," in [4], pp. 395–405.

Inagaki, T. K., K. Inoue, and H. Akashi: "Interactive Optimization of System Reliability under Multiple Objectives," *IEEE Transactions on Reliability*, vol. 27, no. 4, 1978, pp. 264–267.

Isermann, H.: "Duality in Multiple Objective Linear Programming," in [34], pp. 274–285.

———: "The Enumeration of All Efficient Solutions for a Linear Multiple-Objective Transportation Problem," *Naval Research Logistics Quarterly*, vol. 26, no. 1, 1979, pp. 123–139.

———: The Enumeration of the Set of All Efficient Solutions for a Linear Multiple Objective Program," *Operational Research Quarterly*, vol. 28, no. 3, 1977, pp. 711–725.

———: "Existence and Duality in Multiple Objective Linear Programming," in [27], pp. 64–75.

———: "A Note on Proper Efficiency and the Linear Vector Maximum Problem," *Operations Research*. vol. 22, no. 1, 1974, pp. 189–199.

———: "The Relevance of Duality in Multiple Objective Linear Programming," in [25], pp. 241–262.

———: "On Some Relations Between a Dual Pair of Multiple Objective Linear Programs," *Zeitschrift für Operations Research*, vol. 22, 1978, pp. 33–41.

———: "Some Remarks on Optimising and Satisficing in Multiple Criteria Decision Problems," in D. J. White and K. C. Bowen (eds.), *The Role and Effectiveness of Theories of Decision in Practice*, Crane, Russak & Co., New York, 1975, pp. 43–51.

Jääskeläinen, V.: "A Goal Programming Model of Aggregate Production Planning," *Swedish Journal of Economics*, vol. 71, no. 1, 1969, pp. 14–29.

———: "Strategic Planning with Goal Programming," *Management Informatics*, vol. 1, no. 1, 1972, pp. 23–31.

Jackman, H. W.: "Financing Public Hospitals in Ontario: A Case Study in Rationing of Capital Budgets," *Management Science*, vol. 20, no. 4, part 2, 1973, pp. 645–655.

Jacobson, D. H.: "On Fuzzy Goals and Maximizing Decisions in Stochastic Optimal Control," *Journal of Mathematical Analysis and Applications*, vol. 55, 1976, pp. 434–440.

Jacquet-Lagrèze, E.: "Explicative Models in Multicriteria Preference Analysis," in M. Roubens (ed.), *Advances in Operations Research*, North-Holland Publishing, Amsterdam, 1977, pp. 213–218.

———: "How We Can Use the Notion of Semi-Orders to Build Outranking Relations in Multi-Criteria Decision Making," *Revue METRA*, vol. 3, 1974, pp. 59–86.

———: "Modelling Preferences among Distributions Using Fuzzy Relations," in H. Jungermann and G. De Zeeuw (eds.), *Decision Making and Change in Human Affairs*, D. Reidel, Dordrecht, 1977.

Jahn, J.: "The Haar Condition in Vector Optimization," in [7], pp. 128–134.

Jaikumar, R.: "A Heuristic 0-1 Algorithm with Multiple Objectives and Constraints," in [4], pp. 745–748.

Jain, R.: "A Procedure for Multi-Aspect Decision-Making Using Fuzzy Sets," *International Journal of Systems Science*, vol. 8, 1977, pp. 1–7.

Johnsen, E.: "Experiences in Multiobjective Management Processes," in [33], pp. 135–152.

———: "Multiobjective Management of the Small Firm," in [34], pp. 286–298.

Johnson, E. M., and G. P. Huber: "The Technology of Utility Assessment," *IEEE Transactions on Systems, Man, and Cybernetics*, vol. SMC-7, 1977, pp. 311–325.

Johnson, L. E., and D. P. Loucks: "Interactive Multiobjective Planning Using Computer Graphics," in [31], pp. 89–97.

Joksch, H. C.: "Constraints, Objectives, Efficient Solutions and Suboptimization in Mathematical Programming," *Zeitschrift für die gesamte Staatswissenschaft*, vol. 122, no. 1, 1966, pp. 5–13.

———: "Mathematical Aspects of a Multi-Objective Optimization Model Proposed by Leininger et al.," *Accident Analysis and Prevention*, vol. 3, no. 3, 1971, pp. 209–213.

Juralewicz, R. S.: "Interpersonal Dimensions of Decision Making in a Cross-Cultural Setting," in [4], pp. 749–752.

Kafarov, V. V., G. B. Lazarev, and V. I. Avdeev: "Multicriterial Problems in the Control of Complex Chemical-Engineering Systems," *Soviet Physics Doklady*, vol. 16, no. 5, 1971, pp. 344–345.

Kantariya, G. V.: "Optimal Choice of Strategy Based on Compromise Agreement among Alternative Selection Criteria," *Engineering Cybernetics*, vol. 12, no. 1, 1974, pp. 39–42.

Kapur, K. C.: "Mathematical Methods of Optimization for Multi-Objective Transportation Systems," *Socio-Economic Planning Science*, vol. 4, no. 4, 1970, pp. 451–467.

Karlin, S.: *Mathematical Methods and Theory in Games, Programming and Economics*, vol. 1, Addison-Wesley, Reading, Mass., 1959, pp. 216–217.

Karwan, K. R., and W. A. Wallace: "A Comparative Evaluation of Conjoint Measurement and Goal Programming as Aids in Decision Making for Marine Environmental Protection," in [7], pp. 135–149.

Keefer, D. L.: "Allocation Planning for R and D with Uncertainty and Multiple Objectives," *IEEE Transactions on Engineering Management*, vol. 25, 1978, pp. 8–14.

——: "Applying Multiobjective Decision Analysis to Resource Allocation Planning Problems," in [34], pp. 299–320.

—— and C. W. Kirkwood: "A Multiobjective Decision Analysis: Budget Planning for Product Engineering," *Journal of the Operational Research Society*, vol. 29, no. 5, 1978, pp. 435–442.

—— and S. M. Pollock: "Approximations and Sensitivity in Multiobjective Resource Allocation," *Operations Research*, vol. 28, no. 1, 1980, pp. 114–128.

Keen, P. G. W.: "The Evolving Concept of Optimality," in [25], pp. 31–58.

Keeney, R. L.: "The Art of Assessing Multiattribute Utility Functions," *Organizational Behavior and Human Performance*, vol. 19, 1977, pp. 267–310.

——: "Concepts of Independence in Multiattribute Utility Theory," in [4], pp. 62–71.

——: "A Decision Analysis with Multiple Objectives: The Mexico City Airport," *Bell Journal of Economics and Management*, vol. 4, 1973, pp. 101–117.

——: "Evaluating Multidimensional Situations Using a Quasi-Separable Utility Function," *IEEE Transactions on Man-Machine Systems*, vol. MMS-9, no. 2, 1968, pp. 25–28.

——: Evaluation of Proposed Pumped Storage Sites," *Operations Research*, vol. 27, 1979, pp. 48–64.

——: "Examining Corporate Policy Using Multiattribute Utility Analysis," *Sloan Management Review*, vol. 17, no. 1, 1975, pp. 63–76.

——: "An Illustrated Procedure for Assessing Multiattributed Utility Functions," *Sloan Management Review*, vol. 14, no. 1, 1972, pp. 37–50.

——: "Multiplicative Utility Functions," *Operations Research*, vol. 22, no. 1, 1974, pp. 22–34.

——: "Quantifying Corporate Preferences for Policy Analysis," in [27], pp. 293–304.

——: "Quasi-Separable Utility Functions," *Naval Research Logistics Quarterly*, vol. 15, 1968, pp. 551–565.

——: "Risk, Independence and Multiattributed Utility Functions," *Econometrica*, vol. 41, no. 1, 1973, pp. 27–39.

——: "A Utility Function for Examining Policy Affecting Salmon on the Skeena River," *Journal of the Fisheries Research Board of Canada*, vol. 34, 1977, pp. 49–63.

——: "A Utility Function for the Response Times of Engines and Ladders to Fires," *Urban Analysis*, vol. 1, 1973, pp. 209–222.

——: "Utility Functions for Multiattributed Consequences," *Management Science*, vol. 18, no. 5, part 1, 1972, pp. 276–287.

——: "Utility Independence and Preferences for Multiattributed Consequences," *Operations Research*, vol. 19, no. 4, 1971, pp. 875–893.

—— and G. L. Lilien: "A Utility Model for Product Positioning," in [34], pp. 321–334.

—— and K. Nair: "Nuclear Siting Using Decision Analysis," *Energy Policy,* September 1977.

—— and ——: "Selecting Nuclear Power Plant Sites in the Pacific Northwest Using Decision Analysis," in [2], pp. 298–322.

—— and A. Sicherman: "Assessing and Analyzing Preferences Concerning Multiple Objectives: An Interactive Computer Program," *Behavioral Science*, vol. 21, no. 3, 1976, pp. 173–182.

—— and E. F. Wood: "An Illustrative Example of the Use of Multiattribute Utility Theory for Water Resource Planning," *Water Resources Research*, vol. 13, no. 4, 1977, pp. 705–712.

Kendall, K. E.: "Multiple Objective Planning for Regional Blood Centers," *Long Range Planning*, vol. 13, no. 4, August 1980, pp. 98–104.

Keown, A. J.: "A Chance-Constrained Goal Programming Model for Bank Liquidity Management," *Decision Sciences*, January 1978, pp. 93–106.

—— and C. P. Duncan: "Integer Goal Programming in Advertising Media Selection," *Decision Sciences*, vol. 10, no. 4, 1979, pp. 577–592.

—— and J. D. Martin: "A Chance-Constrained Goal Programming Model for Working Capital Management," *Engineering Economist*, vol. 22, no. 3, Spring 1977, pp. 153–174.

—— and ——: "An Integer Goal Programming Model for Capital Budgeting in Hospitals," *Financial Management*, Autumn 1976, pp. 28–35.

—— and B. W. Taylor: "A Chance-Constrained Integer Goal Programming Model for Capital Budgeting in the Production Area," *Journal of the Operational Research Society*, vol. 31, no. 7, 1980, pp. 579–589.

——, ——, and C. P. Duncan: "Allocation of Research and Development Funds: A Zero-One Goal Programming Approach," *Omega*, vol. 7, no. 4, 1979, pp. 345–354.

Khairullah, Z. Y., and S. Zionts: "An Experiment with Some Algorithms for Multiple Criteria Decision Making," in [7], pp. 178–188.

Killough, L. N., and T. L. Souders: "A Goal Programming Model for Public Accounting Firms," *Accounting Review*, vol. 48, no. 2, April 1973, pp. 268–279.

Kirkwood, C. W.: "Parametrically Dependent Preferences for Multiattributed Consequences," *Operations Research*, vol. 24, 1976, pp. 92–103.

——: "Social Decision Analysis Using Multiattribute Utility Theory," in [34], pp. 335–344.

——: "Superiority Conditions in Decision Problems with Multiple Objectives," *IEEE Transactions on Systems, Man, and Cybernetics*, vol. SMC-7, no. 7, 1977, pp. 542–544.

Klahr, C. N.: "Multiple Objectives in Mathematical Programming," *Operations Research*, vol. 6, no. 6, 1958, pp. 849–855.

Klahr, D.: "Decision Making in a Complex Environment: The Use of Similarity Judgements to Predict Preferences," *Management Science*, vol. 15, no. 11, 1969, pp. 595–617.

Klinger, A.: "Improper Solutions of the Vector Maximum Problem," *Operations Research*, vol. 15, no. 3, 1967, pp. 570–572.

——: "Vector-Valued Performance Criteria," *IEEE Transactions on Automatic Control*, vol. AC-9, no. 1, 1964, pp. 117–118.

Klock, D. R., and S. M. Lee: "A Note on Decision Models for Insurers," *Journal of Risk and Insurance*, vol. 16, no. 3, September 1974, pp. 537–543.

Knoll, A. L., and A. Engelberg: "Weighting Multiple Objectives—The Churchman-Ackoff Technique Revisited," *Computers and Operations Research*, vol. 5, no. 3, 1978, pp. 165–177.

Knutson, D. L., et al.: "A Goal Programming Model for Achieving Racial Balance in Public Schools," *Socio-Economic Planning Sciences*, vol. 14, no. 3, 1980, pp. 109–116.

Kojima, M.: "Duality between Objectives and Constraints in Vector Maximum Problems," *Journal of Operations Research Society of Japan*, vol. 15, no. 1, 1972, pp. 53–62.

——: "Vector Maximum Problems," *Keio Engineering Report*, vol. 24, no. 4, 1971, pp. 47–61.

Koopman, B. O.: "Fallacies in Operations Research," *Operations Research*, vol. 4, no. 4, 1956, pp. 422–426.

——: "The Optimum Distribution of Effort," *Operations Research*, vol. 1, no. 2, 1953, pp. 52–63.

Koopmans, T. C.: "Analysis of Production as an Efficient Combination of Activities," in T. C. Koopmans (ed.), *Activity Analysis of Production and Allocation*, Cowles Commission Monograph 13, Wiley, New York, 1951, pp. 33–97.

——: "Objectives, Constraints, and Outcomes in Optimal Growth Models," *Econometrica*, vol. 35, 1967, pp. 1–15.

Korhonen, P., J. Wallenius, and S. Zionts: "A Bargaining Model for Solving Multiple Criteria Problem," in [7], pp. 178–188.

Kornbluth, J. S. H.: "Accounting in Multiple Objective Linear Programming," *Accounting Review*, vol. 49, no. 2, 1974, pp. 284–295.

————: "Duality, Indifference and Sensitivity Analysis in Multiple Objective Linear Programming," *Operational Research Quarterly*, vol. 25, no. 4, 1974, pp. 599–614.

————: "The Fuzzy Dual: Information for the Multiple Objective Decision Maker," *Computers and Operations Research*, vol. 4, 1977, pp. 65–72.

————: "Ranking with Multiple Objectives," in [34], pp. 345–361.

————: "A Survey of Goal Programming," *Omega*, vol. 1, no. 2, 1973, pp. 193–205.

————: "Using Duality Theory for Identification of Primal Efficient Points and for Sensitivity Analysis in MOLP: A Comment," *Journal of the Operational Research Society*, vol. 30, no. 3, 1979, pp. 285–287.

———— and R. E. Steuer: "On Computing the Set of all Weakly Efficient Vertices in Multiple Objective Linear Fractional Programming," in [7], pp. 189–202.

Krajewski, L. J., and J. C. Henderson: "Decision Making in the Public Sector: An Application of Goal Interval Programming for Disaggregation in the Post Office," in L. P. Ritzman et al. (eds.), *Disaggregation, Problems in Manufacturing and Service Organizations*, Martinus Nijhoff, Boston, 1979.

Krasnenkar, A. S.: "Method for Local Improvements in Vector-Optimization Problem," *Automation and Remote Control*, vol. 36, 1975, pp. 419–422.

Krueger, R. J., and J. P. Dauer: "Multiobjective Optimization Model," *SIAM Review*, vol. 20, 1978, p. 629.

Kuhn, H. W., and A. W. Tucker: "Nonlinear Programming," in J. Neyman (ed.), *Proceedings of the Second Berkeley Symposium on Mathematical Statistics and Probability*, University of California Press, Berkeley, 1951, pp. 481–491; also in P. Newman (ed.), *Readings in Mathematical Economics*, Johns Hopkins University Press, Baltimore, 1968, pp. 3–14.

Kumar, P. C., and G. C. Philippatos: "Conflict Resolution in Investment Decisions: Implementation of Goal Programming Methodology for Dual-Purpose Funds," *Decision Sciences*, vol. 10, no. 4, 1979, pp. 562–576.

————, ————, and J. R. Ezzell: "Goal Programming and the Selection of Portfolios by Dual-Purpose Funds," *Journal of Finance*, vol. 33, March 1978, pp. 303–310.

Kumbaraci, T. E.: "The Judgment of Improvement—Choice for Decisions Relating to Medical Efficacy," in [4], pp. 753–754.

Kunreuther, H.: "Extensions of Bowman's Theory on Managerial Decision-Making," *Management Science*, vol. 15, no. 8, 1969, pp. B415–B439.

Kuzimin, I. V., E. O. Dedikov, and B. Y. Kukharev: "Choice of Global Solution Criterion in Problems with Several Objective Functions," *Soviet Automatic Control*, vol. 7, no. 4, 1974, pp. 59–62.

Kvanli, A. H.: "Financial Planning Using Goal Programming," *Omega*, vol. 8, no. 2, 1980, pp. 207–218.

Kwak, N. K., and M. J. Schniederjans: "A Goal Programming Model for Improved Transportation Problem Solutions," *Omega*, vol. 7, no. 4, 1979, pp. 367–370.

Ladany, S. P., and M. Aharoni: "Maintenance Policy of Aircraft According to Multiple Criteria," *International Journal of Systems Science*, vol. 6, no. 11, 1975, pp. 1093–1101.

Landsberger, M., and A. Subotnik: "Optimal Behavior of a Monopolist Facing A Bicriteria Objective Function," *International Economic Review*, vol. 17, no. 3, 1976, pp. 581–600.

Larichev, O. I.: "Man-Machine Procedures for Decision Making (Review)," *Automation and Remote Control*, vol. 32, no. 12, part 2, 1971, pp. 1973–1983.

————: "Method for Evaluating R & D Projects," *Automation and Remote Control*, vol. 33, no. 8, 1972, pp. 1356–1360.

————: "A Practical Methodology of Solving Multicriterion Problems with Subjective Criteria," in [2], pp. 197–208.

LaValle, I. H.: "On Admissibility and Bayesness When Risk Attitude But Not the Preference Ranking Is Permitted to Vary," in [4], pp. 72–83.

Lawrence, K. D., and J. J. Burbridge: "A Multiple Goal Linear Programming Model for Coordinated Production and Logistics Planning," *International Journal of Production Research*, vol. 14, no. 2, March 1976, pp. 215–222.

────── and J. I. Weindling: "Multiple Goal Operations Management Planning and Decision Making in a Quality Control Department," in [7], pp. 203–217.

Lee, S. M.: "Goal Programming," in *Encyclopedia of Computer Science and Technology*, vol. 9, Marcel Dekker, New York, 1978, pp. 83–104.

──────: "Interactive Integer Programming: Methods and Applications," in [34], pp. 362–383.

──────: "Goal Programming for Decision Analysis of Multiple Objectives," *Sloan Management Review*, vol. 14, no. 2, 1973, pp. 11–24.

──────: "Decision Analysis Through Goal Programming," *Decision Sciences*, no. 2, 1971, pp. 172–180.

────── and M. M. Bird: "A Goal Programming Model for Sales Effort Allocation," *Business Perspectives*, vol. 6, no. 4, 1970, pp. 17–21.

────── and D. L. Chesser: "Goal Programming for Portfolio Selection," *Journal of Portfolio Management*, vol. 6, no. 3, 1980, pp. 22–26.

────── and E. R. Clayton: "A Goal Programming Model for Academic Resource Allocation," *Management Science*, vol. 18, no. 8, 1972, pp. B395–B408.

────── and L. S. Franz: "Optimising the Location-Allocation Problem with Multiple Objectives," *International Journal of Physical Distribution and Materials Management*, vol. 9, no. 6, 1979, pp. 245–255.

────── and V. Jääskeläinen: "Goal Programming: Management's Math Model," *Industrial Engineering*, vol. 3, no. 2, 1971, pp. 30–35.

────── and A. J. Lerro: "Capital Budgeting for Multiple Objectives," *Financial Management*, vol. 3, no. 1, 1974, pp. 58–66.

────── and ──────: "Optimizing the Portfolio Selection for Mutual Funds," *Journal of Finance*, vol. 28, no. 5, 1972, pp. 1087–1101.

────── and L. J. Moore: "Multi-Criteria School Busing Models," *Management Science*, vol. 23, no. 7, 1977, pp. 703–715.

────── and ──────: "Optimizing University Admissions Planning," *Decision Sciences*, vol. 5, no. 3, July 1974, pp. 405–414.

────── and ──────: "A Practical Approach to Production Scheduling," *Production and Inventory Management*, vol. 15, no. 1, 1974.

────── and ──────: "Optimizing Transportation Problems with Multiple Objectives," *AIIE Transactions*, vol. 5, no. 4, 1973, pp. 333–338.

────── and R. L. Morris: "Integer Goal Programming Methods," in [25], pp. 273–289.

────── and R. Nicely: "Goal Programming for Marketing Decisions: A Case Study," *Journal of Marketing*, vol. 38, no. 1, 1974, pp. 24–32.

────── and A. J. Wynne: "Separable Goal Programming," in [21].

──────, E. R. Clayton, and B. W. Taylor: "A Goal Programming Approach to Multi-Period Production Line Scheduling," *Computers and Operations Research*, vol. 5, no. 3, 1978, pp. 205–211.

──────, J. Van Horn, and H. Brisch: "A Multiple Criteria Analysis Model for Academic Policies, Priorities, and Budgetary Constraints," in [7], pp. 218–237.

Legasto, A. A.: "A Multiple-Objective Policy Model: Results of an Application to a Developing Country," *Management Science*, vol. 24, no. 5, 1978, pp. 498–509.

Lehmann, R., and W. Oettli: "The Theorem of the Alternative, the Key-Theorem, and the Vector-Maximum Problem," *Mathematical Programming*, vol. 8, no. 3, 1975, pp. 332–344.

Leitmann, G.: "Some Problems of Scalar and Vector-Valued Optimization in Linear Viscoelasticity," *Journal of Optimization Theory and Applications*, vol. 23, no. 1, 1977, pp. 93–99.

────── and W. Schmitendorf: "Some Sufficient Conditions for Pareto-Optimal Control," *Journal of Dynamic Systems, Measurement and Control*, vol. 95, no. 3, 1973.

Levanon, Y., and U. Passy: "Condensing Multiple Criteria," in [34] pp. 449–461.

Lhoas, J.: "Multi-Criteria Decision Aid Application to the Selection of the Route for a Pipe-Line," in M. Roubens (ed.), *Advances in Operations Research*, North-Holland Publishing, Amsterdam, 1977, pp. 265–273.

Lin, J. G.: "Maximal Vectors and Multi-Objective Optimization," *Journal of Optimization Theory and Applications*, vol. 18, no. 1, 1976, pp. 41–64.

———: "Multiple Objective Optimization: Proper Equality Constraints (PEC) and Maximization of Index Vectors," in [18], pp. 103–128.

———: "Multiple-Objective Problems, Pareto-Optimal Solutions by the Method of Proper Equality Constraints," *IEEE Transactions on Automatic Control*, vol. AC-21, 1976, pp. 641–650.

——— "Proper Equality Constraints and Maximization on Index Vectors," *Journal of Optimization Theory and Applications*, vol. 20, no. 2, 1976, pp. 215–244.

———: "Proper Inequality Constraints and Maximization of Index Vectors," *Journal of Optimization Theory and Applications*, vol. 22, no. 4, 1977, pp. 505–521.

———: "Three Methods for Determining Pareto-Optimal Solutions of Multiple-Objective Problems," in Y. Ho and S. Mitter (eds.), *Directions in Large-Scale Systems*, Plenum, New York, 1976, pp. 117–138.

Lin, S. A. Y.: "Dynamic Growth of the Firm under Uncertainty with Multiple Goals," in [4], pp. 755–759.

Lin, T. W.: "An Accounting Control System Structured on Multiple Objective Planning Models," *Omega*, vol. 8, no. 3, 1980, pp. 375–382.

———: "Application of Goal Programming in Accounting," *Journal of Business Finance & Accounting*, vol. 6, no. 4, 1979, pp. 559–577.

Lin, W. T.: "Multiple Objective Budgeting Models: A Simulation," *Accounting Review*, vol. 53, January 1978, pp. 61–76.

———: "A Survey of Goal Programming Applications," *Omega*, vol. 8, no. 1, 1980, pp. 115–117.

Lockett, A. G., and A. P. Muhlemann: "A Problem of Aggregate Scheduling: An Application of Goal Programming," *International Journal of Production Research*, vol. 16, no. 2, 1978, pp. 127–136.

Loucks, D. P.: "An Application of Interactive Multiobjective Water Resources Planning," *Interfaces*, vol. 8, no. 1, November 1977, pp. 70–75.

———: "Planning for Multiple Goals," in C. R. Blitzer, P. B. Clark, and L. Taylor (eds.), *Economy-Wide Models and Development Planning*, Oxford University Press, London, 1975, pp. 213–233.

Lucas, H. C., and J. R. Moore: "A Multiple-Criterion Scoring Approach to Information System Project Selection," *INFOR*, vol. 14, no. 1, 1976, pp. 1–12.

MacCrimmon, K. R.: "An Overview of Multiple Objective Decision Making," in [4], pp. 18–44.

——— and M. Toda: "The Experimental Determination of Indifference Curves," *Review of Economic Studies*, vol. 36, no. 4, 1969, pp. 433–450.

——— and D. A. Wehrung: "Trade-off Analysis: The Indifference and Preferred Proportions Approaches," in [2], pp. 123–147.

McGinnis, L. F., and J. A. White: "A Single Facility Rectilinear Location Problem with Multiple Criteria," *Transportation Science*, vol. 12, 1978, pp. 217–231.

McGrew, D. R., and Y. Y. Haimes: "Parametric Solution to the Joint System Identification and Optimization Problem," *Journal of Optimization Theory and Applications*, vol. 13, no. 5, 1974, pp. 582–605.

McMillan, C.: *Mathematical Programming*, Wiley, New York, 1975, chap. 4.

Mahoney, F. J.: "The Design of Regression Experiments with Multiple Objectives," in [4], pp. 760–763.

Major, D. C.: "Benefit-Cost Ratios for Projects in Multiple Objective Investment Programs," *Water Resources Research*, vol. 5, no. 6, 1969, pp. 1174–1178.

———: "Multiobjective Redesign of the Big Walnut Project," in R. De Neufville and D. Marks (eds.), *Systems Planning and Design*, Prentice-Hall, Englewood Cliffs, N. J., 1974, pp. 322–337.

———: *Multiobjective Water Resource Planning*, Water Resources Monograph 4, American Geophysical Union, Washington, D.C., 1977.

Marks, D. H.: "Water Quality Management," in A. Drake, R. Keeney, and P. Morse (eds.), *Analysis of Public Systems*, M.I.T., Cambridge, Mass., 1972, pp. 356–375.

Marschak, J.: "Guided Soul-Searching for Multi-Criterion Decisions," in [33], pp. 1-16.

Marshall, H. E.: "Cost Sharing and Multiobjectives in Water Resource Development," *Water Resources Research*, vol. 9, no. 1, 1973, pp. 1-10.

Martin, W. S., and A. Barcus: "A Multiattribute Model for Evaluating Industrial Customer's Potential," *Interfaces*, vol. 10, no. 3, June 1980, pp. 40-44.

Marzollo, A., and W. Ukovich: "On Some Broad Classes of Vector Optimal Decisions and Their Characterization," in [19], pp. 281-324.

Masakazu, K.: "Vector Maximum Problems," *Keio Engineering Report*, vol. 24, 1971, pp. 47-64.

Masser, I., P. W. J. Batey, and P. J. B. Brown: "Sequential Treatment of the Multi-Criteria Aggregation Problem: A Case Study of Zoning System Design," in I. Masser and P. Brown (eds.), *Spatial Representation and Spatial Interaction*, Studies in Applied Regional Science, vol. 10, Martinus Nijhoff, Boston, 1978.

Medanic, J.: "Minimax Pareto Optimal Solutions with Application to Linear Quadratic Problems," in [19], pp. 55-124.

Mehta, A. J., and A. K. Rifai: "Application of Linear Programming vs. Goal Programming to Assignment Problem," *Akron Business and Economic Review*, Winter 1976, pp. 52-55.

Meisel, W. S.: "Tradeoff Decisions in Multiple Criteria Decision Making," in [4], pp. 461-476.

Merkurev, V. V., and M. A. Moldavskii: "A Family of Convolutions of a Vector-Valued Criterion for Finding Points in a Pareto Set," *Automation and Remote Control*, vol. 40, no. 1, part 2, January 1979, pp. 87-97.

Miller, D. L., and D. M. Byers: "Development and Display of Multiple Objective Project Impacts," *Water Resources Research*, vol. 9, no. 1, 1973, pp. 11-20.

—— and S. P. Erickson: "The Impact of High Interest Rates on Optimum Multiple Objective Design of Surface Runoff Urban Drainage Systems," *Water Resources Bulletin*, vol. 11, no. 1, 1975, pp. 49-59.

Minnehan, R. F.: "Multiple Objectives and Multigroup Decision Making in Physical Design Situations," in [4], pp. 506-516.

Mitroff, I. I.: "On Being Consistent: The Management of Inquiry as a Multi-Criteria Decision Problem," in [25], pp. 291-300.

Moinpur, R., and J. B. Wiley: "Application of Multi-Attribute Models of Attitude in Marketing," *Journal of Business Administration*, vol. 5, no. 2, 1974, pp. 3-16.

Monarchi, D. E., C. C. Kisiel, and L. Duckstein: "Interactive Multiobjective Programming in Water Resources: A Case Study," *Water Resources Research*, vol. 9, no. 4, 1973, pp. 837-850.

——, J. E. Weber, and L. Duckstein: "An Interactive Multiple Objective Decision-Making Aid Using Nonlinear Goal Programming," in [33], pp. 235-253.

Moore, J. M.: "The Zone of Compromise for Evaluating Lay-Out Arrangements," *International Journal of Production Research*, vol. 18, no. 1, 1980, pp. 1-10.

Moore, J. R., and N. R. Baker: "Computational Analysis of Scoring Models for R and D Project Selection," *Management Science*, vol. 16, no. 4, 1969, pp. B-212-B-232.

Moore, L. J., B. W. Taylor, and S. M. Lee: "Analysis of a Transshipment Problem with Multiple Conflicting Objectives," *Computers and Operations Research*, vol. 5, no. 1, 1978, pp. 39-46.

Morris, P. A., and S. S. Oren: "Multiattribute Decision Making by Sequential Resource Allocation," *Operations Research*, vol. 28, no. 1, 1980, pp. 233-252.

Morris, W. T.: *Engineering Economic Analysis*, Reston Publishing, Reston, Va., 1976, chap. 7.

Morse, J. N.: "Reducing the Size of the Nondominated Set: Pruning by Clustering," in [31], pp. 55-66.

——: "A Theory of Naive Weights," in [34], pp. 384-401.

—— and R. Clark: "Goal Programming in Transportation Planning: The Problem of Setting Weights," *Northeast Regional Science Review*, vol. 5, 1975, pp. 140-147.

—— and E. B. Lieb: "Flexibility and Rigidity in Multicriterion Linear Programming," in [7], pp. 238-251.

Moscarola, J.: "Multicriteria Decision Aid: Two Applications in Education Management," in [34], pp. 402-423.

Moskowitz, H., G. Evans, and I. Jimenez-Lerma: "Development of Multiattribute Value Function for Long-Range Electrical Generation Expansion," *IEEE Transactions on Engineering Management*, vol. EM-25, no. 4, 1978, pp. 78–87.

Muhlemann, A. P., and A. G. Lockett: "Portfolio Modeling in Multiple-Criteria Situations under Uncertainty: Rejoinder," *Decision Sciences*, vol. 11, no. 1, 1980, pp. 178–180.

———, ———, and A. E. Gear: "Portfolio Modeling in Multiple-Criteria Situations under Uncertainty," *Decision Sciences*, vol. 9, no. 4, 1978, pp. 612–626.

Mukai, H.: "Algorithms for Multicriterion Optimization," *IEEE Transactions on Automatic Control*, vol. AC-25, no. 2, April 1980, pp. 177–186.

Mundlak, Y., and Z. Volcani: "The Correspondence of Efficiency Frontier as a Generalization of the Cost Function," *International Economic Review*, vol. 14, no. 1, 1973, pp. 223–233.

Muralidharan, R., and Y. C. Ho: "A Piecewise-Closed Form Algorithm for a Family of Minmax and Vector Criteria Problems," *IEEE Transactions on Automatic Control*, vol. AC-20, no. 3, 1975, pp. 381–385.

Naccache, P. H.: "Connectedness of the Set of Non-Dominated Outcomes in Multicriteria Optimization," *Journal of Optimization Theory and Applications*, vol. 25, 1978, pp. 459–467.

Nakayama, H.: "Subjective Programming in Multi-Criterion Decision Making," in [7], pp. 252–265.

———, Y. Karasawa, and S. Dohi: "Subjective Programming Applied to Optimal Operation in Automated Warehouses," *International Journal of Systems Science*, vol. 11, no. 4, 1980, pp. 513–525.

———, T. Tanino, and Y. Sawaragi: "An Interactive Optimization Method in Multicriteria Decisionmaking," *IEEE Transactions on Systems, Man, and Cybernetics*, vol. SMC-10, no. 3, March 1980, pp. 163–169.

Narisimhan, R.: "Goal Programming in a Fuzzy Environment," *Decision Sciences*, vol. 11, no. 2, 1980, pp. 325–336.

Narula, S. C., and J. F. Wellington: "Linar Regression Using Multiple Criteria," in [7], pp. 266–277.

Neely, W. P., R. M. North, and J. C. Fortson: "Planning and Selecting Multiobjective Projects by Goal Programming," *Water Resources Bulletin*, vol. 12, no. 1, 1976, pp. 19–25.

Negoita, C. V.: *Management Applications of System Theory*, Birkhäuser Verlag, Basel, 1979, pp. 136–143.

——— and M. Sularia: "A Selection Method of Nondominated Points in Multicriteria Decision Problems," *Economic Computation and Economic Cybernetics: Studies and Research*, vol. 12, no. 2, 1978, pp. 19–23.

Neumann, S.: "Calibration of Distributed Parameter Groundwater Flow Models Viewed as a Multiple-Objective Decision Process under Uncertainty," *Water Resources Research*, vol. 9, 1973, p. 1006.

Nijkamp, P.: "A Multicriteria Analysis for Project Evaluation: Economic-Ecological Evaluation of a Land Reclamation Project," *Papers of the Regional Science Association*, vol. 35, 1975, pp. 87–111.

——— and P. Rietveld: "Conflicting Social Priorities and Compromise Social Decisions," in I. G. Cullen (ed.), *Analysis and Decision in Regional Policy*, Pion, London, 1979, pp. 153–177.

——— and ———: "Multilevel Multiobjective Models in a Multiregional System," in [21].

——— and ———: "Multi-Objective Programming Models: New Ways in Regional Decision-Making," *Regional Science and Urban Economics*, vol. 6, 1976, pp. 253–274.

——— and J. Spronk: "Analysis of Production and Location Decisions by Means of Multicriteria Analysis," *Engineering and Process Economics*, vol. 4, 1979, pp. 285–302.

——— and ———: "Interactive Multiple Goal Programming: An Evaluation and some Results," in [7], pp. 278–293.

——— and ———: "Multicriteria Analysis: Theory and Reality," in [21].

——— and J. B. Vos: "A Multicriteria Analysis for Water Resource and Land Use Development," *Water Resources Research*, vol. 13, no. 3, 1977, pp. 513–518.

Nurminen, M. I., and A. Paasio: "Some Remarks on the Fuzzy Approach to Multi-Goal Decision-Making," *Finnish Journal of Business Economics*, special ed. 3, 1976, pp. 291–302.

Nutt, P. C.: "Comparing Methods for Weighting Decision Criteria," *Omega*, vol. 8, no. 2, 1980, pp. 163–172.

Odom, P. R., R. E. Shannon, and B. P. Buckles: "Multi-Goal Subset Selection Problems under Uncertainty," *AIIE Transactions*, vol. 11, no. 1, 1979, pp. 61–69.

Ölander, F.: "Search Behavior in Non-Simultaneous Choice Situations: Satisficing or Maximizing?," in D. Wendt and C. Vlek (eds.), *Utility, Probability, and Human Decision Making*, D. Reidel, Boston, 1975, pp. 297–320.

Olech, C.: "Existence Theorems for Optimal Problems with Vector-Valued Cost Function," *Transactions of American Mathematical Society*, vol. 136, 1969, pp. 159–180.

Olenik, S. C., and Y. Y. Haimes: "A Hierarchical-Multiobjective Method for Water Resources Planning," *IEEE Transactions on Systems, Man and Cybernetics*, special issue on Public Systems Methodology, 1979, in press.

Oppenheimer, K. R.: "A Proxy Approach to Multi-Attribute Decision Making," *Management Science*, vol. 24, no. 6, 1978, pp. 675–689.

Ören, T. I., and C. Y. Ören: "Solution Selection Techniques for Decision Making in Complex Systems," in [4], pp. 764–767.

Orne, D. L., A. Rao, and W. A. Wallace: "Profit Maximization with the Aid of Goal Programming for Speculative Housing Estate Developers," *Operational Research Quarterly*, vol. 26, no. 4, 1975, pp. 813–826.

Osteryoung, J. S.: "Multiple Goals in the Capital Budgeting Decision," in [4], pp. 447–457.

Osyczka, A.: "An Approach to Multicriterion Optimization Problems for Engineering Design," *Computer Methods in Applied Mechanics and Engineering*, vol. 15, 1978, pp. 309–333.

Ozernoi, V. M.: "Using Preference Information in Multistep Methods for Solving Multiple Criteria Decision Problems," in [7], pp. 314–328.

—— and M. G. Gaft: "Multicriterion Decision Problems," in [2], pp. 17–39.

Pascual, L. D., and A. Ben-Israel: "Vector-Valued Criteria in Geometric Programming," *Operations Research*, vol. 19, no. 1, 1971, pp. 98–104.

Passy, U.: "Cobb-Douglas Functions in Multiobjective Optimization," *Water Resources Research*, vol. 14, 1978, pp. 688–690.

—— and Y. Levanon: "Manpower Allocation with Multiple Objectives—The Min Max Approach," in [7], pp. 329–343.

Pasternak, H., and U. Passy: "Bicriterion Mathematical Programs with Boolean Variables," in [4], pp. 327–348.

Pau, L. F.: "Two-Level Planning with Conflicting Goals," in [27], pp. 263–273.

Payne, H. J., E. Polak, D. C. Collins, and W. S. Meisel: "An Algorithm for Bicriteria Optimization Based on the Sensitivity Function," *IEEE Transactions on Automatic Control*, vol. AC-20, no. 4, 1975, pp. 546–548.

Pearman, A.: "Approaches to Multiple Objective Decision Making with Ranked Criteria," in I. G. Cullen (ed.), *Analysis and Decision in Regional Policy*, Pion, London, 1979, pp. 136–152.

——: "A Weighted Maximin and Maximax Approach to Multiple Criteria Decision Making," *Operational Research Quarterly*, vol. 28, 1977, pp. 584–587.

Perlman, M. D.: "Jensen's Inequality for a Convex Vector-Valued Function on an Infinite-Dimensional Space," *Journal of Multivariate Analysis*, vol. 4, 1974, pp. 52–65.

Peschel, M., and C. Riedel: "Use of Vector Optimization in Multiobjective Decision Making," in [2], pp. 97–122.

Philip, J.: "An Algorithm for Combined Quadratic and Multiobjective Programming," in [27], pp. 35–51.

——: "Vector Maximization at a Degenerate Vertex," *Mathematical Programming*, vol. 13, no. 3, 1977, pp. 357–359.

——: "Algorithms for the Vector Maximization Problem," *Mathematical Programming*, vol. 2, no. 2, 1972, pp. 207–229.

Philippatos, G. C.: "Behavioral Implications of Discrepancies in Expectations Between the Firm and Its Stockholders with an Application to Dividend Policies," in [4], pp. 768–770.

——: "On the Specification of Viable Financial Goals," *Managerial Planning*, vol. 20, no. 1, 1971, pp. 11–16.

Philipson, R. H., and A. Ravindran: "Application of Goal Programming to Machinability Data Optimization," *Journal of Mechanical Design*, vol. 100, 1978, pp. 286–291.

Pitkanen, E.: "Goal Programming and Operational Objectives in Public Administration," *Swedish Journal of Economics*, vol. 72, no. 3, 1970, pp. 207–214.

Podrebarac, M. L., and S. S. Sengupta: "Parametric Linear Programming: Some Extensions," *INFOR*, vol. 9, no. 3, 1971, pp. 305–319.

Polak, E.: "On the Approximation of Solutions to Multiple Criteria Decision Making Problems," in [33], pp. 271–282.

—— and A. N. Payne: "On Multicriteria Optimization," in Y. C. Ho and S. K. Mitter (eds.), *Directions in Large-Scale Systems*, Plenum, New York, 1976, pp. 77–94.

Pollatscheck, A.: "Personnel Assignment by Multiobjective Programming," *Zeitschrift für Operations Research*, vol. 20, no. 5, 1976, pp. 161–170.

Powell, J., and R. Vergin: "A Heuristic Model for Planning Corporate Financing," *Financial Management*, vol. 4, no. 2, 1975, pp. 13–20.

Price, W. L.: "Goal Programming and a Manpower Problem," in P. L. Hammer and G. Zoutendijk (eds.), *Mathematical Programming in Theory and Practice*, North-Holland Publishing, New York, 1974, pp. 395–416.

——: "An Interactive Objective Function Generator for Goal Programmes," in [27], pp. 147–158.

——: "Solving Goal-Programming Manpower Models Using Advanced Network Codes," *Journal of the Operational Research Society*, vol. 29, no. 12, 1978, pp. 1231–1240.

—— and W. G. Piskor: "The Application of Goal Programming to Manpower Planning," *INFOR*, vol. 10, no. 3, 1972, pp. 221–231.

Pruzan, P. M.: "Is Cost Benefit Analysis Consistent with the Maximization of Expected Utility?" in J. R. Lawrence (ed.), *Operational Research of the Social Sciences*, Tavistock Publications, London, 1966, pp. 319–336.

——: "Measures of Performance for 'Significant' Planning Problems," *Erhvervsøkonomisk Tidsskrift*, vol. 2, 1966, pp. 91–100.

—— and J. T. R. Jackson: "On the Development of Utility Spaces for Multi-Goal Systems," *Erhvervsøkonomisk Tidsskrift*, vol. 27, no. 4, 1963, pp. 257–274.

Pun, L.: "Multicriteria Decision-Aid-Making in Production-Management Problems," in [7], pp. 344–373.

Radner, R.: "Satisficing," in G. Marchuk (ed.), *Optimization Techniques: IFIP Technical Conference*, Springer-Verlag, New York, 1975, pp. 252–263.

Rae, A. N.: "A Note on the Solution of Goal Programming Problems with Preemptive Priority," *New Zealand Operational Research*, vol. 2, no. 1, 1974, pp. 34–39.

Rapoport, A.: "Interpersonal Comparison of Utilities," in [33], pp. 17–43.

Rasmusen, H. J.: "Multilevel Planning with Conflicting Objectives," *Swedish Journal of Economics*, vol. 76, no. 2, 1974, pp. 155–170.

Reeves, G. R.: "A Note on Quadratic Preferences and Goal Programming," *Decision Sciences*, vol. 9, no. 3, 1978, pp. 532–534.

Reggiani, M. G., and F. E. Marchetti: "The Pseudometric View in Problems Involving Vector-Valued Performance Criteria," *Alta Frequenza*, vol. 43, no. 7, 1974, pp. 462–467.

Reid, R. W., and S. J. Citron: "On Noninferior Performance Index Vectors," *Journal of Optimization Theory and Applications*, vol. 7, no. 1, 1971, pp. 11–28.

—— and V. Vemuri: "On the Noninferior Index Approach to Large-Scale Multi-Criteria Systems," *Journal of the Franklin Institute*, vol. 291, no. 4, 1971, pp. 241–254.

Ritzman, L., J. Bradford, and R. Jacobs: "A Multiple Objective Approach to Space Planning for Academic Facilities," *Management Science*, vol. 25, no. 9, 1979, pp. 895–906.

Ritzman, L. P., and L. J. Krajewski: "Multiple Objectives in Linear Programming—An Example in Scheduling Postal Resources," *Decision Sciences*, vol. 4, no. 3, 1973, pp. 364–378.

Rivett, B. H. P.: "Indifference Mapping for Multiple Criteria Decisions," *Omega*, vol. 8, no. 1, 1980, pp. 81–94.

———: "Multidimensional Scaling for Multiobjective Policies," *Omega*, vol. 5, no. 4, 1977, pp. 367–379.

———: "The Use of Local-Global Mapping Techniques in Analysing Multi-Criteria Decision Making," in [7], pp. 374–388.

Rödder, W.: "A Duality Theory for Linear Vector Optimum Problems," in M. Roubens (ed.), *Advances in Operations Research*, North-Holland Publishing, Amsterdam, 1977, pp. 405–407.

———: "A Generalized Saddle-Point Theory as Applied to Duality Theory for Linear Vector Optimization Problems," *European Journal of Operational Research*, vol. 1, 1977, pp. 55–59.

———: "A Satisfying Aggregation of Objectives by Duality," in [7], pp. 389–399.

Rom, W. O., and M. S. Hung: "Application of Primitive Sets to Multi-Criteria Optimization Problems," *Journal of Mathematical Economics*, vol. 7, no. 1, 1980, pp. 77–90.

Rosenblatt, M. J.: "The Facilities Layout Problem: A Multi-Goal Approach," *International Journal of Production Research*, vol. 17, no. 4, 1979, pp. 323–332.

Rosinger, E. E.: "Interactive Algorithm for Multiobjective Optimization," in [7], pp. 400–404.

———: "Duality and Alternative in Multiobjective Optimization," *Proceedings of American Mathematical Society*, vol. 64, no. 2, 1977, pp. 307–313.

Ross, G. T., and R. M. Soland: "A Multicriteria Approach to Location of Public Facilities," *European Journal of Operational Research*, vol. 4, no. 5, 1980, pp. 307–321.

Roy, B.: "A Conceptual Framework for a Prescriptive Theory of 'Decision-Aid'," in [25], pp. 179–210.

———: "From Optimization to Multi-Criteria Decision Aid: Three Main Operational Attitudes," in [27], pp. 1–34.

———: "How Outranking Relation Helps Multiple Criteria Decision Making," in [4], pp. 179–201.

———: "A Multicriteria Analysis for Trichotomic Segmentation Problems," in [21].

———: "Partial Preference Analysis and Decision-Aid: The Fuzzy Outranking Relation Concept," in [2], pp. 40–75.

———: "Problems and Methods with Multiple Objective Functions," *Mathematical Programming*, vol. 1, no. 2, 1971, pp. 239–266.

———: "Why Multicriteria Decision Aid May Not Fit In with the Assessment of a Unique Criterion," in [33], pp. 283–286.

——— and E. Jacquet-Lagrèze: "Concepts and Methods Used in Multicriterion Decision Models: Their Applications to Transportation Problems," in H. Strobel, R. Genser, and M. M. Etschmaier (eds.), *Optimization Applied to Transportation Systems*, IIASA, Laxenburg, Austria, 1977, pp. 9–26.

Roy G. G.: "A Man-Machine Approach to Multicriteria Decision Making," *International Journal of Man-Machine Studies*, vol. 12, no. 2, 1980, pp. 203–215.

———: "A Multicriteria Approach to Regional Planning Problems," *Environment and Planning*, vol. 6, 1974, pp. 313–320.

Ruefli, T. W.: "A Generalized Goal Decomposition Model," *Management Science*, vol. 17, no. 8, 1971, pp. B505–B518.

———: "Linked Multi-Criteria Decision Models," in [4], pp. 406–415.

Saaty, T. L.: "Exploring the Interface Between Hierarchies, Multiple Objectives and Fuzzy Sets," *Fuzzy Sets and Systems*, vol. 1, no. 1, 1978, pp. 57–68.

Sakawa, M.: "An Approximate Solution to Linear Multicriteria Control Problems through the Multicriteria Simplex Method," *Journal of Optimization Theory and Applications*, vol. 22, no. 3, 1977, pp. 417–427.

———: "Multiobjective Optimization by the Surrogate Worth Trade-off Method," *Journal of the Operational Research Society*, vol. 31, no. 2, 1980, pp. 153–158.

————: "Multiobjective Reliability and Redundancy Optimization of a Series-Parallel System by Surrogate Worth Trade-off Method," *Microelectronics and Reliability*, vol. 17, 1978, pp. 465–467.

————: "Solution of Multicriteria Control Problems in Certain Types of Linear Distributed-Parameter Systems by a Multicriteria Simplex Method," *Journal of Mathematical Analysis and Applications*, vol. 64, 1978, pp. 181–188.

———— and R. Narutaki: "Multi-Objective Optimization in Decentralized Management of Development in Large Production Organizations," *International Journal of Systems Science*, vol. 8, 1977, pp. 9–16.

———— and Y. Sawaragi: "Multiple-Criteria Optimization of Pollution Control Model," *Journal of Systems Science*, vol. 6, no. 8, 1975, pp. 741–748.

———— and ————: "Multiple-Objective Optimization for Environment Development Systems," *Journal of Systems Science*, vol. 6, no. 2, 1975, pp. 157–164.

———— R. Narutaki, and T. Suwa: "Optimal Control of Linear Systems with Several Cost Functionals through a Multicriteria Simplex Method," *International Journal of Control*, vol. 25, no. 6, 1977, pp. 901–914.

Salama, A. I. A., and V. Gourishankar: "Optimal Control of Systems with a Single Control and Several Cost Functionals," *International Journal of Control*, vol. 14, no. 4, 1971, pp. 705–725.

———— and M. H. Hamza: "On the Optimization of Static Systems with Several Cost Measures," *IEEE Transactions on Automatic Control*, vol. AC-17, no. 1, 1972, pp. 170–172.

Salih, K.: "Goal Conflicts in Pluralistic Multi-Level Planning for Development," *International Regional Science Review*, vol. 1, 1975, pp. 49–72.

Salkin, G. R., and R. C. Jones: "A Goal Programming Formulation for Merger Strategy," in S. Eilon and T. R. Fowkes (eds.), *Applications of Management Science in Banking and Finance*, Gower Press, London, 1972.

Salukvadze, M. E.: "On the Existence of Solutions in Problems of Optimization under Vector-Valued Criteria," *Journal of Optimization Theory and Applications*, vol. 13, no. 2, 1974, pp. 203–217.

————: "Linear Programming Problem with a Vector-Valued Performance Criterion," *Automation and Remote Control*, vol. 33, no. 5, part 1, 1972, pp. 794–799.

————: "Optimization of Vector Functionals, I. The Programming of Optimal Trajectories," *Automation and Remote Control*, vol. 32, no. 8, 1971, pp. 1169–1178.

————: "Optimization of Vector Functionals, II. The Analytic Construction of Optimal Controls," *Automation and Remote Control*, vol. 32, no. 9, part 1, 1971, pp. 1347–1357.

Salvia, A. A., and W. R. Ludwig: "An Application of Goal Programming at Lord Corporation, " *Interfaces*, vol. 9, no. 4, 1979, pp. 129–133.

Sarin, R. K.: "Interactive Evaluation and Bound Procedure for Selecting Multi-Attributed Alternatives," in [25], pp. 211–224.

————: "Ranking of Multiattribute Alternatives with an Application to Coal Power Plant Siting," in [7], pp. 405–429.

Sartoris, W. L., and M. L. Spruill: "Goal Programming and Working Capital Management," *Financial Management*, vol. 3, no. 1, 1974, pp. 67–74.

Sawaragi, Y., K. Inoue, and H. Nakayama: "Multiobjective Decision Making with Applications to Environmental and Urban Design," in [2], pp. 358–366.

Sayeki, Y., and K. H. Vespers: "Allocation of Importance in a Hierarchical Goal Structure," *Management Science*, vol. 19, no. 6, 1973, pp. 667–675.

Schiemenz, B.: "Possibilities to Consider Multiple Criteria in Decision Situations," in [27], pp. 274–292.

Schilling, D.: "Dynamic Location Modelling for Public-Sector Facilities: A Multicriteria Approach," *Decision Sciences*, vol. 11, no. 4, 1980, pp. 714–724.

Schmee, J., E. Hannan, and M. P. Mirabile, "An Examination of Patient Referral and Discharge Policies Using a Multiple Objective Semi-Markov Decision Process," *Journal of the Operational Research Society*, vol. 30, no. 2, 1979, pp. 121–129.

Schmidt, J. W., and G. K. Bennett: "Economic Multiattribute Acceptance Sampling," *AIIE Transactions*, vol. 4, no. 3, 1972, pp. 194–199.

Schmitendorf, W. E.: "Cooperative Games and Vector-Valued Criteria Problems," *IEEE Transactions on Automatic Control*, vol. AC-18, no. 2, 1973, pp. 139-144.

—— and G. Moriarty: "A Sufficiency Condition for Coalitive Pareto-Optimal Solutions," in [18], pp. 163-172.

Schönfeld, K. P.: "Some Duality Theorems for the Non-Linear Vector Maximum Problem," *Unternehmensforschung*, vol. 14, 1970, pp. 51-63.

Schroeder, R. G.: "Resource Planning in University Management by Goal Programming," *Operations Research*, vol. 22, no. 4, 1974, pp. 700-710.

Schwartz, L. E.: "Uncertainty Reduction Over Time in the Theory of Multiattributed Utility," in [4], pp. 108-123.

Schwartz, S. L., and I. Vertinsky: "Multi-Attribute Investment Decisions: A Study of R&D Project Selection," *Management Science*, vol. 24, no. 3, 1977, pp. 285-301.

——, ——, and W. T. Ziemba: "R&D Project Selection Behavior: Study Designs and Some Pilot Results," in [27], pp. 136-146.

——, ——, ——, and M. Bernstein: "Some Behavioural Aspects of Information Use in Decision Making: A Study of Clinical Judgements," in [27], pp. 378-391.

Sealey, C. W.: "Financial Planning with Multiple Objectives," *Financial Management*, Winter 1978, pp. 17-23.

Seiford, L., and P. L. Yu: "Potential Solutions of Linear Systems: The Multi-Criteria Multiple Constraint Levels Program," *Journal of Mathematical Analysis and Applications*, vol. 69, no. 2, June 1979, pp. 283-303.

Seinfeld, J. H., and W. Z. McBride: "Optimization with Multiple Performance Criteria," *I & EC Process Design and Development*, vol. 9, no. 1, 1970, pp. 53-58.

Sengupta, S. S., M. L. Podrebarac, and T. D. H. Fernando: "Probabilities of Optima in Multi-Objective Linear Programmes," in [4], pp. 217-235.

Shachtman, R.: "Generation of the Admissible Boundary of a Convex Polytope," *Operations Research*, vol. 22, no. 1, 1974, pp. 151-159.

Shapiro, J. F.: "Multiple Criteria Public Investment Decision Making by Mixed Integer Programming," in [27], pp. 170-182.

Shapley, L. S.: "Equilibrium Points in Games with Vector Payoffs," *Naval Research Logistics Quarterly*, vol. 6, no. 1, March 1959, pp. 57-61.

Shepard, R. N.: "On Subjectively Optimum Selection Among Multiattribute Alternatives," in M. W. Shelly and G. L. Bryan (eds.), *Human Judgments and Optimality*, Wiley, New York, 1964, pp. 257-281.

Shim, J. K., and J. Siegel: "Sensitivity Analysis of Goal Programming with Pre-emption," *International Journal of Systems Science*, vol. 11, no. 4, April 1980, pp. 393-401.

—— and ——: "Quadratic Preferences and Goal Programming," *Decision Sciences*, vol. 6, no. 4, 1975, pp. 662-669.

Sinha, N. K., V. Temple, and J. C. Rey: "A Vector Cost Function for Efficient Adaptation," *International Journal of Control*, vol. 16, no. 6, 1972, pp. 1107-1120.

Slovic, P.: "Analyzing the Expert Judge: A Descriptive Study of a Stockbroker's Decision Processes," *Journal of Applied Psychology*, vol. 53, no. 4, 1969, pp. 255-263.

—— and S. Lichtenstein: "Comparison of Bayesian and Regression Approaches to the Study of Information Processing Judgment," *Organizational Behavior and Human Performance*, vol. 6, 1971, pp. 649-774.

Smith, C. J.: "Using Goal Programming to Determine Interest Group Disutility for Public Policy Choices," *Socio-Economic Planning Sciences*, vol. 14, no. 3, 1980, pp. 117-120.

Smith, L. H., R. W. Lawless, and B. Shenoy: "Evaluating Multiple Criteria—Models for Two Criteria Situations," *Decision Sciences*, vol. 5, no. 4, 1974, pp. 587-596.

Smith, R. D., and P. S. Greenlaw: "Simulation of a Psychological Decision Process in Personnel Selection," *Management Science*, vol. 13, no. 8, 1967, pp. B409-B419.

Snyder, W. W.: "Economic Policy and Multiple Objective Decision Making Lessons from the Postwar Period," in [4], pp. 771-733.

Soland, R. M.: "Multicriteria Optimization: A General Characterization of Efficient Solutions," *Decision Sciences*, vol. 10, no. 1, 1979, pp. 26-38.

Soyster, A. L., and B. Lev: "An Interpretation of Fractional Objectives in Goal Programming as Related to Papers by Awerbuch, et al., and Hannan," *Management Science*, vol. 24, no. 14, 1978, pp. 1546-1549.

——, ——, and D. I. Toof: "Conservative Linear Programming with Mixed Multiple Objectives," *Omega*, vol. 5, no. 2, 1977, pp. 193-205.

Spivey, W. A., and H. Tamura: "Goal Programming in Econometrics," *Naval Research Logistics Quarterly*, vol. 17, no. 2, 1970, pp. 183-192.

Spronk, J.: "Capital Budgeting and Financial Planning with Multiple Goals," in [21].

Srinivasan, V., and G. L. Thompson: "Alternate Formulations for Static Multi-Attribute Assignment Models," *Management Science*, vol. 20, no. 2, 1973, pp. 154-158.

Stadje, W.: "On the Relationship of Goal Programming and Utility Functions," *Zeitschrift für Operations Research*, vol. 23, no. 1, 1979, pp. 61-69.

Stadler, W.: "Preference Optimality and Applications of Pareto Optimality," in [19], pp. 125-226.

——: "Sufficient Conditions for Preference Optimality," in [18], pp. 129-148.

Stainton, R. S.: "Production Scheduling with Multiple Criteria Objectives," *Operational Research Quarterly*, vol. 28, no. 2, 1977, pp. 285-292.

Stalford, H. L.: "Criteria for Pareto Optimality in Cooperative Differential Games," *Journal of Optimization Theory and Applications*, vol. 9, no. 6, 1972, pp. 391-398.

Stancu-Minasian, I. M.: "Stochastic Programming with Multiple Objective Functions," *Economic Computation and Economic Cybernetics Studies and Research*, vol. 1, 1974, pp. 49-67.

Starr M. K., and L. H. Greenwood: "Normative Generation of Alternatives with Multiple Criteria Evaluation," in [25], pp. 111-128.

—— and I. Stein: *The Practice of Management Science*, Prentice-Hall, Englewood Cliffs, N.J., 1976, unit 5.

—— and M. Zeleny: "MCDM—State and Future of the Arts," in [25], pp. 5-29.

Stedry, A. C., and A. Charnes: "Investigation in the Theory of Multiple Budgeted Goals," in C. P. Bonini, R. K. Jaedicke, and H. M. Wagner (eds.), *Management Controls: New Directions in Basic Research*, McGraw-Hill, New York, 1964, pp. 186-204.

Stern, R. J., and A. Ben-Israel: "An Interior Penalty Function Method for the Construction of Efficient Points in a Multiple-Criteria Control Problem," *Journal of Mathematical Analysis and Applications*, vol. 46, no. 3, 1974, pp. 768-776.

—— and ——: "On Linear Optimal Control Problems with Multiple Quadratic Criteria," in [4], pp. 366-372.

Steuer, R. E.: "ADBASE: An Adjacent Efficient Basis Algorithm for Vector-Maximum and Interval Weighted–Sums Linear Programming Problems," *Journal of Marketing Research*, vol. 12, 1975, pp. 454-455.

——: "A Five Phase Procedure for Implementing a Vector-Maximum Algorithm for Multiple Objective Linear Programming Problems," in [27], pp. 159-169.

——: "Goal Programming Sensitivity Analysis Using Interval Penalty Weights," *Mathematical Programming*, vol. 17, no. 1, 1979, pp. 16-31.

——: "An Interactive Multiple Objective Linear Programming Procedure," in [25], pp. 225-239.

——: "Multiple Objective Linear Programming with Interval Criterion Weights," *Management Science*, vol. 23, no. 3, 1976, pp. 305-316.

——: "Vector-Maximum Gradient Cone Contraction Techniques," in [34], pp. 462-481.

—— and F. W. Harris: "Intra-Set Point Generation and Filtering in Decision and Criterion Space," in [31], pp. 41-53.

—— and A. T. Schuler: "An Interactive Multiple Objective Linear Programming Approach to a Problem in Forest Management," *Operations Research*, vol. 26, no. 2, 1978, pp. 254-269.

—— and M. J. Wallace: "A Linear Multiple Objective Programming Model for Manpower Selection and Allocation Decisions," in A. Charnes, W. W. Cooper, and R. J. Niehaus (eds.), *Management Science Approaches to Manpower Planning and Organization Design*, North-Holland Publishing, Amsterdam, 1978, pp. 193-208.

Sullivan, R. S., and J. A. Fitzimmons: "A Goal Programming Model for Readiness and the Optimal

Replacement of Resources," *Soci-Economic Planning Sciences*, vol. 12, no. 5, 1978, pp. 215–220.

Sundaram, R. M.: "An Application of Goal Programming Technique in Metal Cutting," *International Journal of Production Research*, vol. 16, no. 5, 1978, pp. 375–382.

Taft, M. I., and A. Reisman: "A Proposed Generalized Heuristic Algorithm for Scheduling with Respect to n-Interrelated Criterion Functions," *International Journal of Production Research*, vol. 5, no. 2, 1966, pp. 155–162.

Takeda, E., and T. Nishida: "Multiple Criteria Decision Problems with Fuzzy Domination Structures," *Fuzzy Sets and Systems*, vol. 3, no. 2, pp. 123–136.

Tamura, K.: "A Method for Constructing the Polar Cone of a Polyhedral Cone, with Applications to Linear Multicriteria Decision Problems," *Journal of Optimization Theory and Applications*, vol. 19, no. 4, 1976, pp. 547–564.

—— and S. Miura: "On Linear Vector Maximization Problems," *Journal of the Operations Research Society of Japan*, vol. 20, no. 3, 1977, pp. 139–149.

Tanino, T., and Y. Sawaragi: "Stability of Nondominated Solutions in Multicriteria Decision-Making," *Journal of Optimization Theory and Applications*, vol. 30, no. 2, 1980, pp. 229–253.

—— and ——: "Duality Theory in Multiobjective Programming," *Journal of Optimization Theory and Applications*, vol. 27, no. 4, 1979, pp. 509–529.

Tauxe, G. W., D. M. Mades, and R. R. Inman: "Multiple Objectives Analysis by Dynamic Programming," *Transactions of American Geophysical Union*, vol. 59, 1978, p. 1073.

Taylor, B. W., and A. J. Keown: "A Goal Programming Application of Capital Project Selection in the Production Area," *AIIE Transactions*, vol. 10, 1978, pp. 52–57.

—— and ——: "Planning Urban Recreational Facilities with Integer Goal Programming," *Journal of the Operational Research Society*, vol. 29, 1978.

——, K. R. Davis, and R. M. North: "Approaches to Multiobjective Planning in Water Resources Projects," *Water Resources Bulletin*, vol. 11, no. 5, 1975, pp. 999–1008.

Taylor, R. L.: "Consistent Multiattributed Decision Procedures," in [4], pp. 774–778.

Tell, B.: "An Approach to Solving Multi-Person Multiple-Criteria Decision-Making Problems," in [34], pp. 482–493.

——: "A Comparative Study of Four Multiple-Criteria Methods," in [27], pp. 183–197.

——: "The Effect of Uncertainty on the Selection of a Multiple-Criteria Utility Model," in M. Roubens (ed.), *Advances in Operations Research*, North-Holland Publishing, Amsterdam, 1977, pp. 497–504.

——: "Factor Analysis—A Method for Reducing the Number of Criteria in a Multiple-Criteria Model," *Omega*, vol. 6, no. 5, 1978, pp. 451–454.

Terry, H.: "Comparative Evaluation of Performance Using Multiple Criteria," *Management Science*, vol. 9, no. 3, 1963, pp. 431–442.

Tersine, R. J.: "Organizational Objectives and Goal Programming: A Convergence," *Managerial Planning*, vol. 25, no. 2, 1976, pp. 27–40.

Thiriez, H., and D. Houri: "Multi-Person Multi-Criteria Decision-Making: A Sample Approach," in [27], pp. 103–119.

Thomas, H., and A. R. Lock: "An Appraisal of Multi-Attribute Utility Models in Marketing," *European Journal of Marketing*, vol. 13, no. 5, 1979, pp. 294–307.

Togsverd, T.: "Multi-Level Planning in the Public Sector," in [27], pp. 201–214.

Tomlinson, J. W. C., and I. Vertinsky: "Selecting a Strategy for Joint Venture in Fisheries: A First Approximation," in [27], pp. 351–363.

Törn, A.: "A Sampling-Search-Clustering Approach for Exploring the Feasible/Efficient Solutions of MCDM Problems," in [31], pp. 67–79.

Trippi, R. R.: "On the Evaluation of Investment Proposals Having Multiple Attributes," *Naval Research Logistics Quarterly*, vol. 21, no. 2, 1974, pp. 327–332.

Van Wassenhove, L. N., and L. F. Gelders: "Solving a Bicriterion Scheduling Problem," *European Journal of Operational Research*, vol. 4, no. 1, 1980, pp. 42–48.

Vedder, J.: "Multiattribute Decision Making Under Uncertainty Using Bounded Intervals," in [4], pp. 93–107.

————: "Planning Problems with Multidimensional Consequences," *Journal of the American Institute of Planners*, vol. 36, no. 2, 1970, pp. 112–119.

Vehovec, M.: "Simple Criterion for the Global Regularity of Vector-Valued Functions," *Electronics Letters*, vol. 5, 1969, pp. 680–681.

Velichenko, V. V.: "Sufficient Conditions for Absolute Minimum of the Maximal Functional in the Multi-Criteria Problem of Optimal Control," in G. Marchuk (ed.), *Optimization Techniques: IFIP Technical Conference*, Springer-Verlag, New York, 1975, pp. 220–225.

Vemuri, V.: "Multiple Objective Optimization in Water Resource Systems," *Water Resources Research*, vol. 10, no. 1, 1974, pp. 44–48.

Villarreal, B., M. H. Karwan, and S. Zionts: "An Interactive Branch and Bound Procedure for Multicriterion Integer Linear Programming," in [7], pp. 448–467.

Vincke, P.: "A New Approach to Multiple Criteria Decision-Making," in [27], pp. 341–350.

Vinogradskaya, T. M., and M. G. Gaft: "An Exact Upper Bound for the Number of Nonsubordinate Solutions in Multicriterion Problems," *Automation and Remote Control*, vol. 35, no. 9, 1974, pp. 1474–1481.

Viswanathan, B., V. V. Aggarwal, and K. P. K. Nair: "Multiple Criteria Markov Decision Processes," in [25], pp. 263–272.

Volpato, M.: "Estimating the Common Cost of a Good When the Local Costs Are Known in the Countries of a Community," in [19], pp. 325–350.

Wacht, R. F., and D. T. Whitford: "A Goal Programming Model for Capital Investment Analysis in Nonprofit Hospitals," *Financial Management*, vol. 5, no. 2, 1976, pp. 37–47.

Walker, J.: "An Interactive Method as an Aid in Solving Bicriterion Mathematical Programming Problems," *Journal of the Operational Research Society*, vol. 29, no. 9, 1978, pp. 915–922.

————: "An Interactive Method as an Aid in Solving Multi-Objective Mathematical Programming Problems," *European Journal of Operational Research*, vol. 2, 1978, pp. 341–349.

Wallenius, H., J. Wallenius, and P. Vartia: "An Approach to Solving Multiple Criteria Macroeconomic Policy Problems and an Application," *Management Science*, vol. 24, no. 10, 1978, pp. 1021–1030.

Wallenius, J.: "Comparative Evaluation of Some Interactive Approaches to Multicriterion Optimization," *Management Science*, vol. 21, no. 12, 1975, pp. 1387–1396.

———— and S. Zionts: "A Research Project on Multicriterion Decision Making," in [2], pp. 76–96.

———— and ————: "Some Tests of an Interactive Programming Method for Multicriterion Optimization and Attempt at Implementation," in [27], pp. 319–331.

Walters, A., J. Mangold, and E. Haran: "A Comprehensive Planning Model for Long-Range Academic Strategies," *Management Science*, vol. 22, no. 7, 1976, pp. 727–738.

Waltz, F. M.: "An Engineering Approach: Hierarchical Optimization Criteria," *IEEE Transactions on Automatic Control*, vol. AC-12, no. 2, 1967, pp. 179–180.

Warford, J. J., and D. S. Julius: "Multiple Objectives of Water Rate Policy in Less Developed Countries," *Water Supply Management*, vol. 1, 1977, pp. 335–342.

Wedley, W. C., and A. E. J. Ferrie: "Duality and Vector Optima for Polyhedral Sets-Reply," *Journal of the Operational Research Society*, vol. 30, 1979, p. 84.

Wehrung, D. A., D. S. P. Hopkins, and W. F. Massy: "Interactive Preference Optimization for University Administrators," *Management Science*, vol. 24, no. 6, 1978, pp. 599–611.

Weiner, N. S.: "Multiple Incentive Fee Maximization: An Economic Model," *Quarterly Journal of Economics*, vol. 77, no. 4, 1963, pp. 603–616.

Welam, U. P.: "Comments on Goal Programming for Aggregate Planning," *Management Science*, vol. 22, no. 6, 1976, pp. 708–712.

Welling, P.: "A Goal Programming Model for Human Resource Accounting in a CPA Firm," *Accounting, Organization and Society*, vol. 2, April 1977, pp. 307–316.

Wendell, R. E., and D. N. Lee: "Efficiency in Multiple Objective Optimization Problems," *Mathematical Programming*, vol. 12, no. 3, 1977, pp. 406–414.

————, A. P. Hurter, and T. J. Lowe: "Efficient Points in Location Problems," *Journal of Mathematical Analysis and Applications*, vol. 49, no. 2, 1975, pp. 430–468.

————, ————, and ————: "Efficient Points in Location Problems," *AIIE Transactions*, vol. 9, no. 3, 1977, pp. 238–246.

Werczberger, E.: "A Goal Programming Model for Industrial Location Involving Environmental Considerations," *Environment and Planning*, vol. 8, 1976, p. 173.

————: "The Versatility Model in Decision Making under Uncertainty with Regard to Goals and Constraints," in [21].

Wheeler, B. M., and J. R. M. Russell: "Goal Programming and Agricultural Planning," *Operational Research Quarterly*, vol. 28, no. 1, 1977, pp. 21–32.

White, C. C., and K. W. Kim: "Solution Procedures for Vector Criterion Markov Decision Processes," *Journal of Large-Scale Systems*, vol. 1, no. 2, 1980, p. 129.

———— and A. P. Sage: "A Multiple Objective Optimization-Based Approach to Choicemaking," *IEEE Transactions on Systems, Man, and Cybernetics*, vol. SMC-10, no. 6, 1980, pp. 315–326.

White, C. M.: "Multiple Goals in the Theory of the Firm," in K. E. Boulding and W. A. Spivey (eds.), *Linear Programming and the Theory of the Firm*, Macmillan, New York, 1960, pp. 181–201.

White, D. J.: "Multi-Objective Interactive Programming," *Journal of the Operational Research Society*, vol. 31, no. 6, 1980, pp. 517–523.

————: "Generalized Efficient Solutions for Sums of Sets," *Operations Research*, vol. 28, no. 3, 1980, pp. 844–846.

————: "Optimality and Efficiency I," *European Journal of Operational Research,* vol. 4, no. 5, 1980, pp. 346–355.

————: "Duality and Vector Optima for Polyhedral Sets," *Journal of the Operational Research Society*, vol. 30, 1979, pp. 81–83.

Wiedemann, P.: "Planning with Multiple Objectives," *Omega*, vol. 6, no. 5, 1978, pp. 427–432.

Wierzbicki, A. P.: "Basic Properties of Scalarizing Functionals for Multiobjective Optimization," *Mathematische Operationsforschung und Statistik*, ser. Optimization, vol. 8, no. 1, 1977, pp. 55–60.

————: "The Use of Reference Objectives in Multiobjective Optimization," in [7], pp. 468–486.

Wilcox, J. W.: *A Method for Measuring Decision Assumptions*, M.I.T., Cambridge, Mass., 1972.

Wilhelm, J.: "Generalized Solution Principles and Out-Ranking Relations in Multi-Criteria Decision-Making," *European Journal of Operational Research*, vol. 1, no. 6, 1977, pp. 376–385.

———— and G. Fandel: "Two Algorithms for Solving Vector-Optimization Problems," *Automation and Remote Control*, vol. 37, 1976, pp. 1721–1727.

Williams, F. E.: "On the Evaluation of Intertemporal Outcomes," in [4], pp. 429–438.

Winterfeldt, D. von: "Multi-Criteria Decision Making: Comments on Jacquet-Lagrèze's Paper," in D. Wendt and C. Vlek (eds.), *Utility, Probability, and Human Decision Making*, D. Reidel, Boston, 1975, pp. 113–117.

———— and G. W. Fischer: "Multiattribute Utility Theory: Models and Assessment Procedures," in D. Wendt and C. Vlek (eds.), *Utility, Probability, and Human Decision Making*, D. Reidel, Boston, 1975, pp. 47–85.

Wright, P. L., and F. Barbour: "Phased Decision Strategies: Sequels to an Initial Screening," in [25], pp. 91–110.

Yager, R. R.: "Extending Nash's Bargaining Model to Include Importances for Multiobjective Decisionmaking," *IEEE Transactions on Systems, Man, and Cybernetics*, vol. SMC-10, no. 7, July 1980, pp. 405–407.

————: "Fuzzy Decision Making Including Unequal Objectives," *Fuzzy Sets and Systems*, vol. 1, no. 2, 1978, pp. 87–96.

————: "Multiple Objective Decision Making Using Fuzzy Sets," *International Journal of Man-Machine Studies*, vol. 9, no. 4, 1977, pp. 375–382.

Yntema, D. B., and W. S. Torgerson: "Man-Computer Cooperation in Decisions Requiring Common Sense," *IRE Transactions on Human Factors in Electronics*, vol. HFE-2, 1961, pp. 20–26.

Yu, P. L.: "Behavior Bases and Habitual Domains of Human Decision/Behavior—Concepts and Applications," in [7], pp. 511–539.

———: "A Class of Solutions for Group Decision Problems," *Management Science*, vol. 19, no. 8, 1973, pp. 936–946.

———: "Cone Convexity, Cone Extreme Points, and Nondominated Solutions in Decision Problems with Multiobjectives," *Journal of Optimization Theory and Applications*, vol. 14, no. 3, 1974, pp. 319–376.

———: "Decision Dynamics with an Application to Persuasion and Negotiation," in [25], pp. 159–178.

———: "Domination Structures and Nondominated Solutions," in [19], pp. 227–280.

———: "Introduction to Domination Structures in Multicriteria Decision Problems," in [4], pp. 249–261.

———: "Toward Second Order Game Problems: Decision Dynamics in Gaming Phenomena," in [34], pp. 509–528.

——— and G. Leitmann: "Compromise Solutions, Domination Structures and Salukvadze's Solution," *Problems of Control and Information Theory*, vol. 2, no. 3-4, 1973, pp. 183–197.

——— and ———: "Compromise Solutions, Domination Structures, and Salukvadze's Solution," *Journal of Optimization Theory and Applications*, vol. 13, no. 3, 1974, pp. 362–378.

——— and ———: "Confidence Structures in Decision Making," *Journal of Optimization Theory and Applications*, vol. 22, no. 2, 1977, pp. 265–285.

——— and ———: "Nondominated Decisions and Cone Convexity in Dynamic Multicriteria Decision Problems," *Journal of Optimization Theory and Applications*, vol. 14, no. 5, 1974, pp. 319–377; also in [18], pp. 61–72.

——— and L. Seiford: "Multistage Decision Problems with Multicriteria," in [21].

——— and M. Zeleny: "Linear Multiparametric Programming by Multi-Criteria Simplex Method," *Management Science*, vol. 23, no. 2, 1976, pp. 159–170.

——— and ———: "The Set of All Non-Dominated Solutions in Linear Cases and a Multicriteria Simplex Method," *Journal of Mathematical Analysis and Applications*, vol. 49, no. 2, 1975, pp. 430–468.

——— and ———: "The Techniques of Linear Multiobjective Programming," *Revue Française d'automatique, d'informatique, et de recherche opérationelle*, vol. 8, no. V-3, 1974, pp. 51–71.

Zadeh, L. A.: "Optimality and Nonscalar-Valued Performance Criteria," *IEEE Transactions on Automatic Control*, vol. AC-8, no. 1, 1963, pp. 59–60.

———: "Outline of a New Approach to the Analysis of Complex Systems and Decision Processes," in [4], pp. 686–725.

Zeleny, M.: "Adaptive Displacement of Preferences in Decision Making," in [25], pp. 147–158.

———: "The Attribute-Dynamic Attitude Model (ADAM)," *Management Science*, vol. 23, no. 1, 1976, pp. 12–26.

———: "A Case Study in Multiobjective Design: De Novo Programming," in [21].

———: "Compromise Programming," in [4], pp. 262–301.

———: "A Concept of Compromise Solutions and the Method of the Displaced Ideal," *Computers and Operations Research*, vol. 1, no. 4, 1974, pp. 479–496.

———: "Conflict Dissolution," *General Systems Yearbook*, vol. 21, 1976, pp. 131–136.

———: "Descriptive Decision Making and Its Applications," in R. L. Schultz (ed.), *Applications of Management Science*, vol. 1, JAI Press, Greenwich, Conn., 1981, pp. 327–388.

———: "Games with Multiple Payoffs," *International Journal of Game Theory*, vol. 4, no. 4, 1976, pp. 179–191.

———: "On the Inadequacy of the Regression Paradigm Used in the Study of Human Judgment," *Theory and Decision*, vol. 7, 1976, pp. 57–65.

———: "MCDM Bibliography—1975," in [33], pp. 291–321.

————: "Multicriteria Simplex Method: A Fortran Routine," in [33], pp. 323–345.

————: "Multidimensional Measure of Risk: Prospect Rating Vector (PRV)," in [34], pp. 529–548.

————: "Multiple Objectives in Mathematical Programming: Letting the Man In," in [31], pp. 1–4.

————: "The Pros and Cons of Goal Programming," *Computers and Operations Research*, in press.

————: "Satisficing, Optimization, and Risk in Portfolio Selection," in F. Derkinderen and R. Crum (eds.), *Readings in Strategies for Corporate Investment*, Pitman Publishing, Boston, 1981.

————: "A Selected Bibliography of Works Related to Multiple Criteria Decision Making," in [4], pp. 779–796.

————: "The Theory of the Displaced Ideal," in [33], pp. 153–206.

———— and J. L. Cochrane: "A Priori and A Posteriori Goals in Macroeconomic Policy Making," in [4], pp. 373–391.

Zimmermann, H. J.: "Fuzzy Programming and Linear Programming with Several Objective Functions," *Fuzzy Sets and Systems*, vol. 1, no. 1, 1978, pp. 45–56.

Zionts, S.: "Integer Linear Programming with Multiple Objectives," *Annals of Discrete Mathematics*, vol. 1, 1977, pp. 551–562.

————: "MCDM—If Not a Roman Numeral, Then What?" *Interfaces*, vol. 9, no. 4, 1979, pp. 94–101.

————: "Methods for Solving Management Problems Involving Multiple Objectives," in [7], pp. 540–558.

———— and D. Deshpande: "Energy Planning Using a Multiple Criteria Decision Method," in [21].

———— and ————: "A Time Sharing Computer Programming Application of a Multiple Criteria Decision Method to Energy Planning—A Progress Report," in [34], pp. 549–560.

———— and J. Wallenius: "Identifying Efficient Vectors: Some Theory and Computational Results," *Operations Research*, vol. 28, no. 3, 1980, pp. 785–793.

———— and ————: "An Interactive Programming Method for Solving the Multiple Criteria Problem," *Management Science*, vol. 22, no. 6, 1976, pp. 652–663.

Zrnovský, P.: "The Possibilities of Multigoal Optimization in Network Analysis," *Ekonomicko-matematický Obzor*, vol. 8, 1972, pp. 174–190.

Additional references

Benson, H. P.: "Vector Maximization with Two Objective Functions," *Journal of Optimization Theory and Applications*, vol. 28, no. 2, 1979, pp. 253–257.

Bitran, G. R.: "Linear Multiple Objective Problems with Interval Coefficients," *Management Science*, vol. 26, no. 7, 1980, pp. 694–706.

Czap, H.: "The Dependency of Automatically Designed Multicriterion Decisions on Scale Transformations," *European Journal of Operational Research*, vol. 5, no. 1, 1980, pp. 51–55.

Hannan, E. L.: "Nondominance in Goal Programming," *INFOR*, vol. 18, no. 4, 1980, pp. 300–309.

Hobbs, B. F.: "A Comparison of Weighting Methods in Power Plant Siting," *Decision Sciences*, vol. 11, no. 4, 1980, pp. 725–737.

Lukka, M.: "An Algorithm for Solving a Multiple Criteria Optimal Control Problem," *Journal of Optimization Theory and Applications*, vol. 28, no. 3, 1979, pp. 435–438.

Musselman, K., and J. Talavage: "A Tradeoff Cut Approach to Multiple Objective Optimization," *Operations Research*, vol. 28, no. 6, 1980, pp. 1424–1435.

Schmitendorf, W. E.: "Optimal Control with Multiple Criteria When Disturbances Are Present," *Journal of Optimization Theory and Applications*, vol. 27, no. 1, 1979, pp. 135–146.

Stadler, W.: "A Survey of Multicriteria Optimization or the Vector Maximum Problem, Part 1: 1776–1960," *Journal of Optimization Theory and Applications*, vol. 29, no. 1, 1979, pp. 1–52.

Stewart, T. J.: "A Descriptive Approach to Multiple-Criteria Decision Making," *Journal of the Operational Research Society*, vol. 32, no. 1, 1981, pp. 45–53.

Tamura, K., and S. Miura: "Necessary and Sufficient Conditions for Local and Global Nondominated Solutions in Decision Problems with Multi-Objectives," *Journal of Optimization Theory and Applications*, vol. 28, no. 4, 1979, pp. 501–523.

Tanino, T., and Y. Sawaragi: "Conjugate Maps and Duality in Multiobjective Optimization," *Journal of Optimization Theory and Applications*, vol. 31, no. 4, 1980, pp. 473–499.

Wendell, R. E.: "Multiple Objective Mathematical Programming with Respect to Multiple Decision-Makers," *Operations Research*, vol. 28, no. 5, 1980, pp. 1100–1111.

INDEX